Third Edition

Foundations of Clinical and Counseling Psychology

Third Edition

Foundations of Clinical and Counseling Psychology

Judith Todd
California State University–Dominguez Hills

Arthur C. Bohart
California State University–Dominguez Hills

WAVELAND
PRESS, INC.
Prospect Heights, Illinois

For information about this book, contact:
    Waveland Press, Inc.
    P.O. Box 400
    Prospect Heights, Illinois 60070
    (847) 634-0081
    info@waveland.com
    www.waveland.com

ISBN 1-57766-292-X

Printed in the United States of America

7 6 5 4 3 2 1

To Dan and Karen

Brief Contents

■ **PART ONE**   *In the Beginning*   *1*
   CHAPTER 1   *Professional Psychology in Context*   *3*
   CHAPTER 2   *Historical Development of Professional Psychology*   *27*

■ **PART TWO**   *Assessment*   *51*
   CHAPTER 3   *Assessment and Diagnosis*   *53*
   CHAPTER 4   *Methods of Intellectual, Cognitive, and Neuropsychological Assessment*   *76*
   CHAPTER 5   *Personality, Behavioral, and Other Forms of Assessment*   *100*

■ **PART THREE**   *Psychodynamic Approaches*   *137*
   CHAPTER 6   *Sigmund Freud and Psychoanalysis*   *139*
   CHAPTER 7   *Interpersonal Approaches to Psychoanalysis*   *170*

■ **PART FOUR**   *Humanistic Approaches*   *201*
   CHAPTER 8   *Client-Centered and Other Person-Centered Therapies*   *203*
   CHAPTER 9   *Gestalt and Other Existential-Humanistic Approaches*   *238*

■ **PART FIVE**   *Behavioral and Cognitive Approaches*   *265*
   CHAPTER 10   *Behavioral Approaches to Therapy*   *267*
   CHAPTER 11   *Behavioral Medicine and Hypnosis*   *306*
   CHAPTER 12   *Cognitive Approaches to Psychopathology and Psychotherapy*   *335*

■ **PART SIX**   *Relational Approaches*   *371*
   CHAPTER 13   *Group Approaches to Treatment*   *373*
   CHAPTER 14   *Marriage, Family, and Child Counseling*   *396*

■ **PART SEVEN**   *Empirical and Theoretical Issues*   *437*
   CHAPTER 15   *Research in Psychotherapy*   *439*
   CHAPTER 16   *Psychotherapy Integration: Convergence in Psychotherapy*   *468*

■ **PART EIGHT**   *Contemporary Issues*   *511*
   CHAPTER 17   *The Psychologist and Contemporary Society: Diversity and Postmodern Issues*   *513*
   CHAPTER 18   *Professional Issues and the Future*   *543*
   APPENDIX   *American Psychological Association Ethics Code, 1992 Version*   *573*

Detailed Contents

Preface   *xix*

■ **PART ONE**   *In the Beginning*   *1*

   CHAPTER 1   *Professional Psychology in Context*   *3*

     THE MENTAL HEALTH PROFESSIONS   5

       Clinical Psychology   *5* / *Counseling Psychology*   *9* / *Clinical Neuropsychology*   *10* / *Educational Psychology*   *11* / *School Psychology*   *11* / *Other Fields in Professional Psychology*   *12* / *Psychiatry*   *14* / *Psychoanalysis*   *15* / *Social Work*   *16* / *Marriage, Family, and Child Counseling*   *17* / *Other Mental Health Professions*   *17*

     PROFESSIONAL PSYCHOLOGY IN PRACTICE   19

       The Team Approach   *20* / *Actual Practice*   *20*

     PSYCHOTHERAPY INTEGRATION   23

   CHAPTER 2   *Historical Development of Professional Psychology*   *27*

     ACADEMIC PSYCHOLOGY   28

     SOCIETY'S TREATMENT OF ITS DEVIANT MEMBERS   30

       Who Is Deviant?   *30* / *From Supernatural to Medical Model*   *31* / *From Medical to Psychological Model: Sigmund Freud*   *34* / *Clinical Psychology*   *37* / *Counseling Psychology*   *38*

     PROFESSIONAL PSYCHOLOGY IN THE TWENTIETH CENTURY   39

       Assessment   *39* / *Interventions*   *43* / *Professional Organizations*   *45*

■ **PART TWO**   *Assessment*   *51*

   CHAPTER 3   *Assessment and Diagnosis*   *53*

     PSYCHOLOGICAL ASSESSMENT   54

Norms and Standardization 55 / Reliability and Validity 55 / The Assessment Process 57 / Issues in Psychological Assessment 59 / Criticisms of Psychological Assessment 63

DIAGNOSIS 65

Reliability and Validity of Diagnosis 66 / The Diagnostic and Statistical Manual 66 / Criticisms of Diagnosis 72

CHAPTER 4 *Methods of Intellectual, Cognitive, and Neuropsychological Assessment 76*

INTELLECTUAL AND COGNITIVE ASSESSMENT 77

The Stanford-Binet 77 / The Wechsler Tests 78 / Other Intellectual and Cognitive Tests 81 / Reliability and Validity of Cognitive Ability Tests 82 / Clinical Use of Intelligence Tests 83

NEUROPSYCHOLOGICAL ASSESSMENT 84

Single Neuropsychological Tests 87 / The Halstead-Reitan Battery 87 / The Luria-Nebraska Battery 89 / The Boston Process Approach 89 / Reliability and Validity of Neuropsychological Tests 90 / Clinical Uses of Neuropsychological Assessment 90

CHAPTER 5 *Personality, Behavioral, and Other Forms of Assessment 100*

THE INTERVIEW 100

The Intake Interview 101 / The Mental Status Exam 101 / The Case History Interview 102 / Pretest and Posttest Interviews 103 / Reliability and Validity of Interviews 103

PROJECTIVE PERSONALITY TESTS 104

The Rorschach 105 / Storytelling Tests 105 / Drawing Tests 107 / Sentence Completion Tests 107 / Reliability and Validity of Projective Tests 108 / Clinical Uses of Projective Tests 109

OBJECTIVE PERSONALITY TESTS 110

MMPI and MMPI-2: An Example of the Empirical Approach 111 / The Millon Tests: Another Example of the Empirical Approach 114 / Eysenck Personality Questionnaire (EPQ): An Example of the Inductive Approach 115 / The Myers-Briggs Type Indicator (MBTI): An Example of the Deductive Approach 115 / Other Psychological Tests of Interest 116 / Reliability and Validity of Objective Tests 118 / Clinical Uses of Objective Tests 118

BEHAVIORAL ASSESSMENT 119

Behavioral Assessment Interviews 120 / Naturalistic Observation 120 / Analogue Observation 121 / Participant Observation 121 / Self-Monitoring 121 / Psychophysiological Measures 121 / Behavioral Questionnaires and Checklists 121 / Product-of-Behavior

Measures   122 / Radical Behavioral Assessment   122 / Reliability and Validity of Behavioral Assessment   122 / Clinical Uses of Behavioral Assessment   123

VOCATIONAL, APTITUDE, AND INTEREST TESTS   123

Strong Interest Inventory   124 / Kuder Occupation Interest Survey   124 / 16PF   125 / Other Tests   125 / Reliability and Validity of Vocational and Interest Tests   125 / Clinical Uses of Vocational and Interest Tests   125

■ **PART THREE**   *Psychodynamic Approaches   137*

CHAPTER 6   *Sigmund Freud and Psychoanalysis   139*

THEORY OF PERSONALITY   140

Hidden Meaning and the Concept of Repression   140 / Metapsychology   142 / Defense Mechanisms   143 / Psychopathology and Anxiety   146 / Developmental Stages and Id, Ego, and Superego   147

PSYCHOTHERAPY   150

Free Association   150 / Therapist Interventions   151 / Therapeutic Conditions of Change   154 / Dreams, Resistance, and Transference   155 / Mechanics of Psychoanalysis   158

RECENT ISSUES IN PSYCHOANALYSIS   158

Spence and Historical Truth Versus Narrative Truth   158 / Child Abuse and the Seduction Theory   159

RESEARCH EVALUATION OF PSYCHOANALYTIC THEORY AND THERAPY   160

Effectiveness of Psychotherapy   160 / Psychoanalytic Personality Theory   162

ENDURING CONTRIBUTIONS OF PSYCHOANALYSIS: TOWARD

CHAPTER 7   *Interpersonal Approaches to Psychoanalysis   170*

THE NEO-FREUDIANS   170

Adler   171 / Jung   172 / Other Neo-Freudians   173

CONTEMPORARY PERSPECTIVES   174

OBJECT RELATIONS THEORY   174

Self-Structure and Integration of Aims   175 / Mahler and Separation-Individuation   178 / Psychopathology   181

KOHUT AND SELF PSYCHOLOGY   182

Psychopathology   185

PSYCHOTHERAPY   186

Self Psychology and Object Relations Theory   186 / Brief Forms of Psychoanalytic Psychotherapy   188 / Summing Up Recent Approaches   191

EVALUATION OF INTERPERSONAL PSYCHOANALYTIC APPROACHES   191
   Research on Psychotherapy   191 / Research on Child Development   192
ENDURING CONTRIBUTIONS OF INTERPERSONAL APPROACHES AT

■ **PART FOUR**   *Humanistic Approaches   201*

CHAPTER 8   *Client-Centered and Other Person-Centered Therapies   203*

MODEL OF THE PERSON   204
   Multiple Realities   205 / The Meaning of Acceptance   206 / Personal Constructs and Values   207 / Process Orientation   208 / Internality, Authority, and Individualism   209

EXPERIENCING   210
   Experiential Knowing   210

PSYCHOPATHOLOGY   212

PSYCHOTHERAPY   214
   Therapeutic Process   214 / Role of the Therapist   216

RECENT DEVELOPMENTS IN PERSON-CENTERED THERAPIES   221
   Gendlin's Experiential Psychotherapy   223 / Process-Experiential Psychotherapy   224

CURRENT STATUS AND NEW DIRECTIONS   226

EVALUATION OF CLIENT-CENTERED THERAPY   227
   Research   227 / Therapeutic Conditions   228 / Experiencing   228 / Task Analysis   229 / Theory   230

ENDURING CONTRIBUTIONS OF THE CLIENT-CENTERED APPROACH

CHAPTER 9   *Gestalt and Other Existential-Humanistic Approaches   238*

THE CONCEPT OF THE RIVER   238

EXISTENTIAL THERAPY   239
   Philosophical Background   239 / Theory of Personality and Psychopathology   241 / Psychotherapy   244

GESTALT THERAPY   245
   Theory of Personality and Psychopathology   246 / Therapeutic Approach   254

MAHRER'S EXPERIENTIAL PSYCHOTHERAPY   258

EVALUATION OF HUMANISTIC APPROACHES   259
   Effectiveness of Therapy   259 / Theoretical Evaluation   260

ENDURING CONTRIBUTIONS OF THE EXISTENTIAL-HUMANISTIC APPROACH:

■ **PART FIVE**   *Behavioral and Cognitive Approaches*   265

CHAPTER 10   *Behavioral Approaches to Therapy*   267

FOUNDATIONS OF BEHAVIOR THERAPY   268
  A Brief History of Behavior Therapy   271 / *Principles of Learning*   272 /
  The Development of Abnormal or Unwanted Behavior   275

BEHAVIOR THERAPY   278

EXPOSURE-BASED TREATMENTS (PAVLOVIAN CONDITIONING
METHODS)   279
  Desensitization   279 / *Extinction*   280 / *Punishment*   280

SKILLS TRAINING (OPERANT CONDITIONING METHODS)   283
  Social Skills Training (Assertion Training)   283 / *Contingency
  Management (Behavior Modification)*   285 / *Self-Management*   290 /
  Punishment   292

SOCIAL LEARNING METHODS   293

OTHER FORMS OF BEHAVIOR THERAPY   293

POSTMODERN BEHAVIOR THERAPY   294
  Functional Analytic Psychotherapy (FAP)   296 / *Acceptance and
  Commitment Therapy (ACT)*   298 / *Dialectical Behavior Therapy
  (DBT)*   298 / *Evaluation of Radical Behavior Therapies*   300

EVALUATION OF BEHAVIOR THERAPY   300
  Criticisms of Behavior Therapy   300 / *Strengths of Behavior
  Therapy*   302

ENDURING CONTRIBUTIONS OF BEHAVIOR THERAPY: TOWARD

CHAPTER 11   *Behavioral Medicine and Hypnosis*   306

FOUNDATIONS OF BEHAVIORAL MEDICINE   307
  The Very Brief History of Behavioral Medicine   309 / *Biofeedback*   310 /
  Interventions in Behavioral Medicine   311 / *Evaluation of Behavioral
  Medicine*   319

FOUNDATIONS OF HYPNOSIS   321
  A Long History Briefly Told   322 / *Theoretical Explanations of Hypnosis*
  322 / *Milton Erickson's Theory of Hypnosis*   323 / *The Cognitive-
  Behavioral View of Nicholas Spanos*   325 / *Hypnosis Interventions*   326 /
  Evaluation of Hypnosis   330

ENDURING CONTRIBUTIONS OF BEHAVIORAL MEDICINE: TOWARD

CHAPTER 12   *Cognitive Approaches to Psychopathology and Psychotherapy   335*

KELLY'S CONSTRUCT THEORY   337

SOCIAL LEARNING THEORY   339
*Situational Specificity of Behavior   340   /   Self-Efficacy   342   /
Contributions to Psychotherapy   343*

ATTRIBUTIONAL APPROACHES   343

BECK'S COGNITIVE THERAPY   345
*Cognitive Therapy for Depression   345   /   Role of Emotion in Cognitive
Therapy   352   /   Cognitive Therapy for Personality Disorders   352*

ELLIS'S RATIONAL-EMOTIVE THERAPY   353
*Causes of Psychopathology   353   /   Therapeutic Methods   355   /
Comparison of Ellis and Beck   357*

MEICHENBAUM'S COGNITIVE BEHAVIOR MODIFICATION   358

SPECIFIC COGNITIVE-BEHAVIORAL TREATMENTS FOR SPECIFIC
DISORDERS   360

RECENT THEORETICAL ADVANCES   361

EVALUATION OF COGNITIVE APPROACHES   362
Effectiveness of Psychotherapy   362   /   Theoretical Evaluation   362

ENDURING CONTRIBUTIONS OF COGNITIVE THERAPY: TOWARD

■ **PART SIX**   *Relational Approaches   371*

CHAPTER 13   *Group Approaches to Treatment   373*

GROUP THERAPY   373
*Forms of Group Therapy Based on Individual Approaches   374   /   Group-
Based Forms of Group Therapy   379*

GENERAL FACTORS OF GROUP STRUCTURE AND PROCESS   382
*Group Dynamics   382   /   Curative Factors in Groups   384   /   Special Uses
of Group Therapy   385*

OTHER KINDS OF GROUPS   389
*Sensitivity Training Groups   389   /   Encounter Groups   389   /   Self-Help
or "Mutual-Support" Groups   391*

ENDURING CONTRIBUTIONS OF GROUP APPROACHES: TOWARD

CHAPTER 14   *Marriage, Family, and Child Counseling   396*

PSYCHOLOGICAL INTERVENTIONS WITH CHILDREN   397
*Psychoanalytically Oriented Therapy   397   /   Client-Centered Therapy
398   /   Play Therapy   398   /   Behavior Therapy   400   /   Behavioral*

Medicine and Hypnosis 400 / Cognitive-Behavior Therapy 401 / Psychopharmacological Interventions 401 / Family Therapy 401 / Group Therapy 402

SEX THERAPY 402

MARITAL AND COUPLES COUNSELING AND THERAPY 404

Psychodynamic Marital Therapies 406 / Behavioral and Cognitive Marital Therapies 406 / Experiential-Humanistic Approaches 408

FAMILY COUNSELING AND THERAPY 409

Murray Bowen and Personal Differentiation 410 / Virginia Satir and Dysfunctional Communication 412 / Minuchin and the Structural Approach 414 / Strategic and Solution-Focused Approaches 415 / Milton Erickson 416 / Modern Strategic and Solution-Focused Therapists 418

EVALUATION OF MARRIAGE, FAMILY, AND CHILD THERAPY 428

Evaluation of Child Therapy 428 / Evaluation of Marital and Family Therapy 428 / Theoretical Evaluation 430

ENDURING CONTRIBUTIONS OF CHILD, SEX, MARITAL, AND FAMILY

■ **PART SEVEN** *Empirical and Theoretical Issues 437*

CHAPTER 15 *Research in Psychotherapy 439*

WHY WE NEED TO STUDY PSYCHOTHERAPY EMPIRICALLY 439

METHODOLOGICAL ISSUES IN PSYCHOTHERAPY RESEARCH 443

Control Groups 443 / Meaning and Measurement of Change 445 / Analogue Designs 449 / Other Research Problems 449

THE EFFECTIVENESS OF PSYCHOTHERAPY 451

Meta-Analysis 453 / Recent Developments in Psychotherapy Research: The Search for Specificity 454

CURRENT RESEARCH CONTROVERSIES AND ISSUES: POLITICS AND PSYCHOTHERAPY 458

Treatment Guidelines and the American Psychological Association Template 458 / Empirically Validated Treatments 460 / Measuring Outcome in Clinical Practice 462

CHAPTER 16 *Psychotherapy Integration: Convergence in Psychotherapy 468*

TYPES OF PSYCHOTHERAPY INTEGRATION 469

Technical Eclecticism 469 / Common Factors 471 / Theoretical Integration 473 / Assimilative Integration 476 / Objections to Psychotherapy Integration 477

Our Views on Integration and Convergence   478

The Basis of All Therapies: The Problem of Access   478 / Strategies for Facilitating Access   480 / Theoretical Reasons for the Access Problem   492 / The Importance of Self-Acceptance   497 / Rigid Schemas as a Major Cause of Psychopathology   498 / Therapy as the Development of a Hypothesis-Testing Attitude   499 / Therapy as the Reorganization of Personal Meaning   499 / Self-Empowerment   500 / The Interpersonal Nature of the Human Being   502

■ **PART EIGHT**   *Contemporary Issues   511*

CHAPTER 17   *The Psychologist and Contemporary Society: Diversity and Postmodern Issues   513*

The Challenge of Diversity   514

The Self Across Cultures   516 / Contributions of Diverse Views of the Self   517

Postmodern Treatment Approaches   518

Multicultural Counseling   519 / Feminist Therapy   523 / Constructivism and Narrative Psychotherapies   527 / Other Issues in Contemporary Treatment Approaches   528

Contemporary Treatment Modalities   531

Brief Therapy   532 / Technology and Counseling   536 / Self-Help   537

CHAPTER 18   *Professional Issues and the Future   543*

Ethical Issues   543

Confidentiality and Privilege   544 / Informed Consent   546

Legal Issues   546

Licensing of Professional Psychologists   547 / Health Care Regulation   547 / Malpractice   548

Professional Issues   551

Competition with Medicine   551 / Defining and "Diagnosing" Mental Disorders   552 / Professional Competence   553 / Hospital Privileges   554 / Prescription Privileges   555 / Treatment Manuals and Empirically Validated Treatments   555

Psychology and Corporate Control of the Health Care System   556

Accountability and Peer Review   557 / Cost-Effectiveness   557 / Cost-Cutting and Rationing   558

The Profession and Society   559

Change Versus Adjustment   559 / Misuses of Mental Health Concepts   560 / Psychological Intervention in Social Problems   561

THE FUTURE   562

   *Changes in Professional Practice   563 / Future Roles for Professional
   Psychologists   563 / Employment Prospects in Psychology   565*

APPENDIX: *American Psychological Association Ethics Code, 1992
            Version   573*

INTRODUCTION   573

PREAMBLE   574

GENERAL PRINCIPLES   575

   *Principle A: Competence   575 / Principle B: Integrity   575 / Principle C:
   Professional and Scientific Responsibility   576 / Principle D: Respect for
   People's Rights and Dignity   576 / Principle E: Concern for Others'
   Welfare   576 / Principle F: Social Responsibility   576*

ETHICAL STANDARDS   577

GLOSSARY   *579*

INDEX   *591*

Preface

At the present time, the field of clinical psychology and psychotherapy is going through unprecedented changes. In this, the third edition of our clinical and counseling psychology text, we focus on updating trends toward the future while retaining the coverage of the topics that have traditionally constituted the field of clinical psychology. Our original goal in writing the first edition was to design an introductory professional psychology text that emphasized psychotherapy while still retaining coverage of other important topics such as assessment, history, and professional, legal, and ethical issues. Our experience was that our students in introductory clinical psychology courses wanted more material on psychotherapy than other texts provided.

In this edition, we build on that foundation by adding or expanding coverage of topics such as brief therapy, the use of the Internet and other electronic innovations in counseling, the development of treatment guidelines and the controversies associated with them, the impact of managed care on the mental health field, the importance of cultural and gender issues, and the expanding use of clinical psychology in the area of behavioral medicine. In addition, we have updated our coverage of the various traditional topics, for example, by adding coverage of some of the new cognitive-behavioral treatments for specific disorders, new radical behavioral approaches to psychotherapy, the increased interpersonal emphasis in psychoanalysis, and developments in the fields of psychotherapy research and psychotherapy integration.

As in the two previous editions, one of our goals has been to write a useful book. It is impossible to learn how to do therapy from a survey-type textbook (or from any book, for that matter). We have opted to focus on presenting a clear, understandable view of how each theoretical perspective regards the person, the person's problems, and how to help the person change. While we could not hope to teach counseling skills, we do hope to give students a "feel" for how therapists of differing persuasions saw their clients and worked with them. We believe that our book gets "inside" the differing perspectives better than any other book.

We also feel that a useful book should be flexible so that individual instructors and readers can use it differently as it suits their needs. We wrote this book so that the chapters can be read in almost any order because of careful cross-referencing and a consistent, eclectic, integrative viewpoint that makes connections between topics.

Finally, a useful book should be readable and enjoyable. We have tried to write the text in an interesting, down-to-earth manner, using case material and everyday examples to flesh out the more abstract theoretical material. Because we like to laugh, we have included several items of humor, believing that humor can "help the medicine go down" and illustrate important points in a vivid an memorable manner.

The current edition tries to capture the flavor of the extensive changes that are occurring in the professions devoted to providing psychological services such as assessment, counseling, and psychotherapy. Major changes in how these services are paid for, such as the fact that now most psychotherapy and counseling is either paid for by insurance companies or provided through health maintenance organizations, affect both how these services are provided and the nature of the services. The individual private practitioner who hangs out his or her "shingle" and works with clients for as long as he or she and the client deem necessary is not exactly a thing of the past, but is an endangered species. Increasingly, psychologists and other types of counselors are working for health maintenance organizations, or getting reimbursed through managed care companies that carefully monitor the length and kind of services provided in order to control and cut costs. As a result, psychotherapy is becoming briefer and more focused. Along with this has come increased pressure for accountability: Health care and governmental agencies want to know that what they are paying for works. We have tried to cover the developments associated with these changes in this edition. For instance, with regard to the issue of accountability, we cover the recent controversy in the American Psychological Association over "empirically validated treatments" both in the chapter on psychotherapy research and in our concluding chapter on the future of clinical psychology.

In keeping with the theme of this edition of dealing with this unprecedented change, we have tried to identify what we see as the important contributions of each approach to psychotherapy that we expect will persist in the twenty-first century. We discuss this at the end of each chapter on psychotherapy.

Our text is written from an eclectic, integrative point of view. We do not believe that any one approach to psychotherapy or counseling can be said to be "the" correct one. Instead, we believe that the practitioner of the future will have theoretical and empirical knowledge of differing points of view and an ability to use "what works" with individual clients.

In keeping with this, we have updated the two chapters on psychotherapy research and on psychotherapy integration. The research chapter is included because we believe it is important that students be aware of the great difficulties involved in sorting out belief and opinion from knowledge about psychotherapy. We are dismayed whenever a student is dogmatically sure that the behavioral approach or the humanistic approach or the systems approach is best. We hope that the research chapter will introduce students to the complexities of how one goes about truly *knowing* something, provide them with an overview of the current (but rapidly changing) state of knowledge, and increase their critical reasoning skills about research and the nature of knowledge.

The psychotherapy integration chapter has been significantly changed and updated. When we were writing our first edition, the field of psychotherapy integration was young (and so were we!). The Society for the Exploration of Psychotherapy Integration was only a year or so old. Since then, the *Journal of Psychotherapy Integra-*

tion has been founded, and numerous books and articles have been published in which attempts are made to integrate various aspects of the differing approaches to psychotherapy. Our chapter on psychotherapy integration in the first two editions was largely our own attempt to provide a theoretical framework for how differing approaches converged.

In the current edition, the psychotherapy integration chapter has been enlarged to review some of the newer attempts at psychotherapy theory integration, as well as to give an updated version of our approach to it. One of us (JT) would like to point out that the other of us (AB) has, since the first edition, become an internationally recognized expert and author in the field of psychotherapy theory integration. Readers of the third edition will benefit from his latest thinking on this topic.

We believe this edition remains suitable for a one-semester course; however, it is designed so that instructors may assign selected chapters if they do not wish to use the whole text. Some might choose, for instance, to emphasize assessment and perhaps not assign all parts of all chapters on psychotherapy. Others might decide that psychotherapy integration or the history of clinical psychology are topics that need not be covered in their course. Generally, the chapters have been written so that they stand on their own, for various topics are carefully cross-referenced. The psychotherapy integration chapter is the one exception; it depends on having read most of the earlier chapters on psychotherapy (with the exceptions of the group therapy and current issues chapters). Due to student demand, we added a glossary of important terms to the second edition, and this feature also helps students with reading chapters assigned in a sequence different from the text.

Although this book was originally written for use in upper division clinical psychology courses, we have since learned that it has been used in a much wider range of contexts. We know of instructors who have used it as a text in graduate courses on personality theory in clinical psychology programs, in graduate courses on counseling theory in education programs, and in upper division counseling psychology classes. We also know of some practitioners in the United States and England who bought the book for their own review, and it would make an excellent reference for all mental health professionals. The usefulness of our text in such different contexts is very gratifying.

A short note on the order of authors is needed. Since our coauthorship was originally an equal endeavor, we decided to list ourselves alphabetically for the first edition and to trade places for the second. However in this edition, instead of switching once again, we have chosen to keep the order of authorship of the second edition. The main reason for this is that Judy has taken primary responsibility for this third edition. A second reason is that we don't want to confuse those who use our book.

Special appreciation goes to our reviewers: Jim Archer, University of Florida, Gainesville; Lenore Defonso, Indiana University, Purdue; Gerald Mohatt, University of Alaska, Fairbanks; Dick Schmidt, California State University, Long Beach; and Mary Anne Watson, University of Colorado, Denver.

We'd like to thank the reviewers of the second edition: Leslie Greenberg, York University, Toronto; Beverly Palmer, California State University, Dominguez Hills; Susan Regas, California School of Professional Psychology, Los Angeles; Robert Rosenbaum, California Institute of Integral Studies, San Francisco; and Jeremy Safran, Derner Institute at Adelphi University, New York.

We also wish to thank reviewers of the first edition: Franz R. Epting, University of Florida; Ruthellen Josselson, Towson State University; Joseph Lyons, University of California, Davis; Beverly L. Palmer, California State University, Dominguez Hills; Lyle Schmidt, Ohio State University; T. Gale Thompson, Bethany College; Donald H. Voss, Slippery Rock College of Pennsylvania; Rudolph L. Zlody, College of the Holy Cross; and Fran Miller. And special thanks go to Janet Nuciforo, our Project Editor, who greatly improved our work.

Judith Todd
Arthur C. Bohart

PART **ONE**

In the Beginning

CHAPTER 1

Professional Psychology in Context

Frank S., age 38, unemployed aerospace worker, sits at home most days, watching TV and drinking beer. He appears glum, says little, and reacts with irritation when his wife or children try to talk to him. While he dozes frequently during the day, he has difficulty sleeping at night; therefore, he is too tired to look for work. Frank's thoughts center on why he can't find work, and when drunk, he occasionally stands on the front porch accusing the neighbors of being "after" him, along with "the others." Mrs. S., who began to work as a cashier when her husband was laid off his job, is beginning to lose patience with his depressed mood, confused thinking, erratic behavior, and constant drinking. She thinks he needs help. If she is correct, what sort of help does he need and who should provide it?

Clinical psychology and counseling psychology are helping professions, specifically, mental health professions. In the United States today many individuals, groups, and institutions offer to help others in many ways. Schools and churches, for instance, attempt to help members of the community by teaching academic skills and moral behavior. Many groups, from weight clinics to seminars on how to become rich and famous, are in the business of changing the behavior of others. The helping methods of counseling and psychotherapy include many techniques used by others, such as advice ("You should give up drinking," "You need to raise your consciousness"); suggestion ("Your Higher Self will appear to help you," "You will not feel like smoking"); and interpretation ("You feel life is meaningless because you haven't accepted Jesus," "You aren't earning riches because of your underlying belief that you don't deserve them").

While clinical psychology and counseling psychology exist in a social matrix with other helping groups, they can nevertheless be distinguished from others in several important ways. Professional psychologists are just that—professional. They have attended recognized universities where they have received extensive postgraduate education and training in research, evaluation, and implementation of helping methods. They are licensed or certified by the state to engage in specific kinds of helping practice. They are guided by a professional code of ethics.

Educated in the graduate departments of universities and independent graduate schools, professional psychologists are unique in the emphasis on research in their training. Clinical psychology as a field was based on what is known as the scientist-practitioner model, a model that incorporates both academic research and applied helping skills as necessary for the profession. Clinical and counseling psychologists employ helping methods and theories that are more likely to have been subjected to empirical research than those of other helpers.

Although professional psychologists are trained to help people and to change behavior, the questions of who needs professional help and what kind of help is needed may be answered differently by the various individuals involved. Take Frank S. as an example. His neighbors may regard Frank as dangerous, needing imprisonment; his minister may see him as weak, needing spiritual help; his wife may see him as sick, needing medical help; and Frank himself may deny that he needs help at all.

Helpers, too, may recommend different types of help, as even professional helpers may disagree on what is needed. A psychiatrist may believe Frank S. suffers from a disease, a literal "mental" illness, requiring proper diagnosis and medication. Psychologists may see him as exhibiting emotional, cognitive, or behavioral disorders requiring psychological intervention. Even within the specialty of clinical psychology, a psychodynamic therapist may view Frank as having unconscious intrapsychic conflicts requiring individual psychotherapy; a cognitive behavior therapist may see him as living in an environment that reinforces his helpless behavior and hopeless cognitions and as needing modifications in his environment and thinking; a psychoneurologist would want to consider the possibility of brain damage; a family therapist might consider Frank's problem as a symptom of family dysfunction; and a community psychologist might regard Frank as reacting to social change and in need of a support group and a job. The answers to the questions of who needs what sort of help, then, will reflect the use of different models and theories of disorder and treatment, as well as competition between helping professions.

The question of who should receive professional help also reflects society's attitudes toward problem behavior. These attitudes change with time. In the eighteenth century in the United States, public drunkenness was considered normal, socially acceptable behavior, and at that time Frank's drinking behavior would not have been considered part of his problems. In the nineteenth century, excessive drinking came to be regarded as a problem, specifically, a sin to be railed against by ministers and temperance workers. By the twentieth century, public drunkenness was a crime, to be controlled through laws and imprisonment. In recent decades, excessive drinking has been regarded as a disorder requiring professional help and now as a disease requiring medical treatment and hospitalization.

When public drunkenness was socially accepted, it was not defined as a problem. Once excessive drinking came to be viewed as a problem of concern to the whole community, how best to prevent and control it raised the difficult issue of balancing traditional values of individual liberty versus the need to control the behavior of certain individuals. Our society is comfortable with depriving of their liberty individuals who engage in behaviors with serious consequences to others, such as murder or assault. Our society seems to prefer trying to use medical treatment or psychological help to control individuals who engage in behaviors with less serious or more ambiguous consequences. In fact, it has been argued that in the United States at present there is a tendency to medicalize social problems that have not been solved by other means. Furthermore, by medicalizing or psychologizing social problems, Americans can continue to regard them as problems of the individuals involved and thereby avoid community responsibility for them and the difficulties of implementing social change. Clinical and counseling psychology allow us to treat social problems while preserving our value of individualism.

Because our society constantly redefines social problems and the types of behaviors that require professional help, the roles of clinical and counseling psychologists are constantly changing. Furthermore, many individuals see themselves as in need of help or treatment. As increasing numbers of problematic behaviors are defined as suitable for psychological treatment, the diversity of roles for professional psychologists has also increased in recent years. The goals, methods, and clientele of professional psychology will continue to change, as we will discuss in Chapter 18. However, let us first try to define and describe the fields of clinical psychology, counseling psychology, and the other mental health professions as they exist in the United States today.

THE MENTAL HEALTH PROFESSIONS

Besides clinical psychology and counseling psychology, there are several other mental health professions (MHPs) that help individuals whose thoughts, feelings, or behaviors are problematic to themselves or to others. The differences among these professions can be examined in terms of their areas of expertise, their education and training requirements, licensing and certification requirements, and even levels of pay and prestige. The type of education required for psychiatrists and psychologists is standard across the United States, but the requirements for the other professional groups vary from state to state. The professional duties of the different MHPs also vary, but in most cases, they overlap.

Clinical Psychology

The field of clinical psychology integrates science, theory, and practice to understand, predict, and alleviate maladjustment, disability, and discomfort as well as to promote human adaptation, adjustment, and personal development. Clinical psychology focuses on the intellectual, emotional, biological, psychological, social, and behavioral aspects of human functioning across the life span, in varying cultures, and at all socioeconomic levels.

This definition appears in a public information brochure published in 1992 by the Division of Clinical Psychology (Division 12) of the American Psychological Association. It appears to cover every aspect of human functioning.

Historically, the existence of clinical psychology as a separate professional field has been tenuous, with much competition between psychiatry and clinical psychology. Just a few years ago there was heated controversy over the right of clinical psychologists to do anything besides psychological assessment and counseling with children. In 1954, the American Medical Association (AMA) declared that psychotherapy was a medical treatment, thus implying that psychotherapy by a psychologist constituted practicing medicine without a license and was therefore illegal. In 1958, the American Psychiatric Association adopted the AMA position and opposed the legal certification of psychologists. The American Psychological Association (APA) threatened to sue the AMA and "the other APA" over these issues. However, these conflicts were worked out by the 1960s. With the liberal funding of mental health programs in that prosperous decade, there was business enough for everyone, and the competition between psychology and psychiatry was reduced. When funds for mental health were greatly reduced in the 1980s, the competition between MHPs again intensified, with many threats to psychology as an independent profession. Furthermore, certain psychologists themselves believe that clinical psychology as currently practiced is of limited value and the field should shift its emphasis to prevention and social action (Albee, 1970).

Education and Training   According to the APA, the term *psychologist* should be used only for individuals with a doctoral degree in psychology. However, increasing numbers of people are earning master's degrees in psychology. What are they to be called? Master's-level psychologists almost always find appropriate employment, and even individuals with a bachelor's degree may hold jobs in agencies or companies that require performing some of the functions of a psychologist. However, their status remains an issue within the APA.

There are two educational models for the profession of clinical psychology. The first, established in 1949 when the American Psychological Association held a conference in Boulder, Colorado, to formulate training requirements for psychology, is known as the **scientist-practitioner model,** also called the **Boulder model** (Shakow, 1949). In this training model, clinical psychology requires both the academic research skills obtained by completing a research dissertation for the doctoral degree and the applied helping skills obtained by supervised internship experience. Clinical psychologists trained according to the scientist-practitioner model are unique among mental health professionals in their knowledge of assessment, evaluation, and the empirical basis for their methods.

The second training model was established in 1973 at the APA training conference held in Vail, Colorado. Because of criticism that research training is irrelevant to the majority of professional practice, the **professional model,** also known unsurprisingly as the **Vail model,** still requires a doctoral degree, but eliminates the academic research requirement for clinical psychology. As a result of the development of this new training model, schools of professional psychology were established as institutions separate from universities, and these graduate schools emphasize clinical training, not research.

At present there are two types of doctoral degrees in clinical psychology, reflecting the two training models. The Ph.D., or Doctor of Philosophy, is awarded by academic departments of psychology in universities upon the completion of a research dissertation. For a Ph.D. in clinical psychology, a year of internship in an APA-approved clinical setting is required in addition to three years of related course work and the research dissertation, for a minimum total of five postgraduate years. A Ph.D. in other areas of psychology, such as social or experimental psychology, is supposed to require three years, since there is less course work and no clinical internship. In many cases doctoral degrees take longer than these minimums.

Professional schools offer the Psy.D., or Doctor of Psychology, and their programs take from four to six years after the bachelor's degree. Recently, some professional schools began offering the Ph.D. as well as the Psy.D., and thus they now require the research component in the form of the doctoral dissertation.

Training requirements for clinical psychology undergo constant evaluation and change as the nature of psychologists' work changes. The APA has held several conferences regarding training since the Vail Conference in 1973 to discuss such issues as the growth of specializations within psychology and the need for core curriculum requirements, but these conferences have not created a coherent new model to add to or replace the scientist-practitioner and professional models.

The increasing diversity of professional psychology means that individuals considering applying to graduate school must do a great deal of research in order to choose the appropriate one. There are reference books on graduate education to assist students in their search, including one published annually by the American Psychological Association. As early as possible in their educational careers, students should write to the graduate schools that interest them and obtain a description of their programs and requirements. Once in graduate school, students are still responsible for seeing to it that they obtain training in the specializations they prefer.

Professional Ethics   The American Psychological Association has established, and constantly evaluates and changes, a professional code of ethics for all its diverse members. The 1992 revision of the code of ethics includes six general principles regarding competence, integrity, professional and scientific responsibility, respect for people's rights and dignity, concern for others' welfare, and social responsibility. In addition there are eight ethical standards that detail the implementation of the general principles in specific situations. The eight standards cover: general standards; evaluation, assessment, or intervention; advertising and other public statements; therapeutic relationships; privacy and confidentiality; teaching, training, supervision, research, and publishing; forensic activities; and resolving ethical issues. The code of ethics for psychologists is shown in more detail in the Appendix and discussed further in Chapter 18.

Licensing and Certification   At present, all states regulate the practice of clinical psychology through licensing, certification, and registration. Licensing of psychologists is a fairly recent phenomenon. Most laws regarding licensure were enacted in the 1950s and 1960s. As psychotherapy became acceptable and even popular, some unscrupulous and untrained individuals were offering to treat the public. Many people believe that individuals seeking psychological help are exceptionally vulnerable and liable to be harmed by inept or exploitative practitioners. At the same time, organized medicine was trying to ensure that only medical doctors treated the public with psychotherapy, and psychologists wanted to legitimize their right to offer psychotherapeutic services to the public. Desires to protect the public and for professional recognition led the psychological community to urge state governments to enact laws to license psychologists.

A **license** is issued to professionals who have demonstrated competence in their field, and it permits them to practice in the state. Regulations vary, but we can use California licensing law, which is similar to that of many states, as an example. California law requires 2,000 hours of supervised clinical practice in a multidisciplinary setting to be obtained within a 24-month period after acquiring a doctoral degree. After candidates apply for a license and verify their education and training, they must take a national multiple-choice examination relating to all areas of psychology, including statistics, research design, and clinical practice. If they pass the written exam, candidates must submit to a one-hour oral examination by two licensed psychologists, in which they are asked about ethics, the law, and clinical practice. After obtaining a license, psychologists retain it by taking mandatory continuing education courses each year. This procedure is supposed to ensure that only ethical, competent people are licensed as psychologists and allowed to offer psychological services to the public.

State **certification** is a weaker form of control than licensure. The state certifies that the person claiming to be a psychologist has indeed completed all the educational and training requirements for the profession, but issuing a certificate does not include evaluating the candidate for competence. Certificates in specialized areas, such as alcoholism counseling, are offered by many public and private educational institutions, and again, these certificates guarantee only that an individual has completed certain course requirements. An interesting point, discussed in more detail later, is that the health industry increasingly prefers to hire or reimburse mental health professionals with certificates over those with licenses.

Registration is a still weaker form of state control. Practicing psychologists merely register their practice with the state. In California, registration is required for psychology trainees and psychological assistants working for agencies or psychologists in private practice. Employed psychologists who are not yet licensed may also be required to register.

Most state licensing and certification laws were enacted during the 1950s and 1960s. Because of criticisms that licensing laws failed to protect the public and merely protected professional psychology from competition, in the 1970s, some states enacted so-called "sunset legislation," which would allow their licensing laws to go off the books, as discussed in Chapter 18. In response to this threat, psychology created a system of self-certification through the *National Register of Health Service Providers in Psychology,* first published in 1975. Psychologists who are licensed or certified in their own states may submit their names for inclusion in the *Register,* which is now published annually. It is easier for insurance companies to consult this national publication when deciding whose fees to reimburse than to check who is licensed in each state.

In addition to licensing or certification, experienced psychologists may seek to become diplomates of the American Board of Professional Psychology (ABPP). To qualify for this diploma, a psychologist must have five years of professional experience, be a member of the APA, hold a Ph.D. from an APA-approved program, submit copies of his or her work, see an unknown patient under observation, and pass an oral examination. Being an ABPP diplomate implies additional competence and professional status for the psychologist.

Employment   Clinical psychologists work in a wide variety of settings and engage in a wide variety of activities. In fact, one of the advantages of the profession is the flexibility to do so many different, interesting things. As we will show later in the chapter, employment may involve private practice, hospitals, public agencies, health maintenance organizations, businesses, universities, schools, or the military, and professional duties range from teaching, research, assessment, psychotherapy, and mental health services to administration, consultation, and supervision. Professional psychologists assess and treat children, adolescents, adults, families, groups, businesspeople and workers, people with neurotic and psychotic disorders, people who abuse alcohol and drugs, smokers, overweight people, prisoners, people with mental retardation, and individuals with brain damage as a result of accidents, strokes, and the like.

Because of the doctoral degree and the extensive training requirements, and because of years of struggle to obtain public recognition and parity with medical doctors, clinical psychologists are the second most prestigious group of MHPs, and they command, on average, the second highest fees.

Counseling Psychology

Although similar in many ways to clinical psychology, counseling psychology is distinguished by requiring a doctoral degree in counseling psychology or counselor education, by stressing certain theories of therapy (such as client-centered therapy, discussed in Chapter 8), and by working with a relatively nondisturbed clientele. Counseling psychologists may assess and counsel individuals or groups regarding their life problems, career plans, relationship issues, academic choices, and the like. They may teach in counseling psychology programs at universities and conduct research on communication, relationships, and the counseling process. They may be consultants for business, education, and mental health institutions, and provide program development. Some counseling psychologists obtain the psychologist's license and work in private practice, while others work in clinics, hospitals, student counseling services, and business in as many diverse roles as clinical psychologists.

Career Counseling   Once called vocational guidance, career counseling has grown in recent decades, in response to advances in theory and assessment and to increased demand for such services in an increasingly complex economy. Early "vocational aptitude" tests tried to determine what sort of job a particular individual was suited for in terms of skills and abilities. Present-day vocational assessment investigates interests and personality as well as skills, and its goal is to match career planning with an individual's interests, abilities, and temperamental suitability for certain jobs so that the person's happiness and personal growth will be enhanced. Career counseling takes a comprehensive, developmental approach to lifelong career planning, helping both individuals beginning to choose their careers and those who change careers later in life because of personal desire or economic need. Career counselors often work in educational settings, where career decisions may determine educational choices, and they may provide a variety of educational services, such as workshops on job searches and résumé writing or training in the social skills needed to apply and interview for jobs.

Personal Counseling   Although counseling psychologists may work with disturbed people, the focus of personal counseling, which may be conducted with individuals or in groups, is supposed to be on the problems and personal growth, adjustment and relationship issues, and developmental or situational crises of adequately functioning people. The goal of personal counseling is to help people through the expected difficulties of life, prevent severe disturbance from developing, and to improve and enhance personal functioning and satisfaction with life.

Marriage, Family, and Child Counseling   Counseling psychologists work with couples (married or not), families, and children to assist them with the expected difficulties of close relationships, including communication, conflict resolution, issues of closeness and trust, and childrearing practices. The theories and intervention methods used in this type of counseling are described in Chapter 13. Counseling psychologists working with couples, families, and children are to be distinguished from the person who obtains a license in Marriage, Family, and Child counseling, a master's-level mental health profession described later in the chapter.

Clinical Neuropsychology

Clinical neuropsychologists also call themselves neurocognitivists or neuroscientists, a labeling issue that reflects the facts that this is a relatively new field and training has been diverse. Although some neuropsychologists began as clinical psychologists, many originally held doctorates in psychophysiology, comparative psychology, cognition, or medicine. Today it is possible to obtain a doctorate in clinical neuropsychology at some universities, and the training parallels that of clinical psychology. Students receive intensive academic education in the research on the relation between brain and behavior, they complete a research dissertation, and they serve in a supervised internship where they are trained to apply their academic knowledge in a work setting.

A large body of research in several disciplines has now been developed for the analysis of the behavioral consequences of central nervous system lesions. The development of quantitative and qualitative neuropsychological procedures has led to clinical applications of this knowledge to the assessment and treatment of a variety of brain and nervous system disorders. A detailed description of neuropsychological assessment is presented in Chapter 4.

In addition to careers in basic research of the brain and its relation to behavior, neuropsychologists find employment in hospitals, medical schools, and universities, and they may also work in private practice. They often engage in assessment, they make treatment recommendations, and they may be involved in rehabilitation. Their clients may be aphasics (people lacking speech), epileptics, children with learning difficulties, stroke victims, accident victims, or individuals with congenital brain abnormalities. It appears that clinical neuropsychology is a growing field for which many psychologists will be needed in the future. Advances in medical treatment now save the lives of many people who would have died in previous decades but who survive with varying degrees of brain damage, such as extremely premature infants or those with head injuries from automobile accidents. Neuropsychology enjoys prestige and relatively high pay, partly because it fits in well with our society's current emphasis on biological causes of disorders.

Educational Psychology

Overlapping with clinical and counseling psychology is educational psychology, which requires an Ed.D., Doctor of Education, degree. There are also master's degrees in educational psychology and counselor education. Training in educational psychology is available from universities with a graduate school of education, department of educational psychology, or other similar unit.

Educational psychologists stress research, assessment, and methods relevant to the educational process. They draw from psychology's scientific knowledge of assessment, learning and motivation, cognition, child development, computers and artificial intelligence, and other areas. They develop theories and methods aimed at improving the educational process, teacher effectiveness, and student learning and motivation, and they develop training programs to implement their methods in the schools. As with other psychological specialties, educational psychology often finds itself involved in conflicts about public policy. Whether children should be bussed to achieve integration, which programs (such as Head Start) are effective and deserving of federal funds, and what is the best and most cost-effective way of improving public education are all important issues that educational psychologists can help address.

Educational psychologists often obtain the psychologist's license and work in schools, universities, private practice, or mental health agencies, in a variety of roles similar to those of clinical psychologists.

School Psychology

The requirements and roles of school psychologists vary from state to state and from school district to school district. Generally, school psychologists have had teaching experience and hold at least a master's degree in school psychology, pupil personnel, or other areas. As the name implies, they work in schools and participate in the evaluation of and intervention with individual pupils, groups of pupils, teachers, administrators, or the educational system itself.

Some school psychologists specialize in one of three areas as psychoeducational, systems change, or developmental specialists. Psychoeducational school psychologists focus on children with learning difficulties, testing such children and making remediation recommendations. When there is money available, such psychologists may also test and design programs for gifted children. Systems change specialists examine interpersonal and group behavior in schools and develop programs to improve the performance of the overall system. Developmental school psychologists design programs to facilitate the growth and education of all children within the school. There may be much overlap with educational psychology.

Other Fields in Professional Psychology

As psychological research and social need lead psychologists to apply their skills to new problems, new specialties are developed. Some of these have previously been considered specialties within clinical psychology, but it is now possible to obtain doctorates in these areas at some universities. In addition to those fields that are descendants of or related to clinical and counseling psychology, described next in the chapter, there are other applied psychology fields that have developed from social and experimental psychology.

Human factors psychologists help design industrial and office environments and machines so that humans can interact with them safely and effectively. Industrial and organizational psychologists consult with business, government, and organizations to help them function more effectively. Furthermore, because graduate training in psychology provides various methodological skills that are "content free" and applicable to many nontraditional job areas, psychologists increasingly find employment as managers, training analysts, database analysts, consumer researchers, personnel researchers, organization effectiveness analysts, program coordinators, computer consultants, and program directors and supervisors (Oskamp, 1988). Although any list of specialties is subject to constant social change, the following are now identifiable special fields within psychology.

Rehabilitation Psychology   The field of rehabilitation psychology is relatively old, and some consider it a precursor to the newer specialty of neuropsychology, which deals with disabilities due to neurological abnormalities. Rehabilitation psychologists focus on individuals with physical, cognitive, developmental, and emotional disabilities, as well as neurological ones. They conduct research on the causes and effects of disability, they assess people with disabilities, and they design and conduct remediation for them. Rehabilitation involves identifying and remediating both personal and environmental factors that impede the disabled person's maximum participation in "normal life" in the community.

Community Psychology   Also a relatively old specialty, community psychology was rather "in" during the 1960s, when there was both money available and optimism about social change. Community psychology differs from clinical psychology and most other specialties in two profound ways. First, it emphasizes the prevention of psychological disorders. Second, it views intervention to be most effective and necessary at the community level. Community psychologists emphasize wholistic theories, such as systems theory, which analyzes community organization and how groups relate to each other, and the ecological approach, which analyzes the relationship between individuals and resources within the community. Community psychology interventions vary widely and may include crisis intervention, client advocacy, improving and integrating community services and support, and political activism. Community psychology is discussed further in Chapter 17.

Forensic Psychology   A relatively new field, forensic psychology involves the application of psychology to issues relating to law and the legal system. Any involvement in the legal system will naturally lead to controversy, and forensic psychology has been subject to much criticism. Nevertheless, the legal system finds many uses for psychologists' expertise, and the field is growing. Training requirements for forensic psychology have not been formally established; some practitioners are clinical psychologists who have expanded their practice and others hold joint degrees in law and psychology. Because of the lack of consistency in training, there are now credentialing programs in forensic psychology. States may credential mental health professionals who perform court-ordered evaluations, and some psychologists may seek to be credentialed by the American Board of Forensic Psychology.

Since the role of forensic psychologists is still evolving, we will list a few things they do now. Forensic psychologists may do psychological assessment for criminal court, as in determining competency to stand trial or other psychological issues, and for dependency court, as in assessing parental suitability for child custody. Forensic psychologists may give expert testimony in a wide variety of matters, such as children's memory in child abuse cases or the effects of posttraumatic stress syndrome in an assault case, but the admissibility of psychologists' testimony varies by judicial jurisdiction. Psychologists are increasingly asked by the courts, both in criminal cases and civil commitments, to predict dangerousness, but their ability to do so is extremely controversial, as discussed further in Chapter 18. Forensic psychologists may prepare briefs for the court summarizing psychological knowledge on a certain issue, treat individuals under court jurisdiction, or conduct research on issues that affect the legal system, such as jury selection, factors influencing jury verdicts, witness memory, and the like. Some are involved in civil commitment hearings and in cases of guardianship for the incompetent. Forensic psychologists may be involved in civil litigation and provide evidence in personal injury or workmen's compensation cases. They may also provide consultation to attorneys, judges, legislators, law enforcement, and the prison system.

Clinical Health Psychology   Similar to behavioral medicine, discussed in Chapter 11, clinical health psychology deals with the application of psychological knowledge to matters of health, but it tends to focus on maintaining and improving general health and wellness, while behavioral medicine tends to focus on preventing and treating specific illnesses. Also a fairly new field, health psychology training standards are not formalized, but some clinical psychologists develop additional specialized knowledge while others obtain doctorates in health psychology. Health psychologists research the relationship between behavior and physical health, and clinical health psychologists apply this knowledge to the assessment and treatment of individuals and groups. Intervention methods in health psychology include behavioral and cognitive programs to help people reduce stress, stop smoking, lose weight, or maintain exercise programs, as well as public education programs and interventions to make organizations more conducive to health.

Clinical Child Psychology and Pediatric Psychology   Although both fields deal with children and there is much overlap, clinical child psychology is mostly concerned with the assessment and treatment of psychologically disordered children, and pediatric psychology deals with problems presented by normal development or with children who are physically ill. As with other specialties, originally clinical psychologists obtained further training in working with children, but now there are doctoral programs with these titles. The theories and intervention methods in clinical child psychology are similar to those in clinical psychology, with the additional consideration of the developmental stages of children. They are covered in detail in Chapter 14.

Some people consider pediatric psychology to be clinical child psychology practiced in a general medical setting or child health psychology. Some pediatric psychologists work with pediatricians and help them deal with such developmental issues as toilet training, sleep difficulties in young children, temper tantrums, separation anxiety, and the like. Others work with ill children and their families in pediatric or hospital settings. Children with catastrophic illnesses or injuries need assessment and interventions to help them deal with painful medical procedures, disfigurement, loss of previous abilities, fears of death, anger or depression over their fate, jealousy of healthy siblings, or a number of other difficult issues. The families of such ill children also need assistance with coping, problem solving, depression, anxieties, or the difficult behavior of ill children or their siblings. Pediatric psychologists also treat children with noncatastrophic illnesses; for example, they may teach diabetic children how to manage their illness and motivate them to stick with their diet. Pediatric psychologists combine knowledge of child development, family functioning, and therapy theories and methods to intervene with the goal of improving the child's health or helping the child and family cope with an ongoing illness.

Psychiatry

Psychiatry is the most prestigious and powerful mental health profession. Psychiatrists are physicians who have specialized in psychiatry, and as physicians, they utilize the medical model. In the medical model, diagnosis is the crucial first step, for only by diagnosing what is wrong can one identify a specific disorder and then search for the underlying cause of it, the discovery of which leads to the development of prevention or cure. Thus, diagnosis is always required, because diagnosis determines the treatment, and treatment cannot begin without an accurate diagnosis. This model is logical and has been highly effective for physical diseases, but difficulties arise when it is applied to psychological, behavioral, and social problems. The medical model has been criticized as being incorrect, authoritarian, leading to labeling and stigmatization, focusing too much on pathologies and deficits, and biasing treatment policies toward psychiatry. While these issues are discussed in more detail in Chapter 3, the point here is that belief in the medical model differentiates psychiatry and psychology and may explain some of the difficulties the two fields have with each other.

As implied, psychiatric training requires an M.D., or Medical Doctor, degree (or other medical degree) from an accredited medical school, followed by an internship and a three-year residency in psychiatry, during which residents provide psychiatric services under the supervision of one or more psychiatrists. Critics of this admittedly rigorous and demanding regimen complain that the majority of it is irrelevant to the practice of psychiatry. Others argue that because organic processes and physical diseases may be part of or must be distinguished from mental disorders, the extensive medical training is necessary. And some argue that all mental illness must ultimately have a biological basis such as a brain abnormality or a biochemical dysfunction and thus medical training is required to treat any psychological disorder.

Psychiatrists are licensed by state medical boards, and they are thus qualified to work in hospitals and agencies and to engage in private practice. Only psychiatrists may prescribe medications, including psychotropic drugs, although this situation may be changing, as discussed in Chapter 18. In most states, only psychiatrists may commit people to mental hospitals against their will. In California, a psychiatric nurse, clinical social worker, or psychologist on a hospital staff may sign commitment papers, but only with the additional signature of a psychiatrist. Until recently, a psychologist's clients who required hospitalization had to admit themselves or the psychologist had to find a psychiatrist willing to treat them. The clients' treatment was taken over by a psychiatrist, and the psychologist usually stopped seeing them during their hospital stay. This situation is changing as discussed in Chapter 18.

Psychiatrists are by law permitted to engage in a variety of forms of psychotherapy, including individual, group, and family therapy. Because they tend to believe that psychological disorders are biologically based and because they have the power to prescribe medication, they may emphasize drug treatments. They may also prescribe electroconvulsive shock therapy, occupational therapy, art therapy, and other forms of treatment in hospitals or out.

Many psychiatrists work in private practice and are affiliated with a hospital; some work exclusively in mental hospitals and hospitals with psychiatric wards. Psychiatrists also work in outpatient mental health clinics, and the director of such community facilities is often a psychiatrist.

Psychiatrists have the highest status and highest rate of pay of all the MHPs, although their status within the medical field may have slipped in recent years. The number of medical graduates pursuing psychiatric residencies has decreased, and compared to other medical specialties, the pay of psychiatrists is considered low.

Psychoanalysis

At the present time in the United States almost all psychoanalysts hold a medical degree and received special psychoanalytic training at a psychoanalytic institute, including taking special courses, seeing patients under a training analyst, and undergoing a long and intensive analysis of their own with an experienced psychoanalyst. The psychoanalytic institutes are independent of medical schools. In other countries, MHPs other than physicians may seek psychoanalytic training and become psychoanalysts. In the United States, social workers and psychologists may take analytic training at certain institutes, and they may engage in analytically oriented psychotherapy, although it remains controversial whether they may call themselves psychoanalysts. Various courts have ruled that the psychoanalytic institutes must admit nonmedical therapists for training, but enforcing these rulings is difficult, as discussed in Chapter 18.

Since psychoanalysis is a long and expensive procedure, psychoanalysts almost always work in private practice. They typically see patients individually several times a week for one to several years. (Psychoanalytic therapy is described in Chapters 6 and 7.) Since most psychoanalysts hold medical degrees, they may prescribe drugs and hospitalize patients if necessary. Their fees are equivalent to those of psychiatrists.

Social Work

Social work is a fairly old mental health profession, older than professional psychology. The roots of social work can be traced back to the support and assistance people give each other in small communities, but in the last century, such community volunteerism began to be delivered through organized charities. Although they often ran completely with volunteers, some charities hired people to do their work full time, and the recognized field of social work began. In the early years of the profession, social workers provided direct services to the disadvantaged portions of the population through organized charities. They helped the needy obtain charitable services, find jobs, get training, get medical treatment, deal with crises, and the like. The practice of social work has changed in recent years, evolving to resemble clinical psychology.

There is a bachelor's degree in social work at some universities, the B.S.W. The master's degree in social work, or M.S.W., requires two years of course work and supervised experience after the bachelor's degree. Licensing (for the LCSW, Licensed Clinical Social Worker) and certification requirements vary greatly from state to state. In some states and in some jobs, social workers need only the bachelor's degree. Although the master's degree is considered the usual requirement for social work, some social workers, especially those working in universities, supervision, and training, obtain a doctoral degree, such as the D.S.W.

Like psychologists, social workers work in a variety of settings, including private practice and hospitals and agencies, and they provide several types of psychotherapy. Some decades ago many social workers became analysts, and many still remain psychodynamically oriented in theory and practice. Today most social workers do intake interviews, make treatment plans, and, most of all, conduct individual and group therapy and counseling.

Also like psychologists, social work has developed a set of specialties. Social workers may specialize in child welfare, family services, protective services, victim assistance, mental health, medical social work, school social work, psychiatric social work, gerontology, and other fields. In addition to individual and group therapy, the interventions of social workers are more likely than those of psychologists to include providing concrete information and direct assistance to clients by, for example, helping them find child or elder care, apply for public assistance, develop a budget or go for debt counseling, search for jobs, obtain legal services, enter an alcohol or drug rehabilitation program, obtain a place in sheltered housing (if they are released prisoners or mental patients), and similar services.

In terms of power, prestige, and pay, social workers generally rank somewhat lower than psychologists. However, fees for social workers in private practice vary greatly, and may be as high as those of psychologists.

Marriage, Family, and Child Counseling

Some states now license or certify a relatively new group of MHPs called marriage, family, and child counselors (MFCCs). In most states, an MFCC requires a master's degree, but some graduate schools now offer a doctoral degree in MFCC. In California, for example, the MFCC license requires 3,000 hours of supervised training and a master's degree in MFCC or its equivalent. An equivalent degree is presently open to interpretation and controversy, so that people with master's degrees in several subjects, such as clinical psychology or pastoral counseling, may be allowed to take the MFCC examination. The MFCC examination has written and oral components that test for knowledge, ethics, and clinical competence.

MFCCs are supposed to engage in marriage, family, and child counseling, according to their expertise. They work in a variety of settings, as well as in private practice.

Since most MFCCs have less training and a lower-level degree, they are usually paid less than psychologists and often less than social workers. Some agencies prefer to hire MFCCs as a way to cut the cost of providing counseling and therapy to the public. While MFCC fees are usually lower than those of psychologists, some energetic and successful MFCCs in private practice command higher fees.

Other Mental Health Professions

Counseling   Some states certify mental health counselors. These individuals may hold bachelor's or master's degrees with various types of training and experience required for the certificate. They engage in various types of group and individual counseling in various service settings. As another example of types of counselors, career counselors generally have a master's degree and work in university counseling and advisement centers to help students decide on and pursue their careers.

Psychological Assistants   Some states allow unlicensed persons to work under the supervision of licensed psychologists as psychological assistants, so they may gain necessary experience. A psychological assistant is employed by a licensed psychologist or psychiatrist to perform limited psychological functions within the assistant's area of competence. In California, the assistant is allowed to perform his or her work only while the supervisor is on the premises, and the supervising psychologist must provide a certain number of hours of face-to-face supervision for every so many hours of work. In addition, the assistant must be registered with the licensing board and be making progress toward an advanced degree in psychology. Supervising psychologists must verify annually to the licensing board that their assistants meet all of these requirements.

Typically, psychological assistants perform limited services, such as administering psychological tests (which are perhaps scored and interpreted by the supervising psychologist), some forms of behavior modification, intake interviews, or play therapy with a child while the employing psychologist sees the parents. Some experienced assistants do individual psychotherapy, in a way similar to private practice, although they are not technically independent practitioners.

Bachelor's-Level Professions   There are several bachelor's-level mental health professions that involve limited forms of counseling other than psychotherapy. Although individuals with a bachelor's degree in psychology find employment in the field, there are other majors that lead to work in mental health, such as human services. Students majoring in human services do course work in topics such as clinical psychology, psychopathology, social work, agency administration, and counseling skills, and they do many hours of fieldwork in many different settings. Human services workers work in agencies providing services for children, the disabled, the elderly, and other disadvantaged portions of the population. They also work in law enforcement, probation, and the prisons. In many ways, the human services worker resembles the social worker of old.

Other bachelor's-level graduates work in hospitals, clinics, and community agencies under a variety of job titles: counselor, alcoholism counselor, intake worker, community worker, recreation leader, group leader, welfare officer, evaluation officer, drug rehabilitation leader, and many others. The job requirements, skill level, and services performed in these positions vary, but often resemble the work of psychologists and other therapists.

There are even jobs in the mental health field for people without a bachelor's degree. For example, the position of psychiatric technician in a hospital requires two years of college. Psych techs, as they are called, usually perform protective or custodial services in hospital wards, but some engage in individual and group counseling with patients. A Certified Alcoholism Counselor (CAC) is not required to hold any degree at all, but must undergo special training in order to obtain the certificate.

Psychiatric Nursing   The profession of psychiatric nursing requires a bachelor's degree in nursing and usually some type of postgraduate course work or training. Psychiatric nurses generally work in mental hospitals and on psychiatric wards, performing nursing duties such as overseeing the administration of prescribed medications and the daily care of patients. Psychiatric nurses may also conduct individual or group counseling and participate in behavior modification programs in the hospital, and some engage in private practice.

Paraprofessional Counseling   Paraprofessional counselors, also called nonprofessional counselors or peer counselors, may have little formal education, but they receive special training in counseling skills to enhance their natural helping abilities. Paraprofessionals generally work in community agencies that treat special populations that are underserved or poorly served by the usual mental health institutions. Often, a paraprofessional counselor is a member of the underserved group. For example, ex-drug addicts may assist drug abusers, and a minority group member may counsel minorities. The use of paraprofessional counselors was encouraged by research in the 1960s that showed that naturally helpful nonprofessionals were as effective in counseling certain groups as psychiatrists and psychologists.

Trainees and Volunteers   Many undergraduate and graduate students in psychology and related fields volunteer to work in mental health and community agencies in order to obtain training and experience in their chosen fields and to be of service to the community. (Nonstudent citizens also volunteer to be of service.) If there are formal ties between the agencies accepting volunteers and the university sending out students, the volunteers may have a formal role with a title such as trainee or intern. In return for giving their time, the trainees receive supervision and in-service training, which help the students to obtain future employment, to get into graduate school, and to explore how well they like the mental health field. Trainees take part in many mental health services, including many activities similar to those undertaken by professional psychologists.

PROFESSIONAL PSYCHOLOGY IN PRACTICE

As all the mental health professions have grown, the overlap in functions and populations served and, to some degree, the competition among the professions have also grown. Clinical psychology is constantly expanding into new areas as research suggests new applications and as society comes to view psychological intervention as the solution to more of its problems. For example, when research discovered that people could learn to control their own brain waves and other autonomic responses thought to be outside of conscious control, this discovery led to behavioral treatments involving biofeedback for migraine headaches, high blood pressure, and other disorders, as discussed in Chapter 11. An example of turning to psychology for a solution to a social problem can be seen in the case of excessive drinking. As church and state failed to control problem drinking, it became defined as a psychological or psychiatric disorder.

Along with growth has come increased contact between professional psychology and the other mental health professions. Often, this contact is cooperative and fruitful, but as has long been the case between psychiatry and clinical psychology, there may be competition and conflict over expertise, methods of treatment, and the right to treat certain groups. Some people, including many MHPs, have come to believe that a system that involves many specialist groups, each with its own methods, training, and regulations, has outlived its usefulness. The time and money spent on competition, legal battles, and replication of services could be better spent on cooperating to solve society's problems. Back in 1983, Raymond Cattell was arguing for greater cooperation between psychiatry and psychology and for an end to the battle for "control of the booming $17 billion a year mental health business." In actual practice the similarities among the various MHPs appear to be greater than their differences.

The Team Approach

In theory, MHPs should work effectively together. In the decade before World War II, the team approach to the treatment of mental illness was developed. The psychiatrist was the head of the team, made most of the treatment decisions, and was responsible for the physical well-being of the patients. The clinical psychologist assessed patients for their intellectual and personality functioning. The social worker coordinated the cases, often did the intake interviews, and worked with the family members of the patients. The provider of actual psychotherapy, if any, varied. You may note the medical bias to this approach, with the psychiatrist as head and the use of words such as mental "illness" and "patients."

The team approach survives today in many agencies and in mental hospitals. Decisions may be made in a more egalitarian fashion today, and psychologists and social workers may be more involved in providing psychotherapy and counseling than in earlier years. More members have been added to the team, including psychiatric nurses, MFCCs, speech therapists, occupational therapists, art therapists, and paraprofessional counselors. Today, clinical psychologists in mental hospitals and in community agencies generally work in departments of psychology, rather than in departments of psychiatry as before, and therefore they may have more independence and status than in earlier years of the team approach.

Even in private practice, cooperation among the different professions is common. A psychologist in private practice may work with a psychiatrist in order to obtain medication or hospitalization for clients when necessary. A psychiatrist may make referrals to a psychologist when patients need assessment or a special kind of treatment. Psychologists, social workers, and MFCCs may refer clients to each other when the clients' problems are outside their areas of expertise or when clients are unable to afford their fees.

Actual Practice

Actual practice may depart from the ideal model just described, and the following section attempts to give a realistic and concrete picture of what the professional practice of psychology is like. The licensing and certification laws of most states explicitly state what psychologists may do. In 1987, the APA approved a revised Model Act for State Licensure of Psychologists, which serves as a model for state laws. This act's definition of the practice of psychology gives a fairly complete description of the roles of psychologists:

> The practice of psychology is defined as the observation, description, evaluation, interpretation, and modification of human behavior by the application of psychological principles, methods, and procedures, for the purpose of preventing or eliminating symptomatic, maladaptive, or undesired behavior and of enhancing interpersonal relationships, work and life adjustment, personal effectiveness, behavioral health, and mental health. The practice of psychology includes, but is not limited to, psychological testing and the evaluation or assessment of personal characteristics, such as intelligence, personality, abilities, interests, aptitudes, and neuropsychological functioning; counseling, psychoanalysis, psychotherapy, hypnosis, biofeedback, and behavior

analysis and therapy; diagnosis and treatment of mental and emotional disorder or disability, alcoholism and substance abuse, disorders of habit or conduct, as well as of the psychological aspects of physical illness, accident, injury, or disability; and psychoeducational evaluation, therapy, remediation, and consultation. Psychological services may be rendered to individuals, families, groups, and the public. The practice of psychology shall be construed within the meaning of this definition without regard to whether payment is received for services rendered. (APA, 1987, p. 2)

There are many different types of employment available to psychologists. Clinical psychologists work in private practice and in mental health agencies. They also work in universities, hospitals, prisons, schools, managed health care organizations, counseling centers, government agencies, halfway houses, nursing homes, police departments, the military, and private companies and businesses. Psychologists are involved in Employee Assistance Programs (EAPs), in which businesses retain mental health professionals to provide treatment of disturbed or troublesome employees, as a way to improve company functioning and profits. The settings in which psychologists find employment are constantly changing and growing.

Psychotherapy and Counseling   In both private and institutional practice, psychologists engage in a variety of types of psychotherapy and counseling, the theories and techniques of which are discussed in detail throughout this book. In addition to individual, group, marriage, and family therapy, the types of interventions clinicians may use include behavior modification, biofeedback, cognitive retraining and rehabilitation, environmental consultation and design, psychoanalysis, and hypnosis, according to their training and expertise. Although it is widely accepted today that psychotherapy may be brief or long term, psychologists introduced shorter forms of psychotherapy than long-term psychoanalysis, which was the only form of therapy available in earlier decades. Some modern interventions require only one or two sessions, but while short-term therapies are emphasized today, long-term psychotherapy is still available, especially for those who can afford to pay for it themselves.

Assessment   In addition to doing psychotherapy and other interventions, clinical psychologists engage in assessment of the psychological factors associated with mental, physical, behavioral, and emotional disorders and of other aspects of human functioning. They utilize interviews, behavioral assessments, and observation, and they are qualified to administer, score, and interpret a variety of tests designed to assess psychopathology, personality development, aptitudes, and intellectual and cognitive functioning. One major difference between the practice of clinical psychology and that of psychiatry is that psychologists are the only MHPs adequately trained in the administration and interpretation of certain psychological tests. Both psychiatry and MFCCs have developed their own tests and use some psychlgical tests, so this distinction may blur.

Teaching and Research   Some psychologists engage in university teaching and research, as well as or instead of assessment and treatment. Working in a university setting may involve teaching courses such as abnormal psychology, introduction to clinical psychology, counseling theory, and many other possibilities. Advising students regarding their course work and their careers, supervising students in fieldwork placements, and supervising student research are also involved. While evaluation research is often conducted in clinical settings, most psychological research is conducted at universities. Research may require writing grant applications and even political lobbying in order to obtain funds necessary to carry out the research, as well as designing measurements and experiments. Some psychologists pursue research careers outside of universities; they direct and conduct research in a variety of government and business settings.

Consultation   Consultation may occasionally be done by professors or therapists or as a full-time private practice by other types of psychologists. By consulting with, advising, and teaching specific skills to such people as teachers or the police, psychologists can help them help many other people, more than a psychologist could help individually. Consultation may be used for mental health goals, as in teaching pediatricians how to recognize child abuse or teaching parents how to modify their children's negative behaviors. Consulting with industry may involve helping businesses organize themselves more effectively, working with management in order to improve company communication, or teaching businesses ways to improve employee morale or reduce employee problems such as absenteeism or alcoholism.

Administration   All psychologists must engage, at least occasionally, in administration. Many people find such tasks aversive, and these skills are rarely formally taught in graduate school. Psychologists in private practice must keep case notes, write assessment reports, bill clients, bill insurance companies, obtain malpractice insurance, deal with the licensing board, and keep financial records. Those working for agencies may not have to do their own billing, but they will have to keep case notes and write a variety of reports to meet the requirements of the agency or its funding sources. Child abuse reporting laws, custody evaluations requiring court testimony, victim assistance laws, changes in Medicare regulations, and many other situations require administration and documentation. Psychologists who direct agencies or their programs will find themselves doing a great deal of paperwork in order to meet legal requirements and to obtain and retain grants and funds. They may find themselves constantly embroiled in struggles with regulatory and funding agencies, and at times, in political lobbying in order to maintain government funding, which is constantly threatened with cuts. Research and university psychologists not only write grant reports; they must also administer them if they receive them. Documentation and careful records are crucial in research.

Administration is a part of the real world of the professional psychologist. Another, the ability to write well, is an advantage to all professional psychologists. Researchers must publish papers, clinicians must write assessment reports, therapists must write treatment reports, and so on. Perhaps even more important, obtaining funding requires writing grant applications both for research and for mental health clinics. Well-written grants are more likely to be funded, and well-written reports and articles reflect favorably on the profession.

Psychology in the Public Forum   One of the advantages of psychology as a career is the possibility to do one or several of many different, interesting activities, from teaching, research, and consultation to psychotherapy, assessment, and community work. As new psychological techniques are developed and as people increasingly seek psychological solutions for their problems, the diversity of psychotherapy and other psychological services offered by MHPs should increase. However, Albee (1970) has long argued that professional psychology should be working to put itself out of business by focusing on the prevention of psychological disorders. He believes that psychologists should stop wasting their expertise providing inefficient and costly psychotherapy to a few individuals, and should focus instead on "giving psychology away" by teaching the public how to help themselves.

In this vein, psychology has become highly involved in the public forum. Rather than emphasizing individual psychotherapy, professional psychology may help more people by educating the public regarding its research findings and its methods, by becoming involved in court proceedings that affect people's mental health, such as cases involving sexual harrassment, and by lobbying the government to alter or enact laws that affect the public. For example, Siegel (1983) suggested that the United States should shift the focus of its handling of the crime problem from capturing and punishing the criminals to providing psychological treatment for the inevitable victims. Weiss (1983) urged psychology to move into the field of behavioral toxicology and environmental health science, including research, assessment, treatment, prevention, and education related to environmental hazards that affect behavior. As psychology develops a solid base of knowledge relevant to issues affecting the public's health and well-being, it has the responsibility to become involved in the public forum and to contribute to society's attempts to address social problems.

As professional psychology grows and becomes increasingly involved in issues of importance to the public, it finds itself both enmeshed in social issues and constrained by social forces. For example, competition between psychology and medicine and among the many mental health professions is acted out through laws and insurance company regulations regarding payment of fees. Many other laws and court rulings affect the practice of psychology. The right of psychologists to pursue psychoanalytic training and the right of MFCCs to use psychological tests are both the result of lawsuits and court rulings that state that to deny psychoanalytic training or the use of tests to certain groups is to engage in unfair restraint of trade and is illegal under antitrust laws. Child abuse reporting laws involve therapists who work with children in the court system. Laws governing the health care industry may mandate mental health coverage or not, may require freedom of choice in the type of therapists or not, and will otherwise directly affect the ability of psychologists to make a living.

As with administration, a possibly unanticipated task is added to the activities of professional psychologists: to keep up to date on a wide variety of legal developments and to be willing to engage in political action or lawsuits to change laws and court rulings that are detrimental to the public or the profession.

PSYCHOTHERAPY INTEGRATION

At the same time as differing psychological theories and techniques are proliferating, there is a growing movement to integrate psychotherapy, to synthesize psychological knowledge instead of specializing. There are three basic approaches to psychotherapy integration. One approach, the **common factors approach,** is to search for the commonalities present in all the therapeutic approaches. For example, it has been suggested that all therapies instill hope, impart information, and model interpersonal skills, while research indicates that all good therapists share such characteristics as warmth and empathy. A second approach to psychotherapy integration, **technical eclecticism,** involves pragmatically selecting techniques that work from all the different approaches, as exemplified by the "multimodal therapy" of Arnold Lazarus. The third approach, **theoretical integration,** is to combine theories, exemplified by an early attempt by Dollard and Miller (1950) to recast psychoanalysis in learning theory terms. Some integrative theorists attempt the difficult task of developing a new, overarching theory that can account for the other psychotherapy theories and unify them all. In Chapter 16 we make our contribution to the common factors and this last approach.

Briefly, we note that all psychotherapies face a common problem, which we call the problem of "access." The problem is that psychological change is difficult. Of course, if it were easy, there would be no need for therapists. Despite saying they want to change and making great efforts to change, people constantly find that they cannot. It appears that these efforts to change do not access or get into and become part of the individual's personal system of thoughts, emotions, and motivations.

One way of understanding the access problem is to imagine the personality as composed of at least two parts: the part that wants to change and the part that gets in the way of change. The therapist's challenge is to speak to, or access, the part of the personality that wants to change and help it, while circumventing the part that doesn't change.

All psychotherapy theories split the personality into parts. These parts are given different labels in different theories, such as id, ego, and superego in psychoanalysis; or cognition, emotion, and behavior in cognitive-learning theory. Modern psychoneurological research suggests that the brain may be composed of a loosely connected set of modules, each with its own organization and way of behaving, so it is possible that these theoretical divisions of the personality have a basis in the physiology of the brain. The psychotherapy theories differ as to which parts of the personality are considered to be enabling or hindering change. For example, psychoanalysis considers the conscious personality to be the part that wants to change and conflicts in the unconscious part to be in the way of change. Other theories, such as client-centered therapy, consider the conscious personality to be the problem, while the individual's ignored or "unconscious" emotions would aid change.

Briefly, we theorize that all psychotherapy techniques are attempts to get around the part of the personality or situation that resists change and to access the part of the personality that favors change. For example, the psychoanalytic technique of free association can be seen as an attempt to sneak into the resistant unconscious and to make its contents conscious. Client-centered therapy's use of empathy can be seen as a way to focus on and empower the individual's ignored emotional side while avoiding the disabling "shoulds" and self-criticism of the person's conscious cognitions. Hypnosis may be viewed as a technique designed to confuse the logical mind so that suggestions can be given directly to other parts of the personality. These examples should become clear as we discuss the different theories in the following chapters.

We discuss psychotherapy integration in Chapter 16, but in the chapters before that we encourage you to try to discover for yourself the similarities and commonalities in the different therapeutic approaches.

IN CONCLUSION

We have tried to give a broad picture of the field in this introductory chapter, but an in-depth understanding of professional psychology requires reading the entire book. Let us give you a preview of what to expect.

Chapter 2 covers the history of psychology as an applied profession. Professional psychology is not a very old profession, and it evolved to its present state because of specific social forces. A review of its historical development may explain some of the current controversies in the field and predict its future development. Chapters 3, 4, and 5 cover diagnosis and assessment, including theories and techniques of measurement and important developments in the field. Chapters 6–14 describe the major therapeutic approaches, perhaps the topic of most interest to our readers. The theories and techniques of such different approaches as psychoanalysis, client-centered and experiential therapies, the behavioral and cognitive approaches, and group and relationship therapies make for fascinating and challenging reading. Chapter 15 addresses the important topic of research in psychotherapy, and Chapters 16–18 cover psychotherapy integration, diversity and contemporary treatment issues, and legal and ethical issues and the future.

We trust that by now you have a good idea of the scope of modern clinical and counseling psychology. We believe that professional psychology is an exciting field precisely because it is constantly changing in response to important social issues. It is part of the process by which we as a people at this point in history are determining the meaning and direction of our lives.

BIBLIOGRAPHY

Albee, G. W. (1970). The uncertain future of clinical psychology. *American Psychologist, 25,* 1071–1080.

American Psychological Association. (1987, February). *Model act for state licensure of psychologists.* Washington, DC: Author.

American Psychological Association. (1992, May). APA continues to refine its ethics code. *The APA Monitor, 23,* 38–42.

American Psychological Association Division 12. (1992). *Clinical psychology.* Oklahoma City, OK: Division of Clinical Psychology Central Office.

Bickman, L., & Ellis, H. C. (Eds.). (1990). *Preparing psychologists for the 21st century: Proceedings of the National Conference on Graduate Education in Psychology.* Hillsdale, NJ: Erlbaum.

Cattell, Raymond B. (1983). Let's end the duel. *American Psychologist, 38,* 769–776.

Dollard, J., & Miller, N. E. (1950). *Personality and psychotherapy.* New York: McGraw-Hill.

Ellis, H. C. (1992). Graduate education in psychology: Past, present, and future. *American Psychologist, 47,* 570–576.

Fagan, T. K. (1986). School psychology's dilemma: Reappraising solutions and directing attention to the future. *American Psychologist, 41,* 851–861.

Fitzgerald, L. F., & Osipow, S. H. (1986). An occupational analysis of counseling psychology: How special is the specialty? *American Psychologist, 41,* 535–544.

Knesper, D. J., Pagnucco, D. J., & Wheeler, J. R. C. (1985). Similarities and differences across mental health services providers and practice settings in the United States. *American Psychologist, 40,* 1352–1369.

Kohout, J., Wicherski, M., & Pion, G. (1991). *Characteristics of graduate departments of psychology: 1988–89.* Washington, DC: American Psychological Association Education Directorate.

Oskamp, S. (1988). Nontraditional employment opportunities for applied psychologists. *American Psychologist, 43,* 484–485.

Shakow, D. (1949). *Report of the Commission on Clinical Training.* Washington, DC: American Psychological Association.

Siegel, M. (1983). Crime and violence in America: The victims. *American Psychologist, 38,* 1267–1273.

Taube, C. A., Burns, B. J., & Kessler, L. (1984). Patients of psychiatrists and psychologists in office-based practice: 1980. *American Psychologist, 39,* 1435–1447.

Watkins, C. W., Lopez, F. G., Campbell, V. L., & Himmell, C. D. (1986). Counseling psychology and clinical psychology: Some preliminary comparative data. *American Psychologist, 41,* 581–582.

Weiss, B. (1983). Behavioral toxicology and environmental health science: Opportunity and challenge for psychology. *American Psychologist, 38,* 1174–1187.

CHAPTER
2

Historical Development of Professional Psychology

Henri D. was a 30-year-old, unmarried farmer who worked hard on his family's farm. During the previous year, he had gradually become more withdrawn and uncommunicative. Now he stayed in bed most days, face turned to the wall, unable to work, unwilling to talk. He had difficulty sleeping and paced the floors at night, occasionally wringing his hands and murmuring that he was damned. No one could determine what was bothering him, and his family and neighbors became quite anxious to have an explanation for his behavior.

In cases of melancholy . . . I conclude it is merely the work of the devil. Men are possessed by the devil in two ways; corporally or spiritually. Those whom he possesses corporally, as mad people, he has permission from God to vex and agitate, but he has no power over their souls. (Martin Luther, *Colloquia Mensalia*, quoted in Coleman, 1972)

As is already clear from Chapter 1, professional psychology currently exists in a complex social matrix, and it developed historically from a complex set of social forces. Examining the history of the field will help explain why the practice of professional psychology is organized the way it is and why certain issues are important and still problematic. Understanding the history of the field may help us predict and plan for the future.

Modern professional psychology evolved as the synthesis of two distinct trends in the history of Europe and the United States. Its current theories and practices, its controversial issues, and its status as a field of endeavor can be more easily understood by examining those two historical forces. One trend is the development of psychology as an independent academic discipline within universities. The other is the failure of other institutions and professions to deal adequately with deviant members of society. These two forces came together in the individualistic, pragmatic United States of the twentieth century to develop a unique scientific and applied field, professional psychology.

ACADEMIC PSYCHOLOGY

Modern academic psychology developed in Western Europe, and thus, this history will emphasize Europe and the United States. However, the kinds of questions that the academic discipline of psychology studies have interested individuals and scholars of all cultures since ancient times, and complex bodies of philosophy have been developed by other cultures to deal with what we label psychological issues. In Europe, the Middle Ages question of "What is the relation between the pure immortal soul and the corrupt mortal body?" became in recent centuries "What is the relation between the mind and the body?" This fascinating question is still studied in fields such as neuropsychology. How does the mind work? What motivates people to behave the way they do? How can we explain deviant behavior? What can we do about it? How can we all get along together? These are ancient questions of interest to modern psychology and to most people.

Among some ancient peoples, gods and demons were believed to cause everything and provided the answers to the above questions. In the early Christian era, the conflict between God and Satan and the concept of sin provided answers. After universities were founded in Europe in the fifteenth and sixteenth centuries, secular scholars as well as priests began to study these ancient questions, and academic departments of philosophy were formed.

After the Renaissance, the world entered a period of rapid social change brought on by the expansion of knowledge, increases in the population, urbanization, and the Industrial Revolution. Religion no longer seemed adequate to provide the guideposts needed. Science emerged with what seemed to be more adequate explanations for many phenomena through the scientific method of empirical observation, measurement, and experimentation. There was hope that the method would eventually solve all the questions that have long perplexed humankind.

In the nineteenth century, these ancient questions were still in the province of philosophy departments of universities. In the last part of that century, a new discipline, psychology, broke away from philosophy to become a separate academic specialty. It charged itself with studying the same types of problems as philosophers, but by applying the new scientific method. Some scholars in the new field viewed humans as just another natural phenomenon, not special creations in God's image, and others saw them as machines, but psychologists agreed that the nature of humanity and the nature of the mind could best be discovered through empirical measurement and experimentation, not through metaphysics or philosophical argument.

Psychology as an experimental science began in the mid-nineteenth century with the psychophysical experiments of Fechner and Helmholtz in Germany. However, the year 1879 is the generally accepted date for the birth of academic psychology. In that year, Wilhelm Wundt established the first independent psychology laboratory in Leipzig, Germany. Wundt argued that the subject matter of psychology was experience, not the relation of the body and soul, and that the mind alone was a legitimate object of scientific study. While Wundt is considered the first "great mind" in psychology, other scholars at that time were also doing work that became part of psychology. In 1869, Francis Galton in England began his study and measurement of individual differences in attributes and abilities. And in 1875, William James, considered the first American psychologist, equipped part of a small laboratory at Harvard for the study of mental associations.

Even though James began his work before Wundt opened his laboratory, psychology became established as a separate academic discipline in the United States somewhat later than in Europe. Most early American psychologists traveled to Europe for graduate study in psychology. Nevertheless, psychological topics were taught in schools and universities in the United States throughout the nineteenth century under topics such as moral philosophy. For example, *Elements of the Philosophy of Mind, Applied to the Developement of Thought and Feeling* by Elizabeth Secord was published in 1840. However, the first full-scale psychology laboratory in the United States was established in 1883 by G. Stanley Hall at Johns Hopkins University. He also established the first psychology journal, the *American Journal of Psychology,* in 1887. In 1888, James M. Cattell at the University of Pennsylvania held the first professorship in psychology. In 1890, William James published the first book officially devoted to psychology, *The Principles of Psychology.* Hall founded the American Psychological Association (APA) in 1892, and by that time, American universities had established about 20 psychology laboratories.

American psychology as an academic discipline has continued to emphasize the empiricism and experimentation of the scientific method that helped create it, but it has experienced several major shifts in the focus of its subject matter over the years. Early psychology was concerned with the structure and contents of the mind, a view called **structuralism.** Then the focus of psychology became **functionalism,** the study of the functions of the mind, what it does and how. About 1913, the approach called **behaviorism** broke with previous positions. John B. Watson, a major proponent of this view, argued that the proper study of psychology was observable behavior, that the mind cannot be observed. Pavlov's studies in Russia on the conditioned reflex bolstered Watson's position. Like the times in the United States, Watson's behaviorism was mechanistic, materialistic, and positivistic. By the 1920s, behaviorism had largely replaced the study of the mind and individual experience in academic psychology in the United States. B. F. Skinner carried behaviorism further, from the 1940s into the 1980s, with his arguments for strict empiricism and the objective, atheoretical description of behavior without any reference to a mind.

Although it always emphasized experimental empiricism, academic psychology has had to deal with the fact that its graduates have continued since the beginning to find employment in the applications of psychology. Professors, researchers, and students interested in applied psychology were considered suspect, and distinctions in prestige and even promotion were made between the "hard" scientists involved in experimental psychology and the "soft" psychologists interested in practice. This attitude favoring hard science is still evident today, although the scientist-practitioner model described in Chapter 1 and discussed later in this chapter helped legitimize the status of professional psychology.

In recent years, the mind has crept back into academic psychology. Albert Bandura, a prominent psychologist, developed social learning theory in the 1960s, which added the concept of imitation and the influence of other people to behavioristic learning theory. In the 1970s, Bandura began to write about possible internal, or cognitive, variables that affect behavior and learning. He contributed to the development of a currently important body of theory and research called cognitive behaviorism. Swiss biologist Jean Piaget's influential research on cognitive development in infants and children also contributed to the new emphasis on cognition, which is a process of the mind. The growth in numbers and status of clinical psychology and psychotherapy also helped turn attention to the mind. The old conflict over whether the proper study of psychology is the mind or behavior appears to be reaching a synthesis that psychology studies both, that cognition and behavior are related and affect each other.

SOCIETY'S TREATMENT OF ITS DEVIANT MEMBERS

For far longer than academic departments of psychology have existed in universities, society has had to deal with its deviant members. The history of how society has treated its deviants interacted with the developments in academic psychology in the twentieth century to produce a new applied profession, clinical psychology, in the United States, where the individualistic science fit in well with the individualistic values of the culture.

Who Is Deviant?

People who do not conform to the behavior or beliefs of the majority of the members of society have always existed. For the sake of discussion, let us divide such deviant or nonconforming members of society into two types, the disturbed and the disturbing. Disturbing people are bothersome to other people. They may hold politically radical views and foment revolution; they may get drunk and fail to work; they may steal. The way our society is organized in the United States today, extremely bothersome people are handled by the legal system. Laws are supposed to protect the life, well-being, and property of all the members of the community from the harmful acts of the criminal few. The most common method of social control of such people is imprisonment as a form of punishment, isolation, or rehabilitation.

There are also disturbed people. Other people, or they themselves, think that there is "something wrong" with them, but no one is quite sure what it is. They suffer from uncontrollable urges to kill themselves; they are severely anxious for no reason; they see or hear things that others say are not real; they suffer paralysis or weakness when others say they are well; they are troubled by intrusive thoughts; they feel compelled to perform certain acts over and over. In the United States today, such individuals are viewed as being psychologically disordered and in need of treatment by various mental health professionals. In previous ages, disturbed people were sometimes tolerated or even venerated as "seers," but often they were killed, tortured, and locked away, although without doubt, many such individuals were protected and cared for by their families, just as many are today. Our present society has developed a number of ways of dealing with the disturbed, including voluntary or involuntary hospitalization, psychotropic drugs, electroconvulsive shock treatments, group therapy, individual psychotherapy, cognitive behavior modification, psychoanalysis, counseling, pastoral counseling, and medical consultation.

Perhaps the most difficult cases for society are the disturbed disturbing people who don't do anything bad enough to merit prison and yet resist or seem unsuitable for psychological treatment. What of the schizophrenic who stands in the middle of the freeway trying to direct traffic because God told him to? What of the alcoholic executive who functions well in the morning but is drunk all evening? What of the psychopathic person who continually exploits, deceives, and abandons those who love him or her? How is society to help or control the behavior of such individuals, especially if they deny having any problems? As institutions such as the church, the school, the family, the workplace, and even the prison system fail to help or change these people, the community may turn to the mental health professions for solutions. In recent decades, it seems that such social control problems are increasingly defined as being suitable for treatment by the mental health professions.

From Supernatural to Medical Model

The history of how society has arrived at ways of dealing with disturbed and disturbing people is fascinating. We can safely assume that what we call mental illness or emotional disturbance today has always existed. Although described in different terminology according to the times, examples of mentally disturbed individuals abound in history. King Saul of Israel suffered terrible bouts of depression and tried to kill his own son. The Roman emperor Caligula was grandiose and delusional, claimed to be a god, and slaughtered hundreds of people, including the beloved sister he married. King George III was depressed and manic in cycles, and his erratic behavior lost Britain the American colonies. Their behavior as described in whatever terms by their contemporaries would clearly be called symptomatic of mental disorder today.

Demonology Many early peoples, including the early Greeks and Romans, believed that disturbance was caused by the invasion of spirits, gods, or demons, and priests were viewed as the appropriate professionals to treat disturbed individuals. Hippocrates disagreed with the prevailing view and argued that disturbance was due to natural, not supernatural, causes. He believed that most disorders were due to brain pathology, while hysteria in women was due to the wandering of the womb to other parts of the body. He recommended humane treatment for the victims of brain pathology and marriage for the victims of wandering wombs.

Plato wrote that mental disturbance was partly organic, partly moral, and partly divine. Anticipating a modern idea, he believed that dreams represented denied desires. Aristotle raised the possibility that disturbance was due to purely psychological causes, but rejected this hypothesis in favor of organic causes. Galen believed that the causes of disturbance could be either physical or mental.

Although the belief in natural causes of mental disturbance persisted, many Europeans returned to the model of **demonology** in the Dark Ages. They believed that the causes of mental disturbance and some other forms of deviance were wickedness, possession by a devil, or witchcraft, and they returned such problems to the province of religious experts. In the early Middle Ages the clergy treated disturbed individuals by prayer, the laying on of hands, and other relatively benign measures. The monasteries were refuges for the mentally ill, who were usually treated kindly. In the latter part of the Middle Ages the treatment of disturbed people often involved cruelty, torture, and execution.

The end of the Middle Ages was a chaotic period in European history. Natural and manmade disasters abounded—war, plague, the breakup of the feudal system. People were confused and fearful, and they needed explanations for the distressing events around them. The Inquisition, witchcraft, and demonology at least provided explanations and guidelines for what to do. If members of the community were disturbed or disturbing, it was natural to suspect them of practicing witchcraft or of being victims of witchcraft. The suspected persons were then tortured until they confessed to whatever the community expected to hear, usually implicating other members of the community, who were then tortured and confessed, and so on.

Although not all of the victims of the Inquisition were mentally disturbed, some were, and we may wonder how anyone could conceive of torturing an unfortunate disturbed person (or anyone, for that matter). If it is unquestionably believed by the religious experts and all the members of the community that the disordered person is possessed by an evil demon, and if helpful and concerned people want to save that individual's immortal soul, then it becomes logical to make the body such an uncomfortable and miserable place that the demon will want to leave. The person was tortured for his or her own good. The disturbed individual may have welcomed the treatment, for it is common for some severely disturbed people to believe that they are guilty, worthless, and deserving of punishment. This historical example demonstrates the power of what people think, or cognition. It may also suggest the importance of scientific empiricism.

Nineteenth-Century Reform   From the sixteenth through the nineteenth centuries, the care of the mentally disturbed was transferred from the monasteries and dungeons to asylums run by charities and local governments. The conditions in the asylums were not much better than in the dungeons. Inmates were chained, poorly fed, exhibited to the public for a fee, and subjected to various "treatments" such as hot pokers, cold baths, and straitjackets. It seems that the majority of asylum inmates were the poor, violent people, or unwanted but undivorceable wives.

By the eighteenth century, some priests and scholars began to argue openly against the prevailing views and to advocate more humane treatment for disturbed persons. At the end of the eighteenth century, French physician Philippe Pinel was able to convince important people to allow him to try an experiment at the large asylum in Paris: to release the inmates from restraints and to treat them with kindness and decent food and conditions. These changes worked wonders, and most inmates improved dramatically. At the same time in England, William Tuke established a country house where disturbed individuals lived, worked, and rested in a kindly religious atmosphere. And in the United States, reformer Benjamin Rush (1745–1813) encouraged humane treatment of the mentally disordered.

By the nineteenth century, writers and intellectuals were proclaiming the dignity, worth, and equality of all men (only a few included women). The benefits of the scientific revolution were becoming observable in the form of new machines, better hygiene and health care, and improved living conditions for some. In short, the times were changing, and reform was in the air, from abolition to temperance and women's rights.

Dorothea Dix (1802–1887) was an important nineteenth-century reformer. Through extensive traveling and zealous campaigning between 1841 and 1881, she improved conditions in prisons, almshouses, and asylums throughout the United States and Europe. Singlehandedly, she convinced charities and state governments to build at least 32 new mental hospitals in the United States for the care of the retarded and disturbed. She was particularly interested in the care of the "deserving poor," the indigent mentally ill, although the state hospital superintendents, then called alienists, were more interested in attracting affluent lunatics. Dorothea Dix was ahead of her time in giving legislatures detailed analyses of the hidden costs of not building hospitals and treating the needy.

Another contribution to efforts to reform asylums was made by Clifford Beers. Beers was forcibly hospitalized near the turn of the century, and in 1908 he published a book, *A Mind That Found Itself,* in which he described his terrible experiences. He helped form the National Committee for Mental Hygiene and served as its secretary for 30 years.

During the early and middle nineteenth century in the United States, "moral treatment" was used in some mental hospitals, led by the Reverend Dr. Woodward of Worcester State Hospital. The advocates of moral treatment believed that the mentally disturbed were normal people with temporary problems who would benefit from a favorable environment, emotional support, and being involved in work. Recovery rates for moral treatment were reported to be between 70 and 90 percent in the early part of the century, although these figures were later considered inflated in order to obtain funding, a familiar modern problem.

In the latter part of the century, the effectiveness of moral treatment and other treatments in mental hospitals declined because of a number of factors. A major factor was overcrowding, as funds were cut and large numbers of poor immigrants were consigned to the hospitals. The influx of immigrants and the disruptions that accompanied industrialization and expansion also contributed to the difficult social conditions that increased the numbers of individuals who were dealt with by hospitalization. The growing evidence of the ineffectiveness of moral treatment and the mental hospitals set the stage for a new set of authorities to claim the ability to solve the problems of the disturbed, and the medical model of "mental illness" gained credence at the end of the nineteenth century.

The Medical Model   The model of scientific medicine appeared to be a useful way to define and discover solutions to the suffering of the disturbed. Some also saw it as a way to reduce the stigma attached to psychological disturbance. The medical model first takes note of symptoms, such as fever or red spots. The study of symptoms reveals that certain symptoms often appear together in syndromes, such as red spots appearing just after the onset of fever. The study of syndromes may reveal a specific disease process, such as measles. Once a disease can be diagnosed, then its cause, such as a measles virus, may be investigated and discovered. Only after the cause is known can a prevention or treatment, such as a measles vaccine, be developed. Accurate diagnosis must, in this logical system, precede treatment.

Physician Emil Kraepelin (1856–1926) developed the first diagnostic system for mental disorders at the turn of the century. Kraepelin believed that each type of mental illness was a separate and distinct disorder with an organic cause and that the course and outcome of each mental illness were as predetermined as those of measles. Using only his own keen powers of observation and organization, he developed a precise and comprehensive system of diagnostic categories that is still used with some modifications today.

The medical model of mental illness is probably the most widely accepted view of disturbed people today. Its wide acceptance is due to its great success with numerous diseases that have long plagued humankind and to the credibility and power of the medical profession. Because of the success and power of medicine, there is a tendency to define increasing numbers of human problems as medical disorders. To return to an earlier example, at various points in our history excessive drinking has been viewed as acceptable, a sin, a crime, and a disease. When moral exhortation and Prohibition failed to control excessive drinkers, people began to view alcoholism as a disease and to turn to the medical profession to control drinking through medical "treatment." In a similar manner, previous views of disturbed people were not successful in helping or changing them, and a disease model led to hopes for a "cure." Another explanation for the wide acceptance of the medical model of mental illness can be found in the tremendous influence of Sigmund Freud, who was a physician, although he himself believed that his form of psychotherapy should be practiced independently of medicine.

From Medical to Psychological Model: Sigmund Freud

Sigmund Freud (1856–1939) developed the first comprehensive theory of personality development and psychopathology. His influence on twentieth-century thinking has been equated with that of Marx. The impact of his ideas and extensive writings can be seen in the widespread acceptance of some of his ideas today, ideas that are almost taken for granted, such as that childhood experiences affect adult personality or that we defend ourselves against certain thoughts and feelings. He developed the theory and therapeutic techniques of **classical psychoanalysis** (described in Chapter 6), a therapy that survives today in both its original form and in numerous variations, covered in Chapter 7.

Early in his medical career, Freud intended to become a neurologist and pursue research. He went to Paris to study with the famous neurologist Jean Charcot and his student Pierre Janet. Charcot treated those with **hysteria,** such as women with paralyzed healthy limbs or inexplicable yet disabling pains, through hypnosis and suggestion, with impressive success. Back in Vienna, Freud watched his friend and colleague Josef Breuer treat a patient diagnosed as a hysteric with daily sessions of talking and hypnosis, again with what he considered to be impressively successful results. After some time this patient, known as Anna O., began to talk of sexual fantasies regarding Dr. Breuer during her hypnotic trances. At this point, Breuer abruptly terminated treatment, which Freud thought was a mistake. Freud argued that the patient's expression of feelings for the doctor was a necessary part of psychotherapy. In 1895, Breuer and Freud published *Studies in Hysteria,* in which the concept of **transference** in the therapist-patient relationship was described.

Soon most of Freud's medical practice was composed of neurotic women seeking relief. He began by using hypnosis, but soon abandoned it in favor of having the patient simply talk while in a relaxed state on a couch. He directed patients to engage in **free association,** that is, to say freely whatever entered their minds. He found that childhood memories and sexual thoughts were invariably reported. (The sexual content is perhaps unsurprising, given that his women clients were lying on a couch talking intimately to a man!) Freud discovered that when the patient could not free associate, some especially painful memory was later reported. He noticed that patients were helped to free associate and to uncover important material when they discussed their dreams. In 1900, he published his classic work, *The Interpretation of Dreams.* In this book, he presented his theory of neurosis, his concept of the unconscious, and his belief that dreams symbolize repressed desire—conclusions he had deduced from the data of his clinical cases. Although Freud was brilliant in synthesizing and applying these concepts, he did not simply invent them, for ideas about psychology, dreams, and the unconscious were being discussed by the European intellectuals of his day.

At first, Freud thought that neurosis was due to a genuine sexual trauma early in childhood, such as viewing the primal scene of parental intercourse or being sexually molested. These ideas met with considerable resistance and scorn from the medical community, and Freud himself was horrified by them. After a long period of self-analysis, he arrived at the insight that the sexual traumas and memories of his patients might be fantasies. Although somewhat relieved, he was distraught that his theory of neurosis was destroyed. However, he soon came to the conclusion that fantasy can have just as much impact, possibly more, on the small child's developing psyche as real events, and he elaborated his theory of neurosis to include the effect of unconscious conflicts as expressed in fantasies, dreams, and imaginary "screen memories." In recent years, some psychoanalytic writers and other scholars have gone back to Freud's original idea and believe that Freud's patients' difficulties were due to genuine sexual traumas. Particularly in the case of Anna O., many now believe that she was actually molested by her father (Masson, 1984).

In 1909, the ambitious American psychologist G. Stanley Hall daringly invited Freud to speak at Clark University in Massachusetts. He gave five highly influential lectures, now considered classics, which were published in 1910 in the *American Journal of Psychology.* In the United States at that time, only a few people in academic psychology were interested in Freud's ideas; most psychologists and physicians ignored him or considered him a quack. However, the public found Freudian ideas fascinating, and by 1920, over 200 books on psychoanalysis had been published in the United States alone. In the two decades from 1919 until his death in London from cancer of the jaw in 1939, Freud's prominence increased, and there was widespread acceptance of psychoanalytic theory, both by the public and in the psychiatric community.

Academic psychology, on the other hand, continued to view psychoanalysis with even more suspicion than it did applied psychology. Some even considered it a cult to be eradicated. As a young science, psychology felt threatened by the greater

Unbeknownst to Most Historians, Pavlov Got His First Idea from Mrs. Pavlov.

prominence of psychoanalysis. Academic psychology and psychoanalysis developed during the same time, but they were unrelated in aims, methods, and subject matter. The aim of early academic psychology was the scientific study of the normal mind; that of psychoanalysis was the treatment of disturbed individuals. The method of psychology was scientific experimentation; that of psychoanalysis was observation of clinical cases. The subject matter of psychology was normal experience and behavior; that of psychoanalysis was abnormal psychology. Academic psychology finally asserted itself as the true scientific authority by conducting experiments on psychoanalytic hypotheses, so as to have the ability to pass judgment on them. Eventually, just as professional psychology was accepted by academic psychology, psychoanalytic ideas were gradually incorporated into the field. Now there is even a Division of Psychoanalysis (39) in the American Psychological Association.

Psychoanalytic theory was a historical turning point from the late nineteenth-century medical view that the cause of disturbance was organic malfunction of the body to the twentieth-century psychological view that at least some of the causes were to be found in the mind. Once this view was widely accepted, the individualistic United States was ready for the development of clinical psychology. As the twentieth century nears its end, the acceptance of psychological causes of mental disturbance is also waning, and the emphasis is shifting back to biological causes and models of psychological disorders.

Clinical Psychology

Although psychology as an academic discipline began in Europe, psychology rapidly expanded in the United States while remaining a relatively minor area of study in Europe. Clinical psychology developed in the United States, remained an American specialty for decades, and is now exported to Europe and other countries. The popularity of clinical psychology in the United States is partly due to its ability to address certain social problems while preserving the American value of individualism and without necessitating social change.

The end of the nineteenth century found the United States a diverse and prosperous country in certain areas and among certain classes. The country had experienced three decades of official peace after the Civil War. A rapid expansion of the population and a large influx of immigrants allowed the country to be settled from coast to coast. Urbanization and industrialization were underway in all sections of the country. Tendencies toward social reform that had begun with abolitionist, feminist, and temperance movements in the early part of the century had been dissipated in the violence of the Civil War. Cultural values tended toward rugged individualism, competition, and individual achievement. Academic psychology and its scientific study of the individual fit the times well. It only remained for individualistic scientific psychology to be applied to help the casualties of the social forces of the era for clinical psychology to develop as a field.

In 1896, Lightner Witmer established the first psychological clinic at the University of Pennsylvania for the evaluation of children. The founding of this first clinic for psychological services in a university setting established the combined academic and applied approach that is characteristic of clinical psychology. In 1907, Witmer established and edited a journal called *Psychological Clinic.* The *Journal of Abnormal Psychology* also began in 1907, so applied psychologists had two journals for the communication of their ideas and research. About 20 psychological clinics had been established at American universities by 1915. Some included counseling services for students at the universities, but the emphasis was on services for children.

Although clinical psychology flourished in the United States, work in Europe influenced its practice. In 1904, Carl Jung in Switzerland was experimenting with a word association test for the assessment of personality. In 1905, Alfred Binet and Theodore Simon in Paris developed the first intelligence test for children. Swiss psychoanalyst Hermann Rorschach developed his famous inkblot test for the assessment of personality and psychopathology about the same time.

World War I provided a big opportunity for applied psychology to define and prove itself. The U.S. Army needed a way to predict which soldiers would do well and which would not, so that the costs of training and shipping a soldier who would fail could be saved. Psychologists developed the Army Alpha test, the first group test of intelligence. It did a fairly good job of screening recruits. The Army Beta was a non-verbal test for illiterates. At the same time, Robert Woodworth developed the Personal Data Sheet, a pencil-and-paper personality test also useful for screening recruits. By the end of the war, the statistical procedures and standards for establishing the norms, reliability, and validity of psychological tests had been formulated. And by the end of the war, clinical psychology was recognized as a discipline, as reflected in the formation of a clinical section within the American Psychological Association in 1919.

Between the wars, clinical psychology was dominated, as were all mental health professions, by psychoanalysis. The publication of *Counseling and Psychotherapy* by Carl Rogers in 1942 provided the first comprehensive psychological theory and treatment alternative to psychoanalysis, and a framework for clinical psychology to move from assessment into treatment. World War II provided the demand in the form of thousands of returning disturbed soldiers needing treatment. The Veterans Administration provided training funds for clinical psychology.

The professional identity of clinical psychology was solidified in 1949 with the APA conference on graduate education in clinical psychology, held in Boulder, Colorado. Prior to World War II, most early applied psychologists held bachelor's degrees and later, master's degrees. The Boulder conference determined that the degree for a clinical psychologist would now be the Ph.D., with training in both science and practice. The scientist-practitioner model required competence in research, assessment, and psychotherapy.

Counseling Psychology

Counseling psychology shares many of the early roots of clinical psychology and has been subject to the same historical and social forces. The career counseling branch of the field developed in the United States around the turn of the century in response to increasing industrialization and its need for a skilled work force. Frank Parsons is credited with founding the vocational guidance movement. He established the Vocation Bureau in Boston in 1908 and published a book, *Choosing a Profession,* in the same year, followed by *Choosing a Vocation* in 1909. The year 1913 saw the formation of the National Vocational Guidance Association, a precursor to the professional organization of counseling psychology. Parsons emphasized evaluation of individuals coupled with helping them with self-exploration and decision making. As psychological assessment developed through World War I, Parsons included the use of tests in vocational guidance. Partly because of the demand for vocational services created by the Depression, there was a testing boom between the world wars, and many group and individual tests of intelligence, achievement, aptitudes, interests, and personality were developed for use in education and industry.

Vocational guidance began its movement into counseling between the world wars, and as with clinical psychology, World War II provided a major impetus for the growth of the field. In 1942 two books were published that greatly affected counseling psychology: *Counseling and Psychotherapy* by Carl Rogers and *The Dynamics of Vocational Adjustment* by Donald Super. Rogers emphasized helping individuals realize their innate positive potential, and Super conceptualized vocational guidance as involving a developmental, life span process, rather than a single advising event. These works provided the theoretical framework for the application of psychological knowledge and interventions to problems and issues in normal life. World War II provided thousands of returning soldiers needing personal and career counseling, and the Veterans Administration provided training funds to develop needed staff. There were two counseling positions with the V.A., the doctoral-level counseling psychologist (vocational) in the Division of Medicine and Neurology and the subdoctoral counseling psychologist in the Division of Vocational Rehabilitation and Education.

Two conferences helped establish the professional identity of counseling psychology: the Northwestern Conference in 1951 and the Greystone Conference in 1954. These conferences adopted the term *counseling psychology* and developed standards for the training of counseling psychologists. The Division of Counseling Psychology within the APA was formed in 1952. Since then, counseling psychology has grown tremendously, and it shares many theories, research and intervention methods, and values with clinical psychology. We will now turn to a detailed history of the two fields in this century.

PROFESSIONAL PSYCHOLOGY IN THE TWENTIETH CENTURY

The first recognized applied profession in psychology—clinical psychology—was well established in the United States by the end of World War I. Other specialties in professional psychology shared these early roots. World War I provided the initial impetus for the development of professional psychology, but World War II ignited its phenomenal growth in the mid-twentieth century. Growth continued exponentially until the 1980s, when it slowed sharply. In that decade and after, professional psychology became embroiled in a series of interesting professional and social conflicts that presage its role in the twenty-first century.

In order to examine these developments, this century's history of professional psychology will be divided into three topics: assessment, interventions, and professional organizations. A strictly chronological presentation of important historical events is presented in Box 2.1.

Assessment

Psychology's first big public success was assessment. The role of assessment in World War I has already been described. In addition to the short group tests of intelligence and personality for screening soldiers, psychology gained public recognition for its individual intelligence tests for children. While the roots of testing individual differences go back to Galton's work in England in the 1870s, the work of Binet and Simon at the turn of the century in France marks the foundation of modern intellectual assessment.

Intellectual Assessment   In 1904, the Paris school commission asked Binet and his colleague to develop a test that would predict which children would do well in school and which would not, so that something could be done about the latter. They developed a test that sampled school-related skills in a standardized manner, and a child's score could be compared to the scores of other children. Binet's development of the concepts of norms and deviations from norms gave meaning to an individual's test score. Knowing that a child's score on a vocabulary test is 13, for example, does not tell you much, but knowing that the child scored one standard deviation above the mean for children of her or his age does. Binet contributed substantially to the field of intellectual assessment and thus to professional psychology.

BOX 2.1

Important Historical Events in Professional Psychology in Chronological Order

1879 Wundt established first psychology laboratory

1883 Hall established first U.S. psychology laboratory

1887 First psychology journal, *American Journal of Psychology*, founded

1888 First professorship in psychology (Cattell)

1890 William James published *Principles of Psychology*

1892 Hall founded American Psychological Association

1895 Freud and Breuer published *Studies in Hysteria*

1896 Lightner Witmer established first psychological clinic

1900 Freud published *The Interpretation of Dreams*

1905 Binet and Simon published first intelligence test

1907 The *Journal of Abnormal Psychology* began publication

1908 Frank Parsons established the Vocation Bureau in Boston

1909 Freud delivered lectures on psychoanalysis in the United States

1916 Terman developed Stanford-Binet intelligence test

1917 Army Alpha test developed

1919 Clinical section formed within the APA

1920 Watson and Rayner applied learning theory to develop a phobia in Little Albert

1921 Rorschach inkblot test published

1935 Thematic Apperception Test published by Morgan and Murray

1938 Wechsler-Bellevue intelligence test for adults published; Bender-Motor-Gestalt Test published

1942 Carl Rogers published *Counseling and Psychotherapy*, which described client-centered therapy as first major alternative to psychoanalysis; Donald Super published *The Dynamics of Vocational Adjustment*

1943 Minnesota Multiphasic Personality Inventory published by Hathaway and McKinley

1944 APA reorganized into division system; Division of Clinical Psychology (12) formed

1949 Boulder Conference held; scientist-practitioner model of clinical psychology established; Halstead published first neuropsychological test battery

1951 Northwestern Conference held; term *counseling psychology* adopted

1952 Division of Counseling Psychology (17) formed

1954 Greystone Conference held; training requirements for counseling psychology established

1958 Wolpe published *Psychotherapy by Reciprocal Inhibition*

1963 Community Mental Health Act enacted

1973 Vail Conference held; professional model of clinical psychology established

1987 Practice and Science Directorates formed within the APA

1988 American Psychological Society formed

English translations of the Binet-Simon test were used in the United States until Lewis Terman at Stanford greatly modified it and standardized it with American children. The Stanford-Binet was published in 1916 and has been revised and updated three times since then. In 1928, Gessell published his developmental scales for use with babies and young children. In 1939, David Wechsler published the Wechsler-Bellevue, the first satisfactory individual test of adult intelligence. Several revisions of the Wechsler and the addition of versions for children in 1949 and for very young children in 1967 have helped make the Wechsler tests the most used individual intelligence tests today. Other intelligence tests are constantly being developed and marketed, such as the Kaufman Assessment Battery for Children, published in 1983.

Personality Assessment   After psychology had demonstrated its power with intelligence testing, psychologists working in clinics and hospitals began to be asked to help with other problems besides school performance and mental retardation. Psychiatrists and social workers wanted help with differential diagnosis of psychopathology and with understanding personality dynamics. Professional psychology responded with two types of tests, projective and objective.

Projective Tests   Early word association tests were developed by Galton, Jung, and others in the last century, but the most successful projective test was the inkblot test developed by Rorschach and published in his *Psychodiagnostik* in 1921. The test consists of a series of inkblots, and individuals are asked to tell what the blots look like to them. While the title "projective technique" wasn't used until 1939, the assumption behind the Rorschach was that individuals would project their personalities and unconscious conflicts onto the ambiguous ink blots in order to make sense out of them.

In 1935, Christiana Morgan and Henry Murray published the Thematic Apperception Test (TAT), which consists of a series of drawings of people in a variety of situations. Individuals are asked to make up a story about what is going on in the pictures, and again, it is assumed that they must use their own personalities and experiences in order to do so.

In 1938, Lauretta Bender published the Bender-Motor-Gestalt Test, a series of geometric designs to be copied, which is used as a projective test of personality as well as a measure of brain damage. In 1949, Karen Machover published her description of the Draw-A-Person test. Individuals are simply asked to draw a person, and the way they do so is supposed to indicate how they function in some ways and how they perceive themselves.

Despite ongoing controversy over their validity, projective tests have enjoyed widespread acceptance. Developed between the world wars, they continue to be widely used today. Other projective tests have been developed, such as the House-Tree-Person drawing test or the Roberts Apperception Test for Children, but the Rorschach and the TAT continue to be used in assessment and research.

Objective Tests Empirical psychology would not let these psychoanalytically tinged projective measures hog the assessment show. Psychology took the measurement concepts of norms and deviations invented for intelligence tests, applied them to measuring personality, and developed the so-called objective tests. After Woodworth's Personal Data Sheet and his Psychoneurotic Inventory of World War I, the first major empirically derived, pencil-and-paper personality test, the Minnesota Multiphasic Personality Inventory (MMPI), was published by Hathaway and McKinley in 1943. Several scales were developed by giving hundreds of true-or-false statements to many "normal" people and to people who were known to belong to certain diagnostic groups, such as the depressed or the socially introverted; those statements that the diagnostic groups answered differently from the "normals" became the scales. The MMPI was a phenomenal success. It became and remains the personality test most often used in research and in clinical assessment in the world. Not until 1989 was a revision, the MMPI–2, published.

Other objective tests soon followed: the Edwards Personal Preference Schedule in 1954, the California Psychological Inventory in 1957, the Myers-Briggs in 1962, the Beck Depression Inventory in 1972, and the Eysenck Personality Inventory in 1975, among others. New objective tests are constantly being developed and marketed for a wide variety of uses, from assessing childrearing practices to measuring management styles. A recent competitor for the MMPI, in terms of its use in assessing psychopathology, is the Millon Clinical Multiaxial Inventory, developed and constantly revised by Theodore Millon since the early 1980s and designed to give psychiatric diagnoses. Again, despite years of controversy over the reliability and validity of the objective personality tests, the MMPI remains widely accepted and used in a variety of settings today.

Other Forms of Assessment With the success of intelligence tests, psychologists moved into many different types of assessment. As noted, achievement, vocational, aptitude, and interest tests were developed during the 1920s and 1930s by counseling, school, and educational psychologists to help advise students about their careers and to supplement the information gained from the ability tests.

Behavioral assessment was developed during the 1970s to be used with behavior therapy, which is based on learning theory. The techniques of behavioral assessment, such as naturalistic observation, self-monitoring, psychophysiological measures, and the like, are used to identify target behaviors to modify, to identify causal variables so interventions can be made at that point, and to evaluate and modify the interventions.

Neuropsychological assessment grew during the 1970s and 1980s. It involves a set of procedures designed to detect the presence, extent, and type of organic brain damage or neurological impairment in individuals. The oldest test of this type, the Bender-Gestalt, published in 1939, was discussed earlier in the chapter. Involving the copying of a few designs, it is short, quick, and easy to administer, but it merely suggests the presence or absence of organic impairment. Modern tests, though long, complex, and difficult to administer, give a complete picture of the nature of the impairment. The Halstead-Reitan Battery, originally developed in the 1960s, is constantly revised by Ralph Reitan and his colleagues. There are now several quantitative procedures available in neuropsychology, including the Luria-Nebraska Neuropsychological Battery, the Boston Diagnostic Aphasia Examination, and others. Research in neuropsychology is "in" at present, so it receives funding, and new findings will undoubtedly lead to new measures.

Interventions

Psychological interventions for alleviating human misery have a long history. Shamanistic dances to drive evil spirits from the ill could be considered psychological interventions. In the early nineteenth century, Franz Anton Mesmer developed hypnotic techniques to treat a variety of problems, and mesmerism, as it was then called, was used in obstetrics as early as 1831 (Chertok, 1981). Later Charcot and Janet also used hypnosis, as did Freud at first. In the early nineteenth century in the United States, "moral treatment" incorporated group discussions and emotional support.

In the early years of professional psychology, the vast majority of psychologists were involved in assessment. Furthermore, a great deal of their work dealt with children or the so-called "feebleminded." The first two psychology clinics focused on children. As mentioned previously, Lightner Witmer established the first one in 1896 at the University of Pennsylvania in order to help children who exhibited learning difficulties or disruptive classroom behavior. The second, William Healy's child guidance clinic in Chicago, was established in 1909 to deal with delinquents. Parsons' Vocation Bureau, established in 1908, dealt with guiding education and work. Thus, if professional psychologists were involved in treatment at all, it was generally limited to counseling children or youth or to vocational guidance. The child therapists of that day adopted the psychoanalytic model, especially the version developed by Alfred Adler and the play therapy developed by Anna Freud, Sigmund's daughter.

In 1920, John Watson demonstrated that a phobia could be learned, but even though he clearly pointed out that phobias could be treated with behavioristic methods and Mary Cover Jones showed how in 1924, it would be several decades before professional psychology developed behavioral interventions based on learning theory.

In the late 1930s, Carl Rogers (1902–1987) developed his client-centered counseling theory and methods, publishing *Counseling and Psychotherapy* in 1942, but again, it would be several years before his ideas achieved prominence. Furthermore, Rogers made an important contribution to professional psychology by being the first to systematically research his therapy, examining both the theory behind his methods and the process of psychotherapy itself. As an interesting historical aside, at about the same time, and even for a time at the same university, psychiatrist Heinz Kohut was developing a new model of psychoanalysis called **object relations** theory, a model with striking parallels to the theory and methods developed by Rogers. Yet Rogers and Kohut never met (Rogers, personal communication, 1985).

Nevertheless, in terms of psychological interventions with adults, the dominant model in the mental health field at that time was psychoanalysis, and the dominant profession was psychiatry. World War II changed everything.

World War II created an enormous demand for assessment, counseling, and psychotherapy services for hundreds of thousands of soldiers. There was so much business to go around that professional psychology was able to move rapidly into providing psychotherapy and counseling for adults, not just assessment and treatment for children, without encountering much resistance from medicine or other groups. In 1946, the Veterans Administration, the National Institute of Mental Health, and the U.S. Public Health Service began to fund training programs in clinical psychology and counseling psychology at universities. They supported training programs in order to produce more psychologists to provide the many services that the returning soldiers would require for years to come. This financial support contributed greatly to the expansion of psychology as a field.

The decade after World War II saw tremendous strides in professional psychology as it expanded into new and varied research and treatment areas. In 1947, the National Training Laboratory at Bethel, Maine, held its first summer workshop. This event saw the birth of T-groups, or sensitivity training groups, which were designed to help businesspeople improve their communication and productivity through meeting in and examining the process of small groups. As with vocational guidance, therapy-like services were offered to nondisturbed individuals. In 1949, Andrew Salter published *Conditioned Reflex Therapy* and in 1958, Joseph Wolpe published *Psychotherapy by Reciprocal Inhibition,* both of which helped establish behavior therapy as a major alternative to the psychoanalytic view.

The 1960s saw an explosion of diverse theories and techniques. Important therapies at this time included client-centered, humanistic, Gestalt, and behavior therapy, all covered in detail in later chapters. Psychologists were conducting individual, group, marriage, and family therapy. They were involved in the human potential movement, which offered psychological services to nondisturbed people in order to help them reach their full potential. In short, many new ideas were tried. And, as is typical of psychology, many of these new ideas were subjected to research.

The tremendous postwar growth of psychology was due to several factors. The **scientist-practitioner model** bore fruit, for academic research frequently provided new applications of psychological principles and developed new techniques of behavior change. By the early 1960s, the majority of people in the United States were prosperous to a degree never before seen in history, and they could afford a sense of social responsibility for less fortunate individuals. The public turned to psychology for solutions to social problems, because psychology had proved so successful in the two world wars. Psychology also fit in with the still-treasured value of individualism. It was essentially a conservative approach in that problems were defined as being within individuals or, at most, their families, and solutions could be found that did not require change in anyone else, the community, or society. Social problems were addressed solely through the treatment of individuals.

In 1963, President Kennedy signed the Community Mental Health Act, which provided funding for many community-based mental health agencies. The goal of this act was to reduce the population warehoused in large mental hospitals and to allow the mentally disturbed to be treated in their own communities. Psychologists found extensive employment in the agencies and programs funded by the act. The federal government and the Veterans Administration continued to be generous with funds for training psychologists, and research was also liberally funded. This steady flow of money coupled with positive public attitudes contributed to the growth of professional psychology.

The years since this expansive period have been a mix of good and bad for psychology and society. Even during the height of 1960s prosperity, the poor were never provided with services adequate to help them. The community mental health agencies were also inadequately financed, yet the big state mental hospitals closed, forcing many disturbed people into prisons, cheap hotels, or onto the streets. There have been wars, assassinations, and recurring recessions. While the 1980s appeared to be another highly prosperous decade, it was so only for some people, and they did not appear to feel the earlier sense of social responsibility for the disadvantaged. In the 1980s, the government chose to cut spending for mental health research and services, and the poor economy of the early 1990s meant it had to.

Nevertheless, there were advances in research, theories, and methods of intervention during the late 1970s and 1980s. Examples include the development of cognitive behavior therapy, strategic and paradoxical interventions, and family systems therapies, all covered in later chapters. Even before reduced government spending, psychologists were concerned that individual therapies were not a cost-effective way of reaching people and solving social problems. Some psychologists responded to the ineffectiveness of psychotherapy to address social problems by advocating social and political action. Others contributed to the development of community psychology in the 1970s. In this model, interventions are aimed at the prevention of psychological disorders through education, parent training, crisis intervention, or changing parts of the community. The 1980s saw the development of behavioral medicine, or health psychology, another preventive field, in which interventions are aimed at changing people's health-risking behaviors. The appeal of this field is that its interventions are cost-effective: early, relatively inexpensive behavioral interventions prevent the need for later, more costly medical interventions. Demonstrating the cost-effectiveness of its interventions is crucial for the future of professional psychology.

The effects of a poor economy have meant severe criticism and funding cuts for psychology and other mental health professions. Reduced funding has increased competition among professional groups for the few remaining dollars. The 1980s became a period of decreasing growth in the field and a sense of unease over the future of professional psychology. However, the need for cost-effective interventions may well lead to new treatment theories and methods and to new and varied roles for professional psychologists.

Professional Organizations

The development of the field of psychology has been inextricably linked with that of the American Psychological Association. Changes and struggles within the organization reflect both academic and professional developments, as well as changes in society at large. The size of the APA suggests the importance of psychology in the United States today.

As already stated, the APA was founded by G. Stanley Hall in 1892 with 26 or 31 members. By 1900, the APA had 127 members. The field of psychology has, until recently, grown rapidly ever since, with about 1,100 APA members by 1930; 17,000 in 1960; 29,000 in 1970; 60,000 in 1980; and 70,000 in 1990. These numbers appear to be leveling off at present.

The division structure of APA as of 1997 is shown in Box 2.2. It is worth examining this box to see that along with increasing numbers has come increasing diversity in the special interests of APA members. The higher the number of the division, the more recently it was added, so the types of roles for psychologists that have proliferated in recent years can be seen in the later divisions. With over 50 divisions in 1997, it is, in a way, amazing that the APA continues to function as one organization.

The Early Years   The key word in the APA is *American,* and the organization prospered by fitting in well with American society. In the nineteenth century, the rapidly developing sciences began to organize themselves into specialities. G. Stanley Hall invited several colleagues and friends to a meeting in 1892 in order to form a disciplinary society for psychology, the American Psychological Association. The organization held annual meetings for the presentation of papers, the election of officers (unsurprisingly, Hall was the first president), and the election of new members. Annual dues were a whopping three dollars (now about two hundred dollars, depending on the divisions a member joins and still a bargain considering inflation). Journals were published, research was encouraged, and ties were maintained with related disciplines. The APA functioned well to create an identity for scientific psychology.

Since the goals of the APA were scientific, it became involved in professional psychology almost against its will. A Committee on Physical and Mental Tests was formed in 1896, and a Committee on Measurements in 1906. By 1919, there were enough applied psychologists working in various settings that a Section of Clinical Psychology was created within the APA.

World War II   As described earlier, World War II profoundly affected the field of psychology. The APA was reorganized into the division system in 1944, and Division 12 became the Division of Clinical Psychology. As noted, in 1949, the APA Boulder Conference on graduate education in clinical psychology bridged the academic–applied schism in the field and determined the future of clinical psychology as a profession. The Boulder conference determined that the degree for an applied psychologist would be the Ph.D. with training in both science and practice. The scientist-practitioner model required competence in research, assessment, and psychotherapy. The inclusion of psychotherapy was a courageous stance for the APA, considering the opposition of psychiatry at the time. The later Northwestern and Greystone conferences established the training requirements for counseling psychology, as described previously. The Division of Counseling Psychology (17) was formed in 1952.

Other events also affected professional psychology. The first certification law for psychologists was passed in Connecticut in 1945. In 1946, the APA formed the American Board of Examiners in Professional Psychology (later ABPP, described in Chapter 1) to certify the competence of Ph.D. applied psychologists. In 1953, the

BOX 2.2

Divisions of the American Psychological Association as of 1997

1. Division of General Psychology
2. Division on the Teaching of Psychology
3. Division of Experimental Psychology
5. Division of Evaluation, Measurement, and Statistics
6. Division of Physiological and Comparative Psychology
7. Division of Developmental Psychology
8. The Society of Personality and Social Psychology
9. The Society for the Psychological Study of Social Issues
10. Psychology and the Arts
12. Division of Clinical Psychology
13. Division of Consulting Psychology
14. Society for Industrial and Organizational Psychology
15. Division of Educational Psychology
16. Division of School Psychology
17. Division of Counseling Psychology
18. Division of Psychologists in Public Service
19. Division of Military Psychology
20. Division of Adult Development and Aging
21. Division of Applied Experimental and Engineering Psychology
22. Division of Rehabilitation Psychology
23. Division of Consumer Psychology
24. Division of Theoretical and Philosophical Psychology
25. Division for the Experimental Analysis of Behavior
26. Division of the History of Psychology
27. Division of Community Psychology
28. Psychopharmacology
29. Division of Psychotherapy
30. Division of Psychological Hypnosis
31. Division of State Psychological Association Affairs
32. Division of Humanistic Psychology
33. Division of Mental Retardation and Developmental Disabilities
34. Division of Population and Environmental Psychology
35. Division of Psychology of Women
36. Psychologists Interested in Religious Issues
37. Division of Child, Youth, and Family Services
38. Division of Health Psychology
39. Division of Psychoanalysis
40. Division of Neuropsychology
41. American Psychology-Law Society
42. Psychologists in Independent Practice
43. Family Psychology

BOX 2.2 *(continued)*

44. Society for the Psychological Study of Lesbian and Gay Issues
45. Society for the Psychological Study of Ethnic Minority Issues
46. Media Psychology
47. Exercise and Sport Psychology
48. Peace Psychology
49. Group Psychology and Group Psychotherapy
50. Addictions
51. Society for the Psychological Study of Men and Masculinity
52. International Psychology

Note: There is no Division 4 or Division 11. Division 4 was saved for the Psychometric Society, but they decided not to join the APA. Division 11 was Abnormal Psychology and Psychotherapy, but they combined with Division 12 when the APA reorganized in 1946.

APA published its first *Ethical Standards,* a code of ethics designed to protect the public and enhance the professionalism of applied psychology.

Recent Decades   The incredibly rapid postwar growth of professional psychology, discussed earlier, led to further changes in the field and the APA. The 1973 APA conference on education and training in clinical psychology, held this time in Vail, Colorado, developed the professional model as an alternative to the scientist-practitioner model. The APA continues to hold conferences to discuss issues that arise in training as professional psychology changes.

The debate over academic versus applied psychology is far from over. Furthermore, the split between the two factions in the APA has widened. As suggested by Box 2.2, the number of APA divisions that could be considered applied now outweigh the number of strictly scientific divisions. The majority of APA members are professional psychologists. By the 1980s, the scientists began to feel neglected. To scientists, it seemed that the APA was devoting all its energies to issues of importance to clinicians, such as licensing laws, hospital privileges, lawsuits over insurance reimbursement of psychologists' fees, and the like. The APA responded to these charges by assessing clinicians higher dues than scientists and then by forming the Practice Directorate and the Science Directorate in 1987.

A plan to reorganize the APA was voted down by the membership in 1988. As a result, the dissatisfied members left and in that year formed their own professional organization, the American Psychological Society (APS), dedicated to the advancement of scientific psychology. The first APS convention was held in 1988, and the APS now has its own newsletter, *The Observer,* a monthly *Employment Bulletin,* and its own journal, *Psychological Science.* The formation of the APS may result in the APA's becoming a completely professional organization.

There are many who oppose this breakup of psychology. They believe that both sides benefit by one strong, unified organization. Furthermore, they argue, research and applied psychology should continue to inform each other and benefit from each other's input. Many fear that the splintering into special-interest groups predicts the disintegration of the discipline, and they contend that the goal of psychology should be the integration of theory and knowledge. At present, many psychologists belong to both the APA and the APS, a fact that suggests that psychology as a discipline may be able to both specialize and synthesize, as it has in the past.

IN CONCLUSION

This brief history of professional psychology should set the following chapters in context. The majority of this book is devoted to the description, explanation, and analysis of the theories and methods of professional psychology, especially psychotherapy and counseling. As you read these chapters, remember that the theories and methods under discussion developed at a certain time and place as a result of certain social forces. Once you have gained a comprehensive understanding of the field of professional psychology by reading the following chapters, we will return in the last chapter to some of the social and professional issues raised by this history. The meaning of the current important legal, ethical, economic and professional issues facing the field will be discussed with the hope of helping you to understand the future of professional psychology.

BIBLIOGRAPHY

Alexander, F. G., & Selesnick, S. T. (1966). *The history of psychiatry.* New York: Harper & Row.

Beers, Clifford W. (1908). *A mind that found itself.* New York: Longmans.

Benjamin, L. T. (1986). Why don't they understand us? A history of psychology's public image. *American Psychologist, 41,* 941–946.

Benjamin, L. T. (Ed.). (1992). The history of American psychology. *American Psychologist, 47,* 109–335.

Benjamin, L. T. (1996). Introduction: Lightner Witmer's legacy to American psychology. *American Psychologist, 51,* 235–236.

Benjamin, L. T., & Dixon, D. N. (1996). Dream analysis by mail: An American woman seeks Freud's advice. *American Psychologist, 51,* 461–468.

Chertok, L. (1981). *Sense and nonsense in psychotherapy: The challenge of hypnosis.* New York: Pergamon Press.

Coleman, J. C. (1972). *Abnormal psychology and modern life* (4th ed., p. 33). Glenview, IL: Scott, Foresman.

Dawis, R. (1992). The individual differences tradition in counseling psychology. *Journal of Counseling Psychology, 39,* 7–19.

Deutch, A. (1952). *The mentally ill in America* (2nd ed.). New York: Columbia University Press.

Ellis, H. C. (1992). Graduate education in psychology: Past, present, and future. *American Psychologist, 47,* 570–576.

Gollaher, D. (1995). *Voice for the mad: The life of Dorothea Dix.* New York: Free Press.

Guthrie, D. J. (1946). *A history of medicine.* Philadelphia: Lippincott.

Lewis, N. D. C. (1941). *A short history of psychiatric achievement.* New York: Norton.

Masson, Jeffrey M. (1984). *The assault on truth: Freud's suppression of the seduction theory.* New York: Farrar, Straus & Giroux.

Meier, M. J. (1992). Modern clinical neuropsychology in historical perspective. *American Psychologist, 47,* 550–558.

Rogers, C. (1942). *Counseling and psychotherapy.* Boston: Houghton Mifflin.

Rorschach, H. (1921). *Psychodiagnostik.* Bern: Bircher.

Rosen, G. (1962). *Madness in society.* New York: Harper & Row.

Russell, W. L. (1941). A psychopathic department of an American general hospital in 1808. *American Journal of Psychiatry, 98,* 229–237.

Schoeneman, T. J. (1982). Criticisms of the psychopathological interpretation of witch hunts: A review. *American Journal of Psychiatry, 139,* 1028–1032.

Stone, S. (1937). Psychiatry through the ages. *Journal of Abnormal and Social Psychology, 32,* 131–160.

Super, D. (1942). *The dynamics of vocational adjustment.* New York: Harper.

Super, D. (1955). Transition: From vocational guidance to counseling psychology. *Journal of Counseling Psychology, 2,* 3–9.

Szasz, T. (1961). *The myth of mental illness.* New York: Harper & Row.

Tourney, G. (1967). A history of therapeutic fashions in psychiatry, 1800–1966. *American Journal of Psychiatry, 124,* 784–794.

Watson, R. I. (1963). *The great psychologists.* Philadelphia: Lippincott.

Zilboorg, G., & Henry, G. W. (1941). *A history of medical psychology.* New York: Norton.

PART **TWO**

Assessment

CHAPTER
3

Assessment and Diagnosis

Several people are quietly riding the noon bus downtown when suddenly, a middle-aged, well-dressed man stands up and begins to shout incomprehensibly and wave his arms about. Most passengers try to ignore him, but one asks him what is wrong and another mumbles at him to be quiet. He gives no reply, but sits back down for a few moments, quietly shaking. He stands again, staggers up and down the aisle twice, pointing his finger and glaring at a few passengers. This time, the passengers try different responses: glaring back, shaking their heads, cowering, and telling him to calm down. After sitting quietly for a few moments more, he stands, shouts, and seems to throw himself to the floor. What should the others do now?

As you read this description, you undoubtedly began thinking, "What is going on here? What is wrong with this man?" It seems obvious that something *is* wrong, but it is not clear what. Nevertheless, what the passengers will do depends on what they think is wrong. How can they assess this man's behavior and decide what to do? Most chose to observe him. One asked him to tell her what he thought was wrong, and others gave him orders to see if he could understand and would obey. Some may have concluded that he was a lost foreigner, others that he was drunk, crazy, or ill.

All people engage in assessment and diagnosis every day of their lives. A young woman meets a young man, looks him over, asks him a few questions about his zodiac sign and his interests, and observes his reactions to her. On the basis of this assessment procedure, she may diagnose him as a "nerd," a "hunk," or a "nice guy" and then try to predict whether she should go out with him. A parent observes that his 3-year-old doesn't throw a ball well, cries easily when frustrated, and says things such as "Listen! The birds are waking the sun up!" On the basis of these observations, he concludes that his child is "stupid" and "slow" and predicts that she will have trouble in school. Another parent, making the same observations, concludes that her child is "creative" and "clever" and will do well in school. We all need to observe others, categorize them, and make predictions about their behavior so we can understand them and guide our behavior toward them.

In these examples, the observations are informal and haphazard, the categories used contain value judgments (nerd and stupid), and the predictions may well be wrong. Assessment in psychology, on the other hand, is supposed to be systematic, objective, and accurate. Clinical psychology has applied the scientific method of empirical observation and measurement to the very human activities of trying to assess and predict others. Clinical psychologists' training in measurement theory, statistics, and research methods helps them collect accurate psychological information about individuals and make appropriate predictions and recommendations based on that information. Although we have pointed out that all people try to assess others, we should also point out, before we begin to discuss the topic, that not all psychologists use or even believe in formal psychological assessment.

PSYCHOLOGICAL ASSESSMENT

We can define psychological assessment as the process of collecting information in a systematic, objective, empirical way about individuals' intellectual functioning, behavior, or personality so that predictions and decisions about them can be made. Parents may need to know a child's current level of intellectual functioning so they can decide what type of special education, if any, they should obtain for their child. A behavior therapist may need to assess the frequency, intensity, and precipitating events of a target behavior such as smoking in order to plan a treatment program. A court may order an assessment of a prisoner's personality to determine whether that person is competent to stand trial. These examples are just a few of the uses of psychological assessment.

The process of psychological assessment is complex. The most common method of assessment, used by professional psychologists and everyone else, is the interview. It is possible to gather useful information and data by conversing with a person and asking pertinent questions. Because of their special training in science and experimentation, psychologists have developed additional methods of assessment, namely, tests. A psychological test is any procedure or method used to obtain information during the process of assessment. Often, tests are regarded as methods of collecting samples of behaviors under standardized conditions, and as such, the results are subject to methods of data analysis.

Psychological tests vary in how they are constructed, administered, scored, and interpreted and in what they are supposed to measure. There are group and individual intelligence tests, which may be short or long, with sections that test vocabulary, arithmetic, logical reasoning, and other abilities. Personality tests may involve true-or-false responses to a series of statements about life, or they may require making up stories about pictures or supplying the endings to incomplete sentences. Whatever their form, psychological assessment procedures have certain characteristics in common. They are designed to serve specific purposes and to measure specific aspects of people, they attempt to be as objective as possible, and they are subject to empirical verification.

A review of test construction theory, scaling methods, and the rules of empirical verification is beyond the scope of this book. We assume that you have already studied research methods and measurement. However, certain measurement concepts should be reviewed, namely, test standardization and norms, and test reliability and validity, in order for you to understand and evaluate psychological tests.

Norms and Standardization

In order to attach meaning to their scores, many psychological assessment instruments are standardized and utilize the concept of norms. When a psychological test is constructed, it is given to a large number of representative people. The scores of this standardization group become the test norms, that is, how most people perform on the test. The score of a particular individual who later takes the test can then be compared to the test norms. It is then possible to say that this individual scores so much higher or so much lower than most people (most people being represented by the standardization group), and thus, the person's score is placed in a meaningful context. For example, to know that Mr. Smith scored 34 on an anxiety test is basically meaningless. If we know that among a standardization group of 200 people the mean score on the anxiety test was 33.5, then we also know that Mr. Smith is about average in the degree of anxiety he reports.

Reliability and Validity

Reliability and validity help psychologists know if tests meet the criteria for scientific acceptability. **Reliability** refers to the "trustworthiness" or consistency of a measuring device; that is, is the same result obtained every time the measure is used, even when different people use it? If you use a yardstick to measure your desk and find that it is 38 inches wide, you will find that it is still 38 inches wide when you measure it the next day or if someone else measures it—the yardstick is therefore a very reliable measuring device. People trust it, and they will believe you when you tell them how wide your desk is.

Evaluating the reliability of a psychological measurement is more difficult. Several methods for determining test reliability have been developed. All of them involve a statistic called the correlation coefficient, r, which varies from 0 to 1.0. As the name implies, a correlation reveals to what degree two things vary together. If $r = 0$, the two variables are completely unrelated, or independent of each other. An r of 1.0 would mean the two behave identically. If you measure 10 objects with your yardstick and your friend measures the same ten objects with her yardstick, you can subject your answers and her answers to a correlation and see if they vary in the same way. That is, if your yardstick says something is large and another thing is small, does her yardstick result in measures in the same direction? It is likely that the correlation between your measurements and your friend's will be about $r = .98$. It is unlikely that it would be a perfect 1.0, because small errors in measurement always occur.

There are several types of reliability, but we will cover *test-retest, split-half,* and *observer* reliability. In test-retest reliability, the question is, does the test give the same answer at different times? A large group of people is given a psychological test, and a month later the same people are given the test again. The correlation between their answers the first time and their answers the second is the test-retest reliability for that measure. With split-half reliability, also called *internal consistency,* the question is, do different parts of the test give the same results? A large group of people is given a psychological test at one time, and the test itself is split in half, often into odd-numbered and even-numbered test items. The correlation between the two halves of the test is the measure of the test's internal consistency. In observer reliability, also called *interrater reliability,* the question is, do different people using the same measuring device come up with similar answers? If two psychiatrists diagnose the same disordered person, do they agree? If two psychologists give the same individual the Rorschach inkblot test, do they come up with similar interpretations of the results?

Validity refers not to the measuring system itself but to the appropriateness of the interpretation of the results of the measurements; that is, does the measuring device really measure what the person using it says it is measuring? What is really being measured with psychological tests is highly controversial. Validity refers to the meaning of the results of the measurement, that is, the appropriateness or accuracy of the interpretation of those results.

Several methods for evaluating validity have been developed, many of which also involve the correlation statistic. *Face validity,* which doesn't, is an appealingly simple way of determining validity. Does the test look like it is measuring what its developer says it measures? For example, items such as "Do you feel worried at times?" on a test of anxiety make it appear to have face validity. *Predictive validity* addresses how well test scores predict the behavior that the test should predict if it is indeed measuring what it purports to measure. Do people who score high on an anxiety test later act worried and agitated under stress while those who score low remain calm? *Concurrent validity* can be determined by the correlation of a test's scores with those of another, better-known or already well-researched test. A group of people may be administered a new anxiety scale as well as the older, well-established Taylor Manifest Anxiety Scale (TMAS), and the correlation between the two sets of scores would indicate the concurrent validity of the new measure. *Construct validity* involves the relationship of a test to other test scores and behaviors that would be predicted by theory. For example, high anxiety is theoretically linked to poor performance under pressure, and if scores on a test of anxiety can be shown to be related to school grades in a theoretically predicted way, then construct validity may be demonstrated.

Most measurement experts agree that a test cannot be valid unless it is also reliable. It is, however, possible for a method of measurement to be reliable but not valid. For example, suppose that you measure your desk with a plastic tape measure that over years of use has stretched. When you or anyone else uses this tape to measure your desk several times, it gives consistent results—it is reliable. However, concluding that your desk is 38 inches wide is inappropriate, and other people using yardsticks to measure your desk will disagree with you.

As the next chapters show, a great deal of controversy is generated over the validity of psychological tests. A major reason for the controversy is that test results have consequences in the real world, in that decisions about people are made based on test scores. In fact, Messick (1995) proposed a unified concept of validity that included its consequential aspects. An important example is the use of intelligence tests, which are highly reliable, in the public schools. If a test purporting to measure intelligence is used to disproportionately assign minority children to special education classes, then people will argue that the test does not really measure intelligence, but rather a set of skills that white children are taught by their families and culture but minority children are not.

The Assessment Process

Psychological tests and measurements are used for many different purposes: in research, for diagnostic purposes, to determine intellectual functioning, to detect personality dynamics, to reveal family dynamics, to design behavioral interventions, to evaluate psychotherapy outcomes, to screen candidates for jobs, to help individuals decide on a vocation, and more. The clinical assessment of individuals, however, is a complicated process, and psychological tests are only part of it. It is similar to the scientific process of formulating hypotheses, designing measures to test the hypotheses, collecting data, and interpreting the results. Psychological assessment involves framing a question about an individual, deciding how best to examine the possible explanations, collecting data through interviews and with appropriate psychological tests, analyzing the results of data collection, integrating and interpreting the results in terms of how they answer the original question, and making predictions and recommendations based on the analysis and interpretations.

The Referral Question   Individual psychological assessment is conducted only when someone needs to know something about a specific individual. While psychologists may occasionally decide to assess their own clients, in general, assessment is initiated by a referral question from other professionals. Teachers, physicians, social workers, psychiatrists, speech therapists, or others may ask psychologists for assistance in evaluating and understanding the difficulties of individuals with whom they are working.

It is important to obtain a clear understanding of the nature of the question from the referral source. Only with a clear, concrete, specific question can the assessment process begin. An important part of psychologists' expertise is knowing what tests to use for what purposes. Appropriate requests for assessment from psychiatrists, schools, or the courts should ask one or more questions about the client and leave the choice of assessment methods to the professional judgment of the psychologist.

Test Administration and Scoring (Collecting Data)   Once the psychologist has an appropriate referral question about an individual, the psychologist begins the process of collecting data, or gathering information. Psychologists frequently begin by interviewing the individual involved and possibly his or her family members. Information will be collected from other sources if possible, such as previous physical or psychiatric evaluations, school reports, and the like. If psychological tests are used, they are generally administered along with other relevant tests in a test battery.

The test battery consists of all the tests that can help answer the referral question. After all, a single test result in isolation is meaningless, and only when it is substantiated by other results can a meaningful conclusion be drawn. For example, a single high score on the TMAS is not evidence of a disorder, but coupled with certain signs on the Rorschach inkblot test and elevated scores on certain Minnesota Multiphasic Personality Inventory (MMPI) scales, it can be seen as part of the evidence for a diagnosis of an anxiety disorder.

The referral question determines the type of assessment. In a differential diagnosis, the psychologist is being asked to determine which of two or more possible things is wrong with a client when the client's symptoms present a confusing or conflicting picture. One of us tested a young man several years ago at a Veterans Administration hospital. He appeared to be psychotic, but not all of his symptoms fit a diagnosis of schizophrenia, so psychological assessment was requested. The psychological tests indicated organicity, that is, a physical disorder of the brain. There was no other evidence of a brain problem, no evidence of an injury, nothing indicating a tumor. The admitting psychiatrist was about to prescribe Thorazine, but on the basis of the results of the psychological tests, ordered a brain scan instead. An unsuspected hematoma was discovered. The appropriate medication for this condition is blood-thinning drugs, not Thorazine, which would have resulted in serious harm. Within a few weeks this young man was discharged as "cured."

Psychologists are often requested to do intellectual assessments, usually of children who are having some kind of problem in school. (The intellectual level of adults may be assessed for vocational counseling purposes, if it is suspected that an organic process is lowering their competence, or if it is important to know their current level of functioning during or after a mental illness.) The evaluation of a child having difficulty in school will include interviewing the child and the parents and collecting other available information, especially school reports. Children may do poorly in school because of organic problems (such as difficulty with perceptual-motor coordination) or because of emotional problems, as well as because of low intelligence. A typical test battery for such a case might include a Wechsler intelligence test, an achievement test to assess current grade-level performance, a test to rule out organicity, and one or more other tests, including personality tests to assess emotional factors.

Interpreting the Data   After administering and scoring psychological tests, the psychologist must interpret the test results and integrate the findings in order to develop a comprehensive picture of the psychological functioning of the individual and his or her difficulties and strengths. It has been said that interpretation is the clinician's most important skill. Unfortunately, while we will describe the major psychological tests and their uses in the next chapter, the procedures for scoring and interpreting the tests are beyond the scope of this book. Postgraduate course work and hundreds of hours of supervised experience are necessary to become competent in these tasks.

A psychologist's theoretical orientation will determine the types of interpretations made. Suppose, for example, a client says one of the Rorschach inkblots looks like a squashed witch. A clinician with a psychoanalytic orientation may say this response indicates the client's unconscious hostility toward her mother. Another clinician from a different theoretical perspective may regard this response as suggesting a lack of contact with reality, because the blot does not look anything like a squashed witch. A behavioristic psychologist may consider the response irrelevant. Regardless of theoretical orientation, all psychologists must make inferences in order to move from their assessment data to predictions and recommendations.

The Psychological Assessment Report   After scoring the tests, making interpretations, and formulating predictions and recommendations, the psychologists must communicate their findings to others, particularly the referral source. This is generally done in the form of a psychological assessment report (example reports are shown in Box 4.4 and Box 5.2 in the following chapters). Most psychologists develop a standardized way of writing their assessment reports. Sometimes the agencies where they work require the report to be in a certain form. Psychological assessment reports vary greatly, according to the theoretical orientation of the writer, the needs of the client, the nature of the information sought, and the person who will read and use the report. As the final step in the assessment process, reports of the findings should be useful, understandable, and helpful.

Ethics in Assessment   Psychologists have certain ethical obligations when engaged in psychological assessment. As in all situations, including psychotherapy and teaching, psychologists must serve the best interests of the client. This ethical principle includes obtaining the individual's consent before assessment, fully explaining the nature and purposes of psychological assessment procedures to clients, and revealing the results of such assessments to them in a helpful way. In addition, clients should be informed of their right not to be tested or to discontinue testing at any time and of the limits to confidentiality.

Like all psychological information, the information obtained by psychological assessment must be protected and kept confidential, except under special circumstances such as when the client is a danger to others or when the testing is ordered by the court. The client owns the information, and it may be released to another professional, the courts, an agency, or a school only with the written consent of the client or the client's parent or guardian.

Issues in Psychological Assessment

Although an in-depth discussion of controversies about the proper way to construct a psychological test is beyond the scope of this book, some important issues in assessment must be addressed.

Patterns of Test Usage   Over the years, interviews and certain psychological tests have remained in consistent use. Lubin, Larsen, and Matarazzo (1984) surveyed over 200 clinical psychologists as to which psychological tests they used most frequently. Craig and Horowitz (1990) conducted a similar survey a few years later. Box 3.1 lists the 10 most frequently used tests from these surveys, and we will discuss each in detail in the following chapters. It is interesting that the two surveys show such similar results. A third survey of over 400 agencies employing psychologists (Piotrowski &

BOX 3.1

Ten Most Frequently Used Individual Psychological Tests, 1982 and 1988

In 1982, Lubin, Larsen, and Matarazzo (1984) surveyed over 200 psychologists who worked in psychiatric hospitals, community mental health centers, schools for the mentally retarded, counseling centers, and Veterans Administration hospitals. The psychologists were asked to rank order the psychological tests most frequently used at their agencies. In 1988, Craig and Horowitz (1990) conducted a similar survey. They asked the directors of training at 38 settings, including community mental health clinics, institutions for the retarded, psychiatric facilities, and Veterans Administration hospitals, to indicate the tests used at their sites. The two lists are quite similar and the tests on them are old, facts which suggest that psychological test usage remains stable.

1982 Survey	1988 Survey
Wechsler Adult Intelligence Scale	Wechsler Adult Intelligence Scale—Revised
Minnesota Multiphasic Personality Inventory	Thematic Apperception Test
Bender-Motor-Gestalt Test	Bender-Motor-Gestalt Test
Rorschach	Rorschach
Thematic Apperception Test	Draw-A-Person Test
Wechsler Intelligence Scale for Children	Minnesota Multiphasic Personality Inventory
Peabody Picture Vocabulary Test	Sentence Completion Tests
Sentence Completion Tests	Wechsler Intelligence Scale for Children—Revised
House-Tree-Person Drawing Test	Wide Range Achievement Test
Draw-A-Person test	House-Tree-Person Drawing Test

Keller, 1989) found essentially the same pattern of test usage, except for the addition of the Beck Depression Inventory, as the two surveys in Box 3.1. It appears that psychological test usage remains quite consistent, perhaps even resistant to change, over the years.

Furthermore, most of the frequently used tests are quite old. Seven of the tests in Box 3.1 were developed between 1920 and 1950. The Rorschach was developed in the 1920s; the Thematic Apperception Test and the Bender-Gestalt in the 1930s; and the first Wechsler, the Minnesota Multiphasic Personality Inventory, and the Draw-A-Person in the 1940s. New psychological tests are constantly being developed and marketed. In fact, the market is so flooded with new tests that psychologists may feel unable to evaluate them adequately, and so they stick with the old standbys. They use these old tests despite continuing controversy over the reliability and validity of some of them.

The two lists presented in Box 3.1 point out a discrepancy in belief between academic and applied psychologists regarding projective tests, which are personality tests based on the psychoanalytic tradition. Academic psychologists are quite critical of projective tests, citing research that shows poor reliability and validity of these tests. Nevertheless, half of the top 10 tests in actual use are projectives (Rorschach, Thematic Apperception Test, Sentence Completion Tests, House-Tree-Person, and Draw-A-Person). Lubin, Larsen, and Matarazzo (1984) noted that

> Psychological test usage shows only a modest relationship to test quality as judged by academic psychologists. . . . Despite the fact that surveys of university clinical faculty consistently show that the majority of them express negative attitudes toward the clinical value of projective techniques and recommend against increasing the amount of time devoted to teaching projectives at the university . . . , several of these instruments . . . still rank among the top 10 in frequency of use in 1982. (p. 453)

The same statement holds for today.

Clinical Versus Statistical Prediction   In the 1950s, Paul Meehl (Meehl, 1954, 1956) started a controversy that threatened to tear clinical psychology apart when he presented convincing evidence that statistical interpretation of test results is better than clinical interpretation. Clinical prediction refers to the complicated, deductive process by which professional psychologists use their extensive training and clinical experience to integrate and interpret the results of psychological tests. Statistical prediction refers to the application of empirically derived arithmetic rules or actuarial tables for the same purposes. According to Meehl, a statistical table—or today, a computer—can do the same thing as a trained clinical psychologist and do it better. If there is empirical evidence that certain test scores predict certain behaviors, then the "interpretation" of test results does not take any particular skill other than looking up in a table what a score means. Many clinicians find this idea unacceptable (Matarazzo, 1986).

Over the years there have been many studies to try to settle this controversy. A typical study gives a group of clinical psychologists some test results and asks them to make certain predictions about the individuals based on their clinical interpretation of the test results. The same set of results is subjected to statistical interpretation, predictions based on empirical data about what scores predict what behaviors. Then the two types of predictions are compared as to which is most accurate. After years of such studies, Meehl's original conclusion still stands: Where appropriate statistical information exists, clinical interpretation cannot improve on it. The key phrase is "where appropriate statistical information exists," since statistical predictions will only be as good as the empirical evidence on which they are based.

Meehl and others argue that psychologists' efforts should be directed toward collecting the empirical evidence necessary to create manuals or "cookbooks" for psychological tests so as to make good statistical interpretations and predictions.

They claim that training in clinical interpretation should be dropped. It is now proposed that therapy also be done according to "cookbooks," another proposal embroiled in controversy, as discussed in Chapter 18.

Some critics argue that the whole statistical versus clinical prediction controversy is irrelevant because neither process is very accurate. They argue that the most accurate predictions can be made using only a person's past behavior as a basis. For example, an experimental study may demonstrate that several clinical psychologists can examine psychological test results of 100 prisoners and predict which ones will return to crime on release with about 30 percent accuracy. A statistical rule applied to the same test results may be able to hit about 40 percent accuracy. This finding may be interesting to academicians, but it is certainly not exciting when we realize that released prisoners return to crime about 60 to 80 percent of the time. Simply predicting that all prisoners will return to crime will result in an accuracy rate of 60 percent. And it is a lot cheaper and quicker than either clinical judgment or statistical methods.

However, accuracy of prediction is not the only important criterion in assessment. Utility and the problem of base rates must be considered. If a certain hospital ward contains almost 90 percent schizophrenics, a test that identifies schizophrenia with even 80 percent accuracy is not useful, because the base rate of schizophrenia in the ward is so high. Furthermore, ethics and the social consequences of certain decisions for specific individuals are often more important than an accurate prediction. Take suicide, for example. Only about 2 percent of callers to a suicide prevention hot line actually make a suicide attempt (Farberow & Schneidman, 1961). If all we were interested in was accurate prediction, we could simply predict that all callers would not attempt suicide and hang up on them. After all, we would be right 98 percent of the time, an incredibly high level of predictive validity. Obviously, though, the consequences of the 2 percent error are not acceptable in the case of suicide. Thus, questions and procedures have been developed to identify callers at high risk for suicide, so preventive actions can be taken. This assessment procedure has poor accuracy, that is, it results in a high rate of false-positive errors by incorrectly identifying persons who would not attempt suicide as suicide-attempters. Nevertheless, we conclude that the assessment procedure in this case is valuble and even cost-effective.

The Use of Technology in Assessment   Like every other field, professional psychology makes increasing use of computers and other modern technology in its work. Probably the earliest use of computers or computer-like machines was scoring test answers, since machines can quickly scan answer sheets and print out scores. Now there are computer programs to administer a variety of psychological tests. In a computerized administration, the directions for taking the test appear on the screen first; then, as each item appears, the client presses certain keys to respond.

Computer administration of psychological tests clearly saves time for psychologists, who don't have to be present at all while clients take the tests. Some psychologists argue that it also results in more valid scores; first, because when using the keyboard, clients are less likely to become confused or make mistakes than when marking their answers on a form, and second, because they may be more likely to be honest with the impersonal machine. Others say computers may affect validity negatively, but in any case, there is insufficient research on this question. One drawback of computers is that clients, particularly upset or disturbed ones, may be intimidated by having to use a computer. However, computer administration is so clear and simple that most people lose their discomfort quickly (Moore, Summer, & Bloor, 1984), and many even start to enjoy themselves.

Computer programs have been developed to interpret the results of tests as well. These programs are supposedly based on extensive research and use empirically derived rules to interpret individual test results. The evidence favoring statistical over clinical prediction suggests that computer interpretations of tests may be more accurate than those of individual psychologists, because computers can store and integrate far more empirical data than most people can learn and remember. Nevertheless, because clients are individuals and may be exceptions to empirical rules, all ethical computerized reports carry the caution that they are only to be used by psychologists who know the client being evaluated and who have the expertise to evaluate the reported results.

Computers are also used to compose and print psychological assessment reports. Some programs score the test, interpret the scores according to built-in empirical rules, and then compose and print out the report. In addition, human services agencies and psychologists in private practice, like many businesses, use computers to keep files, bill clients, and keep accounts.

Other technology, such as scanners and fax machines, can be incorporated into the scoring, interpretation, and reporting of psychological tests. For example, the Child Behavior Checklist has forms that can be faxed to the University of Vermont College of Medicine for scoring, and software is available for psychologists to scan the forms themselves. In addition, information on psychological tests for sale is available by E-mail and on the World Wide Web.

Not everyone is enthusiastic about the increasing use of technology in psychology. Some critics fear that psychological "interpretations" printed out by a computer will appear to have greater "scientific value" than they truly have or that such printouts might be misused by nonprofessionals. Some believe that the computerized assessments have not been sufficiently validated (Matarazzo, 1986, 1992). Others fear that the increasing use of computers in psychology will increase risks to the confidentiality of psychological information. However, methods of safeguarding computer data are constantly being developed, and we can assume that psychologists will make use of them to keep the information obtained in the course of their professional duties as confidential as they have in the past. At any rate, increasing use of technology in both assessment and therapy appears to be inevitable.

Criticisms of Psychological Assessment

Psychological tests and assessment procedures have been criticized since they were first developed. Criticisms of the way tests are constructed may be of interest to academics, but we will address the cost-effectiveness of assessment and the validity and possible misuses of certain psychological tests.

Even if it is generally agreed that psychological tests are reliable and valid, they can still be criticized as not cost-effective if a simpler, less expensive way of doing the same thing exists. We have already discussed the clinical versus statistical prediction controversy and the evidence that appears to show that empirically derived statistical rules for pencil-and-paper test results are just as good, if not better, at making clinical predictions as interpretation by individual psychologists. Using computers to interpret tests may be more cost-effective than using expensive psychologists.

Many critics have argued that psychological tests are open to misuse. The most well-known controversy over the use of psychological tests has to do with intelligence tests. The alleged misuse of intelligence tests is directly related to issues of their validity. Intelligence tests have been used to place certain students in institutions or special education classes. If the tests do not appropriately and validly measure intelligence, then it is possible that at least some individuals so placed do not belong there. If the tests in fact measure acquired knowledge or level of education or cultural values, then minority group members in particular may be discriminated against if the tests are used to make such decisions about them, because they may not have had equal education and their culture may be different (see Helms [1997] for an excellent discussion of this issue).

The controversy over the validity and misuse of intelligence tests has been brought into court. The California State Supreme Court in 1979 in the case of *Larry P. v. Wilson Riles and the Board of Education* ruled that intelligence tests were biased in favor of middle-class white children and against minority groups. Larry P. was an African American child assigned to special education classes on the basis of his score on an intelligence test. Special education classes contain far more minority group students than their proportion in the population. Larry P.'s parents argued that this disproportionate assignment of minority students to special education classes constituted discrimination and denied Larry P. an equal education. The California State Supreme Court agreed, determining that the scientific evidence for the validity of intelligence tests was inadequate, and ruling that schools could no longer assign students to special education classes on the basis of their intelligence test scores alone, that they had to take into account other information as well. While the court and many others believe that Larry P.'s case represented a misuse of psychological tests, others such as Lambert (1981) believe that the court was wrong, and that intelligence tests are a valid way to make such educational decisions and less prejudicial than teachers' judgments and other methods. Interestingly enough, by the end of the 1980s, the use of IQ tests in determining special education placement had been almost entirely eliminated in California and other states, but the proportion of minority children in such classes was even greater than in the 1970s. In 1988, a group of African American parents went to court in order to *obtain* IQ testing for their children, arguing that *not* allowing the use of such tests was discriminatory, and in 1992, a federal judge in California lifted the ban on IQ testing of African American children.

The most frequently used personality test of all, the Minnesota Multiphasic Personality Inventory, is also a frequent target of criticism. Its very success and popularity may lead to its misuse, as people try to apply it in situations for which it was not designed. Originally developed in order to diagnose mental disorders, the MMPI was (and sometimes still is) used to make employment and personnel decisions without adequate research to test its validity for those kinds of decisions. Individuals applying for jobs or promotions may rightfully complain that they cannot see the relevance of MMPI test items to either the job they want or their competence to do it.

Employers may respond that they do not want to hire and train a disturbed or unstable individual who will be unable to do the job properly or will quit or cause other problems.

In 1991, a California state appeals court in a class action suit against Target Stores (*Saroka v. Dayton Hudson Corporation, dba Target Stores*) prohibited employers from requiring job applicants to take the MMPI, because certain questions in it about religion and sex are not job related and violate the individual's constitutional right to privacy (Hager, 1991). This decision was appealed to the California Supreme Court, and the American Psychological Association filed an *amicus curiae,* or friend-of-the-court, brief. The APA believed the court needed to be educated in how the MMPI was constructed (described in Chapter 4), because the crucial point is that responses to groups of items, not specific items themselves, are related to job performance. However, in late 1993, the Court prohibited Target from using the test for five years and awarded damages to those denied employment. The use of the MMPI or similar tests to deny employment or promotions would appear to be open to the criticism of misuse and to be an issue that will continue to appear in the courts.

DIAGNOSIS

One of the traditional goals of psychological and psychiatric assessment is to reach a diagnosis of the patient's disorder. Diagnosis involves determining that a certain disorder is present or identifying a specific disorder that best matches an individual's symptoms. In differential diagnosis, the goal is to distinguish a diagnosis from other disorders, and assessment may be necessary in order to distinguish which of two or more possible diagnoses best matches the client's conflicting symptoms. In functional diagnosis, assessment focuses on the types and severity of specific deficits, as well as strengths, in order to design treatment interventions.

As discussed in earlier chapters, the medical model holds that the first step in dealing with a disordered individual is to make a diagnosis, so the cause of the problems can be discovered and a treatment can be scientifically developed. In this model, diagnosis determines the type of treatment prescribed, although this may not be what happens in actual practice. This emphasis on diagnosis as a logical first step may seem simplistic compared to professional psychology's complex process of assessment as a method for developing a comprehensive picture of the intellectual, personality, and behavioral functioning of an individual. Furthermore, some psychologists argue that diagnosis as practised in the United States has no validity for other cultures, and some theoretical approaches reject diagnosis and assessment entirely. Nevertheless, it is important for psychologists to understand diagnosis and to know the diagnostic categories commonly used by psychiatry, because of the power of physicians and the prevalence of the medical model. Controversies over diagnosis reflect both scientific disagreements and competition between psychology and psychiatry (Gorenstein, 1984).

The German physician Emil Kraepelin developed the first modern classification system for mental illnesses at the turn of the century. He carefully observed which symptoms tended to go together and gave a label to each set of symptoms. He believed that each disorder had a separate cause and a definite, predictable course and outcome. Kraepelin's original nosology, or system of classification, has held up well over time. The first *Diagnostic and Statistical Manual of Mental Disorders* (DSM), published by the American Psychiatric Association in 1952, was basically an expanded version of Kraepelin's categories, and even later revisions of the DSM retained many of these original categories.

Psychiatry's diagnostic system has grown in complexity and numbers of categories. The first DSM contained 60 types and subtypes of mental illness. The first revision (DSM-II), published in 1968, listed 145 categories. The second revision (DSM-III), published in 1980, contained approximately 205 separate conditions, including such "disorders" as tobacco dependence, binge eating, sexual dysfunctions, and adjustment reactions. Albee (1985, p. 61) noted, "Clearly the more human problems that we label mental illnesses, the more people that we can say suffer from them. And, a cynic might add, the more conditions therapists can treat and collect health-insurance payments for."

Reliability and Validity of Diagnosis

Diagnosis can be looked at as a nominal scale of measurement, that is, a measuring scale that names items or puts them into categories (sorting eggs into white, brown, and speckled categories is an example of a nominal scale). Thus, we can assess the reliability and validity of any system of diagnosis. There are serious problems with the reliability of diagnosis of mental disorders, especially with interrater reliability. Many studies have documented that different diagnosticians often reach different diagnoses for the same patients (Nobins & Helzer, 1986). For one thing, the more categories there are, the more room for disagreement there is. For example, how does a diagnostician distinguish between agoraphobia with panic attacks, social phobia, panic disorder, and generalized anxiety disorder? Or between schizophreniform disorder and schizoaffective disorder? Agreement between diagnosticians tends to be higher for broad categories, such as neurosis versus psychosis or schizophrenia versus organic brain damage, than for narrow categories such as those just mentioned.

The validity of diagnosis may be even more important and more controversial than reliability. The medical model implies that diagnosis is tapping "real" underlying organic disorders. But there is a great deal of debate about the existence of "mental illnesses" (Gorenstein, 1984; Szasz, 1961). Some argue that there is no such thing, that what are being labeled in diagnosis are problems in living, reactions to high levels of stress, poor social competence, faulty social learning, communication disorders, and the casualties of poor parenting, abuse, exploitation, and poverty. Albee (1985, p. 61) has noted that political ideology is implicated in this debate. As he said, "Conservatives strongly favor a constitutional-organic disease explanation, largely because no major social change is called for if the problems are all inside the skin." Liberals favor an environmental view of psychological disorders, because helping the disturbed by changing social conditions can justify their goal of increasing social justice. A "scientific" resolution to the debate over the validity of diagnosis and the medical model of mental illness is probably unlikely.

The Diagnostic and Statistical Manual

As already mentioned, the first DSM was published by the American Psychiatric Association in 1952. It was next revised in 1968 as the DSM-II. Another revision, the DSM-III, was published in 1980, partly as an attempt to solve the problems with the reliability and validity of the DSM-II, discussed below. An interim revision, the DSM-III-R, was published in 1987, and the DSM-IV was published in 1994.

A major change occurred between the DSM-II and the DSM-III. The DSM-II categories were short, vague, and contained much psychiatric and psychoanalytic jargon. They required a high degree of inference about the patient's internal state, as in this description of phobic neurosis: "Phobias are generally attributed to fears displaced to the phobic object or situation from some other object of which the patient is unaware" (American Psychiatric Association, 1968, p. 40). Because of the level of inference required, the reliability of the DSM-II was low. The DSM-III attempted to correct these defects by basing categories on "objective" criteria and observable behavior, so that all observers would be able to agree on whether a given person exhibited a specific behavior or not. A diagnosis is reached when a given person exhibits so many of the listed behaviors for a specific category. In this way, it was hoped, diagnosis would be more reliable.

In addition, the DSM-III tried to take into account the complexity of psychological disorders by including more variables in each diagnosis. It was based on what is called a **multiaxial model**, still used in the DSM-IV. Any single patient can be evaluated and categorized along five independent dimensions, or axes, which are summarized in Box 3.2. Axis I contains the clinical syndromes, or typical diagnostic labels for mental disorders, such as adjustment reaction of adolescence, bipolar depression, and schizophrenia. Axis II deals with personality disorders, such as narcissistic and borderline personality disorder, and certain developmental disorders, such as mental retardation. Axis I diagnoses cover what are supposed to be relatively temporary disorders, while Axis II covers those that are present early and are relatively enduring characteristics that are more difficult to change. Axis III assesses physical disorders and conditions, such as injuries or chronic illnesses that may affect the course of a mental disorder. Axis IV is designed to measure the severity of psychosocial stressors, and Axis V estimates both the current and the highest level of adaptive functioning in the past year. Patients are categorized on all five axes, which are supposed to be independent of each other. For example, a person may exhibit both a phobia (Axis I) and a dependent personality disorder (Axis II). The remaining axes attempt to take into account the patient's physical and social context, coping skills, and level of previous functioning. See Box 3.2 for an example DSM category and a typical diagnostic decision tree.

While an improvement over the DSM-II, the DSM-III had no clear or consistent theoretical or empirical basis. In fact, the manual stated that "DSM-III is generally atheoretical with regard to etiology" and that disorders "are described at the lowest order of inference necessary to describe the characteristic features of the disorder" (American Psychiatric Association, 1980, p. 7). Although many professionals criticized the DSM-III's atheoretical stand, others regarded it as a strength, as an attempt to remain as objective and behavioral as possible. Nevertheless, an implicit medical model was still evident in many categories, while others seemed to be more behavioral or environmental. These problems have continued with the subsequent revisions of the DSM.

In trying to reduce the need for inferences, diagnostic criteria have a tendency to become very long. For example, the DSM-III said that histrionics are "vain." The DSM-III-R described behavioral manifestations of vanity, such as "constantly seeks

---

B O X   3 . 2

Understanding the DSM-IV

The DSM-IV, like the DSM-III and the DSM-III-R, employs a multiaxial model. Each of the axes refers to a different class of information, and the resulting diagnosis is supposed to be quite complete. The multiaxial system is supposed to ensure that certain types of disorders, aspects of the environment, and areas of functioning that might otherwise be overlooked are considered in evaluating an individual. The first axis contains the types of disorders usually handled by the mental health professions, such as phobias, anxiety disorders, and schizophrenia, while the second covers more enduring difficulties, such as mental retardation or personality disorders such as antisocial personality disorder. The majority of the DSM-IV is devoted to describing the categories on these two axes. The five axes used in the DSM-IV are:

Axis I: Clinical Syndromes

Axis II: Developmental Disorders and Personality Disorders

Axis III: Physical Disorders and Conditions

Axis IV: Psychosocial and Environmental Problems

Axis V: Global Assessment of Functioning

A diagnosis should include a statement for each axis. It is possible for an individual to show behaviors that would be classified as two or more disorders on any one axis, and, of course, as two or more disorders on different axes. As noted, Axis I is for the various mental disorders, and each diagnostic category is assigned a specific number. Axis II, for the developmental and personality disorders, also has a specific number for each category. Axis III requires a medical diagnosis. For Axis IV, there is a checklist of nine broad categories of psychosocial and environmental problems, such as problems with the primary support group, housing, occupation, or education. Axis V requires a global assessment of the individual's functioning. There are two types of global assessments made: level of functioning at time of evaluation and highest level of functioning during the past year. The GAF rating is based on a hypothetical continuum of mental health, ranging from 0 for highly disturbed to 100 for perfect mental health. Here is an example diagnosis:

Axis I: 300.21 Panic Disorder with Agoraphobia
           303.90 Alcohol Dependence

Axis II: 301.60 Dependent Personality Disorder (provisional, rule out Borderline Personality Disorder)

Axis III: Alcoholic cirrhosis of liver

Axis IV: Psychosocial problems: anticipated retirement and change in residence, with loss of contact with friends

Axis V: Current GAF: 40

Highest GAF past year: 55

Reaching this type of diagnosis is a logically complicated process. The DSM-IV includes decision trees to guide the process. Part of the decision tree for the differential diagnosis of anxiety disorders is presented here:

Symptoms of irritation and excessive anxiety or worry, avoidance behavior, or increased arousal not attributed to a psychotic disorder? If yes, go to:

Organic factor that initiated and maintained the disturbance has been established? If yes, go to organic decision tree. If no, go to:

Recurrent panic attacks? If no, go to:

Fear of being in certain places in case of an incapacitating or extremely embarrassing symptom? If yes, diagnosis is agoraphobia without panic disorder. If no, continue with tree.

Back to recurrent panic attacks, if yes, go to:

Fear of being in certain places in case of having a panic attack? If yes, diagnosis is panic disorder with agoraphobia. If no, diagnosis is panic disorder without agoraphobia.

... praise," "is overly concerned with physical attractiveness," and "is uncomfortable in situations in which he or she is not the center of attention." In order to provide enough observable, behavioral criteria to adequately describe a diagnostic characteristic, the DSM may become cumbersome and impractical.

Furthermore, in the guise of being "objective," many DSM labels contain latent and not-so-latent value judgments. Many critics claim that the DSM is biased toward seeing all behavior as symptomatic of some disorder or other. Others (Kaplan, 1983) have argued that it is biased in a sexist direction in that certain male behavior is seen as normal or "human," while certain female behavior is viewed as deviant. There are diagnostic labels for primarily feminine behaviors, such as dependent personality disorder, without complementary diagnoses for masculine behaviors, such as an "independent personality disorder" (Caplan, 1987a, 1991). Furthermore, critics say, the process of adding and deleting categories in the DSM is more political than scientific (see Box 3.3). For example, homosexuality was considered a disorder in the DSM-II, but because the lesbian and gay community organized itself to summarize the research evidence showing that homosexuals were as well adjusted as heterosexuals and to fight its inclusion as a disorder, it was removed from the DSM-III.

B O X   3 . 3

Controversies over Revising the DSM

The professional and political conflicts involved in developing a system of diagnosis of mental disorders became quite public during the 1987 revision of the DSM-III, known as the DSM-III-R, and continued through the next few years until the publication of the DSM-IV. *The Diagnostic and Statistical Manual of Mental Disorders* is published by the American Psychiatric Association, and critics charge that it is biased toward the therapeutic theories and professional needs of psychiatry. For decades, psychologists, social workers, and others have complained that they are not sufficiently consulted in the process of developing the diagnostic categories for the DSM.

At least three new categories proposed for the DSM-III-R and the DSM-IV aroused particularly strong opposition from psychologists, social workers, feminists, and others. These three were originally called masochistic personality disorder, premenstrual dysphoric disorder, and paraphilic rapism. Feminist critics called the original language for these categories "antifemale" and argued that they could easily be used to re-inforce negative attitudes toward and discrimination against women.

Along with other groups, the Committee on Women in Psychology (1985) of the American Psychological Association charged that the psychoanalytic term *masochistic personality disorder* would be disproportionately applied to persons who engaged in apparently self-defeating behaviors and who stayed in situations that appeared to be harmful to them. For example, women whose husbands beat them would be considered to have a psychopathological conditon, while the aggressive husbands would not. The APA Committee on Women (1985) stated,

> A large and well-developed body of research in the area of victimization would suggest that many of the criteria of this proposed diagnosis are, in fact, normative responses to the experience of having been victimized. . . . In a worst-case scenario, it is possible to imagine a battered woman with children who leaves her batterer and files for custody of the children, but loses it because she is diagnosed as having Masochistic Personality Disorder, while her batterer (for whom there exists no corollary diagnosis) appears more "normal" and functional. (pp. 1, 5)

In response to such criticisms, the name of this category was changed to "self-defeating personality disorder" in order to make it equally applicable to men. Many groups continued to oppose its inclusion, but it ended up being included.

The proposed category of premenstrual dysphoric disorder (PMDD) would obviously be applied only to women, and critics charged that it attempted to create a mental disorder for the known gynecological disorder of PMS, or premenstrual syndrome. The American Psychiatric Association Committee on Women, the Committee on Women of the American Psychological Association, the National Association of Social Workers, and others opposed this category. Defenders of the category argued that it would help women by legitimizing the monthly depression of those who have it and by allowing them to receive treatment for it. Critics continued to oppose the inclusion of this category, because it creates a gender-specific mental disorder, it reinforces stereotypical views of women as victims of "raging hormones," it can be used as a "scientific excuse" against women in the workplace, and there is insufficient evidence for it, among other objections. It was placed in the DSM-III-R appendix, but was dropped in the DSM-IV. Instead, a depressive personality disorder was added.

The category of paraphilic rapism would appear likely to be used to diagnose mostly men, yet feminists objected strongly to it. In addition to citing research that did not support the creation of such a category, the Committee on Women of the American Psychological Association (1985, p. 5) stated, "It appears to add little to the understanding of individuals who engage in sexual assault. Additionally, it would seem to provide an instant insanity plea for anyone charged with rape." At one point the name was changed to "paraphilic coercive disorder," but finally the category was dropped.

Some people argue that paraphilic rapism was dropped to placate feminist critics so that self-defeating personality disorder could be retained. Defenders of the DSM state that they create, change, keep, or eliminate various categories based on "scientific evidence," but critics still contend that "science" is being used to cover up a very political process. What do you think?

DSM-IV Work began on the DSM-IV in 1988 to prepare for its publication in 1994. Several DSM Task Forces and Work Groups proceeded through three stages of empirical documentation. The first stage involved reviewing the literature regarding specific problems with the DSM-III-R diagnoses. Once specific issues and areas were thus identified, the second stage attempted to reanalyze existing research in order to resolve the problems. Finally, the third stage conducted research trials to evaluate the reliability of the diagnoses and to evaluate the adequacy, reliability, and validity of proposed revisions. This process was funded in part by the MacArthur Foundation.

You can see from the description of the process that the development of the DSM-IV was supposed to be scientific and empirical. Criticisms that the process of adding and deleting categories in the DSM-III-R were more political than scientific, as discussed in Box 3.3, have continued with the DSM-IV. Furthermore, critics say the DSM revision process occurs so frequently that it disrupts research and does not allow sufficient empirical review of the diagnostic system to develop. The frequent changes without sufficient research increase the probability that theoretical and political biases will affect the development of diagnostic categories.

Criticisms of Diagnosis

Psychologists have been very critical of the use of the DSM in diagnosis. Smith and Kraft (1983) surveyed over 500 American Psychological Association psychologists for their opinions of the DSM-III. The majority clearly disavowed the DSM-III, saying they would prefer a new nosology based on better empirical research than that cited in the DSM-III. Many view the DSM-IV in the same negative light. Most psychologists believe that categories of behavior derived from good empirical evidence free of the medical model would lead to a more valid and reliable diagnostic system than the DSM.

Some people criticize the whole notion of diagnosis, regardless of the system, because diagnosing or classifying various disorders often leads to labeling. These critics argue that labeling people gives us a false sense of doing something helpful and useful, that labels always contain hidden value judgments, that labels are a way of controlling or devaluing others by objectifying them and making them "different," and that there is no mental "illness" or disorder to label anyway (Szasz, 1961).

Others believe that labels or diagnoses stigmatize a person, who may then be affected by a "self-fulfilling prophecy." Once people know that someone has been diagnosed as "schizophrenic" or "paranoid," they may act differently toward that per-

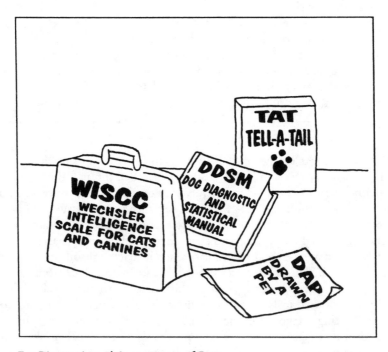

For Diagnosis and Assessment of Pets

son and induce the very behavior the label leads them to expect. Indeed, Farina and his colleagues have demonstrated that people both expect mental patients to be highly unpredictable (Farina & Fisher, 1982) and behave differently around them (Farina, Holland, & Ring, 1966). Rosenhan's (1973) study of "sane" graduate students admitted to mental hospitals demonstrated how others then construed all their behavior as evidence of abnormality.

Diagnosis is also criticized as being a mechanism of social control. The medical model and its attendant system of diagnosis is perceived by some critics to be a way for society to allow mental health professionals to become the social control agents of various irritating deviant members of society. If an irritating deviant, such as a loud drunk, is labeled as having the "illness" of "alcohol dependence," then doctors and psychiatrists are the proper authorities for controlling that behavior. The ultimate in the use of medicalization for social control can be seen in a diagnostic category proposed for inclusion in the DSM-IV, that of "adjustment reaction with maladaptive denial of physical illness" (Strauss, Spitzer, & Muskin, 1990, p. 168). On the one hand, there may well be some people with AIDS or other diseases who deny their illness and refuse treatment in a way that is harmful to themselves or others. However, with this new diagnosis, if physicians say someone is ill and they deny they are ill, then that is proof that they are ill with "maladaptive denial." Substitute the words "possessed by a demon" for the word "ill" and you have the same irrefutable system of logic that fueled the Inquisition.

It can be argued that diagnosis by itself is neither totally desirable nor totally undesirable. The question is, do the benefits of diagnosis outweigh the drawbacks? Some medical labels, such as venereal disease or AIDS, carry a social stigma, but a correct diagnosis of such diseases has positive benefits, such as correct treatment and possible cure. Much research demonstrates the social stigma attached to mental illness labels. Is there any evidence that diagnosis has positive consequences, such as determining the type of treatment to be administered?

Unfortunately, it often appears that in practice, individuals receive the form of treatment that is available, regardless of their diagnosis. Psychiatrists are especially criticized for prescribing medication too often simply because they have the power to do so. In hospitals with group therapy and occupational therapy, most patients receive group therapy and occupational therapy, whether they are schizophrenic or manic-depressive, whether they have a character disorder or are neurotic. Often, what type of treatment clients receive depends on such factors as whether other family members can make the appointment times, whether a certain kind of therapist has any free patient hours, or whether someone at the hospital wants to try a new kind of therapy on certain problems.

Despite the criticisms of diagnosis and the DSM, it seems likely that the recent trend to medicalize mental disorders will ensure that psychologists will often be involved in assessment in order to help make diagnoses. Thorough knowledge of the diagnostic process, the latest DSM, and the scientific or political process by which it is developed are essential for professional psychologists. It is still possible that psychologists will organize themselves and their body of scientific knowledge in order to create an alternative and, we trust, superior system of classifying psychological disorders.

IN CONCLUSION

This chapter described the theory and general methods of psychological assessment. It also discussed the reliability and validity, cost-effectiveness, and social uses or misuses of psychological tests. Because clinical psychologists are trained to research, develop, administer, score, and interpret psychological tests, tests will remain an important part of professional psychology. Through constant research and the help of computers to analyze and integrate this research, psychological tests will continue to improve and find new applications. Because people have always wanted to be able to predict human behavior in many situations, the tests will continue to be used and possibly misused. Educating the public, as well as students of psychology, about the nature and meaning of psychological tests may become an important ethical obligation of psychologists.

In the next two chapters we will consider specific tests and assessment techniques used in intellectual, cognitive, and neuropsychological assessment, and then, in personality, behavioral, and other types of assessment.

BIBLIOGRAPHY

Albee, G. (1985, February). The answer is prevention. *Psychology Today,* 60–64.

American Psychiatric Association. (1968). *Diagnostic and statistical manual of mental disorders* (2nd ed.). Washington, DC: Author.

American Psychiatric Association. (1980). *Diagnostic and statistical manual of mental disorders* (3rd ed.). Washington, DC: Author.

American Psychiatric Association. (1987). *Diagnostic and statistical manual of mental disorders* (3rd ed. rev.). Washington, DC: Author.

American Psychiatric Association. (1994). *Diagnostic and statistical manual of mental disorders,* (4th ed.). Washington, DC: Author.

APA Committee on Women in Psychology. (1985, October). *Statement on proposed diagnostic categories for DSM-III-R.* Washington, DC: American Psychological Association.

Butcher, J. (Ed.). (1987). *Computerized psychological assessment: A practitioner's guide.* New York: Basic Books.

Caplan, P. (1987a). The name game: Psychiatry, mysogyny, and taxonomy. *Women and Therapy, 6,* 187–202.

Caplan, P. (1987b). The psychiatric association's failure to meet its own standards: The dangers of "self-defeating personality disorder." *Journal of Personality Disorders, 1,* 178–182.

Caplan, P. (1991). How *do* they decide who is normal? The bizarre, but true, tale of the DSM process. *Canadian Psychology, 32,* 162–170.

Craig, R. J., & Horowitz, M. (1990). Current utilization of psychological tests at diagnostic practicum sites. *The Clinical Psychologist, 43,* 29–36.

Farberow, N. L., & Schneidman, E. S. (1961). *The cry for help.* New York: McGraw-Hill.

Farina, A., & Fisher, J. D. (1982). Beliefs about mental disorders: Findings and implications. In G. Weary & H. Mirels (Eds.), *Integrations of clinical and social psychology* (pp. 144–195). New York: Oxford University Press.

Farina, A., Holland, C. H., & Ring, K. (1966). The role of stigma and set in interpersonal interaction. *Journal of Abnormal Psychology, 70,* 421–428.

Gorenstein, E. E. (1984). Debating mental illness: Implications for science, medicine, and social policy. *American Psychologist, 39,* 50–56.

Gould, S. J. (1981). *The mismeasure of man.* New York: Norton.

Hager, P. (1991, October 29). Court bars psychological tests in hiring. *Los Angeles Times,* p. A20.

Helms, J. (1997). The triple quandary of race, culture, and social class in standardized cognitive ability testing. In D. Flanagan, J. Genshaft, & P. Harrison (Eds.), *Contemporary intellectual assessment.* New York: Guilford Press.

Kaplan, M. (1983). A woman's view of DSM-III. *American Psychologist, 38,* 786–792.

Lambert, N. M. (1981). Psychological evidence in *Larry P. v. Wilson Riles:* An evaluation of the evidence by a witness for the defense. *American Psychologist, 36,* 937–952.

Lubin, B., Larsen, R., & Matarazzo, J. (1984). Patterns of psychological test usage in the United States: 1935–1982. *American Psychologist, 39,* 451–454.

Matarazzo, J. (1992). Psychological testing and assessment in the 21st century. *American Psychologist, 43,* 484–485.

Matarazzo, J. D. (1986). Computerized clinical psychological test interpretations: Unvalidated plus all mean and no sigma. *American Psychologist, 41,* 14–24.

Meehl, P. E. (1954). *Clinical versus statistical prediction: A theoretical analysis and review of the evidence.* Minneapolis: University of Minnesota Press.

Meehl, P. E. (1956). Wanted—A good cookbook. *American Psychologist, 11,* 263–272.

Meehl, P. E. (1965). Seer over sign: The first good example. *Journal of Experimental Research in Personality, 1,* 27–32.

Messick, S. (1995). Validity of psychological assessment: Validation of inferences from persons' responses and performances as scientific inquiry into score meaning. *American Psychologist, 50,* 741–749.

Moore, N. C., Summer, K. R., & Bloor, R. N. (1984). Do patients like psychometric testing by computer? *Journal of Clinical Psychology, 40,* 875–877.

Nobins, L. N., & Helzer, J. E. (1986). Diagnosis and clinical assessment: The current state of psychiatric diagnosis. In M. R. Rosenzweig & L. W. Porter (Eds.), *Annual review of psychology* (pp. 55–69). Palo Alto, CA: Annual Reviews.

Piotrowski, C., & Keller, J. W. (1989). Psychological testing in outpatient mental health facilities: A national study. *Professional Psychology: Research and Practice, 20,* 423–425.

Rosenhan, D. (1973). On being sane in insane places. *Science, 179,* 180, 250–258, 365–369.

Smith, D., & Kraft, W. A. (1983). DSM-III: Do psychologists really want an alternative? *American Psychologist, 38,* 777–785.

Spitzer, R., Williams, J., & Skodol, A. (1980). DSM-III: The major achievements and an overview. *American Journal of Psychiatry, 137,* 151–164.

Strauss, D., Spitzer, R., & Muskin, P. (1990). Maladaptive denial of physical illness: A proposal for DSM-IV. *American Journal of Psychiatry, 147,* 1168–1172.

Sundberg, N., Tyler, L., & Taplin, R. (1973). *Clinical psychology: Expanding horizons.* Englewood Cliffs, NJ: Prentice-Hall.

Szasz, T. (1961). *The myth of mental illness: Foundations of a theory of personal conduct.* New York: Harper & Row.

Widiger, T. A. (1991a). Definition, diagnosis, and differentiation. *Journal of Personality Disorders, 5,* 42–51.

Widiger, T. A. (1991b). DSM-IV reviews of the personality disorders: Introduction to special series. *Journal of Personality Disorders, 5,* 122–134.

Widiger, T. A., Frances, A., Pincus, H., & Davis, W. (1991). DSM-IV literature reviews: Rationale, process, and limitations. *Journal of Psychopathology and Behavioral Assessment, 12,* 189–202.

CHAPTER 4

Methods of Intellectual, Cognitive, and Neuropsychological Assessment

LaTisha M., age 8, rarely attends school, where she is in the third grade, because of headaches and stomachaches. Although she did well in kindergarten, she began to have difficulty with learning to read in the first grade. When she was in second grade, LaTisha was pushed from some playground equipment and sustained a head injury, which went untreated. LaTisha's mother has six other children, and she rarely has time to pay attention to LaTisha except when she complains of illness. The school is beginning to demand that LaTisha's mother get some help for her, but the mother does not know where to begin.

What can be done to help this child? Before we can answer this question, we need to evaluate several aspects of her current functioning. Because her difficulties are related to school, it seems reasonable to assess her intellectual and cognitive abilities. Because of the headaches and the head injury, neuropsychological assessment would also be appropriate. Obviously, the stomachaches and headaches require a separate physical examination. Finally, because of the hints of emotional and family problems, personality assessment should be included. It may also be necessary to request other information, such as school reports, and further evaluations, such as by a speech pathologist or educational psychologist. Although covered in the next chapter, interviews with the mother and the child before and after any assessment procedure are necessary. This chapter focuses on a portion of any complete psychological assessment, the portion dealing with tests of cognitive and neuropsychological functioning.

INTELLECTUAL AND COGNITIVE ASSESSMENT

Although covering the years of controversy over the definition of intelligence is beyond the scope of this book, let us briefly point out two points of contention. Early researchers considered intelligence to be a general factor (g-factor) or characteristic that was manifested in a wide range of behaviors. Later psychologists have argued that intelligence is a collection of different kinds of abilities, all relatively independent of each other. The first view holds that a person of high intelligence will be superior to others in many different ways, while in the second view, a person may be high in logical intelligence but low in artistic intelligence. The second controversy has to do with whether intelligence is inherited and relatively unchangeable or it is environmentally determined and can be improved.

However intelligence is defined, psychologists have developed a number of tests designed to measure it. In response to the above issues, some have argued that a better term for intelligence tests is cognitive ability tests (CATs) and that they should simply be regarded as a systematic way to gather samples of school-related skills and behaviors in a structured setting.

The Stanford-Binet

The first so-called intelligence scale was published in 1905 (Binet & Simon, 1905). At the turn of the century, the Paris school system had asked Alfred Binet and his colleagues to develop a test that would predict which children would do well in school and which children would not, so something could be done about the latter. Note the assumption that if children fail to benefit from schooling, it must be because of some (measurable) defect in the children, not because of any inadequacy in the educational system. Many critics think that the tests are still used to label and discriminate against children, rather than to change education or tailor it to individuals' needs.

Binet did as he was asked, and he did it brilliantly. He developed tests that directly sampled the skills needed in school, such as verbal comprehension, numerical skills, logical reasoning, visual discrimination, and the like. He developed standardized tests of these skills and administered them in standardized ways to many children. Because of this standardization, the performance of different children could be compared directly.

In addition, he developed the concept of age norms. He noted how many children of a particular age in a standardization group passed specific test items. Test items that half of 6-year-olds passed were called 6-year items. By this means, the scores of children could be directly compared across ages. A 9-year-old who passed the 6-year items and failed the 7-year items was considered to be the intellectual equal of an average 6-year-old.

Binet's test was modified in the United States by psychologists at Stanford University (Terman, 1916). It is still in use today as the Stanford-Binet Intelligence Scale, Form LM (Terman & Merrill, 1973) and the more recent Stanford-Binet Intelligence Scale, Fourth Edition, published in 1986 (Thorndike, Hagen, & Sattler, 1986).

The Stanford-Binet is administered individually by a trained psychologist. It can be used to test individuals from age 2 years to adult. The raw scores of the standardization groups are statistically transformed by a formula into IQ (intelligence quotient) scores, which are presented in tables in the test manual. A particular testee's raw scores are then compared to the tables to obtain an IQ. An IQ of 100 represents the average or mean score for an age group. The standard deviation is set at 16. If a particular individual achieves an IQ score of 116 on the Stanford-Binet, we know that she or he scored one standard deviation above the mean of the standardization group of the same age, or about 84 percent higher than most people of that age.

Up until the Fourth Edition, the Stanford-Binet produced only one overall IQ score, so it was difficult to assess an individual's strengths and weaknesses. Furthermore, the test items were different for each age. For example, a 3-year-old might be asked to identify body parts on a picture of a child, copy paper folded into a shape, match geometric designs, copy a circle, and determine whether two drawings match or not, while an 8-year-old might be asked to define words, compute math problems, and do analogies. Critics viewed this situation as unsound, because in fact different skills, perhaps even different types of intelligence, were tested at different ages.

The Fourth Edition made major changes in the Stanford-Binet. There are now four general classes of tests, each with several kinds of subtests for ages 2 to adult. The four types of tests are verbal reasoning, quantitative reasoning, abstract/visual reasoning, and short-term memory. It is now possible to analyze a person's strengths and weaknesses, but because some of the subtests still differ for different ages, the Stanford-Binet is still criticized for evaluating intelligence differently at different ages. On the other hand, one of the strengths of the test is that it can be used with such a wide age range, and it is quite possible that there are developmental differences in the organization of cognitive skills and intelligence at different ages so that different types of tests would be required.

The Wechsler Tests

The Wechsler intelligence scales are now used more often than the Stanford-Binet. Beginning in the 1940s and making later revisions, David Wechsler and his colleagues have developed an intelligence test for children ages 5 to 16, the Wechsler Intelligence Scale for Children (WISC), later revised as the WISC-R (Wechsler, 1974) and revised again in 1991 as the WISC-III (Wechsler, 1991); one for adults, the Wechsler Adult Intelligence Scale, Revised, or WAIS-R (Wechsler, 1981); and another for children ages 4 to 6, the Wechsler Preschool and Primary Scale of Intelligence or WPPSI (Wechsler, 1967), revised in 1989.

The structure of all the Wechsler tests is alike. They are divided into two parts: verbal subtests, which assess verbal skills such as vocabulary and comprehension, and performance subtests, which tap nonverbal skills such as putting puzzles together and copying designs. Unlike the Stanford-Binet, which contains different subtests for different ages, all individuals are tested on the same subtests, which contain items of increasing difficulty so that older or brighter people answer more items within each subtest. A summary of the subtests in the WISC-III is presented in Box 4.1. Most of the subtests of the WAIS-R are quite similar, but more difficult, while the WPPSI contains similar, but simpler and more concrete test items in each subtest.

BOX 4.1

Subtests of the WISC-III

VERBAL SUBTESTS

Arithmetic
A series of arithmetic problems that the child solves mentally and responds to orally.

Comprehension
A series of orally presented questions that require the child's solving of everyday problems or understanding of social rules and concepts.

Digit Span
A series of orally presented number sequences that the child repeats verbatim for Digits Forward and in reverse order for Digits Backwards. This test is optional and not administered in every case.

Information
A series of orally presented questions that tap the child's knowledge about common events, objects, places, and people.

Similarities
A series of orally presented pairs of words for which the child explains the similarity of the common objects or concepts they represent.

Vocabulary
A series of orally presented words that the child orally defines.

PERFORMANCE SUBTESTS

Block Design
A set of modeled or printed two-dimensional geometric patterns which the child replicates using two-color cubes.

Coding
A series of simple shapes or numbers, each paired with a simple symbol. The child draws the symbol in its corresponding shape or under its corresponding number, according to a key.

Mazes
A set of increasingly difficult mazes, printed in a response booklet, that the child solves with a pencil. This subtest is optional and not administered in every case.

Object Assembly
A set of puzzles of common objects, each presented in a standardized configuration, that the child assembles to form a meaningful whole.

BOX 4.1 *(continued)*

Picture Arrangement
A set of colorful pictures, presented in mixed-up order, that the child re-arranges into a logical story sequence.

Picture Completion
A set of colorful pictures of common objects and scenes, each of which is missing an important part that the child identifies.

Symbol Search
A series of paired groups of symbols, each pair consisting of a target group and a search group. The child scans the two groups and indicates whether or not a target symbol appears in the search group. This test is optional, but often administered.

From Wechsler, D. (1991). *WISC-III Manual.* New York: The Psychological Corporation.

Like the Stanford-Binet, the Wechsler tests are based on the norms of large standardization groups for each age, and the raw scores are transformed through a statistical formula into IQ scores, which are summarized in tables. The mean of the Wechsler IQ is set at 100, but the standard deviation is set at 15. Three IQ scores are calculated for an individual: the verbal IQ, the performance IQ, and the full-scale IQ. Furthermore, the raw scores of each subtest are transformed into standardized "scaled scores" with a mean of 10 and a standard deviation of 3. These subtest scaled scores can be profiled in order to compare relative strengths and weaknesses. Thus, it is possible to obtain a great deal of information about a specific testee.

For example, if a person had a full-scale IQ score of 100, we know that he or she performed at the mean for his or her age group, or better than 50 percent of people his or her age, but this does not tell us much. If we know that this individual scored 115 on the verbal part of the test and 85 on the performance part, then we know that he or she scored one standard deviation above the mean, or better than 84 percent of most people, in verbal skills, but one standard deviation below the mean, or better than only 16 percent of most people, on the performance skills. Furthermore, we can examine subtest scores for even more information about an individual's strengths and weaknesses. A scaled score of 16 on one verbal subtest means that person scored two standard deviations above the mean in that particular area, which might be significant compared to the same person's scaled score of 7 on a performance subtest. In fact, differences in Wechsler subtest scores are used diagnostically in assessment of learning disabilities and neuropsychological disorders.

The 1991 WISC-III contains several important changes from the earlier Wechsler tests. While the age-related norms were updated, the test items were also revised to make them more interesting to children; items that were unfair to certain cultural groups were eliminated; and a new subtest, Symbol Search, was added. Furthermore, the WISC-III was subjected to much research and factor analysis, and four factors, or clusters of scores, were found. As might be expected, given the division of the tests into Verbal and Performance subtests, the first two and the strongest factors are Verbal Comprehension and Perceptual Organization. Two other factors are called Freedom from Distractibility and Processing Speed. It is now possible to obtain IQ-like scores on these four indexes, in addition to the Verbal, Performance, and Full Scale IQ scores. Thus, the WISC-III produces a great deal of information about intellectual functioning that can be used to help diagnose learning difficulties and design helpful interventions.

Other Intellectual and Cognitive Tests

There are many other intelligence scales, some with special uses. For example, the Peabody Picture Vocabulary Test—Revised or PPVT-R (Dunn, 1959), revised in the 1980s, can be used to test children and adults who have a problem speaking English, perhaps because they are not native English speakers or because they have a speech disorder. Test takers are presented with four pictures and asked to point to the picture that represents a certain word. The vocabulary is different for different age groups. For example, children may be asked to point to a "car," while adults may be asked to point to "imbibe" or "bovine." The raw scores are converted to IQ scores, which compare fairly well to the IQs from other tests. This test is short and easy to administer, and it may provide a better estimate of a speech-disordered person's intellectual functioning than a Wechsler test.

An addition to the field of intellectual assessment of children is the Kaufman Assessment Battery for Children or K-ABC (Kaufman & Kaufman, 1983). It is suitable for children ages 2 to 12. This test has two unique features. It tries to assess the functions of the right and left hemispheres of the brain, and it tries to separate the measurement of skills or "intelligence" from that of fact-oriented or acquired knowledge. The separation of measurements is an attempt to answer the frequent criticism that intelligence tests really measure cultural and acquired knowledge and are therefore biased in favor of middle-class, white people. The test has three sections. The Sequential Processing scale involves the solution of problems presented in a serial or temporal order (a left-hemisphere function); the Simultaneous Processing scale requires the integration and synthesis of problem materials (a right-hemisphere function); and the Achievement scale assesses scholastic achievement or grade-level performance.

Another example of a cognitive ability test is the Woodcock-Johnson Test of Cognitive Abilities, or WJ-R (Woodcock & Johnson, 1989). Based on a theory of fluid and crystallized abilities, this test assesses eight areas: Fluid Reasoning, Visual Processing, Processing Speed, Long-Term Retrieval, Comprehension-Knowledge, Auditory Processing, Short-Term Memory, and Quantitative Ability.

Achievement tests are frequently given with intelligence tests. It is often important to know how the level of global functioning measured by the intelligence tests compares to the level of academic achievement. Discrepancies, such as a child with a high IQ and low achievement, require explanation. There are many group and individual achievement tests, but the Wide Range Achievement Test, Third Edition, or WRAT-3, (Jastak & Jastak, 1965), revised in 1993, is an example. It is short and straightforward in administration and scoring. It assesses three areas of achievement: reading, spelling, and arithmetic. An individual's scores in the three areas are both age normed and transformed into grade equivalents.

Reliability and Validity of Cognitive Ability Tests

It is generally agreed that properly administered intelligence tests are highly reliable, by both split-half and test-retest measures of reliability. For the Stanford-Binet, internal consistency correlations were reported to be in the .80s and .90 range, and test-retest correlations for intervals of two to eight months were reported from the .70s to the low .90s. Wechsler reported higher reliabilities for his tests, with internal consistency for the WAIS-R ranging from .93 to .97 and test-retest reliabilities for short intervals ranging from the .70s to the high .90s.

It should be pointed out that the intelligence tests were constructed so that they would be reliable. Careful standardization and using transformed scores contribute to these tests' reliability. After all, they were designed so that they would measure what was assumed to be an enduring characteristic. When it comes to specific individuals, most people will score rather similarly when given IQ tests at different times, except for young children, whose motivation and cooperation may change greatly. A 12-year-old's IQ will generally be quite similar to his or her IQ at 13; the IQs at ages 12 and 20 will be less similar but still close. However, an individual may show large changes in IQ scores over time if there are changes in any number of important variables, such as health, motivation, mood, type of education, or psychological disorder.

The validity of intelligence tests is much more debatable, as discussed in Chapter 3. Recall that validity refers to the accuracy or appropriateness of the interpretation of the results of a test: Do IQ tests really measure intelligence, as they are often interpreted to do? Naturally, the answer to this question depends on the definition of intelligence. The theoretical argument over the nature of intelligence becomes important outside of academia when the lives of individuals are affected by decisions based on intelligence test scores.

Like many subsequent psychologists, Binet developed a pragmatic definition of intelligence—it was whatever the tests he was constructing measured. Spearman (1904) originated the theoretical definition of intelligence as a unitary factor, which became known as general intelligence or g factor. He considered intelligence to be an innate, global capacity that runs through and accounts for all the different skills and abilities a person may have. Although Wechsler's tests divide intelligence into verbal and performance skills, he, like Spearman, defined intelligence as "the aggregate or global capacity of the individual to act purposefully, to think rationally, and to deal effectively with his environment" (Wechsler, 1974, p. 3).

Other researchers have refuted the idea of intelligence as a unitary factor, and many, among them Gardner (1983) and Piaget and his colleagues (Flavell, 1963), have argued that there are types of intelligence that are not being measured by current intelligence tests. Furthermore, they have evidence that children's cognitions are qualitatively different at different developmental stages so that an intellectual test given to all ages cannot assess these important differences. Gardner (1983) identified at least seven different kinds of intelligence: linguistic skills, logical and mathematical skills, visual and spatial conceptualization, musical skills, bodily kinesthetic skills, interpersonal skills, and intrapersonal knowledge. Each kind of intelligence functions semiautonomously and has its own form of memory, learning, and perception. Gardner argued that our culture values only the first two kinds of intelligence and they are what intelligence tests measure, not "true" intelligence.

One type of evidence used to assess the validity of intelligence tests is predictive validity. What do the tests predict? Career success? Happiness? Income potential? No, they predict school grades, because they sample school-related tasks and skills. And what do school grades predict? College grades. And college grades predict graduate school grades. Do these grades predict success or income? The evidence is mixed (Ceci & Williams, 1997). Validity becomes a special concern when cognitive ability tests are applied outside their culture of origin. It can be argued that ability tests can be considered items of symbolic culture (Greenfield, 1997) that are constructed within racial, cultural, and socioeconomic contexts (Helms, 1997). In that case, the racial, cultural, and socioeconomic characteristics of the test-maker, test-giver, and test-taker will influence test results and can undermine test validity. Given the increasing cultural diversity of the United States, this possibility becomes an important issue.

The question of the validity of intelligence tests is important because of the social uses to which the tests are put. Although IQ tests are often used to help children receive the most appropriate and helpful educational experiences they can, they are at times used to label certain people, to lay the blame for their failure in school on them rather than on the educational system, and to assign minority group children disproportionately to special education classes, as was discussed in the case of *Larry P.* in the last chapter. If these tests do not really measure intelligence, if there are indeed many types of intelligence that people could use if the culture valued them, then these uses of intelligence tests represent a social injustice. Test validity is more than a theoretical issue of interest to psychologists; it has real-life consequences for some people and for society.

The controversial nature of the validity of intelligence tests came to public, as well as professional and academic, attention with the publication of a book called *The Bell Curve* (Herrnstein & Murray, 1994). One chapter of this book argued that racial differences in IQ are inherited, and this point sparked a great deal of public and scientific debate. Although not many addressed the point that there is little evidence for the existence of "races" in the first place, many have argued that there is little evidence for the book's thesis (Neisser et al., 1996) and that there are major errors in the book's statistical analyses (Fischer et al., 1996).

Clinical Use of Intelligence Tests

At present, in clinical practice, the Wechsler scales are used more frequently than the Stanford-Binet or any other intelligence test. Although psychologists have rapidly embraced the WISC-III, they have been resistant to changing to the Stanford-Binet IV, partly because it seems difficult to administer. The Stanford-Binet is most likely to be used to assess children under the age of 5. The occasion to test such young children arises largely when there is reason to suspect mental retardation and the parents are trying to obtain special services.

The WAIS-R is often used to assess adults who have lost some degree of cognitive functioning because of illness or injury. In such cases, it is necessary to estimate the prior level of intelligence by the person's amount of education and occupational level and possibly by asking family members. The comparison of present intellectual strengths and deficits to the estimated prior intellectual level can be useful diagnostically and in planning treatment or rehabilitation.

The WISC-III is widely used for a variety of purposes. It is useful in differential diagnosis and in identifying causes of difficulties in school, as seen in the case of Jimmy S. in the psychological assessment report in Box 4.4. The WISC-III may be helpful in several ways in the case of LaTisha M. The WISC-III may suggest evidence of psychoneurological disorder or a learning disability, and other kinds of interventions could be planned. On the other hand, if in fact she performed well in all areas of the test, then the reasons for her school difficulties are not intellectual deficits, and other evaluations would be necessary. Achievement tests would be useful at this point. Whether her achievement scores were appropriate for her intellectual level or much lower than would be expected is important in explaining her school difficulties.

Many psychologists regard intelligence tests as methods for gathering behavioral observations in different structured settings. They observe how the child copes with the stress of the test, the kinds of verbal answers given, and the nonverbal behavior and physical coordination demonstrated during performance tests. Jimmy S. exhibited a great deal of motor activity throughout the WISC-III, behavior that suggested either anxiety or hyperactivity, and it is possible that LaTisha M. may exhibit anxiety by complaining, refusing to answer, or losing concentration during certain subtests. If she were to put puzzles and block designs together in a rapid, systematic fashion, it would lead to different conclusions than if she did them slowly, in a haphazard, poorly planned, or uncoordinated manner.

The content in responses to certain questions can be analyzed in terms of what they imply about the child's worldview, social perceptions, attitudes, and the like. Jimmy S. revealed a surprisingly positive attitude toward the police in his reply to the question asking about why we have police. A completely different social perception would be revealed if LaTisha M. were to answer the same question by saying that "We don't need them. They just hurt you." The Picture Arrangement subtest is especially useful in eliciting social attitudes. In this test, the child is asked to arrange mixed-up cartoon panels in the proper order so that the pictures "tell a story." While this test taps sequential logic, it is also interesting to ask children to tell the story, especially if the order they give is incorrect. Additional information about their reasoning and their understanding of social relationships and implicit social rules can thus be obtained.

These few examples give an idea of how the intellectual tests are used in clinical practice, but the tests can reveal a great deal more in the hands of a highly trained, skilled psychologist. Assessment of children with learning disabilities almost always includes the WISC-III, and researchers are finding ways to analyze WISC subtest scores for what they indicate about specific forms of neurological impairment, as discussed in the following section.

NEUROPSYCHOLOGICAL ASSESSMENT

The field of neuropsychology studies the relation between brain and behavior, and neuropsychological assessment involves a set of procedures designed to detect the presence, extent, and type of organic brain damage or neurological impairment in individuals through evaluating the behavior that is related to brain functioning. As researchers learn more about the brain and its contribution to behavior, and even behavior's effect on the brain, physiological and neurological factors must be taken into account in all forms of assessment, including personality assessment, and we can expect that neuropsychological assessment will become an increasingly important part of the occupation of psychologists. In fact, the field has grown so quickly that Division 40 (Clinical Neuropsychology) was the fastest-growing division in the APA during the 1980s, with a 533 percent increase in membership from 1980 to 1990.

Another, unfortunate reason for the growth in neuropsychological assessment is the increase in brain damage in our society. Because of advances in medical technology, the lives of severely head-injured people are being saved. This same advanced medical technology saves the lives of babies born prematurely or otherwise damaged to mothers too poor to obtain adequate prenatal care or nutrition. We will not address the issue of a society that pays a fortune for emergency medical care to save the lives of babies who would not be damaged if it would pay for less costly preventive care, but we will simply point out that these social forces and medical changes are increasing the need for clinical neuropsychologists.

Research on the brain has grown exponentially in the last century, and especially rapidly in the last two decades with the technological development of computerized ways of imaging and studying the brain. The earlier work on split brains, which demonstrated different skills in the right and left hemispheres of the brain, is well-known enough that people make remarks such as "That artist is so right brain." Of course, in real brains the hemispheres are connected and work together, so the concept of hemispheric dominance is somewhat misunderstood by the public. Nevertheless, recent findings in brain science are fascinating.

A controversial issue throughout history has been whether functions are localized in certain parts of the brain or whether the brain is *equipotential* and any part can have any function. As usual, the final answer seems to be both. Although many functions are localized, the brain is highly plastic, with a great deal of individual variation, and it appears that if part of the brain is destroyed, other parts can take over its functions, at least in some cases. One of our graduate students suffered severe brain damage at birth so that only a thin outer layer of brain tissue remained intact, yet this student achieved well-deserved A grades.

Because some functions are localized to some degree in specific parts of the brain, the location of a brain injury will determine the nature of the resulting behavioral deficits. While Gazzaniga (1985) has gathered years of extensive evidence that the brain is a loosely connected set of modules, each with its own way of functioning, clinical psychoneurologists at present look at brain organization in terms of large portions of the brain. For example, the right and left hemispheres of the brain differ in that certain abilities related to sequential reasoning, vocabulary, and detail analysis appear to be preferentially handled in the left hemisphere of the brain in most individuals, while abilities related to wholistic reasoning, spatial relations, and implied meanings appear to be handled by the right. However, it is important to keep in mind that the brain normally functions as a unit and requires all its parts for any one function.

You may be wondering why we need neuropsychological assessment, given the number of medical tests for brain damage. Computers and technology allow the development of new ways to study the brain. Matarazzo (1992) argued that even intelligence tests in the future will be biologically based when there is sufficient knowledge about brain-behavior functions. At present, there are X rays, EEGs, CAT scans, PET scans, and nuclear magnetic resonance techniques. Although these are powerful tests, there are problems of interpretation with them. Because the brain is plastic, injuries to certain parts of the brain do not necessarily predict the type of behavioral deficits that will result. Neuropsychological assessment is necessary in order to determine the exact nature of behavioral deficits in any kind of brain disorder so treatment can be planned (see Box 4.2).

The causes of brain damage are many. Accidents are a leading cause of brain trauma. Blockages of blood vessels in the brain, known as vascular accidents or strokes, can cause certain parts of the brain to die, as can a cerebral hemorrhage, or rupturing of the blood vessels, and brain tumors. Degenerative diseases, such as Alzheimer's, are well-known causes of organic brain disorders. A variety of environmental toxins harm the brain, as in mercury and lead poisoning. Nutritional deficiencies also harm the brain, especially in children. Lack of oxygen during difficult births, and toxins, diseases, and poor nutrition during pregnancy are important causes of damage to the developing nervous system and brain.

Symptoms of brain disorder also vary. Disturbances in perception, inability to smell, slurring of speech or inability to speak, a change in coordination, headaches, a sudden change in emotional reactivity, or a deterioration in intellectual functioning

---

BOX 4.2

Some Examples of Disorders of Learning and Memory Associated with Neurologic Injury

Temporal Lobe.   Left temporal lobe damage is associated with impaired memory for verbal material, while damage to the right temporal lobe is linked to an inability to recall nonverbal material, such as faces or geometric drawings.

Frontal Lobe.   Damage to the upper middle frontal lobe is associated with inhibition of information processing. Front lesions are linked to a disinhibition of stimulus-response reactions, characterized by impulsivity and hyperactivity.

Parietal Lobe.   Parietal lobe damage has been associated with impaired performance of order memory tasks for auditory and visual information.

Cerebral Cortex.   Injuries of the cerebral cortex have been associated with distractibility.

Cerebellum.   In laboratory studies, damage of the cerebellum is associated with loss of previously learned conditioned responses in animals.

From: Lauerman, J. (1992, May/June). Neurologic impairment: Understanding the effects on learning. *Headlines,* pp. 12–15.

all may indicate the presence of neurological damage. These symptoms must be differentiated from similar ones seen in some psychoses or even malingering. Other types of brain impairment are subtle and may become evident only when complex tasks are encountered, as in learning to read. It is obviously important to understand the cause of such symptoms so appropriate treatment can be developed.

Single Neuropsychological Tests

Because of the complexity of the brain and of brain-behavior relations, neuropsychological testing is also complex, generally requiring the use of several types of tests. However, in previous decades, single tests were developed to detect the general presence or absence of brain damage. All of the short, single neuropsychological tests involve drawing and copying designs.

The oldest neuropsychological test is the Bender-Motor-Gestalt Test (Bender, 1938). Short and easy to administer, it involves copying geometric designs, a task commonly incorporated into psychoneurological test batteries. It consists of a series of nine geometric designs, each on a small card. The test taker is given a blank sheet of paper and a pencil and asked to copy the designs as they are presented one at a time. The test taker must be able to perceive the design and then draw it, hence a measure of visual-motor coordination. The copied designs are scored for their accuracy and their preservation of the **gestalt,** or overall form, of the designs. Designs that are poorly done considering the age of the child would suggest that there is impairment in the child's visual-motor coordination, which would be due to some organic brain dysfunction. However, the Bender-Gestalt is no longer considered an adequate test of neuropsychological functioning.

The Beery Buktenica Developmental Test of Visual-Motor Integration (VMI), published in 1989, may be used in place of the Bender-Gestalt. It also involves copying designs, and three of the designs are the same as those in the Bender-Gestalt. However, all the designs are contained in a booklet, the designs are arranged in order of difficulty, and specific scoring criteria and extensive age-related norms have been developed. Some examples of VMI designs are shown in Box 4.3.

Another figure copying test, the Rey-Osterrieth Complex Figure (Osterrieth, 1944), is also in use. The child copies one very complicated geometric drawing with different colored pencils so that his or her strategy for copying the design can be analyzed for specific types of neurological deficit.

The Halstead-Reitan Battery

The Halstead-Reitan Battery is a complicated but comprehensive set of tests originally developed by Halstead and continually revised by Reitan and his colleagues (Reitan, 1966; Reitan & Davison, 1974). It is probably the most widely used test in neuropsychological assessment. To give you an idea of just how comprehensive it is, Reitan recommends allowing eight hours just to administer the test! Obviously, the testing should be broken up into two or more sessions. Because of the long administration time, technicians sometimes administer all or parts of the test, leaving the intricacies of interpretation to the neuropsychologist.

BOX 4.3

Some Drawings from the VMI Developmental Test of Visual-Motor Integration

The drawings below represent six of those included in the VMI Developmental Test of Visual-Motor Integration. The drawings by the 10-year-old girl are not perfect, but they are accurate representations of the designs she was told to copy. The drawings by the 11-year-old boy show some errors commonly made by children with learning disabilities. The designs are drawn awkwardly, with much pressure on the pencil, lines drawn over each other several times, and lines drawn not very straight. In the design in the upper left, the partial square is rotated and runs into the circle. In the design in the upper right, the arrows to do not properly join the lines. In the design in the lower right, the circle is not round, the point of contact between circle and square is poorly drawn, and the square lacks two proper corners. Such errors are given certain scores, according to criteria in the VMI manual, and scores can be compared to age norms.

Drawn by an 11-year-old boy with learning difficulties:

Drawn by a 10-year-old girl with no learning difficulties:

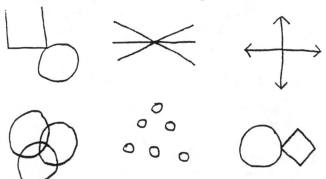

The Halstead-Reitan includes several procedures: an intelligence test; aphasia tests; copying tasks; a memory test; tactile, visual, and auditory discrimination tests; speech, rhythm, and fine motor coordination tasks; form board problems; and more. New tests are occasionally added. Directions and research on the test are published in a variety of papers, and Reitan training workshops are offered to psychologists and physicians.

The Luria-Nebraska Battery

Based on the work of Russian Alexander Luria, the Luria-Nebraska Neuropsychological Battery (Golden, Hammeke, & Purisch, 1980), like the Reitan, undergoes constant modification. The battery consists of over 250 items divided into 11 content scales, from which 3 overall scales are derived. For example, the Tactile scale, a content scale, measures touch localization and tactile recognition by asking patients to do things such as tell where they are being touched with a pencil. Another content scale, the Memory scale, measures types of memory deficits by asking patients to do things such as repeat back a short story. The three derived scales are the Pathognomonic, which contains items from throughout the battery that detect the presence or absence of brain damage; the Left Hemisphere, which contains items from parts of the battery that reflect left-brain function; and the Right Hemisphere, which contains items that reflect right-brain function. The Luria-Nebraska has been criticized for its theoretical foundations and for methodological flaws in its standardization.

The Boston Process Approach

A group of neuropsychologists, physicians, and other professionals at Boston University School of Medicine have developed an approach to neuropsychological assessment of children with learning difficulties, known as the Boston process approach. They utilize a variety of well-known and new assessment techniques, but they interpret the results of these measures in terms of a theory that emphasizes the process by which the patient solves the problems presented by the tests. They emphasize that the meaning of test scores is context-dependent, including the contexts of age, sex, socioeconomic class, developmental history, genetic background, handedness, developmental level, emotional style, and even the interactional style with the examiner. They consider behavior deficits to reflect the *intact* portion of the brain doing its best in the absence of the damaged portion of the brain, so that strengths, not just deficits, are examined.

Traditional neuropsychological tests and the WISC-III are analyzed in terms of this brain-world, context-dependent model. Among the many tests used in the Boston approach, children may be asked to perform difficult motor tasks, such as walking on the sides of the feet. How well children perform such tasks for their age and what sorts of behaviors are elicited by the stress of the tasks can provide trained observers with much information about the children's neurological functioning. Among the contextual variables taken into consideration in the process approach, the functioning of the examiner-child dyad is examined. For example, if the examiner feels her space is invaded, then the child may have a social problem; if the examiner finds herself using very simple speech, then the child may have a language deficit; or if the examiner begins talking louder and louder, the child may need an audiologist.

Reliability and Validity of Neuropsychological Tests

There are special problems in determining the reliability of neuropsychological tests. Because they take so long to administer, a thorough evaluation may take place over several days, so internal consistency becomes essentially a measure of test-retest reliability. Organic patients may be deteriorating or (preferably) improving, so that their performance will differ on subsequent tests. In spite of these problems, some studies (Golden, Hammeke, & Purisch, 1980) indicate that reliability is adequate.

Validity of neuropsychological tests can be examined by several criteria. One measure of validity is the tests' ability to pinpoint the location of brain lesions, as determined by brain scans, the results of neurosurgery, or autopsy, as well as their ability to differentiate organicity from psychosis or other diagnoses. Predictive validity would include the effectiveness of interventions based on the test results. Studies (reviewed by Goldstein, 1984) indicate fairly good validity for the Reitan, although that of the Luria-Nebraska has been criticized (Adams, 1984).

Clinical Uses of Neuropsychological Assessment

Typically, neuropsychological assessment is used with adults to assess stroke patients, head injury victims, or people with aphasia, amnesia, brain tumors, epilepsy, or senility, and with children to assess learning disabilities. In addition to use in medical research, neuropsychological tests are used for diagnosis, prognosis, differential diagnosis, and planning of patient care and rehabilitation. With children, they are used to evaluate the specific deficits involved in learning disabilities so that individually tailored educational intervention plans can be made.

As research advances and as knowledge of brain function improves, neuropsychology will continue to develop new tests and procedures to evaluate learning disabilities and other behavioral consequences of brain impairment. Appropriate interventions can be implemented only from a comprehensive picture of the nature of cognitive impairment. For example, it may be well known that stroke patients have suffered specific kinds of brain damage, but neuropsychological assessment evaluates the precise kinds of cognitive impairment, such as short-term memory loss or word retrieval difficulty, that are present so that appropriate interventions, such as memory retraining and speech therapy, can be designed. In the Boston model, behavior is assessed as a reflection of the intact brain coping with the damage, so that interventions are oriented to developing and training the intact part to compensate for the impairment.

Neuropsychological assessment is important in differential diagnosis. In elderly patients, for example, evidence of cognitive impairment may be erroneously interpreted as reflecting an organic disease when actually, cognitive abilities have been compromised by a psychiatric disorder such as depression. Costly and inappropriate treatments may be tried, and the failure to treat the depression may result in greater cognitive loss. With both LaTisha M. and Jimmy S., it is important to know if their difficulties in school are due to psychosocial problems or to specific learning disabilities, because very different treatment recommendations would be made in either case.

Although the Boston process approach is achieving national recognition, the Halstead-Reitan and Luria-Nebraska are the most commonly used neuropsychological test batteries. A national survey of over 200 psychologists trained in both batteries found that 51 percent preferred the Halstead-Reitan and 23 percent preferred the Luria-Nebraska (Guilmette & Faust, 1991).

IN CONCLUSION

The intelligence tests remain psychology's big success. They are the most frequently used individual psychological test in clinical practice. They have been constructed such that they have the highest reliability of all psychological tests, although questions about their validity remain controversial. Neuropsychological assessment is poised to become psychology's next big success. Already extremely useful in diagnosing and designing interventions and rehabilitation for the increasing numbers of brain-injured people in our society, neuropsychological tests will improve in reliability, validity, and clinical utility as current research continues to help us understand brain structure and functioning and to pinpoint brain and behavior connections.

BOX 4.4

Example Evaluation Report

PSYCHOLOGICAL EVALUATION REPORT

Name: Jimmy S.

Address: 200 Main, Downtown, CA

Date of birth: November 20, 1980

Age: 12 years, 2 months

Gender: Male

Grade level: 5

Dates of testing: 1/18/98

Place of testing: Downtown Child Guidance Clinic

Tests administered: Wechsler Intelligence Scale for Children—III,
Bender-Motor-Gestalt Test
Wide Range Achievement Test—3

BOX 4.4 *(continued)*

Administered by: Lisa Dee, Ph.D.
　　　　　　　　 Licensed Clinical Psychologist

Referral: Parents requested assessment because school recommended it, for an explanation of Jimmy's poor performance in school.

> The privacy of this report is protected by law. This report may contain data or comments that should be interpreted by those trained in psychological assessment procedures to prevent misunderstandings about the findings or recommendations. Scores reported herein reflect functioning during this session and may or may not relate to later functioning.

PRESENTING PROBLEM

The mother of Jimmy S. requested psychological assessment for her son because of school difficulties, both academic and interpersonal. Jimmy does reasonably well in math and physical education, but fails all other subjects. At 12 years of age, he reportedly reads at the first-grade level, and he has been held back from grade promotion twice so that he is now in the fifth grade instead of the seventh. Jimmy is involved in frequent fights with other boys. He also complains of frequent intense, prolonged headaches, often accompanied by nausea.

BEHAVIORAL OBSERVATIONS

Jimmy S., a small, good-looking 12-year-old Caucasian American boy, arrived for the testing session dirty and disheveled, clad only in shorts and sandals despite the cold day. Jimmy began the testing enthusiastically, saying he was "good at tests." He was attentive at first, but soon he began to engage in continuous motor activity, jumping up and sitting back down, thumping the table as though playing drums, humming and singing, reciting rap songs complete with obscenities under his breath, and strumming an imaginary guitar. He alternated between paying attention and being inattentive.

Most of this activity occurred during the verbal subtests of the WISC-III. During Block Design and Object Assembly, Jimmy was focused and efficient. He examined the test materials carefully and manipulated the materials systematically. In contrast, during Picture Arrangement and Symbol Search, his approach to the tasks was inattentive and haphazard. He appeared to be guessing and just trying to "get it over with." Symbol Search was given last, and he may have been tired and eager to end the testing session.

SOCIAL HISTORY

An interview with the three adults in Jimmy's family revealed the following information. Jimmy's family is unconventional in a number of ways. Jimmy and his three younger sisters have fathers who are identical twins, both "married" to their mother for 15 years. No one in the family knows which brother fathered which child, and all the children call both men "Dad." The parents appeared to be articulate and intelligent, enjoying talking, telling jokes, and arguing about politics. They said they are all drug-addicted, and they reported using cocaine, methamphetamines, and marijuana, sometimes in front of the children. The mother said she continued using drugs throughout all her pregnancies.

The financial status of the family is precarious. At times they have been homeless, but now they are living in one motel room in a poor neighborhood. They reported that their sources of income include welfare, food stamps, collecting aluminum cans, doing odd jobs in the neighborhood, selling drugs, and prostitution of the mother. The family reported that as their economic situation has worsened, Jimmy has become very enterprising in finding odd jobs in the neighborhood. He apparently is an extremely hard worker, and they have come to depend on his income.

The parents were not able to remember anything unusual in Jimmy's birth and early development. One of his fathers was abusive of him when he was small, and broke his arm at age 6. Jimmy was placed in a foster home, and was returned home after the father "mended his ways" and cut back on his drug use. They denied any abusive behavior with Jimmy at present. Jimmy became sexually active at age 10, but the parents seemed unconcerned about this behavior. They noted that they engage in sex in front of the children. They expressed no alarm over his smoking marijuana. Their attitude seemed to be, "Boys will be boys." They also seemed unconcerned about Jimmy's headaches.

The parents were very concerned about his difficulties with reading and other academic subjects, and they were especially angry and worried about his fighting and "getting in trouble" in the neighborhood. Last year Jimmy set several small fires and stole small items from local stores. Because he appears charming, winsome, and younger than his age, Jimmy was able to talk himself out of being arrested for some of these offenses. The parents claimed he had stopped this behavior.

The parents said Jimmy spends a great deal of time playing Nintendo and watching television, as well as working at odd jobs. According to them, he enjoys art and making collages and plays in a junior soccer league. The parents reported that they always manage to get Jimmy to soccer and school. However, because of family moves, Jimmy has had to change schools approximately four times.

BOX 4.4 *(continued)*

EVALUATION RESULTS
Wechsler Intelligence Scale for Children—III

Verbal Tests		Performance Tests	
Test	Scaled Score	Test	Scaled Score
Information	9	Picture Completion	14
Similarities	9	Picture Arrangement	11
Arithmetic	12	Block Design	15
Vocabulary	8	Object Assembly	15
Comprehension	12	Coding	10
(Digit Span)	4	(Symbol Search)	4

Verbal Score	100	50th percentile
Performance Score	120	91st percentile
Full-Scale Score	110	75th percentile
Verbal Comprehension Index	100	50th percentile
Perceptual Organization Index	119	90th percentile
Freedom from Distractibility Index	90	25th percentile
Processing Speed Index	86	18th percentile

A WISC-III Verbal score of 100, a Performance score of 120, and a Full-Scale score of 110 place Jimmy currently in the high-average range of cognitive functioning overall, but in the average range in verbal skills and superior range in performance skills. The 20-point difference between Jimmy's Verbal and Performance scores is generally considered within the clinically significant range, and suggests the possibility of learning disability or some degree of organic impairment. While Jimmy's Verbal score is low compared to his superior Performance score, it is still in the average range and inconsistent with Jimmy's reported first-grade reading ability.

Jimmy's highest subtest scores were on Block Design (15), Object Assembly (15), and Picture Completion (14), scores that suggest excellent spatial relations ability, visual synthesis, and visual analysis, with a good eye for detail. These strengths may contribute to his interest in art. Jimmy's next highest subtest scores were on Arithmetic (12), confirming his mathematical ability, and on Comprehension (12), indicating good verbal reasoning and a good sense of what is socially appropriate. Jimmy's score on Picture Arrangement (11) indicates adequate sequential reasoning and social sense. His visual memory and perceptual-motor coordination also appear to be adequate, as seen in his average score (10) on Coding.

Jimmy's lowest scores were on Digit Span (4) and Symbol Search (4). Given strengths Jimmy shows in other areas, these extremely low scores appear discrepant and suggest difficulties with attention, a short-term memory deficit, anxiety, tiredness, or lack of motivation. Jimmy's other relatively low scores, compared to his high scores, were Information (9), Similarities (9), and Vocabulary (8), possibly indicating lack of a consistent education, relatively weak abstract verbal reasoning, and poor verbal memory. These lower scores suggest difficulties with verbal information processing and are consistent with Jimmy's reading difficulties, which may be due to a learning disability in verbal perception and processing.

Consistent with the difference between his verbal and performance scores, Jimmy's Verbal Comprehension Index is much lower than his Perceptual Organization Index. Nevertheless, the Verbal Comprehension Index is still within the average range and does not appear to account for poor school performance. However, both the Freedom from Distractibility and Processing Speed Indexes are below average. It may be a combination of distractibility and a verbal-processing deficit that hinders Jimmy's reading and verbal learning ability.

Jimmy gave some interesting responses to the Comprehension questions, responses that may reveal some of his problem areas. One of the advantages of paperback books is "If you get hit with one, it won't hurt as much." In Jimmy's world, even books may be potentially dangerous. Criminals are imprisoned because "If they're not they'll just keep right on breaking the law." Perhaps this response reflects Jimmy's observation of his parent's illegal behavior. The purpose of the police is to "protect us, control crazy people and criminals." At this point, Jimmy announced that he wanted to be a policeman when he grew up. It is possible that Jimmy experiences the world as a dangerous place and longs to be the one in control.

Wide Range Achievement Test—3

Consistent with the parents' report of his school performance, Jimmy achieved a grade-level equivalent of 1.7 on reading, 6.2 on arithmetic, and 2.6 on spelling on the WRAT–3. Thus, there is a clinically significant difference between his achievement in school-related subjects and his intellectual scores. With an average Verbal score and an average Verbal Comprehension Index, Jimmy should be able to read and spell at grade level.

Bender-Motor-Gestalt Test

Jimmy's performance on the Bender-Gestalt was immature for his age. He rotated three designs, and drew all but the most difficult one

BOX 4.4 *(continued)*

awkwardly with large circles for dots and recrossing of lines. Jimmy made 8 errors, according to the Koppitz scoring method, and the norm for age 10–11 is 0 to 3.6 errors. Seven of his eight errors were similar to those made by brain-injured children. The heavy lines drawn over each other may indicate anxiety, tiredness, or insecurity, but his overall performance is suggestive of difficulty in perceptual-motor coordination. Although his Coding score on the WISC-III is average, it was low in the context of Jimmy's other rather high performance scores and may not be inconsistent with a perceptual-motor problem. Although the Bender-Gestalt and low scores on the Freedom from Distractibility and Processing Speed Indexes together suggest organic brain damage, any organicity must be subtle and does not appear to interfere with his functioning as indicated in his superior Performance and average Verbal scores. Nevertheless, the possibility of a psychoneurological disorder should be further investigated, especially considering Jimmy's severe headaches and his mother's drug use during pregnancy.

Many of Jimmy's Bender-Gestalt designs were rotated and drawn off-kilter. Besides suggesting organicity, such drawings may also indicate that straight living and orientation have little importance to Jimmy.

SUMMARY

Jimmy exhibited several strengths in his psychological testing. He is personable and charming, with a good knowledge of socially appropriate behavior. His superior Performance score and average Verbal score on the WISC-III indicate that Jimmy has the ability to perform adequately in school. However, the testing also suggests that Jimmy has several cognitive difficulties. He appears to be distractible and to have difficulty processing information, especially verbal information. The large difference between his Verbal and Performance scores and the discrepancy between his low achievement scores and strong intellectual scores together suggest a learning disability or possible organic impairment. The Bender-Gestalt also suggests an organic impairment, but it appears to be subtle and not to interfere with his overall intellectual functioning. Jimmy's headaches and his prenatal and postnatal exposure to illegal drugs are causes for concern, given this suggestive evidence for organicity. A comprehensive neuropsychological assessment is needed in order to determine the extent and nature of any neurologically based learning disability and in order to plan appropriate interventions.

The present assessment does not provide evidence that adequately explains Jimmy's poor school achievement. He has adequate intelligence to do grade-level work. The evidence for organic impairment suggests that it is limited and does not sufficiently interfere with his intellectual ability that it can explain his poor school performance.

Jimmy's distractibility may be a result of anxiety or a stressful environment, as well as neurological impairment. Jimmy lives in an unstable environment, and there are suggestions that he finds it threatening. The fact that he was abused severely enough to break his arm at age 6, a crucial age for learning to read, suggests that emotional trauma may play a part in his learning difficulties. Further assessment of Jimmy's personality and behavior is recommended in order to determine other explanations for his school difficulties and to plan interventions.

Finally, the parents should request that the school design an Individualized Educational Plan (IEP) for Jimmy to address his learning difficulties. Supportive individual tutoring in reading and spelling appears to be necessary, but further psychoeducational assessment is necessary for specific recommendations. It appears that frequent school changes may account for the lack of an IEP earlier.

DIAGNOSIS
Deferred.

RECOMMENDATIONS
THE USE OF STANDARDIZED ASSESSMENT MEASUREMENTS SHOULD NOT BE EMPLOYED AS THE SOLE CRITERION IN DEVELOPING A TREATMENT PLAN OR IN THE PLACEMENT OF AN INDIVIDUAL.

In order to determine the nature and extent of Jimmy S.'s learning disability and possible organic impairment, a thorough physical examination, including hearing and vision testing, is necessary. A neuropsychological assessment emphasizing verbal information processing and verbal memory is also necessary.

Further assessment of Jimmy's personality and behavior is recommended.

An IEP at school is necessary. Further psychoeducational assessment is recommended for determining specific educational interventions. At a minimum, supportive individual tutoring is recommended.

BIBLIOGRAPHY

Adams, K. M. (1984). Luria left in the lurch: Unfulfilled promises are not valid tests. *Journal of Clinical Neuropsychology, 6,* 455–458.

Adams, R. L., Parsons, O. A., Culbertson, J. L., & Nixon, S. J. (1996). *Neuropsychology for clinical practice: Etiology, assessment, and treatment of common neurological disorders.* Washington, DC: APA Press.

Bender, L. (1938). A visual motor gestalt test and its clinical use. *American Orthopsychiatric Association, Research Monographs,* (3).

Binet, A., & Simon, T. (1905). Méthodes nouvelles pour le diagnostic du niveau intellectuel des anormaux. *L'Anée Psychologique, 11,* 191–244.

Ceci, S., & Williams, W. (1997). Schooling, intelligence, and income. *American Psychologist, 52,* 1051–1058.

Dunn, L. M. (1959). *Peabody Picture Vocabulary Test.* Minneapolis: American Guidance Service.

Fischer, C. S., Hout, M., Jankowski, M. W., Lucas, S. R., Swindler, A., & Voss, K. (1996). *Inequality by design: Cracking The Bell Curve myth.* Princeton, NY: Princeton University Press.

Flavell, J. A. (1963). *The developmental psychology of Jean Piaget.* Princeton, NJ: Van Nostrand.

Gardner, H. (1983). *Frames of mind: The theory of multiple intelligences.* New York: Basic Books.

Gazzaniga, M. (1985). *The social brain: Discovering the networks of the mind.* New York: Basic Books.

Golden, C. J., Hammeke, T., & Purisch, A. (1980). *The Luria-Nebraska battery manual.* Los Angeles: Western Psychological Services.

Goldstein, G. (1984). Comprehensive neuropsychological assessment batteries. In G. Goldstein & M. Hersen (Eds.), *Handbook of psychological assessment* (pp. 141–178). New York: Pergamon Press.

Gould, S. J. (1981). *The mismeasure of man.* New York: Norton.

Greenfield, P. (1997). You can't take it with you: Why ability assessments don't cross cultures. *American Psychologist, 52,* 1115–1124.

Guilmette, T., & Faust, D. (1991). Characteristics of neuropsychologists who prefer the Halstead-Reitan or the Luria-Nebraska Neuropsychological Battery. *Professional Psychology: Research and Practice, 22,* 80–83.

Helms, J. (1997). The triple quandary of race, culture, and social class in standardized cognitive ability testing. In D. Flanagan, J. Genschaft, & P. Harrison (Eds.), *Contemporary intellectual assessment.* New York: Guilford Press.

Herrnstein, R. J., & Murray, C. (1994). *The bell curve: Intelligence and class structure in American life.* New York: Free Press.

Hersen, M., Kazdin, A. E., & Bellack, A. S. (Eds.). (1983). *The clinical psychology handbook.* New York: Pergamon Press.

Holmes, J. M. (1988). *Assessment of developmental learning disorders: A neuropsychological approach.* New York: Basic Books.

Jastak, J. F., & Jastak, S. P. (1965). *The Wide Range Achievement Test: Manual of instructions.* Wilmington, DE: Guidance Associates.

Kaufman, A. S., & Kaufman, N. L. (1983). *K-ABC: Kaufman Assessment Battery for Children.* Circles Pines, MN: Guidance Services.

Lauerman, J. (1992, May/June). Neurologic impairment: Understanding the effects on learning. *Headlines,* pp. 12–15.

Mackenzie, B. (1984). Explaining race differences in IQ: The logic, the methodology, and the evidence. *American Psychologist, 39,* 1214–1233.

Matarazzo, J. (1992). Psychological testing and assessment in the 21st century. *American Psychologist, 47,* 1007–1018.

Meier, M. J. (1992). Modern clinical neuropsychology in historical perspective. *American Psychologist, 47,* 550–558.

Neisser, U., Boodoo, G., Bouchard, T. J., Boykin, A. W., Brody, N., Ceci, S. J., Halpern, D. F., Loehlin, J. C., Perloff, R., Sternberg, R. J., & Urbina, S. (1996). Intelligence: Knowns and unknowns. *American Psychologist, 51,* 77–101.

Osterrieth, P. A (1944). Le test de copie d'une figure complexe. *Archives de psychologie, 30,* 206–356.

Reitan, R. M. (1966). A research program on the psychological effects of brain lesions in human beings. In N. R. Ellis (Ed.), *International review of research in mental retardation* (pp. 57–90). New York: Academic Press.

Reitan, R. M., & Davison, L. A. (1974). *Clinical neuropsychology: Current status and applications.* Washington, DC: Winston.

Snyderman, M., & Herrnstein, R. J. (1983). Intelligence tests and the Immigration Act of 1924. *American Psychologist, 38,* 986–995.

Spearman, C. (1904). "General intelligence," objectively determined and measured. *American Journal of Psychology, 15,* 201–293.

Terman, L. M. (1916). *The measurement of intelligence.* Boston: Houghton Mifflin.

Terman, L. M., & Merrill, M. A. (1973). *Stanford-Binet Intelligence Scale, 1972 norms edition.* Boston: Houghton Mifflin.

Thorndike, R., Hagen, E., & Sattler, J. (1986). *Guide for administering and scoring the fourth edition.* Chicago: Riverside.

Wechsler, D. (1967). *Manual for the WPPSI.* New York: Psychological Corporation.

Wechsler, D. (1974). *Manual for the WISC-R.* New York: Psychological Corporation.

Wechsler, D. (1981). *Manual for the WAIS-R.* New York: Psychological Corporation.

Wechsler, D. (1991). *WISC-III manual.* New York: Psychological Corporation.

Woodcock, R. W., & Johnson, M. B. (1989). *Woodcock-Johnson Tests of Cognitive Ability: Standard and supplemental batteries.* Chicago: Riverside Publishers.

CHAPTER
5

Personality, Behavioral, and Other Forms of Assessment

Steven G., a 23-year-old undergraduate, requests services at a large community mental health center. His presenting complaints include an inability to think clearly, poor grades, excessive tiredness, anxiety, worry, and fears of speaking in class and in social situations. He states that he had a few sessions of counseling at his university's student health service, but they did not help. He believes he needs long-term psychotherapy, but he isn't certain what kind of therapy he needs or whether anyone can really help him.

There are methods of psychological assessment for many different purposes. In the case of Steven G., there are several questions that psychological tests might help answer. Does he exhibit symptoms that match a known diagnostic label? What sort of personality characteristics does he have? What is the nature of his anxieties, worries, and social fears? What is going on in his family life and environment that might be contributing to his problems? What are his career plans and do they suit his strengths and interests? What kind of therapy would best help him?

This chapter examines several methods of psychological assessment, including their theoretical and empirical foundations, their reliability and validity, and their clinical uses. The best place to begin is with the oldest assessment method known, the interview.

THE INTERVIEW

Despite all the technology and tests being developed, old-fashioned interviewing as a method of assessment is showing a resurgence in popularity. Professionals have made the apparently surprising discovery that clients may well tell them what they want to know if they simply ask them, so many psychologists and psychiatrists do interviews for a variety of reasons. Interviews are useful when clients are first seen, in assessments, and in diagnosis. Their use in psychotherapy is well known.

A good psychological interview both obtains information and helps the client. Interviews are goal-oriented, and the interviewer bears the responsibility for guiding the interview so that all necessary information is obtained while at the same time rapport and good communication with the client are established. Questions should be asked matter-of-factly with a nonjudgmental attitude, and the interviewer should listen and observe carefully. Most interviews require privacy, generally in the confines of a quiet, professional office, but interviews outdoors and in other settings are possible. If a great deal of information is given, unobtrusive note-taking may be necessary. Standardized protocols for conducting different types of interviews have been developed and published.

The Intake Interview

Intake interviews, conducted when a client first contacts a therapist or a hospital or agency for services, are conducted for two purposes: to determine the nature of the individual's problems and to decide whether the psychologist or agency has the competence and facilities to help with such problems. These interviews usually take 45 to 90 minutes and can follow a structured, question-and-answer format or be relatively unstructured. There are many outlines or protocols available for structured interviews. Most professionals seem to prefer a semistructured interview that follows their own outline or one required by their agency, while allowing for variation as determined by the particular case and their theoretical orientation. For example, all interviewers must obtain information about the individual's symptoms, but a psychoanalyst might want information on defenses and ego structure, and a behaviorist would want information on environmental circumstances. The results of the interview may be utilized to make a diagnosis, prognosis, or treatment plan, so a sufficient amount of relevant information must be elicited to meet these purposes.

Besides identifying data such as name, age, address, family members, educational or occupational status, and the like, the information sought in an intake interview will focus on the presenting problem, that is, what brought the individual in for services. It will include the client's description of her or his problems and symptoms, when they began, what brought them on, and what the client has tried to do about them. Questions about the client's past psychological history, medical history, and personal history may also be asked. Any information from other sources, such as school reports or psychological tests, if available, may be collected. The goal is to obtain as much information as possible in order to determine the next step to be taken to help the client.

The Mental Status Exam

The mental status examination is the formal part of an interview that assesses the client's current mental functioning. It is often conducted when individuals are seen in an emergency room or admitted to a psychiatric ward. Usually fairly structured, this interview may include clinical tests such as asking the patient to repeat a series of digits backward, to answer questions about current events, or to subtract 7 from 100 serially. The typical mental status exam tries to cover the following areas:

1. General appearance and behavior. Is the person neat or disheveled, walking straight or not, alert or stuporous, avoiding eye contact, slow moving or agitated?
2. Speech and thought. Is the person's speech coherent, understandable, excessive, nonexistent? Is thinking logical, peculiar, confused, grandiose?
3. Consciousness. Is the person conscious, clear, confused?
4. Mood and affect. Is the person's prevailing mood sad, elated, irritable, appropriate, inappropriate?
5. Perception. Is the person hallucinating, and if so, when?
6. Obsessions and compulsions. Does the person engage in repetitive behavior or reveal intrusive thoughts? If so, are they seen as real or symptomatic?
7. Orientation. Does the person know what time, day, year it is?
8. Memory. How are the person's long-term and short-term memory?
9. Attention and concentration. Is the person distracted, preoccupied, able to concentrate?
10. General information. Can the person name the president, six large states, the capitals of a few countries?
11. Intelligence. What level of education has the person attained? Are the questions in number 10 answered well?
12. Insight and judgment. Does the person seem to have insight into his or her current situation? (Judgment often seems to be assessed by whether persons agree that they are in need of treatment!)

The Case History Interview

Sometimes done during an intake interview, the case history interview attempts to elicit the client's personal and family history and social situation. The purpose is to provide a broad background and context for the individual's current difficulties, and the range of material covered in such interviews is also quite broad. Most adults provide their own social history, but in the case of children, people who are retarded, or people who are incompetent, parents, family members, or caretakers may be interviewed.

Besides identifying data, the presenting problem, and information about current difficulties, the case history interview will ask individuals about most of the following areas:

1. Their present situation. How they spend their time, descriptions of their family members and significant others, their work, recreation, and interests, and any changes in these areas in the recent past or near future.

2. Family history. Descriptions of their parents and siblings, their childhood, their role in the family, early family conflict, and early recollections.

3. Birth and development. Term and conditions of birth, developmental milestones, any evidence of child abuse, and major childhood events.

4. Health. Childhood diseases, other illnesses or injuries, drug and alcohol use, and current health.

5. Education. How they did in school, difficulties encountered, and achievements.

6. Work history. Past jobs, reasons for changing jobs, and attitudes toward work and money.

7. Sexual development. Attitudes toward sex, evaluation of sex life, and any sexual traumas, such as rape or childhood sexual abuse.

8. Marriage and current family. Marriages and divorces, how they met the current spouse, children, a description of their family functioning, and perhaps a comparison of this family with their family of origin.

9. A self-description. Their own assessment of their strengths and weaknesses, what they would do if suddenly free of their problems.

10. Other information. What they have already tried to do to solve their problems, their view of the future, and any information they wish to add.

Pretest and Posttest Interviews

If the above interviews indicate that psychological tests would be useful in assessing the client's problems, it is helpful to interview the person before and after the testing. A pretest interview helps establish the rapport and trust needed for the testing process. It should also explain the testing procedures to the client, including the kinds of tests to be administered, their purposes, and how the results will be used. Most people hold various preconceived notions about psychological tests, and care must be taken to elicit and correct any misperceptions, to answer clients' concerns, and to allay their fears.

After subjecting a person to several possibly disquieting psychological tests, it is ethical and humane to have a posttest interview in order to give the client feedback. It may be necessary to explain the tests again (most people are too anxious to listen well the first time) and to go over the client's misperceptions and concerns again, and to address any new questions or fears the testing may have raised. Although there is professional disagreement about how much people should be told about their own test results, we believe that sensitive feedback coupled with a thorough explanation of the tests and their limits can be very therapeutic. We have also found it useful and helpful to ask clients to offer their own interpretations of what they think their test results mean.

Reliability and Validity of Interviews

The reliability of interviews will depend on how structured they are and how reliability is assessed. For example, interrater reliability of diagnoses reached through the Mental Status Exam is fairly good, but the interrater reliability of diagnoses with less structured interviews is low. Because people change and because different interviewers will ask different questions, test-retest reliability of interviews can also be quite low. Having a clear goal in mind, establishing a precise definition of what is being assessed, developing specific interview questions to elicit the information sought, and providing appropriate training for interviewers all improve the reliability of interviews (see, for example, Hodgins & el-Guebaly, 1992; Williams et al., 1992).

The validity of interviews is assessed in a variety of ways, depending on the purposes of the interview and the theoretical orientation of the evaluator. For example, one measure of predictive validity examines the correctness of the diagnosis reached through an interview and the success of the treatment plans it leads to (see Malgady, Rogler, & Tryon, 1992). Studies on validity have not been positive, but in actual practice, numerous treatment decisions and diagnoses are reached with interviews.

PROJECTIVE PERSONALITY TESTS

Two major types of personality tests have been developed in the United States. The oldest type is the projective test. Test takers are given an ambiguous stimulus, such as a picture of a scene, an inkblot, or an unfinished sentence, and are asked to tell a story about the scene, say what the inkblot looks like, or finish the sentence. There are no objectively right or wrong answers to guide them. Clients must "project" their own thoughts, beliefs, and feelings onto the stimulus in order to make sense out of it. This is known as the projective hypothesis. The projective hypothesis also assumes that test takers will reveal their unconscious personality dynamics in their projected responses, because the ambiguity of the test and the test directions make it impossible to fake or to become guarded or defensive in their responses.

The other type of personality test is the objective or structured test. These tests usually require people to answer written questions with a pencil, hence their other name, pencil-and-paper tests. The answers required are usually short, such as true or false or agree or disagree, so that objective tests may take less time to administer and score than projective tests. Projective tests are somewhat like essay examinations, in which test takers must create their own answers from what they have in their minds, while objective tests are rather like multiple-choice examinations, in which test takers choose from among a limited number of given answers.

As you might guess from the projective hypothesis, projective tests grew out of the psychoanalytic tradition (see Chapter 6) and were designed for the purpose of identifying the nature of psychological disturbance. Carl Jung first experimented with this idea at the turn of the century, when he developed a word association test to detect patients' unconscious conflicts and personality dynamics. The most famous projective test, the Rorschach inkblot test, was developed by Herman Rorschach, a Swiss psychoanalyst, in the 1910s (Rorschach, 1921). The second most popular projective test, the Thematic Apperception Test (TAT), was created in the 1930s (Murray, 1938). The Draw-A-Person test (DAP) was developed in the 1940s (Machover, 1949); the House-Tree-Person test (HTP) was a later extension. Sentence completion tests were constructed in the 1940s and 1950s (Rohde, 1957). It is apparent that the most frequently used projective tests are quite old.

Because they came from the psychoanalytic tradition, projective tests are based on certain theoretical assumptions. The people who developed the tests began with the assumption that what is bothering disturbed individuals is unconscious and must be discovered by indirect means. They also assumed that these unconscious difficulties centered on sex, aggression, early family relationships, and other specific issues. Thus, for the Rorschach, the inkblots chosen had portions that resembled sex organs, blood, and the like, while the TAT pictures portrayed conflicted relationships, childhood experiences, and the like. Projective tests were constructed from theory, not from empirical research.

The Rorschach

The Rorschach test consists of 10 inkblots printed on cards. Rorschach chose inkblots because they do not depict anything realistic and therefore would require persons trying to "see" something in them to project their own internal thoughts and feelings onto them. He made his inkblots just the way one usually makes inkblots—by dropping some ink in the middle of a piece of paper and folding it in half, thereby spreading the ink in a symmetrical pattern. However, Rorschach had specific theoretical reasons for choosing the shape, color, and order of presentation of his inkblots. For example, he started with an all-black, fairly easy inkblot, one that is often seen as a bat or a butterfly. His second card contained the addition of some red ink parts, which he supposed would throw test takers off guard and stimulate deep emotional responses. How they handled this stress and integrated the parts of the blot would indicate their coping abilities and degree of personality integration or disintegration.

The Rorschach is administered by psychologists to clients individually. The psychologist presents the ten inkblot cards in the designated order one by one, and asks the client to tell what each might be. After the client responds to all 10 blots, the psychologist conducts the inquiry part of the test and asks the client to tell what aspect of each blot, such as its shape, color, or texture, made it look like that.

After the Rorschach is administered, it is scored and interpreted according to a complex system. There has been much controversy among competing systems as to the best way to score and interpret. In addition to Rorschach's original methods, Beck (1945), Klopfer (Klopfer & Kelley, 1942), Exner (1991), and others have developed scoring methods and interpretation rules, with Exner's system the most popular at present. Exner has spent years validating his system with extensive research, and he continues to modify and improve his system based on his empirical work. Even though the scoring and interpretation of the Rorschach is complex and beyond the scope of this book, you can easily imagine how a person whose response to the first card is "A raging dragon with his intestines hanging out" differs in important ways from someone whose response is "It looks like a butterfly."

Storytelling Tests

Perhaps because storytelling has been a human activity since ancient times, there are many projective tests based on storytelling. As already noted, the oldest and most frequently used storytelling test is the Thematic Apperception Test. There are special versions of the TAT for use with African or Hispanic Americans, and other such tests include the Children's Apperception Test (CAT), the Blacky Pictures, which depict dogs, the Make A Picture Story (MAPS), which involves making up the picture as well as the story, and the Picture Projective Test (PPT), which uses photographs.

The Thematic Apperception Test (TAT)   The TAT consists of 31 cards with drawings of people in various scenes. Because the TAT is supposed to be a projective test, the pictures are not drawn with photographic realism, but are in fact quite vague in many details to allow for individual projection. Certain pictures are supposed to elicit certain themes or issues that psychoanalysts assume to be important, such as authority, gender, and family relationships. In practice today a subset of 10 cards is generally given to individuals in a traditional order. Some psychologists develop preferences for certain cards over others, or they may vary the cards according to the nature of the test taker or the diagnostic question. For example, there is a card depicting a person alone at a window in a darkened room. This card is not often used, but psychologists may choose to use it if they are testing depressed and possibly suicidal individuals, for it tends to "pull" themes of loneliness, sadness, and sometimes suicide.

Like the Rorschach, the TAT is administered by psychologists to clients individually. Clients are directed to make up a story about each picture, to tell how the story begins, what is going on in the picture, what the characters are thinking and feeling, and how the story ends.

Differing systems for scoring and interpreting the stories have been developed for use in research or personality assessment. Interpretation depends on the psychologist's theoretical orientation. Those with a psychoanalytic orientation will analyze the stories for recurring themes of sex, aggression, and early family relationships. Others will examine the stories as to how the issues of nurturance or achievement are handled in certain cards that pull these motives, degree of social appropriateness or maturity, how well-organized and coherent the stories are, adequacy of reality testing, and other variables.

Recently, a different method of dealing with the TAT, the Apperceptive Personality Test, has been developed (Silber, Karp, & Holmstrom, 1990). Instead of making up any story they wish, test takers fill out a questionnaire with specific questions about the characters in the story. The questionnaire results in several scores that yield information about the personality. Although sufficient research on the norms, reliability, and validity of this test has not yet been done, it represents an interesting combination of traditional storytelling and questionnaire methods.

Roberts Apperception Test for Children   The Roberts Apperception Test for Children, published by McArthur and Roberts in 1982, is now preferred by many clinicians for assessing children. It consists of 27 line drawings depicting family situations, of which generally only 16 or fewer are administered to any one child. There are different drawings for use with girls or boys, and the pictures are designed to elicit specific issues, such as a picture of a child at a desk with books for school attitudes or a child watching parents admire a baby for sibling rivalry issues. There is a separate set of 27 drawings for use with African American children.

Drawing Tests

The Draw-A-Person test is generally administered individually, but it may be given in groups. The administration of this test is simplicity itself. The psychologist gives clients a blank piece of paper and a pencil and asks them to draw a whole person. If clients express doubt, the psychologist may explain that this is not a test of artistic ability and any kind of whole person will do. They are then given another piece of paper and asked to draw a whole person of the opposite sex. Most people draw a person of their own gender first. Some psychologists ask their clients to describe the personalities of the persons they drew and to indicate their age, occupation, and other details.

While the administration is simple, the interpretation of the DAP is complex and subject to controversy. For example, a large head is supposed to represent an emphasis on intellect, and sketchy lines on the head are supposed to represent anxiety about intellect. The validity of such interpretations is debatable. Nevertheless, the DAP is an interesting test, and you might want to try it yourself. Draw a person and see if you can figure out what it says about you. For example, common sense would suggest that if you draw a smiling person it indicates something different about you at this time than if you drew a sad or angry person.

The House-Tree-Person test is similar in many ways to the DAP. Clients are given a blank sheet of paper and a pencil and told to draw a picture with a house, a tree, and a person in it. The relations between the house, tree, and person are supposed to indicate how people view their world and themselves in it. Another version of this test has people draw the house, tree, and person on separate sheets of paper. Differing theoretical assumptions regarding what the house, tree, and person symbolize affect the interpretation of the test. For example, some psychologists believe the house symbolizes the mother and the tree the father, while others think the house reflects the nurturing side of the personality and the tree the achieving side.

The Kinetic Family Drawing (KFD), often used with children, involves having people draw a picture of everyone in their family doing something. The way the family members are depicted, their relative sizes, their facial expressions, and the relations between them may be quite revealing of how individuals see their families. For example, a child who draws her mother, father, and brothers all together in one room, with herself to the side, may feel left out or rejected by her family.

The Bender-Motor-Gestalt Test, described in Chapter 4, is sometimes interpreted to indicate characteristics of the personality. For example, someone who copies the designs quickly and confidently may differ from someone who copies them slowly and laboriously by counting the dots and curves in the lines. Some psychologists make symbolic interpretations as well, such as considering disconnected parts of designs as indicating distance in relationships or overlapping designs as indicating difficulty with boundaries. However, the validity of this use of the Bender-Gestalt has not been demonstrated.

Sentence Completion Tests

There are several sentence completion tests available, the Rotter Sentence Completion Test (Rotter & Rafferty, 1950) being perhaps the best known. Clients are asked to finish series of incomplete sentences, such as "Mothers are . . . ," "I hate . . . ," "I am very good at . . . ," "Girls are best because . . . ," or "Life can be very. . . ." The tests may be administered individually in oral form, with the psychologist reading the sentence beginning to the client, or they may be administered in written form, with the test takers writing down the completions. Again, there are several ways of scoring and interpreting these tests. You can easily imagine how a child who says "I am very good at nothing" differs in important ways from a child who says "I am very good at school and baseball."

Reliability and Validity of Projective Tests

It is difficult to measure the reliability and validity of projective tests, because the tests are scored, interpreted, and used in so many different ways, depending on the theoretical assumptions employed. Internal consistency may be considered irrelevant because it is assumed that different inkblots or different TAT pictures reflect different issues, and test-retest reliability may also be considered irrelevant because it is assumed that people change with time and in different situations. Most criticism is directed at interrater reliability, because it appears from years of research that different psychologists analyzing the same set of Rorschachs or TATs may well produce widely divergent interpretations, even when using the same scoring system. Exner (1991) has tried to address this problem by making his scoring rules very precise and explicit and basing their interpretation on empirical research, and he reports reasonable levels of reliability with his methods. However, reviews of research have concluded that projective tests do not demonstrate adequate reliability (Wierzbicki, 1993).

How to measure the validity of these tests is extremely controversial also because of differing theoretical assumptions. Should validation hinge on the content of responses, on what they are supposed to symbolize, or on some other criterion? After all, what are these projective tests purporting to measure? For example, it is assumed that people "identify" with the protagonists in their stories and thus reveal their own personalities in the behavior of the story hero. However, it is also possible that the hero represents cultural stereotypes, what test takers think the test giver wants to hear, or even how test takers wish they were, but are not.

It is relatively easy to criticize the validity of projective tests, because their interpretation depends on the theoretical framework of the tester. For example, a psychologist with a psychoanalytic orientation may try to use the Rorschach to reach conclusions about a patient's ego strength or unconscious defenses. Behaviorists would reject the validity of such an interpretation, because they do not accept the existence of the ego or the unconscious. They would not accept this interpretation even if empirical research demonstrated that people with poor ego strength could be differentiated from people with good ego strength. Even psychologists within similar theoretical frameworks may disagree with each other's interpretations of projective tests.

Also controversial is whether projective tests have validity for cultures other than the Western tradition of psychoanalysis. On the one hand, projective tests, being vague stimuli, may elicit universal themes; all cultures tell stories, for instance. On the other hand, it is unlikely that the meaning of stories or perceptions is universal across cultures. See Dana (1993) for discussion of this issue. Research on the validity of projective tests is extremely mixed, but generally unsupportive. The evidence for symbolic interpretations of the tests appears to be especially low. Interpretations of test behavior, such as drawing impulsively or telling incoherent stories, are closer to the data than symbolic interpretations, and appear to have adequate validity in terms of predicting other, similar behavior. A literature review of studies on the TAT concluded that it does not exhibit adequate validity (Keiser & Prather, 1990). Studies by Exner and his colleagues (reviewed by Erdberg & Exner, 1984) have demonstrated the validity of specific sorts of Rorschach interpretations, such as quality of reality testing. Nevertheless, after reviewing the research on the Rorschach and the TAT, Wierzbicki (1993, p. 84) concluded, "As was the case with the Rorschach, reviews of the empirical evidence concerning the reliability and validity of the TAT have repeatedly shown that its clinical use has far outdistanced its scientific status." The same can be said of the DAP.

Clinical Uses of Projective Tests

Despite low demonstrated reliability and validity, projective tests continue to be used extensively in clinical practice. Half of the top 10 psychological tests shown in Box 3.1 in Chapter 3 are projective measures. Psychologists continue to use these tests for several reasons. First, there are the natural human tendencies to resist change and to attend to validating instances and not to disconfirming evidence. We described in Chapter 3 how one of us tested a young man who had been diagnosed as schizophrenic and found evidence of organicity on the Rorschach, a result that saved this man from inappropriate and damaging drug treatment. Another time, one of us tested a man who had been severely depressed, but requested discharge from the mental hospital. Despite appearing to be improved, he showed evidence on the Rorschach of continuing severe depression. The psychiatrist in charge of the case chose to ignore this evidence and released the man, who promptly bought a gun and shot himself to death the very next day. Such dramatic and fateful experiences may be more convincing of the usefulness of projective tests to practitioners than dozens of empirical studies, even though drawing conclusions based on a few personal experiences is not rational or scientific.

Second, professional psychologists use projective tests only in conjunction with other methods of assessment, as in a test battery. Projectives are interpreted tentatively and used as a source for hypotheses about a person, hypotheses that must be confirmed by other evidence. Often, in reporting the results of projectives, psychologists try to indicate the evidence for their inferences and interpretations, as do the reports in Boxes 4.4 and 5.2.

There are at least four levels of inference used in making interpretations of projective tests. First, the level closest to the data of observable behavior is the task level. Some psychologists consider projective tests to be simply an opportunity to collect behavioral samples in a structured way. They will ask, how do individuals cope with and solve the problem presented by the test task? Do they work quickly or slowly, stick to the obvious or get creative, respond coherently or in a confused manner, include all the elements or leave some out? Second, the transactional aspects of the testing situation can be interpreted. How does the individual relate to the tester, with cooperation or resistance, with enthusiasm or anxiety, with overt or covert hostility?

Third, the representational level of the test results, such as the types of things seen in the Rorschach or the content of TAT stories, can be analyzed. Are realistic or frightening things seen in the Rorschach? What is the nature of relationships as portrayed in TAT stories? Do the characteristics portrayed represent perceptions, wishes, or simply imaginitive creations? Finally, interpretations at the symbolic level will depend on theoretical orientation, and this level requires the largest leaps in inference. Does using black as a color on the Rorschach indicate depression? Does drawing a large head on the DAP indicate an emphasis on intellect? As noted above, the validity of projective tests is dubious, especially at the symbolic level of interpretation.

As implied by the example questions above, projective tests are often used to assess emotionally disturbed people in order to make a diagnosis or a differential diagnosis, to evaluate the nature and extent of the disturbance, or to make treatment plans. In the case of Steven G., projective tests might be useful in determining the nature of his mental confusion and the nature and severity of his other complaints. The Rorschach may suggest whether his confusion is a result of anxiety, lack of reality testing, or some organic disorder. The TAT may reveal his attitudes and feelings about important social relationships, so that the possible causes of his fear of speaking in class or to others could be investigated. In the case of LaTisha M., such tests may also help distinguish whether her difficulties are emotional or organic and reveal her perceptions of the problems in her family. As might be expected, the usefulness of these tests will depend on the clinical skill, as well as the theoretical orientation, of the psychologists using them.

Some psychologists make use of projective tests in therapy. Collecting TAT stories during a series of therapy interviews is a good way to get children involved in talking with the therapist and exploring important issues indirectly and safely. The KFD can also be used in therapy with children as a way to talk about their family relationships. Some family therapists ask the entire family to draw one large KFD, and their drawing and how they go about making it can serve as topics for discussion.

OBJECTIVE PERSONALITY TESTS

There are many objective pencil-and-paper tests used in research and personality assessment. They are an economical use of the psychologist's time. Clients can answer the test questions by themselves, without any interaction with the psychologist after initial instructions are given, and answers can be written on machine-scorable answer sheets, which lend themselves to computer analysis, as described in the last chapter.

Burisch (1984) distinguished three major approaches to objective personality scale construction: external, inductive, and deductive. In the external approach, also known as the *empirical approach,* the test constructors know that people differ, but not how, so they determine the difference(s) empirically. They invent a lot of test items, give them to people who are known to differ in some way (say, anxious people and relaxed people), and then make their test up from items the two groups answer differently. In the *inductive approach,* the constructors "discover" laws or personality structure by giving many people many test items and then subjecting their responses to mathematical analyses that determine which items go together. In the *deductive approach,* constructors have a theory or definition of what they want to measure before they begin, and their theory or definition guides the choice of test items. They choose test items because they look like they fit, or they may ask the opinions of experts as to what items they should use. The differences in these three ways of constructing psychological tests will become clear as specific tests are discussed.

MMPI and MMPI-2: An Example of the Empirical Approach

The Minnesota Multiphasic Personality Inventory (MMPI), the personality test most frequently used by both professional and research psychologists, is an example of the empirical or external approach. The MMPI has a scale called Depression. People who were known to be depressed were compared to people who were not. Since it was not known how they were different, both groups answered hundreds of items, and the items that depressed people answered differently from nondepressed people were put in the Depression scale. There was no theoretical reason why depressed people should answer the items differently from the nondepressed—it was just an empirical observation that they did. Therefore, the items must measure something about depressed people, whatever it is, and they were put together in a Depression scale. Answers to these Depression items were then statistically transformed into scale scores with a mean of 50 and a standard deviation of 10.

The MMPI was developed by Hathaway and McKinley in the late 1930s and early 1940s (Hathaway & McKinley, 1943). It was originally developed to diagnose adult psychopathology in psychiatric and medical settings, but it is now used for many other purposes with individuals over 16 years old. (There is the MMPI-A for use with adolescents.) The MMPI consists of several hundred statements about life, opinions, likes and dislikes, family events, and similar things, about which people must make a forced choice between true or false, as the items apply to them. MMPI items range from statements such as "I like mechanics magazines" and "I am happy most of the time" to "I am worried about sex matters" and "At times I have a strong urge to do something harmful or shocking." Students (and psychologists, too) often have fun making up MMPI-like test items. See Box 5.1 and try to make up a few yourself.

Despite its tremendous success, there were complaints about the MMPI. With 566 items, it was very long. Some of the items are seen as intrusive and possibly offensive. Since the MMPI scales were developed by comparing "abnormal" groups to "normal" Minnesotans from the 1930s, the norms for what is considered a "high" score appeared to be out of date. For example, a 1930s Minnesota farmer was not likely to have a high score on the Schizophrenia scale unless there was actually something seriously wrong with him. Today a high score for a college student who once experimented with drugs might not indicate any serious disorder. Another criticism was that the standardization group was composed of mostly rural white people, so that the norms did not apply to today's urban, multiethnic populations. Although the standardized norms were out of date and irrelevant to some groups, both "clinical lore" and computer programs had come through empirical research to take this kind of variation into account.

Nevertheless, the MMPI was revised in 1989 as the MMPI–2. Some offensive items were deleted, some items were updated, and norms based on new, multiethnic

---

BOX 5.1

New, Improved MMPI Items

A favorite pastime of psychologists is developing new MMPI items. Over the years we have collected quite a few from various sources, including our students. The wording of these items is quite similar to many genuine MMPI items. Here are a few.

I like mechanics.

Cauliflower makes me sad.

I am not troubled by thoughts of housework.

I am sure most people would pick their noses if they thought they could get away with it.

I am excited by committee meetings.

As a child I was often an imaginary companion.

I feel like jumping off low places.

I think I would like the work of a chicken plucker.

I am bored by thoughts of death.

Sometimes I have difficulty remembering what I have done after hours of watching television.

I am not afraid to wash clothes.

My mother's third cousin was a good man.

I have used floor wax to excess.

Pedestrians are not to be trusted.

I cannot read or write.

My navel is always cold.

I like to kill gnats.

Some people never smell me.

Sometimes I find it hard to know what to say at an orgy.

Piercing screams make me nervous.

I am afraid of finding my self.

---

standardization groups were developed. Some new scales were added, including two posttraumatic stress disorder scales. The basic structure of the test remained the same.

As presently used, the MMPI and the MMPI–2 are divided into 10 empirically derived clinical scales:

1. Hypochondriasis (somatic problems and physical complaints)
2. Depression (sadness, hopelessness, depression)

3. Hysteria (using repression and denial as defenses)

4. Psychopathic Deviate (active family conflict, or possibly antisocial behavior, such as impulsivity, poor judgment, disregard for authority)

5. Masculine-Feminine (nontraditional sex role attitudes and behavior)

6. Paranoia (suspiciousness, hostility, and aloofness)

7. Psychasthenia (anxiety, phobias, obsessiveness)

8. Schizophrenia (being unconventional, withdrawn, confused, unusual in one's thinking)

9. Mania (impulsivity, optimism, high energy, impatience)

10. Social Introversion (nonsociability)

In addition to the 10 clinical scales, the test has four validity scales:

? (the number of omitted items)

L (a tendency to lie or present oneself in a favorable light)

F (an unusual items scale, suggesting a tendency to exaggerate difficulties)

K (defensiveness)

These four scales represent an attempt to build checks for validity into the assessment device itself. Obviously, if individuals fail to answer many items, it reduces the validity of their answers. The L scale is composed of socially desirable items that no one ever does, such as "I read all of the editorials in the newspaper every day." People who endorse many of these items are apparently trying to present themselves in a socially favorable way. This tendency to lie may reduce the validity of their answers. The F scale is composed of unusual items that are rarely marked by anyone. People who endorse many of these items may be "faking bad," confused, or unable to read. The K scale is supposed to measure the personality trait of defensiveness. It is added to the scores of some of the other scales as a corrective factor.

In recent years, many new scales have been constructed empirically from the original MMPI test, such as the Ego Strength and Anxiety scales. Because the MMPI was originally designed to detect psychopathology, the titles of the original 10 scales, as you can see, have negative connotations that are not appropriate for the many uses to which the MMPI is now put. Psychologists generally try to avoid the titles and refer to the scales by numbers.

In addition to the scores on individual scales, psychologists interpret the *profile* of the scores. The clients' scores on all the scales are drawn on a graph so that the peaks and valleys of the high and low scores can be seen, as in Fig. 5.1. This profile can then be interpreted according to clinical inferences or according to empirically derived rules. The MMPI was designed so that it could be interpreted with a "cookbook" of empirical rules, such as an early manual by Dahlstrom and Welsh (1960) and a later one by Duckworth and Anderson (1994). The individual's two or three highest scores are coded as a combination; the person in Figure 5.1 represents a 4-2-6 combination. These combinations of scores can then be looked up in the

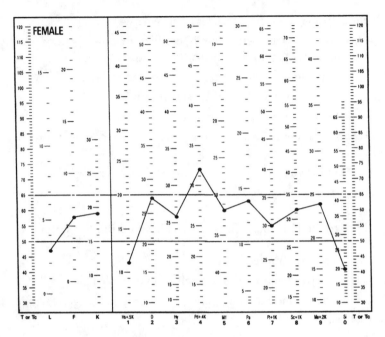

Figure 5.1 **Example MMPI-2 profile.**

Source: Minnesota Multiphasic Personality Inventory-2. Copyright © by the Regents of the University of Minnesota, 1942, 1943 (renewed 1970), 1989. This profile form 1989. All rights reserved. "MMPI-2" and "Minnesota Multiphasic Personality Inventory-2" are trademarks owned by the University of Minnesota.

"cookbook," which will summarize research on other individuals with that profile. Interpretation may consider several other aspects of the profile, including low scores. A high score on any one scale can be modified by high or low scores on other scales. For example, a high score on scale 4 suggests a tendency to be rebellious and to act out in socially unacceptable ways. However, a low score on scale 9 (energy) would attenuate this tendency, while a high score would increase it.

The Millon Tests: Another Example of the Empirical Approach

The Millon tests are recent competitors of the MMPI. The Millon Clinical Multiaxial Inventory (MCMI) is similar to the MMPI in its construction and purpose. The MCMI is shorter, with 175 items compared to over 500 for the MMPI-2. The scores and profiles on 20 scales are designed to give diagnoses that are similar to those in the DSM-IV. While the 20 MCMI scales are empirically derived, as are the MMPI scales, the comparison group for each scale was not "normals," but the general psychiatric population. Thus, the MCMI is appropriate only for diagnosing psychopathology.

In addition to the MCMI, there are the Millon Adolescent Personality Inventory (MAPI) and the Millon Behavioral Health Inventory (MBHI). Each test is designed for use with specific patient populations in clinical settings, so the Millon tests may be more useful than the MMPI in certain cases. The Millon tests continue to be researched and revised by Millon and others. For example, the MCMI-II has two new personality disorder scales and revised versions of several test items that proved insufficiently discriminating.

The Millon tests are best scored and interpreted by computer. The computer-generated report gives the clinician a list of possible diagnoses on Axes I and II of DSM-IV, a personality description based on both Millon's personality theory and empirical factors, and recommendations for treatment and therapy. Some have accused Millon of making his tests scorable and interpretable only by his computers as a way to control the market for his tests and to increase his profits, but Millon argues that he controls his tests for ethical reasons and to ensure that the latest research is always used.

Eysenck Personality Questionnaire (EPQ): An Example of the Inductive Approach

In the second type of approach to personality scale construction, the inductive approach, a personality structure and its test are "discovered" by giving huge numbers of people huge numbers of test items and subjecting the responses to a statistical procedure called factor analysis. Factor analysis discovers responses that consistently go together and therefore presumably measure some "real" aspect or dimension of personality. What that dimension is may be inferred by examining the content of the items that statistically go together. The Eysenck Personality Questionnaire (EPQ) was developed using just this method.

The EPQ is supposed to measure three fundamental dimensions of personality, which Eysenck "discovered" through factor analysis and labeled Extraversion-Introversion, Neuroticism, and Psychoticism. Extraversion-Introversion is supposed to have a physiological basis in the reactivity of the voluntary nervous system, so that extraverts prefer a great deal of stimulation and introverts do not. The dimension of Neuroticism is supposed to have a physiological basis in the reactivity of the autonomic nervous system, which includes emotion. People high on Neuroticism exhibit strong emotional reactions and easily develop fears, while low scorers do not. The dimension of Psychoticism reflects lack of socially appropriate behavior. Specific diagnostic categories are plotted in the three-dimensional "space" of these three scales. For example, a person with agoraphobia should be low on Extraversion, high on Neuroticism, and moderate on Psychoticism.

While it is a fairly important research questionnaire, the EPQ is not used much by American professional psychologists, who seem to prefer measures with several scales and complex profiles to one with three basic dimensions. However, Matarazzo (1992) predicted that psychological assessment in the next century will be more biologically based than today, so that tests such as the EPQ, which assumes biological substrates for its measures, may become more common in clinical practice.

The Myers-Briggs Type Indicator (MBTI): An Example of the Deductive Approach

The deductive approach to personality scale construction assumes that a great deal is already known from theory, and possibly other research, about the personality characteristics to be measured. This theoretical knowledge governs the formulation of the test items. A good example of this type of test is the Myers-Briggs Type Indicator (MBTI) (Myers, 1962, 1977).

The Myers-Briggs is based on Jung's theory of the basic dimensions of the personality. In his theory, and on the test, there are four theoretically independent dimensions of personality: Extraversion-Introversion, Sensing-Intuition, Thinking-Feeling, and Judging-Perceptive. Items for the test were developed because they appeared or were judged by experts to measure these theorized dimensions.

The Myers-Briggs has a 126-item version (Form G) and a 166-item version (Form F). An individual's responses are scored so as to result in a "profile" of the four dimensions. For example, a person with an ENFP profile would be high in Extraversion, Intuition, Feeling, and Perceptive. The manual lists all the possible profiles and describes this one as a person who prefers to be with others, looks for options rather than known facts, makes judgments according to personal values rather than logic, and prefers spontaneity over careful planning. In addition to the cookbooklike manual, there are other, more sophisticated ways to interpret the Myers-Briggs (Willis, 1987).

Other Psychological Tests of Interest

Beck Depression Inventory (BDI)   As the name implies, the Beck Depression Inventory was developed in the 1960s and 1970s by Dr. Aaron Beck, a cognitive behaviorist discussed in Chapter 12, to assess the presence and severity of depression in adults and adolescents. This test, revised in 1996 as the BDI-II to be more in line with DSM-IV criteria for depression, consists of 21 groups of 4 statements, each describing more severe versions of a depressive symptom. For example, the first group of four statements is as follows:

0 I do not feel sad.

1 I feel sad.

2 I am sad all the time and I can't snap out of it.

3 I am so sad or unhappy that I can't stand it.

Other groups of statements deal with pessimism, past failure, agitation, worthlessness, loss of energy, concentration difficulty, loss of pleasure, guilt, crying, and other symptoms of depression. Test takers are given written instructions to circle the statement in each group that best describes how they have been feeling during the past two weeks. Points are assigned to each statement in a group, with 0 being no symptom and 3 being the most severe statement of the symptom. Points are summed, so that scores on the BDI range from 0 to 63. Although the test is not normed in the way the MMPI is, a score of 29 or more is generally considered to indicate severe depression. The BDI has been subject to extensive research, and it has found wide application in clinical practice.

California Psychological Inventory (CPI)   Constructed in a way similar to the MMPI, the CPI is designed to measure dimensions of "normal" personality. It consists of 462 true-false items, almost 200 of them taken directly from the MMPI. There are 20 scales to measure such "normal" personality characteristics as dominance, sociability, self-acceptance, independence, tolerance, achievement via conformance, intellectual efficiency, and flexibility. While these scales were constructed empirically like the MMPI scales, factor analysis of the scales resulted in three "vectors" of personality: (1) an external or internal interpersonal orientation, (2) a norm-favoring or norm-questioning perspective, and (3) higher or lower levels of self-realization.

NEO PI-R The NEO Personality Inventory—Revised, based on the five-factor theory of personality (Costa & McCrae, 1992), is supposed to allow a comprehensive assessment of adult personality. A great deal of personality research agrees that five empirically derived factors can account for most of the variance in personality tests—Neuroticism, Extraversion, Openness to Experience (the NEO), Agreeableness, and Conscientiousness. (Note the similarity to Eysenck's factor analysis and that of the CPI.) Within each of the five factors or domains, there are six facets. For example, the facets of Extraversion are Warmth, Gregariousness, Assertiveness, Activity, Excitement-Seeking, and Positive Emotions. The makers and users of this test, which was originally developed as a measure of the "normal" personality, are researching clinical uses for it.

This paper-and-pencil test consists of 240 statements about the self to which the individual indicates strongly agree, agree, disagree, or strongly disagree. These responses are assigned points and summed for raw scores on the five factors and their facets. Based on a representative sample of 500 women and 500 men similar in characteristics to the overall U.S. population, these raw scores are normed and can be profiled and then interpreted, somewhat like the MMPI.

For example, suppose a man scores quite low on the Agreeableness factor, such that his score is lower than those of 75% of the people in the normative sample. It can be said that this person tends to be cynical, skeptical, and antagonistic in his interpersonal relations. If, as early research suggests (Costa & McCrae, 1992), antagonism as reflected in a low score on the A factor predicts an increased risk of coronary disease, then potentially useful, early treatment plans can be developed. The empirical basis of this test appears to be sound, although its clinical uses remain to be developed.

Q-Sort Developed by Stephenson (1953), the Q-sort or Q-technique was researched and popularized by Carl Rogers (Rogers & Dymond, 1954), who used it as a measure of self-concept and to develop and evaluate his client-centered approach to counseling (see Chapter 8). The Q-sort consists of about 100 small cards, each containing a statement such as "I am likable," "I am honest with friends," and "I make strong demands on myself." The individual is asked to sort the statements into nine piles from least like the self to most like the self, first as representing the real self and then as representing the ideal self. Rogers used the discrepancy between the two sorts as a measure of psychological maladjustment.

Repertory Grid George Kelly (1955) invented the repertory grid assessment technique as a way to develop and evaluate his cognitive theory of personality and his therapy techniques (see Chapter 12). The psychologist asks the client to name several people important in her or his life, and then goes through various pairs of these people asking how they are alike and how they are different. In this way, the psychologist builds up a picture of the cognitive constructs the individual uses to make sense of her or his social world. The resulting "cognitive constructs" can be analyzed for how appropriate and flexible they are and whether certain inappropriate or rigid cognitions are contributing to the person's difficulties so that interventions can be designed.

Reliability and Validity of Objective Tests

The internal consistency and reliability of objective personality tests range from low to moderately high, depending on the type of test. For example, the reliability of the computer-scored MMPI may be quite high. Internal consistency of the separate scales is in the .70s, and even test-retest reliabilities range from the .50s to the .90s. Although individuals change, it is not unusual for a person to show a certain MMPI profile one year and to have almost the same profile the next. Some researchers believe that the test-retest reliability of a personality test may be irrelevant. They assume that it is human nature to change both over time and from situation to situation, so it is not reasonable to expect measures of human nature (i.e., personality) to stay the same (i.e., be reliable).

Burisch (1984) reviewed 15 studies that directly compared the validity and effectiveness of the three approaches to personality test construction. In all cases, the different approaches were found to produce personality tests with similar levels of validity and effectiveness. However, it is obviously cheaper and quicker to make up short deductive and self-rating tests, which are also simpler to administer and score. The cost-effectiveness of tests must be considered in addition to their validity.

Arguments over the validity of objective tests such as the MMPI, the Millon tests, and others would seem open to settlement by empirical studies. For example, in terms of using the tests to make diagnoses, some independent researchers (Bonato et al., 1988; Dana & Cantrell, 1988; Widiger, Williams, Spitzer, & Frances, 1985) argue that the MCMI does not validly assess DSM categories on Axis II, while others (Millon, 1985) claim that the body of evidence supports its validity.

While it may remain forever debatable whether the MMPI is really measuring "hypochrondriasis" or "psychasthenia" (whatever that is), there are literally thousands of studies demonstrating that the MMPI can adequately predict many things, such as neurosis versus psychosis or whether someone will benefit from a certain kind of treatment. MMPI profiles can also predict which alcoholics will recover and which chronic pain sufferers will benefit from surgery, to give just a few examples. The MMPI is often used to make these kinds of predictions with a fair degree of success. Several hundred new studies on the MMPI are published every year, so it would appear to have acceptable validity, at least for a substantial number of researchers in the United States. As with projectives, the use of objective tests in other cultures is questionable.

Clinical Uses of Objective Tests

Objective personality tests are used for a variety of purposes, besides the typical goal of diagnosis and differential diagnosis. New applications of the MMPI are being researched all the time. Many of them appear to be valuable and useful extensions of the test and psychological knowledge. For example, using the MMPI to predict which chronic pain sufferers would benefit from back surgery (Turner, Herron, & Weiner, 1986) would save medical expenses and unnecessary suffering from surgery that won't help. Predicting which form of psychological treatment will best help clients is another example of a beneficial use of objective tests.

In the case of Steven G., an MMPI–2 profile and the Beck Depression Inventory, along with some projective tests, would help clarify personality characteristics and tendencies that contribute to his complaints. If he scored high on both the MMPI–2 Depression scale and the BDI, and if he told sad stories on the TAT and saw black as a color in the Rorschach, then there would be a great deal of evidence to support the hypothesis that his confusion, tiredness, poor grades, and worry are due to a clinical depression. A cognitive behavioral intervention could then be designed to treat the depression. If, on the other hand, there were no signs of depression whatsoever, then alternative explanations could be sought. The MMPI-2 profile and other test scores could be examined for excessive anxiety, obsessiveness, social introversion, and other possibilities.

As with the projective tests, objective tests are sometimes used in therapy. For example, some family therapists ask everyone in a family to take the Myers-Briggs. Each family member's profile is discussed and explained in a way that also educates the family about the nature of different communication styles. When misunderstandings arise, the therapist can point out that they are not anyone's "fault," but rather the result of differing communication styles. Families can learn to problem solve these differences, rather than becoming defensive and placing blame.

In clinical assessment, the MMPI continues to be the test of choice. Clinicians have resisted the switch to the MMPI-2 not only because of the typical human resistance to change, but also because many of them have years of experience with the MMPI, experience that contributes to the body of "clinical lore" they use to interpret the test. Even though the norms are out of date, they know through keeping up with the research and their own use of the test with certain groups how to compensate for that fact. The MMPI-2 would force them to abandon all that knowledge and start over. Some have even criticized the MMPI-2 as not yet being adequately researched, not being a genuine improvement, and being merely a marketing ploy to "give the publisher more control over this widely used psychology tool" (Rodgers, 1992, p. 13). Defenders, of course, say that modification of the MMPI was necessary and long overdue (Butcher, 1992).

BEHAVIORAL ASSESSMENT

Although the techniques of behavioral assessment are quite old, its recognition as a separate type of assessment is recent. No books on the subject were published before the mid-1970s, but now there are many. Two journals in the field, *Behavioral Assessment* and *Journal of Behavioral Assessment,* were founded in 1979. Since then, research and applications of behavioral assessment have proliferated, and the field continues to expand and change.

Behavioral assessment is derived from the empirical and theoretical foundations of behaviorism and behavior therapy (covered in Chapter 10). Behaviorists do not accept the traditional concept of the personality, and radical behaviorists deny it exists. Behaviorists look at people in terms of their behaviors in specific situations.

Rather than assessing underlying personality characteristics, they examine interactions between behaviors and situations. Rather than looking for "signs" of enduring personality characteristics, they examine "samples" of behavior and situations.

In *functional analysis,* behaviorists analyze the stimuli that precede a behavior and the consequences that follow it. Behaviors are precipitated by certain stimuli or situations, and they are learned and maintained because of their consequences. Only by identifying the conditions that elicit a behavior and the consequences that maintain it can appropriate interventions to change that behavior be designed, all without making inferences about the "personality" of the behavior-emitter.

Furthermore, behaviorists assume that behavior has multiple causes, that the environment and the person interact to cause behavior (reciprocal determinism), that individuals have behavioral skills as well as deficits, and that mediational variables such as social support systems, cognitive coping strategies, past experiences, and physiological responses or disorders are important in determining behavior. The functional analysis of behavior attempts to study all these factors, because the assessment of any one factor in isolation will result in an inadequate or incorrect conclusion. Because of its ties to academic behaviorism and its empirical hypothesis-testing paradigm, behavioral assessment values quantification of variables, objective observation, and assessment and intervention within controlled conditions. Therefore, behavioral assessors obtain information about the rate, duration, and intensity of target behaviors and the conditions under which they occur.

Most behaviorists would agree that methods of behavioral assessment include interviews, various kinds of observation, exposure-based methods, self-monitoring, psychophysiological measures, and behavioral questionnaires. Although more controversial, neuropsychological assessment, projective methods, intelligence tests, computer-assisted assessment, and other techniques may also be included in behavioral assessment. Because behavioral assessment is a rapidly growing and changing field, any list of its methods would soon be outdated, but we can describe some of the techniques most widely used today.

Behavioral Assessment Interviews

All behavioral interventions require some form of interview before they are attempted. The behavior therapist must first ask clients the nature of their problems and when and where they occur. Interviews are necessary to define the problem(s), target the behavior(s), and set therapy goals. Compared to nonbehavioral interviews, behavioral interviews tend to be more structured, more focused on overt behavior, more oriented to environmental causes of behavior, less interested in the past, and more quantitative.

Naturalistic Observation

In this method, two or more trained observers enter the client's natural environment (home, classroom, hospital ward) and systematically record the occurrence or nonoccurrence of predefined behaviors. Behaviors to be sampled in this way are carefully selected and defined prior to observation. They may be undesirable behaviors to be decreased, desirable behaviors to be increased, or behaviors with causal significance to be analyzed. For example, observers may go into the homes of obese individuals to observe their eating patterns or into bars to observe the drinking behavior of alcoholics.

Analogue Observation

Observations of behavior are made in a controlled environment that is different from but similar or analogous to the client's natural environment. Role-playing is a form of analogue observation often used to assess social skills. A shy client may role-play a scenario of being more assertive with the therapist role-playing the client's boss or date. The behavior avoidance test (BAT) is another type of analogue assessment. Clients are asked to approach a feared object, such as a snake or hypodermic needle, and their behavior is carefully observed and recorded.

Participant Observation

A family member or other involved person who is not professional is asked to monitor the target behavior. For example, parents may be asked to keep a record of all instances of tantrums thrown by their difficult child.

Self-Monitoring

Clients are asked to observe and record the occurrence or nonoccurrence of their own predefined behaviors. Smokers may be asked to record all cigarettes smoked, when, where, what they were doing as they smoked, how much they did or did not enjoy it, and what they were thinking about when they decided to smoke.

Psychophysiological Measures

The increasing popularity of biofeedback and behavioral medicine has contributed to the development of psychophysiological techniques in behavioral assessment. Measures of brain waves, eye movements, skin temperature, pulse, muscle tension, respiration, penile erections, skin conductance, and blood pressure have been used in the behavioral assessment of headaches, phobias, high blood pressure, pain, anxiety, smoking, sexual dysfunctions, compulsions, and many other problems.

Behavioral Questionnaires and Checklists

Behavioral clinicians utilize a number of self-report techniques. Written questionnaires, symptom inventories, behavior checklists, and rating scales are often used in behavioral assessment. For example, a questionnaire could be used to collect information on what, when, where, how much, and how often someone eats. A fear survey may ask people to indicate the presence or intensity of the fear of different objects. Or a rating scale could ask clients to rate their levels of anxiety in different example situations. Compared to personality questionnaires, behavioral question-naires tend to be shorter, more specific, and more focused on the occurrence and fre-quency of behaviors than on enduring traits. They are a quick and inexpensive way to screen clients and to obtain preinterview and preintervention data.

One behavioral assessment method that is frequently used in both research and the clinical assessment of children is the Achenbach Child Behavior Checklist (CBCL), developed in the 1980s by Edelbrock and Achenbach. Having both teacher report and parent report versions, the behavior checklist consists of over 100 normal and problematic behaviors with brief descriptions. The teacher or parent checks the behavior if it occurs and rates whether it occurs sometimes or often. The listed be-haviors are clustered into meaningful scales for which extensive age-related norms have been developed. In the teacher's report version, there are six adaptive scales, such as Working Hard and Behaving Appropriately, and nine behavior problem scales, such as Anxious and Aggressive. The profile, or pattern of high and low scores on the various scales, can be analyzed for behavioral strengths and weaknesses in order to design and focus appropriate interventions. The CBCL is also useful for as-sessing improvement as a result of therapy.

Product-of-Behavior Measures

Product-of-behavior measures are records of data generated by the target behaviors themselves. For example, weight is often used as a product-of-behavior measure of eating behavior. Such assessments have the advantage of being objectively measurable and easily obtained as a byproduct of the behaviors to be modified by the interven-tion procedures.

Radical Behavioral Assessment

The radical behaviorists, discussed in Chapter 10, claim to base their methods on Skinner's principles, but their therapy ends up looking more like traditional psy-chotherapy than behavior therapy. Radical behaviorists utilize all of the above behav-ioral assessment methods, but they emphasize the unique individual in her or his his-torical and environmental context. Thus, their relatively idiographic approach to behavioral assessment leads to the frequent use of self- monitoring or other methods that are designed for specific individuals and are not standardized. For example, an agoraphobic would be periodically asked to complete a standard one-mile walk with specific stopping points to rate anxiety. The radical behaviorists emphasize "clinically relevant behavior" and how it functions in its context. For example, there can be no universal definition of social skills in radical behaviorism. A behavior is socially skilled if it functions as a skill in a specific situation in relation to certain other people when performed by an individual with a specific learning history.

Reliability and Validity of Behavioral Assessment

Because of the strong empirical foundation of behaviorism, the reliability of behav-ioral assessment methods is high. In general, the more structured and objective the assessment procedure, the higher its reliability will be. Thus, more structured interviews, such as those used in behavioral assessment, result in higher reliability than unstructured ones. In the case of observations, careful training of the observers is crucial for interrater reliability.

As you might expect, the validity of the empirically derived behavioral assessment methods are mostly well researched. Furthermore, the results of such research lead to changes in the methods in order to improve validity. Many studies (reviewed by Ciminero, Calhoun, & Adams, 1984) indicate good reliability and validity for behavioral assessment, while others (Haynes, 1984) suggest that at least some methods have not been adequately researched for reliability and validity. The ultimate test of the predictive validity of the behavioral assessment methods is, of course, whether they lead to effective behavioral interventions, as discussed in Chapter 15 on research on therapy outcomes.

Clinical Uses of Behavioral Assessment

Behavioral assessment is used most often in conjunction with behavior therapy. A general list of purposes, in addition to empirical research, would include identifying target behaviors to modify, identifying alternative (desirable) behaviors to replace or reduce undesirable ones, identifying causal variables so interventions can be made at that point, developing a functional analysis of the entire environmental and social situation in which the client is embedded, designing intervention strategies, and evaluating and modifying the intervention(s).

In the case of LaTisha M., the CBCL may be used to indicate behavioral strengths and weaknesses. In her case, it may be more useful for trained observers to go to her school to observe her behavior and its antecedents and consequences in that situation and to her home to observe the same. It is possible that certain frightening situations elicit illness behaviors that are rewarded with attention and sympathy from the teacher, the mother, or even siblings and friends. An intervention designed to reduce the attention she receives for illness behaviors and to increase the attention she receives for assertive and independent behaviors could be designed.

In the case of Steven G., various symptom checklists and a fear survey schedule might be useful in clarifying the exact nature of his anxieties and fears. Observing Steven role-play a public speaking situation in front of two therapists or fellow clients would help determine the variables that maintain his fear, or it may reveal deficits in Steven's social skills. Requiring Steven to self-monitor his thoughts while role-playing public speaking may clarify the role of negative cognitions in his fears. All of these measures could lead to the development of appropriate interventions to reduce his fears, to reduce his negative cognitions, and to reward and increase his social skills.

VOCATIONAL, APTITUDE, AND INTEREST TESTS

Professional psychologists are involved in many other forms of assessment, from measuring physiological responses to assessing organizational dynamics and making employment decisions. This chapter cannot cover them all, but we will cover one final area. Assessment of vocational skills and potentials, aptitudes, and vocational and life interests is often done by counseling and educational psychologists.

Vocational, aptitude, and interest tests are used to help parents, schools, and individuals make educational and vocational decisions. They are supposed to measure people's talents, interests, and potentials, characteristics that should be related to what sorts of education and careers they would do well in. They are not intelligence tests, which supposedly measure a global ability to do well in school (some view this as "scholastic aptitude"). And they are not achievement tests, which are supposed to measure level of performance already achieved in various subjects. Rather, these tests attempt to identify specific talents or unknown potentials or patterns of interests to predict how individuals will "fit" in certain careers or educational programs.

These tests, especially aptitude tests, have been criticized for serving gatekeeper functions. The most common use of aptitude tests is in college admissions. Universities require minimum scores on the Scholastic Aptitude Test (SAT) of the College Entrance Examination Board for entrance, and the real-life consequences of this test are well known. Television viewers watched Bart Simpson's aptitude test go to be scored at an institute very similar to the College Board, and the sign over the door said "Determining Your Destiny Since 1923."

Nevertheless, many individuals desire assistance in "discovering" their talents and making career decisions. There are many group and individual vocational and interest tests designed to help them do so. Among the best known—and the ones most often used by professional psychologists—are the Strong Interest Inventory and the Kuder Occupation Interest Survey.

Strong Interest Inventory

First developed in the 1920s, the Strong Interest Inventory was constructed using the empirical method of contrast groups, like the MMPI, and new norms were developed in the 1980s. It includes over 300 items, such as "Watching an open-heart operation," "Sports pages in the newspaper," and "Outspoken people with new ideas," for which test takers indicate their interest by marking "Like," "Indifferent," or "Dislike." These items were administered to national samples of 200 to 300 women and 200 to 300 men in nearly 100 different occupations. The contrast sample consisted of several hundred women and men not identified by occupation. Their answers were compared to the answers of those in different occupational groups to identify those test items that statistically distinguished each occupational group from the general group. It is assumed that if an individual's answers on the Strong inventory match the interest patterns of certain occupational groups, then that person would be likely to find satisfaction in that vocation. There are also 23 Basic Interest scales on the Strong, and these scales indicate low, moderate, and high interest in categories such as nature, science, art, religious activities, and sales.

Kuder Occupation Interest Survey

Begun in the 1930s and published in several different forms, the Kuder Occupation Interest Survey is composed of 100 triads of work-related activities, such as "Read lessons to a blind student," "Keep records of experimental results," and "Interview people in a survey of public opinion." For each triad of activities, the test taker indicates the most preferred and least preferred activity. This procedure results in a rank ordering of preference for the different kinds of activities, and the individual's pattern of ranked interests can be related to certain college majors and to occupational groups to indicate possible educational and career goals.

16PF

Originally developed by Cattell as a personality test, the 16PF (16 Personality Factors) has also been utilized in career counseling. Although several versions of the test have been developed, it typically consists of nearly 200 different types of items, some being questions about interests, some being tests of cognitive ability, and others being MMPI-type items about personal characteristics and beliefs. Among the 16 personality scales on the test are warmth, dominance, rebelliousness, and compulsivity. Methods and norms for making occupational predictions about certain patterns of scores have been developed. Rather than revealing preferred interests and activities, as the Strong and Kuder do, the 16PF may reveal whether individuals will be happy in certain occupations and whether their personalities or behavioral styles will fit well with certain career requirements.

Other Tests

There are numerous other tests used in vocational and career counseling and assessment. There are other interests tests, such as the Career Assessment Inventory or the Career Occupational Preference System. There are tests of mechanical abilities, such as the Bennett Mechanical Comprehension Test; tests of spatial ability, such as the Minnesota Form Board; tests of artistic talents, social intelligence, managerial talent, and many others. A comprehensive career assessment will include interviews, interest tests, personality tests, possibly intelligence tests, and other tests the psychologist deems necessary for the particular individual. Counseling and thoroughly reviewing the results of the tests are part of the vocational assessment process.

Reliability and Validity of Vocational and Interest Tests

According to the research done for their manuals, the reliability of both the Strong and the Kuder tests is high—in fact, close to the reliability of intelligence tests. Because aptitude and interest tests are used to make long-term decisions about education and careers, it is important that their predictive validity be high. According to several studies, between one-half and three-fourths of subjects in studies on predictive validity choose college majors (Hansen & Swanson, 1983) or enter careers (Campbell, 1966; Spokane, 1979) that would be predicted by their scores on the Strong. The Kuder predicts careers accurately about half the time (Zytowski, 1976). While a 50% correct prediction rate may not seem high, it does, in fact, represent good predictive validity for a psychological test.

Clinical Uses of Vocational and Interest Tests

Steven G.'s difficulties may be due to a mismatch between his interests and aptitudes and his chosen college major. His poor grades and anxieties may be due to trying to pursue a major or a career for which he is unsuited, perhaps because his parents expect him to or perhaps because he is unaware of his own preferences. Giving Steven vocational and interest tests would help him examine his aptitudes and abilities, his interests and preferences, and his educational and career options, and it may reveal another explanation for his difficulties.

IN CONCLUSION

Because of their use in both research and professional practice and the constant development and revision of psychological tests, the enduring popularity of objective personality tests seems assured. Furthermore, a great deal of research demonstrates the clinical utility of the MMPI for a multitude of purposes. Vocational and interest tests also remain vital in both research and clinical practice. The fate of the projective tests seems more questionable. Projective tests produce a wealth of fascinating data, and they may lead to interesting interpretations and hypotheses, as demonstrated in the report on Jimmy S. in Box 5.2. However, their validity and cost-effectiveness remain problematic. Future developments in personality assessment may include empirically based neuropsychobiological measures.

BOX 5.2

Example Evaluation Report

Name: Jimmy S.

Address: 200 Main, Downtown, CA

Date of birth: November 20, 1980

Age: 12 years, 3 months

Gender: Male

Grade level: 5

Dates of testing: 2/30/98

Place of testing: Downtown Child Guidance Clinic

Tests administered: Roberts Apperception Test for Children
Kinetic Family Drawing (KFD),
House-Tree-Person (HTP),
Achenbach Child Behavior Checklist (CBCL)

Administered by: Lisa Dee, Ph.D.
Licensed Clinical Psychologist

Referral: Previous assessment of intellectual functioning resulted in recommendation of personality and behavioral assessment to help explain poor school performance.

The privacy of this report is protected by law. This report may contain data or comments that should be interpreted by those trained in psychological assessment procedures to prevent misunderstandings about the findings or recommendations. Scores reported herein reflect functioning during this session and may or may not relate to later functioning.

PRESENTING PROBLEM

The mother of Jimmy S. originally requested psychological assessment for her son because of school difficulties, both academic and interpersonal. Previous testing revealed that Jimmy reads and spells well below grade level in spite of average to superior intellectual abilities. Distractibility, slowness in processing, poor verbal memory, and possible subtle neuropsychological impairment may explain his school difficulties, but personality and behavioral assessment was recommended in order to investigate other explanations.

BEHAVIORAL OBSERVATIONS

Jimmy's mother "forgot" to bring him for two appointments for this assessment. Nevertheless, during this testing session, Jimmy's behavior was markedly different from that reported earlier. He arrived rather neatly dressed, after having had lunch. In spite of the fact that this session lasted almost three hours, Jimmy was patient and attentive throughout. He showed no evidence of anxiety, and appeared to enjoy the tests. He did not exhibit any of the excessive activity shown in the earlier testing.

SOCIAL HISTORY

Please see earlier report of 1/18/98 assessment.

EVALUATION RESULTS

Roberts Apperception Test for Children

Jimmy's stories about the Roberts pictures were quickly told and averaged about 150 words each. He refused to elaborate beyond his original story, saying "That's it" or "That's all" at the end. Rather than narrating stories in the third person, Jimmy spoke as the characters in the story, indicating which character was speaking by changes in accents and deep voices for males and high voices for females. In this way, he was able to comply with the directions for the test (to tell what is going on in the picture, what led up to it, what the characters are thinking and feeling, and how the story ends) without doing so explicitly. Although about half the stories had simple, clear plots, about half were confused and disjointed. These disorganized stories may suggest that Jimmy was tired or confused. They may reflect that Jimmy has a disorganized approach to life or lives in a chaotic environment.

Seven of Jimmy's twelve stories told of things being "hard." "Another day's work is just so hard," "Since your dad just died, it's going to

BOX 5.2 *(continued)*

be hard," and "Without electricity it's going to be hard" are examples. Things were "hard" largely because of economic difficulties: a father who "only makes minimum wage," a father who died and left no money, a boy who "gets small pay." This constant theme may reflect Jimmy's feelings that his own life is hard and his worries about his family's financial situation. The story endings suggest Jimmy sees few options other than to continue working hard without much reward.

Three of Jimmy's stories contained explicit references to sex, unusual in the stories of 12-year-old boys. His story for a picture of an older couple embracing, which usually pulls pleasant stories of golden wedding anniversaries and the like, was this: "I can hold you tight next to me. I can feel you're getting big. . . . I think I'm ready, but I didn't get my birth control pills this week. . . ." In the two other stories, sex was used as a distraction from the hard life. Jimmy's stories may reflect his own sexual experiences or his observation of the way his parents use sex.

Two stories contained a wish to have a baby. In one story a male character stated, "I wish one day I could have a baby, just like that lady over there." In another story, a female character stated, "I better have a baby so I can have a little hoodlum to keep me company." This unusual theme could be interpreted in several ways. These statements could be Jimmy's way of referring indirectly to sex or trying to make a joke. They could represent an unconscious wish to be a baby and be taken care of or to have a baby and have someone for him to love. It is also possible that Jimmy is concerned that his mother may have another baby.

Three of Jimmy's stories were inappropriately violent. One story had several gory deaths of cats, even though no cats were pictured: "I wanted to kill that cat and feed its brains to my dog," "I stuck my cat in a doberman pinscher's mouth," and "I ran over that cat—see the stains the ugly bastard left on my car." This story ended with "And now we are done with the case of the cat squished like a pancake." In another story, a son intended to shoot his father because "My dad's in a bad way. . . . I think he'd be happier. He wouldn't have to suffer." In the third story, a woman stated, "Oh, my, I shouldn't have killed that man. . . . I just know the cops are going to get me this time. . . . I will have to shoot myself, too. I'm feeling very sad and lonely now. I don't have no more family. I killed them, too." These stories may be Jimmy's attempt to joke or perhaps to express indirect anger over having to take the tests. On the other hand, it appears that once an aggressive act enters Jimmy's stories, it has a tendency to become excessive. This tendency may reflect Jimmy's observation of the nature of violence in his home or neighborhood, or it may reflect Jimmy's own inability to limit his aggressive feelings or his fear that he cannot.

Overall, the Roberts suggests that Jimmy may see the world as a chaotic, confusing place, where life is hard and there are few options. He seems to have difficulty limiting his sexual and aggressive feelings, as they enter his stories inappropriately and then become excessive. He appears to feel ambivalent about authority, complying with directions indirectly and telling hostile stories. He seems to be (appropriately) worried about the finances and stability of his family.

Kinetic Family Drawing

The figures in Jimmy's KFD are well proportioned and carefully drawn, but anything but kinetic. They are drawn in a row, each standing passively staring straight ahead. Jimmy said that they were "looking at Mickey Mouse." The lack of activity in the picture may represent Jimmy's resistance to instructions ("Draw everyone in your family doing something") or his view that his family is passive or inactive. From left to right, the drawings represent his 7-year-old sister, his 5-year-old sister, himself, one father, the second father, and the year-old baby sister. It is interesting that the mother was left out, and when asked about her, Jimmy said she was "down at the liquor store, hanging out." This deletion may indicate that Jimmy does not feel close to his mother or feels that she is not there for him. He may feel closer to his fathers.

The figures were all drawn similarly, even the baby, with long hair, neutral facial expressions, and hands behind the back, with some notable exceptions. The neutrality and lack of hands suggest that Jimmy views his family as passive, inactive, and perhaps helpless, powerless, or ineffective. The father next to Jimmy was drawn with a hand, and it is a large, rather ominous-looking hand. The large hand coupled with the somewhat threatening expression on the face may reflect Jimmy's fear of his father's abuse. The drawing of Jimmy is the only one with short hair, a smile with bared teeth, and blank eyes. The smile with bared teeth may be interpreted as anxiously placating or denying of aggression. It may also represent a "grin and bear it" attitude. The blank eyes may be interpreted perhaps as Jimmy's wish to avoid really looking at his surroundings or his life.

The two fathers are dressed in gang outfits, possibly as symbols of unconventionality or rebellion. Jimmy drew himself dressed in the shirt and cap of a specific gang in his neighborhood. When asked, Jimmy stated he hates that particular gang. Jimmy appears to be ambivalent about his and his parents' degree or type of rebellion.

Overall, the KFD suggests a lack of cohesiveness and involvement between the family members. The mother is not available, and the one father appears threatening. Again, difficulties or ambivalence around the expression of aggression or rebellion are suggested.

House-Tree-Person Drawing Test

For the HTP, Jimmy drew from left to right a very small tree with a knothole in the trunk, a slightly larger, but barren house, and a tiny little boy, again with blank eyes. The knothole is consistent with Jimmy's history of

BOX 5.2 (c o n t i n u e d)

abuse. The small boy may reflect low self-esteem or a low sense of entitlement. The blank eyes may again suggest denial or avoidance. If a psychodynamic inference is made with the assumption that the house represents the mother and the tree the father, then it may be that Jimmy wishes his mother would be big and strong and protect him from his father. Or it may be that she does protect him. The fact that she was the one who brought him for assessment suggests the latter interpretation, but her absence in the KFD suggests the former. It is possible that she is inconsistent in her support.

Achenbach Child Behavior Checklist

Although the mother originally requested assessment of Jimmy, she failed to complete the parent version of the CBCL. Her constant "forgetting" to complete the checklist is consistent with her unexplained failure to keep two previous assessment appointments.

Jimmy's teacher completed the Teacher's Report Version. According to her behavior ratings, Jimmy's scores were in the clinical range on three scales. Jimmy was high on Inattentive (T = 77), and he was rated as often being hyperactive, often fidgeting, often underachieving, often being inattentive, and often having difficulty learning. He was high on Aggressive (T = 71), and he was rated as often humming and making odd noises, often arguing, often showing poor peer relations, often disrupting class, and easily frustrated. He was high on Self-destructive (T = 71), and he was rated as often lying, often doing messy work, and sometimes stealing and being unclean. He was somewhat high on Unpopular (T = 66), and he was rated as having poor peer relations and not being liked. He was in the average range on the following scales: Social Withdrawal, Anxious, Obsessive-Compulsive, and Immature.

Jimmy's behavior was rated overall as being impulsive, hyperactive, inattentive, and aggressive. Although he is rated as self-destructive, his tendency is to externalize his aggression, and this aggressiveness may make him disliked by his peers. Despite his inattentiveness and self-destructiveness, he is not seen as immature, anxious, dependent, or withdrawn. This may be due to pseudomaturity and counterdependence as having to be an adultlike figure in his undependable family and to contribute to his family's finances.

SUMMARY

Jimmy exhibited several strengths in his psychological testing. He is personable and charming, with a good knowledge of socially appropriate behavior. He demonstrates initiative, both in telling creative stories and in obtaining odd jobs. Previous testing revealed average to superior intellectual abilities in contrast to low achievement in reading and spelling.

The personality testing indicated alternative explanations for Jimmy's learning problems. Jimmy's distractibility may be a result of anxiety or a stressful environment, as well as neurological impairment. Jimmy lives in a threatening and unstable environment, and he may cope with this by denial, avoidance, sexual acting out, and aggression.

He seems to have difficulty limiting his aggressive feelings once they are stimulated. The aggression in his stories is also found in ratings of his behavior, so it appears that his aggressive fantasies and feelings find expression in his behavior. This is also consistent with parental complaints about his fighting with other boys.

Jimmy appears to have low self-esteem and to be searching for protection and care in a life that is hard and a constant struggle. He seems to have been neglected and abused by his parents, and their failure to meet his needs may be the source of his anger and aggression.

Jimmy appears to be ambivalent about authority, exhibiting some indirect noncompliance and wanting to be a policeman while portraying himself as a gang member. This ambivalence may be a result of observing his parents break the law while telling him to obey the rules and not fight. He may identify with policemen as a subtle rebellion against or criticism of his parents, who consider the police their enemy, or as a way to help him control his aggression.

It is difficult to be optimistic about Jimmy's future. The parents are unlikely to seek further assessment or therapy for their son, because of their distrust of the system and their lack of money. Given recent reductions in funding for schools, it seems unlikely that the school system will be able to provide the special education and support that Jimmy probably needs. Since Jimmy is already highly involved in the drug culture through his parents, his ability to resist continuing drug use would appear compromised. His low self-esteem, distractibility, impulsiveness, and anxiety would seem to make him vulnerable to stress, possibly acting out with sex or aggression.

However, Jimmy has strengths, such as a relatively high level of intellectual functioning in several areas, physical attractiveness, and an appealing personality. If he can learn to find more socially acceptable means for expressing his anxious and aggressive feelings, he may be able to benefit from interventions by school authorities and remedial education.

PROVISIONAL DIAGNOSIS

Axis I: Conduct Disorder, mild
          (Child is also anxious)

Axis II: Developmental Reading Disorder
          Attention-deficit/Hyperactivity Disorder, mild

BOX 5.2 *(continued)*

Axis III: Frequent headaches, possibly migraine
Diagnosis deferred, pending medical examination

Axis IV: Psychosocial stressors: Overcrowded living quarters, harsh parents, parental drug abuse, poverty

Axis V: Serious impairment in school functioning

RECOMMENDATIONS

THE USE OF STANDARDIZED ASSESSMENT MEASUREMENTS SHOULD NOT BE EMPLOYED AS THE SOLE CRITERIA IN DEVELOPING A TREATMENT PLAN OR IN THE PLACEMENT OF AN INDIVIDUAL.

Previous recommendations for a thorough physical examination, including hearing and vision testing, and neuropsychological assessment still stand. The previous recommendations for a school IEP and psychoeducational assessment remain crucial.

The results of the present assessment indicate that individual and family therapy are to be strongly recommended.

Individual psychotherapy for Jimmy S. is strongly recommended in order to help him develop higher self-esteem, control his anger, reduce his self-destructive and inappropriate behavior, and pay attention at school so that he can utilize his good intellectual abilities to develop social and work-related competencies. This treatment probably needs to be relatively long term. At the end of 18 months of treatment, Jimmy can be reassessed with the Children's Psychological Inventory as a measure of self-esteem and the CBCL as a measure of inattention, aggression, and self-destructiveness in order to see if the treatment goals are being reached. Measures of achievement may be used to indicate if he is learning to pay attention and develop competencies.

Family therapy is strongly recommended to help the parents become more consistent in both nurturing and setting limits for Jimmy. If trust could be established and the parents' resistance to authority overcome, psychoeducational interventions could be aimed at increasing their concern over Jimmy's inappropriate sexual acting out and drug use and helping them learn appropriate ways to limit such behaviors. Since they are already concerned about his fighting, they could be taught specific techniques for discouraging such behavior and rewarding desired behavior. Given the nature of the family, another realistic goal may be to support the mother in being more protective and nurturant of Jimmy perhaps by spending more time with him. The family should be encouraged to reduce the discrepancy between what they tell Jimmy to do and what they do in front of him. If they can be taught behavioral methods that help them feel more competent as parents, they may be more motivated to do so. Achieving these therapy goals depends on the parents' willingness to attend therapy regularly.

BIBLIOGRAPHY

Archer, R. (1992). *MMPI-A: Assessing adolescent psychopathology.* Hillsdale, NJ: Lawrence Erlbaum.

Beck, A. T. (1972). *Depression: Causes and treatment.* Philadelphia: University of Pennsylvania Press.

Beck, S. (1945). *Rorschach's test.* New York: Grune & Stratton.

Bonato, D. P., Cyr, J. J., Kalpin, R. A., and others. (1988). The utility of the MCMI as a DSM-III Axis I diagnostic tool. *Journal of Clinical Psychology, 44,* 867–875.

Burisch, M. (1984). Approaches to personality inventory construction: A comparison of merits. *American Psychologist, 39,* 214–227.

Butcher, J. N. (1987). *Computerized psychological assessment: A practitioner's guide.* New York: Basic Books.

Butcher, J. N. (1992, March). MMPI–2: A step in the right direction. *The National Psychologist,* p. 12.

Butcher, J. N., Dahlstrom, W. G., Graham, J. R., Tellegen, A., & Kaemmer, B. (1989). *Minnesota Multiphasic Personality Inventory (MMPI-2). Manual for administration and scoring.* Minneapolis: University of Minnesota Press.

Campbell, D. P. (1966). Occupations ten years later of high school seniors with high scores on the SVIB life insurance salesman scale. *Journal of Applied Psychology, 50,* 369–372.

Campbell, D. P., & Hansen, J. C. (1981). *Manual for the SVIB-SCII* (3rd ed.). Palo Alto, CA: Stanford University Press.

Ciminero, A. R., Calhoun, K. S., & Adams, H. E. (Eds.). (1984). *Handbook of behavioral assessment* (2nd ed.). New York: Wiley.

Costa, P. T., & McCrae, R. R. (1992). *Revised NEO Personality Inventory (NEO PI-R) and NEO Five-Factor Inventory (NEO-FFI): Professional manual.* Odessa, FL: Psychological Assessment Resources.

Dahlstrom, W. G., & Welsh, G. S. (1960). *An MMPI handbook: A guide to use in clinical practice and research.* Minneapolis: University of Minnesota Press.

Dana, R. (1993). *Multicultural assessment perspectives for professional psychology.* Boston: Allyn & Bacon.

Dana, R. H., & Cantrell, J. D. (1988). An update on the Millon Clinical Multiaxial Inventory (MCMI). *Journal of Clinical Psychology, 44,* 760–763.

Duckworth, J., & Anderson, W. (1994). *MMPI and MMPI-2 interpretation manual.* Bristol, PA: Accelerated Development.

Erdberg, P., & Exner, J. E. (1984). Rorschach assessment. In G. Goldstein & M. Hersen (Eds.), *Handbook of psychological assessment* (pp. 227–298). New York: Pergamon Press.

Exner, J. E. (1991). *The Rorschach: A comprehensive system: Vol. 2. Interpretation* (2nd ed.). New York: Wiley.

Hansen, J. C., & Swanson, J. L. (1983). Stability of interests and the predictive and concurrent validity of the 1981 Strong-Campbell Interest Inventory. *Journal of Consulting Psychology, 30,* 194–201.

Hathaway, S., & McKinley, J. (1943). *The Minnesota Multiphasic Personality Inventory.* New York: Psychological Corporation.

Haynes, S. N. (1984). Behavioral assessment of adults. In G. Goldstein & M. Hersen (Eds.), *Handbook of psychological assessment* (pp. 337–386). New York: Pergamon Press.

Hodgins, D., & el-Guebaly, N. (1992). More data on the Addiction Severity Index: Reliability and validity, with the mentally ill substance abuser. *Journal of Nervous and Mental Disease, 180,* 197–201.

Hogan, R., Hogan, J., & Roberts, B. W. (1996). Personality measurement and employment decisions: Questions and answers. *American Psychologist, 51,* 469–477.

Keiser, R., & Prather, E. (1990). What is the TAT: A review of ten years of research. *Journal of Personality Assessment, 55,* 800–803.

Kelly, G. A. (1955). *The psychology of personal constructs: A theory of personality* (2 vols.). New York: Norton.

Klopfer, B., & Kelley, D. (1942). *The Rorschach technique.* Yonkers, NY: World Book.

Kuder, G. F. (1966). *General manual: Occupation Interest Survey—Form DD.* Chicago: Science Research Associates.

Machover, K. (1949). *Personality projection in the drawing of the human figure: A method of personality investigation.* Springfield, IL: C. C. Thomas.

Malgady, R., Rogler, L., & Tryon, W. (1992). Issues of validity in the Diagnostic Interview Schedule. *Journal of Psychiatric Research, 26,* 59–67.

Matarazzo, J. (1992). Psychological testing and assessment in the 21st century. *American Psychologist, 47,* 1007–1018.

Millon, T. (1983). *Millon Clinical Multiaxial Inventory Manual.* Minneapolis: National Computer Systems.

Millon, T. (1985). The MCMI provides a good assessment of DSM-III disorders: The MCMI-II will prove even better. *Journal of Personality Assessment, 49,* 379–391.

Millon, T., Green, C. J., & Meagher, R. B. (1982). *Millon Adolescent Personality Inventory.* Minneapolis, MN: National Computer Systems.

Millon, T., Green, C. J., & Meagher, R. B. (1982). *Millon Behavioral Health Inventory Manual.* Minneapolis, MN: National Computer Systems.

Murray, H. A. (1938). *Explorations in personality.* New York: Oxford University Press.

Myers, I. B. (1962). *Manual: The Myers-Briggs Type Indictor.* Palo Alto, CA: Consulting Psychologists Press.

Myers, I. B. (1977). *Supplementary Manual: The Myers-Briggs Type Indicator.* Palo Alto, CA: Consulting Psychologists Press.

Rodgers, D. A. (1992, March). The MMPI–2: Improvement or marketing ploy? *The National Psychologist,* p. 13.

Rogers, C. A., & Dymond, R. F. (Eds.). (1954). *Psychotherapy and personality change: Coordinated research studies in the client-centered approach.* Chicago: The University of Chicago Press.

Rohde, A. R. (1957). *The sentence completion method.* New York: Ronald Press.

Rorschach, H. (1921). *Psychodiagnostik.* Bern: Bircher.

Rotter, J. B., & Rafferty, J. E. (1950). *The Rotter Incomplete Sentences Blank.* New York: Psychological Corporation.

Silber, D., Karp, S., & Holmstrom, R. (1990). Recommendations for the clinical use of the Apperceptive Personality Test. *Journal of Personality Assessment, 55,* 790–799.

Spokane, A. R. (1979). Occupational preferences and the validity of the Strong-Campbell Interest Inventory for college women and men. *Journal of Counseling Psychology, 26,* 312–318.

Stephenson, W. (1953). *The study of behavior: Q-technique and its methodology.* Chicago: University of Chicago Press.

Turner, J., Herron, L., & Weiner, P. (1986). Utility of the MMPI Pain Assessment Index in predicting outcome after lumbar surgery. *Journal of Clinical Psychology, 42,* 764–769.

Widiger, T. A. (1991). DSM-IV and personality disorders: Introduction to special series. *Journal of Personality Disorders, 5,* 122–134.

Widiger, T. A., Williams, J. B., Spitzer, R. L., & Frances, A. (1985). The MCMI as a measure of DSM-III. *Journal of Personality Assessment, 49,* 366–378.

Wierzbicki, M. (1993). *Issues in clinical psychology.* Boston: Allyn & Bacon.

Williams, J., Gibbon, M., First, M., Spitzer, R., & Davies, M. (1992). The Structured Clinical Interview for DSM-III-R (SCID): II. Multisite test-retest reliability. *Archives of General Psychiatry, 49,* 630–636.

Willis, C. G. (1987). Myers-Briggs Type Indicator. In D. Keyser & R. Sweetland (Eds.). *Test critiques compendium.* Kansas City: Test Corporation of America.

Zytowski, D. G. (1976). Predictive validity of the Kuder Occupational Interest Survey: A 12- to 19-year follow-up. *Journal of Counseling Psychology, 3,* 221–233.

PART **THREE**

Psychodynamic Approaches

CHAPTER
6

Sigmund Freud and Psychoanalysis

I treated a young lady who suffered for six years from an intolerable and protracted nervous cough. . . . Every other remedy had long since shown itself powerless, and I, therefore, attempted to remove the symptom by psychic analysis. All that she could remember was that the nervous cough began at the age of fourteen while she boarded with her aunt. She remembered absolutely no psychic excitement during that time, *and did not believe there was a motive for her suffering* [italics added]. Under the pressure of my hand, she at first recalled a large dog. She then recognized the memory picture; it was her aunt's dog which was attached to her, and used to accompany her everywhere, and without any further aid it occurred to her that this dog died and that the children buried it solemnly; and on the return from this funeral her cough appeared. I asked her why she began to cough, and the following thought occurred to her: "Now I am all alone in this world; no one loves me here; this animal was my only friend, and now I have lost it. . . ." That was, therefore, the pathogenic idea: People do not love her, everybody else is preferred; she really does not deserve to be loved, etc. (Freud, 1895/1937, pp. 204–205)

. . . [O]ne analysand with marked obsessive-compulsive problems, based as is usually the case on an unconsciously maintained anal orientation to himself and his world, would at times grunt, groan, and writhe on the analytic couch in his efforts to force out some of his thoughts and feelings; finally he would appeal to the analyst explicitly for help in "getting it out." Upon analysis, this conduct proved to be a reenactment of his ambivalence during and after toilet training with respect to holding on to or letting go of his stools; it was also a reenactment of his conflictual retentive-expulsive actions in other areas of his life. In his childhood he often had ended up requiring help from his mother in completing his evacuations. It also emerged that he derived some secret masturbatory pleasure from the considerable and prolonged anal stimulation occasioned by his intermediate "paralysis." (Schafer, 1978, pp. 36–37)

The idea that a neurotic is suffering from a sort of ignorance, and that if one removes this ignorance by telling him facts (about the causal connection of his illness with his life, about his experiences in childhood, and so on) he must recover, is an idea that has long been superceded, and one derived from superficial appearances. . . . if knowledge about his unconscious were as important for the patient as the inexperienced in psychoanalysis imagine, it would be sufficient to cure him for him to go to lectures or read books. . . . (Freud, 1910/1963, p. 93)

Psychoanalysis had been the most influential approach to psychotherapy. Originally developed by Sigmund Freud, psychoanalysis has provided many insights into both the process of psychotherapy and the nature of psychopathology. Many of Freud's insights have been incorporated into other approaches to psychotherapy that may diverge widely from psychoanalysis in other respects.

Psychoanalysis has spawned a host of creative offshoots. Taken all together, these are called the "psychodynamic" set of views. Psychodynamic views of the person hold that the personality is an organized system of forces and counterforces. Different dynamic theorists may disagree on what forces in the personality are important, but all usually include the need to protect against psychologically painful wishes, thoughts, feelings, or experiences as one of the major forces that drives the person. One of the major ways this is done is to deny painful aspects of the self or personality and keep them from awareness. Some of the theorists who have developed out of psychoanalysis are Jung, Adler, Rank, Reich, Sullivan, Horney, Fromm, Erickson, and Hartmann. More recent developments are object relations theory and Kohut's self psychology. In this chapter we will look at Freud's view of psychopathology and psychotherapy ("classical" psychoanalysis). In the next chapter we will consider the views of those who have followed Freud, examining in some detail object relations theory and self psychology.

THEORY OF PERSONALITY

Hidden Meaning and the Concept of Repression

The core idea in Freudian psychoanalysis can be seen in the first two quotations at the start of the chapter. In both cases, the client's overt symptomatology (the cough in the first case and the difficulty in "getting it out" in the second) is actually not the problem. Rather, the symptoms are expressions of meanings hidden deep in the personality structure. The hidden meaning of the cough has to do with feelings of loss, of being alone, and of being unlovable. The second client's difficulty in getting his feelings and thoughts out is an expression of underlying conflicts over the act of defecation. The idea that overt behavior contains hidden meanings (Cameron & Rychlak, 1985) implies that there is a kind of "secret code" to overt behavior that must be deciphered if we are to help the client modify his or her actions. It is not sufficient to treat the symptoms themselves. Treating the overt behavior will be useless unless the hidden meanings are dealt with. In order to deal with them the client must become aware of them, and that is the ultimate goal of Freud's psychoanalysis. However, as the last quote at the start of the chapter indicates, intellectual knowledge about hidden meanings is not sufficient for therapeutic change to occur. Therapy must include the reexperiencing of the feelings and affects that accompany the hidden meanings. For instance, it would not be enough for the woman to know intellectually that conflicts about being lonely and being unlovable were underlying her cough. She would have to experience the feeling of being alone and unlovable for her awareness of these hidden meanings to be therapeutic. We will discuss why this is so later.

Most of Freud's original work was done with patients who used to be diagnosed as suffering from the neurotic disorder of conversion hysteria. In the current edition of the *Diagnostic and Statistical Manual of Mental Disorders* (DSM-IV), the terms *neurotic* and *conversion hysteria* no longer appear. Conversion hysteria is now called *conversion disorder.* Because for Freud (and, indeed, for many modern psychoanalysts) the concept of neurotic disorders was so important, we will briefly describe it. Basically neurotic disorders are disorders in which individuals have one or two symptoms that interfere with their functioning, but otherwise they are in touch with reality. This differs from psychosis, in which individuals are "out of touch" with reality, and personality disorders, in which individuals have pervasive characterological difficulties in the personality.

In **conversion disorders,** clients suffer from one or more physical symptoms that mimic physical illnesses. For instance, a client may lose sight or hearing or speech, with no detectable physical cause for the loss. In fact, tests will often reveal that the client's eyes respond to light, ears to sound, and so on. Breuer and Freud (Freud, 1895/1937) originally treated conversion disorders with hypnosis. Under hypnosis the client was asked to recall when the particular symptom began. They found that the symptom was associated with an emotionally charged, forgotten memory. When this memory was recovered, the symptom would vanish. For instance, Anna O., Breuer's most famous client, developed the symptom of being unable to drink out of a glass and swallow water. The incident she had forgotten was one in which she had unexpectedly discovered her maid allowing a dog to drink out of a glass. Anna O. recalled feeling repulsed and disgusted. With the recovery of the memory, and her disgust, the symptom vanished, and she was able to drink easily from a glass.

It was such experiences with clients that led to Freud's view of psychopathology and then to his theory of personality. The client suffers from a symptom that disrupts the client's life. The symptom seems irrational and inexplicable; it does not appear to make sense. Furthermore, the client is unable to control the symptom consciously. However, there is a reason for the symptom at another, nonconscious level. Thus, the overt symptom is a disguised manifestation of a hidden meaning. In particular, the underlying meaning involves an emotional conflict of some sort. Though the emotional conflict is not in consciousness, it nevertheless manifests itself in overt behavior.

We may now ask why this memory is forgotten. Why was Anna O. unable to recall the dog's drinking out of the glass? Freud's answer was that such things are forgotten because they are painful and thus are blocked out of consciousness. Freud arrived at this conclusion by finding that some clients seemed to resist remembering the feelings that had been forgotten. From this, Freud ultimately developed the concept of **repression,** that is, some emotionally conflictual material is excluded from consciousness because of its painful nature.

But why did the excluded material continue to influence behavior? Why was it not simply hidden and forgotten? Freud's answer was that it remains active because it is emotionally charged. It "clamors" for expression. Breuer and Freud used the term *strangulated affect* to capture this idea. The method of cure was to make these emotions available to consciousness, thereby allowing them expression and discharge. This idea is usually called *emotional catharsis.* Freud later abandoned the idea that catharsis is what makes therapy work, but he retained the idea that unconscious material remains active because it has a kind of "charge" (or "energy") attached to it.

You now have the basics of Freud's view of psychopathology and personality. Certain conflictual material is excluded from consciousness because it is too painful. However, because it is emotionally charged, it remains active in the personality, resulting in overt behavioral symptoms. Full awareness (including allowing oneself to experience the emotions consciously) results in alleviation of the symptoms. These are Freud's theoretical hypotheses to explain the observations that recovery of forgotten, emotionally charged memories seemed to be related to the disappearance of hysterical symptoms. We mention this because other theorists have other ways of explaining these observations.

Metapsychology

With this in mind, we will now look at how Freud extended the above ideas to a whole theory of personality and psychopathology. We will be discussing Freud's **metapsychology,** which is what is most disputed by many modern psychoanalytic theorists and practitioners. The metapsychology consists of Freud's belief that the personality is fundamentally an energy system whose business is the regulation and discharge of both sexual and aggressive energy and his belief that the mind consists of three processes or structures: the id, the ego, and the superego.

As Freud extended his work, he began to find that the removal of symptoms in his hysterical clients did not effect a total cure. Other symptoms would pop up. This led Freud to believe that the ultimate causes of the person's problems lay deeply buried in the personality. In the second quote at the start of the chapter the man's problems in "getting it out" are not based on a single, emotionally charged memory, but on the repression of a whole set of experiences with toilet training when he was a child. As Freud continued to delve into the buried memories of his clients, he came to believe that psychological problems were not usually the result of a few highly charged emotional memories (traumatic memories), but rather the result of patterns of repression of meanings and associated experiences in early childhood.

In addition, Freud believed that many of the buried memories revolved around sexual themes. It is now unclear to what extent Freud actually found these themes in his client's repressed memories and to what extent he went looking for them (see Masson, 1985). It is known that theorists both prior to and at the time of Freud (including Freud's friend Wilhelm Fleiss) were speculating that many psychological problems had their origins in sexual repression (Ellenberger, 1970). Freud was working during the Victorian era, a time of sexual repression, and it would not be surprising if sexual conflicts figured prominently among the emotional difficulties people had. Further, it was also about this time that Freud began his own self-analysis and began to uncover themes of repressed sexuality in himself. As a result Freud began to believe that repressed sexuality lay at the core of psychopathological behavior. His clients' reports of early childhood sexual experiences with adults led to the formulation of his seduction theory. This theory held that it was the repression of actual traumatic memories of childhood molestations that caused neurotic behavior. However, Freud began to believe that many of these seductions had in fact not taken place. This led to the crucial idea that what had been repressed were not memories of actual experiences, but memories of primitive sexual wishes and fantasies that were too painful for the individual to acknowledge consciously.

Freud later developed the idea of the regulation of aggressive energy in the form of what he called the death instinct. He believed we each have competing "life" (or sexual) instincts and "death" instincts. The death instinct is supposedly an impulse to die or to return to inert matter. It is turned outward as aggression, as a defense to keep us from killing ourselves. Many analytic theorists do not accept the concept of the death instinct, though they may believe in an aggressive instinct. For our purposes, we will mainly talk about the development and regulation of sex and aggression, not the death instinct.

If, during development, various infantile sexual or aggressive wishes and fantasies are unacceptable to consciousness, they will be repressed (pushed out of consciousness). Repression leads to fixation, that is, if some wish is repressed, the developmental "stream" is arrested at that point. The infantile wish, with its accompanying energy, remains alive and active. The "trick" for the personality is to find an outlet for the repressed wish and simultaneously to keep it unconscious and hidden. The way to do this is to let the wish out in a disguised form. Much of personality—overt behaviors, values, beliefs, goals, job and mate choices, recreational choices—consists of disguised outlets for primitive, childhood repressed wishes and conflicts. It is not only people with psychological problems who have repressed wishes and fantasies, but all of us. For Freud, personality was the system of controls and restraints we develop in the first five or six years of life to regulate and channel our repressed primitive wishes, fantasies, and conflicts. Our early childhood experiences are the primary determinant of our current personality functioning. To quote a typical psychodynamic viewpoint (Adelson & Doehrman, 1980),

> [Psychoanalysis] holds that in truly important moments of one's life one is unwittingly held captive by the past. Whom we marry and how the marriage fares; the work we choose and how well we do it; whether we have children and when and how we raise them and feel about them; when we become ill and how we survive or fail to—all these and other vital events of the life course can be understood in depth only after we have a sufficient understanding of the personal past. (p. 100)

Defense Mechanisms

Although all of us have repressed wishes, most of us, while we may have our troubles, do not develop persistent neurotic symptoms. Nor do we become alcoholics or consistently act in impulsive or self-destructive ways. Whether or not we end up relatively "symptom free" depends on how our personalities regulate our repressed wishes and fantasies. For Freudians, that ultimately depends on the crucial, formative experiences with the family in early childhood.

Perhaps the most socially adaptive way of handling repressed wishes and conflicts is sublimation. In sublimation, the repressed desire is channeled into some socially acceptable outlet. For instance, aggressive feelings may be channeled into being a highly competitive athlete. Sexual wishes associated with defecation and the anal stage of development (discussed below) may be channeled into creative activity, such as painting and sculpting. Or, early childhood wishes and conflicts may get channeled into founding the most influential of all theories of personality and psychopathology (see Box 6.1).

But sometimes we are unable to sublimate. Then we must rely on **defense mechanisms** that distort reality to some slight degree. The concept of defense is a pervasive one in psychoanalytic theory. Psychoanalysis holds that the most fundamental factor in psychic development is avoidance of painful or threatening information. Repression is the fundamental way most of us have of avoiding painful information. In order to maintain repression, and to try to protect the ego from anxiety, we utilize defense mechanisms.

Denial is the simplest of these. Denial is the refusal to recognize the real nature of one's behavior. A person may act quite seductively, for instance, but deny there is any sexual intent to his behavior. Another person may exhibit symptoms of anger, such as a flushed face, angry expression, and angry tone of voice, yet deny that she is angry. Denial is the mechanism most commonly used by alcoholics. Long past the time when friends, neighbors, employers, and doctors have told an alcoholic that he has a drinking problem, the alcoholic will deny that he has a problem.

BOX 6.1

Freud's Defenses

Freud's wish to restore and preserve an early idealized image of his mother ran through his life like a red thread, influencing his reconstruction of his early childhood history, his choice of a field of study, his important adult relationships, and his theoretical ideas. The defensive operations which Freud employed to protect the idealized version of his mother from invasion by a deep unconscious ambivalence conflict fatefully left their mark on his theory of psychosexual development and its central metapsychological reifications, in which the sources of evil were internalized, hostility was displaced onto the father, and the split-off bad maternal image was relegated largely to the psychology of the girl. (Stolorow & Atwood, 1979)

Stolorow and Atwood are not "classical" psychoanalysts, who see everything in terms of sex and aggression. Nevertheless, they do use Freudian concepts of how early childhood conflicts may determine adaptive adult behavior to analyze Freud's life and work.

Rationalization is giving a plausible and acceptable reason for one's behavior and feelings in order to hide one's real motives. A rationalization we frequently heard in college was from male students who would claim that they bought *Playboy* magazine "for the articles" (but, of course, they never bought any other magazine with similar articles and stories). Alcoholics often combine rationalization with denial. For each lapse into excessive drinking, the alcoholic will have an excuse. It was because she was depressed or she had to join the office party and so on.

With **projection,** the individual attributes to others the wishes, aims, and motives he cannot accept in himself. If a person has a lot of repressed hostility, she may see other people as dangerous and hostile. She may adopt a defensive, suspicious view of other people and be constantly on the lookout to protect herself from their malicious intentions and purposes. If a person has repressed his sexual impulses, he may angrily criticize what he sees as everyone else's preoccupation with sex. Projection allows some gratification of the repressed impulses by allowing them into consciousness, but protects the individual by ascribing the impulses to other people.

Most of us are familiar with **displacement.** In displacement, we deflect our feelings onto another less threatening target. Often we do this consciously. We get angry at our boss and come home and yell at our kids. With true displacement, however, this is done unconsciously. We actually believe we are angry at our kids and deny that our anger is toward our boss.

In **reaction formation,** the individual acts in a way that is diametrically opposite to what she unconsciously wants. Thus, if a person has a good deal of unconscious hostility, she may act like an uncompromising pacifist on the surface or she may strongly condemn contact sports or violence on television. Conversely, a person with strong repressed dependency needs may intensely value toughness, physical violence, and contact sports. We should point out that neither being a lover of violent sports nor being a pacifist is necessarily a reaction formation against unconscious impulses. Perhaps a better index of reaction formation would be the rigidity with which beliefs are held, an unwillingness to tolerate or even consider different points of view. For psychoanalysis, rigidity of belief systems is usually a sign of defensiveness. A conflict area can often be identified by the degree of emotion invested in surface issues associated with it. The person cannot be flexible because she is protecting herself in that area. A fully functioning person is able to consider other points of view, even though she may come to identify strongly with one particular perspective.

With **intellectualization,** the individual "understands" and acknowledges that he "must have" certain repressed impulses. Knowledge of the impulses, but not the impulses themselves, is thereby allowed into consciousness. For instance, a client may intellectually accept that she had incestuous feelings toward her father, while still repressing the actual feelings and impulses themselves.

With **compensation,** the individual deals with frustration and inadequacy in one area by investing in another area. Thus, an individual who has underlying feelings of physical inadequacy as a male (he is not athletic or handsome) may compensate by becoming highly competent at intellectual pursuits. Conversely, an athlete who feels intellectually inferior may overinvest in his athletic skills.

According to psychoanalytic theory, defense mechanisms involve mild distortions of reality, but they are functional and necessary. In fact, all of us need to be able to regulate negative, conflictual feelings in order to function. Denial, for instance, may be important in certain professions, such as the military, where one must be able to "deny" one's fear in order to function. Intellectualization may help emergency room physicians deal with the very painful experiences they face. There are more or less mature defenses (Vaillant, 1977). More mature defenses are means whereby we control our conflictual fears and negative emotions, but which actually allow us to behave productively and effectively. For instance, Vaillant considers altruism to be a mature defense.

However, if defenses become too rigid or are overused, they may unduly constrict the individual's functioning. And what happens when an individual's defenses fail— when they fail either to provide a sufficient outlet for unconscious impulses or when they fail to control the warded-off feelings, wishes, and impulses, and these threaten to break into consciousness? It is at this point that neurotic symptoms appear.

Psychopathology and Anxiety

For Freud, neurotic anxiety appears when one's defenses begin to break down. It is a signal that forbidden unconscious impulses are breaking into consciousness. Generalized anxiety disorder and panic disorder, in which free-floating anxiety is experienced, are examples. The person is overwhelmed by anxiety and cannot pin down any particular cause because the cause is unconscious: The anxiety is a signal of danger from within.

Other neurotic disorders also develop when unconscious impulses get intensified and threaten to break into consciousness. Symptoms develop that, like the defense mechanisms, allow some expression of the unconscious impulses, but disguise their nature. But because more extreme measures are now needed, the symptoms that develop are likely to be socially dysfunctional. For example, in order to control unconscious conflicts over sexuality, an individual may develop a phobia about being outside in crowds (where he is afraid he might unconsciously "lose control"). If unconscious hostile and rebellious impulses are threatening to break through, a person might carry "rule following" to the extreme or develop elaborate obsessive-compulsive rituals to control the impulses. She may wash her hands 200 times a day in order to quell anxiety by washing away those "dirty," unconscious, hostile, rule-breaking impulses.

Why does this happen? Usually it happens because some event intensifies a person's unconscious conflicts. If a person has strong unconscious hostility, he may shy away from situations in which he might be tempted to lose control. He may avoid, as an example, being in situations where he has the power to take out his hostility on others. Being in such a situation may provide so much unconscious temptation that he needs to develop some neurotic symptomatology to keep his defenses in order. For instance, suppose this person is a lawyer who is made a judge with the power to impose sentences. The possibility that his unconscious hostility may now come out in harsh, punitive judgments may be so threatening that he breaks down.

What happens if neurotic symptoms don't work as defenses? What happens if even they fail in keeping unconscious material out of consciousness? The person may then experience a psychotic episode, which can essentially be seen as a disintegration of the ego (the ego is discussed in the next section). Unconscious material now floods into consciousness. While Freudian psychoanalysis attempts to help the average neurotic to gain insight into his defenses, with psychotics, the Freudian approach is the opposite. It tries to shore up defenses and restore the ego.

Developmental Stages and Id, Ego, and Superego

We have now seen how repression and other defense mechanisms function to keep material unconscious and how psychopathology develops when they do not work. Now we will look at personality development both in terms of Freud's concept of the mind and various stages of development.

Freud held that there are three "structures" or components to the mind: the ego, the id, and the superego. At birth, the person is all **id.** The id is the biological storehouse of primitive impulses. It is all "want." Since it is pure desire, it has no concept of reality—others don't exist, reality doesn't exist, and time doesn't exist. At birth, the infant has no concept of itself as a separate human being, of others as human beings, of itself and the world as separate, of time, or of the difference between reality and fantasy.

The first stage of personality development, which lasts from birth to about 1 1/2 or 2 years, is the oral stage. It is called oral because during this stage, the mouth is the primary erogenous zone, that is, sexual gratification is gained primarily through oral stimulation. This is why the infant not only nurses, but is constantly putting things into its mouth.

The most crucial thing that happens at the oral stage is the beginning of the development of the **ego.** The ego develops both as a result of biological maturation and as a result of interaction with environmental demands. At birth, the infant is all id, but soon learns that its needs will not automatically be met whenever it wants. As a result, the infant begins to develop a concept of reality. It must learn to develop a concept of itself as separate from the world. It must develop concepts of external "objects" that will help it gain gratification. Objects are any things that populate the external world. Among the objects that an infant must form concepts of to view reality accurately are chairs, tables, floors, cribs, bottles, spoons, and so on. Among the most important object concepts the child needs to form are concepts of other people. In forming concepts of objects and of the external world, the child needs to realize that fantasies and reality are separate. The ego can be thought of as the "executive" part of the personality. It is the part that learns to perceive reality accurately in order to help the id get its demands met as effectively as possible. If at this stage (through severe neglect, extreme overindulgence, inconsistent experience) a strong ego does not begin to develop, the person will be predisposed to having psychotic experiences under stress in later life. Other oral fixations (the stopping of the developmental process in the oral stage) may lead to dependency, alcoholism, overeating, or a constant need to be loved and "nourished" by others.

The ego continues to develop during the anal stage, which lasts from about age 1 1/2 to 3. In this stage of personality development, the anus becomes the primary erogenous zone, and the child gains sexual gratification through the act of defecation. Parents' attempts at toilet training will be interpreted as infringements on the child's freedom to indulge in instinctual gratification. Thus, the anal stage is when the issue of socialization becomes prominent. The developing ego must learn to control and regulate impulses. The child is confronted with the need to regulate its bodily activities in order to follow societal rules and will experience anger at the parents for imposing restrictions on gratification of its bodily pleasures.

If the anger is repressed, the child may become on the surface a rigid, orderly, rule-following person, concerned with cleanliness. Underneath is a great deal of "dirty" anger. This is the anal-retentive pattern. For the anal-retentive, rules and rituals become defense mechanisms for binding and controlling unconscious hostility. In addition, the individual may engage in undoing rituals to overcome unconscious guilt over the buried anger and rebellion. Undoing rituals are like atonements. Undoing can be used to overcome unconscious guilt over sexuality as well, as when individuals need to shower or wash their hands after making love. The ritualistic nature of defenses developed at this stage lay the basis for obsessive-compulsive neurosis, in which individuals may have to shower for hours a day or engage in other extreme undoing rituals.

If the anger is not repressed, the child may repetitively act out his anger, constantly trying to prove his independence. In effect he is "defecating all over everyone," and this is the anal-expulsive pattern.

The phallic stage is the most important one, according to Freud. It is the stage during which the third component of mental functioning—the superego—develops. It occurs between the ages of 4 and 6. Though most of Freud's clients were women, the phallic stage is named after the male and is one example of why Freud has often been accused of being sexist. During the phallic stage, sexuality becomes localized in the genitals. Of particular importance during this stage is the Oedipus complex. The male child presumably begins to develop sexual feelings toward his mother and wants some kind of sexual contact with her. As a result of this, he views his father as a rival and may harbor primitive fantasies of wanting to murder his father and take his place. However, the male child becomes afraid that if the father finds out about these feelings and wishes, the father will castrate him. This castration anxiety leads the child to repress both his rivalrous feelings toward his father and his lustful feelings toward his mother.

The way the male child resolves the Oedipal crisis is to identify with his father (and be able to possess his mother vicariously as a result). This identification leads both to an adoption of the male sex role and to the development of the **superego.** The superego is formed out of the internalized (or "introjected") values of the parent. It consists of both the parent's moral values (essentially the "conscience") and a perfectionistic standard of what a good person should be like (the "ego-ideal"). If the values of the superego are harsh or unrealistic, the individual will be constantly plagued with feelings of guilt and failure. The individual may have a need to punish himself and may set up situations where others are rejecting or punitive. The individual may unconsciously cause painful accidents to happen and, in the extreme, may have unconscious suicidal wishes that get expressed in self-destructive acts (for instance, through reckless driving).

The "female Oedipus complex"(sometimes called the Electra complex) is similar in its general outlines to that of the male. However, there are some important differences. According to Freud, little girls note that they are missing something that little boys have. This is called penis envy. The girl's desire for her father is not only sexual, but is based on the desire to obtain a penis as well. Because girls do not fear being castrated, there is less fear to lead to repression. As a result, girls develop less strong superegos than boys (Freud, 1925/1961). Girls resolve penis envy by identifying with the mother and accept the ability to have a baby as a substitute for a penis.

Between age 6 and adolescence is the latency stage, during which the child is busy regulating the repressed impulses from the Oedipal period. Psychoanalytically, this is why children at this age are often so fascinated with rules and the establishment of order in their lives. At adolescence, the genital stage, the upsurge of sexuality reawakens Oedipal conflicts. The adolescent's task is to not allow incestuous feelings to surface into consciousness. Rebelliousness against the parents and intense love affairs with peers are ways of distancing and redirecting the incestuous wishes so that they do not become conscious. If handled effectively, these desires will be tamed and sublimated, and adult personality established.

With the phallic stage, the three major mental structures are all established. The mind can almost be thought of as a kind of stage with three actors on it. The three voices are in constant contention, and psychopathology can be seen as the conflict among them. The ego bears the brunt of coordinating the primitive wishes of the id, the limitations imposed by reality, and the moral restrictions of the superego. Repression complicates matters. Primitive wishes and impulses are repressed and kept out of conscious awareness, partly to satisfy the moral values of the superego. Repression weakens the ego's ability to deal realistically with the world. A particularly harsh superego may lead to extreme and debilitating repression. On the other hand, a particularly weak superego may lead to psychopathic behavior.

Not only are primitive wishes and fantasies repressed, but parts of the ego itself are unconscious. This is necessary for repression to occur. After all, repression is a kind of unconsciously "deliberate" avoidance of painful material. If this avoidance were conscious, it would not work, so the act of avoiding itself must be performed unconsciously. As one of our children said about something she was trying to forget, "I have to forget that I've forgotten, too. Otherwise I'll remember it." Therefore, repression means that forces unknown to the ego may be controlling behavior. As a result, the person will engage in behavior for reasons unknown to the conscious ego. Such behavior will be consciously experienced as "irrational" or "ego-alien." It is such an experience that often propels a person to seek therapy.

To sum up, the Freudian view of personality and psychopathology is that both ultimately rest on unconscious self-deception. Behavior is under the control of hidden meanings that are hidden because they are too painful to consciousness to be acknowledged and known. For Freud, these hidden meanings revolve around primitive sexual and aggressive impulses. As part of this self-deception, we must also, of necessity, distort external reality via defense mechanisms such as projection and displacement. Thus, most of us live in a world where objective reality is obscured by shadows from our past. These shadows also distort our perception of our own inner reality of feelings, thoughts, and motives. Each of us lives in a reality of our own construction, contrived to protect us from painful self-knowledge. Therefore, none of us lives fully in touch with external or internal reality. For most of us, the distortions are compatible enough with social reality that we are generally functional. For some of us, the distortions are discrepant enough, and the resulting behavior deviant enough, that our behavior is dysfunctional and in need of treatment.

PSYCHOTHERAPY

The goal of classical Freudian psychoanalysis is to "lift repression" (Freud, 1937/1963). Freud said, "Where id was there shall ego be" (1924/1964). However, it is rarely the case that all repression is lifted. Often, some repression is lifted and some is reworked so that it is not so incapacitating (Freud, 1937/1963). Following from this, the goal of psychoanalysis is insight into and conscious awareness of the hidden meanings influencing behavior. This involves overcoming resistance, which is the main work of therapy.

How does awareness and the lifting of repression cure? Before therapy, the ego is not able to control behavior effectively because it is being guided by forces of which the ego is unaware. When the ego becomes aware of these forces, they can be controlled consciously and channeled into suitable outlets. It is important to note that insight does not eliminate the previously unconscious primitive impulses. A man's awareness that he has primitive wishes to kill his father and sleep with his mother does not relieve him of these impulses, but it does allow him to control them, rather than being controlled by them. Luborsky (1984, p. 20) said that what changes in psychoanalysis is the function that controls and regulates a wish or need, but "the wish, need or intention . . . changes relatively little." (In Chapter 7 we will look at some recent psychoanalytic theorists' views of what happens when a person gains insight.)

While the impulses themselves may change relatively little, learning that these impulses are there helps people discriminate between reality and their primitive wishes, fantasies, and feelings. A person may come to therapy because he feels that people in authority are always putting him down. In therapy he may find that he is displacing onto authority figures unconscious perceptions of his father. He may discover that he could never face up to perceiving his father as critical because he would then have to face up to all the buried anger he has toward him. He can now separate what people in authority are really saying and thinking from what he is displacing onto them. Thus, an important consequence of lifting repression is the ability to see reality more clearly.

The ultimate goal of therapy for Freud is to facilitate the individual's ability to love and work (Ekstein, 1974). Freud did not believe that the goal of therapy is to make a person "happy." In fact, he saw therapy as "replacing neurotic misery with common unhappiness" (1918/1955). One of the major achievements of therapy is an increase in the person's capacity to tolerate ambivalence and conflict or to live with "uneasiness" (Bettelheim, 1982). In relegating happiness to a secondary place among goals for healthy functioning, Freud's thought is compatible with many other theorists, including Rogers, Perls, and Beck.

Free Association

So how does classical psychoanalysis go about facilitating insight? Originally, Freud used hypnosis. However, he abandoned hypnosis early in his work. For a while he used a technique in which he placed his hand on the client's head to "suggest" that they remember (see the second quote at the start of the chapter). Eventually he abandoned this, too, in favor of the method of free association.

You might be thinking that hypnosis seems like the answer. Hypnotize patients, ask them to recover memories from early childhood, and therapy should be easy and quick. Why spend years in psychoanalysis? But Freud did not think this would work. The reason is that finding the buried memories is but a part of the therapeutic process. More important is going through the process of confronting yourself, learning how to dig into your past, and learning how to face up to your defenses. Using the easy magic of hypnosis to leapfrog defenses and resistances to get to "the truth" is bad therapy. You might be able to leapfrog these obstacles, but Freud wants you to clear the roads of them, so to speak. Thus, psychoanalysis needs to be a process done with relatively full awareness. After all, what you want is to be able to relate to yourself in a fully conscious way. You need to learn to do this by slowly and painstakingly confronting obstacles to full awareness as they arise. As you work through and discard or modify each obstacle or defense, you do indeed get closer to the buried childhood memories. But in addition, you have already become less defensive and more flexible and better able to tolerate painful self-knowledge.

Freud devised a technique to allow the person to stay conscious: *free association.* He believed that nothing psychological happens by chance. This is called "psychic determinism." Any thought that appears in consciousness is there for some reason. No matter how trivial or irrelevant, it is likely to be connected to some unconscious dynamic material. Normally, people control their stream of thoughts. For example, in conversations with others, we focus our thoughts and what we say on the conversation. We screen out, ignore, or do not give verbal expression to irrelevant thoughts and to thoughts that we judge to be socially inappropriate because they are hostile, sexual, or embarrassing. Freud wanted to relax the censoring activity that accompanies normal consciousness, so that deeper dynamic associations to surface thoughts could become conscious. So he instructed his patients to say whatever came to mind, regardless of how apparently irrelevant or inappropriate it was. In order to facilitate this, the client would lie on a couch, and Freud would sit behind him. This was presumed to reduce the demands of a normal social situation, where one converses face to face and does not let one's mind wander to whatever associated thoughts come up.

Suppose a client is discussing how loving his wife is and what an ungrateful wretch he is for not being more attentive to her. Suddenly he thinks of something that seems totally irrelevant—how much he hates spinach. It may turn out, through subsequent exploration, that it is no mere chance that this thought surfaced at that point. There may be an unconscious link between "spinach" and "wife." Perhaps the wife is so "loving" that he feels she treats him like a child. Since "being made to eat your spinach" is a fairly common image associated with being a child, the thought of spinach at that point makes sense. After this link is established, further exploration might uncover feelings of being smothered, and still further exploration, feelings of anger, and finally, feelings of being castrated. The unconscious is seen to follow a kind of emotional logic in how one thought flows into another. Topics are organized together based on their emotional associations, and it is this organization that the analyst hopes to tap into. But what does the analyst do while the client free associates?

Therapist Interventions

Psychoanalytic interventions are largely a matter of timing. Good analytic interventions first prepare a context for insight to develop and then facilitate the development of that insight. At first, the therapist will do relatively little other than listen. She may ask questions such as "What does spinach remind you of?" or "What else comes to mind?" Such questions will help the client explore his experience, and eventually, certain aspects of the client's experience will become more crystallized and focused.

When the context is sufficiently crystallized and developed, the analyst may broach an interpretation. An interpretation is a response designed to increase client insight. It attempts to bring into consciousness some thematic material that is unconscious. For the context to be sufficiently crystallized, the topic under discussion must have been explored enough for certain themes to be nearly apparent to consciousness. In addition, at the moment an interpretation is made, the context must be "affectively" alive, that is, the emotions associated with the underlying themes must be present or nearly present in consciousness. Put another way, a good interpretation works when it relates to something that is currently "on your mind," something you are currently "working on." Most of us have had the experience of being emotionally involved in talking about a problem (say, about our boss). At that moment, if a friend makes a response such as "He sounds like a real idiot" or "I bet you feel you can't show your real stuff around him," it will very likely feel relevant at that moment and help us crystallize our feelings about the boss. But if the same comments are made an hour later, when we are thinking about something completely unrelated, they will feel pallid, flat, and useless.

There are two general kinds of interpretations, vertical and horizontal (Bellack, 1954). A **horizontal interpretation** identifies common themes in apparently unrelated aspects of the client's experience. A **vertical interpretation** relates aspects of current experience to "deeper" childhood experiences. For instance, suppose several experiences surface in which the spinach-hating client reports that his wife and secretary are constantly "taking care of him." The analyst might make a horizontal interpretation: "You seem to feel uneasy about all these situations in which women 'take care of you,' and I wonder if it is because they make you feel a little like a child." A vertical interpretation (usually made much later in therapy after the affective context has been prepared) might relate the client's dislike of being treated like a child to feelings of having been overmothered (and thus demasculinized or "castrated") as a child.

Interpretations are supposed to be short and couched in concrete, vivid, everyday language. Both of these requirements relate to the need for an interpretation to have a concrete emotional impact (we will discuss this later). In addition, interpretations are supposed to address material that is near the surface of consciousness. We have already mentioned that interpretations are made only when sufficient material has been examined by client and therapist so that the common underlying theme is apparent. After the client has related several instances of feeling disgruntled at his wife's taking care of him, the theme that he feels he is being treated like a child almost pops out, and it is at this point that interpreting this to the client will facilitate therapeutic insight.

Interpretations need to deal with material that is already nearly in consciousness so that therapy proceeds gradually. One cannot simply jump to a deep vertical interpretation, for instance, that the client is suffering from castration anxiety. There are three reasons for this. First, one goal of psychoanalysis is to gradually work through the blockades the person has constructed against awareness of the unconscious impulses. Deeper material is presumably more anxiety provoking and better defended.

It is easier and less anxiety provoking to recognize that "I feel my wife treats me like a child" than it is to realize that "I felt overmothered and castrated as a child." As the client gradually confronts deeper and deeper material, the ability to tolerate the anxiety associated with deeply buried memories increases (this process is not unlike that of systematic desensitization, discussed in Chapter 10).

The second reason for proceeding gradually has to do with the plausibility of the interpretation (Fisher, 1956). After only one example of feeling disgruntled at his wife's taking care of him, it might not seem plausible to the client if the analyst were to jump in with, "You feel angry with your wife because she always treats you like a child." It would be even more implausible to say, "Your disgruntlement with your wife is based on feeling castrated as a child." Once the client accepts that he dislikes feeling treated like a child by his wife, it might seem more plausible to him that he may have felt overmothered as a child.

The third reason insights must be acquired gradually is that insight is therapeutic only if it is affectively meaningful. (We will discuss this in the next section when we discuss the therapeutic conditions of change.)

What happens if interpretations are badly done? (We hope this section will discourage you from playing amateur psychoanalyst with yourself, friends, or relations.) We have said that the affective context for an interpretation must be carefully prepared. If the client, for instance, were to say to his wife, "Don't tell me to eat my spinach!" it would do no good for her to retort, "You are rebelling against me only because you didn't feel like a man when your mother told you what to do." Not only

Using Interpretation with Pets.

is the interpersonal atmosphere a very unsafe one for the client to consider the truth of such a remark, but the careful exploration needed to make such an interpretation therapeutically useful has not been done. Such an interpretation, even if true (and, of course, without the exploration, you don't know it's true—you're only guessing) will not be therapeutic. All the intervening resistances to insight have not been worked through, and the result of such an interpretation might be only to make the client more defensive.

Breaching defenses too quickly may make the client feel bad about himself. The client has presumably been overmothered as a child. This may make him unusually sensitive to criticism from mother figures. But, of course, all he knows is that he feels bad about himself when his wife criticizes him. His conscious context, then, is to take comments about himself as criticisms. So when a mother figure (his wife) tells him he was overmothered as a child, he will not take this as an insight-gaining, repression-lifting interpretation, but as a criticism. While this might be especially true if the interpretation is done by someone close to the person, the same thing can happen with inappropriately timed interpretations done by analysts. Thus, interpretations that go too deep too fast will not be therapeutic. They may actually be harmful, may lead to overwhelming anxiety, and could result in disintegration of the ego and increased psychopathology.

Therapeutic Conditions of Change

It is possible for people to have knowledge about themselves that is totally useless to them in terms of therapeutic change. Such knowledge, even if accurate, may actually shore up defenses, rather than lead to their disappearance. This happens if the knowledge is in the form of an intellectual insight. Freud found early (see the third quote at the beginning of this chapter) that the knowledge that transforms is knowledge that is affectively meaningful. Put another way, insights that are acquired without an accompanying emotional experience will not be therapeutic. For instance, somewhere at the basis of your character, according to psychoanalytic theory, are Oedipal feelings. If you are a male, somewhere deep inside you is primitive lust toward your mother and hatred toward your father. If you are a female, you harbor hidden feelings of lust toward your father and hatred toward your mother. Yet we venture to guess that most of you have no awareness of such feelings. Presuming that analytic theory is true, such buried feelings play a role in whatever personal failings you may have. Now, we have just told you that those feelings are there in you. You have acquired (if you believe us) intellectual insight. Have you noticed any magical transformations in yourself? Have you suddenly found all your conflicts or self-doubts vanishing? Probably not.

The reason is that your knowledge is purely intellectual, abstract, and hypothetical. What you know is that you must have hated your father or mother. That is different from experientially knowing that you hated your father or mother. You have no direct awareness of such feelings, no direct personal memories of hating your father or mother (or lusting after one or the other). To acquire therapeutic insight is to relive the emotion of hating. To remember your personal experience of the feelings will be to reexperience them in the therapeutic context. Thus, you must recover the deepest and most personal part of your memories—your feelings—in order for insight to be therapeutic.

Even after a person achieves early childhood insights that are accompanied by emotional reexperiencing, there is no magical change. But how can this be so, since we said that the goal of psychoanalysis is to lift repression? We have already partially answered this in our discussion of why Freud abandoned hypnosis. Basically, feelings and behavior must be worked through. The working-through phase of therapy is the longest. Clients must learn how derivatives of early childhood feelings have been woven into the fabric of their whole lives. They need to examine specific events to find where the unconscious feelings are coloring and distorting their perceptions of situations and relationships. For example, you might examine an instance of anger at your boss to see if unconscious hatred of a parent is coloring your reactions. Insight does not magically lead to change. It is rather a precondition to change, because change actually occurs during the working through process.

Television and movie portrayals of instantaneous and magical therapeutic change are seriously distorted. A client has a hysterical symptom, such as blindness. The doctor discovers the reason—the client saw his wife in the arms of another and became hysterically blind to deny what he saw. The doctor confronts the client with the truth. The patient resists: "No! No!" The doctor repeats the truth, more loudly. Finally the patient faces up to it: "You're right! . . . I can see!" Most therapists agree that change is slow and gradual. In a small survey of over 30 therapists of all persuasions done by one of us (Bohart, 1979), only one therapist reported a case in which change was sudden and instantaneous as a result of an insight.

Dreams, Resistance, and Transference

We have now seen that the major therapeutic tool of psychoanalysis is interpretation. We have also seen that insight must be accompanied by emotional reliving and working through in order to be therapeutic. Now we will discuss three sources of data that the analyst uses in facilitating therapeutic change. For Freud, dreams were the "royal road to the unconscious." Freud believed that dreams express unconscious wishes and conflicts in symbolic form. Therefore, they can be used to acquire insight. The client is asked to free associate to the dream symbols in order to discover their unconscious meaning.

Resistance provides another general source of data about repression. The basic phenomenon is that no matter how much people may consciously wish to change (especially if their symptoms are painful), unconsciously, they do not wish to change. To change is to undo the repression that protects them from painful unconscious memories, and therefore, they will unconsciously resist treatment.

Resistance manifests itself in many ways in therapy. It may show up in difficulties in free association ("I can't think of anything at all to say"), in missing or being late for appointments, or in wasting most of the appointment talking about trivia. A client may try to seduce the therapist, literally or figuratively, to keep the therapist from forcing confrontation with the unconscious. Aside from literal sexual seduction, a person may try flattering the therapist, buying her gifts, or wanting to be

"friends" outside of therapy. The client may resist by belittling or berating the therapist or by deciding therapy is a waste of time or through a temporary "flight into
health," insisting that problems are solved after a few sessions.

The phenomenon of resistance to change is noted by therapists of most persuasions. However, there are different ways of interpreting the cause of resistance, as
you shall see later on in this book. The psychoanalytic interpretation of resistance is
that it occurs because the client is unconsciously avoiding the pain of facing unpleasant buried memories.

The analyst may confront resistance. Confrontation is essentially a kind of interpretation in which the therapist attempts to make the client aware of what the client
is really doing and the consequences of the behavior. For example, the therapist may
present the possibility that there is some underlying motive to the client's repeated
missed appointments. Good confrontation, as with good interpretation in general,
does not force insight. The client may be confronted with the idea that something
underlies the missed appointments, but then the client and therapist will explore to
find out what it is.

Confrontation is a response that is especially susceptible to misuse. It is too easy
for the therapist to use confrontations as punishments or manipulations. For instance, a client may really feel therapy is not working. For the therapist to say, "You
only feel that because unconsciously you don't want to get well" could be a dangerous response. It may manipulate the client into staying in therapy when indeed it
isn't working. It would be more appropriate in such a situation for the therapist to be
more open-minded and help the client explore the possibility that resistance underlies the desire to terminate, rather than to assume that is the reason.

We have saved the **transference** relationship for last because it is actually the
most important part of psychoanalysis. As you'll recall, overt relationships to people
and to the world are derivatives of unconscious conflicts. In particular, the way
adults perceive and relate to significant others is almost invariably tinged by unconscious feelings and wishes they had toward the significant others in their early childhood. Thus, people transfer onto others feelings and reactions they had toward their
parents. This is done not only to use other people as outlets for disguised wishes,
feelings, and fantasies, but also as a defense against recognition of these wishes and
fantasies. A man may sublimate his lustful feelings toward my mother by transferring
them onto other women in his adult life. And by having an outlet for these feelings,
he is able to maintain the repression so that he never has to face up to their true nature. This partly explains why people may get involved in the same kind of destructive relationship time and again. For instance, the client who was overmothered may
continually seek out women who dominate him and with whom he can feel simultaneously protected and rebellious.

The therapist, as part of a significant relationship, becomes a target for transference of significant emotional themes from childhood. The client, for instance, may
see any friendly, helpful gestures by the analyst as signs that the analyst will
"mother" and protect him. Certainly he will wish for the analyst to mother and protect him. To the extent that he initially sees the analyst as fulfilling these infantile
wishes, he will see the analyst as wonderful and therapy as wonderful. This is positive

transference. However, as soon as the analyst does not act in accord with his unconscious wishes and fantasies, he may begin to feel lost, frightened, and even angry. If the client begins to feel angry toward the analyst, this is negative transference. Even if he unconsciously is able to see the analyst as the all-protective mother, he may exhibit negative transference toward the analyst. After all, unconsciously, he both likes the safety of being overmothered and resents feeling emasculated. So he may begin to see the analyst as trying to belittle him.

In order to use the transference therapeutically, the analyst attempts to remain relatively anonymous and neutral in demeanor. It is often said that the analyst attempts to act like a "blank screen" onto which the client can transfer images of childhood relationships. This does not mean that the analyst acts like a personality-less robot. It simply means that she does not share her personal reactions to things. She may nevertheless convey warmth and empathy to the client and not be phony or assume a false facade. By remaining relatively neutral in expressing opinions and judgments, the analyst allows the transference to become clear. If the client accuses the analyst of being critical of him, this must be a transference since the analyst has not expressed judgments.

Therapist neutrality is also designed to frustrate the client's unconscious desires for the therapist to provide gratification for the client's unconscious wishes. This also fosters transference.

The transference relationship is so important therapeutically because the client acts out the core of his neurotic problems right in therapy. Insight into the unconscious dynamics of these problems can be acquired as the problems are lived out and experienced directly. We have already seen that interpretations are most effective if timed to coincide with affectively alive context, and the transference relationship is certainly that. The client feels treated like a child by experiencing the analyst as treating him like a child, and in this affective context, he may gain insight into how he constructs reality.

In order to handle the transference relationship well, the analyst must be careful not to let her personal reactions intrude. However, in order to do this, the therapist must be aware of her own countertransference. Remember that all people have unconscious memories that color their current experiences. If therapists are to react clearly and objectively to their clients, they must be aware of what kind of unconscious transference relationships they are projecting onto their clients. If the therapist has an unconscious need for approval, for instance, she may be devastated by a client's negative transference and may react in a way that has no therapeutic benefit or even impedes the process. In order to be aware of countertransference, the psychoanalyst must undergo a training analysis herself.

Recently, a shift in psychoanalytic thinking has occurred in that analysts now believe that countertransferential reactions are therapeutically useful. The analyst must still be able to separate out his or her own personal reactions from more "objective" perceptions of the client, but personal reactions can often provide important clues to what clients are thinking and feeling, and to what may be going on with them at an unconscious level. Thus, analysts now try to understand their countertransferential reactions, and use them to develop hypotheses about the client.

Mechanics of Psychoanalysis

Classical Freudian psychoanalysis is a lengthy affair. Freud himself often saw clients six days a week and complained that the one-day break would set the analysis back. Modern analysts usually see clients three to five times a week. A full-fledged analysis usually lasts several years. Furthermore, since analysis is never complete, clients often return periodically (Malcolm, 1981).

Because it is believed that making too many concessions to the client, such as allowing sessions to run long or going for walks, may increase resistance, the client is seen in a fairly rigid format. He is usually billed for missed appointments, rarely allowed more than the traditional "50-minute hour," and rarely seen in settings other than the therapist's office.

At approximately $120 (as of 1997) an hour several times a week over a period of years, classical psychoanalysis is obviously expensive. Its high cost is part of the reason for the development of modern shortened versions. We will discuss these short-term approaches to psychoanalytic therapy in Chapter 7.

RECENT ISSUES IN PSYCHOANALYSIS

Spence and Historical Truth Versus Narrative Truth

Freud likened his therapy to archeology. The therapist is like the archeologist who searches for ancient relics of lost civilizations, digging down through layer upon layer of ever more ancient civilizations until he reaches the bottom. The therapist engages in a kind of psychic excavation of the personality, seeking buried "truths" from the deepest layer of early childhood.

Based on this archeological model, analysts have believed that the memories clients ultimately uncover (often after years of analysis) represent historical truth, that is, they are actual memories of what really happened to the client or what the client really fantasized about as a child. Spence (1982), himself a psychoanalyst, challenged this view. We cannot reproduce all of Spence's argument here, but basically it is that psychoanalysis cannot be said to be uncovering historical truth. Rather, it has to do with replacing old, dysfunctional stories about one's past, with new, more functional stories. This view is not only advocated by Spence, but by many other modern analysts, including Roy Schafer (1992), whose recent book is entitled *Retelling a Life.*

Many of these authors draw on psychological research which has demonstrated that memory is reconstructive. What is remembered in the present is influenced at least as much by our present state of mind as it is by what happened in the past. Therefore, our memories of childhood are always interpretations of what our childhood was like rather than the literal, "historical" truth.

Most of us are aware by now that what we see in any particular scene is partially determined by how we are looking at it. Different observers can see the same scene quite differently and give differing accounts of it. In psychoanalysis, a crucial change is the acquisition of a different interpretive scheme. Most of us do not have a view of the world that includes constructs such as "Children sexually lust after their parents." We learn in psychoanalysis to see the world through such an interpretive framework, and that interpretive framework is then brought to bear on our own memories. Do we actually "recover" memories of having lusted after our parents? Or, do we learn to see our behavior and interpret our feelings as meaning that we lusted after our parents?

Spence points out that this is simply undecidable. There is no way to verify empirically the "truth" or "falsity" of these memories. Indeed, in some sense, the question of truthfulness is meaningless. What is meaningful is the fact that the interpretive scheme we learn in psychoanalysis creates more of a sense of order in our experience.

Narrative truth has to do with how well an explanation makes an individual's "life story" a sensible coherent whole. But what purpose does this kind of "truth" serve? Fingarette (1963) suggests that the development of a coherent explanation for symptoms reduces anxiety. A coherent explanation helps "make sense" of behavior. By itself the consequent reduction in anxiety helps the individual to manage behavior better. Having a sensible explanation for a symptom robs it of its "power," so to speak. The person is not so frightened or mystified by it and is therefore more confident that she can control it without letting it disrupt her life. In addition, a good explanation will suggest ways of coping. In some sense, whether or not your overreaction to criticism is actually due to how your father treated you is beside the point, but having that explanation helps you cope. You might be able to say to yourself, "Oh, there I go again. Now remember. Part of this is my father, so let me just stop a minute and sort out what is real here."

The obvious problem with Spence's view is that it makes people wonder if just any old explanatory system can work. In work with some rural clients who were not psychologically sophisticated, Kelly (see Chapter 12) made up interpretations, based on no particular theory, and found that they could be therapeutic. We do not believe, however, that any old explanation will do. The explanation has to be "plausible," and we take this to mean that it must "fit the facts." As long as an interpretation is plausible and fits a client's memories of experience, that may be all that is needed for therapy to occur.

Narrative views of psychoanalysis are controversial (Eagle, 1984; Westen, 1990). However, they are controversial primarily if taken to an extreme: that there is no historical truth in a person's reconstruction of his childhood. A reconstruction of childhood is a current perspective, interpretation, and "story" about one's past, and it most likely must contain elements of historical truth in order to be therapeutically effective.

Child Abuse and the Seduction Theory

Early in Freud's work, he believed that his patients were suffering from repressed memories of actual traumatic events of having been sexually abused, or "seduced," as children. He later came to believe that most of his clients had not actually been abused, but that what had been repressed were infantile wishes and desires.

Masson (1984), as well as others such as Alice Miller (Greif, 1992), have argued that the seduction theory was correct and that Freud's clients probably had been molested as children. Summit (1987) has argued that some of Freud's early work was a masterful description of the relationship of child abuse to psychopathology. However, Freud changed his mind. Summit says that during Freud's time, it was taken as ridiculous on the face of it that adults did such things to children. Thus, when Freud came out with his seduction theory, he was heavily criticized. Sometime thereafter Freud revised his theory so that instead of presenting a radical view of adults as sexual molesters, he presented a radical view of children as having sexual lusts and fantasies. Freud then saw his patients not as suffering from real abuse, but from their own infantile wishes.

Masson (1984) goes on to accuse Freud of having modified his point of view in order to make his views acceptable to his medical colleagues. The implication is that Freud "sold out" on the truth in order to buy acceptance. Many others, such as Summit, have pointed out that at the time in Victorian Vienna, people simply were unaware of the extent of child abuse. Freud's rejection of the child abuse theory, therefore, would not represent intellectual dishonesty so much as ignorance about and denial of abuse.

The importance of the controversy lies in how we view clients' problems. Are they a response to real traumatic events, or are they simply a result of fantasies? Briere (1989) mentions that there are cases of abused women going to therapists who tell them that their abuse memories are "really" fantasies of what they unconsciously wanted! In light of recent information about the prevalence of childhood sexual abuse, it does not seem improbable that many "Oedipal fantasies" were indeed memories based on actual childhood experiences. Some researchers now believe that childhood abuse is at the heart of a variety of disorders, including some anxiety disorders, some depressions, borderline personality, and multiple personality (e.g. Briere, 1989).

Of course, it need not be an either/or issue. The key event in psychopathology from a Freudian standpoint is that in using mechanisms such as repression, individuals cut off from conscious experience aspects of themselves. In some sense, it may not matter whether these cut-off elements are fantasies or memories of actual events.

RESEARCH EVALUATION OF PSYCHOANALYTIC THEORY AND THERAPY

Once upon a time, one of the most telling criticisms that could be launched against psychoanalysis was the lack of research done to investigate its premises. However, in recent years, this situation has changed significantly (Westen, 1990). Especially with regard to the study of psychotherapy, there are now a number of vigorous research projects on various aspects of psychoanalytic theory and psychotherapy in both the United States and Europe. In the next section, we will review research findings relevant to several psychoanalytic premises, from both psychoanalytic and nonpsychoanalytic investigators.

Effectiveness of Psychotherapy

Because classical psychoanalysis, in which the client is seen three to five times a week for several years, is the most intensive of all approaches to psychotherapy, some of its advocates have concluded that it is therefore the most effective. Fine (1973), for instance, says, "Psychoanalysis was the first psychotherapeutic system that had any value. Currently it is the most complete, the most highly developed, the one with the greatest theoretical sophistication and *by far the most effective*" (p. 30, italics ours). However, we must point out that length and intensiveness do not necessarily make a therapy more effective.

How effective is long-term, intensive psychoanalysis? The answer is that there is no evidence that it is more effective than other therapies, including short-term psychoanalytic approaches. In fact, until very recently, there was no evidence for its effectiveness at all. A study of psychoanalysis at the Menninger Clinic (Kernberg, Burstein, Coyne, Applebaum, Horwitz, & Voth, 1972) involved 42 clients over a 20-year period. Some were seen in regular analysis (an average of 835 hours), others in a shorter version of psychoanalytic therapy (an average 289 hours). For the most part, there was no evidence that clients who had regular analysis improved more than clients who had the short-term analysis, though there were some clients for whom regular analysis did work better. However, recently, Blatt and Ford (1994) have found some evidence that long-term, intensive psychoanalysis of the object relations variety (see Chapter 7) can be effective.

While evidence for the effectiveness of long-term psychoanalysis is sparse, there is evidence that psychoanalytically oriented psychotherapy is effective. From the results of their **meta-analysis** of many studies of psychotherapy, Smith, Glass, and Miller (1980) calculate an average "effect size" of 0.69 for psychoanalytic approaches. They also find an effect size of 0.89 for dynamic-eclectic therapies, which are therapies based on dynamic principles, but more eclectic in techniques than psychoanalysis. Basically, the larger the effect size, the more substantial the amount of change. The highest effect sizes calculated have been around 1.0 for some of the behavior and cognitive therapeutic techniques. (We will explain an effect size in more detail in Chapter 15.) To date, no therapy has demonstrated an effect size sufficiently higher than the others to conclude that it is superior. The effect sizes mentioned for psychoanalytic approaches are in the average range, meaning these approaches are indeed effective and about as effective as other approaches. Several other studies have suggested that short-term psychoanalytically oriented therapy is effective (Luborsky, Singer, & Luborsky, 1975).

Some psychoanalytic proponents claim that their therapy is superior because it cures the underlying disorder, while other approaches are superficial. This argument rests on the assumption that psychological problems are grounded in deep early childhood experiences that must be worked through in order for change to occur. However, evidence (Nicholson & Berman, 1983) suggests that many so-called superficial treatments are quite effective and that their positive benefits persist long after therapy has been terminated. Long-term, in-depth therapy may have other positive benefits in addition to symptom removal, but therapy can remove symptoms without deep exploration.

Aside from the question of its effectiveness, is there any evidence for some of the key components of psychoanalytic therapy? Orlinsky, Grawe, and Parks (1994) summarize a number of studies which show that interpretation is usually, but not always, positively associated with therapeutic outcome. Henry, Strupp, Schacht, and Gaston (1994) summarize a series of studies on interpretations of the client's transferential reactions to the therapist and conclude that transference interpretations can be damaging if there are too many of them, and are more likely to elicit client defensiveness; but can be effective if they are accurate, delivered with low frequency, and given to relatively high-functioning clients. Fitting in with this, the suitability of an interpretation to the client's problem appears to be important to the effectiveness of an interpretation (Messer & Warren, 1990).

With regard to transference, Luborsky, Crits-Christoph, and Mellon (1986) have also studied transference reactions in therapy and find evidence to support several of Freud's formulations. For instance, a client's core relationship problems were found to manifest themselves in a variety of relationships in the client's life and in relationship to the therapist. There was also evidence that this relationship theme could be found in the client's memories of early childhood. Other evidence from Luborsky and his colleagues indicates that therapy alters the transference relationship, though it does not entirely eliminate it (Luborsky, Crits-Cristoph, & Barger, 1991).

Psychoanalytic Personality Theory

We now turn to a brief evaluation of psychoanalytic hypotheses on personality and psychopathology. The concept of the unconscious is central to psychoanalytic formulations. Evidence for the existence of some kind of unconscious ("nonconscious") information processing now seems convincing (Greenwald, 1992), although whether it functions the way Freud said it did remains to be determined. Shevrin and Dickman (1980), after reviewing a variety of models of consciousness, suggest that all information processing happens first at the nonconscious level, and only later and secondarily do some aspects show up as conscious ideation. However, psychoanalysis assumes that some things are unconscious because they have been repressed. Repression has not been extensively researched, partly because of the difficulty of studying things such as repression in the laboratory (Feshbach, Weiner, & Bohart, 1996). At the same time, the possibility of something like repression is compatible with several modern cognitive versions of the unconscious (Bowers & Meichenbaum, 1984; Shevrin & Dickman, 1980). In studies in which words are presented to subjects at a very rapid exposure speed and the subjects are asked to report what they saw, subjects do not recognize certain emotionally charged words as rapidly as neutral words, even though the words can be shown to have been perceived unconsciously (Kostandov & Arzumanov, 1977; Shevrin, 1973).

For psychoanalysis, the content of the unconscious includes material from early childhood. In a series of studies, Silverman (Silverman & Weinberger, 1985) has presented sentences to subjects at a speed so rapid that perception was subliminal (not producing a sensation that is consciously perceived). In one study, for instance, subjects who unconsciously saw the sentence "beating dad is okay" did better at playing darts than did subjects who saw the sentence "beating dad is wrong."

There is also evidence for defensive processes. Morokoff (1985) had female subjects view an erotic videotape. They were asked to report how arousing they found the tape. A physiological measure of vaginal activity was also taken. It was found that women who had high levels of guilt over sex reported that they did not find the videotapes arousing, even though the vaginal measure showed that they had found it even more arousing than had women who were low in feelings of guilt over sex.

There has recently been a great deal of controversy over the concept of repression with respect to the recovery of memories of childhood sexual abuse. Many believe that childhood sexual abuse experiences are so traumatic that people repress them, either partially or entirely. These memories sometimes surface in psychotherapy, especially if the therapist has encouraged the client to search for them. The problem is that the recovery of memories in therapy cannot be taken as reliable evidence for the existence of repression because some have argued that therapists are capable of suggesting or implanting such memories. However, there is evidence to suggest the possibility that memories of childhood sexual abuse can be lost or forgotten. Williams (1992) studied 100 women who, as children, had been sexually abused. Their abuse had been carefully documented at the time because they had been taken to hospital emergency rooms for treatment and for collection of evidence. The women were located and interviewed 17 years later, and it was found that 38% of them did not remember the abuse. On the other hand, there is also evidence to suggest that memories can be implanted in therapy. Loftus (1993) found that it was possible to successfully implant a false memory in a 14-year-old boy of having been lost in a shopping mall as a little child.

Overall, the concept of repression remains controversial and awaits further empirical clarification.

Personality Development   One of the cornerstones of psychoanalytic theory is the idea that children around the age of 5 or 6 experience the Oedipal conflict of sexually desiring their parent of the opposite sex, while viewing the parent of the same sex as a rival. To date there is no empirical evidence supporting the idea of an Oedipus complex in children, and many experts on child development reject the idea (e.g., Brophy, 1977). They argue that to the extent that a child does experience Oedipal feelings, it is a response to a real situation being set up by dysfunctional parenting, rather than something all children undergo.

We have seen that many psychoanalytic thinkers consider childhood events to be the primary determinant of the most important aspects of adult functioning. In this chapter, we consider the question of whether adult personality is indeed formed in early childhood. At the end of Chapter 7, we will consider the further questions of whether problems in early childhood are the causes of adult psychological problems, and whether the "foundational" view of personality is valid.

Basically, evidence does not support the hypothesis that personality is largely finished or formed in early childhood. Chess and Thomas (1984), for instance, studied a sample of children from infancy into adulthood. Chess (1979) concluded that

> We now have to give up the illusion that once we know the young child's psychological history, subsequent personality and functioning are *ipso facto* predictable. On the other hand, we now have a much more optimistic vision of human development. The emotionally traumatized child is not doomed, the parents' early mistakes are not irrevocable. (p. 112)

Livson and Peskin (1980), based on their developmental studies, conclude "neither past nor present, neither childhood nor adolescence, nor any era of adulthood is fixed in its effects or of higher priority in its contribution" (p. 84). These research studies suggest that while early childhood is one important time of life, it is not necessarily more important than any other. They also suggest that early effects on personality can be modified and even undone by later events.

Vaillant (1977) has studied a sample of males from late adolescence into mid-adulthood, and has found evidence for significant changes in personality as people mature past their adolescence. More recently, McCrae and Costa (1990) conclude from their research, as well as their review of other research, that personality continues to develop into early adulthood and only finally becomes "fixed" around age 30.

The fact that personality in general continues to grow and change into early adulthood, however, does not preclude the possibility that certain characteristics do remain relatively stable from childhood onward. Block and Block (1980) have found evidence of stability from early childhood on in what they call "ego control" and "ego resiliency," that is, the degree to which the individual can control and regulate impulses and feelings, and the degree to which the individual exhibits flexibility in coping.

Is Character Structure as Fixed as Freudian Theory Presumes?   There is another implication of the view of personality as something that is primarily fixed. Classical Freudian psychoanalytic theory holds a largely intrapsychic view of behavior. That is, a person's present behavior problems (as well as other, more normal aspects of that person's personality) derive primarily from internal factors such as character traits that have been developed and fixed in early childhood. Such a view minimizes the impact of current situations on a person's behavior, implying that behavior largely reflects a person's internal personality dynamics. Thus, if someone seems obsessed with detail at work, Freudian theory assumes that this reflects an underlying character trait of orderliness, which developed during the anal stage of development. It would be expected that this person would appear to be orderly in a wide variety of other situations in his or her life: at home, while making travel arrangements, on vacations, perhaps even during sex.

This view is to be contrasted to other views we consider in this book that ascribe progressively more importance to the here-and-now situation in creating psychopathology. In the next chapter, you shall see that for one modern variant of psychoanalysis, self psychology, the here-and-now interpersonal situation plays an important role in determining a person's behavior. For self psychology, a person's transferential reactions to the therapist in therapy are not simply a manifestation of that person's unconscious personality dynamics, but are a complex interpersonal event, coshaped by the person of the therapist and the dynamics of the client. Similarly, Paul Wachtel's integrative psychodynamic perspective (to be covered in Chapter 16) ascribes significant importance to the here-and-now situation as well as to intrapsychic factors from childhood.

To what degree does the pervasiveness in behavior implied by classical psychoanalytic theory exist? Do people exhibit the degree of orderliness in widely differing situations in their lives that this view implies? Do individuals diagnosed as having a borderline personality disorder, for instance, characteristically act borderline, in situation after situation, relatively independent of what is going on? Kroll (1988) has noted that borderline behaviors wax and wane. People labeled borderline may act borderline in some situations and not others. They may act borderline at some times and not others. Further, individuals diagnosed as having a borderline personality disorder at one point may, even within a few years, be diagnosed as having some other kind of personality disorder. The point is that the borderline's behavior does not exhibit the degree of stability that a traditional view of personality structure might imply. In general, there has been a great deal of controversy over the years concerning the degree to which behavior primarily reflects a person's character versus the degree to which it primarily is a result of the situations people are in. The current consensus is that people are probably more changeable than a traditional view of character structure implies, but that there is some consistency in personality. At the same time, behavior is also significantly influenced by the situation (Feshbach, Weiner, & Bohart, 1996).

The same applies to psychological problems. While some problems may primarily owe their existence to early childhood factors, others appear to be heavily influenced by a person's current situation, with early childhood factors playing only a secondary role, or no role at all. Many would argue that present events, such as stress, play a major role in creating adult psychopathology (Bloom, 1984). Many cases of depression appear to reflect here-and-now factors more so than childhood factors. Brown and Harris (1978) attribute 80 to 90% of the causes of depression in women to "provoking agents" such as loss, poor housing, and family alcoholism. Also, vulnerability to depression is greatly enhanced by the lack of a good social support network. This is not to say that childhood events are of no importance. Brown, Harris, and Bifulco (1986) found that death of a parent enhanced vulnerability to depression in these women. Nevertheless, the stresses in adulthood appear to play a significant role, although a vulnerability may be created by a childhood event. As another example, Hobfall (1989) has argued that women who stay in abusive relationships are not doing so primarily because of individual personality factors (though low self-esteem can play a role), but because of problems in current resources. Many women stay in abusive relationships because they do not have the here-and-now resources to leave.

In sum, research suggests that personality in general is not fixed in early childhood as Freud assumed and that many behavior and psychological problems are more influenced by current situations than classical Freudian theory has assumed. At the same time this does not rule out the importance of early childhood in the creation of certain aspects of psychological disorder. We shall consider this issue more fully in the next chapter.

IN CONCLUSION

Freud has had such an enormous impact on our Western intellectual tradition in general (including the fields of psychology, philosophy, literature, and history) that it would be impossible to discuss all facets of his influence here. Among his many contributions are a major theory of personality, and a whole set of ideas about how to help people change. It would be inaccurate to say that Freud "created" psychotherapy, because many of the ideas and processes had been around before he was. However, Freud can be said to be the foremost figure in having formalized all these diverse ideas and processes into the discipline of psychotherapy. In a generic form, many of Freud's insights about the nature of the change process have held up, although Freud's interpretations of these insights have been challenged. Many of the "common factors" among the differing approaches to psychotherapy (see Chapter

16) were first given prominence by Freud. For instance, Freud noted that sheer intellectual knowledge was not sufficient to produce personal change, that the affective, feeling side of the personality was important, that nonconscious processes and lack of personal awareness played a significant role in behavior, that what happened in the therapeutic relationship was an important part of the change process, and that helping people to "free their minds" from rigid constrictions imposed by learned ways of thinking and perceiving was central to change. In addition, Freud called attention to the importance of self-deception and the avoidance of painful feelings, wishes, and thoughts in personal functioning. He also alerted us to how childhood experiences can have significant impact on adult behavior. Even as interpersonal views of psychoanalysis (see Chapter 7), existential-humanistic views (see Chapters 8 and 9), cognitive views (see Chapter 12), and strategic views (see Chapter 13) put their own spin on many of these insights, they are following the path first started on by Freud.

In particular, we believe therapists in the twenty-first century will still be utilizing the following insights of Freud. First, they will continue to utilize the insight that childhood experiences play a role in some (though perhaps not all) psychological problems. They will use this insight to understand how a person's early experiences may have led him or her to make personal developmental compromises and to adopt coping strategies that made sense when the person was a child, but that now get in the person's way. They will use this understanding to identify important life themes in the individual's life, themes that indicate the nature of the person's enduring struggles. Second, they will continue to use the insight that at least some psychological problems have unconscious components that the person does not have access to or understand. Such components may not be involved in every problem, but knowing that such unconscious components can exist will help clinicians cope with cases in which they do play a major role. Third, they will be aware that clients often bring their problems into the therapy situation (transference) and that problems can therefore be worked with in an *in vivo* sense. This insight converges with the emphasis on the relationship in existential-humanistic and some cognitive and behavioral approaches. Fourth, they will be aware that their own personal reactions (countertransference) can be used therapeutically. Once again, this insight already forms a component of some existential-humanistic and cognitive-behavioral approaches. Fifth, they will be aware that one of the major blocks to therapeutic progress is the client's defensive need to protect him- or herself in the therapy session. Helping clients find ways of reducing their need for self-protection so that they can "come out" and engage their energies in the pursuit of change will continue to be one of the major tasks of therapists. Sixth, they will continue to be aware that the development of self-awareness is one of the major components involved in personal change, and that awareness must not be just intellectual awareness, but experiential awareness as well.

BIBLIOGRAPHY

Adelson, J., & Doehrman, M. J. (1980). The psychodynamic approach to adolescence. In J. Adelson (Ed.), *Handbook of adolescent psychology*. New York: Wiley.

Bellack, L. (1954). *The TAT and CAT in clinical use*. New York: Grune & Stratton.

Bettelheim, B. (1982). *Freud and man's soul*. New York: Vintage.

Blatt, S. J., & Ford, R. Q. (1994). *Therapeutic change: An object relations perspective.* New York: Plenum.

Block, J., & Block, J. (1980). The role of ego-control and ego-resiliency in the organization of behavior. In W. A. Collins (Ed.), *Minnesota Symposium on Child Development* (Vol. 13). Hillsdale, NJ: Erlbaum.

Bloom, B. L. (1984). *Community mental health: A general introduction* (2nd ed.). Monterey, CA: Brooks/Cole.

Bohart, A. (1979). *Personal paradigms, resistance, and change in psychotherapy.* Paper presented at the Western Psychological Association Convention, San Diego, CA.

Bowers, K. S., & Meichenbaum, D. (1984). *The unconscious reconsidered.* New York: Wiley.

Breuer, J., & Freud, S. (Eds.). (1937). *Studies in hysteria.* Boston: Beacon Press. (Original work published in 1895)

Briere, J. (1989). *Therapy for adults molested as children.* New York: Springer.

Brophy, J. (1977). *Child development and socialization.* Chicago: Science Research Associates.

Brown, G. W., & Harris, T. O. (1978). *Social origins of depression.* New York: Free Press.

Brown, G. W., Harris, T. O., & Bifulco, A. (1986). Long-term effects of early loss of parent. In M. Rutter, C. E. Izard, & P. B. Read (Eds.), *Depression in young people: Developmental and clinical perspectives* (pp. 251–296). New York: Guilford.

Cameron, N., & Rychlak, J. F. (1985). *Personality development and psychopathology* (2nd ed.). Boston: Houghton Mifflin.

Chess, S. (1979). Developmental theory revisited. Findings of longitudinal study. *Canadian Journal of Psychiatry, 24,* 101–112.

Chess, S., & Thomas, A. (1984). *Origins and evolution of behavior disorders.* New York: Brunner/Mazel.

Eagle, M. N. (1984). *Recent developments in psychoanalysis: A critical evaluation.* New York: McGraw-Hill.

Ekstein, R. (1974). Psychoanalytic theory: Sigmund Freud. In A. Burton (Ed.), *Operational theories of personality.* New York: Brunner/Mazel.

Ellenberger, H. F. (1970). *The discovery of the unconscious.* New York: Basic Books.

Feshbach, S., Weiner, B., & Bohart, A. (1996). *Personality.* Lexington, MA: Heath.

Fine, R. (1973). Psychoanalysis. In R. J. Corsini (Ed.), *Current psychotherapies.* Itasca, IL: Peacock.

Fingarette, H. (1963). *The self in transformation.* New York: Harper & Row.

Fisher, S. (1956). Plausibility and depth of interpretation. *Journal of Consulting Psychology, 20,* 249–256.

Freud, S. (1937). Psychotherapy of hysteria. In J. Breuer & S. Freud (Eds.), *Studies in hysteria.* Boston: Beacon Press. (Original work published 1895)

Freud, S. (1955). Lines of advance in psycho-analytic theory. In J. Strachey (Ed.), *The standard edition of the complete psychological works of Sigmund Freud* (Vol. 17). London: Hogarth Press. (Original work published 1918)

Freud, S. (1961). Some psychical consequences of the anatomical distinction between the sexes. In J. Strachey (Ed.), *The standard edition of the complete psychological works of Sigmund Freud* (Vol. 19). London: Hogarth Press. (Original work published 1925)

Freud, S. (1963). Analysis terminable and interminable. In P. Rieff (Ed.), *Sigmund Freud: Therapy and technique.* New York: Crowell-Collier. (Original work published 1937)

Freud, S. (1963). Observations on "wild" psychoanalysis. In P. Rieff (Ed.), *Sigmund Freud: Therapy and technique.* New York: Crowell-Collier. (Original work published 1910)

Freud, S. (1964). The dissection of the psychical personality. In J. Strachey (Ed.), *The standard edition of the complete psychological works of Sigmund Freud* (Vol. 22). London: Hogarth Press. (Original work published 1924)

Greenwald, A. G. (1992). New look 3: Unconscious cognition reclaimed. *American Psychologist, 47,* 766–779.

Greif, G. (1992). Alice Millers' revision of psychoanalysis. *Psychotherapy, 29,* 310–317.

Henry,W. P., Strupp, H. H., Schacht, T. E., & Gaston, L.(1994). Psychodynamic approaches. In A. E. Bergin & S. L. Garfield (Eds.), *Handbook and psychotherapy and behavior change* (pp. 467–508). New York: Wiley.

Hobfall, S. (1989). Conservation of resources: A new attempt at conceptualizing stress. *American Psychologist, 44,* 513–524.

Howard, G. S. (1991). Culture tales: A narrative approach to thinking, cross-cultural psychology, and psychotherapy. *American Psychologist, 46,* 187–197.

Kaplan, L. J. (1984). *Adolescence: The farewell to childhood.* New York: Simon & Schuster.

Keen, S., & Fox, A. (1973). *Telling your story.* New York: Doubleday.

Kernberg, O. F., Burstein, E. D., Coyne, L., Appelbaum, A., Horwitz, L., & Voth, H. (1972). Psychotherapy and psychoanalysis: Final report of the Menninger Foundation's psychotherapy research project. *Bulletin of the Menninger Clinic, 36,* 1–276.

Kostandov, E., & Arzumanov, Y. (1977). Averaged cortical evoked potentials to recognized and non-recognized verbal stimuli. *Acta Neurobiologiae Experimentalis, 37,* 311–324.

Kroll, J. (1988). *The challenge of the borderline patient.* New York: Norton.

Livson, N., & Peskin, H. (1980). Perspectives on adolescence from longitudinal research. In J. Adelson (Ed.), *Handbook of adolescent psychology.* New York: Wiley.

Loftus, E. F.(1993). The reality of repressed memories. *American Psychologist, 48,* 518–537.

Luborsky, L. (1984). *Principles of psychoanalytic psychotherapy: A manual for supportive-expressive treatment.* New York: Basic Books.

Luborsky, L., Crits-Cristoph, P., & Barger, J. (1991). University of Pennsylvania: The Penn Psychotherapy Research Projects. In L. E. Beutler & M. Crago (Eds.), *Psychotherapy research: An international review of programmatic studies* (pp. 133–141). Washington, DC: American Psychological Association.

Luborsky, L., Crits-Cristoph, P., & Mellon, J. (1986). Advent of objective measures of the transference concept. *Journal of Consulting and Clinical Psychology, 54,* 39–47.

Luborsky, L., Singer, B., & Luborsky, L. (1975). Comparative studies of psychotherapies. *Archives of General Psychiatry, 29,* 719–729.

Maccoby, E. E. (1980). *Social development.* New York: Harcourt Brace Jovanovich.

Malan, D. H. (1980). *Toward the validation of dynamic psychotherapy.* New York: Plenum.

Malcolm, J. (1981). *Psychoanalysis: The impossible profession.* New York: Vintage.

Masson, J. M. (1984). *The assault on truth: Freud's suppression of the seduction theory.* New York: Farrar, Straus & Giroux.

Masson, J. M. (Ed.). (1985). *The complete letters of Sigmund Freud to Wilhelm Fliess 1887–1904.* Cambridge, MA: Harvard University Press.

McCrae, R. R., & Costa, P. T. (1990). *Personality in adulthood.* New York: Guilford.

Messer, S. B., & Warren, S. (1990). Personality change and psychotherapy. In L. Pervin (Ed.), *Handbook of personality* (pp. 371–398). New York: Guilford.

Mischel, W., & Peake, P. K. (1982). Beyond déjà vu in the search for cross-situational consistency. *Psychological Review, 89,* 730–755.

Morokoff, P. J. (1985). Effects of sex guilt, repression, sexual "arousibility," and sexual experience on female sexual arousal during erotica and fantasy. *Journal of Personality and Social Psychology, 49,* 177–187.

Nicholson, R. A., & Berman, J. S. (1983). Is follow-up necessary in evaluating psychotherapy? *Psychological Bulletin, 93,* 261–278.

Orlinsky, D. E., Grawe, K., & Parks, B. K. (1994). Process and outcome in psychotherapy. In A. E. Bergin & S. L. Garfield (Eds.), *Handbook and psychotherapy and behavior change* (pp. 270–378). New York: Wiley.

Schafer, R. (1978). *Language and insight.* New Haven: Yale University Press.

Schafer, R. (1992). *Retelling a life.* New York: Basic Books.

Shevrin, H. (1973). Brain wave correlates of subliminal stimulation, unconscious attention, primary- and secondary-process thinking, and repressiveness (Monograph 30). *Psychological Issues, 8,* 56–87.

Shevrin, H., & Dickman, S. (1980). The psychological unconscious: A necessary assumption for all psychological theory? *American Psychologist, 35,* 421–434.

Silverman, L. H., & Weinberger, J. (1985). Mommy and I are one: Implications for psychotherapy. *American Psychologist, 40,* 1296–1308.

Singer, J. L. (1984). *The human personality.* New York: Harcourt Brace Jovanovich.

Smith, M. L., Glass, G. V., & Miller, T. I. (1980). *The benefits of psychotherapy.* Baltimore: Johns Hopkins University Press.

Spence, D. P. (1982). *Narrative truth and historical truth: Meaning and interpretation in psychoanalysis.* New York: Norton.

Stolorow, R. D., & Atwood, G. E. (1979). *Faces in a cloud: Subjectivity in personality theory.* New York: Aronson.

Summit, R. (1987, January 16). *Introduction to the problem of child abuse.* Paper presented at the Child Abuse Reporting Course, Harbor-UCLA Medical Center, Torrance, CA.

Vaillant, G. (1977). *Adaptation to life.* Boston: Little, Brown.

Westen, D. (1990). Psychoanalytic approaches to personality. In L. Pervin (Ed.), *Handbook of personality* (pp. 21–65). New York: Guilford.

Williams, L. M. (1992). Adult memories of childhood abuse: Preliminary findings from a longitudinal study. *The Advisor: American Professional Society on the Abuse of Children, 5,* 19–21.

CHAPTER
7

Interpersonal Approaches to Psychoanalysis

I n recent decades, a revolution has taken place within psychoanalysis. This revolution has consisted of the increasing influence of object relations theory and self psychology. The shift to these two perspectives within the psychoanalytic camp is important because these perspectives overlap with other important perspectives on psychotherapy. Object relations theory, with its emphasis on internal representations of the self and of others, shares commonalities with cognitive theory. Self psychology, with its emphasis on empathy and the interpersonal nature of the person, shares commonalities with both humanistic and systems theories.

These two perspectives continue developments that began almost as soon as Freud first articulated his views in the early 1900s. It did not take long for dissenters to appear within the ranks of Freud's own inner circle. First Alfred Adler and then Carl Jung broke with Freud's emphasis on the human being as primarily a creature driven by sexual and aggressive impulses. Later, many other theorists, such as the neo-Freudians Eric Fromm, Erik Erickson, and Karen Horney, dissented from some of Freud's basic views. These perspectives set the stage for the development of the modern perspectives of object relations theory and self psychology. First we shall briefly review the contributions of some of these early dissenters. Then we shall consider object relations theory and self psychology in some detail. Finally, we shall consider a related development: that of brief forms of psychoanalytic psychotherapy.

THE NEO-FREUDIANS

There have been so many creative offshoots from traditional Freudian psychoanalysis that we cannot consider them all here. In this chapter, we will briefly review the contributions of Jung and Adler, perhaps the two most famous theorists to develop out of psychoanalysis.

Adler

Alfred Adler (1929/1964) was Freud's contemporary and a respected psychiatrist in his own right when he studied with Freud. He subsequently rejected many of Freud's ideas. Like many others, Adler rejected Freud's emphasis on sexuality and the unconscious as crucial forces in personality development. He called the system he developed "individual psychology."

Adler emphasized the unique individuality of each personality. In contrast to Freud, who viewed the personality as fundamentally split into conflicting components, Adler saw the personality as unified. Adler also focused on the conscious side of the personality. Like later ego analysts, Adler believed that the strivings of a rather rational, organized self accounted for much behavior. He emphasized people's thoughts and beliefs and how they affected behavior. He felt that the relationship of this self to other people ("social interest") and the striving of this self toward future goals ("fictional finalism") were also important. Adler stressed the ongoing social environment as a cause of behavior more than Freud did. For this reason, some view Adler as one of the forerunners of the community psychology movement (see Chapter 17).

Adler is perhaps best known for his concepts of the inferiority complex and striving for superiority. He began with the idea of "organ inferiority." He argued that people born with certain physical defects (such as deafness, poor vision, lameness) would organize their personalities around compensating for the feelings of inferiority engendered by the defect. Later he came to believe that feelings of inferiority as a result of being a small, weak child are universal. Some individuals would successfully compensate for their feelings of inferiority and achieve a great deal, while others would fail to do so and would develop feelings of insecurity or grandiosity or other symptoms. The negative personality characteristics surrounding the attempt to deal with these feelings were called an **inferiority complex.**

For Adler, the basic dynamic motivating force within the personality is striving for superiority. This basic force is normal and inborn and continues throughout life. All people strive for self-esteem, perfection, and completion in all their behaviors. This dynamic force results in achievement and fulfillment in most individuals, although each expresses these strivings in different ways. Some strive for superiority by being successful in their occupations, others by being loving or creative. Disturbed individuals may express their strivings for superiority in less desirable ways, such as becoming tyrannical at home or being viciously competitive. Unlike Freud, Adler was an optimist, and he believed that the normal, inborn motivation for humans is a prosocial striving for accomplishment and achievement.

Adler's approach to therapy was active, kindly, and "commonsensical." He appealed to his patients' rationality and supported their general strivings and goals. Part of his treatment of neurotic behavior was to help his patients choose more socially effective means of pursuing their general goals. He often worked with children, and he would invite family members, teachers, and other involved adults to attend therapy sessions. He would support the child and explain the child's view to the surrounding adults, somewhat like family therapists do today. He also tried to make the child's and the family's goals explicit, so they could all agree to work together.

This brief summary cannot do justice to Adler's theory, which also included a personality typology and extensive discussion of people's styles of life. Style of life referred to the person's individuality, ways of handling problems, methods of compensation for feelings of inferiority, and specific goals and ways of achieving them. Like Freud, Adler believed the style of life was set in early childhood and continued in the same direction throughout adulthood. Adler began the notion that people's earliest memory indicates the basic direction of their life. (The earliest memory of one of us is taking a nap!)

Although Adler still has followers with their own journal, *The American Journal of Individual Psychology,* his system never became as famous and popular as Freud's. However, his ideas were important precursors of many currently popular ideas—an emphasis on the social nature of the person, an emphasis on how people construe their personal realities, and an emphasis on an individual's personal vision of his or her future and his or her goals.

Jung

Carl Jung (1933, 1956) studied under Freud when he was just beginning his psychiatric practice. Like Adler, he disagreed with Freud's emphasis on sexuality. His extensive theory of personality, called analytical psychology, was considerably more mystical and philosophical than Freud's. However, his therapeutic practices were generally similar to Freud's. Jung emphasized dreams even more than Freud. The kinds of interpretations he made also focused on symbolic and archetypal meanings underlying behavior, in addition to meanings from early childhood.

Like Freud, Jung believed that psychic energy coursing through personality structures causes behavior. However, while this energy derives from biological processes, it is not particularly sexual. This energy motivates behavior whose goal is the actualization and fulfillment of the self, an idea similar to Adler's striving for superiority. In this respect, Jung's theory presaged both recent developments in psychoanalysis and humanistic approaches.

Like Freud and unlike Adler, Jung emphasized unconscious determinants of behavior. He divided the unconscious into two parts—the personal unconscious and the collective unconscious. The personal unconscious contains repressed and forgotten memories from infancy and childhood. It is unique to the individual, depending on the types of childhood experiences the individual had.

The collective unconscious is transpersonal and shared by all human beings. It is the foundation of the entire personality structure and contains inherited memory traces embedded in the brain. These include memories from humankind's ancestral past and prehuman nature. For example, humans are predisposed to know God, since the memory traces of countless preceding generations' experiences of God are in the collective unconscious. Jung wrote that the collective unconscious contains centuries of wisdom and experience.

Archetypes are the "primordial images" or "universal thought forms" found in the collective unconscious. After centuries of experiencing similar issues, the human brain evolves archetypes to deal with each issue. Like all evolutionary structures, archetypes help us survive. Some archetypes are so important to our evolutionary survival that they have formed important subsystems within the personality structure. Jung wrote especially about the persona, shadow, anima-animus, and self archetypes. To simplify greatly, the persona is the socially conventional mask we all wear; the shadow is the darker, animal side of human nature; anima represents the feminine in men and animus represents the masculine in women; and the self is our striving for unity and wholeness. Jung wrote extensively about the self and its strivings for actualization.

Jung developed a complex personality typology of eight major types based on two major life orientations—extraversion and introversion—coupled with four psychological functions—thinking, feeling, sensing, and intuiting. Extraversion is an outer-directed orientation to life; introversion is inner directed. A person could be a thinking introvert, who spends all her time alone reading philosophical works; a feeling extravert, who constantly creates emotional scenes with other people; a feeling introvert; and so on.

Jung's impact has perhaps been greater in fields other than psychology. His importance to philosophy, art, literature, metaphysics, and history is acknowledged by many. His ideas are complex, unsystematic, and subjective. An idea such as the collective unconscious is untestable and in its pure form is not accepted as a scientific hypothesis today. However, many cognitive psychologists do believe there may be inborn ways of organizing information, somewhat like archetypes.

Other Neo-Freudians

Many highly creative therapists and theorists have arisen from the psychoanalytic perspective. These include Karen Horney (1945), Harry Stack Sullivan (Mullahy, 1952), and Erik Erikson (1968). What is common to all these theorists is a greater emphasis on the importance of relationships to others in determining personality and psychopathology than is found in classical Freudian theory. Horney's three orientations to life—moving toward people, moving away from people, and moving against people—stress relationships. Erikson saw development in interpersonal terms. For instance, the key development at Freud's oral period is for Erikson the development of "basic trust." Furthermore, Erikson saw development as continuing throughout the life span, instead of being largely completed by age 5. His approach has become increasingly influential in the field of developmental psychology. Harry Stack Sullivan believed that we develop a concept of the "good me" based on what is acceptable to our parents. Those aspects of ourselves that we consider to be the "bad me" are split off from consciousness. With his emphasis on the "good me" and the "bad me" and their development as a result of relationships to others, Sullivan was a precursor of object relations theory.

Along with a greater emphasis on the importance of interpersonal relations in the development of personality, these theorists also generally placed greater emphasis on the ego than did Freud. For Freud, the ego developed out of the id, and its main function was to mediate between the id and reality. Erickson and Sullivan, as well as others such as Heinz Hartmann (1964), saw the ego as having greater autonomy. They saw humans as consisting of more than the management of sexual and aggressive instincts. In this respect, these theorists were also precursors of the developments to be considered next.

CONTEMPORARY PERSPECTIVES

Two major developments in recent years have significantly changed the face of psychoanalytic theory. These two developments can be said to represent the most potent influences in the field of psychoanalytic theory at the present time. They are object relations theory (Cashdan, 1988; Hamilton, 1988), and self psychology (Kohut, 1984; Stolorow, Brandchaft, & Atwood, 1987). Both view the development of a stable, cohesive self or identity as fundamental and relationships with people as crucial in this development. Both focus on the importance of interpersonal patterns in understanding an individual's psychological problems. These two approaches now constitute the predominant influences on the current psychoanalytic scene. Further, their influence is seen in other approaches to psychotherapy, such as cognitive therapy, and in fields as diverse as social psychology and developmental psychology.

These developments continue trends noted in the previous section. For Freud, psychological development was primarily a matter of mastering and regulating sexuality and aggression. Relationships with "objects" in the environment, including other people, ultimately only occurred because at some unconscious level they served the purpose of discharging sexual or aggressive drives. Love of another person, for instance, could be for the purposes of gaining unconscious gratification of sexual drive, even if that gratification were obtained only in highly disguised forms. Or, it could be a defense against unconscious aggressive wishes. In addition, all forms of "higher" human activity, such as learning, studying, writing novels, composing music, or exploring science, are also unconscious, displaced forms of dealing with sex and aggression. Thus the "higher" in human behavior is really an expression of the "lower"—more basic biological impulses—as is the need for relatedness to others. Psychotherapy becomes the process of helping people become aware of the roots of their problems in early childhood sexual and aggressive wishes and fantasies.

We have already noted how various theorists who followed Freud discounted Freud's emphasis on sex and aggressive wishes and impulses in various ways. Most gave greater importance to ego functioning than Freud did, and saw the "higher" activities of the human, such as art, philosophy, or science, as arising from an "autonomous ego," rather than as being derivatives of sexual and aggressive wishes. In a similar manner, many emphasized the importance of interpersonal relationships in human life for their own sake, over and above sexual and aggressive aspects. Sullivan, for instance, believed that it was the interpersonal context that was most important to people's development, and Adler believed that concern for others was crucial to full human development.

OBJECT RELATIONS THEORY

According to Harry Guntrip (1973), important precursors of object relations theory were Melanie Klein (1932/1975) and Harry Stack Sullivan. Other important figures (see St. Clair, 1986) associated with this approach are D. W. Winnicot, W. R. D. Fairbairn, Otto Kernberg, Margaret Mahler, and James Masterson (Masterson, 1981, 1985). Object relations theorists generally reject part or all of Freud's metapsychology, that is, his concept of id, ego, and superego and the idea that the personality is an energy-regulating device. Some substitute a rather complex metapsychology of their own, which we will only briefly touch on later.

Self-Structure and Integration of Aims

> A person is a whole self and so unique that it is impossible to find, among all the millions of human beings that have existed and do exist, any two who are exactly alike. When a baby is born, he contains a core of uniqueness that has never existed before. The parents' responsibility is not to mold, shape, pattern, or condition him, but to support him in such a way that his precious hidden uniqueness shall be able to emerge and guide his whole development. (Guntrip, 1973, p. 181)

It is apparent from this quote that we have come a long way from Freud. Whereas Freud saw development in terms of regulating and expressing sexuality (and later, aggression), object relations theory focuses on the development of a separate, differentiated, integrated, cohesive self. Certainly the regulation of sexuality and aggression is an important issue for the development of a differentiated, cohesive self, but so are hunger and needs for closeness, attention, competence, mastery, and others.

Object relations theory is thus more comprehensive than Freud's psychoanalysis. Sex and aggression are important, but they are only a part of the whole story. A fully developed self is unique. It is also creative, flexible, and self-regulating. It is true to itself, and behavior flows from its own plans and schemes, rather than from some externalized image of how it should be (a "false self"). The most crucial factor in the development of a true self is relationships to other people, particularly the mother. As we said in the previous chapter, relationships with other people are seen by psychoanalysts as a subcategory of relationships with objects in general. Hence, even though the object relations theorists are most interested in relationships with people, they call them "object relations." Now read the following quote with the understanding that the word people can be substituted for object and see what it means to you. "The entire process of growth, disturbance, and restoration of wholeness as an ego or personal self depends upon the ego's relations with objects, primarily in infancy, and thereafter in the unconscious . . . interacting with object-relations in real life" (Guntrip, 1973, p. 95).

Along with the emphasis on the development of the self in the context of relationships to other people comes a deemphasis of Freud's view of the mind as composed of id, ego, and superego. For Freud, the id was a biological repository of primitive sexual and aggressive energies. But if sex and aggression are energies that build up and clamor for discharge, people have a need to act aggressively or sexually regardless of what is going on in their lives. For Freud, relationships with other people are based on their being sources of need gratification. It is important for an individual to be liked or loved by other people, because people are vehicles of sexual gratification. All motives, such as the need to achieve, to have power over others, to have positive self-esteem, to be loved, are all ultimately secondary to the basic needs of discharging and regulating sexuality and aggression.

Many object relations theorists reject the view that sexuality and aggression are instinctual energies that build up and clamor for discharge (Eagle, 1984; Guntrip,

1973). They believe that both sex and aggression have a biological component, but neither are instincts in the generally accepted meaning of the word, that is, they are not energies that build up and need to be discharged or reduced. In rejecting an energy model of motivation, object relations theory is in accord with most modern views of needs and motivations (Weiner, 1980). According to Guntrip, sex is better thought of as a biologically based appetite. An appetite may increase in intensity if a person is not able to engage in the desired activity, but there is no energy that builds up if the person does not engage in it. For example, if one has an interest or "appetite" for going to classical music concerts, one's desire to go may increase if one has not been for a while, but there is no buildup of "classical music energy." Freud's energy idea implies that people need to discharge the energy in order for pleasure to occur. Such a view makes orgasm the ultimate goal of sexual activity and makes any sexual activity without orgasm appear to be ultimately incomplete. This is quite out of keeping with modern views of sexuality. In fact, this view is now seen as one of the causes of sexual problems. Sexual activity and becoming aroused may be experienced as pleasurable whether or not they lead to orgasm. If sex is an energy that needs to be discharged and dissipated, then this does not make sense. If sex is an appetite, then it does make sense.

Similarly, if aggression is an instinctual energy, then we as species would periodically have to act aggressively in order to dissipate this energy. But while most modern theorists believe there is a biological basis to aggression, they hold that it is a response to threat rather than instinctual energy. We may learn to enjoy aggression for its own sake, but that is because aggression, like sex, can come to serve other needs in the personality. There is no aggressive energy that needs to be discharged.

If the self is the focus of development, and not sex and aggression, then what is the self? Morris Eagle (1984) defined the self

> as a biologically evolved adaptive hierarchical structure coordinating a wide range of subordinate functions. In as complex a system as a person, one would expect the evolution of a superordinate structure whose main functions would include the coordination and fulfillment of a wide range of the person's interests and needs. (p. 207)

Thus, the self is an organization that attempts to coordinate a host of goals, desires, aims, and values. For instance, at any given moment you may have a host of conflicting aims and goals. You may feel hungry, tired, bored with your studies. Yet you may have the goal of passing the test tomorrow, which may relate to other goals of becoming a psychologist, pleasing your parents, maintaining your self-esteem. You may also have a desire to please your spouse, who wants to go out, or to pay attention to your children. The individual needs an organizational structure that can prioritize competing aims, desires, and feelings and bring some coherence to how the individual goes about meeting them. That is what the self is and what it does.

Eagle goes on to suggest that some of our aims are infantile and some are not available to conscious awareness, having been split off and disavowed, usually in early childhood. He sees persons as

> attempting to carry out a variety of aims—some in conflict with each other and others harmoniously, some infantile and others more mature, and all with varying de-

grees of conscious awareness and of acknowledgment as one's own aims, ranging from full conscious awareness and acknowledgment to total lack of awareness and disavowal. (p. 123)

Disowned or disavowed aims imperil adequate functioning of the self.

A superordinate structure or self-organization which excludes and dissociates a wide range of strivings and aims does not adequately reflect one's welfare and is therefore carrying out its adaptive functions poorly. (p. 207)

Thus, if persons have disavowed certain primitive wishes in early childhood, their self-organization cannot function adequately. These wishes still influence their behavior, but cannot be integrated and coordinated with other aspects of their personality because they are not available to awareness.

Sex and aggression, in this view, are aims or desires, not instincts. As such, they need to be integrated with other aims and desires. Sex, as an appetite, may become integrated with other aspects of the self so that it comes to serve a variety of other needs of the self. And it takes on many meanings. It becomes part of the functioning of the self and takes a place in the whole system of personal values and meanings. For Freud, many of our "higher" aims, such as success, self-esteem, and closeness, are ultimately in the service of sexual energy discharge; for Guntrip, Eagle, George Klein, and others, it is just the reverse. Sexual activity may be a means of achieving closeness and intimacy, a way of proving attractiveness or self-worth, an "achievement" activity, or an act of rebellion. Klein (1976) says that sexual cravings are not the naggings of undischarged sexual tension, but represent the failure to actualize some self-value that has become symbolized by sexual activity. Thus, sexual tension usually has more to do with an individual's needs for closeness, acceptance, or achievement than it does with some pure need for "sex." After all, if it were just a need for "sex," one could masturbate. The point is that in the human there really isn't something so simple as a need for sex. Rather, sex becomes an activity through which a whole range of other needs and values are expressed.

This way of looking at the self provides a better explanation of what happens in therapy than classical analytic theory. Classical analytic therapy makes repressed impulses conscious, but then what? You can't go have sex with your mother or father. All you can do is make sure these impulses don't distort your view of the world. But what do you do with them? In object relations theory, aims are influenced by their place in the whole self-structure and take on different meanings depending on how they are integrated into the personality. The problem with repression is that certain primitive childhood aims are split off from the self-structure and therefore not given a chance to be integrated effectively. Conscious awareness in therapy allows these aims to be integrated in the adult self and therefore modified.

Consider a client who gets in touch with infantile rage toward his father, who often slighted him. In classical analytic therapy, what does a person now do with this rage? We have had clients get in touch with such rage, only to feel worse, saying, "Now what do I do?" Our answer was that the rage needs to be worked through until the client can "let go" of it. This may involve forgiving the father, which itself involves relinquishing demands that the father (or all people, including oneself) be perfect. It also involves recognizing the father's humanness. Finally, it involves the realization that the client is now an adult and no longer needs to feel so threatened by such slights. These learnings fundamentally alter the rage so that it either goes away or becomes considerably less intense.

We will now look at one of the most commonly accepted object relations views of the development of the self.

Mahler and Separation-Individuation

Margaret Mahler (Mahler, 1968; Mahler, Pine, & Bergman, 1975) conducted observational studies of mothers and children to arrive at her model of development. For her, development is primarily a matter of separation and **individuation,** that is, the child must separate herself from other objects and the external world and develop a sense of her own uniqueness as an individual. According to Mahler, the child in the first month of life is in the stage of *normal autism.* In this stage, the infant is only fleetingly attentive to external reality, being more preoccupied with internal stimuli. The infant could be described at this stage as *narcissistic.* She has no interest in the external world; in fact, she does not even have a concept of the external world. External objects, such as the mother, are not seen as external objects, and their presence may only be dimly sensed as an accompaniment of need gratification. The infant may believe that her desires are all that is needed to make the mother magically appear to satisfy them.

From the second or third month, the child begins to attend to the world. At this stage, known as *normal symbiosis,* the child cannot distinguish between her own efforts to get her needs met and the mother's responses to her needs. The child may now be aware of external stimuli, particularly of those associated with the mother, but the child does not perceive the mother as an external object (a separate person). In effect, the child experiences herself as fused with the mother, as sharing a common boundary with the mother. When the mother feeds the child, for instance, the child perceives the mother's arm and the bottle as part of her own body feeding herself. Thus, when the mother does not immediately gratify the infant's hunger, the child perceives her own self as inflicting pain and frustration.

At about 4 months of age, the separation-individuation process proper begins. The first phase of the process, from about 4 months to 10 months, involves the infant's development of a sense of *bodily separation* from the mother. Through his activities, the child begins to realize that he and the mother are physically separate. This realization, however, is anxiety provoking, and the child will periodically "check back" with the mother in order to reassure himself of her presence. The next phase, from about 10 to 14 months, is that of *practicing.* Early practicing involves gradual acquisition of motor skills that allow further separation from the mother. Practicing proper begins when the infant begins to walk. This is the peak period of the child's omnipotence. The child acts as if he is on top of the world, and can master anything, as a whole new world is opened up to him by his ability to move around. However, this sense of omnipotence is still linked to the psychological presence of the mother as the child's "security blanket."

Before we discuss the next phase, we should discuss the mother's activity during the whole maturation process. For development to be successful, the child must experience "good enough mothering" (Winnicot, 1965). A good enough mother is not a perfect mother who meets all of the child's needs, but rather a mother who is "good enough" to postively encourage and support the development process in the child. A good mother enjoys her child and is comfortable holding him. Mahler believes that how and when a mother holds her child conveys to the child a whole host of attitudes. As the child begins to separate and individuate, the mother is neither too distant nor too close. An overprotective, smothering mother holds a child when she needs comforting rather than when the child needs comforting. This behavior may stifle the child's initiative and moves toward autonomy. It inhibits the child's ability to develop a sense of himself as separate from the mother and to develop his capacity for independent judgment. A distant, rejecting mother may also be harmful because she does not provide a safe place of support to which the child can return after venturing out into the world. The child needs both a sense of support from the mother as he challenges the world and some freedom to explore. A distant, rejecting mother may allow freedom, but provide no support. Her child will never successfully separate and individuate because he will forever long for union with her. He will fantasize union with the mother because that is the only way he can control his own anxiety in response to his mother's abandonment or neglect.

One other factor of good enough mothering is that the mother be able to act as a "holding environment" (Winnicot, 1965) or a "container" for overwhelming emotions the infant might feel. When the infant is experiencing anger or pain or fear the mother can "hold," soothe, and contain these feelings so that the infant feels safe and is not overwhelmed by them. This allows the infant to learn how to master these strong emotions himself.

It is particularly important that the mother effectively balance support and freedom in the next phase of separation-individuation, that of *rapprochement,* which occurs from about 14 to 24 months. Some object relations theorists hypothesize that many different kinds of psychopathology, including borderline personality disorder and eating disorders such as bulimia, have their roots in this developmental phase. During rapprochement, the child becomes more aware of her separateness from the mother. Her joyous sense of omnipotence vanishes as she begins to recognize her separateness. She begins to feel small, deflated, weak, and helpless. This is the beginning of the rapprochement crisis. The child must master the fact of her separateness from the mother. In addition, it is during this time that the child becomes aware of gender differences, and thus, analytic theorists see it as the beginning of a person's identity as a male or female.

During rapprochement, splitting is used as a defense mechanism. All object relations theorists discuss splitting. However, some assume that it begins to happen earlier in development than Mahler, according to whom it primarily occurs during rapprochement. For these other theorists, such as Cashdan (1988), splitting is the first and most primary way we evaluate and judge the world, separating things into "good" and "bad" based on our affective responses to them—that is, how much they please or displease us. Thus, the roots of splitting may develop earlier than the rapprochement period.

For Mahler, as the child begins to form a representation (or image) of the mother as a separate person, the child is confronted with some painfully contradictory information. Mother is good, a rewarding source of pleasure and support, but she is also bad, a frustrating source of criticism, punishment, and saying no. It is too painful for the child to perceive the "good" mother as having bad qualities, so the image of mother is split in two. When mommy is being nice, the child's image is of the "good mother"; when she is being critical, the image is of the "bad mother." In other words, the mother is perceived as all good or all bad, depending on how she is acting, and the two images are not integrated. Similarly, the child splits his own self-image into the "good me" and the "bad me." When the child is being praised by the mother, he feels good and sees himself as all good. When he is being criticized, he feels bad and sees himself as all bad, rotten through and through.

The point here is that the child's self-image is unfinished. First, the child judges himself completely in terms of how the mother is responding to him: He is bad if she is critical of him. Second, the child engages in global, either-or thinking: I cannot be both good and bad at the same time; I am either all bad or all good. Thus, the child does not have an integrated image of a whole self, consisting of good and bad aspects. Similarly, the child does not have an integrated image of the mother or, by extension, of people in general.

A concrete example of splitting is when the baby feels weak and helpless and reaches out to the mother. Suppose the mother is unable to respond to these needs appropriately. The baby is helpless and cannot afford to get angry at the mother. So the baby "splits off" her helpless, needy baby side. She must also split off her anger toward the mother because it is too threatening to be angry at the mother. It is better to feel "bad" than to feel weak and needy and angry at the mother. In later life, this person will have difficulty in interpersonal relationships, immediately feeling "bad" about herself whenever someone else doesn't meet her needs, or even contradicts or disagrees with her.

All children use splitting as a defense mechanism at a certain point in development, but it is crucial that the child develop whole object representations and emotional object constancy. With good enough mothering, the child eventually overcomes her defensive need to separate good and bad images of the mother. She will be able to unify them into an image of a whole person. She will also be able to develop whole object representation of her self-image. Then, when her mother is critical of her, she will not see the mother as all bad, nor will she see herself as all bad. By extension, as an adult, she will not completely devalue people just because they do something that displeases her, nor will she idealize them just because she feels attracted to them, and expect them to be perfect in her terms and to meet all her needs. Because she is able to see people as having both good and bad qualities, she will develop emotional object constancy, that is, she will be able to maintain a constant emotional reaction toward someone. Being able to separate a person's actions from the person, she will be able to continue to love the person, even if the person engages in some behavior that displeases her.

In addition to being able to maintain positive feelings toward a person, it is sometimes necessary to be able to maintain negative feelings toward someone. For instance, battered women are often unable to maintain negative feelings toward their husbands. As soon as the husband apologizes and acts repentant, the wife "forgets" her negative reaction to him.

The achievement of emotional object constancy and whole object representations happens during the final phase of the separation-individuation process. This phase of *consolidation of individuality* occurs at 24 to 36 months. The person who achieves these goals can maintain self-esteem even in the face of failing at something, can continue to like and prize others even if they do not live up to expectations, can maintain a "good self" image without needing to please others continually. The person will be able to continue to develop his or her true self, that is, to separate his or her own intentions, perceptions, and goals from others.

Psychopathology

We have already mentioned some of the things that can go wrong during this sequence of separation-individuation. A person may fail to establish whole object representations and emotional object constancy. The individual may be unable to form stable, enduring relationships, constantly fluctuating from intense love and involvement to intense disappointment. He may be unable to establish a stable, cohesive identity in terms of an integrated set of goals, values, and self-perceptions. This may lead to unstable vocational pursuits—frequent job changes and inability to settle on and pursue some career. The individual may exhibit a pattern of impulsiveness as the result of these instabilities. Because the individual has not developed a stable inner self, he may need constant emotional stimulation from outside to feel alive and involved. Thus, he may invest himself in casual or promiscuous sex, use of drugs, and gambling. Because he has not learned emotional object constancy, his emotional responses may be intense but momentary. He may be afflicted with intense feelings of hostility that come and go. If he does not completely establish a sense of self as a separate object—if he feels fused with the mother—he will continually search for the "ecstasy" of the fusion experience. He may seek intense, immediate personal encounters (such as promiscuous or casual sex) in which he can temporarily experience that sense of fusion, but then when he is alone, he will feel depressed, empty, and abandoned.

An individual who exhibits a pattern of impulsive behavior, anger and depression, intolerance of being alone, and identity problems is likely to fit the criteria for borderline personality disorder in the DSM-IV. While there is controversy over both the definition and cause of this condition (Clarkin, Marziali, & Munroe-Blum, 1992), it is the disorder on which recent object relations theorists have focused. Borderline personality involves the failure to establish a healthy identity.

Object relations theory, like most psychoanalytic theories, postulates a structural model of personality development. However, instead of focusing on personality traits as defenses against unconscious sexual and aggressive wishes, these theorists focus on the development of the ego, most specifically, on a subset of the ego: the self. For them, what is most important is that one develop a good "working model" of the self inside, which includes good working models of relating to others as well.

As part of ego development, stable core images of the self and of others must be formed early. This constitutes the foundation of later personality development. These stable, core images are of the self-in-relation-to-mother. It is important to note their interpersonal nature: they are not of self alone, but of self-relating-to-mother. In other words, we first develop an image of self as part of relationships, and only later begin to synthesize out from all these images of self-in-relationship an image of self as "its own thing." If early childhood relationships with the mother (and later with the father) are dysfunctional, then the child develops flawed models of both the self and of relationships. These models persist and influence later adult behavior. For object relations theorists, it could be said that personality is primarily interpersonal, that is, it consists of stable patterns of relating to others. If we have had "good enough mothering," we will carry into adulthood effective prototypes of how to relate to others. If we have had dysfunctional parenting, we will carry forward flawed models. Thus, for object relations theory, it is the real relationship with the mother that plays an important role in devleopment.

There seems to be a lack of consensus among various object relations theorists as to what degree they hold to the Freudian idea that personality is basically "finished" in early childhood. Certainly all believe that early childhood is a "critical period" within which certain things must happen in order for later development to proceed normally. Thus, if early relationships with the mother are dysfunctional and the child never successfully separates or resolves splitting, the child will move onward in development with a fundamentally flawed ego that will not be "repaired" by the ordinary course of later events. For object relations theory, as for Freud, the more severe the adult behavior problem, the earlier the problem occurred and the more fundamental are the flaws in personality.

However, some theorists seem to believe (Hamilton, 1988) that if infancy and early childhood go well, then the person can use these healthy "working models" to build on, and the person will continue to develop and grow, incorporating later learnings into these working models. In other words, the person is not "all finished" by age 3 or 5. Other object relations theorists seem to emphasize that early models of relationships are highly influential in shaping adult relationships no matter what has happened since, suggesting, more along the lines of Freud, that the basics of personality are laid down in early childhood (Meissner, 1978).

KOHUT AND SELF PSYCHOLOGY

The other major new approach to psychoanalysis to develop is that of self psychology. Self psychology is sufficiently revolutionary compared to other analytic theories that some writers treat it as a unique perspective in its own right, rather than as a form of psychoanalysis (Messer & Warren, 1990). Self psychology is also much closer to the humanistic theories of client-centered therapy (Chapter 8) and existentialism (Chapter 9) than other psychoanalytic approaches (Kahn, 1985; Tobin, 1990).

For Heinz Kohut (1971, 1977), the growth of a stable, cohesive, unique self is the basic issue in personality development. Other issues, such as how the parents handle toilet training during the anal stage or how they react to the child during the phallic stage, make sense only if we see them in terms of this process, and psychopathology is seen as a result of the thwarting of that process.

Self-objects are crucial in the person's development of a cohesive self. A self-object can be thought of as a person who supplies an important set of functions for the developing self, though some writers have stressed that it is more appropriate to talk about self-object functions than about self-objects, since the crucial things are really the functions themselves.

Consider a small infant within the first year of life. At that point, according to Kohut, he has no "self" (though he does have the innate potential to develop a self).

At that point in development, his sense of self is fragmented and incoherent. It is through the responses of important caretakers that he begins to develop an organized core "nuclear" sense of self, along about the second year of life. The caretaker engenders this development by providing certain functions that the infant is unable to provide for himself. The most basic mode of such support is through empathy. The mother, through her empathic responses to the infant, conveys to him that he is a self: unique, distinctive, and worthy of being understood and responded to.

The mother also supports the child's developing self by helping the child with tension regulation, that is, by providing for the child's basic needs. More importantly, the mother provides psychological support. In order to develop a cohesive self, the child must develop mature ambitions, ideals, and positive self-esteem. He must develop the ability to support himself in the face of frustration and to nurture and empathize with himself. If the mother is unable to respond when the infant is experiencing some troubling emotion such as anger or anxiety, those troubling emotions will not be integrated into the developing self-structure, and will trouble the individual the rest of his life, threatening psychological disorganization when they are reawakened (Stolorow, 1992).

Initially, these self-supportive functions are provided by the mother, if the child is lucky enough to have good mothering. Early in childhood, the child will have grandiose and exhibitionistic needs for attention and admiration. In order for the child to develop a sense of her own self-worth, the mother must engage at this stage in empathic **mirroring**—that is, the mother must be able to experience and respond to the child's "look at me" behavior with appreciation and joyfulness. If the child rarely or never gets empathic mirroring, then she never has the kind of appreciative support she needs to grow. Anyone who has been around small children will have experienced their "look at me" behavior. One must be "properly appreciative" in order for the children to develop a sense of their own self-worth.

At the same time, mothers (and other self-objects, such as fathers) are not always available to provide empathic mirroring. Mother may be busy, or Father may be tired. There will be inevitable failures in empathic mirroring. However, if a self-object always provided empathic mirroring, the child would never learn to take over this function herself. In optimal development, the periodic failures of empathic mirroring allow the child to learn to provide her own self-support. At times when the mother is unavailable, the child can model the mother's empathic response and "talk" internally to herself as the mother would. Put in Kohut's terms, a "transmuting internalization" occurs, in which the function of self-support provided by the mother gets internalized and built into the individual's own self-structure. Optimal empathic mirroring from the mother leads to a modulating and softening of the grandiose and exhibitionistic tendencies of the child, and the development of healthy, mature self-esteem, ambitions, and assertiveness.

The very young child also has a need to idealize his caretakers. As adults, we can still have this need. When we are learning in a new area, for instance clinical psychology, we may have a tendency to idealize and then pattern ourselves after certain figures, say, Freud, Rogers, or Kohut. These figures embody our ideals, and it is through them that we develop our own ideals. As adults, of course, we are not directly soothed by these figures, but the presence of someone whom we can idealize is emotionally soothing.

For a child, it is reinforcing to the self-image and self-esteem to be soothed and nurtured by someone who is idealized. Thus, idealizing the mother helps the child feel good about himself. If the mother is empathic, the child will eventually develop the ability to soothe himself. He will also internalize the ideals of the parents. Further, he will grow out of the need to idealize the mother and, by extension, other individuals as well. As the child develops the ability to soothe himself, he no longer needs to see the person who soothes him as perfect.

Another need that the young child has is to feel a similarity to other people and a feeling of belonging ("twinship"). As adults, for instance, we experience this twinship need when we are pleased to meet someone who we feel is a great deal like ourselves. The child's ability to develop this aspect of herself has to do with her ability to establish sociable relationships with others.

The development of these three "poles" of the self—the grandiose, exhibitionistic pole; the idealizing pole; and the twinship pole—leads to the achievement of a cohesive nuclear self by sometime in the third year of life if all goes well. This cohesive self includes the functions of both healthy self-assertiveness and an internalized image of parental goals and ideals. This process of "self-structuralization" leads to a child who will ultimately be able to regulate her own emotions, be assertive, take responsibility for herself, pursue and develop her own ambitions and goals, form healthy relationships with others, empathically minister to her own self when distressed, and empathically relate to others.

Once we have achieved a healthy nuclear self, do we no longer need other people? No, according to Kohut. Self psychology is not a theory of separation-individuation as is object relations theory, where the healthy outcome is a separate, autonomous self (Tobin, 1990). To the contrary, the healthy self exists in an *intersubjective field* (Stolorow, 1992). That is, the healthy self always exists in relation to others. There is no such thing as a self completely separate from other people. Thus, all of us will continue to need support from others throughout our lives. We will continue to need empathy, connectedness in the form of twinship relationships, people to idealize, and so on. These functions mature with age, that is, they take more mature forms, but they don't disappear.

Self psychology thus postulates a radically different view of the human being in contrast to Freud, object relations theory, and most traditional Western theories of the self. Its view is compatible with modern feminist interpretations of the self, recent developments in the view of the self in client-centered therapy (see Chapter 8), the "field" view of the self postulated by Gestalt theory (see Chapter 9), and systems views of the self (see Chapter 14).

To quote Mitchell (1988),

> the basic unit of study is not the individual as a separate entity . . . but an interactional field within which the individual arises and struggles to make contact and to articulate himself . . . Mind is composed of relational configurations. (pp. 3–4)

That is, your experience of self in any given moment is always a product of your history plus whom you are with at the moment. Even if you are alone, your mind is basically relational, which means that emotionally you are never really alone, because everything you are doing is always relational, at least mentally. The meanings that you apply to what you are doing are always grounded in your past and present relationships with others, even if they are not present. You may be at home painting a picture, but even that is an intersubjective experience in that you are always implicitly planning to show it to others, seeing it through the eyes of others (as well as through the eyes of yourself), and so on. There simply is no such thing as a separate, developed, autonomous "self" from which your behavior flows independent of the context of others.

Thus, developing a "nuclear self" is not quite the same as becoming separated and individuated as in object relations theory. A cohesive, functional, nuclear self is really a structured set of interactive functions: the ability to make decisions, to choose ideals and goals, and so on.

Psychopathology

Psychological problems occur when parents or other caretakers do not provide the supportive, empathic context for the development of a coherent nuclear self. The self remains fragmented, and the child never develops certain of these important self-functions, such as the ability to set goals or soothe the self. As an adult, these disturbed self-functions will manifest themselves in disturbed relationships, both with others and with one's work.

For instance, the child who does not receive healthy empathic mirroring at an early age may develop a narcissistic personality disorder. This disorder is characterized by an incessant need to be the center of attention and to be loved and admired. The person also has fantasies of unlimited success. Some narcissistic people, who have not successfully internalized an idealized image of their parents, may continually search to merge with people whom they can idealize. The self-esteem of narcissistic individuals depends on the availability of people who can admire them or of people they can identify with and idealize. When they do not have these things, or when they engage in behaviors that are less than admirable, they respond with shame and rage rather than with the more mature emotion of guilt.

It is important to realize that the adult is not simply "acting like an infant" whose development has been arrested at a very early age. The adult's narcissistic behavior is an attempt at the present time to get the kind of emotional support he needs in order to resume growing. In other words, dysfunctional adult behavior is not merely a repetition of childhood behavior; it is an active attempt to cope, to get what is needed to grow, in the present.

In fact, contrary to object relations theory, where psychopathological behavior is simply a manifestation of an immature ego, for self psychology, psychopathology is a manifestation of the particular interpersonal relationship the person is in. Pathological behavior is not merely a manifestation of primitive, immature ways of viewing the self and the world, as it is in object relations theory, but rather, the individual's desperate attempts in the present to get what he needs to grow.

Kohut's (1984) version of the Oedipus complex is different from Freud's. Kohut assumes that the child enters the Oedipal stage joyfully if she has had a healthy environment until then. For Kohut, the primary issues of the Oedipal stage are not sex and aggression, but affection and assertiveness. The young male child begins to explore his affectional capacity in relation to his mother and his assertive capacity in relation to his father. The converse happens for the female child.

At this age, assertion and aggression are often not sufficiently differentiated for the child, and neither are sex and affection. As a result, if the parents handle the situation badly, assertion degenerates into aggression and affection degenerates into sexual wishes. Thus, according to Kohut, the Oedipus complex as Freud portrayed it is actually not universal, but a product of poor parental management. If the mother has conflicts over sexuality herself, she may be put off or threatened by her child's affectional moves. Her sense of threat may inadvertently sexualize these affectional moves for the child. Similarly, if the father is threatened by the child's assertion, then the situation may become a competitive, rivalrous one, leading to feelings of hostility toward the father.

For Kohut, castration anxiety is actually a metaphor for disintegration anxiety. Anxiety is fear of the self's disintegration or a sense of the self as disintegrating, in contrast to Freud's view of anxiety as a signal that the repressed is about to break through into consciousness. Kohut's view of penis envy should also be mentioned. For Kohut, penis envy in the girl is a result of failure on the part of parents and culture to prize the uniqueness and individuality of the female. It is a metaphor for the girl's diminished sense of self due to her parents' and society's masculine bias.

Even if as children people receive adequate empathic responding from their parents, they continue to need self-objects throughout their lives. One of Kohut's interesting ideas is that anyone who supports a person's self-development can function as a self-object. For instance, you may find one theorist in this book that you really resonate with. That theorist will be a self-object for you. As you read about that theorist and find your developing ideas mirrored and supported in the theorist's work, that mirroring and support will further the development of your own ideas. Rock stars are often self-objects for teenagers, and for young adults it is often a respected teacher or supervisor. Of course, we all want self-objects in our romantic relationships—someone who "prizes" us and likes us for who we are.

PSYCHOTHERAPY

Self Psychology and Object Relations Theory

There are several similarities between object relations and self psychological approaches to therapy. First, both approaches stress the importance of therapist empathy. Empathy is used in classical psychoanalysis, but its primary use is to help the analyst gain insight into the client. In contrast, both object relations and self psychological approaches assume that empathic failures in childhood have contributed to the adult client's problems. Therefore, it is important that the therapist provide empathy as a way of helping the client "contain" strong unruly emotions and affects, and integrate them into the personality. For these approaches, empathy itself is a major vehicle of therapeutic change. This is particularly true in self psychology (Rowe & Mac Isaac, 1991), where the provision of empathy by the therapist actively institutes a condition for maturation and growth of the self.

Second, most therapists in both approaches value insight into childhood roots of adult problems, but to a lesser degree than in classical psychoanalytic therapy. It is helpful to learn how one's adult problems are based on parenting failures in childhood. However, the corrective experience of the here-and-now therapy relationship itself is also valued. Masterson (1981), an object relations therapist, calls therapy an "experiment in individuation." Change occurs through the experiential reliving of early childhood conflicts in therapy, and through that reliving, the maturational process is freed for the individual to develop a more differentiated and cohesive self. For some object relations therapists, such as Cashdan (1988), insight into the past plays very little role, and therapy is primarily concerned with helping clients gain insight into how they are unconsciously structuring present relationships.

According to Kohut, when pathological early childhood experiences are revived and reworked in therapy, the therapist can provide the empathic conditions missing in childhood (including the occasional failures of empathy necessary for transmuting internalizations to occur). In these circumstances, "the accretion of psychological structure that optimally should have occurred during normal development is now belatedly occurring in the therapeutic milieu" (Kahn, 1985, p. 900).

Guntrip (1973) has perhaps most forcefully expressed the idea that through the experiential quality of the therapy relationship, growth can be achieved.

> I cannot think of psychotherapy as a technique but only as the provision of the possibility of a genuine, reliable, understanding, and respecting, caring personal relationship in which a human being whose true self has been crushed by the manipulative techniques of those who only wanted to make him "not a nuisance" to them, can begin at last to feel his own true feelings, and think his own spontaneous thoughts, and find himself to be real. (p. 182)

Third, these therapeutic approaches advocate the selective use of therapist self-disclosure. For instance, the therapist may reveal her feelings of ignorance or clumsiness in attempting to understand the client. Or the analyst may reveal her own occasional needs to use the client as a self-object (Wolf, 1983). For Kohut, a parent may have been unable to provide empathy because his or her own self-development was incomplete. As a result, he or she may have been more interested in gaining emotional support from the child, rather than in giving it to the child. Self-disclosure by the therapist may help the client realize that the therapist is not there to use the client for her own needs. This may help the client to overcome feelings of resistance and defensiveness and, therefore, to grow (Wolf, 1989):

> Since in essence, resistance is nothing but fear of being traumatically injured again, the decisive event of its analysis is the moment when the analysand has gained courage from these self-revelations of the analyst to know that the analyst does not need to feed on the patient to achieve cohesion and harmony. (pp. 500–501)

Guntrip also clearly believes that the therapist should be a real person in therapy, at least more so than in traditional analytic therapy. In a somewhat related fashion, Masterson (1981) will abandon therapeutic neutrality to confront clients with the destructiveness of some of their behavior.

Fourth, both approach the transference relationship differently than classical psychoanalysis. For Freud, transference relationships were ultimately patterns of resistance. For self psychologists, they may involve resistance, but they are also expressions of the self's needs from early childhood. Needs for mirroring and for idealizing will be expressed in therapy. In the mirroring transference, the infantile, grandiose self demands continual empathic approval and attention from the therapist. In the idealizing transference, the client wishes for the therapist to be the all-powerful person who can fix all the client's problems. While it is acceptable for the analyst to provide some mirroring, it is often through failures in empathy that these two transferences get resolved. Through failures in empathy, the patient is reminded of the unempathic parent. These experiences are then relived, but because they are relived in the context of an overall empathic relationship, growth of the self occurs.

For object relations therapists, a major key is to work with the *projective identifications* of the client. Projective identification is a defense mechanism in which the client projects unwanted aspects of the self onto another person, and then attempts to control those unwanted aspects via interactions with that other person. Suppose you are unconsciously uncomfortable with your sexual desires. You may project them onto another person, and then see that person as being sexual and seductive toward you. Now you are able to feel sexual, because the other person is acting sexually toward you. With projective identification, the individual may unconsciously manipulate the other person into actually acting out the unconscious projection. Thus, the individual may act unconsciously sexual in order to manipulate the other person into being sexual toward them. Another example of projective identification is that of a prison inmate who, at Christmas, felt lonely, and so he called his wife to "cheer her up" (Robert Rosenbaum, personal communication, June 1993). In other words, he projected his loneliness onto his wife and then tried to control those feelings by taking action toward her.

Thus, projective identification creates a specific kind of transferential relationship in which the client unconsciously tries to manipulate the therapist into feeling and acting in a way that the client unconsciously needs. An important part of object relations therapy is to make the client aware of how he or she is unconsciously "setting up" certain kinds of interpersonal patterns (Cashdan, 1988).

Finally, the goal of both object relations therapy and Kohut's therapy is similar. That goal is the development of the self. For object relations theory, this includes separation of the self from the mother and forming differentiated and integrated representations of both the self and of others. According to Masterson, this manifests itself in increased client autonomy and the ability of the client to take responsibility for himself and manage his life in a constructive manner. In addition, it should lead to a capacity for creativity, intimacy, and flexibility. For Kohut, the goal of therapy is the development of a cohesive self that has realistic ambitions and goals, is able to be creative, intimate, and flexible, and is able to make its own judgments and maintain its own self-esteem.

Brief Forms of Psychoanalytic Psychotherapy

We now turn our attention to a related development in psychoanalysis, that of relatively brief forms of psychotherapy. Among the problems associated with classical psychoanalytic therapy are its lengthiness and its expense. This is also true to some

Projective Identification from Pets.

extent of object relational treatment of borderline personality and of Kohut's treatment of narcissistic personality. In contrast, Luborsky (1984) has outlined his supportive-expressive approach to psychoanalytic psychotherapy. This relatively brief form of psychotherapy can be practiced on an open-ended basis or on a time-limited basis, in which case it usually lasts less than 25 sessions. Strupp and Binder (1984) have developed a time-limited dynamic therapy that lasts 25 to 30 sessions. There are other approaches to brief psychoanalytic psychotherapy (reviewed in Strupp and Binder), but we will focus on these two. Among the virtues of these approaches is that both have been presented as psychotherapy treatment manuals. This relatively recent innovation in writing about psychotherapy developed because of the need to standardize treatment for purposes of doing research on psychotherapy. The treatment manuals are somewhat more concrete and specific in describing treatment than many other writings on psychoanalysis.

What is common to most brief forms of psychodynamic therapy is that they focus on dysfunctional interpersonal relationship patterns, as opposed to early childhood sexual and aggressive wishes. Strupp and Binder's time-limited dynamic therapy is based on the assumption that earlier difficulties with significant others have given rise to patterns of interpersonal relatedness that originally served a self-protective function but are now anachronistic, self-defeating, and maladaptive. Central to these problems are deficiencies in self-esteem, inability to form satisfying interpersonal relationships that gratify the person's needs for closeness, and interferences with autonomous adult functioning (Strupp & Binder, 1984, pp. xiii–xiv).

In childhood, the person experiences a disturbed pattern of interpersonal relationships, from which he develops organizing themes that form a rigid, habitual way of construing and acting in current relationships. These patterns are hidden from the self because of "the ubiquitous human tendency to hide from oneself painful experiences and their aftermath" (p. 32). The client unconsciously believes these patterns will bring him security and nurturance in current relationships. Relationships are defensively distorted in order to protect the self as the person strives to achieve these primitive, unconscious forms of intimacy. Time-limited dynamic therapy attempts to identify and concentrate on these "focal issues."

Strupp and Binder believe that these central relationship issues will manifest themselves in the therapeutic relationship and that the reexperiencing of them in the transference relationship will be therapeutic. The therapist attempts to help the client become aware of the symbolic meanings of his or her behavior, but this needs to be done when "an appropriate affective context exists" (1984, p. 136). At the same time intellectual reconstruction of the past is deemphasized. In fact, Strupp and Binder assume that it is impossible to really recover the past. The most important quality of a therapeutic relationship is that it is a human one. Learning occurs not through acquisition of abstract knowledge, but "rather it is the result of a human experience in which he or she feels understood and in which this understanding is given new meanings" (1984, p. 45). While it is true that transference involves bringing past relationships into the current, therapeutic relationship, Strupp and Binder assume that the client's feelings toward the therapist also include some real aspects of the here-and-now relationship. The therapist is to use her own feelings as signals of how the client is attempting to structure their relationship. Empathic listening is important, and the therapist is encouraged to engage in honest self-disclosure if necessary and appropriate.

Luborsky's supportive-expressive psychoanalytically oriented therapy is similar. It is based on the assumption that a core conflictual relationship theme (CCRT) is at the center of a person's problems. This relationship theme developed from early childhood experiences, but the client is unaware of it and its relation to childhood experiences. Therapy is oriented toward increasing the client's awareness of the theme. It is assumed that the client will have better control over behavior if he knows more about what he is doing at the unconscious level. This knowledge is acquired through reliving childhood experiences. Interpretations must be done only with strands of the CCRT that are close to awareness and not heavily defended against in the therapeutic moment. As we have said, knowledge alone does not change previously unconscious wishes and needs. However, it does lead to an increased ability to master and control them consciously. Luborsky says that the change "may be considered to have enabled the person to function at a higher level of organization" (1984, p. 21). The transference relationship is important in that the CCRT will probably be lived out and enacted in relationship to the therapist. A supportive, empathic relationship is considered crucial, and Luborsky speculates that compared to the acquisition of insight, the relationship may be the more potent therapeutic factor.

Luborsky's supportive-expressive psychotherapy begins with a "socialization interview" in which the client is told how psychotherapy proceeds, what is expected of the client, and what the therapist will do. In the initial, supportive phase of therapy, the therapist attempts to listen nonjudgmentally, demonstrate acceptance and understanding, support defenses and activities that bolster positive functioning, and encourage a "we" feeling. In the expressive phase, the therapist is more active: listening, responding, and listening further.

In general, the brief forms of psychoanalytic psychotherapy are utilized with relatively "more healthy" clients, that is, clients who may have some significant symptoms, but whose functioning in general is relatively adequate. Other brief psychodynamic approaches include those of Davanloo, Mann, and Malan (reviewed in Strupp & Binder, 1984).

Summing Up Recent Approaches

As we have pointed out, object relations therapy, Kohut's therapy, and the brief therapies have some common themes. First, they place greater emphasis on the curative power of the therapeutic relationship itself than did classical psychoanalysis. Second, they place less emphasis on change through insight and reconstruction of the past and more emphasis on change through reliving significant early childhood relationship issues in the context of therapy. Third, they allow the therapist to be more flexible than in classical analysis and encourage the therapist to provide empathy as a vehicle of therapeutic change and to use self-disclosure, when therapeutically appropriate, to help overcome resistance. Finally, all emphasize the importance of ruptures in interpersonal relationships as being the cause of psychological problems, and the repairing of interpersonal relationship patterns as being the cure.

EVALUATION OF INTERPERSONAL PSYCHOANALYTIC APPROACHES

After a brief mention of psychotherapy research, our evaluation below primarily focuses on object relations theory and its hypotheses about early childhood and about self-representations in psychopathology. We particularly focus on the issue of the extent to which early childhood is foundational in influencing later development.

Research on Psychotherapy

There is relatively little research on interpersonal psychodynamic approaches to psychotherapy. A study we reviewed in the last chapter on intensive long-term psychoanalytic psychotherapy is specifically a study of object relations therapy. This study found evidence for its effectiveness (Blatt & Ford, 1994) for clients with personality disorders. A combined interpersonal psychodynamic/humanistic approach has been shown to be effective with depression (Shapiro, 1995). A meta-analysis of research on brief psychodynamic psychotherapy approaches has shown them to be as effective as nonpsychodynamic approaches (Crits-Christoph, 1992) for a variety of problems. This latter is a particularly important finding in an era of brief therapy and managed care.

Research on Child Development

Both Freud's classical version of psychoanalysis and the modern interpersonal approaches place a heavy emphasis on the impact of early childhood on the development of personality and psychopathology. Both adopt a "foundational view," that is, that early experiences form a strong or weak foundation for later development. In the previous chapter, we reviewed research findings suggesting that, in general, personality is not fixed in early childhood, and that many forms of psychopathology are influenced in important ways by here-and-now situational factors. In this chapter, we will take a closer look at development in the first few years of life. We first evaluate several aspects of Margaret Mahler's view of development. In so doing, we shall consider the work of Daniel Stern (1985). We then take a broader look at the impact of the first few years of life on later development, and in so doing, consider attachment theory.

Mahler's Separation-Individuation Model of Development   Mahler held that during the first month of life the infant lived in an "autistic shell," unresponsive to the outer world. We now know from a great deal of infant research that this is not true. Infants are highly responsive to the external world from birth on, and that capacity grows rapidly within the first few months of life.

More importantly, the idea that infants do not have a separate sense of self and experience themselves as fused with their mothers also does not appear to be true. To quote Ulric Neisser (1988), a cognitive scientist,

> Certainly by 3 months of age (and probably from birth), the infant perceives much the same sort of world that we do: a world of distinct, solid, and permanent objects of which she herself (or he himself) is one. . . . The old hypothesis that a young infant cannot tell the difference between itself and the environment, or between itself and its mother can be decisively rejected. (p. 7)

Stern (1985), in an influential psychoanalytic view of child development, also has argued that evidence does not support the idea that infants ever confuse themselves with their mothers. Stern believes that everything we know about infants supports the idea that infants have a sense of self as a separate entity from near birth onward.

Stern argues that there are several different senses of self, and that they develop at different times. The most basic sense of self, that of the self as a physically distinct entity, which is the source of its own actions and experiences, develops very early, within the first few months. Later, around 18 months of age, the young child begins to develop the ability to think about herself in the form of concepts, and begins to develop a concept of self. Stern argues that it is at this level of the self that the things object relations theorists talk about might happen. That is, as the child begins to develop concepts about his own traits and characteristics, his own values and beliefs, the child might confuse his view of himself with his mother's views of him.

Stern further argues that the process of separation-individuation is not something that begins and ends in the first three years of life, but is something that people continue to work on and struggle with throughout their lives.

Stern's work has also demonstrated how early childhood influences might persist into adulthood. Stern gives several examples of children's interactions with mothers who are acting dysfunctionally, and how these interactions might create enduring patterns. For instance, one mother persistently forced her child to look at her and engage in play when the child clearly was feeling overstimulated and was trying to avoid her. The result was a child who (a) hadn't learned how to terminate interactions that were stressful and overwhelming, and therefore (b) might enter interpersonal situations with an avoidant, defensive stance. In another case, the only way a young child could get his depressed mother to interact with him was by very actively pursuing and initiating contact. A few years later. this child was already a "social clown," trying to be the life of the party in social interactions.

Stern's work has not as yet traced the persistence of these patterns into late childhood or adulthood. So it is not known whether these patterns will persist. However, Stern's work is one of the first empirical demonstrations of how early interaction patterns with the mother could establish interpersonal patterns that might persist.

In sum, Mahler's description of the developmental sequence of the child appears to have some flaws in it. Children do not appear to confuse themselves with their mothers at a basic level. Further, they are highly responsive to environmental stimulation even at birth. On the other hand, Daniel Stern's work provides models of how very early interactions with adult caretakers might establish long-standing dysfunctional relationship patterns.

Are Early Experiences Foundational in Creating Psychopathology?   There is a pervasive view in our culture, influenced by psychoanalytic views, that very early childhood (around the first two years of life) is of crucial importance in terms of later development. Presumably, early "damage" during this period can irrevocably harm the person (unless the person goes into therapy), creating serious personality problems in later life. Many object relations theorists, for instance, argue that borderline personality disorder results from damage occurring within the first two years of life, particularly at the rapprochement stage. To what degree is it true that very early experiences are generally foundational in this sense?

With respect to borderline personality disorder, Mahler (1971) herself concluded that parental conflict during the rapprochement period was not the primary cause of borderline personality disorder. She noted in the sample of subjects she had followed into adulthood someone who had become borderline even though the rapprochement period had been nonconflictual, and others who had had highly conflictual rapprochement periods who did not become borderline. In general, researchers now reject the idea that borderline personality disorder is a product of a specific developmental failure at a specific time of life in a specific process, such as separation-individuation (Marziali, 1992). The development of borderline personality disorder is a complex process involving constitutional, biological, and many environmental factors (Marziali, 1992).

Other research suggests that what happens during the first two years of life is not generally as foundational as object relations theorists suppose (Kagan, 1996). As we noted in Chapter 6, researchers on child development now believe that no one developmental period is any more primary, foundational, or crucial in development than any other one. Kagan (1984) cites several studies which show that neglect within the first two years of life need not leave permanent damage if children later receive good supportive home environments. Gaensbauer and Harmon (1982) found that abused infants separated from their parents and placed with nurturing foster mothers were able to respond with considerable adaptability and resilience.

Werner and Smith (1982) followed a large sample of children from infancy into adulthood. They conclude

> As we watched these children grow from babyhood to adulthood, we could not help but respect the self-righting tendencies within them that produced normal development under all but the most persistently adverse circumstances. (p. 159, as quoted in Kagan, 1996)

What this means is that the idea that early events create a kind of damage to internal psychological structures which then persists relatively unchanged unless modified by intensive psychotherapy is not necessarily true. Other evidence shows that problems in childhood do not necessarily continue into adulthood. Several researchers have looked at the issue of whether pathology in childhood portends pathology in adulthood. Their conclusion is that neurotic and adjustment disorders do not portend psychological difficulty in adulthood, whether or not the child has had therapy (Cass & Thomas, 1979; Dohrenwend, Dohrenwend, Gould, Link, Neugebauer, & Wunsch-Hitzig, 1980; Eme, 1979). For instance, Dohrenwend and his colleagues conclude that "most neurotic children become normal adults" (p. 23).

At the same time, there is evidence of some occasions in which early aspects of personality do seem to predict to later psychopathology. Block, Block, and Keyes (1988) found that low ego control at ages 3 to 4 predicted marijuana use at age 14. Briere (1989) has noted that the more severe childhood sexual abuse is at an earlier age, the more likely the person is to have residual adult problems.

Bowlby's **attachment theory** (Hamilton, 1985) is one psychoanalytic view of development that has been intensively researched. Bowlby assumes that infants are biologically predisposed to form attachments with adult caretakers. This is because infants could not survive very long on their own, so it has been evolutionarily advantageous that they form bonds with adult caretakers. Similarly, adults are biologically predisposed to form bonds with their children. The attachment bond between infant and mother is a joint product of both of them. That is, mothers may find some infants more "cute and cuddly" than others, and bond more easily with them. On the other hand, no matter how cute and cuddly an infant is, some mothers may be inept at forming good, secure attachment bonds.

A good attachment bond with the mother provides a "secure base" from which the growing infant can gradually move out to explore the world. It also provides a context in which the infant develops an internalized "working model" of relationships with people. If the relationship with the mother is dysfunctional, the infant's working model of relationship with others will be dysfunctional. It is assumed that these working models persist into adulthood. A child whose relationship with the mother has been such that she got attention only when she was quiet and passive, will assume that adults will like her only when she is quiet or passive.

Attachment theory has been extensively researched (Paterson & Moran, 1988). Several studies have shown correlations between being insecurely attached to the mother in infancy and later problems in social relationships in elementary school. Several retrospective studies have found that adults with various kinds of problems recall having had insecure attachments with their mothers in childhood. Thus, there is some evidence that insecure attachments in infancy may be associated with later problems. However, there is no evidence to date that shows that actual observations of insecure attachments in infancy by researchers are associated with actual pathological behavior in adulthood years later. Nor is there any evidence as to how early attachment problems are associated with later behavior problems. Do early attachment problems cause the development of dysfunctional internal working models? Or, do early attachment problems interfere with the learning of various social skills, which in turn interferes with the further learning of social skills at school? Or, are early attachment problems simply a measure of a dysfunctional parent-child relationship that persists into the school years and is continuing to contribute to social and personality problems?

In sum, the evidence does not support the idea that very early childhood experiences are as formative in determining personality and psychopathology as object relations theory has held. Negative early experiences do not necessarily leave indelible marks that are not erasable without intensive therapy. To the contrary, there is evidence that children are resilient and that as long as they get good support and parenting somewhere along the line, early damage can often be repaired.

On the other hand, research by Stern and attachment theorists suggest ways in which early experiences may persist and influence later development. We believe that the question is not simply "Does early experience influence adult behavior?" but rather, "Under what conditions does early experience persist into adulthood? When it does, how and in what form does it influence adulthood, and how does it interact with later developmental experiences?" This question awaits further research.

If we talk about childhood experiences more broadly (and not just limit ourselves to the first few years of life), then there is good evidence that childhood experiences play a role in the genesis of many forms of psychopathology. However, here we are assuming that the child has had a "continous envelope" of negative experiences throughout a sizable time span, or that the child has been exposed to considerable psychological trauma such as extensive and repeated child abuse.

For instance, abuse experiences have particularly been associated with the development of at least some borderline personality disorders (Briere, 1989; Links, 1992; Marziali, 1992), as well as with the development of a variety of other problems (Briere, 1989). Briere (1989) has argued that the symptoms of borderline personality disorder, such as impulsiveness; inability to form stable, lasting relationships; lack of a stable, organized identity; and so on, are natural consequences of living through the terrifying experience of having been sexually abused.

Similarly, in one study of girls raised in institutions, Rutter (1986) found that "adverse experiences in childhood were associated with substantially worse psychosocial outcomes in early adult life" (p. 8). However, Rutter also found that "marriage to . . . a well-functioning man who provided a supportive relationship was associated with a marked improvement in functioning. Good experiences in adult life can lead to important psychosocial gains" (p. 8). The loss of a parent can predispose a child to depression in adulthood. However, Rutter (1986) suggests that the long-term effects of a death on a child

> probably stem as much from factors consequent upon the death as from the death it-self. These other factors include such hazards as the break-up of the home, frequent changes of caretaker, changes in family roles, financial and material disadvantage, the effects of bereavement on the surviving parent, and the arrival of a stepparent.

Thus, the loss may affect development because it creates a continuous envelope of adverse experiences, such as family and financial instability.

Some research (Garmazy, 1986; Weintraub, Winters, & Neale, 1986) has also found that depression in the parent affects the development of the child. In sum, negative childhood experiences are implicated in the genesis of psychopathology. However, the genesis of both personality and most forms of psychopathology is probably a complex process that involves many experiences over time and does not generally appear to be the product of specific events or interactions at specific times.

Object Relations Theory, Self-Representations, and Psychopathology Object relations theory holds that psychopathology is a result of disturbed representations of self in relation to others, and that this results from negative childhood experiences. There is some evidence supporting the object relational idea that individuals diagnosed as having a borderline personality disorder do have less complex and less developed internal representations of people than do "normal" individuals (Westen, Lohr, Silk, Gold, & Kerber, 1990) and that having less complex and well-developed internal representations of people is associated with pathogenic developmental experiences such as neglect and abuse (Westen, Ludolph, Block, Wixom, & Wiss, 1990).

Similarly, Blatt and Wild (1976) reviewed studies suggesting that individuals with less well-developed boundary concepts exhibit more psychopathology. Boundary concepts have to do with the ability to tell where one object begins and another leaves off (e.g., be able to tell where the self begins and the other person leaves off). For instance, Blatt and Ritzler (1974) measured boundary disturbances with the Rorschach inkblot test. They found that schizophrenics with more severe disturbances exhibited greater difficulties in reality testing.

Silverman and Weinberger (1985) report on research in which the sentence "Mommy and I are one" was presented to subjects at a speed so rapid that it was subliminal (not producing a sensation that is consciously perceived). In a series of studies this subliminal perception was found to reduce psychopathological symptoms and to improve performance on mathematics tests. In one study (Palmatier & Bornstein, 1980), smokers receiving behavior therapy were broken into two groups. One group received several subliminal exposures to the "Mommy and I are one" message in addition to the behavior therapy. This group had a much higher rate of maintaining abstinence from smoking than the group that did not receive this message. Similar results have been found with treatment of a variety of other disorders (see Silverman & Weinberger, 1985, pp. 1, 301).

In sum, there is evidence supporting the object relational hypothesis of disturbed representations of self in relation to others in individuals with psychological problems.

ENDURING CONTRIBUTIONS OF INTERPERSONAL APPROACHES AT THE MILLENNIUM

Interpersonal approaches to psychoanalysis have revolutionized psychoanalytic theory and had signficant influence on nonpsychoanalytic theory. The idea that psychological problems occur at least in part because of disturbed interpersonal relationships is widely accepted. Interpersonal approaches provide models of relationships and self development in childhood that help clinicians develop detailed descriptions of adult pathology. Many therapists in practice find that such conceptualizations help them, particularly with difficult, "personality-disordered" clients (Tobin, 1990). Underlying these formulations are attempts to outline the emotional conflicts and tempests involved in primary relationships with the self and others, and interpersonal psychoanalytic accounts vividly capture these conflicts and tempests. Attachment theory in particular has become and will continue to be an important theory in the study of child development, and ongoing research on that theory holds promise of helping us to understand just how early relationships may affect adult psychopathology.

Interpersonal approaches have facilitated the development of brief forms of psychodynamic therapy. These forms rely on identifying problematic interpersonal themes in an individual's life. The presence of these themes can also be looked for in the transference relationship with the therapist. Identification of such a "core conflictual relationship theme" (Luborsky, 1984) helps focus the therapist's efforts. Research currently supports the effectiveness of brief forms of psychodynamic therapy.

The focus on interpersonal relationships has also led to the development of other new, psychodynamic theories, which we did not have space to review in this chapter. These include approaches such as the work of the Mount Zion group (Weiss, Sampson, & The Mount Zion Psychotherapy Research Group, 1986) who hold that clients in therapy engage in unconscious "testing" to try to undo dysfunctional beliefs learned in early childhood, and Horowitz's (1987) "states of mind" model, which holds that at any given moment, our behavior is guided by the state of mind we are in, and that state of mind is made up of internal models of ourselves in relationship. Wachtel's integrative cyclical psychodynamic theory (reviewed in Chapter 16) also fits into this group.

Interpersonal models have also brought psychodynamic thinking closer to other approaches. Their emphasis on the development of internal models of the self and of relationships brings them close to cognitive theories. Their focus on the here-and-now relationship in therapy brings them close to humanistic theories. And self psychology's focus on the mutual relationship between therapist and client brings that theory closer to systems theories (Chapter 14) and feminist theories (Chapter 17). As such, interpersonal psychodynamic theories are having an impact on nonpsychoanalytic approaches. In sum, interpersonal psychodynamic theories appear to be the wave of the future in psychodynamic theorizing.

BIBLIOGRAPHY

Adelson, J., & Doehrman, M. J. (1980). The psychodynamic approach to adolescence. In J. Adelson (Ed.), *Handbook of adolescent psychology.* New York: Wiley.

Adler, A. (1964). *Social interest: A challenge to mankind.* New York: Capricorn Books. (Original work published 1929)

Blatt, S. J., & Ford, R. Q. (1994). *Therapeutic change: An object relations perspective.* New York: Plenum.

Blatt, S. J., & Ritzler, B. A. (1974). Thought disorder and boundary disturbances in psychosis. *Journal of Consulting and Clinical Psychology, 42,* 370–381.

Blatt, S. J., & Wild, C. (1976). *Schizophrenia: A developmental analysis.* New York: Academic Press.

Block, J., Block, J. H., & Keyes, S. (1988). Longitudinally foretelling drug usage in adolescence: Early childhood personality and environmental precursors. *Child Development, 59,* 336–355.

Briere, J. (1989). *Therapy for adults molested as children.* New York: Springer.

Cashdan, S. (1988). *Object relations therapy.* New York: Norton.

Cass, L. K., & Thomas, C. B. (1979). *Childhood psychopathology and later adjustment: The question of prediction.* New York: Wiley.

Chess, S., & Thomas, A. (1984). *Origins and evolution of behavior disorders.* New York: Brunner/Mazel.

Clarkin, J. F., Marziali, E., & Munroe-Blum, H. (Eds.). (1992). *Borderline personality disorder: Clinical and empirical perspectives.* New York: Guilford.

Crits-Christoph, P. (1992). The efficacy of brief dynamic psychotherapy: A meta-analysis. *The American Journal of Psychiatry, 149,* 151–158.

Dohrenwend, B. P., Dohrenwend, B. S., Gould, M. A., Link, B., Neugebauer, R., & Wunsch-Hitzig, R. (1980). *Mental illness in the United States.* New York: Praeger.

Eagle, M. N. (1984). *Recent developments in psychoanalysis: A critical evaluation.* New York: McGraw-Hill.

Eme, R. F. (1979). Sex differences in childhood psychopathology: A review. *Psychological Bulletin, 86,* 574–595.

Erikson, E. (1968). *Identity: Youth and crisis.* New York: Norton.

Gaensbauer, T. J., & Harmon, R. J. (1982). Attachment behavior in abused/neglected and premature infants. In R. R. Emde & R. J. Harmon (Eds.), *The development of attachment and affiliative systems.* New York: Plenum Press.

Garmazy, N. (1986). Developmental aspects of children's responses to the stress of separation and loss. In M. Rutter, C. E. Izard, & P. B. Read (Eds.), *Depression in young people: Developmental and clinical perspectives* (pp. 297–324). New York: Guilford.

Guntrip, H. (1973). *Psychoanalytic theory, therapy, and the self.* New York: Basic Books.

Hamilton, N. G. (1988). *Self and others: Object relations theory in practice.* New York: Aaronson.

Hamilton, V. (1985). John Bowlby: An ethological basis for psychoanalysis. In J. Reppen (Ed.), *Beyond Freud: A study of modern psychoanalytic theorists.* (pp. 1–28). Hillsdale, NJ: Analytic Press.

Hartmann, H. (1964). *Essays on ego psychology.* New York: International Universities Press.

Horney, K. (1945). *Our inner conflicts.* New York: Norton.

Horowitz, M. J. (1987). *States of mind* (2nd ed., p. 26). New York: Plenum.

Jung, C. G. (1933). *Modern man in search of a soul.* New York: Harcourt Brace Jovanovich.

Jung, C. G. (1956). *Two essays on analytical psychology.* New York: New American Library (Meridian Books).

Kagan, J. (1984). *The nature of the child.* New York: Basic Books.

Kagan, J. (1996). Three pleasing ideas. *American Psychologist, 51,* 901–908.

Kahn, E. (1985). Heinz Kohut and Carl Rogers: A timely comparison. *American Psychologist, 40,* 893–904.

Klein, G. S. (1976). *Psychoanalytic theory: An exploration of essentials.* New York: International Universities Press.

Klein, M. (1975). *The psycho-analysis of children.* New York: Delta. (Original work published 1932)

Kohut, H. (1971). *The analysis of the self.* New York: International Universities Press.

Kohut, H. (1977). *The restoration of the self.* New York: International Universities Press.

Kohut, H. (1984). *How does analysis cure?* Chicago: University of Chicago Press.

Links, P. S. (1992). Family environment and family psychopathology in the etiology of borderline personality disorder. In J. F. Clarkin, E. Marziali, & H. Munroe-Blum (Eds.), *Borderline personality disorder: Clinical and empirical perspectives* (pp. 45–66). New York: Guilford.

Luborsky, L. (1984). *Principles of psychoanalytic psychotherapy: A manual for supportive-expressive treatment.* New York: Basic Books.

Mahler, M. (1968). *On human symbiosis and the vicissitudes of individuation: Vol. 1. Infantile psychosis.* New York: International Universities Press.

Mahler, M. (1971). A study of the separation-individuation process and its possible application to borderline phenomena in the psychoanalytic situation. *Psychoanalytic Study of the Child, 26,* 403–424.

Mahler, M., Pine, F., & Bergman, A. (1975). *The psychological birth of the human infant.* New York: Basic Books.

Marziali, E. (1992). The etiology of borderline personality disorder: Developmental factors. In J. F. Clarkin, E. Marziali, & H. Munroe-Blum (Eds.), *Borderline personality disorder: Clinical and empirical perspectives* (pp. 27–44). New York: Guilford.

Masterson, J. F. (1981). *The narcissistic and borderline disorders: An integrated developmental approach.* New York: Brunner/Mazel.

Masterson, J. F. (1985). *The real self: A developmental, self, and object relations approach.* New York: Brunner/Mazel.

Meissner, W. W. (1978). The conceptualization of marriage and family dynamics from a psychoanalytic perspective. In T. J. Paolino & B. S. McCrady (Eds.), *Marriage and marital therapy: Psychoanalytic, behavioral and systems theory perspectives* (pp. 25–88). New York: Brunner/Mazel.

Messer, S. B., & Warren, S. (1990). Personality change and psychotherapy. In L. Pervin (Ed.), *Handbook of personality* (pp. 171–398). New York: Guilford.

Mitchell, S. (1988). *Relational concepts in psychoanalysis.* Cambridge, MA: Harvard University Press.

Mullahy, P. (1952). *The contributions of Harry Stack Sullivan.* New York: Hermitage Press.

Neisser, U. (1988). Five kinds of self-knowledge. *Philosophical Psychology, 1,* 35–59.

Palmatier, J. R., & Bornstein, P. H. (1980). The effects of subliminal stimulation of symbiotic merging fantasies on behavioral treatment of smokers. *Journal of Nervous and Mental Disease, 168,* 715–720.

Paterson, R. J., & Moran, G. (1988). Attachment theory, personality development, and psychotherapy. *Clinical Psychology Review, 8,* 611–636.

Rowe, C. E., & Mac Isaac, D. S. (1991). *Empathic attunement: The technique of psychoanalytic self psychology.* Northvale, NJ: Jason Aronson.

Rutter, M. (1986). The developmental psychopathology of depression: Issues and perspectives. In M. Rutter, C. E. Izard, & P. B. Read (Eds.), *Depression in young children: Developmental and clinical perspectives* (pp. 3–32). New York: Guilford.

Shapiro, D. A. (1995). Finding out how psychotherapies help people change. *Psychotherapy Research, 5,* 1–21.

Silverman, L. H., & Weinberger, J. (1985). Mommy and I are one: Implications for psychotherapy. *American Psychologist, 40,* 1296–1308.

St. Clair, M. (1986). *Object relations and self psychology: An introduction.* Monterey, CA: Brooks/Cole.

Stern, D. N. (1985). *The interpersonal world of the infant: A view from psychoanalysis and developmental psychology.* New York: Basic Books.

Stolorow, R. D. (1992). Closing the gap betwen theory and practice with better psychoanalytic theory. *Psychotherapy, 29,* 159–166.

Stolorow, R., Brandchaft, B., & Atwood, G. (1987). *Psychoanalytic treatment: An intersubjective approach.* Hillsdale, NJ: Analytic Press.

Strupp, H. H., & Binder, J. L. (1984). *Psychotherapy in a new key: A guide to time-limited dynamic psychotherapy.* New York: Basic Books.

Tobin, S. A. (1990). Self psychology as a bridge between existential humanistic psychology and psychoanalysis. *Journal of Humanistic Psychology, 30,* 14–63.

Weiner, B. (1980). *Human motivation.* New York: Holt, Rinehart and Winston.

Weintraub, S., Winters, K. C., & Neale, J. M. (1986). Competence and vulnerability in children with an affectively disordered parent. In M. Rutter, C. E. Izard, & P. B. Read (Eds.), *Depression in young people: Developmental and clinical perspectives* (pp. 205–222). New York: Guilford.

Weiss, J., Sampson, H., & The Mount Zion Psychotherapy Research Group. (Eds.). (1986). *The psychoanalytic process.* New York: Guilford.

Werner, E. E., & Smith, R. L. (1982). *Vulnerable but invincible.* New York: McGraw-Hill.

Westen, D., Lohr, N., Silk, K., Gold, L., & Kerber, K. (1990). Object relations and social cognition in borderlines, major depressives, and normals: A TAT analysis. *Psychological Assessment: A Journal of Consulting and Clinical Psychology, 2,* 355–364.

Westen, D., Ludolph, P., Block, M. J., Wixom, J., & Wiss, F. C. (1990). Developmental history and object relations in psychiatrically disturbed adolescent females. *American Journal of Psychiatry, 147,* 1061–1068.

Winnicot, D. W. (1965). *The maturational processes and the facilitating environment.* New York: International Universities Press.

Wolf, E. S. (1983). Concluding statement. In A. Goldberg (Ed.), *The future of psychoanalysis: Essays in honor of Heinz Kohut.* New York: International Universities Press.

PART **FOUR**

Humanistic Approaches

CHAPTER
8

Client-Centered and Other Person-Centered Therapies

I had been working with a highly intelligent mother whose boy was something of a hellion. The problem was clearly her early rejection of the boy, but over many interviews I could not help her to this insight. I drew her out, I gently pulled together the evidence she had given, trying to help her see the pattern. But we got nowhere. Finally, I gave up. I told her that it seemed we had both tried, but we had failed, and that we might as well give up our contacts. She agreed. So we concluded the interview, shook hands, and she walked to the door of the office. Then she turned and asked, "Do you ever take adults for counseling here?" When I replied in the affirmative, she said, "Well then, I would like some help." She came to the chair she had left, and began to pour out her despair about her marriage, her troubled relationship with her husband, her sense of failure and confusion, all very different from the sterile "case history" she had given before. Real therapy began then, and ultimately it was very successful.

This incident was one of a number which helped me to experience the fact . . . that it is the client who knows what hurts, what directions to go, what problems are crucial, what experiences have been deeply buried. It began to occur to me that unless I had a need to demonstrate my own cleverness and learning, I would do better to rely upon the client for the direction of movement in the process. (Rogers, 1961, pp. 11–12)

Rogers's method brought it home that the decisions a person must make are inherently that person's own. No book knowledge enables another person to decide for anyone. That goes for life decisions and life-style as well as, moment by moment, what to talk about, feel into, struggle with. Another person might make a guess, but ultimately personal growth is from the inside outward. A process of change begins and moves in ways even the person's own mind cannot direct, let alone another person's mind. (Gendlin, 1984, p. 297)

These two quotes capture the "prime directive" of the client-centered approach to psychotherapy. The client-centered approach originated with Carl Rogers in the early 1940s, with the publication of his book, *Counseling and Psychotherapy.* In later years, Rogers and his colleagues began to broaden the application of client-centered principles from psychotherapy to areas such as education, medicine, and organizational psychology. In the last few years of his life, Rogers devoted his efforts to the promotion of world peace by facilitating group encounters between warring factions in different countries, such as between Blacks and Whites in South Africa, or Protestants and Catholics in Northern Ireland (see Chapter 13).

With the expansion of client-centered ideas to areas other than psychotherapy, the client-centered approach broadened to emphasize a general view of human nature, and Rogers renamed his approach **person-centered.** The person-centered philosophy has since spawned several new approaches to psychotherapy. In this chapter, we shall consider client-centered theory, the practice of client-centered therapy, and the practice of two other therapies derived from client-centered ideas, those of Eugene Gendlin's (1996) "experiential psychotherapy" and the "process-experiential" psychotherapy of Leslie Greenberg, Laura Rice, and Robert Elliott (1993).

MODEL OF THE PERSON

The fundamental concept of client-centered therapy is to respect and facilitate the self-propelled and self-generated growth process in the individual. Perhaps it is easier to explain this by describing some of the things a traditional client-centered therapist does not do. First, the therapist does not give specific advice about solving problems ("Why don't you try being honest with her?"). Second, the therapist does not give general advice on strategies for living ("You should live in the here and now"). Third, the therapist does not judge or condemn ("It is all right to get angry with your mother"; "You are a bad person for having gotten drunk"). Fourth, the therapist does not label ("You are a psychotic"). Fifth, the therapist does not develop a treatment plan for the client ("First we will work on your lack of assertiveness, then on your anxiety"). Sixth, the therapist does not interpret the meaning of the client's experience ("You are not really angry at me; you are really angry at your father").

The fundamental concept, that the therapist is to respect and facilitate the self-propelled growth process in the individual, is based on two premises. The first premise is that there are many possible personal realities. No one is in a position to judge someone else's reality as being less correct, more distorted, or less adequate than someone else's reality (Rogers, 1980). The second premise is that if the personal reality of an individual is respected by others and a basic trust is demonstrated toward that person, then a self-propelled growth process will move in a positive, life-affirming direction.

Multiple Realities

Most people believe that somewhere "out there" is "a" reality, and ultimately, there is one correct way of viewing it. For instance, most of us would agree with the Freudian view that people misperceive and distort reality from time to time. Certainly we would think that a person who thought that people on television talk shows were secretly talking about him or who saw things no one else did was distorting reality.

At the same time, most people are aware that there are different ways of experiencing reality. Is there, for instance, a "correct" way of experiencing anchovy pizza? We are personally convinced that those who like anchovy pizza are distorting reality, but they would probably say the same about us. It is clear that people accept differences in tastes in music, clothing, and food, and in preferences for hobbies, choice of careers, and so on.

However, different cultures have different ideas about how people should live. Although they may accept differences within limits, they do have ideas about what is appropriate, or correct, in different settings. For instance, there are very few settings in our culture in which it is correct, or even acceptable, to be nude. The list of "correct" and "incorrect" ways to live is quite extensive and includes both moral and legal rules.

Thus, while people recognize that there are variations in how individuals experience certain aspects of reality, they believe that everyone should experience some aspects the same way, the "correct" way. If someone does not experience one of these aspects in that way, they are said to be "distorting" reality or are "out of touch." Many of Freud's notions are based on this idea. For instance, the concept of transference assumes that patients distort their perceptions of the psychoanalyst by transferring onto the analyst feelings they had toward their parents. The defense mechanisms are also Freudian concepts that include the idea of distortion or misperception of reality. Cognitive therapy (see Chapter 12) also includes the idea that client problems are based on distortion of reality. A person's depression may be a result of an overfocus on the negative, for instance.

Rogers argued that there are multiple realities. To believe that someone is out of touch with reality or is distorting it is to believe that there is a correct way of viewing reality. Rogers believed that reality is relative to each person's point of view and, therefore, there is no possible way for any human to determine which is the "correct" view, if indeed there is a correct view. Rogers was therefore a "constructivist" (we discuss constructivism in more detail in Chapter 14).

This premise sounds simple, but it can lead to disturbing questions. Must we respect the reality of a Hitler? What about a woman who believed her child was possessed by the devil and threw her out of a tenth-story window? To deal with this issue, we will turn to Rogers's second premise.

The Meaning of Acceptance

What about respecting the reality of a Hitler or the woman who killed her child? If we trust the experience of all clients, could the therapist not end up supporting and facilitating murder, child abuse, rape, robbery, or other acts most of us see as negative? Rogers's (1967) answer to this is that the self-actualization or growth process is positive:

> I find it significant that when individuals are prized as persons, the values they select do not run the full gamut of possibilities. I do not find, in such a climate of freedom, that a person comes to value fraud and murder and thievery. (p. 26)

Rogers asserted that individuals who are prized and trusted will naturally choose "prosocial" values. He believed this because he believed that there was an internal process, called the actualization process, which would unfold in positive, prosocial directions *if* given the proper interpersonal conditions.

Rogers believed that accepting and trusting others led to their growing by moving toward more concern and caring for others, not merely toward self-actualization. What does it mean to prize, trust, or accept another's experience? Does this mean the therapist should agree with the way clients view the world, or support and positively reinforce any behavior? What if the therapist disagrees with the clients' views and sees their behavior as destructive?

For Rogers, to accept or trust another's reality does not mean to agree with it or approve of it. It means to acknowledge nonjudgmentally that it is what the other actually perceives. Put another way, an accepting attitude means listening nonjudgmentally. A patient (labeled paranoid schizophrenic by the hospital) may say that the police are always following him around in helicopters and that he is planning to retaliate by blowing up the police station. Does acceptance mean saying "I agree with you. Go to it"? No. It means acknowledging that the client really does experience the police as out to get him. Wanting to blow up the police station is a logical (but not reasonable!) outcome of the way the client is experiencing the world. Either agreeing with the client or telling him that he is wrong or crazy would be making a judgment.

But as the therapist does not agree that the police are out to get him and certainly does not want him to blow up the police station, what does he or she do? Rogers distinguished between accepting another's way of experiencing the world and accepting his or her behavior. A parent can accept and understand a child's desire to stick her finger in a flame (it is bright, it is pretty, the child is curious), while certainly not allowing the child to go through with the act. Thus, one can respect and accept another's experience of the world while not supporting or encouraging certain behaviors that might flow from it. An example of a lack of acceptance would be a parent who not only stops a child from putting her finger in the flame, but tells the child she is wrong or bad for even wanting to do this.

A therapist might want to go further than restraining destructive behavior and express disagreement with the client's experiencing. How is this done? Eugene Gendlin (1967) suggests that therapists can express a viewpoint if they offer it as their own. They would not say, "You are wrong" or "You are crazy for seeing the police as dangerous," but they might say, "I don't agree with you. I don't see the police as out to get you." The latter way of expressing a viewpoint implies a respect for and acknowledgment of the client's perspective that the former does not.

In sum, the prime directive of client-centered therapy is to accept and respect the experience of the client. This means acknowledging that there are multiple possible ways of viewing reality. Acceptance requires neither approval of the client's perspective or actions nor agreement with them.

Because of his emphasis on respecting the world view of each individual client, Rogers was against labels. He preferred that the therapist relate to the client as another person rather than as a "schizophrenic" or an "obsessive-compulsive." Psychiatric labels carry the implication that there is something "wrong" with the person (e.g., a "borderline personality disorder"). In addition to being judgmental, labels tend to pigeonhole and categorize. Therefore, they may blind the therapist to the uniqueness of the individual.

Personal Constructs and Values

Personal constructs is a term borrowed from George Kelly (1955). Kelly's idea was that people organize their lives in terms of their constructs, or concepts, about people, events, and even physical reality. Values can be considered a subset of constructs that have a positive or negative component. People have private values about what constitutes attractive physical appearance and how important physical appearance is, what constitutes a good romantic partner and and how important it is to have a romantic partner. They have moral values about killing, telling the truth, and stealing. They have conventional values about being a good member of society, driving on the right side of the road, and wearing clothes in public. Examples of personal constructs and values are (1) I tend to be a hardworking person (a construct about the self); (2) I believe Carl Rogers's ideas about human nature are wrong; (3) That person is a rat!; (4) People who don't look at you while they are talking are trying to hide something; (5) It is wrong to feel angry toward one's parents.

Congruent with his belief in multiple realities, Rogers believed it is important that people hold their personal constructs and values tentatively. He said that in the early stages of therapy, "personal constructs are rigid, and unrecognized as being constructs, but are thought of as facts" (1961, p. 134), but later, "the ways in which experience is construed are much loosened" (1961, p. 141). Finally, in the highest stage of development, "personal constructs are tentatively reformulated, to be validated against further experience, but even then, to be held loosely" (1961, p. 153).

To put it another way, Rogers seemed to be advocating that people act like good scientists in regard to their personal beliefs and treat personal constructs as hypotheses, rather than as fixed, objective facts. Values and beliefs about themselves and others are all to be treated as imperfect formulations about reality. As with scientific theories, they may be mistaken, and people must be open to challenging even their most deeply held values if they run into experiences that call them into question. This does not mean one cannot be committed to a set of values or personal constructs. Scientists may be committed to a point of view, but still hold open the possibility that future experience may prove them wrong.

To hold personal constructs tentatively means to move away from rigid, absolute "shoulds" (Rogers, 1961, p. 168). If individuals see their values as fixed, unchanging facts, then they must follow them. They have no choice. Rogers wanted people to choose their values on the basis of what makes sense to them, not to adopt values because some authority said that is how one should be. He wanted individuals to challenge and test their values to see if they make sense. Chosen values lose their "should-like" quality; they become something the person wants to do because they make sense to the person. Rogers believed values are meaningful only if so chosen.

Process Orientation

Rogers saw fully functioning individuals as process oriented. This has two meanings. To be process oriented means to see life as a process of becoming and to focus on doing. People are creatures whose nature is characterized by change, which means that the fully functioning person is continually open to the reevaluation of values, goals, and attitudes about life. In this regard, the individual does not even have a fixed "self." As the individual grows and changes, more complex, differentiated, and organized forms of self-organization evolve. In some important sense, you are not the same person you were when you were 14 years old, and your attitudes, values, and self-concept have undergone some alteration to reflect this change. Of course, there are probably also many continuities. For instance, perhaps you valued achievement at age 14 and still do. But your view of what achievement is has probably altered (perhaps from being a rock star or a famous athlete to getting a good job as a psychologist). Further, you have probably been learning to coordinate your striving for achievement with other aims and goals (such as maintaining a relationship, or pursuing a personally meaningful avocation such as music or drama). Therefore, while you are still "the same" in many ways, you are also different.

A process orientation also involves focusing attention on the doing of things rather than on their outcomes (Rogers, 1961, p. 171). Being overly focused on the outcome of actions can lead to excessive preoccupation with self-evaluation. People are inclined to evaluate themselves in terms of success or failure: "I am a good person" if I succeed; "I am a bad person" if I fail. This excessive preoccupation with evaluation draws attention away from the process of doing and prevents people from investing all their energies in the doing of the activity. Paradoxically, by focusing on how well they are succeeding, they may increase their odds of failure. This does not mean they do not have to try to do things well. For instance, to play a guitar, you have to finger the right chords. But if you are worried about the final outcome, that is, whether you will be judged a success or a failure, you are actually drawing attention away from the doing (from the moment-to-moment business of fingering the right chords), and as a result, you may do poorly. From Rogers's perspective, people should focus on what they did "wrong" not to evaluate (I was bad), but only to learn how to improve.

People who are overly concerned about the outcomes of their actions are probably concerned with whether they are good or bad people. To ask whether "I am good or bad" or whether "I have good traits or bad traits" is to treat yourself as if you have a fixed self. From a Rogerian perspective, it is no better to have a fixed positive self-concept than to have a fixed negative self-concept. Fully functioning individuals would have no fixed beliefs about themselves at all and in this sense may not even think about their "self" at all. In other words, if you never worry about whether your successes or failures mean you are good or bad and if you focus on how you are doing this task at this moment, then you are concerned with learning from your success or failure, but not whether you are good or bad.

Internality, Authority, and Individualism

Rogers's emphasis on individual views of reality led him to reject authority. No one possesses the correct answers as to how others should live their lives. This includes parents, the school system, society at large, and religion. Does this mean people should not ever listen to authority? No. But they should not accept what authorities say simply because they are the authorities. People must always take responsibility for listening to and evaluating any idea, no matter what its source, to see if it makes sense to them. Adopting an idea only because a teacher, parent, religious leader, or therapist says it is so may lead to conflict between the adopted value and what a person feels. Fully functioning individuals are autonomous, self-directed, and congruent, that is, their behavior arises from a chosen set of values that are congruent, or in accord with, their perceptions and experience.

Recently, some client-centered therapists have argued that Rogers's emphasis on individualism and autonomy is a value-laden reflection of Western, masculine world values, and is not in keeping with the values of many other cultures in the world, or with the values and experience of females in Western culture (Holdstock, 1990; O'Hara, 1992). These writers are part of a recent intellectual trend that argues that Western psychology's emphasis on the importance of individualism, autonomy, self-direction, having firm self-boundaries, directing oneself from within, and being separate reflects certain cultural values rather than reflecting truth about the nature of human beings. They point out that in many other cultures, the boundary of the self is fluid, is not fixed where the individual's body ends, and often extends to include one's family and even one's social group. In many cultures "I" am my family or my group. Behavior is a product of a field of forces, of which the individual is a part, rather than emerging primarily from processes within the individual. These authors would argue that being influenced by others is a natural part of being human. One's sense of self is intimately linked to one's relationships, and the idea of a separate, autonomous self may be a myth. For them, freedom to be oneself would mean finding oneself within the matrix of one's relationships with others, rather than by separating oneself from such a matrix.

This view paradoxically fits with other aspects of Rogers's views while contradicting his emphasis on individuality and autonomy. Rogers held a "field" view of human functioning, and Rogers himself certainly believed that optimal functioning included care and respect for the uniqueness and empowerment of all people. That is, he believed that people's behavior arose from a field of forces (see the related views of Gestalt therapy, Chapter 9, and systems theory, Chapter 14), of which factors inside the person are only a part. Yet, in his desire to support and respect the uniqueness of individuals, he sometimes wrote as if we could completely separate ourselves from the influence of others.

To put these ideas together, some modern person-centered theorists would hold that becoming oneself only has meaning when it happens in the context of continuous dialogue, interaction with, and concern and respect for others. The trick is to "be oneself" and be interdependent on others, to be both "I" and "We" at the same time.

EXPERIENCING

As noted above, the fully functioning person holds constructs tentatively, does not adopt them just because they are offered by an authority, and continually evaluates them against his or her own experience to see if they make sense. But what is this "experience" against which values and constructs are checked?

You may have heard that it is good to "get in touch with feelings." Often, client-centered therapy is seen as emphasizing this process, and one of the techniques of client-centered therapy is called *reflection of feelings.* Yet actually, it is more accurate to say that client-centered therapists want us to "listen to our experience."

Freud was the first to point out that an affective component seems to be necessary for psychotherapy to work. This is not surprising, since problems are frequently based on the fact that bodily or emotive responses are incongruent with intellectual beliefs. You may feel like eating, though intellectually you decide you should lose weight. Or you might intellectually decide it would be good for you to study, but you find yourself wanting to watch TV. Since the bodily or affective level seems to be so integrally involved in personal problems, it is not surprising that psychotherapy must involve it in some way. Clearly, if we were able to decide intellectually what was good for us and always and easily put it into operation, few therapists would be needed (see Chapter 16). But exactly how the emotive or bodily component plays a role in psychotherapy and mental health is open to debate. For Freud, it was a matter of "getting in touch with" primitive childhood fantasies that carry an emotional charge. In other therapies, such as primal therapy (Janov, 1970), it is a matter of getting in touch with a buried reservoir of pain and then expressing and discharging it. In many existential or humanistic approaches, it is a matter of "getting in touch with feelings," which means being willing to acknowledge and label one's anger, sadness, or fear.

Client-centered therapy, based primarily on Gendlin's theory of experiencing (Gendlin, 1969), has a somewhat different view of the role of the affective component. Experiencing is a broader construct than "emotion." People are said to experience feelings. The goal of client-centered therapy is to help clients become able to experience feelings and to listen to their experience. In the process of experiencing a feeling, it is more important to listen to the experience of the feeling than to the feeling itself.

Experiential Knowing

What is experience? That's a difficult question, and perhaps we can begin to answer it by appealing to your "experience." Let us break down "knowing," or acquiring of knowledge, into two components. The first is intellectual and verbal. This is the kind of knowing you are engaged in right now. You are reading words and thinking about what they mean. The second kind of knowing is experiential. This is knowing that seems more visceral, gut level, sensory, and nonverbal. The difference is not hard to illustrate. Reading a description of being kissed romantically is not the same as experiencing being kissed romantically. There is a kind of "knowing" about being kissed romantically that is beyond what can be conveyed in words. In fact, if one were to try to describe what it feels like to be kissed romantically, the words would come from the experience. They are attempts to verbally encode the experience and, as such, they can never do more than convey part of it. What one knows about being kissed romantically at an experiential level will always be more than one can put into words.

The nonverbal, bodily way of knowing includes the processing of sensory and muscular information. Emotions are bodily events and may be particularly important guides to bodily ways of knowing. However, we know more things in an experiential or bodily way than emotions. We can know how we feel, but we also know how things taste, how some things feel when we touch them, and how it feels to know how to play the guitar.

If you were asked to describe what it feels like to be kissed romantically, you would probably try to describe the bodily sensations that are associated with the experience. You might use metaphors and analogies: "It feels like you are melting for a moment," "It feels like two parts being joined together," "There is a sense of quickening, or excitement, a sense of letting go." Similarly, in describing being rejected, you might say, "It feels like I was kicked in the gut" or "It feels like I was thrown out the door." Again, you are using metaphorical language to try to "capture" that set of bodily sensations that were your experience of being rejected.

"Getting in touch with feelings" for a client-centered therapist, then, means listening to and trying to capture the felt meanings of experience. It does not mean identifying emotions, though that may be a useful route into experiential knowing. More important is the nonverbal sense of what objects and events are felt as meaning. If you feel loved, that probably includes a whole set of experiences you have shared with the person who you feel loves you. If you feel anger, that is because you are experiencing the interaction with another person as anger provoking. Thus, paying attention to feelings is important because they are an indication of how you are experiencing a particular situation or relationship.

What is true for each individual is what that individual knows experientially. This does not mean it is objectively true or experientially true for other people. For instance, you may know that you experience eating anchovy pizza as unpleasant, even if it is judged good by others. Since there is little societal pressure to like anchovy pizza, you are allowed to "follow your own feelings" in the matter. But what happens when an individual's experiential sense disagrees with something society holds to be objectively true and seems to care about? For instance, what if your experiential sense is that you care little about financial success, but society says you should care about it and evaluates you on the basis of it? Rogers seemed to believe that people will be affected more by their experiential sense than by their intellectual beliefs. If they do not actually "follow" their experiential sense, they will still be influenced by it in experiencing conflict between it and what they think they "should" do.

Did Rogers believe that people should always follow their experiential sense? Remember, this is different from emotions. For instance, if I am feeling anger, does that mean I should express or act out my anger? No. To experience anger means to experience a situation as anger provoking. If I experience the situation as anger provoking, does that mean it is anger provoking? Again, the answer is no. That is certainly how I am construing the situation at an experiential level, but that does not necessarily mean my construction of the situation is objectively true. Yet, at the same time, I have little control over my experiencing the situation that way. The crucial thing is to listen to it. While it may be inaccurate in an objective sense, it is nevertheless how I am experiencing the situation at a gut level. Furthermore, it may be correct, because I may have picked up cues from the situation at a gut level of which I was not consciously aware.

Listening means trying to capture the meaning of experience. For instance, you might say, "I feel you dislike me." There are some psychologists who would say that such a statement is inaccurate. Rather, you should say, "I think you dislike me." However, to say "I feel you dislike me" is to say that your experience around this person is like your experience around people who have later proven to dislike you. And you may experience this even though intellectually you have no evidence that this person dislikes you. You could express this as "I think you like me, but I feel as if you don't."

It is against this experiential sense of things that the individual's personal constructs are to be checked to see if they "make sense." While Rogers did not claim that a person's experiential sense is always correct, he did believe that dialogue between the conceptual and experiential levels was necessary. These two levels are different, equally valuable "voices" or perspectives, and both need to be listened to and integrated to make the best possible decisions for the self. A person may be able to resolve incongruence by listening to the experiential level to try to grasp the meanings implicit in it. Gendlin suggests that such a process leads ultimately to an integration of the intellectual and experiential in regard to whatever issue is at hand.

PSYCHOPATHOLOGY

From the client-centered perspective, psychopathology occurs when individuals do not hold constructs tentatively, do not listen to experience, and, as a result, are not able to creatively grow and change. When individuals are functioning optimally and encounter a problem, failure, or a personal setback, they are able to listen to their experience, search for what is new or different in this situation compared to their old constructs, and use that information to creatively learn and evolve. In other words, they are able to function more intelligently, and both Zimring (1990) and Van Balen (1990) have argued that client-centered therapy works by helping individuals function more intelligently.

When people proceed dysfunctionally, they are unable to listen to their experience, and so cannot discern what is new and different in this situation, and therefore cannot learn and form creative new ways of dealing with life's problems. This happens because such people experience incongruence between what they think ought to be and what they experience. Ultimately, all forms of psychopathology—anxiety, depression, alcoholism, rigid behavior, psychotic episodes—result from such incongruence.

Thus, psychopathology results from not accepting or listening to that important source of information about how one finds oneself in the world—one's experience. The case of Janet is an example. Janet appeared to be distant, unemotional, and unfriendly. She was planning to be a doctor. Then, one day she was very different. She was friendly and warm. She said that she had finally admitted to herself that she did not want to be a doctor and had changed her major to art. From a Rogerian perspective, Janet had adopted the ideal that she should be a doctor. In order to pursue this goal, she had consistently denied her own feelings and her own experiential sense of what she enjoyed, what felt meaningful to her. It affected her whole personality.

The above should not be construed to mean that you should never take a class that you find boring. Even though a class may be boring, it might be experientially meaningful to take it anyway, because you know at a feeling level that the class fits your goals. Rather, you should pay attention to the experience of a class as boring to see what it means. Does it mean that this class is boring, or is it that you are feeling bored with the whole field? If it is the latter, you may wish to reevaluate your career goals.

Why do people not listen to their experience? Rogers said that this occurs because in childhood, people are taught that their acceptance or worth as individuals is dependent on their meeting someone else's standards. Children are born with a primitive and undifferentiated **organismic valuing process** through which they directly experience what is meaningful or life-enhancing for them. The valuing process will grow and differentiate if children are allowed to stay in touch with it. However, parents and schools teach rules as to what children should be and think, and the question of whether those rules make sense to the children is never raised. In fact, if children protest that the rules do not make sense, they may well be punished.

For Rogers, emotional disturbance is caused by child-rearing practices that do not convey positive regard for the child. By putting conditions of worth on the child, the parent forces the child to ignore its organismic valuing and thereby creates incongruence. It is this incongruence that causes trouble in development. Incongruence occurs when the child does not trust or listen to her own internal capabilities for experiencing and making judgments about what are the best and most effective things to do and ways to be. A condition of worth is basically a message conveyed to the child that "you as a whole person only have worth when you conform to my ideas of what you should be."

Rogers thought that the organismic valuing process is the innate way that humans have to learn positive or prosocial behavior and that it can become a reliable, valid, and important source of information and guide to action. Humans find it innately rewarding or reinforcing to be kind to each other, to relate to each other, to be affectionate and helpful, and so forth. It is only when the child learns to ignore organismic valuing that behavior goes awry.

Rogers did not advocate letting children follow only those rules or perceptions that make sense to them. For instance, Rogers was not saying that the child has the right to stick her finger in a flame because the rule against doing it doesn't make sense to her. However, insisting that the child follow the rule should be done without telling her that she is bad or wrong or stupid for wanting to stick her hand in the flame. Even if there are occasions when children have to conform to a rule that does not make sense to them, at the very least, the parent tries to convey positive regard and not to invalidate the child's experience.

If children are told that their experiential sense is bad or wrong often enough, they will begin to distrust it, perhaps even to deny it. They will become "other-directed" and depend on authorities to tell them what is correct. They will adopt rules and perspectives in a rigid, either/or manner and lose the ability to be spontaneous or creative, and to effectively self-regulate and evolve. Then, when life poses challenges to them, they are unable to rely on their own internal resources for self-change and growth, and may experience various forms of psychological breakdown instead.

PSYCHOTHERAPY

Therapeutic Process

The process of psychotherapy for Rogers is the restoration of the individual's ability to use all of him- or herself to creatively and intelligently cope with life's challenges. This occurs primarily through the process of self-acceptance. If clients can adopt a nonjudgmental, self-accepting attitude toward themselves, then they can learn to tune into their experiential sense of things. As this occurs, they hold constructs more tentatively and become more flexible, less structure-bound, and more autonomous.

This view of therapy does not mean that clients will automatically or magically find answers to all their questions. For Rogers, life is a continual growth process in which people are periodically challenged to develop and expand their skills in living. "Self-actualized" people are not perfect, are not always happy, are not even always congruent with themselves. Rather, they are people who accept the fact that they will be periodically challenged, and at those times, are willing to reevaluate their personal constructs. They are willing to face the anxiety and disorganization attendant on the struggle to solve a new life problem and move ahead. Rather than "self-actualized," it would be more accurate to call them "self-actualizing." Rogers said, "I believe they would consider themselves insulted if they were described as 'adjusted,' and they would regard it as false if they were described as 'happy' or 'contented,' or even 'actualized'" (Rogers, 1961, p. 186). They know they will not do everything perfectly and that there will be times of unhappiness. But because they view life as a process rather than expecting it to be some fixed state of bliss, they try to learn from their mistakes and to live with the unhappy times in order to move forward.

The ability to trust all of their inner life, feelings as well as thoughts, does not mean that they magically find the right answer to life dilemmas. Rogers said, "[One's] organism would not by any means be infallible. It would always give the best possible answer for the available data, but sometimes data would be missing . . ." (Rogers, 1961, p. 191). A person may feel confusion because a major life decision, such as getting divorced, must include many pros and cons. If the individual can experience the pros and cons (I enjoy being around her, but I enjoy not having to answer to someone), then he can have a direct experiential sense of the whole conflict. But that experiential sense will not be one clear feeling, such as "leave" or "stay." Rather, it will include the whole experience of the situation and how one experiences one's goals. Gendlin says the person experiences the problem as a kind of "all that."

Tuning into one's whole inner experience of the problem, then, means focusing one's attention on all the "inner voices" that constitute the different sides of the problem and listening empathically to all of them. As a person does this, different meanings separate out, and the person begins to get in touch with how he experientially weighs components of the dilemma (My enjoyment of her feels more important than my desire for freedom). In addition, as the person attends to how each component of the dilemma feels, a kind of constructive process takes place. According to Gendlin, as the person attempts to capture experiential meanings in words or images, there is a kind of momentary experiential resolution of some aspect of the problem and a "felt give" or sense of relief. Ultimate problem resolution is made up of many such momentary bits of integration, building on one another. Thus, for Gendlin and Rogers, one important aspect of therapy could be said to be a creative process of synthesizing new, more complex, and more integrated ways of perceiving and experiencing the self and the world. Resolution of particular problems flows from this, often by finding creative ways of synthesizing what appear to be "either/or" aspects of experience into "and"s. For instance, a client may feel "either I stay single in order to have as sexually free a life as I want and lose the positive aspects of being married, or I get married and have those positive aspects, and lose the freedom to have multiple sexual relationships." This may seem like an irresolvable conflict between two mutually contradictory choices. However, as the client listens to his experience, he may find an "and" between the two apparently conflicting poles. He may discover that there are ways to incorporate a feeling of diversity within his marriage in such a way that his needs for the adventure of playing around are satisfied.

The creative aspect of client-centered therapy needs to be emphasized. The goal of the process really is to liberate and facilitate the client's creativity. Clients find creative new solutions to their life dilemmas that neither therapist nor client could have predicted in advance. Following work of the Nobel prize–winning chemist Ilya Prigogine (Prigogine & Stengers, 1984) who found that systems threatened with disorganization can often spontaneously leap to a higher level of organization, client-centered therapists believe that individuals who are struggling with problems in their lives can, under the proper therapeutic conditions, evolve new, more integrated, creative syntheses that help them find new ways of handling problems.

Client-centered therapists therefore do not presume to know what the proper solutions are for their clients. Rather, they believe in providing optimal conditions under which the clients' own creative capacities for self-regulation and self-evolution can operate. For instance, sexual abuse is currently being seen as one important cause of some adult psychological problems, such as borderline personality disorder (Briere, 1989). There are many therapists who, if they believe that their client has been sexually abused, believe that therapy must focus on the abuse as the major issue. Thus, the therapist makes the decision for the client as to what needs to be worked on in order for the client to improve.

In contrast, a client-centered therapist seeing an abuse victim would work with whatever problem the client wanted to work on, in the belief that as the client's own self-creating and self-restoring capacities get mobilized, the client will spontaneously begin to deal with the abuse himself when it is necessary for him to face it in order to creatively move forward.

To sum up, the process of psychotherapy includes two elements. First, clients learn to listen to and accept their experience. As they do this, they become more flexible and more self-directed and begin to hold constructs tentatively. Second, the acceptance of all inner experience mobilizes the client's own creative, self-evolutionary, self-restorative capacities, allowing the client to forge creative new solutions to her life problems, and to develop new, more integrative and organized ways of dealing with life.

Role of the Therapist

There has been an evolution in the role of the client-centered therapist (Hart, 1970). In the 1940s, the therapist was to remain relatively anonymous and create a warm, accepting climate in which the client would feel free to engage in self-exploration. In the 1950s, therapist empathy was stressed. The therapist was not only to convey warmth, but also to make an active effort to understand the client's subjective experience. A technique called *reflection of feelings* was developed, in which the therapist mirrors back to the client the therapist's understanding of the client's subjective experience. The stereotypical picture of the client-centered therapist is based on this period.

In the late 1950s and early 1960s, there was a further evolution. Rogers (1957) published a paper suggesting that it is the therapeutic relationship itself that is therapeutic. More important than the therapist's professional training, theoretical point of view, or techniques are certain personal qualities. Therapists who have these qualities will be effective; those who do not have them will not be. This bold and far-reaching statement implied that a person could be a psychiatrist, a psychologist, or a barber and be an effective therapist if the person had certain crucial personal qualities. It also implied that the crucial qualities were independent of whether the person was a Freudian, Rogerian, Jungian, or behaviorist.

What are these personal qualities? Rogers listed several in 1957, but they have generally been reduced to three major groups: nonpossessive warmth, empathic understanding, and genuineness (we use the names given them by Truax and Carkhuff, 1967). We will discuss each quality in turn and try to identify its therapeutic value.

Nonpossessive Warmth   **Nonpossessive warmth** is a general name for a quality or set of qualities called, variously, unconditional positive regard, prizing, acceptance, respect, caring, or even nonpossessive love (Rogers, 1965). These all refer to the following: First, the therapist must positively prize or care for the client. Second, this caring must be nonpossessive, a quality related to the idea of acceptance. Third, the therapist must not only care for clients in a nonpossessive way, but must also treat them with respect as autonomous individuals, equal in value to the therapist.

Caring is probably therapeutic because it builds trust and is a motivator. Clients are more likely to reveal themselves to, take chances with, and try hard for someone they feel cares about them.

Nonpossessiveness is related to acceptance. Possessive caring is caring with an attempt to control the other. Being nonpossessive in therapy means acknowledging clients' autonomy, accepting their choices, and not imposing one's will on them. As we have stated before, acceptance does not mean approval. It means responding to others nonevaluatively, acknowledging and listening to them nonjudgmentally. Possessive parents or lovers are always either approving or disapproving of the behavior of the child or of the romantic partner. Nonpossessiveness contributes to therapeutic effectiveness because most people are averse to feeling controlled or judged by another. Feeling controlled or judged may motivate clients to rebel or make them feel unsafe.

Respect for clients' individuality and autonomy goes hand in hand with nonpossessive acceptance. The therapist's attitude of respect reinforces clients' belief in themselves as capable of making decisions for themselves. Some parents seem to care for their children in a way that does not include respect. For example, by being overprotective, they convey the message that the children are incompetent to take care of themselves. Respect also implies trust in the client. An attitude of trust should increase the clients' trust in themselves and in the therapist, with a resultant lowering of defenses. As respect and trust increase, so will clients' openness to communications from the therapist.

Empathic Understanding   The term "empathy" has many different meanings in the psychological literature (Bohart & Greenberg, 1997). For some it refers to an emotional sharing between two people. Others believe themselves to be empathic if they are warm, concerned, and showing that they care. However, for client-centered therapy, empathy is primarily a matter of *understanding* the other person's point of view. Empathic understanding involves the ability to enter clients' worlds and to see things from their frame of reference. This is more difficult than it may seem. To be accurately empathic, one must be able to *decenter,* a concept borrowed from the work of Piaget (Cowan, 1978). Decentering is the ability to step outside of one's own perspective and, through imagination, guess at how things would look and feel from someone else's perspective. For adults, it is relatively easy to imagine how someone else is seeing the physical world. For instance, it is not hard for students to imagine what the classroom looks like physically to the professor as he or she lectures, even though the students are not at the podium. It is quite another thing for students to imagine how a teacher is experiencing the lecture material and the classroom situation. The experiencing of any given situation is based on how the person is construing that situation, which is based on that person's prior experiences. Since everyone's experiences are different to some extent, it may be difficult for one person to guess how another is construing a situation. It may be relatively easier if the two people are similar in many ways (Henschel & Bohart, 1984). The greater the difference in prior experience, the greater the difficulty in achieving empathy. Yet true empathic ability is probably demonstrated more in situations when a person is trying to grasp the experience of someone quite different (Henschel & Bohart, 1984), perhaps even somebody he does not like, approve of, or agree with. This also means that therapists must be careful not to mistake recalling their own experiences for having an empathic response. True empathy is not how you would feel if you were in the client's shoes, but an attempt to guess at how she feels, that is, how you would feel if you were she, in her shoes.

How does a therapist "be" empathic? We have described empathy as an ability, but it is not something that one simply "has." Rather, empathy is an active process, a skill that must be practiced. Rarely will a person have a magical flash of insight in which the person just "knows" how another is experiencing the world. Usually, a person can achieve that knowledge only through a laborious process of listening, adjusting guesses, and listening some more. Here is how it goes. The client has said that he has been dumped by his girlfriend. You make a guess at what he is experiencing, based on your own experience in such situations and your general knowledge of the experience of others in such situations. You state your guess, and then you listen to see if you have guessed right. You will know from the client's response. This response will be not only what the client says, but his body language. If the client says, "Yes, that's it!" then you probably hit it. If the client hesitates and says, "Yes, that must be it," then you know you didn't. If your guess is accurate, the client will know right away. It will "feel right" to him. If the client has to hesitate, then at an experiential level, what you said did not feel right, even though at an intellectual level the client decides it "must be right." So you listen, and based on what cues the client gives back to you, you make another guess, and then you listen further.

Achieving empathic understanding can take time because it requires clarifying communication between the therapist and the client. Empathy involves learning the client's private language. For example, when the client says "My girlfriend dumped me," you may take that to mean "I feel rejected," but perhaps the meaning the client attaches to that statement and wants to convey to you is "People always mistreat me." Therefore, empathy is normally achieved over a period of time in therapy. Empathy will develop more quickly if therapists are willing to suspend judgment and their own private way of interpreting words and behaviors.

Reflection of feeling is a technique that was developed in the 1950s as a means for the therapist to convey empathic understanding of the client back to the client. A reflection may start out "It sounds like you feel . . ." or "You're saying that . . ." but it may also simply be an empathic restatement of what the therapist thinks the client is experiencing. Reflection of feeling is actually a misnomer. Several studies have shown that Carl Rogers only referred to feelings about 25% of the time in his reflections, and even then his purpose was to check his understanding of the client's experience, not to empathize at a feeling level. Most often, his reflections focused on meaning. A far more accurate name for the technique would be "reflection of the meaning in subjective experience." To give an example:

CLIENT: I failed the test! Boy, does that screw things up! I'm behind on my other classes, but now I'm going to have to devote extra time to this one.
REFLECTION (OF FEELING):   Oh no! It feels so threatening to have failed that test. And now to have to study extra, that's so frustrating and overwhelming!
REFLECTION (OF MEANING):   Failing the test means you're going to have to change your plans, and devote more time than you would have to that class, and you're behind already.
REFLECTION (OF FEELING AND MEANING):   It almost sounds like you're feeling a little desperate. How can I get caught up on my other classes, and devote extra time to this one?

Notice that the reflections do more than repeat what the client just said. Often, people think of reflecting as nothing but parroting, as in the following parody:

CLIENT: I'm feeling depressed today.
COUNSELOR: You're feeling depressed today.

CLIENT: I think I'll kill myself.
COUNSELOR: You think you'll kill yourself.
CLIENT: I'm going to jump out the window.
COUNSELOR: You're going to jump out the window.
CLIENT: I'm jumping out the window.
COUNSELOR: You're jumping out the window.
SOUND FROM BELOW: Plop!
COUNSELOR: Plop!

Good reflections do not simply repeat back to the client what the client has already said. At the very minimum, they paraphrase. For instance, a simple paraphrasing of the client's statement about being depressed might be, "You're feeling down today." Most reflections, however, go beyond what the client actually said to try to capture more of the flavor of the client's experience than the client put into words. The presumption is that the client's words summarize or convey a fraction of the client's total experience in the moment. Good reflections guess at what some related aspects of that experience might be. In the examples of reflections, each one goes beyond the client statement to make a guess at what the client is experiencing at the moment but did not say. For instance, the first reflection presents a guess that the client is feeling frustrated and overwhelmed, although this was not stated by the client. The reflection is a step in the constructive activity of empathic understanding. If the client responds to the reflection with "Boy! That's for sure!" the therapist guessed correctly and may have moved closer to the therapeutic goal of being able to guess what it feels like to be that client. If the client says, "No, it's more like I'm feeling picked on by life. I'm being treated unfairly," then the therapist has also moved forward in gaining an understanding of the client's subjective world.

Reflection differs from interpretation (see Chapter 6) in that while both guess at the meanings that underlie the client's statement, reflection tries to stay with meanings that are within the client's current awareness. Interpretation attempts to uncover hidden meanings of which the client is unaware. For instance, an interpretation to the client's statement about failing the test might be, "Is it possible that your failing the test means that you don't really like that class?"

Empathy and reflection are presumed to be therapeutic for the following reasons. First, empathy, along with warmth, creates a sense of trust. Second, feeling understood is often by itself therapeutic. Simply knowing that someone else can understand what they feel may make people feel less alone and more "normal." Third, empathy and reflection focus clients' attention on their inner experience. In effect, they train clients to listen to and to try to capture the meanings in their own experience. Thus empathy is directly training the skill Rogers believed is so important in living.

Genuineness   The third important quality for therapists to possess is genuineness. Other words associated with this quality include congruence, honesty, authenticity, openness, and self-disclosure. Genuine people are congruent. This means that their outer actions are congruent with some facet of their inner thoughts and feelings. Put another way, what they say and what they do are accurate reflections of some aspect

Using Reflection with Pets.

of what they are currently thinking and feeling. In this sense, they can also be called honest and authentic. However, genuineness must be distinguished from the terms openness and self-disclosure, although they are related. Self-disclosure and openness are more like things people do. They disclose their problems to another; they are open about private thoughts and feelings with one another. However, people can be genuine and not open or not self-disclosing. And people can self-disclose and be incongruent or phony. Suppose we asked you to tell us about your sexual fantasies. You might feel that it is none of our business. You might act congruently with that feeling and choose not to tell us. In that case, you are being genuine, but you are not being open and self-disclosing about your sexual fantasies. Conversely, you might feel it is none of our business, but because some psychologist told you that the healthy person is open and self-disclosing, you go against your feelings and tell us. In this case you are being open, but you are being incongruent and you are not being genuine or congruent.

People never express or act on everything they are thinking and feeling. They always select. While a professor lectures to a class, she may be simultaneously experiencing (1) a desire to communicate ideas on the class topic, (2) a concern that the students understand what is being said, (3) hunger, (4) anger at her landlord, and (5) dislike of the awful shirt the man in the first row is wearing. If the professor were to try to express or act on all these things, her behavior would be confused and confusing. Instead, she selects those parts of her experience relevant to the situation to express in behavior. It is relevant to act on a desire to communicate and on a concern for the students. It is irrelevant to interject "I'm hungry" or "That darn landlord!" or "That's an awful shirt!" Is the professor being phony because she does not say these things? No. She is being congruent, because what she does say and do is an accurate reflection of the part of her experience that is relevant to the situation. As we said before, people always select. We never act on or verbalize everything we're thinking and feeling. If we did, we would engage in unending monologues and no one else would get a word in edgewise.

While therapists should always be genuine, they should only selectively and judiciously self-disclose. Generally, they should self-disclose only when it is relevant to the therapeutic interaction. Then they need to self-disclose in ways that facilitate the therapeutic process. Gendlin (1968) states that when the therapist does self-disclose, it must be done in a way that is more growth-producing than self-disclosures made by "the person on the street." Many people in everyday life are "honest" in insensitive, critical, and disparaging ways. In therapy, the therapist must give feedback in a way that promotes growth. This includes making "I" statements instead of "you" statements ("I am uncomfortable with the way you are treating your child" versus "You are a terrible parent"), giving specific information in a nonblaming way, and often noting the positive as well as the negative.

Genuineness is therapeutic in combination with warmth and empathy because it promotes a genuinely positive, growth-oriented relationship in which clients can learn to trust and listen to themselves. In addition, self-disclosure appears to be therapeutic for several reasons. First, there is a modeling effect. If the therapist wishes the client to open up, then some gesture of opening up on the therapist's part might provide a model. The therapist is also modeling the idea that one doesn't have to be perfect. Second, by being genuine and by selectively self-disclosing, the therapist is demonstrating trust in the client ("Gee, the therapist trusts me enough to share some private things with me"). Third, self-disclosure can give immediate feedback to the client on the impact of his behavior. Fourth, self-disclosure can create a sense of empathy. Judiciously timed, selective self-disclosure about the therapist's own experiences can demonstrate empathy and understanding of the client's feelings. Fifth, if the therapist's self-disclosures are offered tentatively, this gives therapist and client the opportunity to explore together what is going on in the relationship and to clarify each other's perceptions.

RECENT DEVELOPMENTS IN PERSON-CENTERED THERAPIES

Rogers's statement that therapy is a function of the quality of the relationship, the emphasis on the qualities of warmth, empathy, and genuineness, and Gendlin's theory of experiencing changed the client-centered approach for many of its followers from a specific set of therapeutic techniques to a philosophy of therapy (Lietaer, 1990). Many therapists believed that they could use any technique—behavioral, gestalt, analytic—as long as they maintained the qualities of a good therapeutic relationship and as long as the technique was used only when it was experientially meaningful for the client. With this change, the client-centered approach became a model for the eclectic practice of therapy for many therapists. Hart (1970) discusses an informal study in which tapes of various client-centered therapists were identified by expert listeners as representing a range of other therapies, such as Adlerian or rational-emotive.

This shift from a specific way of practicing therapy to a general philosophy of the person, along with the application of Rogers's ideas to education, medicine, childrearing, and international relations, eventually resulted in Rogers's changing the name of his approach to "the person-centered approach." Person-centered theory holds to the following general hypotheses: First, there is a belief in the intrinsic potential of each person to creatively grow in life-enhancing directions. Each person is ultimately the expert on his or her own process of development, and the person-centered theorist has trust in each person's capacity for self-development, self-righting, and self-creation. Second, there is a belief that the provision of the three therapeutic conditions of warmth, empathy, and genuineness is most fundamental in providing the conditions under which this client capacity for self-growth can function. Within this general framework, a number of different approaches to psychotherapy have evolved. First, we shall discuss the evolution of different ways to practice client-centered therapy itself.

Traditional client-centered therapy is a nondirective process in which the therapist empathically listens to the client explore. The therapist may also self-disclose, but the major activity of the therapist is to empathically listen to and reflect the client's communications. The therapist is a companion on the client's journey, and it is believed that by being a good companion, the therapist helps the client alter that journey in more growthful directions. The therapist is nondirective in two important ways. First, the therapist does not direct the client to focus on specific content or kinds of issues. That is, the therapist does not direct the client to explore childhood, childhood abuse, family relationships, or the client's dysfunctional cognitions. Second, the therapist does not generally provide directions for how the client is to explore. That is, the therapist does not try to direct the process of therapy, either. The client chooses what to talk about, how to talk about it, when to shift to something else, when to focus on feelings, when to talk about thoughts, when to talk about the past, and so on. Ultimate faith is placed in the client's ability to feel his or her way into the right directions for creative growth and to explore in the manner that best suits the client.

Rogers's emphasis on the therapeutic conditions of warmth, empathy, and genuineness as necessary and sufficient for therapy to take place led many client-centered therapists to expand how they practiced. This was especially true because of the increased emphasis on therapist genuineness. If you as the therapist are listening to your client discuss his problems with assertion, and the thought crosses your mind that there is a method—assertion training—that might be of assistance to your client, and you keep that thought to yourself because you are trying to be "nondirective," then you might be acting ingenuinely. Thus, in the name of genuineness, therapists began to share some of their own thoughts on clients' issues when they were sensitively relevant to what the client was dealing with. This meant that the therapist might mention the possibility of assertion training to the client, for instance. Many client-centered therapists began to incorporate techniques and ideas from other approaches into their practice, though the stance of the therapist was not one of the expert "fixing" the client, but one of a "companion sharing with" the client.

With this shift, the old stereotype of all client-centered therapists as simply reflecting client feelings no longer held. Despite the shift toward a more active therapist role, client-centered therapists still held to the belief that it was ultimately the client who would choose what was good for him or her. The therapist was more like a "consultant" who offered empathy, genuineness, and warmth, as well as ideas, feedback, and suggestions. Below we consider two other approaches that are person-centered in their philosophy but are more active, directive, and structured than traditional client-centered therapy.

Gendlin's Experiential Psychotherapy

According to Eugene Gendlin (1996), therapy is effective when it impacts in a directly experiential manner. Gendlin and his colleagues (1967) studied the therapy process by rating samples of successful and unsuccessful therapy. They concluded that when therapy worked, the client was, on the average, engaging in an experiencing process, and when therapy did not work, the client was not.

For Gendlin and his colleagues, engaging in an experiencing process is the activity of focusing inwardly on felt experience, listening empathically to it, and letting words and concepts come from that experience. In other words, it is the process of listening to and articulating one's inner, felt meanings. Clients may explore their problems in intellectual, abstract ways that will have no concrete, felt, therapeutic effect. Or, they may explore by constantly referencing their own inner experiential reactions. This is when therapy happens.

The experiential psychotherapist, according to Gendlin, tries to guide the client to focus on her inner experiencing in a therapeutically productive way. What is talked about is not important. Rather, how the client is exploring is what is crucial. Does the client "feel" what he or she is talking about, and is the client able to refer inwardly to that "feel" and talk from that "feel"? Gendlin called the ability to do this "focusing" ability. He went on to develop a specific technique called **focusing** (Gendlin, 1996) to facilitate it. Focusing is a structured procedure in which clients silently refer inwardly, try to suspend intellectual analysis, and then quietly listen in order to sense or feel what their experience is saying to them. When words come from their experience, rather than being applied to their experience by intellectual thought from above, a felt shift in experienced organization occurs. Clients experience a sense of something coming more clearly into focus that they can feel is right for them. The focusing process is one of repeated steps. Clients may not get "the answer" to their problems all at once. However, over time, focusing leads to greater clarity about what is bothering them, with the development of a more subtle and differentiated way of responding to the problem.

Gendlin and his colleagues suggested that all therapists are being helpful when they facilitate such an experiencing process, be they psychoanalytic, cognitive, or behavioral. Therapists can use many different techniques to facilitate this experiencing process. They can respond empathically; they can self-disclose; they can use ideas and concepts from other theories, such as object relations theory or psychoanalysis; or they can use techniques from other approaches, such as gestalt and behavioral techniques. The only criterion is that the idea or technique not be imposed on the client, but only used if it is experientially meaningful for the client.

Gendlin's experiential therapy is one of the person-centered therapies because Gendlin believes that the therapist's warm, empathic, and genuine "being with" the client is fundamental. Gendlin trusts the client's own inner process to develop wise solutions. However, Gendlin is more directive than a traditional client-centered therapist in that he specifically responds in a manner designed to more efficiently facilitate the experiencing process.

Process-Experiential Psychotherapy

An important theoretical development in person-centered theory was the work of Wexler and others (Wexler & Rice, 1974) to apply an information-processing interpretation to client-centered therapy. Despite Rogers's emphasis on feelings, there has always been a cognitive, information-processing flavor to Rogers's theorizing. For instance, getting in touch with feelings is seen informationally:

> Often I sense that the client is trying to listen to himself, is trying to hear the *messages and meanings* which are being communicated by his own physiological reactions. . . . He comes to realize that his own inner reactions and experiences, the *messages* of his sense and viscera, are friendly. He comes to want to be close to his *inner sources of information.* (Rogers, 1961, p. 174, italics ours)

> This leads to the client's having access to all of the available data in the situation. . . . He could permit his total organism, his consciousness participating, to consider each stimulus, need, and demand, its relative intensity and importance, and out of this complex weighting and balancing, discover that course of action which would come closest to satisfying all his needs in the situation. (Rogers, 1961, p. 190)

Thus, the work of Wexler and his colleagues is an extension of an idea already implicit in Rogers's own work.

Wexler (1974) suggests that the therapist is a "surrogate information processor." What therapists do is direct clients' attention to ignored or neglected aspects of information (that is, feelings and experience), help clients sort out and differentiate relevant from irrelevant aspects of this and other information, and then help clients integrate the information into new and more effective cognitive structures for interacting with reality. Empathy responses are seen as active shapers and facilitators of information processing. They draw out the implications in what clients say, focus attention on selected aspects of client communication, and model and suggest ways of integrating or synthesizing differing themes in what clients say.

Following up on this work, Greenberg, Rice, and Elliott (1993) have recently developed a comprehensive integrative approach to psychotherapy called **process-experiential psychotherapy.** Their approach is an integration of basic person-centered theory with cognitive psychology and ideas from both Gestalt therapy (see Chapter

9) and Gendlin's experiential therapy. Their basic theory is that psychological problems occur because clients are unable to pay attention to the information available in their own emotional reactions. If clients are able to access emotions and emotional meanings, they will be able to reorganize the cognitive belief structures and the emotional patterns that have been guiding their dysfunctional reactions.

Process-experiential psychotherapists are systematic in how they intervene to help clients grow and change. They look for **therapeutic markers** to help them decide exactly how to intervene at a particular moment. A therapeutic marker is some kind of behavior exhibited by the client that signals or marks that the client is struggling with a particular kind of emotional problem or "task." The therapist then picks an intervention that will best help the client explore and resolve that particular emotional processing task.

One kind of marker is called a *problematic reaction point.* Clients who exhibit this marker talk about some kind of incident in which they have said or done something about which they feel self-critical. This marker leads to the use of the intervention called *evocative unfolding.* The therapist guides clients to explore the incident in vivid detail, using empathic reflections that are designed to be highly vivid and evocative of the experience of the scene itself. As clients are able to vividly reenter the scene, they discover the way they are viewing the situation that triggered their reaction. This helps clients resolve the problematic feelings. In addition, clients are able to reevaluate that way of construing things and change it if necessary. We consider this process in more detail under the heading of "task analysis" later on in this chapter.

A second kind of marker is the *split.* Here clients exhibit a split between a "want" and a "should." One part says "you should be studying" and the other part says "I don't want to study." The process-experiential therapist uses the gestalt "two-chair" technique (see Chapter 9) to help clients resolve the split. Clients role-play one side of the split, the "should" side, in one chair, then switch chairs and answer from the other side, the "I don't want to" side. As clients go back and forth, talking from each side, the "should" side begins to soften, it becomes less of a harsh critic, and begins to express the fears and the concerns that underlie the should (e.g., "I'm afraid that if you don't study you won't get good grades and then that makes me feel vulnerable about our future"). As this happens, the "should" and "want" sides begin to move toward some kind of compromise. For instance, the person begins to get a sense of personally wanting what will come from studying, which begins to turn the "should" of studying into a "want." Also, the person validates the side that doesn't want to study but would rather relax or have fun, and some reasonable compromise between these two wants begins to emerge.

A third marker is *unfinished business,* the discussing of problematic experiences with someone in the clients' past life, such as in a past relationship or with a parent. Once again clients are asked to make up a dialogue, this time between themselves and the person they have unfinished business with. Thus, a client may role-play a dialogue between herself and her father, shifting chairs and taking both sides. This usually helps clients come to terms with the problems generated in their relationship with the other person.

As with Gendlin's experiential psychotherapy, process-experiential therapists believe that the therapist must be warm, empathic, and genuine. Further, they also believe that it is the clients who actually find the resolutions to their problems. Process-experiential therapists believe, however, that the systematic use of interventions at specific marker points help clients in the exploratory process.

CURRENT STATUS AND NEW DIRECTIONS

While only a minority of therapists currently identify themselves as client-centered in a pure sense, Carl Rogers has been rated as the most influential of all psychotherapists, including Freud (Smith, 1982). This is because his ideas have influenced many therapists who are eclectic or of other theoretical orientations. Rogers's emphasis on the importance of the therapeutic relationship has been almost universally adopted. Many believe that the relationship is the primary curative factor, even if they are not client-centered in orientation. Of the basic therapeutic conditions, empathy is now seen as an important therapeutic quality in recent theoretical developments in psychoanalysis (see, for example, Kohut's approach, discussed in Chapter 7).

Following from Rogers's emphasis on a therapeutic relationship, training programs designed to increase individuals' "skill" at communicating warmth, empathy, and genuineness have been developed. Communication skills training programs have been used with students, housewives, people looking for jobs, and hospitalized mental patients. Goodman's (1984) SASHA tapes for teaching basic communication skills and Gordon's (1984) efforts to teach effective parenting, leadership, and teaching skills are approaches in the same direction. Many of these programs have been used to train paraprofessional counselors, and many client-centered therapists have been interested in "giving psychology away" to everyone. Gendlin has developed techniques for training the ability to focus in order that individuals may use their experience to grow and change in their private lives (Gendlin, 1981).

In the 1970s, Rogers's own efforts turned to the use of encounter groups. Encounter groups are groups of individuals in which openness, honesty, and feedback among participants are encouraged. In the last years of his life, Rogers utilized encounter groups to increase understanding among Blacks and Whites in South Africa, Protestants and Roman Catholics in Northern Ireland, and other disparate groups (Rogers & Ryback, 1984). He also did work in the Soviet Union (Rogers, 1987). Rogers believed that if world leaders could communicate on a more personal level, chances for world peace and understanding would be increased.

The recent development of process-experiential psychotherapy has already had an impact on the field of psychotherapy; in particular, Leslie Greenberg's work on emotion (Greenberg & Safran, 1987) has been a major contributor to the increasing interest in emotion in both cognitive and psychoanalytic circles.

Currently there is some controversy in the field of client-centered therapy between those who advocate more of a "pure traditional" approach to client-centered therapy, and those who are willing to use techniques such as experiential and process-experiential therapies. Traditional client-centered therapists believe that these approaches are no longer truly nondirective, and in that sense no longer truly client-centered, which is why some (Brodley, 1988b) have argued that there is a family of person-centered therapies, of which pure client-centered therapy is one member, and process-experiential and experiential therapies are other members.

EVALUATION OF CLIENT-CENTERED THERAPY

Research

Carl Rogers has often been seen as the "father of psychotherapy research," and client-centered therapy is the most well-researched of the experiential-humanistic approaches. The meta-analysis by Smith, Glass, & Miller (1980) found client-centered therapy to be effective, with its average level being in the same range as psychoanalytic, transactional analytic, and many other approaches. A more recent meta-analysis also confirmed its effectiveness (Elliott, 1996). Some recent research studies have compared various versions of client-centered therapy to behavioral approaches (Grawe, Caspar, & Ambuhl, 1990) and psychodynamic approaches and have found client-centered therapy to be equivalent in effectiveness to these other approaches. For instance, Eckert and Biermann-Ratjen (1990) compared client-centered with psychodynamic group therapy in the treatment of personality-disordered clients and found equivalence in effectiveness. In another study, client-centered therapy for depression led to changes equivalent to those brought about by cognitive therapy (Greenberg & Watson, in press). Ends and Page (1957) found that a client-centered group therapy approach as an adjunct to inpatient hospital treatment for alcoholism led to higher rates of abstinence at an 18-month follow-up than either a psychodynamic group therapy approach or a learning-based approach. Overall, studies have found client-centered therapy to be effective with a wide range of disorders, including anxiety disorders, personality disorders, and even with some schizophrenics (Bohart, 1995).

Rogers and Sanford (1985) summarized research done in foreign countries on psychotherapy, the teacher-student relationship, and the use of encounter groups. These studies are reported as demonstrating the effectiveness of the person-centered approach. Specifically, teachers high in the facilitative (therapeutic) qualities were found to be more effective. The encounter groups were utilized with a variety of populations, from neurotic students to businesspersons to cancer patients. Generally, these participants gained positive benefits from their encounter experiences.

Research on process-experiential psychotherapy has found that it is equivalent in effectiveness to cognitive therapy (the current "treatment of choice") for the treatment of depression (Greenberg & Watson, in press). Other research has shown that it is useful for helping people who were sexually abused as children to resolve feelings of unfinished business (Paivio & Greenberg, 1995). There are a number of studies demonstrating the empirical effectiveness of Gendlin's focusing technique for the treatment of conditions as diverse as borderline personality disorder and cancer (Greenberg, Elliott, & Lietaer, 1994). In general, Greenberg, Elliott, and Lietaer conclude that client-centered, experiential, and related approaches such as gestalt therapy are equivalent in effectiveness to other major therapeutic approaches for a wide range of disorders.

In sum, a substantial body of evidence demonstrates the effectiveness of the person-centered therapies for a wide range of disorders.

Therapeutic Conditions

The hypothesis that high therapeutic conditions of warmth, empathy, and genuineness are both necessary and sufficient for therapy has been extensively explored. Originally, it was believed that the evidence was strong that high levels of these therapist qualities were related to therapeutic effectiveness (Truax & Mitchell, 1971). However, critical reanalyses of some of this data led to more cautious conclusions being drawn. For instance, Mitchell, Bozarth, and Krauft (1977) concluded that the evidence is mixed, though it "does seem to suggest that empathy, warmth, and genuineness are related in some way to client change but . . . their potency and generalizability are not as great as once thought" (p. 481). Recent tabulations of studies by Orlinsky, Grawe, and Parks (1994) demonstrate that there definitely is a relationship between warmth (or what they call "therapist affirmation"), empathic understanding, and genuineness or congruence (or what they call "therapist self-relatedness") and positive therapeutic outcome. However, the relationship is not strong enough to state that it is either *necessary* or *sufficient* for change to occur. Nevertheless, Rogers appears to have been correct in believing that these qualities play a role in facilitating change. At a broader level, Rogers's hypothesis that the major curative factor in therapy is the relationship has been repeatedly supported (Krupnick et al., 1996; Lambert, 1992)

Experiencing

Gendlin's hypothesis that clients who are working with their inner experiencing in a productive way in therapy will be more likely to benefit from therapy has been extensively researched. Several studies on client-centered therapy found that clients who were high in this ability appeared to benefit more from therapy (Gendlin, Beebe, Cassens, Klein, & Oberlander, 1968). Other studies on other kinds of therapy have produced mixed results, though on balance, higher levels of client experiencing have been associated with therapeutic change (Klein, Mathieu-Coughlan, & Kiesler, 1986).

Gendlin and his colleagues (Gendlin et al., 1968) suggested that their analysis of the data on client-centered therapy found that the ability to relate to one's experience did not increase to any great extent over the course of therapy. Instead, it appeared that people high in this ability had entered therapy with high levels. Therapy then helped them to utilize this ability to change, but it did not teach the ability. It was because of these results that Gendlin developed his "focusing" procedure as a way of facilitating the experiencing process in those who were not good at it when they entered therapy. However, this particular finding—that clients who do well in therapy enter it with higher levels of experiencing—has been disputed (Brodley, 1988a).

Gendlin and his colleagues noted an important distinction between two ways of having a "here-and-now" focus in therapy. Many existential and humanistically oriented therapists (see Chapter 9) believe the client should be discouraged from talking about past events (as in psychoanalysis) and that therapist and client should focus on the client's current feelings and perceptions of the therapist, herself, and other group members in group therapy. Yet, when Gendlin and his colleagues attempted to measure here-and-now focus in this sense, it turned out not to relate to positive change. In other words, therapy that focused on issues and feelings arising from the therapy context was not more successful than therapy that allowed discussion of issues outside of that context, such as the client's past. Similarly, Lieberman, Yalom, and Miles (1973) found that encounter groups that allowed clients to "bring in outside material," rather than keeping a here-and-now focus on interactions within the group, were more successful.

In contrast, Gendlin found that a different kind of here-and-now focus did relate to positive change. Clients who were experientially involved in the here and now in whatever they were talking about (for instance, the past) were more likely to experience positive change.

Other research on the ability to relate to oneself experientially (or to focus) has found that it relates to creativity (Gendlin, 1969) and even to longevity in elderly people (Gendlin, 1981).

Task Analysis

A movement in psychotherapy research has been to study the sequence of specific events in psychotherapy, using what is called a "task analytic" approach (Rice & Greenberg, 1984). Rice and Saperia (1984) studied "evocative unfolding," which is a specific and well-defined approach to client-centered empathic responding. It is based on the belief that clients describe situations and their reactions to them in a highly condensed form.

Suppose a client brings in the following "problematic reaction": She was in a conversation with a friend, suddenly blurted out something hostile, then felt embarrassed afterward. When she relates this incident to the therapist, she condenses it into a few sentences. Through evocative unfolding, the therapist has the client try to vividly recapture the experience. With that as a basis, the client is led through an exploration of the experience, focusing both on her internal reactions and what was going on in the situation.

During this process, meanings implicit in the client's reaction to the situation become clear. In addition, the client usually realizes that her reaction to the situation represents a broader way she has of reacting to other situations as well. This leads to a reprocessing of the experience, and some therapeutic movement or gain. For example, the client, in vividly recalling the incident, might realize that she had been perceiving the other person in the situation as challenging her intellectual competence. She might become aware that this had led her to feel that she was being "put down," although she was not completely aware of her perception or her feeling at the time. Her blurting out an insult now no longer seems so unexpected and inexplicable. In addition, she might also realize that she has a tendency to perceive herself as being criticized or rejected whenever someone seems to disagree with her.

Rice and Saperia (1984) studied the process of evocative unfolding by having undergraduate psychology students meet with therapists for two sessions. In one session, they dealt with a problematic reaction that they had experienced. In the other, the students met with the same therapist, but the therapist responded in a more traditional, unstructured, client-centered way. Some students had evocative unfolding first and the traditional approach second, while others had the reverse. The study found that evocative unfolding led to more therapeutic resolution than the traditional client-centered approach. In addition, by tape-recording the interactions and studying the sequence of therapeutic events that occurred, general support was found for the model of how evocative unfolding worked.

Task analysis has become a major research strategy and a wide range of studies have been done on various therapeutic "tasks." For instance, recently, Watson and Greenberg (1996) showed positive relationships between resolving internal conflict and resolving problems with significant others ("unfinished business") and positive change in therapy for depression.

Theory

Client-centered theory is primarily a theory of personality *process* than it is of personality *structure*. That is, it is a theory of the person as an active, organizing process moving toward the future. It focuses on how people, when they are functioning most effectively, are continually and actively using their own experience to revise their personal constructs, to change, and to create better ways of dealing with life. However, in this focus, client-centered theorists have provided few ideas of how individuals remain the same. We have seen in the evaluation of psychodynamic theories that people probably change more than these theories assume. However, it is also the case that they remain the same in various ways, and client-centered theory has not developed models of what is enduring in personality, as have psychodynamic theories.

Another problem with client-centered theory is that the client-centered therapist's intense focus on the individual tends to result in a view that all psychopathology arises from the client's inability to trust himself. First, such a view ignores biological factors. Second, it ignores the possibility that social, ecological, and systems factors may create psychopathology, even in people who are congruent. As an example, Haney, Banks, and Zimbardo (1973) found that some students who were otherwise free of any apparent signs of psychopathology became brutal or experienced psychological breakdowns when put in the roles of guard or prisoner in a mock prison setup. Finally, Watzlawick, a family systems theorist (see Chapter 14), has argued that often, pathological behavior arises from being congruent. He suggests that pathological behavior is behavior that has worked in the past, but is dysfunctional in the current situation, although the person does not recognize this. When things continue to go wrong, the person tries harder to make things go right by increasing the behaviors that worked in the past. Increasing the now dysfunctional behaviors simply makes matters worse. Yet the person is behaving in what appears to him to be a congruent manner; he's doing what he believes.

Still another problem has been an intense individualistic orientation in client-centered therapy. Rogers (1977) believed that social changes do not result from attempts to change society at a collective level, but from creating personal change within individuals. Yet the individual and society are two parts of a balanced system. In order to create self-actualizing people, it would seem that we must therefore change society, not just try to foster actualization in individuals. But to change society, we must understand all political, cultural, and social forces that are involved. Rogers tended to ignore or distrust this level of analysis.

There are other problems with the Rogerian focus on the self. These problems are shared with other theories such as object relations theory, gestalt, and existentialism. All of these theories in one form or another see the fundamental event in the development of mental health as the development of an integrated, autonomous, separate, actualized self. It is assumed that only an autonomous, actualized self can maturely relate to others. Therefore, for all these theories, good relationships to other people follow self-actualization. However, it has been argued that the emphasis on individuation and development of selfhood is culture-specific and may reflect the high value Western cultures place on individualism. In contrast, Asian personality theories (Pedersen, 1983), for example, stress the development of the person through relationships. What Asian theories see as healthy, Western theories tend to see as unhealthy: an "other" orientation, the positive value of dependency, and so on. And the reverse is true; for some Asian theories, "self" doesn't really even exist, and an emphasis on self-actualization is contrary to optimal development. Similarly, many modern feminist theorists (e.g., Jordan, Kaplan, Miller, Stiver, & Surrey, 1991) have argued that the emphasis many theories place on development of separateness and autonomy over interdependence and connectedness to others reflects a masculine cultural bias. Whether there is a correct theory, we do not know. The important thing is to realize that emphasis on self-actualization and autonomy may reflect "actualization" of cultural values as much as it reflects "fundamental truth" about personality development.

In terms of psychotherapy, client-centered therapy is the purest of the "discovery-oriented" approaches. Discovery-oriented approaches to therapy begin with the idea that change ultimately occurs through clients making their own individual discoveries of their own individual "truths." Psychoanalytic therapy is primarily a discovery-oriented approach, but psychoanalytic therapists have some specific ideas about what clients need to discover in order to change, and so have some directive elements to them. Some client-centered therapists adopt a radical nondirective stance, believing that if the therapist directs the client in any way, he gets in the way of the client's own self-directed growth process. It is because of this that the therapist wishes to encounter the client free of preconceptions in order to relate to the unique person that the client is. Because of this, most client-centered therapists do not want to diagnose. Nor do they wish to make treatment plans for the client. Many client-centered therapists do not even like Gendlin's focusing approach or the process-experiential approach because they are *structured* discovery-oriented approaches. That is, while the ultimate goal is still for the client to discover his or her own truth and solution, process-experiential therapists and those who follow Gendlin's approach believe the therapist can facilitate discovery by structuring therapy with the use of certain techniques.

This radical nondirective stance makes it philosophically difficult for some client-centered therapists to use techniques and procedures when they might be helpful. For instance, with a client with a sexual difficulty, there are techniques that can be useful. Yet Rogers himself, with his increased emphasis on the therapist's genuineness later on in his life, was acceptant of client-centered therapists who believed that they could suggest and utilize techniques without imposing on the self-directed growth process of the client. It does not appear that there is anything inherently contradictory about a therapist suggesting a technique, if she does it in a way that truly respects the client's right to (a) say no if it does not fit, and (b) learn from it in his or her own way. Similarly, there is nothing inherently contradictory about labeling and diagnosing, and treating clients as unique individuals. The issue depends on how therapists use their constructs. To use client-centered theory itself, it depends on whether therapists hold their constructs tentatively. It is unfortunately true that diagnosis has been used to label and pigeonhole clients by therapists who fail to recognize them as individual, unique persons. If the therapist holds her constructs tentatively, using them as tools to "get to know" the client, rather than as fixed truths about the client, then constructs about the client should not obscure the client's uniqueness.

A further, practical problem with the radical nondirective stance is that it does not fit well with the current managed care environment (see Chapter 18), where therapists are expected to diagnose their clients and to develop treatment plans for them. Therapists who truly want to practice in a traditional client-centered way may have to practice outside of the health care establishment.

IN CONCLUSION

There are two major insights of Rogers's that we believe will continue to play an important role in how therapy is conducted in the twenty-first century. First is the importance of the therapeutic relationship, which research has supported as the most important healing element provided by therapy. Other approaches to therapy are increasingly taking the relationship into account. Rogers's emphasis on empathy has spread from a focus on its importance in the therapeutic relationship to an increasing interest in its growth-producing potential in parenting relationships (Feshbach, 1997) and in society at large (Goleman, 1996).

The second major insight concerns the client's own self-healing potential, or what Rogers called "self-actualization." While most therapists do not use the term self-actualization, it seems clear that clients have an enormous capacity for self-healing and self-righting (Bohart & Tallman, 1996). To quote Bergin and Garfield (1994), based on the most comprehensive review of psychotherapy research to date,

> Another important observation regarding the client variable is that it is the client more than the therapist who implements the change process. . . . Rather than argue over whether or not "therapy works," we could address ourselves to the question of whether or not "the client works!" . . . As therapists have depended more upon the client's reources, more change seems to occur. (p. 826)

Orlinsky, Grawe, and Parks (1994, p. 278), based on their comprehensive research review, say " . . . we view psychotherapy as 'the activation through the process of interpersonal communication of a powerful endogenous therapeutic system [in the client] that is part of the psychophysiology of all individuals and the sociophysiology of relationships' (Kleinman, 1988, p. 112)." Therapists of many persuasions are increasingly coming to trust, rely on, and utilize clients' own creativity and self-healing capacities (Bohart & Tallman, in press; Gold, 1994), and this is particularly true of therapists who follow brief, "solution-focused" approaches (Duncan, Hubble, & Miller, 1997). For instance, Duncan et al. (1997) have shown in a study of "impossible cases"—clients who have repeatedly failed to have been helped by prior therapy—that the therapist's reliance on the client's frame of reference and own creativity led to the occurrance of change. Thus, as therapists learn to utilize clients' own self-healing potentials more, we believe they will become more effective (Bohart & Tallman, in press).

Gendlin has contributed an integrative model for the underlying process of change in psychotherapy. In addition, he has done extensive research on experiencing, which is currently one of the most well-substantiated constructs in terms of relating to change in psychotherapy. It is likely that in the twenty-first century, therapists will be, in one way or another, facilitating an experiential process as part of effective therapy.

Greenberg, Rice, and Elliott's (1993) process-experiential psychotherapy is a unique integration of the more systematic therapy formats of cognitive and behavioral approaches with the client-centered belief in a self-propelled growth process. Further, these authors have contributed the idea of therapeutic markers, which is being adopted by therapists of many persuasions, and the development of the research approach of task analysis. Several of their techniques and procedures have already found their way into the armamentarium of other therapy approaches. As a specific, brief, structured experiential-humanistic approach, process-experiential therapy is more compatible with the current managed care climate than is "pure," open-ended client-centered therapy, and is currently being empirically validated.

BIBLIOGRAPHY

Bergin, A. E., & Garfield, S. L. (1994). Overview, trends, and future issues. In A. E. Bergin & S. L. Garfield (Eds.), *Handbook and psychotherapy and behavior change* (pp. 821–830). New York: Wiley

Bohart, A. C. (1990). A cognitive client-centered perspective on borderline personality development. In G. Lietaer, J. Rombauts, & R. Van Balen (Eds.), *Client-centered and experiential psychotherapy in the nineties* (pp. 599–622). Leuven, Belgium: Leuven University Press.

Bohart, A. C. (1995). The person-centered therapies. In A. Gurman & S. Messer (Eds.), *Essential psychotherapies.* New York: Guilford.

Bohart, A. C., & Greenberg, L. S. (1997). *Empathy reconsidered.* Washington, DC: American Psychological Association.

Bohart, A., & Tallman, K. (in press). *The client as active self-healer.* Washington DC: American Psychological Association.

Borkovec, T. D., & Mathews, A. M. (1988). Treatment of nonphobic anxiety disorder: A comparison of nondirective, cognitive, and coping desensitization therapy. *Journal of Consulting and Clinical Psychology, 56,* 877–884.

Briere, J. (1989). *Therapy for adults molested as children.* New York: Springer.

Brodley, B. T. (1988a, May). *Does early-in-therapy experiencing level predict outcome?* Paper presented at the Second Annual Meeting of the Association for the Development of the Person-Centered Approach, New York.

Brodley, B. T. (1988b). Responses to person-centered versus client-centered? *Renaissance, 5,* 1–2.

Cowan, P. A. (1978). *Piaget: With feeling.* New York: Holt, Rinehart and Winston.

Duncan, B. L., Hubble, M. A., & Millerr, S. D. (1997). *Psychotherapy of "impossible cases."* New York: Norton.

Eckert, J., & Biermann-Ratjen, E.-M. (1990). Client-centered therapy versus psychoanalytic psychotherapy. Reflections following a comparative study. In G. Lietaer, J. Rombauts, & R. Van Balen (Eds.), *Client-centered and experiential psychotherapy in the nineties* (pp. 457–468). Leuven, Belgium: Leuven University Press.

Elliott, R. (1996). Are client-centered/experiential therapies effective? A meta-analysis of outcome research. In U. Esser, H. Pbast, G. W. Speierer (Eds.), *The power of the person-centered approach: New challenges-perspectives-answers* (pp. 125–138). Koln, Germany: Verlag.

Ends, E. J., & Page, C. W. (1957). A study of three types of group psychotherapy with hospitalized male inebriates. *Quarterly Journal of Studies in Alcoholism, 18,* 263–277.

Feshbach, N. D. (1997). Empathy: the formative years, implications for clinical practice. In A. Bohart & L. Greenberg (Eds.), *Empathy reconsidered* (pp. 33–59). Washington DC: American Psychological Association.

Gendlin, E. T. (1967). Therapeutic procedures in dealing with schizophrenics. In C. R. Rogers, E. T. Gendlin, D. J. Kiesler, & C. B. Truax (Eds.), *The therapeutic relationship and its impact: A study of psychotherapy with schizophrenics* (pp. 369–400). Madison: University of Wisconsin Press.

Gendlin, E. T. (1968). The experiential response. In E. Hammer (Ed.), *Use of interpretation in treatment.* New York: Grune & Stratton.

Gendlin, E. T. (1969). Focusing. *Psychotherapy: Theory, Research and Practice, 6,* 4–15.

Gendlin, E. T. (1981). *Focusing.* New York: Bantam Books.

Gendlin, E. T. (1984). The politics of giving therapy away: Listening and focusing. In D. Larson (Ed.), *Teaching psychological skills: Models for giving psychology away* (pp. 287–305). Monterey, CA: Brooks/Cole.

Gendlin, E. T. (1996). *Focusing-oriented psychotherapy: A manual of the experiential method.* New York: Guilford.

Gendlin, E. T., Beebe, J., Cassens, J., Klein, M., & Oberlander, M. (1968). Focusing ability in psychotherapy, personality, and creativity. In J. M. Shlien (Ed.), *Research in psychotherapy* (Vol. 3). Washington, DC: American Psychological Association.

Gold, J. R. (1994). When the patient does the integrating: Lessons for theory and practice. *Journal of Psychotherapy Integration, 4,* 133–158.

Goleman, D. (1996). *Emotional intelligence.* New York: Bantam.

Goodman, G. (1984). SASHA tapes: Expanding options for help-intended communication. In D. Larson (Ed.), *Teaching psychological skills: Models for giving psychology away* (pp. 271–286). Monterey, CA: Brooks/Cole.

Gordon, T. (1984). Three decades of democratizing relationships through training. In D. Larson (Ed.), *Teaching psychological skills: Models for giving psychology away* (pp. 151–170). Monterey, CA: Brooks/Cole.

Grawe, K., Caspar, F., & Ambuhl, H. (1990). Differentielle psychotherapieforschung: Vier Therapieformen im Vergleich. *Zeirschrift für Klinische Psychologie, 19,* 287–376.

Greenberg, L. S., & Safran, J. D. (1987). *Emotion in psychotherapy.* New York: Guilford.

Greenberg, L. S., & Watson, J. (in press). Experiential therapy of depression: Differential effects of client-centered relationship and active experiential interventions. *Psychotherapy Research.*

Greenberg, L. S., Elliott, R., & Lietaer, G. (1994). Research on humanistic and experiential psychotherapies. In A. Bergin & S. Garfield (Eds.), *Handbook of psychotherapy and behavior change* (4th ed.). New York: Wiley.

Greenberg, L. S., Rice, L. N., & Elliot, R. (1993). *Facilitating emotional change: The moment-by-moment process.* New York: Guilford.

Greenberg, L. S., & Safran, J. D. (1987). *Emotion in psychotherapy.* New York: Guilford.

Haney, C., Banks, C., & Zimbardo, P. (1973). Interpersonal dynamics in a simulated prison. *International Journal of Criminology and Penology, 1,* 69–97.

Hart, J. T. (1970). The development of client-centered therapy. In J. T. Hart & T. M. Tomlinson (Eds.), *New directions in client-centered therapy* (pp. 3–22). New York: Houghton Mifflin.

Henschel, D. M., & Bohart, A. C. (1984). Egocentric versus decentered empathy (Summary of paper presentation). In G. I. Lubin & M. K. Poulsen (Eds.), *Piagetian theory and its implications for mental health. Proceedings: Ninth through twelfth Interdisciplinary Conference.* (Vol. 2). Los Angeles: University of Southern California.

Holdstock, T. L. (1990). Can client-centered therapy transcend its monocultural roots? In G. Lietaer, J. Rombauts, & R. Van Balen (Eds.), *Client-centered and experiential psychotherapy in the nineties* (pp. 109–121). Leuven, Belgium: Leuven University Press.

Janov, A. (1970). *The primal scream.* New York: Dell.

Jordan, J. V., Kaplan, A. G., Miller, J. B., Stiver, I. P., & Surrey, J. L. (Eds.). (1991). *Women's growth in connection: Writings from the stone center.* New York: Guilford.

Kelly, G. A. (1955). *The psychology of personal constructs: A theory of personality* (2 vols.). New York: Norton.

Klein, M. H., Mathieu-Coughlan, P., & Kiesler, D. J. (1986). The experiencing scales. In L. S. Greenberg & W. Pinsof (Eds.), *The psychotherapeutic process: A research handbook* (pp. 21–72). New York: Guilford.

Kleinmann, A. (1988). *Rethinking psychiatry.* New York: Free Press.

Krupnick, J. L., Sotsky, S. M., Simmens, S., Moyher, J., Elkin, I., Watkins, J., & Pilkonis, P. A. (1996). The role of the therapeutic alliance in psychotherapy and pharmacotherapy outcome: Findings in the National Institute of Mental Health Treatment of Depression Collaborative Research Project. *Journal of Consulting and Clinical Psychology, 64,* 532–539.

Lambert, M. J. (1992). Psychotherapy outcome research. In J. C. Norcross & M. R. Goldfried (Eds.), *Handbook of psychotherapy integration* (pp. 94–129). New York: Basic Books.

Lieberman, M. A., Yalom, I. I., & Miles, M. B. (1973). *Encounter groups: First facts.* New York: Basic Books.

Lietaer, G. (1990). The client-centered approach after the Wisconsin project: A personal view on its evolution. In G. Lietaer, J. Rombauts, & R. Van Balen (Eds.), *Client-centered and experiential psychotherapy in the nineties* (pp. 19–46). Leuven, Belgium: Leuven University Press.

Mitchell, K. M., Bozarth, J. D., & Krauft, C. C. (1977). A reappraisal of the therapeutic effectiveness of accurate empathy, nonpossessive warmth, and genuineness. In A. S. Gurman & A. M. Razin (Eds.), *Effective psychotherapy: A handbook of research.* New York: Pergamon Press.

O'Hara, M. M. (1992, April). *Selves-in-Context: The Challenge for Psychotherapy in a Postmodern World.* Invited Address at the Conference of the Society for the Exploration of Psychotherapy Integration, San Diego, CA.

Orlinsky, D. E., Grawe, K., & Parks, B. K. (1994). Process and outcome in psychotherapy. In A. E. Bergin & S. L. Garfield (Eds.), *Handbook of psychotherapy and behavior change* (pp. 270–378). New York: Wiley

Paivio, S., & Greenberg, L. S. (1995). Resolving unfinished business: Experiential therapy using empty chair dialogue. *Journal of Consulting & Clinical Psychology, 63,* 419–425.

Pedersen, P. B. (1983). Asian personality theory. In R. J. Corsini & A. J. Marsella (Eds.), *Personality theories, research, and assessment.* Itasca, IL: Peacock.

Prigogine, I., & Stengers, I. (1984). *Order out of chaos: Man's new dialogue with nature.* New York: Bantam.

Rice, L. N., & Greenberg, L. S. (Eds.). (1984). *Patterns of change: Intensive analysis of psychotherapy process.* New York: Guilford.

Rice, L. N., & Saperia, E. P. (1984). Task analysis of the resolution of problematic reactions. In L. N. Rice & L. S. Greenberg, (Eds.), *Patterns of change: Intensive analysis of psychotherapy process.* (pp. 29–66). New York: Guilford.

Rogers, C. R. (1942). *Counseling and psychotherapy.* Boston: Houghton Mifflin.

Rogers, C. R. (1957). The necessary and sufficient conditions of therapeutic personality change. *Journal of Consulting Psychology, 21,* 95–103.

Rogers, C. R. (1961). *On becoming a person.* Boston: Houghton Mifflin.

Rogers, C. R. (1965). *Client-centered therapy* (Film No. 1). In E. Shostrom (Ed.), *Three approaches to psychotherapy* (Three 16-mm color motion pictures). Santa Ana, CA: Psychological Films.

Rogers, C. R. (1967). Toward a modern approach to values: The valuing process in the mature person. In C. R. Rogers & B. Stevens (Eds.), *Person to person: The problem of being human.* New York: Pocket Books.

Rogers, C. R. (1970). *Carl Rogers on encounter groups.* New York: Harper & Row.

Rogers, C. R. (1977). *Carl Rogers on personal power.* New York: Delacorte.

Rogers, C. R. (1980). Do we need "a" reality? In C. R. Rogers, *A way of being.* Boston: Houghton Mifflin.

Rogers, C. R. (with R. Sanford). (1987). *Inside the world of the Soviet professional.* Unpublished manuscript.

Rogers, C. R., Gendlin, E. T., Kiesler, D. J., & Truax, C. B. (1967). *The therapeutic relationship and its impact: A study of psychotherapy with schizophrenics.* Madison: University of Wisconsin Press.

Rogers, C. R., & Ryback, D. (1984). One alternative to nuclear planetary suicide. In R. F. Levant & J. M. Shlien (Eds.), *Client-centered therapy and the person-centered approach: New directions in theory, research, and practice* (pp. 400–422). New York: Praeger.

Rogers, C. R., & Sanford, R. C. (1985). Client-centered psychotherapy. In H. I. Kaplan & B. J. Sadock (Eds.), *Comprehensive textbook of psychiatry* (Vol. 4). New York: Praeger.

Smith, D. (1982). Trends in counseling and psychotherapy. *American Psychologist, 37,* 802–809.

Smith, M. L., Glass, G. V., & Miller, T. I. (1980). *The benefits of psychotherapy.* Baltimore: Johns Hopkins University Press.

Speierer, G. W. (1990). Toward a specific illness concept of client-centered therapy. In G. Lietaer, J. Rombauts, & R. Van Balen (Eds.), *Client-centered and experiential psychotherapy in the nineties* (pp. 337–360). Leuven, Belgium: Leuven University Press.

Truax, C. B., & Carkhuff, R. (1967). *Toward effective counseling and psychotherapy: Training and practice.* Chicago: Aldine.

Truax, C. B., & Mitchell, K. M. (1971). Research on certain therapist interpersonal skills in relation to process and outcome. In A. E. Bergin & S. L. Garfield (Eds.), *Handbook of psychotherapy and behavior change.* New York: Wiley.

Van Balen, R. (1990). The therapeutic relationship according to Carl Rogers: Only a climate? A dialogue? Or both? In G. Lietaer, J. Rombauts, & R. Van Balen (Ed.), *Client-centered and experiential psychotherapy in the nineties* (pp. 65–86). Leuven, Belgium: Leuven University Press.

Watson, J. C., & Greenberg, L. S. (1996). Pathways to change in the psychotherapy of depression: Relating process to session change and outcome. *Psychotherapy, 33,* 262–274.

Wexler, D. A. (1974). A cognitive theory of experiencing, self-actualization, and therapeutic process. In D. A. Wexler & L. N. Rice (Eds.), *Innovations in client-centered therapy* (pp. 49–116). New York: Wiley.

Wexler, D. A., & Rice, L. N. (Eds.). (1974). *Innovations in client-centered therapy.* New York: Wiley.

Zimring, F. (1990). Cognitive processes as a cause of psychotherapeutic change: Self-initiated processes. In G. Lietaer, J. Rombauts, & R. Van Balen (Eds.), *Client-centered and experiential psychotherapy in the nineties* (pp. 361–380). Leuven, Belgium: Leuven University Press.

CHAPTER
9

Gestalt and Other Existential-Humanistic Approaches

I have forsaken an earlier position . . . because even the earlier position was only a pause on the way. What lasts in thinking is the way. (Martin Heidegger, 1959, p. 98)

Lose your mind and come to your senses. (Fritz Perls)

We have already considered one of the most important existential-humanistic approaches in the work of Carl Rogers. In this chapter, we will look at the two other major approaches in this perspective, existential therapy and gestalt therapy, and briefly consider Mahrer's experiential approach.

THE CONCEPT OF THE RIVER

Of all the major approaches, the existential-humanistic approach places the most emphasis on the person as the author of his or her own life. For this approach, the very essence of the person is the freedom to shape and reshape his or her own life and identity. The personality is viewed as a continual process of growth and change. The individual never possesses a fixed self, or character structure, or identity. People are "open systems," continually interacting with the environment, taking in information, and growing and changing as they creatively deal with a continual influx of information. The most appropriate metaphor for the personality in the humanistic approaches is "the river." Although the river can be said to have an identity, it is never the same from one moment to the next or one place to the next. Its nature at any given moment is influenced by where it has been, where it is going, where it is now, and what happens to it at any time in the past or present.

Humanists believe that if early childhood events are still influencing a person it is because the person, as the author of her own fate, is still allowing (often unconsciously) them to do so. Personality is not so much something that is built up inside from experiences as it is something that the person actively maintains through choices. The radical emphasis on growth, change, and choice means the humanistic approaches place a heavy emphasis on creativity and the individual's reaching his or her full potential.

Humanistic approaches also generally see the human being holistically. No part of the human is disowned or seen as somehow "lower" or "less human" than other parts. Humanists generally reject Freud's view of the person as split into relatively "higher" (ego) functions and relatively "lower" or more primitive (id) functions. Sex and aggression are not seen as primitive, selfish impulses in and of themselves. They are primitive and selfish only if the person chooses to express them that way. If owned and acknowledged, these parts can play creative, life-actualizing roles in personality development. By the same token, the emotional and intuitive functions are not seen as things to be controlled. Subjectivity, fantasy, and intuition are all regarded as sources of growth and creativity.

Many of the approaches within the humanistic perspective either trace their roots to a philosophical movement called existentialism or reflect ideas compatible with it. For this reason, we will begin this chapter with a brief survey of ideas from the existential philosophical tradition, concentrating on the work of Edmund Husserl, Martin Heidegger, and Jean-Paul Sartre.

EXISTENTIAL THERAPY

Philosophical Background

Phenomenology is the philosophical approach associated with Edmund Husserl (1964). Husserl's goal was to suspend acceptance of all concepts about reality in order to get to things that could not be doubted about reality: pure phenomena. Imagine looking at all things that come into your consciousness as though they were images on a movie screen. Imagine examining them while suspending all judgment about what they are, what they mean, or what they consist of. To the extent that you can do this, you approximate what Husserl was striving for. For instance, you see someone acting "crazy." Can you suspend your judgment that he is acting "crazy"? Can you suspend your tendency to characterize his behavior at all? It is impossible to suspend all preconceptions, but the phenomenologists tried to approach this ideal. Their cry was "To the things themselves!"

One example of the **phenomenological method** in psychology is the work of R. D. Laing (1967). Laing wished to study schizophrenia without any preconceptions. So he suspended the idea that the schizophrenic is mentally ill, crazy, or incomprehensible. In trying to look at the schizophrenic without preconceptions, Laing concluded that the typical Western view of schizophrenia was based on the world view and preconceptions of those judging the schizophrenic as ill or disordered. Laing proceeded to arrive at a very different view. Basically, he argued that schizophrenia can be a growth experience wherein the schizophrenic, by shedding a false, socially imposed identity and descending into madness, is able to reclaim his or her own true inner potential. If this process is respected and supported rather than judged and interfered with (for instance, with the administration of drugs), the schizophrenic can come back to reality as a more whole person than before. Laing's views have not generally found favor among Western psychiatric professionals. However, there is some evidence that for some schizophrenics, treating them as being on a growth experience can be beneficial (Mosher, Menn, & Matthews, 1975). More importantly for our purposes, whether or not we agree with Laing's views on schizophrenia, his work makes us aware that each of us does see the world through the lens of our preconceptions, and that if these are suspended, we might arrive at new and different perspectives.

Martin Heidegger's philosophy was based on Husserl's phenomenological approach, but went in a different direction (Frings, 1968; Schmitt, 1969). He held that humans, in contrast to objects, exist as interactive entities with reality. People are activities rather than fixed objects, in constant dialogue with their surroundings. At any given moment, the individual is a creative construction of both past history and current situation. As a result, the individual is never the same from moment to moment. Heidegger would have considered the belief in a fixed personality structure, including the various labels such as borderline, passive, or narcissistic personality, to be an inauthentic way of relating to ourselves and others. People do not "have" personalities; they constantly create and re-create their personalities through their choices and actions.

Inauthenticity is an attempt to deny the existence of choice. Jean-Paul Sartre (1956) suggested that people become anxious when they face the fact that they are responsible for themselves and their choices. The concept of a fixed identity reduces anxiety. Thinking of myself as a "good" person becomes a substitute for examining my behavior and making choices on the basis of rightness or goodness. If I define myself as a borderline personality, then I no longer have to consider myself responsible for my impulsive acts. In order to avoid the anxiety of choice, we all seek fixed identities, such as "being a doctor" or "being an honorable man." Yet what really counts is not who we are, but what we do, that is, how we choose to behave.

Every time people make choices they open up new possibilities both in themselves and in the world. For example, if I act cruelly toward someone, I "bring out" the negative in myself and, perhaps, reciprocally in that person. If I act caringly, I may allow potential positive aspects to come forth.

Humans are thus the creatures through which reality "knows" itself. An individual's actions allow what has previously been only potential, or "hidden," in reality to be articulated. The most important kind of knowing is knowing how. Knowing how is the kind of knowing involved in doing. For instance, learning how to play the guitar brings forth potential in the player and musical potential in an object. Intellectual knowing about facts is less useful. Therapy should involve learning how to be human, rather than learning about oneself, that is, about one's past. People need to learn how to listen to themselves, how to be in tune with their nature as creatures in transition.

With this brief summary of its philosophical basis, we will now look at existential psychotherapy. We will not concentrate on different existential theorists by name, but we will list here some of the important names: Ludwig Binswanger (1963), Medard Boss (1963), Rollo May (Schneider & May, 1995), J. F. T. Bugental (1976), Salvador Maddi (Kobasa & Maddi, 1983), and Irving Yalom (1981). A closely related approach is Victor Frankl's (1963) logotherapy.

Theory of Personality and Psychopathology

For the existential approach, the primary fact of human existence is that people are free to create their own meaning and identity in life. But can anyone be anything he or she wants? The answer is obviously no. There are limits. People must accept finiteness as a fundamental fact of existence. Humans are finite in two senses: Reality imposes limits and everyone ultimately dies. Reality places limits on people in several ways. We are limited by our biology and by the time and place into which we are born. Being born with a handicap, into a starving Ethiopian family, or as a black slave in 1800 would all impose certain limitations.

But there are two ways of thinking about limits: to see them as restricting freedom or to see them as making the experience of freedom of choice meaningful. Limits and freedom are two sides of the same coin. There could be no freedom without limits. If you could choose to be anything you wanted at any time, then both freedom and choice would lose all meaning. If you could have anything you wanted at any given moment, then you would never really have to choose.

Thus, freedom and choice are mutually interdependent. The individual is free within the limitations imposed by the facts of his existence to create life in any way he can. The individual is free to choose how he will deal with limits. He can view them as immutable barriers and give up, or accept them as challenges. If you lose the use of your legs in an automobile accident, you can withdraw from activities or you can learn to maneuver in a wheelchair and continue with your life. Some limitations cannot be transcended. If you are in prison sentenced to be executed, you may be unable to escape or get the sentence changed. However, you can still choose how you spend your last days, and how you approach death. The challenge is to do as much as possible with what one has. Each individual can be creative and forge something meaningful out of whatever life has given him. Existentialists call the courage to face up to adverse circumstances in life the "courage to be" (Tillich, 1952).

The individual's choices not only create the meaning of her life and being, but also influence the meaning of events surrounding her. The existential view can properly be considered a "field" or "systems" view of behavior. As the meaning of a word is determined by the rest of the sentence it is embedded in and the meaning of a sentence may change if one word is changed, the meaning of any event in an individual's life is determined by the whole web of meanings she has attributed to herself and the world. How the individual sees herself and the world may change if the meaning of some important event in her life changes.

Therefore, people create the structure of their own lives, and each choice moves them along their life paths. But at any moment they can choose to alter the path. Right now your choice to continue reading this chapter is in some sense "creating" who you are. In reading this chapter, you are acting on your perception of your interests and values at this moment. Perhaps you are a student planning a career in psychology, but perhaps you are not a good student. Perhaps you feel awkward around others and have low self-esteem. If, as you read, you grow more and more bored, you might toss the book away and go change your major the next day. Perhaps you change to dentistry. Pursuing dentistry, you associate with different people and take different courses. Now you may find new aspects of yourself opening up. Your values may change and your self-image may improve. You discover that you are so interested in dentistry that you do well academically. Instead of feeling stupid, you now see yourself as motivated and capable. Before, you may have seen yourself as awkward, dull, and romantically undesirable. Now you find yourself talking with enthusiasm to another person who is interested in dentistry, and romantic sparks begin to fly. Your self-image in that area begins to change also.

If people create their life structure and identity through their choices, why does anyone choose a miserable or self-defeating existence? One answer to this is that they are often unaware that they are choosing. They may not have had any experiences that allow them to realize that they have a choice in how they move through life. A woman who grows up in a family and community where the message is that a woman's place is in the home may accept that message as objectively true. She will not see the possibility of any choice over her role as a woman.

Many existential theorists also stress the denial of the possibility of choice. According to May and Yalom (1984), people deny choice because of anxiety. They point out that existentialism is a "depth psychology," similar to psychoanalysis, but what is hidden is the possibility of choice, rather than sexual and aggressive impulses. To avoid anxiety, people avoid their own potential. Often, they try to actualize an image of what society says they ought to be. They ought to be businesspeople rather than artists, married rather than single, heterosexual rather than homosexual, religious rather than nonreligious, or whatever. They deny the possibility of choosing to be anything other than what society says they should be. And they become anxious if they sense that they may not fit these images. They deny themselves knowledge of their true wants and goals in order to try to fit these images.

But these attempts to avoid anxiety don't always work, and anxiety may be a signal that an individual is living an inauthentic existence. Two cases illustrate this point. A man was going for his doctorate because his parents strongly wanted a Ph.D. in the family. About three years into his graduate program, just about the time he had to pass three comprehensive exams to advance to his dissertation, he became anxious and depressed. The interesting thing was that he became anxious and depressed after passing the first two exams with outstanding performances. He found he could not even study for the third. An existential view would be that as the man approached completion of his degree, the lack of fit between that goal and his own feelings grew more pronounced. After a stormy period of depression, anxiety, and several suicide attempts, he finally took an "existential leap" and dropped out of school. He got a job teaching handicapped children and his depression and anxiety vanished, and when last heard of, he was living a normal life. In this case, anxiety and depression were signals of inauthencity, rather than repressed instincts (psychoanalysis), dysfunctional cognitions (cognitive approaches), or conditioning (behavioral approaches).

Another case was a woman in an unfulfilling marriage. She was distant, cold, and reserved, seemed vaguely "out of touch" all the time, and was usually somewhat negative and depressed. Some friends described her as a basically negative person who liked to see the worst in the world. Finally, on facing up to the lack of fit between herself and her marriage, she left it. By taking this "existential leap," she was able to move out of living an inauthentic existence, and this freed up other aspects of her personality. She became more warm, open, and vital.

For existentialists, anxiety results from denial of one's authenticity and potential. But we said earlier that it was to avoid anxiety that people deny their ability to choose in the first place. According to existentialists, people deny their ability to choose to avoid the basic anxiety associated with human finiteness. For existentialists, anxiety is unavoidable. To live is to have to choose. But to have to choose is to face up to the basic uncertainty of life. Whenever we make a choice, we are literally betting our lives. By choosing to read this book and to pursue your college career, you are betting that a college degree will be good for you in some way. The problem is that you may bet on a career only to find there are no jobs available in your field when you graduate. Or there may be jobs, but you discover that you want to change fields or that you aren't as talented in your field as you would have liked. To live authentically is to face up to the fact that there are no "safe" choices in life. And, eventually you will die. If you happen to have made "wrong" choices, time may run out before you can rectify things. Thus, death is the ultimate source of anxiety, and the ability to face up to one's own death is a precondition to authentic living.

Existentialists do not hold that one choice is necessarily superior to another. Any choice involves risk. The woman mentioned above was taking a risk by leaving a marriage (she might be unhappier outside it; she might have been able to work things out), and she was taking a risk by staying in it (she might miss a happier existence; she might not be able to work things out). Telling yourself "I must get a Ph.D.," or "I must stay married," or "I must remain a full-time housewife" reduces anxiety. Then you do not have to make a choice either way. But even though you do not know it, you are making a choice—you are choosing not to face up to the reality of your situation. Other ways you might deny the reality of choice is by drinking too much or taking drugs. You might become dependent, hoping others will make choices for you. You can pretend the future doesn't exist and become an impulsive creature of the moment, thereby denying that choice has some future impact. From an existential perspective, all psychopathology results from an attempt to deny choice.

The inauthentic person does not integrate the past, present, and future in his or her choices. He may avoid choice by thinking in terms of the future: "I'll be myself as soon as I've gotten a good job" or "a good relationship." He may idealize others, thus denying the basic imperfection and uncertainty of life. Or, he may pursue happiness. Victor Frankl (as quoted in May & Yalom, 1984) said that happiness is something that cannot be pursued, it is something that can only ensue. In other words, happiness is a by-product of creative involvement in the world. The "more we deliberately search for self-satisfaction the more it eludes us, whereas the more we fulfill some self-transcendent meaning happiness will ensue" (May & Yalom, 1984, p. 380). Finally, the person living an inauthentic life will often have stereotyped and undifferentiated values, probably swallowed whole from others rather than authentically chosen. As a result, inauthentic patterns of living often consist of attempts to force oneself and the world into rigid, preconceived patterns. Often, the values are treated as objectively real, and the person does not even realize they are chosen.

Psychotherapy

The existential approach is really more of a point of view on psychotherapy than a specific psychotherapeutic approach. The existentially oriented therapist can use any technique or approach, as long as it is used in a way compatible with existential ideas. Some of the earlier existentialists, like Ludwig Binswanger, were psychoanalytic in many respects. Some modern existential therapists practice more like gestalt therapists, others more like client-centered therapists. Nevertheless, there are some general ideas and principles of existential therapy.

The ultimate goal of existential therapy is to get the client to become aware of his or her own goals in life and to make authentic choices. Therapy can be seen in all cases as helping clients "de-restrict" themselves, as helping people to grow. In order to do this, clients must confront themselves and what they have been avoiding. This means confronting their own anxiety and, ultimately, their own finiteness. Often, it is the deepest potentialities that are denied in order to control anxiety. To choose potential is to take a risk, but there will be no richness in life, no joy, unless people confront the possibility of loss, tragedy, and ultimately, death.

One of the first things a client needs to do is to expand awareness. That means to become aware of the potential she is denying, the means she is using to maintain the denial, the reality that she can choose, and the anxiety associated with choice. In order to help her do this, the therapist uses the two basic tools of empathy and authenticity. Empathy is used as a form of the phenomenological method. The therapist attempts to respond to the client without preconceptions. An empathic and nonjudgmental attitude may allow the client's inner world to come to the surface.

The other important tool is the therapist's own authenticity. If the goal of therapy is for the client to be authentic, then it is important that the therapist model authenticity. To be authentic, the client has to learn that he does not have to play roles, that he does not have to be perfect or what he is "supposed" to be, that he does not have to deny aspects of his own experience, and that he can take risks. Therefore, the therapist must model these qualities and try to be a "real" person in therapy. But what does it mean for the therapist to be "real" in therapy? We considered this question in our discussion of genuineness in Chapter 8. It is important because we are aware of a number of instances in which, in our opinion, the concept of "realness" in therapy has been abused by individuals labeling themselves "existential therapists."

In existential therapy, being real or authentic means that therapists share their immediate impressions and reactions to the client with the client. In essence, it is a matter of giving the client immediate personal feedback. However, during the 1960s and 1970s, there were therapists who misapplied this idea and gave feedback in harmfully confrontive ways (Lieberman, Yalom, & Miles, 1973). Effective and helpful feedback is first "owned" by the therapist, that is, presented as his or her personal reaction and not as the objective truth about the client. Second the therapist acknowledges that it *is* his or her perception, that is, it could be unique and idiosyncratic to the therapist. Third, it is given in the form of an "I" statement, which is framed in a way to give specific helpful feedback rather than in a blaming or criticizing way (e.g., "I get bored when you focus on describing what your wife is doing wrong rather than giving me your personal feelings and reactions" versus "You're talking nothing but dry, intellectualized drivel").

Fourth, effective confrontations and shared personal reactions are most helpful when they address clients' strengths—that is, rather than merely tell clients what they are doing wrong, the therapist gives them a sense of what he or she thinks they are capable of doing right.

Beyond empathy and authenticity there are few techniques that are specifically existential. However, Frankl's logotherapy, which is generally considered a form of existential therapy, has contributed two: paradoxical intention and de-reflection (Frankl, 1963). Paradoxical intention is similar to paradoxical intervention, used by family therapists (see Chapter 14). The client is urged to wish for the very thing she fears or to engage in the behavior she fears. Thus, a person with a fear of germs would be instructed to deliberately get herself dirty.

De-reflection, used in cognitive-behavioral approaches, is based on the premise that focusing too much on problems exacerbates them (as an example, think of the last time you tried to get a melody out of your head). The therapist tries to shift the client's attention. This is not to teach the client to deny or repress. Rather, if the client's attention can be directed to positive aspects of his or her life, the negative will not loom so large and may fade away. The best cure for shyness, for instance, is to get so involved in a social situation that you "forget" to worry about how you are being seen by others.

We now turn our attention to a therapeutic approach that is closely related to both existential and client-centered approaches theoretically, but differs substantially in its practice.

GESTALT THERAPY

> In 1970 a terminally ill Fritz Perls was in bed in a hospital in Chicago. At about nine o'clock that evening he kind of half got up with all this paraphernalia attached. The nurse said, "Dr. Perls. You'll have to lie down." He sort of went back down and then almost sat up and swung his legs out a bit. Again she said, "You must lie down." He looked her right in the eye and he said, "Don't tell me what to do," fell back, and died. (Robert Shapiro, as quoted in Shepard, 1975, p. 192)

If there was ever an apostle of "doing your own thing" among the major theorists of psychotherapy, it was Fritz Perls. We have already seen that the existential approach emphasizes the individual's choosing his or her own values and life path. For Perls, this emphasis on individual self-determination and responsibility was central (see Box 9.1). Perls has been virtually synonymous with gestalt therapy and is considered by many to be its founder (or "finder," as Perls said).

Actually, gestalt was cofounded by Perls, his wife, Laura Perls, and a philosopher, Paul Goodman. Perls became the most visible figure and achieved almost guru status on the West Coast in the late 1960s. For many years, people thought of gestalt

---

BOX 9.1

Fritz Perls's Gestalt Prayer

I do my thing, and you do your thing
I am not in this world to live up to your expectations
And you are not in this world to live up to mine.
You are you, and I am I.
And if by chance we find each other, it's beautiful.
If not, it can't be helped.

Source: Fritz Perls, as quoted in Shepard, 1975, p. 3.

---

therapy in terms of Fritz Perls. Yet there is a good deal of diversity among therapists who identify with the gestalt approach, and many do not share Perls's emphasis on "rugged individualism." In fact, Perls's individualistic emphasis actually contradicts other aspects of gestalt theory, as we shall explain. While Perls was preaching rugged individualism on the West Coast, other gestalt therapists, especially those in the eastern United States, were developing a form of gestalt that emphasized interaction and "contact" over "doing your own thing."

Theory of Personality and Psychopathology

Gestalt therapy is a field theory (Kaplan & Kaplan, 1985) in that it holds that one must look at the total configuration of interrelationships in a person's life to understand his behavior. This configuration includes the person's past experiences, beliefs and values, expectations, current momentary desires and needs, current structure of life, including where he lives, his relationships and work, and finally, the immediate situation he is in at the moment. The word **gestalt** (German for "shape" or "form") refers to this configuration of integrated parts.

The state of every element in a field is determined in part by its interaction with every other element in the field. A simple analogy would be a stew. Carrots in a stew made with lamb will taste different from carrots in a stew made with beef. Beef in a stew made with carrots will taste a little different from beef in a stew without carrots, and so on. Thus, the nature of each element in the stew is partly determined by the whole configuration of the stew, and the whole configuration is determined by the interaction of the elements.

This is also true of people, according to gestalt. Psychologically, a person exists at each moment in a field consisting of past experiences, self-image, beliefs, values, attitudes, hopes and fears for the future, significant relationships, career, neighborhood, material possessions, and culture. The field also includes the person's current biological state, momentary needs and desires, and immediate situation (the physical environment, the people present, what is going on). Behavior and experience will be determined at any given moment by the interaction of all these elements. Because there is always some change in some element of this field, the individual is never exactly the same person as he was at any time before. Every day you sit down to breakfast something will be different, if only that you have another day's experience to throw into the "stew." But in addition, the people around you will have changed, and there may be some changes, however small, at work also.

Such a view is a nonlinear perspective on the causes of behavior, experience, and identity. It is the entire configuration that determines behavior, experience, and identity; they cannot be attributed to any one element in the configuration. A linear view traces behavior directly to one or several elements. Suppose a woman is acting rebellious at work. Classical psychoanalysis might hold that her rebellion is caused by the childhood trauma of having an overcontrolling and domineering father. A cognitive view might hold that her rebellion is caused by her dysfunctional belief that she must have her own way. A behavioral view might hold that it is caused by the situational factor of having coworkers who reinforce acting rebellious around the boss. According to gestalt theory, these three factors, plus others, may all be part of the equation of what is leading to the behavior.

Let us look at another set of examples of how the person experiences the current situation in terms of all the other elements in the field. If you are hungry, you will be acutely aware of the presence or absence of food in the situation; if you are in class, your hunger may change your experience of the situation, so that the psychology professor's highly interesting lecture may seem boring and trivial. Or, if you believe psychology is irrelevant to your future plans, you may experience the lecture as boring and trivial. Or, if your past experience has included a large number of academic failures, you may believe that whether you listen in class or not is irrelevant to how well you will do on the test, and you may find it difficult to experience the lecture as involving. Conversely, your hunger, which you experienced as pressing in the classroom situation, may fade completely into the background if the terribly attractive fellow student you have had a secret crush on for weeks suddenly comes over and asks if you would help with today's lecture notes.

The past will take on different roles in a person's current behavior depending on the other elements present. There is no simple linear relationship between the past and the present. The same past experience may play a destructive, disintegrative role in one "stew" and a constructive, integrative role in another. Your past failure experiences in class may interact destructively with usual classroom situations. They may contribute to a configuration that leads you to behave self-destructively by not paying attention and by believing that you will probably fail anyway. But the same set of experiences may interact in a quite different manner with a different classroom situation. Suppose as part of the psychology class, you are assigned to spend 10 hours at a child care center. While there, you notice a child who seems to be having trouble with the class material and who seems to have a negative self-image as a result. Your own experience leads you to establish an immediate empathy with the child. Through your support and empathy, the child begins to change for the better, both in terms of his self-image and in terms of his performance. This, in turn, increases your own feelings of competence. You return to class with a more positive self-image, a greater sense of motivation, and perhaps now begin to do better yourself. The role played by the past, as with any other element, in the stew of your current experience, changes as a function of all other elements present and how those elements blend together.

All the elements we have been discussing form a dynamic whole with each here-and-now situation. The situations individuals live in from moment to moment are, in some sense, part of them. Who they are at any given moment is partially determined by the situation. The "self," from this point of view, is not an internal structure existing somewhere within the person. Rather, it is an ever-shifting, ever-changing part of the ongoing organizational field of experience. The self is really a concept that is part of the stew. It is a concept that helps people to organize the field of their experience in an adaptive way. As with any other concept, its meaning will shift and change in response to other elements present. For example, our bodies are usually incorporated as part of our selves, but sometimes we experience our bodies as alien, particularly if "they" do things we don't like, such as eat or drink too much or get too emotional to function smoothly. Different events, situations, and sensations will be incorporated into the self at different times. Children, for instance, define themselves partially in terms of where they live, who their parents are, and what schools they attend (Montemayor & Eisen, 1977). At a football game, you may function as if your self includes your team. If they win, you feel enhanced; if they lose, you feel defeated.

Therefore, the self exists at the contact boundary between the person and the current situation. An important part of healthy functioning is the ability to draw appropriate contact boundaries between the self and the world. For example, a person who includes too much as part of his self might take too much responsibility for others or feel guilty if things don't go well for others. However, these boundaries shift and change from moment to moment. What is a good, solid, separate boundary in one moment (for instance: between doctor and patient) may become a dysfunctional boundary in another moment when merging and intimacy are involved (for instance, when the doctor is with her romantic partner).

Contact   The process of healthy functioning rests on the idea of maintaining healthy, full, and open contact with one's experiential field. That means staying in contact with what is present in the moment in oneself, and staying in contact with what is present in the moment in the situation. When a person is able to stay in full contact with self and situation, she is able to fully and creatively utilize all aspects of herself to make the best choices possible for herself at that time, given her needs, her values, her goals, and the natural constraints and limits present in the self and the situation. If a man has wrongly been condemned to death, and is waiting on death row for his sentence to be carried out, he can make the most creative choices for himself at that time by staying in full contact with both himself and his situation. He may be able to work through the feelings of hopelessness and rage that he has been having. And, if there is any productive way of dealing with those feelings, such as by contacting his lawyer, or perhaps by helping and comforting others, he will be able to do it. He may not be able to alter his circumstances, but he can find the best possible way of "being himself" given the constraints of the situation.

Full contact can best be thought of in terms of a fluid flow of information. That is, the person's attention is not fixated on one part of his or her experience to the exclusion of other parts. Rather, attention is free to scan the whole field of experience.

Often, individuals are unable to find creative solutions to their problems because they overfocus their attention on certain parts of their experience. Early experiments with animals found that very hungry animals were so overfocused on food that they were unable to "creatively" find ways around barriers to get to that food. Instead they would simply try to break through the barrier over and over (Bruner, 1986).

In a like manner, one of us had a client who had been an executive in a big corporation, but had been laid off when the corporation went bankrupt. He was so overfocused on the idea of finding exactly the same kind of job that he had begun to lapse into despair when his efforts of several months to find such a job had led nowhere. He said he felt he had come to a dead end in a road. There was a big wall and no way to get over it. The therapist attempted to "free up" his attention by asking him to imagine that he was facing a big wall at the end of a road. What does one do? After a few moments, he thought: "Well, one can back up and find a way around that wall." The therapist and the client worked with confronting dead ends metaphorically with this analogy for the rest of the session. Soon after this session, the executive announced that he had found a job in the newspaper doing something different than he had been doing, and at a lower salary, but that he had decided to apply for it. He did apply for and get that job, and the happy ending of this story is that he was ultimately able to get back into a position comparable to the one he had originally held.

Overfocused attention that limits full contact can be caused by many factors: rigidly held values and goals, overly intellectual attempts at problem solving, unacknowledged needs and emotions, and the use of various defense mechanisms. These should be thought of as ways of trying to make or maintain contact with self and world, albeit in dysfunctional ways. For instance, unacknowledged needs and emotions may be a way of trying to maintain contact with people you care about, who you are afraid will reject you if you do acknowledge such needs and emotions.

There is an obvious similarity here between the ideas of gestalt and the ideas of psychoanalysis. That is, disowning or not acknowledging certain parts of oneself, or using defense mechanisms, interferes with effective functioning. The difference is that gestalt emphasizes that these are things the person is actively doing in the moment to try to keep his or her life organized and flowing along, albeit in dysfunctional ways. Disowning, then, is something one does on a moment-to-moment basis. In contrast, in classical psychoanalysis, repression of needs and emotions is something that was done and completed in childhood. Freud likened repression to locking things up in a storehouse. Thus, in contrast to psychoanalysis, gestalt emphasizes the here-and-now activity of disowning. Further, it emphasizes the "life-giving" purpose behind it—to try to maintain some kind of functional contact with one's life situation at the present time.

Organismic Self-Regulation   Gestalt therapists believe that if the individual is able to maintain full, open contact with self and situation in each moment, that individual will be able to make effective choices. They have held that there is a natural organismic self-regulating process by which the whole person can integrate all the available internal and external information so as to "know" or "sense" what is an optimal direction to go in at any given moment. Within the field of a person's experience, whatever is the most important direction for the client to go in will be-come "figural," that is, will stand out against the "ground" of the rest of his or her ex-perience. These are often incomplete gestalts, or unfinished business. For instance, hunger is an incomplete or unfinished part of the field of experience, and it will have a tendency to become figural. However, it will become figural only if it is the most pressing incomplete gestalt present. In our earlier example, hunger became figural during a lecture, but if an attractive classmate asks for help with lecture notes, hunger may temporarily recede into the background as the less pressing of the incomplete gestalts in your current field.

Some incomplete gestalts come from the past. If a woman has a good deal of unre-solved anger toward her father, this may "lurk" in the background until the proper sit-uation brings it forth. Then, as she is dealing with a boss who reminds her of her father, that unfinished business may become figural, influencing her reactions to her boss.

Why is it that most people often don't spontaneously choose what is organismi-cally best? As we have noted, full functioning involves full contact, and that involves full awareness. All barriers to or breakdowns of full functioning can be attributed to things that interfere with full awareness in a given moment. Through full awareness, all the organism's resources are available so that the person's field of experience will organize itself in the best manner possible given the circumstances. According to Simkin and Yontef (1984), the "field will form itself into the best gestalt that global conditions will allow." If full, free attention is available, the person's subjective expe-rience will therefore fluidly shift and flow to best integrate what is happening in each new situation with the person's short-term and long-term goals and needs. Psycho-logical problems are due to interferences with this natural tendency. In other terms, pathology is an interference with the person's creative problem-solving capacity.

The issue is one of availability. Is what is going on both inside and outside avail-able to awareness? Full awareness does not mean being aware at any given moment of everything going on. Attention will flow back and forth, depending on what gestalts form. At times, a person will be in a "contact" mode, and attention will be fo-cused on the situation. At other times, attention will flow more to "inner" thoughts and feelings, and the person will be in a "withdrawal" mode. In the fully functioning person there is a continual flow of awareness between these two poles. If the person attends to the present field, that is, if he is present-centered, he will not ruminate over why he didn't do what he should have done or wonder why he can't seem to do what he should do. The individual will not stop the flow of his awareness by excessively dwelling on thoughts about how he is functioning, or his problems. His full attention will be directed into what he can best do in this moment to move further along his life path.

Open contact allows the individual's full, organismic capacity to "know" to oper-ate. That is, functional knowing is a whole-body affair, not just a matter of intellectual, cognitive analysis. We not only know with our thoughts, but with our intuition and "guts" as well, and intuitive, gut-level knowing is often wiser than intellectual knowing.

While most gestalt therapists value gut-level knowing, many do not carry it to such an extreme as did Fritz Perls, who often sounded anti-intellectual. For instance, he once said, "Intuition is the intelligence of the organism, and intellect is the whore of intelligence" (Perls, 1969, p. 22). The quote from Perls at the beginning of this chapter also captures the anti-intellectual flavor of Perls's form of gestalt. However, most gestalt therapists value both intellectual, rational thinking, and organismic, gut-level knowing.

Abstracting and symbolizing are natural self-regulatory functions, if abstractions and symbols arise from experience. Since experience represents organismic wisdom, abstractions and symbols that arise from experience help organize and integrate experience. However, the kind of abstraction or symbolizing that is most useful for personal change is synthetic rather than analytic, integrative rather than dissective; that is, it is creative, synthesizing knowing, rather than the kind of analytic dissection that we usually equate with thinking. For instance, there are two ways to "know" a poem. One way is to try to experience the poem, and then try to capture your experience in words. The other way is to try to dissect and analyze it. What does this symbol mean? What is the author trying to say? What is the structure of the poem? We are usually taught in school to approach poetry analytically, but from a gestalt perspective, that kind of knowing by itself is useful neither for understanding poetry nor for understanding ourselves.

We have seen that gestalt values full, present-centered awareness, but living in the here and now does not mean pretending that the past did not exist or that the future will not occur. It simply means being fully present in one's awareness of both outer and inner experience, which allows people to bring all of their resources to bear on best coping with the flow of their lives as they are being lived in the present moment. It means to live in the moment, but not for the moment. People's experience will include relevant aspects of their past, as well as relevant aspects of their future goals. If people are fully present, these will all be organismically integrated into their current field of experience.

Psychopathology   What gets in the way of being able to be fully functioning in this manner? People are born with the ability to organismically self-regulate, but they lose it if they learn to split experience up and to categorize rigidly. Categorizing our experience can be helpful as long as we recognize that categories are conceptual tools that help us cope with life and not rigid, absolute fixed realities. It is useful to categorize our experience into "inner" ("inside me") and "outer" ("outside" in the environment). It is useful to categorize part of our experience as "thinking" and part as "feeling." However, the problem is that people are taught to think of these categories as real. In other words, they learn to apply their category systems rigidly and do not even recognize that they are category systems. Therefore, they believe that self and environment are literally and rigidly separate, that feeling and thinking are separate and different, and so on. To make matters worse, they are also taught to categorize some of their experience as "bad" or "sinful."

People are also taught to regulate behavior by external rules and to distrust their feeling and intuition. As a result, they come to believe that the only "good" way to function is to be intellectual, objective, and rational. Both because of the "shoulds" they learn and the labeling of some experience as "bad," they may completely disown some of their experience. For instance, we may completely disown our angry feelings, because it is "bad" to feel anger and we "should" always be kind.

Our upbringing therefore creates splits in our experience. How do these splits affect functioning? In essence, they limit our ability to flexibly adjust to reality. They become rigid organizing principles for our experience. What Freudians call defense mechanisms are organizing principles for gestalt theorists. Take projection as an example. A person projects onto others parts of herself that she has disowned. According to Kaplan and Kaplan (1985), a gestalt way of looking at projection is that the individual organizes her experience of the world so that certain aspects are not included in her concept of "me." But as she organizes her concept and experience of "me," she simultaneously determines how she will organize her experience and concept of others. For example, if she denies and disowns her own assertiveness (perhaps because she was punished for it as a child), she will probably experience and define herself as "weak," "helpless," and "passive." She may simultaneously attribute "strength" and "dominance" to others, because, in relation to her passivity, others will appear especially dominant and assertive. If she denies her own assertiveness, she may further organize her experience of the world so that she believes she must "please" others in order to get along. By splitting up her world, she then "sees" in others what she expects to be there based on her own rigid way of categorizing her experience. A client may "see" the therapist as rejecting or demanding because she "sees" herself as worthy of rejection or as a passive victim of others.

Another defensive organizing principle is introjection. Introjections are rules that are taken whole into how a person organizes his experience, but are not integrated with the rest of his personal rules and values. Thus, they are experienced as external to the self. Usually, what the person wants to do is experienced as "me," while what he ought to do is experienced as an external rule or demand. Parental and societal rules and demands are often introjections. The "top dog-underdog" conflict, described a bit later, exemplifies this conflict.

Responsibility   The splitting of experience and denial interfere with the person's spontaneous ability to regulate himself. The person must instead rely on external guidelines rather than on his own ability to organismically self-regulate. Thus, he is not "response-able." By being "response-able," gestalt theory means taking responsibility for yourself and being present-centered. If you have followed the discussion so far, you can see how they are related. To be fully aware of your inner and outer situation is to be able to make optimum choices for yourself at any given moment.

The word responsibility has several meanings. It is important to keep in mind the gestalt meaning we have just given. Otherwise, the idea of "taking" responsibility for oneself can be misused, and it has been by some humanistic therapists, including Perls himself. In gestalt theory, responsibility rests on the person's ability to make choices for herself and this is often something that therapy helps the client reclaim. That is, it is not always there (at least experientially, for the client) when the client enters therapy. The client learns to take responsibility, meaning that the client reclaims or acquires the power to make choices for herself through the therapy process.

However, the word responsibility has other connotations in our society. To say "I am responsible" for something often means you are to blame for it, it is your fault, or you are the cause of it. In this sense, some depressed individuals take too much responsibility for themselves, rather than too little. They see themselves at fault for just about everything. The meaning of responsibility is sometimes confused by some therapists. A therapist might view a schizophrenic as being responsible for being schizophrenic, and we know of clients who have been accused of "choosing" to be schizo-phrenic, in a way that is blameful and shame inducing. Similarly, some holistic health practitioners even blame people who have cancer, telling them that in some way they have "chosen" to have cancer, through their life decisions. Such a way of getting clients to take responsibility is not helpful. It is disempowering rather than empower-ing. To borrow an adage from feminist therapy (see Chapter 17), it is important to distinguish between how a person's problems developed in the past, and what the person can do about them now. The person needs to take responsibility to now solve them. That does not mean the person was responsible for their development.

There have been other cases in which therapists have abused the concept of re-sponsibility by leading clients to believe that to be responsible for themselves means that they have no responsibility to others. In one such case, a client abandoned her preteenage children to go off and "find herself." The client rationalized her action by saying that the children had to "be responsible for themselves."

Perls himself was guilty of this misapplication of the concept of responsibility. It flowed from his overemphasis on self-sufficiency. Perls confused self-support with self-sufficiency. To be fully in touch with one's organismic experiencing so that one makes optimal choices is to be self-supporting. However, as Simkin and Yontef (1984) point out, there is a difference between being self-supporting and being self-sufficient. As we have said, the self-supporting person makes choices so that his behavior is har-monious and congruent with himself and with his environment. A self-supporting per-son is able to know when he needs help from others and able to ask for it.

Using Gestalt with Pets.

In contrast, Perls seemed to be preoccupied with maintaining his independence from others, as the story about his death and his gestalt prayer illustrate. The gestalt prayer presents a noninvolved image of interpersonal relationships. Despite Perls's stated emphasis on the "I-thou" nature of relationships with others, he remained quite distant and uninvolved with his clients. The "I do my thing . . . you do your thing" idea is an image of ships passing in the night, which, if they just happen to be sailing along on the same course, sail along together for a while. But that is not an image of involvement. The prayer implies, "I don't want your wishes, demands or desires to infringe on me in any way. I want to be free to do my own thing, with no responsibility to you."

The odd thing about this image of insularity is that it contradicts gestalt theory, which holds that a person is an interactive creature. The essential nature of a relationship is, by gestalt's own view, sharing. If a person is sharing, then the other person's wishes and needs will influence and be important to him. The other's needs may even become figural at times, with the person's own needs receding into the background. For instance, if a person you care for is sick, you may let your own needs temporarily recede into the background. Perls's "do your own thing" idea is actually a violation of gestalt itself, and in the years since his death, there has been a movement away from it within gestalt (see Simkin & Yontef, 1984).

Therapeutic Approach

The gestalt goal is not to help the client resolve the particular problem that he or she brings to therapy. The gestalt belief is that the presenting complaint is merely a symptom of a style of living that is the true problem. The focus of gestalt therapy is to increase the individual's ability to maintain full contact and awareness with the current situation, and through that, to reclaim his or her power to make effective choices. Remember that what gestalt means by an "increase in awareness" is not the acquisition of insight. The goal is to increase the client's ability to stay present-centered and be aware in the moment. For this reason, gestalt is a kind of "behavioral existentialism," in that the goal of therapy is to increase the client's "behavior" of maintaining full contact.

As a result, gestalt is a highly experiential therapy. Gestalt does not proceed like verbal therapies, where the therapist and client sit around and talk about the client and his or her problems. In fact, some gestalt therapists see "talking about" problems as an avoidance of here-and-now experiencing, and they will not allow it to take place. They believe that some talking is a cover-up for experiencing. This does not mean that all talking is banned. It is desirable that clients express their feelings toward the therapist or to group members in a group therapy situation and that they express and formulate their present awareness. However, attempts to sit around and talk about one's childhood or one's family life will often be interrupted.

Not all gestalt therapists prohibit talking about one's problems. Some will engage in "conversation" with the client, as long as the conversation is fresh and alive and is a way of creating contact between therapist and client. Polster (1987), for instance, is interested in the "stories" people develop about themselves. Polster is particularly interested in having his clients "flesh out" their stories with concrete details.

Often, clients come into therapy with only story "titles," such as "I'm a failure." Such a title is an abstract, intellectual, global statement, distant from experience. As the client fleshes out the story that goes with this title, he or she gets in touch with the concrete experiences that have led to that global conclusion. Getting in touch with the concrete experiences allows the client to change how the story is evolving, whereas staying with the title leads nowhere.

Some "talking about" that clients engage in is called rehearsing. Often, clients will talk about what the future might bring: "What if I am rejected?" "What if I fail the test?" Such rehearsing can be an avoidance of here-and-now experiencing. Furthermore, it is catastrophizing. Rumination about what the future might bring is, in the gestalt view, one cause of anxiety. Similarly, ruminating about the past can also be an avoidance of here-and-now experiencing.

Instead of having clients talk about problems, the gestalt therapist will interact in ways designed to facilitate full, immediate contact in the here and now. This may include focusing on the here-and-now relationship between the therapist and client. It also can include the use of various exercises that have been developed by gestalt therapists in order to do this. However, gestalt therapists do not like to think of gestalt as a technique-oriented therapy. Resnick (1980) said, "If every technique that any gestalt therapist had ever used before were never used again, true gestalt therapists would barely be affected." Nevertheless, there are a number of techniques or exercises that are commonly used.

Since the main goal of gestalt therapy is to increase contact in the moment, one of the most basic techniques is to have the client simply report what he or she is now aware of in order to train present-centered attention. This will often demonstrate how difficult it is to stay present-centered, as the client will usually stray off into rumination or self-analysis.

Similar to the "now I am aware of" exercise is the "stay with" exercise. The client is instructed to stay with a thought or feeling. Remaining attentive to a feeling may lead to the emergence of some incomplete gestalt or issue the client needs to deal with. Both the "now I am aware of" and the "stay with" exercises can be seen as directly training present-centered attention.

Other techniques enhance the client's experiential focus. Gestalt is a holistic approach, and it is believed that often, nonverbal expression conveys what a client is experiencing more accurately than her words. The client may be asked to exaggerate a gesture or tone of voice to enhance the actual experience of what she is saying. For instance, if the client says in a meek tone of voice, "I feel angry," she may be asked to say it louder. If a client is fooling with his wedding ring as he talks about his depressed feelings, the gestalt therapist may have him exaggerate the gesture and talk from his experience of the gesture: "Now I am slipping my wedding ring on and off my finger. I have a lot of ambivalence about my marriage." If the client is blinking a lot, the therapist may ask him to role-play his eyes: "I am my eyes. I am blinking as fast as I can to hold the tears in."

Another technique is to have a client substitute the phrase "I won't" for "I can't." Often, clients will say, "I can't confront my boss" or "I can't control my sexual feelings." This is a signal that the person is splitting off certain aspects of experience and not being response-able. By saying "I won't confront my boss" or "I won't control my sexual feelings," the individual focuses his attention back to his organis-mic experiencing. He may decide that he does not want to control his sexual feelings or confront his boss, because that is "organismically wise" for him. However, at least now he is able to be response-able.

Perhaps the most well-known experiential exercise used by gestalt therapists is role playing. For instance, to work with a dream, a client will act out parts of the dream. Perls's view was that the parts of a dream, including nonhuman objects such as chairs, cars, or houses, represent different aspects of the self and feelings. One client dreamed of an old road that had fallen out of use when a new superhighway was built nearby. When asked to role-play this road he said, "I'm an old, neglected road. For years I was the center of attention, but even then people used me. They used me and broke me down and then they abandoned me. No one cares about me. I'm just falling apart."

One role-playing exercise is called the "empty chair" (or "two-chair") technique. It is used to help clients resolve internal conflicts and their feeling about conflicts with others. The client sits facing an empty chair. If the problem is an internal con-flict between different aspects of the self, the client is asked to pretend that one side of the conflict is sitting in the chair opposite him. The client role-plays one side. Then the client switches chairs and role-plays the opposite side. If, for instance, you are having a conflict over studying one Sunday afternoon, you would be asked to place the side that watches television in the empty chair and to role-play the side that wants you to study. Then you change chairs and role play the side that wants to watch tele-vision. It might go as follows:

SIDE A: You should study. You'll never graduate and get a good job if you don't. You're bad for wanting to watch television. You just want to do nothing but lie around.

SIDE B: But I only wanted to watch the football game. I need time to relax. I can study later. You demand too much.

The chair-switching continues until some integration between the two sides is achieved.

SIDE A: It's just that I feel so incompetent. I study and study but don't feel I'm get-ting it. Then I get desperate. I'm feeling really vulnerable and scared about my future.

SIDE B: But then I feel like escaping when you feel like that. I don't like feeling in-competent. It's easier to watch TV.

Through the dialogue, the feelings of vulnerability that are the heart of the con-flict emerge. Once you can "own" your feelings, you can deal with them, ultimately freeing you to choose or not to choose to study on any given Sunday afternoon.

The conflict over studying is an example of what Perls called the "top dog-underdog" conflict. The "top dog" is the "should" side, or the "internal critic" side, which is always judging and criticizing the self. The "underdog" is the "want" or "don't want" side. Greenberg (1984) has researched the process of resolution using the two-chair technique. He has found that the critic side starts out expressing itself in terms of shoulds and demands on the other want or don't want side, which Greenberg terms the experiencing side. Eventually, through the role-playing exercise, the critic side begins to soften, and moves away from being a harsh critic. As this happens, the experiencing side moves away from being defensive. The critic side begins to express the feelings of vulnerability that underlie the shoulds and the demands. As that happens, both sides begin to find that they are on the same "side," and some integration is reached.

It is important to note that the goal of gestalt is not to get rid of shoulds, but rather, to own them so that they become choices. A personally chosen "should" feels more like a part of the self, and therefore, the individual feels less "split up" when he or she follows it. For instance, a parent of a newborn may "want" to stay in bed when he begins to cry, but she knows that she should get up and check on him. Because that is a personally chosen, personally meaningful should, she will get up and check on the child, and feel basically good about making that choice.

On the other hand, a should that a person has acquired from parents or society, but that functions more like a voice of someone else telling him what he "should" do or be like, is not experienced congruently, but feels more oppressive and threatening. That kind of should can lead to dysfunctional splits in experiencing.

The same role-playing technique can be used to help a person resolve "unfinished business" with interpersonal conflicts. If, for instance, you are still struggling with feelings that you were neglected and unloved by your father, you would pretend that your father is sitting in the empty chair opposite you. You would role-play your side of the conflict, switch chairs, and role-play your father's side. Again, you would continue the dialogue until some integration occurs. But what is achieved by this role playing? After all, no matter how successfully you use the technique in your therapy sessions, your real father might still act as unloving as ever. But what do you do to contribute to the problem? Perhaps you are in an emotional tangle about your father because you are projecting your expectations onto him. You feel crushed, angry, and depressed when he responds critically to you. Why? Is it possible that this is related to your lack of full acceptance of yourself? If you could fully accept and feel congruent with yourself, then you wouldn't need his approval so much and his rejection of you might be disappointing, but it would not be depressing or devastating. When you role-play your father in the empty chair technique, you may begin to realize that just because he rejects you, you don't have to reject you. You begin to separate out his view of you from your view of you. You begin to take back the power to be in charge of your own life. You may be able to say: "I love you and want you to understand. But if you do not, that is you. I will still love you, but I will not feel bad about myself. I will still feel congruent and whole within myself. I would like your approval, but I do not need it."

There are other gestalt techniques and exercises that we will not present here. The important point is that for many gestalt therapists, techniques are secondary to maintaining full, present-centered contact with the client. While Perls tended to remain distant and uninvolved, many current gestalt therapists respond openly and interactively to their clients. Furthermore, they may integrate ideas from other approaches into their practice.

MAHRER'S EXPERIENTIAL PSYCHOTHERAPY

If you continue on in the field of clinical psychology, you may begin to increasingly encounter the term **experiential psychotherapy.** There is a tendency now to refer to all the existential-humanistic approaches, including client-centered therapy, existential therapy, and gestalt therapy, as forms of "experiential" psychotherapy. This is confusing because there are also a number of specific approaches to psychotherapy that have been named "experiential." In Chapter 8, we discussed Gendlin's experiential psychotherapy, and the process-experiential approach of Greenberg, Rice, and Elliott. Mahrer (1993) has recently noted that there are more than 20 different therapies that include the word "experiential" as part of their name.

Therefore, it is important to keep in mind that when you read about "experiential psychotherapy," the term could be referring to virtually any existential-humanistic approach, or any one of the 20 or more different approaches that specifically call themselves experiential.

What the experiential approaches have in common, in contrast to cognitive-behavioral and psychodynamic approaches, is a relatively stronger emphasis on direct experience in therapy as a key part of the change process. It is only a relative difference, because all therapies are experiential to some degree (see Chapter 16). However, experiential therapies are more likely to stress (a) the activation and experience of emotion; (b) a focus on how people are experiencing their lives, more so than on how they are thinking about their lives; (c) activating the imaginative, experiential side of the personality; (d) the use of experiential activities and exercises, such as gestalt role-play exercises; and (e) a focus on immediate sharing of experience, in one form or the other, between therapist and client.

We shall review one such example of experiential psychotherapy, that of Alvin Mahrer (1989). Mahrer's experiential psychotherapy is based on the idea that the goal is to activate a person's deep inner experiencing potential. Basically, Mahrer assumes that through their upbringing, people develop an operating personality on the "surface." That is the relatively programmed side of the person, through which the person operates on a day-do-day basis. However, this "operating" side of the person often blocks the creative potential for a deeper inner experiencing. Mahrer's goal in therapy is to get people in touch with this deeper inner experiencing.

Mahrer's approach is unusual. He has both client and therapist recline in large easy chairs. Both therapist and client keep their eyes closed throughout the session. Sessions last as long as they have to; that is, there is no fixed time limit, though most sessions usually concluded in about one and a half to two hours.

The client talks about anything he wants, and the therapist tries to facilitate four basic steps. The first step is to try to facilitate the client's being in a moment of very strong experiencing of emotion. This could be anger, sadness, happiness, love, or fear. The most important thing is that strong emotion is accessed. The therapist attempts to do this by trying to put himself in the client's shoes and verbalize the kinds of feelings and emotions he thinks the client is experiencing. The therapist is very dramatic, using loud vocal tone and vivid phrases and images, to try to heighten the client's emotion.

For instance, with a woman client who came in complaining of neck pains (Mahrer, 1989), Mahrer and the client accessed the client's "devilish" side. That brought laughter as the client imagined using her neck pains to get out of going to work.

The second step is to facilitate the appreciation of the inner experiencing that has been accessed. The laughter accessed in step one was associated with the client's "devilish" feelings. This inner experiencing was allowed to be, and the client was allowed to "indulge" in it.

In step three, the goal is to help the client disengage from her normal operating personality, and be able to more fully accept and "be" this inner experiencing. In order to do this, the therapist asks the client to recover memories from childhood where this inner experiencing had been activated. For instance, this client remembered incidents when she had been devilish as a child.

Finally, in step four, using imagination, the client is given a chance to explore what life might be like if she could more fully be this inner experiencing. For instance, with this client, she imagined being "devilish" in her life, quitting her job, and going on a vacation with her husband.

Mahrer's approach to therapy is not explicitly problem oriented. At no time in this therapy session with this client were techniques designed to make the neck pains go away explicitly used, nor was any attempt made to understand the unconscious meaning or the genesis of the neck pains. Yet, after this and several other sessions, Mahrer reports, the pains disappeared. Mahrer's belief is that the goal of his therapy is to access the client's potential for new experiencing, and nothing more. How this becomes concretely instantiated in changing the client's actual life is up to the client. For this reason, Mahrer believes that each of his therapy sessions is a complete "therapy" in itself. There is no continuity from one session to another unless the client brings up the same issue. What is talked about at the next session may be completely unrelated to what was talked about in previous sessions.

EVALUATION OF HUMANISTIC APPROACHES

Effectiveness of Therapy

Smith, Glass, and Miller (1980) found an average effect size of 0.64 for gestalt therapy, which places it around average in effectiveness with most other approaches. Some evidence specifically supports the effectiveness of the gestalt role-playing technique. Bohart (1977) had subjects work on anger conflicts using the empty chair technique. It was found to reduce anger, hostile attitudes, and behavioral aggression more than emotional catharsis procedure or an intellectual analysis procedure. Studies by Greenberg and colleagues (Greenberg, 1984) also demonstrated the efficacy of the empty chair technique in helping a person resolve conflictual feelings. The technique was also found to get the client experientially involved in the therapy process more quickly and immediately than the Rogerian technique of reflection of feelings.

In a recent review of research on "experiential" approaches to psychotherapy in general (including client-centered therapy, gestalt therapy, process-experiential therapy, and related approaches), Greenberg, Elliott, and Lietaer (1994) have concluded that the evidence for the effectiveness of experiential therapies is equivalent to the evidence for the effectiveness of cognitive and other psychotherapies.

We are unaware of any empirical data on existential therapy. A good deal of research has been done on the process of Mahrer's experiential therapy. However, there have been no controlled outcome studies on its effectiveness.

Theoretical Evaluation

The group of existential-humanistic perspectives can be generally criticized in several ways. First, existential-humanistic terminology is vague. Terms such as "living in the here and now," "taking responsibility for oneself," "authenticity," and "staying with one's feelings" are open to a wide range of interpretations. Such vagueness not only leads to widely differing applications of the terms (with some resulting abuses), it also makes it extremely difficult to study existential-humanistic approaches empirically. Further, it is confusing to the beginning therapist. What is "living in the here and now"? How do you know if you are being "authentic"?

A second criticism is the complement of our criticism of psychoanalysis. We criticized psychoanalysis for its overemphasis on the influence of early childhood on personality and the resulting views that personality is fixed and there is therefore little growth and change throughout life. A virtue of the existential-humanistic approach is that it sees the personality as constantly changing. However, this results in an almost complete lack of focus on what remains the same in personality. Existential-humanistic approaches have no language for describing personality structure. Existentialists often write as if people are completely free to remake themselves at any moment. Yet most people are painfully aware of how difficult it is to modify long-standing behavior patterns. In contrast, psychoanalysis has a rich vocabulary for describing various constellations of personality and recognizes that it is not easy to modify ingrained patterns of behavior. The idea that one can "choose" to be whatever one wants at any given moment can be highly distressing to a client. Take as an example a client who feels hollow and depressed when he is alone (one of the symptoms of borderline personality). While it may be true in some theoretical sense that the client is "choosing" to feel that way, the client experiences it as out of his control. To have the client say "I won't feel good when I'm alone" instead of "I can't feel good when I'm alone" may make the client feel even more helpless and guilty. The existential-humanistic overemphasis on the fluidity of human personality is the flip side of the psychoanalytic overemphasis on the fixity of personality.

A third criticism of existential-humanistic approaches is their inconsistent and self-contradictory view of the effects of the environment on behavior. Client-centered therapy, existentialism, and gestalt therapy are all self-identified field theories; that is, they hold that the person exists interactively with the environment. This should mean that the person's current situation would be taken seriously as a partial cause of his or her moment-to-moment behavior. Yet the environment is rarely considered as an influence except in a negative sense. Ricks, Wandersman, and Poppen (1976) said, "Humanistic ignorance of the environment has often led to a naive radicalism, in which the environment is simply treated as an obstacle to self-realization, rather than the arena in which the self will either be realized or lost." We previously made this criticism of client-centered therapy, but it is frequently true of existential-humanistic approaches in general.

As a result of this overemphasis on the possibility of change and underestimation of the environment, humanists do not have ways to explain how situations can influence individuals despite their choices. This sometimes leads to a moralistic flavor in humanistic theorizing, in which, in effect, the client is "at fault" for his problems. He or she has not had the "courage" to rise above the situation and "create" a meaningful life despite environmental limitations. Frankl (1963), for instance, pointed out that some individuals were able to create meaningful existences even in the most extreme circumstances of being in a Nazi concentration camp. However, if we assume that such individuals represent how we all ought to behave, then we have no alternative but to see those who were unable to do this as lacking courage or will or refusing to take responsibility for themselves. In our criticism of psychoanalysis we mentioned some research that finds a correlation between depression in women and adverse circumstances in their life situations (Brown & Harris, 1978). If attributing such depression primarily to early childhood experiences seems overbalanced, it seems equally overbalanced to accuse these women of avoiding choice and not taking responsibility. Humanistic theories don't seem to take into account the fact that some situations are objectively much harder to live in in a creative and actualizing way than others.

Put another way, existential-humanistic approaches see psychological problems as problems of attitude. The problem is that a person has the "wrong" attitudes toward life. If he will only accept responsibility for himself, then he can handle life. What is left out of this approach is the possibility that the individual is doing the best he can given his circumstances and his prior learning history. He may be acting in "good faith," rather than in "bad faith." It may simply be that his view of the world, acquired in an "honest" manner from his upbringing, is limiting. It may also be that he never learned good skills for handling certain situations. Perhaps he avoids not because he lacks courage, but because he lacks skills to cope. Those individuals who handled the concentration camp experience, for instance, may have had the benefit of life experiences (not necessarily favorable ones) that taught them the skills necessary to survive in highly adverse circumstances. Rather than extolling them as being "authentic," and by implication blaming those who did not cope, we might be better off trying to identify the skills these individuals used to survive. It might be possible to teach these skills to others. Existential and gestalt therapists tend to assume that the problem stops with the acceptance of responsibility. But even if the client accepts that he has the power to change, he still needs to learn how to do it. This is especially true if the client's life circumstances are particularly unfavorable.

As previously mentioned, some gestalt therapists in particular, and some existential-humanists in general, can be criticized for adopting an anti-intellectual stance. For Perls "thinking about," "figuring out," and conceptualizing are the "whores" of intelligence, whereas direct experiential, intuitive, gut-level knowing is "real knowing." Presumably, it is our concepts that blind us. However, many cognitive theorists would argue that there is no such thing as "conceptless" knowing. Concepts shape experience, even if they are not consciously thought or verbally articulated. Just because an experience cannot be put into words does not mean it is free of conceptual organization. Cognitive psychologists such as George Mandler (1984) argue that all experience is cognitively constructed, but that only a portion of it is translatable into words.

Furthermore, there are times when what "feels right" may be a less accurate guide to actualizing than what the person thinks is right. For example, a colleague of ours had a client who was raised in an abusive, alcoholic family. For her, what "felt right" was to put up passively with abuse, as she was doing in her marriage. She began to realize intellectually how deadly this was and to work to get out of it. But it was her cognitive analysis of the situation that provided the wisdom and dragged her "reluctant body" and feelings along.

The problem is not a matter of either/or; both intellectual thinking and intuitive or gut-level knowing have their purposes. The problem is that we may learn to overemphasize intellectual knowing at the expense of gut-level knowing. Also, we may learn to treat concepts as more real than the experiences we are using the concepts to describe. The goal is not to eliminate concepts, but rather than realize that concepts are concepts and that we must be open to testing them against experience.

IN CONCLUSION

Existential-humanistic approaches are discovery oriented in their therapy focus. That means that their goal is to provide a context within which clients have the opportunity to consider important personal issues about how they are living life, discover new possibilities for themselves, and create and develop new personal pathways. As such, they are not specifically symptom-focused. Existential-humanistic therapists generally do not look with favor on DSM diagnoses, and prefer to work in an open-ended exploratory fashion, rather than to decide on a specific treatment plan in advance, targeted to removal of client symptoms. As such they do not fit well into the current managed care climate. Yet many clients appear to prefer such approaches, and will even pay out of pocket for them rather than see a brief, symptom-focused therapist through their health care plan. Thus, it is likely that existential-humanistic approaches will flourish outside of the health care system as an alternative therapy for those who want more than symptom removal.

In this regard, existential-humanistic approaches are unique in that they emphasize the whole human being, in the terms that people use to describe and experience their own lives: as creatures who make plans; and have goals, wishes and needs, thoughts and experiences, relationships, and a future. In contrast, psychodynamic approaches emphasize unconscious forces and their impact on conscious experience, and cognitive approaches focus on whether the person's thoughts are logical and scientific. Behaviorism sees the person as a collection of responses, and systems theory sees the person as a "cog" in a system. None of these focuses on the experience of the whole person as an organized, planning entity. It is likely that this aspect of existential-humanistic thought will continue to be of importance.

Existential-humanistic principles have already been incorporated into other approaches, and in that sense will continue to exert influence into the twenty-first century. First, existential-humanistic approaches take growth and change seriously. As such, they give central attention to the creativity of the person. Second, existential-humanists were among the first to take the idea seriously that the person is to some degree the constructor of his or her world. Following from this is an emphasis on choice and individual responsibility. These emphases can now be found in recent psychoanalytic thinking and in cognitive views. Third, existential-humanists were among the first to emphasize the role of meaning, its creation and modification, as a central part of psychotherapy. This also is now a part of most other approaches. Fourth, existential-humanistic thinking was among the first to adopt a "systems" view of personality, emphasizing the interpersonal, interactive nature of the human being. Fifth, approaches such as gestalt have contributed useful techniques to the therapist's "kit."

BIBLIOGRAPHY

Arkowitz, H. (1992, April). [Untitled presentation]. Symposium on "Integrating Experiential, Cognitive, and Behavior Therapies: Theoretical and Clinical Perspectives," Convention of the Society for the Exploration of Psychotherapy Integration, San Diego, CA.

Binswanger, L. (1963). *Being-in-the-world: Selected papers of Ludwig Binswanger.* New York: Basic Books.

Bohart, A. (1977). Role playing and interpersonal conflict reduction. *Journal of Counseling Psychology, 24,* 15–24.

Boss, M. (1963). *Psychoanalysis and Daseinanalysis.* New York: Basic Books.

Brown, G. W., & Harris, T. O. (1978). *Social origins of depression.* New York: Free Press.

Bruner, J. (1986). *Actual minds, possible worlds.* Cambridge, MA: Harvard University Press.

Bugental, J. (1976). *The search for existential identity.* San Francisco: Jossey-Bass.

Fodor, I. (1991, July). *The integration of gestalt and cognitive therapy: Interpreting our ongoing experience.* Workshop presented at the Conference of the Society for the Exploration of Psychotherapy Integration, London.

Frankl, V. E. (1963). *Man's search for meaning: An introduction to logotherapy.* New York: Washington Square Press.

Frings, Manfred S. (Ed.). (1968). *Heidegger and the quest for truth.* Chicago: Quadrangle.

Gendlin, E. T. (1968). The experiential response. In E. Hammer (Ed.), *Use of interpretation in treatment.* New York: Grune & Stratton.

Greenberg, L. S. (1984). A task analysis of intrapersonal conflict resolution. In L. N. Rice & L. S. Greenberg (Eds.), *Patterns of change* (pp. 124–149). New York: Guilford.

Greenberg, L. S., Elliott, R., & Lietaer, G. (1994). Research on humanistic and experiential psychotherapies. In A. Bergin & S. Garfield (Eds.), *Handbook of psychotherapy and behavior change* (4th ed.). New York: Wiley.

Heidegger, M. (1959). Unterwegs zür Sprache. Pfullingen, West Germany.

Husserl, E. (1964). *Cartesian meditations: An introduction to phenomenology.* The Hague, Netherlands: Martinus Nijhoff.

Kaplan, M. L., & Kaplan, N. R. (1985). The linearity issue and gestalt therapy's theory of experiential organization. *Psychotherapy, 22,* 5–15.

Kobasa, S. C., & Maddi, S. R. (1983). Existential personality theory. In R. J. Corsini & A. J. Marsella (Eds.), *Personality theories, research, and assessment.* Itasca, IL: Peacock.

Laing, R. D. (1967). *The politics of experience.* New York: Pantheon Books.

Lieberman, M. A., Yalom, I. D., & Miles, M. B. (1973). *Encounter groups: First facts.* New York: Basic Books.

Mahrer, A. (1989). *How to do experiential psychotherapy: A manual for practitioners.* Ottawa: University of Ottawa Press.

Mahrer, A. (1993). What is "experiencing"?: A critical review of meanings and applications in psychotherapy. *The Humanistic Psychologist, 21,* 2–25.

Mandler, G. (1984). *Mind and body: Psychological stress and emotion.* New York: Norton.

May, R., Angel, E., & Ellenberger, H. F. (Eds.). (1958). *Existence: A new dimension in psychiatry and psychology.* New York: Basic Books.

May, R., & Yalom, I. (1984). Existential psychotherapy. In R. J. Corsini (Ed.), *Current psychotherapies* (3rd ed.). Itasca, IL: Peacock.

Montemayor, R., & Eisen, M. (1977). The development of self-conceptions from childhood to adolescence. *Developmental Psychology, 13,* 314–319.

Mosher, L. R., Menn, A., & Matthews, S. (1975). Soteria: Evaluation of a home-based treatment for schizophrenia. *American Journal of Orthopsychiatry, 45,* 455–469.

Perls, F. S. (1969). *Gestalt therapy verbatim.* Moab, UT: Real People Press.

Polster, E. (1987). *Every person's life is worth a novel.* New York: Norton.

Resnick, R. W. (1980). Foreword. In V. Van De Riet, M. P. Korb, & J. J. Gorrell, *Gestalt therapy: An introduction.* New York: Pergamon Press.

Ricks, D. F., Wandersman, A., & Poppen, P. J. (1976). Humanism and behaviorism: Toward new sysntheses. Reprinted in M. R. Goldfried (Ed.), *Converging trends in psychotherapy: Trends in psychodynamic, humanistic and behavioral practice.* New York: Springer, 1982.

Sartre, J.-P. (1956). *Being and nothingness.* New York: Philosophical Library.

Schmitt, R. (1969). *Martin Heidegger on being human: An introduction to Zein und Zeit.* New York: Random House.

Shepard, M. (1975). *Fritz.* New York: Bantam Books.

Schneider, K., & May, R. (1995). *The psychology of existence.* New York: McGraw-Hill.

Simkin, J. S., & Yontef, G. M. (1984). Gestalt therapy. In R. J. Corsini (Ed.), *Current psychotherapies* (3rd ed., pp. 279–319). Itasca, IL: Peacock.

Smith, M. L., Glass, G. V., & Miller, T. I. (1980). *The benefits of psychotherapy.* Baltimore: Johns Hopkins University Press.

Tillich, P. (1952). *The courage to be.* New Haven, CT: Yale University Press.

Tobin, S. A. (1990). Self psychology as a bridge between existential humanistic psychology and psychoanalysis. *Journal of Humanistic Psychology, 30,* 14–63.

Van De Riet, V., Korb, M. P., & Gorrell, J. J. (1980). *Gestalt therapy: An introduction.* New York: Pergamon Press.

Wheeler, G. (1991). *Gestalt reconsidered: A new approach to contact and resistance.* New York: Gardner Press.

Yalom, I. (1981). *Existential psychotherapy.* New York: Basic Books.

PART **FIVE**

Behavioral and Cognitive Approaches

CHAPTER
10

Behavioral Approaches to Therapy

Much confusion about the etiology of neurotic fear emanates from the assumption that it is quite different from that of normal fear. . . . There is in fact no basic difference. Just as some normal (i.e., appropriate) fears develop on the basis of classical conditioning and some on the basis of information (cognitive learning), the same is true of neurotic fears. What differentiates normal and neurotic fears is the character of the stimulus situation to which the conditioning has occurred. If that stimulus situation is objectively either a source of danger or a sign of danger, the fear is appropriate or "adaptive"; if it is neither, the fear is neurotic. (Wolpe, 1982, p. 27)

A 34-year-old man had a severe fear of being in an automobile. This had started four years previously when his car had been struck from behind while he was waiting for a red light to change. He had been thrust forward so that his head, striking the windshield, had sustained a small laceration. He had not lost consciousness, but a surge of panic had swept over him, brought on by the thought "I am about to die." The fear became connected to the car's interior and spread to all car interiors. During these four years he had been unable to enter a car without great anxiety. Driving was out of the question. That fear was entirely due to classical autonomic conditioning. (Wolpe, 1982, p. 28)

One day you are walking down the hall in the psychology building on campus when a research assistant beckons to you from a laboratory door. "Want to see something weird?" "Okay," you say, following the assistant into the lab. "See anything unusual about this rat?" she says, reaching into a cage and grabbing a fat, glossy, white rat by the scruff of the neck.

"No, it looks like a normal rat," you conclude after a careful examination of 1.5 seconds.

"Well, watch this." She carries the rat over to a large box with lights and wires attached to it. There is no top on the box and it is divided into two compartments with an opening between them. One compartment is painted all white and the other dark brown.

"What will happen if I put the rat in there?"

"Well," you consider, trying to remember what you know about rats, "the rat will probably explore the compartments, and it will probably stay mostly in the dark compartment." (You suddenly remember that rats prefer darkness to light.)

She lowers the rat into the dark side of the box, and almost before its paws can hit the floor, it shoots through the doorway into the white compartment, and there it stays, sniffing around.

"How peculiar," you say, because you are absolutely certain that you recall Professor Lecturn telling the class that rats prefer dark areas. "Maybe it just doesn't know any better," you suggest. "Let's see that again."

Obligingly, the assistant places the rat in the dark compartment again. Again, it rushes to the white side and stays there. She repeats this activity several times, and the rat always runs to the white side without the slightest hesitation. She even inserts a door into the opening between the compartments, which can be opened by a lever in the dark compartment. When she then puts the rat in, it rushes to the lever, pushes it, and scurries through the open door into the white side. Since you (and Professor Lecturn) could not possibly be wrong about normal rat behavior, there must be something wrong with this particular rat. "Wow," you say, "what an abnormal rat!"

"You think so?" the assistant asks. "What if I told you that there used to be an electric grid on the floor of the dark compartment? This rat received a huge electric shock in there."

"I see," you nod knowingly. "But there's no electric grid in there now, so it's impossible for the rat to get shocked again."

"That's the neurotic paradox. The learned behavior remains even though the conditions for the original learning no longer hold."

"Why doesn't the rat eventually learn that no shock is coming?"

"It would under certain circumstances," she admits, "but there are several theories about why it doesn't under these conditions. One possibility is that when the rat runs into the white side, its fear is reduced, which is highly rewarding, so the behavior of running to the white side is constantly being reinforced by fear reduction."

You nod as if you understand and remark, "So this is a perfectly normal rat after all."

"Yes, when you know its learning history."

FOUNDATIONS OF BEHAVIOR THERAPY

The set of therapeutic interventions known collectively as behavior therapy resulted from the application of scientific behavioral theory and methods to the treatment of psychopathology. The foundations of behavior therapy lie in learning theory, and the theoretical assumptions behind behavior therapy techniques begin, like learning theory, with the philosophical belief that methods for dealing with human behavior problems should be based on the scientific method. Another fundamental assump-

BOX 10.1

One Flew Over . . .

Several years ago, a psychologist sat quietly in a staff meeting while two psychoanalytically oriented psychiatrists argued for an hour about the patient they had all seen recently in intake. The patient was an attractive 17-year-old woman who was suffering from anxiety and a severe phobia of birds, which kept her from being able to go out to school or work. One analyst argued strongly that the fear of birds symbolized her fear of heterosexual encounters, since the birds unconsciously represented penises or "cocks." The other analyst argued, equally vociferously, that the fear of birds represented her fear of her latent homosexuality, since at that time and place "bird" was slang for young girl or "chick."

During intake, the psychologist had asked the patient why she thought she was so afraid of birds. The patient immediately described an incident when she was 4 years old and visiting her aunt's farm. As punishment for some naughty act, the aunt locked her in the henhouse for a few minutes. In her attempts to escape from the henhouse, the crying child probably frightened the chickens. She vividly recalled the hens squawking and flying about, hitting her with their wings and scratching her face and arms. She remembered feeling terrified, and she avoided birds ever after.

When the analysts finished arguing, the psychologist ventured to report the client's history. The analysts paused for only a moment before uniting in asserting that the henhouse incident was merely a "screen memory" invented to rationalize the phobia. Nevertheless, the psychiatrists agreed to allow the psychologist and her young colleague to try out a new approach to treatment based on the assumption that the fear was a conditioned response and that unconscious childhood memories need not be dealt with.

The treatment (described in Box 10.3) was successful in that the patient's fear was reduced and she was able to leave her house and obtain a job. It is not known if the young woman developed new or substitute symptoms for the phobia as would be predicted by psychoanalysis, but she did not come back to the agency in the four years the psychologist worked there.

tion is that all behavior is determined and that the variables determining it can be discovered and changed.

Behaviorists differed most drastically from previous theorists of psychotherapy in their insistence that abnormal behavior is not fundamentally different from normal behavior and that the abnormal "symptom" *is* the disorder (see Box 10.1 and Box 10.2 for discussions of the issue of symptom substitution). The same laws of learning

BOX 10.2

Symptom Removal or Symptom Substitution?

Since the 1950s, the debate between behaviorists and psychoanalysts over psychotherapy theory and practice has focused on the issue of symptom substitution. Psychoanalysts believe that neurotic symptoms are expressions of some unconscious internal conflict and that the conflict must be resolved in treatment. Behaviorists believe that internal conflicts, even if they exist, are unimportant; they believe the symptom is the problem, and it is the symptom that can and should be treated. When behaviorists demonstrated empirically that symptoms could be removed with behavioral methods, psychoanalysts countered that symptom removal would merely be followed by symptom substitution. Since the true cause of the neurosis, the internal conflict, was untreated, it would cause new symptoms to appear if others were removed.

In considering the case of the bird-phobic woman in Box 10.1, the psychoanalysts thought that the phobia was caused by her unconscious fear of heterosexuality (or homosexuality) and that treatment should focus on dealing with that unconscious fear, whichever it was. If the bird phobia itself were treated and removed, they argued, she would soon develop another symptom, such as agoraphobia, anxiety attacks, or even sexual acting out or another impulse disorder, because she would still be suffering from her unconscious conflict about sex.

The controversy over symptom substitution is really about which theoretical and therapeutic approach is correct, and it would seem that the issue could be solved empirically. Does symptom substitution occur? After years of research, the answer is a clear "Maybe; sometimes." The question turns out to be difficult to answer.

First, there is little agreement about what constitutes a symptom. Second, it is difficult to distinguish between a symptom that is a replacement and one that is a new problem. How long after therapy is it safe to conclude that a substitute symptom is not going to occur? Most behaviorists follow up cases for six months or a year after treatment, and report few instances of new symptoms, but psychoanalysts argue that it takes longer for symptom substitution to occur. If another symptom does appear after treatment, how is it to be proven that it is caused by the same internal conflict that caused the first one, rather than being a separate problem?

Given these research difficulties, it is probably not surprising that behaviorists continue to report successful symptom removal with little evidence of symptom substitution after six months or a year and psychoanalysts continue to treat unconscious conflicts rather than "mere" symptoms.

apply to all behavior, both "normal" and "abnormal." Abnormal behavior is simply the normal, lawful response to abnormal learning conditions. Abnormal behavior can be changed by changing these learning conditions. In essence, behavior therapy is based on a very optimistic theory.

Early behaviorism also differed from traditional psychotherapy in its opposition to mentalistic notions of the mind and emphasis on objectively observable behaviors and situations. Strict behaviorists, such as B. F. Skinner (1938, 1971), believe that behavior can be explained by the principles of learning and conditioning, without using what goes on in the person's head as an explanation. It is not that behaviorists deny the existence or importance of thoughts and feelings (or genetic predispositions), but rather they think that these internal behaviors should be subject to the same scientific investigation as behavioral factors. Until they are, such factors have no explanatory value, and scientific rigor requires an emphasis on observable behavior.

Most of the basic assumptions in the behavioral view can be seen in the story of the "abnormal" rat at the beginning of the chapter. Mowrer and his associates did a series of experiments similar to the one described in the rat story during the 1940s and 1950s (Mowrer, 1947; Mowrer & Lamoreaux, 1946; Mowrer & Solomon, 1954). Even earlier, in 1920, John B. Watson is supposed to have attempted the first demonstration that "abnormal" behavior is learned in humans as well as rats, and in 1924, Mary Cover Jones demonstrated how such "abnormal" behavior could be unlearned.

A Brief History of Behavior Therapy

Watson reported that in an experiment, he classically conditioned a fear of white rats in 11-month-old Albert (Watson & Rayner, 1920), although some scholars now question the veracity of the tale of Little Albert (Harris, 1979). Prior to Watson's intervention, Little Albert had enjoyed playing with a white rat. Watson paired a loud, frightening noise with handing Little Albert the rat, and he did this a few times. Soon Little Albert cried at the sight of a rat and tried to crawl away, and he showed the same fear reaction to any white, furry object. Watson had demonstrated that an abnormal behavior such as a phobia could be learned. He even wrote, "It is probable that many of the phobias in psychopathology are true conditioned emotional reactions" (Watson & Rayner, 1920, p. 14).

In the case of Little Peter, Mary Cover Jones (1924) demonstrated that phobias could be unlearned. She taught a 3-year-old boy with a fear of rabbits and rats to like them. By bringing a caged rabbit closer and closer while Little Peter was eating, his fear was gradually eliminated, supposedly because the feared object became associated with the pleasure of eating.

Despite these early studies, it was to be several decades before behavior therapy was established as an identifiable school of therapy. There are several reasons for this odd state of affairs. Academic psychologists were interested in establishing the scientific status of their field, not in applications. Clinical psychologists were working in a field dominated by the medical profession and the psychoanalytic viewpoint. It took an outsider, Joseph Wolpe, to popularize behavior therapy in clinical psychology.

Wolpe was (and still is as of this writing) a psychiatrist from South Africa trained in psychoanalysis who became interested in Pavlov's research and theories. Pavlov theorized that fields of excitation and inhibition in the brain caused behavior and that certain kinds of excitation could interfere with or inhibit other responses. Wolpe generalized these ideas to the causes and treatment of phobias. He saw that phobias could be explained as conditioned fear responses. He believed they could be treated by conditioning a new response to the fear stimulus, a response that would interfere with or inhibit the fear response, that is, a response that would be incompatible with the fear response, something that could not be done or felt at the same time as fear. He settled on deep muscle relaxation, also known as progressive muscle relaxation (Jacobson, 1938). Wolpe taught his patients to induce deep muscle relaxation in themselves, and then he gradually introduced verbal images of the phobic object, with the aim of replacing the conditioned fear response with the conditioned relaxation response to the feared stimulus. (This method, also known as **systematic desensitization,** is described in the section on classical conditioning methods of behavior therapy.)

Wolpe achieved good results with his new treatment method, which he described in his *Psychotherapy by Reciprocal Inhibition* (1958). The method was an immediate hit among clinical psychologists, who then turned to their own rich background of behaviorism with new appreciation. Pragmatic American psychologists realized that at last, here was a theory and technology that could challenge psychoanalysis in explanatory and treatment power. This realization coincided with the post–World War II increase in demand for psychological services for people with a wide variety of problems and economic resources. Behavior therapies promised to be a quick, relatively inexpensive, and highly effective way of meeting this increased demand.

Before going further into the types of behavior therapy, we should first review some of the basic principles of behaviorism.

Principles of Learning

There are two basic types of conditioning: classical or respondent conditioning and instrumental or operant conditioning. **Classical conditioning** was first demonstrated by the Russian biologist I. Pavlov in his famous experiments with dogs. Pavlov was actually trying to study digestion when he discovered classical conditioning and then turned to a whole new career in neuropsychology. Each dog was hooked up to a device so that its saliva drained out of a fistula into a beaker to be measured. Pavlov introduced measured amounts of food into a dog's mouth and observed the salivation response, which is the first step in digestion. Soon he noticed that the dogs began to salivate when they saw him approaching with the food, and they even began to salivate at the sight of the experimental harness. While this ruined his digestion research, he became intrigued and began to study this process systematically. He rang a bell immediately before introducing the food into the dog's mouth, and he paired the bell and food several times. Soon the dogs salivated to the sound of the bell, even if no food followed.

In Pavlov's experiment, salivation is the **unconditioned response** to the **unconditioned stimulus** of food. Salivation is the natural or automatic response to food. The bell, rung just before food was given, is the **conditioned stimulus,** and salivating to it, instead of to food, is the **conditioned response.** In other words, salivating to a bell is not a natural, automatic response, but is a conditioned, or learned, one. It has been thought that any stimulus that occurs around an unconditioned stimulus can become associated with it, as the sight of Pavlov and their experimental harness became associated with food for Pavlov's dogs.

Classical conditioning occurs only with behaviors that are automatic, perhaps even unconscious responses to things—for example, reflexes such as salivation and emotions such as fear. The rat described at the beginning of this chapter was classically conditioned to fear the dark compartment. The automatic or unconditioned response to the unconditioned stimulus of electric shock is fear. The cue of the dark compartment was close in time and place to the rat's perception of the shock, so the dark compartment became the conditioned stimulus to the conditioned response of fear.

The most famous example of **instrumental** or **operant conditioning** is B. F. Skinner's bar-pressing rat. In Skinner's experiments, rats learn to press a bar, which releases a pellet of rat chow into a food cup. It is called instrumental because the conditioned response of bar pressing is instrumental in obtaining the reward of food. It is called operant because the behavior being conditioned or learned is operant behavior, that is, behavior that is voluntarily put forth by the organism, rather than an automatic response to a stimulus as in classical conditioning. The response of bar pressing precedes the rewarding stimulus of food. Recall that in classical conditioning, it is the opposite: The conditioned stimulus precedes the conditioned response.

Besides classical and operant conditioning, there is a third type of learning, called **extinction.** Extinction occurs when rewards are no longer delivered after the operant response, and the organism learns to stop making the conditioned response. A rat presses its bar and no food falls into the food cup; the rat is said to be on *extinction.* It may give the bar a few more quick presses—still no food. Gradually, it gives up pressing the bar altogether. Bar pressing has been *extinguished.* Classically conditioned responses can also be extinguished. If Pavlov rang the bell many times without delivering food, the dogs would gradually stop salivating to the bell. Notice that extinction is an active learning process, not simply forgetting or fading. The rat learns that bar pressing does not result in food. A behavior is said to be strongly conditioned, or *resistant to extinction,* if it takes a long time, or many trials of doing the behavior for no reward, to extinguish.

Social learning theorists such as Bandura (1977b) have argued that in addition to classical conditioning, operant conditioning, and extinction, another type of learning, *imitation* or **observational learning,** is important in humans. Humans and other primates are great copiers of others, and it may be that most human learning is a result of imitation. All that is necessary for this type of learning to occur is for the person to observe someone else engaging in the behavior. In many experiments, Bandura (1969) and his colleagues demonstrated that humans will imitate almost anyone, including film and cartoon characters, but they are more likely to imitate models who are warm and nurturant and who have high status and power than to imitate mean, low-status models. They are also more likely to imitate models who are rewarded for their behavior than models who are punished for their behavior.

The reinforcement in operant conditioning has been defined several ways. One seemingly circular definition is that reinforcement is anything that strengthens the behavior that precedes it. "Strengthening," to behaviorists, seems to mean increasing the likelihood of performing a behavior. Any consequence contingent on a behavior that increases the likelihood of that behavior is said to reinforce the behavior.

Currently, a *reward* is defined as either the delivery of a positive stimulus, such as food, or the removal of a negative stimulus, such as turning off a loud noise. Delivering a positive stimulus is also called **positive reinforcement;** removing a negative stimulus, as in stopping a loud unpleasant noise, is called **negative reinforcement.** A *punishment* can also be positive or negative: either the delivery of a negative stimulus, such as an electric shock (and called, just to make things difficult, positive punishment), or the removal of a positive stimulus, such as interrupting beautiful music or docking someone's allowance (called negative punishment). It is a common misconception that positive reinforcement refers to reward and negative reinforcement refers to punishment, an old but no longer correct terminology.

The Nature of Reinforcement   One question that has long puzzled behaviorists is "What constitutes a reward?" Food is obviously a reward to a hungry rat. But rewards are rarely that obvious in human learning, and much of our behavior does not seem to be followed by any obvious reward. In humans, an important reward seems to be the attention of other human beings. We are a social species. We work with people, we talk to them, we go out to lunch, we play cards, we goof off and hang out together. What is the reward? Just the pleasure of interacting with others seems to be enough.

There is evidence that the reward of human attention has drive properties—we need it and are motivated to try to obtain it. In one experiment (Gewirtz & Baer, 1958), children who had been deprived of human attention for 20 minutes worked longer and harder at a subsequent boring marble-dropping task for the simple reward of an adult's saying "Mm-hmm" and "Fine" than children who got lots of attention before the task. This is similar to a food-deprived rat's working longer and harder at bar pressing for food than a well-fed rat. We say the rat is hungry—it has a drive or need for food. People may have a similar need for attention.

Furthermore, if people are deprived of attention, they may resort to unpleasant or "abnormal" behavior to get it. Even if the form of attention they receive for abnormal behavior is disapproval or punishment, it appears that they prefer this to being ignored. Most of you can probably remember a really obnoxious kid in your elementary school who made the other children laugh or bothered them and was repeatedly scolded or threatened by the teacher. When that kid did work quietly, probably everyone ignored him. A child who does not seem able to get enough attention by prosocial methods may resort to disturbing or disturbed behavior in order to get it. Such behavior is called *negative attention seeking,* because both the behavior to get attention and the attention it gets are negative.

Postmodern, radical behaviorists (discussed below) argue that it is futile to try to define what is rewarding for everyone. Food and attention appear to be universal rewards, but they are not. For example, anorexics find food aversive, and very shy people may find attention, even warm praise, to be punishing. Radical behaviorists go back to the earlier definition of reinforcement as any consequence that strengthens a behavior. As such, reinforcement will be different for each individual, depending on that person's learning history and the situational context. In the therapy situation, therapists must pay attention to client behavior in order to determine what reinforces a particular behavior in a specific individual.

Schedules of Reinforcement   Many experiments have studied how the timing of rewards affects the speed and strength of conditioning. Rewards can be given after every instance of an operant response, for a 100 percent reinforcement schedule, or after every few operant responses, for a partial reinforcement schedule. In real life, it is unlikely that rewards ever arrive on a 100 percent reinforcement schedule. In general, 100 percent reinforcement results in faster conditioning than partial reinforcement, but partial reinforcement results in stronger conditioning. The more unpredictable the partial reinforcement schedule, the more resistant the behavior is to extinction. Place a rat who has received food variably for every tenth to twentieth bar press on extinction, and it will take that rat a long time to learn that no food is coming for any bar press.

Human behavior is most often rewarded on some type of variable partial reinforcement schedule, which is probably why it is so difficult to break some bad habits. An hour before dinner, children start whining for snacks. Their parents tell them no, because dinner is almost ready. On the tenth whine, exasperated parents cave in and give the children snacks. Then they wonder why the next night, the children start in whining for snacks before dinner. On a schedule of partial reward, whining has been inadvertently and unfortunately strongly conditioned and made resistant to extinction.

Generalization   Generalization occurs when a response learned under one set of conditions is made in other situations. A child who whines for snacks before dinner and gets rewarded for it may generalize this learning to whining for snacks before lunch, whining for toys as well as snacks, or whining for things at school as well as at home.

Modern learning theory has changed from the principles just described. For example, behaviorists now argue that what the animal is learning in Pavlovian conditioning is not a reflex, but rather *associations* between stimuli. The animal learns which cues predict certain events, and there is evidence that only stimuli that are useful in prediction can be conditioned (Rescorla, 1988; Rachman, 1991; Rapee, 1991). However, since this is not a book on learning theory, we will not cover every aspect of learning, but trust that this review is sufficient to help you make sense of the rest of the chapter.

The Development of Abnormal or Unwanted Behavior

Behaviorists believe that just the basic principles of learning—Pavlovian conditioning, operant conditioning, extinction, imitation, generalization—can account for behavior, both normal and abnormal. Abnormal behavior, bad habits, and other unwanted behaviors are learned in the same way as normal or desired behaviors. Because a behavior that seems odd or abnormal was acquired by the basic learning principles, it will make sense when its learning history is known. And it should be possible to change it by applying those same learning principles.

It is easy to see that phobias might result from experiences like the electric shocking of the rat in the dark compartment. A phobia is a strong fear of something that does not elicit fear in most people. Since most rats prefer dark places, we could say that, compared to other rats, the behavior of the rat that always ran away from the dark looked abnormal. When it is known that the rat had been shocked in the dark compartment, its behavior makes sense. A fear-evoking event may classically condition a phobia in humans as well.

Let us turn to the example of the young woman, described in Box 10.1, who was severely afraid of birds. As a child, she was locked in a henhouse and "attacked" by the frightened chickens. She was classically conditioned to fear chickens, harmless stupid birds that do not ordinarily elicit fear in the human heart. In her case, the sight of chickens was paired with the experience of being locked in a small enclosure with scratching, squawking, flapping, and pecking chickens, an experience that would naturally be frightening to a small child, if not to all of us. The pecking chickens were the unconditioned stimuli for the unconditioned response of fear. That is, fear is the automatic, reflexive response to these stimuli. The sight of chickens, which was paired with the unconditioned stimuli, became the conditioned stimulus for the conditioned fear response. Furthermore, this response generalized, so that the sight of other birds also frightened the girl. She had developed a bird phobia.

Why didn't this fear extinguish with time, as the girl grew up? This phenomenon is the so-called **neurotic paradox.** The conditioned fear remains, even though the original conditions for learning it are no longer present or relevant. The rat's fear of the dark compartment remains even though the electric grid floor has been removed and the rat is no longer shocked when it is placed in the compartment. In the case of the bird-phobic woman, the fear of birds remained even though the fearful event was long in the past and in everyday life, birds don't attack or injure people.

There are several explanations for the neurotic paradox. One possibility is that the amount of time it takes to run away from or avoid the feared stimulus is shorter than the amount of time it takes for real fear to build up and be extinguished. The rat runs away from the dark compartment before it has a chance to learn that it won't be shocked. If the rat were to be locked in the dark compartment, its fear would build up, no shock would follow, its fear would decrease, and the classically conditioned fear of the dark compartment would eventually be extinguished.

Another explanation for the persistence of the phobia is that the operant behavior of running away or avoiding the feared stimulus is repeatedly rewarded with anxiety reduction. When the rat is put in the dark compartment, it starts to feel fear and quickly runs into the white compartment, where it immediately feels better because its fear is reduced. This reward is a so-called negative reinforcement, in that the reduction of the unpleasant fear is rewarding. Thus, the avoidant or phobic behavior is repeatedly rewarded through the reduction of fear, and it will therefore persist. For years, every time the young woman saw a bird, she would feel afraid, walk away from it, and immediately feel better, so that the avoidance of birds was a highly rewarded and well-learned behavior. To summarize, then: A phobia is the result of operantly conditioned avoidance behavior that is rewarded by the reduction of classically conditioned fear.

Behaviorists believe that complex neuroses and other abnormal behaviors, not only phobias, are also learned, and "symptoms" are operant behaviors rewarded by the reduction of classically conditioned fears. Let's look at one more example of how abnormal or unwanted behavior is learned—temper tantrums. Most small children throw one or two temper tantrums at some time or other. This behavior is not abnormal, although it is definitely unwanted. However, some parents inadvertently train their children to throw tantrums excessively, and then it becomes abnormal. Such parents tend to fail to reward desired behavior and to pay attention only to undesired behavior. We have seen that most humans find receiving the attention of other humans highly rewarding. Children will do a lot of things to get their parents' attention: "Look at me! Watch this! See the doggy, Mommy!" A stressed parent may ignore these normal and fairly pleasant attempts to get attention. She may also be so relieved when the child plays quietly by himself that she goes off to rest and so fails to reward this type of "good" behavior with any attention. (It could be said that desired behavior is on extinction.) In stressed families, the level of reward is often low for all behavior. The child may then throw a tantrum, a behavior that is difficult to ignore, especially if it is done in the middle of the supermarket. The parent is forced to pay attention, even if that attention is scolding or punishing, and the child has learned a guaranteed way to get the parent's attention. The parent has rewarded the child for throwing the tantrum by paying attention. In a low-reward family, a child may throw more and more tantrums to get attention until it is a well-learned behavior. The parent has not planned to train the child to throw tantrums, but failing to reward desired behavior and paying attention to undesired behavior has had that result.

By now you have probably thought of some examples of abnormal behaviors that learning theory cannot explain. Not all children in low-reward families learn to throw temper tantrums. It is possible that not all children locked in a henhouse would develop a bird phobia. Not all phobias are associated with an identifiable childhood trauma. Some adults can reason themselves out of early learned fears. Not all survivors of car crashes develop a fear of driving, but some do. How can learning theory account for such individual differences? How can a behaviorist explain such apparently complicated disorders as schizophrenia, which includes hallucinations and bizarre thinking? How could someone learn such a thing as an anxiety neurosis, when the aversive feeling of anxiety is experienced almost all the time?

Behaviorists have developed a number of theoretical and empirical arguments to counter such criticisms. For example, H. J. Eysenck (1967) reported evidence that there are genetic differences in conditionability, which would account for the fact that some people become phobic after car accidents and some do not. In general, behaviorists counter criticisms of their theory by arguing that if we could obtain a sufficiently accurate learning history for each individual, we would find appropriate explanations for her or his behavior. However, a detailed discussion of all the criticisms and defenses of the behavioristic view is beyond the scope of this book. Behaviorists' final argument is that even if we are not certain precisely how all abnormal behavior is learned, we can nevertheless change it by applying learning principles. If behavior is learned, it can be unlearned, and new behavior can be learned.

BEHAVIOR THERAPY

There are behavioral treatment methods based on all the learning principles previously discussed. In addition to Wolpe's method of classically conditioning new responses to feared stimuli, there are behavior therapies based on extinction, classical conditioning of aversive responses, operant conditioning with rewards, imitation, and combinations of these methods. Different forms of behavior therapy have been developed to treat every type of psychological disorder, as well as to modify bad habits, to eliminate unwanted behaviors, and to teach new skills. Behavior therapies have been developed to treat disorders from depression and obsessive-compulsive neurosis to borderline personality disorder, as well as phobias. This chapter will cover only a representative sample of the many behavior therapies currently available.

Behavior therapists agree only that there is no commonly agreed-on definition of behavior therapy. The following definition (Franks & Barbrack, 1983) is, nevertheless, endorsed by the American Association of Behavior Therapists:

> Behavior therapy involves primarily the application of principles derived from research in experimental and social psychology for the alleviation of human suffering and the enhancement of human functioning. Behavior therapy emphasizes a systematic evaluation of the effectiveness of these applications. Behavior therapy involves environmental change and social interaction rather than the direct alteration of bodily processes by biological procedures. The aim is primarily educational. The techniques facilitate improved self-control. In the conduct of behavior therapy, a contractual agreement is negotiated, in which mutually agreeable goals and procedures are specified. Responsible practitioners using behavior approaches are guided by generally accepted principles. (p. 509)

Although they may not define therapy the same way, most behavior therapies do share certain assumptions. All behavior is learned by the same principles. Behavior can be unlearned and changed. Therapy methods are tied to experimentally verified principles of behavior. Research and assessment are integral parts of behavior therapy. Therapy techniques are specified and defined clearly and concretely, so they are testable. The outcome of therapy is evaluated empirically with measurable behavior changes.

All behavior therapies emphasize the importance of the relationship between the therapist and client. Therapy must begin with an interview between therapist and client, in which the nature of the client's problem and its appropriateness for behavioral treatment is assessed. The initial interview may include some of the behavioral assessment techniques described in Chapter 5, such as questionnaires or observations. Trust and understanding between therapist and client are assumed to be essential for the success of the initial interview(s) and for the success of treatment as well. If the therapist is to reward behavior changes, then the therapeutic relationship must have rewarding qualities. Behavior therapists recognize the importance of the nature of the relationship between therapist and client and the role of therapist warmth and empathy to enhance that relationship.

Initially, a detailed history of the client's problems is taken, including when and how the problems began, their frequency (or baseline), what the environmental stimulus of the problems is, and what solutions the client has tried so far. The therapist tries to clarify with the client precisely what the client hopes to accomplish in therapy. The therapist will also try to cast these goals in behavioral terms: What type of behavioral changes will the client and therapist have to see in order to know that therapy has been successful and the goals have been reached?

Once the problems and therapy goals have been defined, the therapist thoroughly explains the therapeutic procedures and their rationale to the client. The therapist may cite research demonstrating the effectiveness of the method with other clients with similar problems. Only when the client completely understands the steps involved in the behavior therapy can the client consent to it. In this sense, the therapist is very much an educator and consultant, and the client is very much an equal partner in the process.

Behavior therapy may involve using more than one method for more than one client problem. In a way, all behavior therapists are eclectic. Despite this variety, most behavior therapies include at least these five steps in their procedures:

- Assess and evaluate the client's problem.
- Choose the best therapeutic method for addressing the problem.
- Educate the client about the method, including exactly what will be done and the likelihood of success.
- Apply the therapeutic method.
- Evaluate the success of treatment.

EXPOSURE-BASED TREATMENTS (PAVLOVIAN CONDITIONING METHODS)

The assumption behind behavior therapies based on Pavlovian conditioning is that abnormal behavior is due to inappropriate, classically conditioned emotions, especially fear and anxiety. These emotions then motivate avoidance and other behaviors that are rewarded by anxiety reduction. Since the Pavlovian methods share the feature of exposing the client in various ways to the feared object, these methods are now called exposure-based treatments. It is also argued that these methods do not work because of classical conditioning, but rather, they work because they increase the individual's sense of coping and mastery. Again, because this is not a book on learning theory, we will leave this issue and move on to a description of the treatments.

Desensitization

Originally called **reciprocal inhibition, systematic desensitization** has already been described as a treatment for phobias, fears, and anxiety, based on classically conditioning a new response that is incompatible with fear and anxiety. The basic idea is that a person cannot be relaxed and afraid at the same time. The client is trained in deep muscle relaxation, a response that is incompatible with fear. In addition, the therapist and client create an anxiety hierarchy. This hierarchy lists aspects of the fear- or anxiety-producing objects, events, or situations from least frightening to most frightening. For example, an anxiety hierarchy for a snake phobia might be a snake in the next county, a snake in the next room, a snake in the same room in an escape-proof cage, a snake on the floor, a snake touching the client. Then the hierarchy and the relaxation are put together to create systematic desensitization. The client is desensitized, that is, made less sensitive, to what he previously found frightening. See Box 10.3 for details.

In vivo (Latin, "in life") **desensitization,** also called *graduated exposure*, is a logical extension of systematic desensitization, and it is often used to assess the success of that procedure. Systematic desensitization relies on imagining the phobic element, and behaviorists have often criticized it as being too cognitive. Furthermore, it is possible that clients could remain relaxed with the image of the phobic element, but become frightened in its actual presence. *In vivo* procedures gradually place the phobic person in contact with the actual feared object or situation.

The possibilities for exposure treatments in the hands of creative therapists are endless. For example, fear of flying is treated by asking the client to engage in behaviors that gradually approach getting on an airplane, such as phoning for a flight reservation, then driving to the airport. The client may be required to sit in an airplane on the ground and then finally to take a short flight. As another example, a technique called cue controlled/active relaxation involves clients learning to *attend* to their feelings of anxiety as a cue to begin their relaxation exercises while they go about their daily lives.

Extinction

Implosive therapy is both an extension of the desensitization work and a direct application of academic research on extinction (Stampfl & Levis, 1973). Rather than conditioning a new response, why not just massively extinguish the fear all in one go? Like the rat kept in the dark compartment, people forced to remain in a frightening situation will have to stop feeling afraid after a while. It is physiologically impossible to remain strongly afraid for more than 20 or 30 minutes. So if a person could be induced to stay in the frightening situation, rather than immediately running away and feeling better, then the fear should extinguish, according to learning research. Implosion involves making the client vividly imagine all aspects of whatever is frightening until he or she becomes relaxed. An *in vivo* version keeps the client in the actual frightening situation until the fear is extinguished and relaxation replaces it. In both cases, the constant presence of a supportive, trusted therapist is crucial.

A technique known as *response prevention* is also considered an extinction procedure. Used to treat obsessive-compulsive disorder and bulimia, the procedure involves exposing the client to the stimuli that elicit the compulsive behavior and then preventing the client from engaging in the response. Because this method requires a great deal of control over the client and because it often elicits anxiety, it is used only in certain cases.

Punishment

Aversion therapy involves the use of an unconditioned aversive stimulus to classically condition fear or aversion to a previously attractive stimulus in order to create an avoidance response or to suppress undesirable or unwanted operant behavior.

BOX 10.3

And One Flew Under . . .

In the systematic desensitization of a phobia, the therapist and client first develop a hierarchical list of phobic situations. Together they work up a list progressing from the least to the most anxiety-provoking situation. There must be enough items on the list so that there are only small increases in anxiety associated with each step. The bird-phobic woman in Box 10.1 and her therapist developed the following anxiety hierarchy:

Looking out of the window at the street

Looking out of the window and seeing one bird in a tree

Looking out of the window and seeing many birds

Walking outside with no birds in sight

Walking outside with one bird down the street

Walking outside with several birds in view

A bird flying near to her

A bird hopping toward her

An injured bird at her feet

Picking up the injured bird

Touching a healthy small bird

Touching a large bird

The next step in systematic desensitization is to train the client in deep muscle relaxation. There are several methods of teaching muscle relaxation, including hypnosis and tape-recorded suggestions. The therapist may train relaxation by directing the reclining client to tense and relax the various muscles of her body, noting the different sensations until she can easily relax all the muscles deeply. The physiological response of muscle relaxation is incompatible with the physiological response of anxiety. Therefore, when the items on the anxiety hierarchy are introduced, the relaxation response should prevent the anxiety response. Additionally, a new response, relaxation, is being conditioned to the anxiety-provoking stimuli.

Once the client has mastered relaxation, the therapist begins to describe items on the anxiety hierarchy, starting with the first item. The therapist invites the client to imagine all the details of an item on the list. The therapist describes sensory details to help make the image vivid and stresses the client's positive feelings. For example, for the item "Walking outside with several birds in view," the therapist may say: "You are walking outside on a beautiful fall day. The sun is shining, you are walking comfortably, and you feel confident and strong. You can hear a breeze

BOX 10.3 (*continued*)

rustling the trees, and you can hear the leaves crunch under your feet as you walk. The air smells fresh. You can hear the cheerful chirping of some small birds in the trees. You keep walking, enjoying their songs. You can see some birds in nearby yards. They are hopping around looking for things to eat. They are very pretty with the sun shining on their feathers. You continue walking past the birds, who do not appear to notice you. You are enjoying your walk in the fresh air, the sunshine, the chirping birds, the beautiful day."

The therapist procedes to cover each item on the anxiety hierarchy, describing the situation in detail, as long as the client remains relaxed. If the client begins to tense her muscles or states that she is experiencing anxious feelings, the therapist may reinstitute muscle relaxation procedures or go back to a less anxiety-provoking item on the hierarchy. It may take several sessions for the client to imagine every item on the anxiety hierarchy while remaining completely relaxed.

The bird-phobic woman was able to complete her anxiety hierarchy in two sessions. *In vivo* desensitization was then used. A bunch of feathers was tied to a clothesline pulley so that she could recline and relax and still pull the feathers closer to her at a speed that was comfortable for her. The therapist helped her remain relaxed by giving relaxation suggestions while she pulled the feathers closer. The therapist also described the feathers vividly as they came closer. When the client felt she could, she touched the feathers, then held them, then brushed them over her arms and face, while the therapist continued to give relaxation suggestions and to describe the feather sensations. Then a caged, tame parakeet was connected to the pulley, and a similar procedure was carried out.

Finally, when the client tolerated the close presence of the caged bird well, the therapist put her hand in the cage and petted the parakeet to model touching a bird. The client was encouraged to do the same, and she was able to do so. The *in vivo* part of the desensitization took three sessions and the client was successfully desensitized to a phobic object.

Electric shock is the most commonly used aversive stimulus, although nausea-inducing drugs have also been used. For example, an electric shock is paired with an alcoholic drink in order to reduce drinking. Through Pavlovian conditioning, the previously attractive stimulus of the drink should become aversive, so that the person will avoid the drink or suppress the operant behavior of drinking.

Aversion therapy has been used in the treatment of bad habits such as smoking, overeating, or nail biting. Except in the treatment of bad habits, aversion therapy alone has not been demonstrated to be an effective treatment. It appears that the aversion gradually wears off or extinguishes and must be periodically reconditioned. However, when used in conjunction with other techniques, aversion therapy appears to be effective in treating smoking and overeating.

Covert sensitization is the use of an imagined stimulus in place of an actual aversive stimulus or punishment to create new learning. Almost the opposite of systematic desensitization, covert sensitization may be used to create classically conditioned anxiety to teach an avoidance response. For example, a dieter may be asked to vividly imagine a favorite food with worms all over it (an aversion stimulus), so that disgust or fear will be conditioned to the food and the person will avoid it in the future. This procedure is similar to the use of aversion, but avoids some of the ethical problems associated with the use of punishment.

SKILLS TRAINING (OPERANT CONDITIONING METHODS)

Behavior therapists who use operant conditioning methods assume that many types of abnormal behavior, such as shyness or even schizophrenic symptoms, are due to a lack of skills or to a poor environment or both. Shy individuals lack the social skills to understand and make contact with other people. It follows that the needed skills can be taught. Abnormal behavior may result from an environment that inadvertently rewards that behavior and fails to reward desirable behavior. Again, such an environment can be changed, mostly by developing the skills of those who deal with the "abnormal" behavior, such as the parent. With operant methods, the collaborative role of the therapist is emphasized. The therapist acts as an instructor or consultant to guide the client or parent in choosing and making changes.

Social Skills Training (Assertion Training)

Assertion training, now called *social skills training,* was originally designed to help shy, retiring people become better able to deal with other people. Assertion therapy includes a variety of training techniques for several social skills and is used with diverse types of clients individually and in groups. It is based on operant conditioning in that operant behaviors that display social skills, such as conversation, asking for dates, and dealing with bosses, are rewarded by praise from the therapist or by the success of the behaviors themselves.

Assertion therapy is widely used to treat shyness. In addition, it has proven useful in teaching mentally retarded adults how to be more effective in a confusing world and how to protect themselves from possible exploitation. It is also used in conjunction with other forms of therapy to train new responses to substitute for abnormal behaviors that are being eliminated.

The social skills taught vary according to what the clients believe they need. Some shy clients wish to learn to make conversation in many social situations. Some clients are not shy, but want to learn to deal more effectively with specific individuals, such as bosses, or in specific situations, such as negotiating a raise at work. Among the skills and situations covered in assertion training are asking for dates, turning down dates, making requests or successfully giving orders to others, refusing requests or orders, starting conversations, making social conversation, negotiation, asking for a raise, dealing with aggressive or difficult coworkers or customers, dealing with sexual harassment, and asserting independence from guilt-inducing parents. For such social skills to be effective, clients must also learn to understand other people's feelings, to be nonjudgmental and uncritical of others, to curb their anger or aversive behavior, and to increase their awareness of the effect of their behavior on others. They must learn to pay attention to the nonverbal behavior of others and to alter their own nonverbal behavior so that it has the effect they intend. For example, shy clients must learn to make eye contact with people during conversation. Social skills are complex, and they must be broken down into specific parts so they can be taught.

The techniques most frequently used to teach these complex social skills are lecture, modeling, and role playing. Assertion therapists describe social skills to their clients, explain how they work, and advise clients what to try. They demonstrate social skills by acting them out in front of the client, saying what they want the client to say, pointing out their own nonverbal behavior. They then ask clients to role-play. The client may role-play the target person, such as a boss or parent, while the therapist plays the client and demonstrates what the client should do. Then the client role-plays his or her own role while the therapist role-plays the target person, so that the client has a chance to rehearse the demonstrated social skills. In groups, clients role-play individuals and social situations for each other. For example, the entire group may pretend to be at a cocktail party, and they practice initiating and carrying on social conversations.

Shaping and covert practice are also sometimes used by therapists to teach social skills. **Shaping,** also called *successive approximation,* involves the client making closer and closer approximations to the desired response. Each step closer to the desired behavior is rewarded with praise from the therapist or group. A shy person cannot be expected to go to a party and start several lively conversations right away. The first step may be simply to go to a party. The next step may be saying "Hello" to just one person, then speaking to two people, and so on. In **covert practice,** the person imagines performing the social skills competently. The shy person is asked to imagine carrying on lively conversations.

An important element of social skills training is *feedback.* As clients rehearse and role-play, the therapist and group members give feedback on the effectiveness of the rehearsed social skills. They point out which aspects of the performance need to be improved and which were done well. The more specific the feedback, the more useful it is. Videotaping the role play is an effective way to give accurate feedback.

The rewarding behaviors of the therapist are an important part of social skills training. Warm praise for successful social skills performance reinforces the behavior. The status, power, warmth, trustworthiness, attractiveness, and other personal attributes of the therapist affect how rewarding the praise will be. The importance of the therapist-client relationship in the effectiveness of behavior therapy is clear.

Most social skills therapy includes practicing the skills in the real world. Specific homework assignments are often given. A shy man may be required to ask a specified woman for a date before the next therapy meeting. A woman may be assigned to say no to at least one request at work by the following week. Such assignments are clear and precise as to what the client is expected to do, and the behavior is practiced beforehand. Usually, the therapist thinks the client has a reasonably good chance at success, but the emphasis is on performing the social skill in the real world, rather than on whether it succeeds or fails. Since the behavior is being done at the direction of the therapist, the therapist will take the blame for failure, but praise the client for success.

For some time, the majority of assertion clients were women. Feminists criticized assertion therapy as reinforcing a masculine way of relating to others, a way that emphasizes confrontation and competition rather than the caring, nonconfrontational way women relate. Defenders of assertion training argue that in a culture that emphasizes passivity, dependence, and nurturance as feminine qualities, women will have difficulty trying to assert their own needs without being labeled aggressive (or "castrating"). Assertion training can be seen as a way of helping women to obtain needed satisfaction and independence. Assertion should not be confused with aggression, and in fact, overly aggressive men are sometimes given assertion training so that they can learn appropriate ways of expressing needs and independence.

Contingency Management (Behavior Modification)

A set of behavioral management techniques known as **contingency management,** also called *behavior modification* or *applied behavior analysis*, utilizes operant conditioning principles. These behavior-changing methods involve simply the planned use of rewards to increase wanted behavior and of extinction to decrease unwanted behavior. The environment is fixed. Rewards are made contingent on desirable behavior and are not given for undesirable behavior. These methods are used in many different settings, including businesses, schools, institutions for the mentally retarded, and prisons. We will describe operant methods used in parent training or child behavior modification, the token economy in mental hospitals, and contingency contracting.

Parent Training Modifying the problem behaviors of children is often accomplished by training the parents to use operant techniques. Therapists teach the parents these techniques in group classes, in couples, or individually with such methods as role playing and videotaping. Basically, parents are taught to reward behavior they want in their children and to remove the rewards for behaviors they don't want. In addition, parents must learn how to communicate clearly to the children what they want done, to be consistent in delivering behavioral consequences, to reduce their own aversive and ineffective parenting behaviors, and to give appropriate rewards. Once again, a seemingly simple operant procedure turns out on examination to require complex behavior changes. Even something as seemingly natural and simple as rewarding a child for being "good" is extremely difficult for some parents to learn. Some parents are opposed to the use of rewards on principle, because they see it as "bribing" the child, who should "want" to be good for goodness' sake. Others have difficulties being warm or affectionate, perhaps because in their own deprived childhoods they never learned how or learned to fear closeness, and so they cannot deliver effective praise. These kinds of problems must be addressed before operant techniques can be used effectively.

There are many programs to train parents to modify their children's behavior. Patterson's program at Oregon Research Institute (Patterson, 1973; Patterson & Chamberlain, 1994; Patterson & Gullion, 1976) is well documented, researched, and evaluated, and it is fairly representative of others. Patterson argues that behavioral disorders in children are a result of parents' reliance on what he calls aversive control, that is, reliance on scolding, punishment, screaming, nagging, and the like to try to control their children. The relatively powerless children engage in disruptive, defiant, or destructive behaviors in an attempt to control their parents, because they learn aversive control from their parents through imitation. These parents also tend to use few rewards, either because they don't know how or they don't feel like being rewarding because of stress or anger. Because of the low level of rewards, the children may engage in aversive behavior just to get their parents' attention. A vicious cycle is set up in which the parents try to control the children with punishment, which makes the children hurt and angry and more likely to be unpleasant too, which makes the parent use more punishment, and so on.

Among some ethnic groups and socioeconomic classes, physical punishment in the form of spanking and hitting is a common and socially acceptable form of child discipline. People from such groups disbelieve or are offended by the insistence of middle-class, White therapists that such punishment should not be used. However, there are sound empirical reasons why physical punishment should be avoided. First, the principle of Pavlovian conditioning indicates that because the parent is paired with pain, the child will come to fear the parent and the parent will lose the ability to be rewarding. Second, the principle of imitation indicates that what children learn when punished is to hit people smaller than themselves. Third, any use of punishment as a method of control always leads to the need for a constant policing function, because children soon learn to discriminate that they should refrain from the undesired behavior only when the parent is around. Finally, parental reliance on punishment leads to the vicious cycle of aversive control described above.

Patterson tries to break this cycle by teaching the parents to increase their use of rewards and to stop all use of punishments and threats. Instead of punishment, extinction in the form of a procedure called time-out, described below, is used. There are several steps in Patterson's program.

The child and the family must be assessed so that an appropriate behavioral program can be designed. Patterson has worked mostly with school-age children with behavior problems of aggressiveness and noncompliance. Similar behavior modification methods have been used to treat temper tantrums, excessive sibling fighting, hyperactivity, disruptive school behavior, stealing and lying, and any sort of frequent unpleasant behavior used as negative attention seeking.

Once the problem has been defined and assessed, Patterson involves both parents and target child in deciding on the behavior modification program. What the child must do is discussed, specified clearly, and agreed on. For example, it might be specified that the child must obey parental requests to do household chores by the second time he is asked. The consequences of behavior are discussed. For example, if the child obeys the first parental request, he will receive a certain reward; if he obeys the second, he will receive a certain other reward; and if he does not comply, he will be placed in five minutes of time-out. Usually, several such concrete behaviors are worked on at once. All of the specified behaviors and consequences may be written down in a behavioral contract, which parents and child sign as an indication of their understanding of the treatment program and their agreement to try it.

The nature of the rewards is open to negotiation. Different children find different things rewarding. Some children prefer monetary rewards, some prefer objects such as toys or bicycles, and others prefer time spent with a parent in an activity of their choice. Parents and children agree on a formula for the distribution of rewards that takes into account the number of behaviors being modified and the frequency with which they occur. For example, each act of compliance with a parental request may be worth 10 cents, or the child must comply with parental requests 90 percent of the time for six weeks in order to get a bicycle. Charts with points or check marks are used to keep track of performance and rewards. The charts are kept in an accessible place, such as on the refrigerator door, and each and every rewarded behavior is noted carefully. Patterson also tries to teach parents to give social rewards such as attention and praise when the points or money or other concrete rewards are given, so that concrete rewards can eventually be eliminated.

Time-out is used to eliminate unwanted behavior or as a consequence for not performing wanted behavior. Unwanted behavior and noncompliance are assumed to be reinforced and maintained by the parental attention they gain. Even if that attention consists of punishment, it seems that some children prefer it to being ignored. So the solution to such problem behavior is to remove the reward in order to extinguish it.

Time-out involves removing children from the rewarding situation to a place where there are no social rewards, and so it can be viewed as an extinction procedure. (It can also be seen as a negative punishment in that it is the removal of something positive.) A bathroom, a porch, even the child's own room or a corner of the living room can be used for time-out. It should be some relatively uninteresting but safe place where children will not be getting attention. In practice, the punishment aspects of time-out are avoided, because the parents are already too reliant on aversive control. Rather, they are taught to be matter of fact and nonthreatening when using time-out.

Time-out should not be frightening, so children should not be locked up and small children should be able to see their parents. Time-out needs to be only a short time, such as five minutes. For very young children two minutes of time-out is a long time. Children have a different sense of time from adults, and five minutes without human attention can seem very long to them. Some therapists suggest giving children a clock or a timer so they can see how long time-out will take.

Some parents express surprise or even outrage that time-out is so short and seems to be such a mild consequence. After all, they have been grounding their children for weeks at a time, although without much success. They need to be convinced that time-out is not a punishment and that five minutes of the removal of social rewards is sufficient. Even children may say, "Oh, time-out! Big deal! What's five minutes?" The first time children must go into time-out, they may well act nonchalant. However, that first time-out is often more difficult than children or parents anticipate. Parents are instructed that they are to add five additional minutes for every instance of unacceptable behavior during time-out. If the child swears, yells, kicks the door, breaks things, leaves the time-out area, or even calls the parent, then five more minutes must be added. That first time-out may well end up being more than 40 minutes long. However, the second time-out is likely to be 20 minutes and subsequent ones only five.

It is essential that parents use time-out consistently for every behavior they agreed it was to be used for. It is also important that it not be viewed as a punishment, used as a threat, or randomly invoked without prior agreement. Parents are encouraged to apply time-out in a matter-of-fact manner, without criticism or yelling. Most parents who apply time-out correctly and consistently find that it does not have to be used often after the first few times. They also find it far more effective than the nagging and yelling and punishments they had tried before. However, because it is difficult to administer time-out properly, especially the first few times, people should not even begin a program utilizing time-out unless they are deeply committed to using it properly and consistently. If time-out is used inconsistently, the child's unwanted behavior ends up receiving partial reinforcement, which only strengthens it.

Evaluation research studies of behavior modification programs such as Patterson's find that it is an effective treatment for child behavior disorders. In addition, parents tend to feel happier and more competent after treatment, as do the children. Parents report that they are able to generalize the principles they learn in treatment to other aspects of child raising and family life. Other behaviors of the child often improve, as well as the treated behaviors. Another frequently reported result is that the behavior of siblings of the treated children also improves (Dangel & Polster, 1984; Forehand & McMahon, 1981).

Parent training can be combined with attempts to modify children's school behaviors. Teachers may agree to keep behavior charts at school, which can be sent home for the parents to reward. For example, for every half hour that children sit and work quietly, the parents can give praise and points toward an agreed-on reward.

Behavior modification principles are sometimes used (and sometimes misused) in classrooms for all the children. Teachers attempt to reward desired child behaviors with praise, gold stars, tickets, and prizes. Teachers also try to implement time-out for disruptive negative attention seeking. Placing the child in time-out outside the classroom can be an effective technique for eliminating such behavior. Using time-out to shame or punish children, making it too long, or keeping children in the classroom during time-out so that they still receive peer attention are common misuses of time-out. However, research indicates that well-conducted behavior management programs in schools are effective in reducing classroom disruptions and increasing the academic progress of all the students (Kiraly & McKinnon, 1984; Klein, Hapkiewicz, & Roden, 1973; O'Leary & O'Leary, 1977).

Token Economy   Token economies are behavior modification programs sometimes used in psychiatric wards in hospitals. They are also used in classrooms and institutions for the mentally retarded. Token economies are based on operant procedures, and rewards are given for desired behavior and not for undesired behavior. Since it is difficult to give actual rewards for each desired behavior, tokens are commonly given to patients instead, hence the name of the programs. When sufficient numbers of tokens are collected, patients can exchange them for designated rewards, such as ten tokens for a pack of cigarettes or five for an extra dessert. Undesirable behavior, such as psychotic talk or failure to show up for therapy appointments, may either be ignored or have a consequence such as being docked tokens.

Positive behaviors commonly rewarded on token economies include getting dressed, shaved, and cleaned up by themselves; arriving at meals on time; engaging in constructive activities, such as socializing or occupational therapy; taking medications without complaining or resisting; cooperating with staff requests; and responding nonpsychotically to questions or conversations initiated by staff or fellow patients. It is argued that learning such behaviors as punctuality and self-care will help patients live better outside the hospital, as well as making the ward easier to manage.

One of the pioneers of token economies, Ted Ayllon, originally used food as a reward (Ayllon & Azrin, 1968). He was allowed to try an experimental behavior modification program on a locked ward of very disturbed schizophrenics, many of whom had been there for many years and some of whom did not even get out of bed or feed themselves. Ayllon thought that it was possible that the schizophrenics were rewarded for this behavior by concerned nurses coming to spoon-feed them in bed. So Ayllon altered the conditions on the ward so that only patients who showed up at the dining room by a certain time were allowed to eat. Despite staff concerns that the very disturbed patients would starve to death, all patients were eating in the dining room within four days.

Everyone would agree that food can be a powerful reward. However, patients' rights advocates have argued that people in mental hospitals have basic rights to care, protection, and treatment, and these rights certainly include the right to eat. So meals are no longer used as rewards in token economies, although some do use special foods or good desserts. The most commonly used reward is cigarettes. Apparently, many mental patients will do quite a lot in order to get cigarettes. The use of health-endangering addictive chemicals such as nicotine is just as ethically questionable as the use of food as a reward, yet cigarette rewards are still used.

Critics have charged that token economies are manipulative methods of social control, used against helpless mental patients. Defenders argue that token economies mimic the real world, in which people have to work for the reward of money. The "real world" argument seems to be substantiated by the fact that in many token economies, there is a flourishing black market in tokens. Patients make counterfeit tokens, play poker with them, steal them, trade them with each other for things, and hoard them, just like people do with ordinary money.

In general, evaluation research on token economies suggests that they are effective in making psychiatric wards fairly pleasant and cooperative places (Ayllon & Azrin, 1968) and that patients on token economies are less likely to return to the hospital than patients on regular wards (Glynn, 1990). However, token economies are not often used on psychiatric wards today. It may be that the expenses of training all ward personnel and needing more personnel than an ordinary ward prevent their use, even though token economies may save money in the long run by reducing rehospitalizations.

Contingency Contracting   Levendusky and his colleagues (1983) reported that **behavioral contracting** worked as well as a token economy in preliminary research. Behavioral contracting, or **contingency contracting,** is the development of an individual behavior modification program for the ward patient by the patient and therapist. The patient is fully informed and actively involved in deciding on the behaviors and rewards to be covered by the program. This type of patient involvement would appear to reduce the potential for manipulation and coercion.

Contingency contracting is also used with many nonpsychotic problems. In contingency contracting, the therapist and client make a formal agreement or contract about certain consequences of certain acts by the client. If the client performs a difficult assignment, such as losing a certain number of pounds or practicing a certain social skill in public, the therapist will give an appropriate reward. For example, a therapist and client may contract that the therapist's fee will be reduced 10% when the client loses 5 pounds, or they may contract that the client will be free to buy a new outfit after a specific weight loss. Some behavior therapists request that clients deposit a sum of money at the beginning of a behavior modification program. The reward may then be to return part of the fee.

The contract may specify punishment-like consequences for certain client behaviors, too. With **response cost,** positive reinforcers are withdrawn to suppress an unwanted behavior. Tokens, points, or privileges may be withdrawn. Or the failure to perform the contracted behavior may result in a "fine." Donation of the sum deposited at the beginning of treatment to a cause the client dislikes may be used as a consequence for failure to comply with the treatment program. For example, a liberal client gives a deposit of $100 prior to treatment, and if he fails to comply with the agreed-on treatment, his money will be given to the Republicans. The potential for creative uses of contingency contracting seems great.

Self-Management

As implied in the name *self-management,* behaviorists can teach individuals to use operant and contingency management techniques to modify their own behaviors, as shown in Box 10.4. Such behavior modification treatments use self-monitoring, self-reward, and techniques of problem solving and coping as well as contingency contracting. Clients set a goal to modify certain behaviors, keep a chart of the frequency and context of the behaviors, and apply appropriate rewards for achieving the goals. It is surprising, but true, that simply recording the frequency of unwanted behaviors often results in their reduction. Perhaps increased awareness of behavior makes it easier to change.

Self-monitoring involves keeping track of the targeted behavior, including when and in what context it occurs. Self-reward allows clients to give themselves a chosen reward. Self-reward follows Grandma's Rule: "First you work, then you play." For example, in smoking-reduction programs, clients keep count of the number of cigarettes smoked and the situations when smoking occurs. If the number of cigarettes falls below a certain number in a day, clients reward themselves with a dinner out, a movie, or whatever. Clients are also trained to reward themselves with self-approval for meeting behavioral goals. People who are trying to modify a bad habit are frequently critical of themselves, and they need to learn to attend to and reward their positive behavior, as is done in cognitive behavior therapy (discussed in Chapter 12).

There are special techniques used in self-management. With **problem-solving training,** clients are taught first to define and assess the problem; second, to recognize their reaction to it, such as anger, which might be part of the problem; third, to

BOX 10.4

Self-Management of Study Habits

Susan F. transferred in her junior year from a community college to a state university and found her grades there dropping. She became anxious, and she could not seem to find the time to study regularly. After reading about self-management in a psychology class, she decided to try to modify her study habits. She defined her problem as an inability to study for longer than about half an hour and a lack of a regular study time. She decided to assess her current study behaviors before attempting to change them.

For one week she kept a chart of her behavior after her classes were done for the day. She made entries every hour, described what she was doing and where, how she felt, and what she was thinking. For example, for Tuesday she had written

4:00   Sitting in living room staring at philosophy book. Feeling lonely, worried. Thinking I'll never get this stuff.

5:00   In the middle of baking chocolate cake in kitchen. Feeling hungry, but happy at prospect of cake. Thinking I should be studying, what's the matter with me?

6:00   After I called Maria, she came over for dinner and cake. Feeling happy, having fun, not lonely. Thinking I better study later or else.

At the end of the week, Susan examined this chart. She noticed a pattern that when she sat down to study, she would begin to feel anxious and lonely and to think that she was stupid. Often she would then find something else to do, especially baking or visiting friends. Later in the day she would be too tired to study, and she would berate herself for her stupidity.

Susan considered several possible solutions to her problem and decided to implement this plan. After classes, she would come home, have a healthy snack such as a banana or apple, rest for 15 minutes, and then study for one hour, a goal that she thought she could accomplish easily. If she began to feel anxious, she would tell herself, "I can easily study for one hour, and studying will improve my grades. I have gotten good grades before, and I can do it again. It's only one hour." If she began to think self-critical thoughts, she would tell herself, "I am an intelligent person, and when I finish studying, I will feel good about myself." When she completed an hour of studying, then and only then would she reward herself with a visit to a friend or a piece of cake after dinner. After five weekdays of keeping this schedule, she planned to reward herself with a nice dinner out with a friend. She continued to keep the behavioral chart in order to keep track of her success with maintaining an hour a day of

---

BOX 10.4 *(continued)*

studying and to make herself substitute calming thoughts when she felt anxious and praising thoughts when she felt self-critical.

At the end of the week, Susan evaluated her success. She was able to keep to her plan. She was tempted to berate herself for studying "only" one hour per weekday, but she decided that she should be proud for accomplishing so much so quickly. She had read that it was important to set achievable goals and to reward oneself for success. The second week, she increased her study time to two hours per weekday, and rewarded herself with two dinners out with friends. The third week, she increased her study time to three hours per weekday, and rewarded herself with a new shirt. By that time, she had had two examinations and the best reward of all, higher grades. Her anxiety had abated, she felt less lonely since her rewards involved visiting friends, and she felt more in control of her life.

---

generate several alternative solutions or responses to the problem; fourth, to evaluate the solutions and decide to act on one; and, fifth, to assess the effect of the attempted solution. *Coping* and *coping imagery exercises* may be part of problem solving. The therapist and client review possible coping strategies for the client's problem, and the client imagines using them in various situations. In reviewing coping strategies, the therapist may teach coping skills that the client lacks or has not thought of before.

In addition to its use in individual therapy, self-management is now often used in business and education. Employees and students are taught self-management techniques in order to improve company functioning and student learning. Furthermore, a structured, modularized teaching program designed to give medicated schizophrenics the information and skills needed to self-manage their illness has been developed by the Veterans Administration (Eckman, Wirshing, Marder, & Liberman, 1992).

Punishment

Delivering punishment for operant behavior is rarely used because of ethical concerns. However, punishment has been used to quickly suppress severely psychotic behavior such as self-injury in retarded or autistic children (Lovaas & Simmons, 1969). Defenders of the practice of shocking autistic children for biting or hitting themselves argue that it is preferable to the amount of injury the child would receive if extinction were used. They agree that punishment should be used only when other methods fail. They also point out that eliminating the psychotic behavior allows the child to make use of other forms of psychotherapy.

Rather than the therapist delivering an actual punishment, the client may be asked to imagine negative consequences (a punishment) to unwanted operant behavior. This technique is similar to the covert sensitization described under aversion techniques. For example, a kleptomaniac may be asked to imagine what would happen if he shoplifted. The therapist may guide his imagery so that he imagines going home with the stolen object, waiting anxiously in his apartment wondering if he will be caught, having the police arrive at his door and arrest him in front of all the neighbors, going to jail, and so on. Another alternative to punishment is response cost, described earlier.

Self-administered punishment is sometimes used to modify bad habits. For example, a cigarette smoker or nail biter may put a rubber band around her wrist and use it to give herself a painful snap every time she reaches for a cigarette or bites her nails. Such a technique may be part of a larger self-management program. A 12-year-old girl we know invented a self-management technique that utilized response cost. To make herself complete reading assignments quickly, she would check the required book out of the library and refuse to return it before she had finished reading it. The threat (and sometimes the payment) of mounting overdue fines motivated her to finish reading the book.

SOCIAL LEARNING METHODS

Like many behavior therapists, those who use social learning methods assume that it is not necessarily important to know the cause of abnormal behavior. They assume that normal behavior can be learned in its place, whatever its causes, through the normal social learning process of imitation or modeling.

Social learning theorists such as Bandura (1977) have extended their concepts of imitation and observational learning to the treatment of behavior disorders such as phobias. Rather than desensitizing or extinguishing fearful feelings, social learning theorists argue that nonphobic behavior can be learned by watching others. Typically, the therapist models the desired behavior for the client, who will learn to engage in the same type of behavior through imitation. For example, a snake phobia is treated by having the client observe the therapist handling a snake. Then the client is encouraged to copy the behavior. **Modeling** is probably an important component of assertion training and other forms of therapy. Through demonstration and role playing, the therapist models appropriate assertive behavior. According to social learning theory, the client learns assertion by observing and imitating the therapist. Even in a talking psychotherapy such as psychoanalysis or client-centered therapy, the client may be learning important relationship skills by observing and imitating the therapist.

Covert modeling, similar to covert practice, is imagining another person engaging in the desired behavior. A therapist may tell a child a story about another child who successfully stops fighting with his siblings and learns other ways to get attention. It is assumed that imagining a successful model facilitates learning new behavior that is similar to the model's.

OTHER FORMS OF BEHAVIOR THERAPY

So many new methods of behavior therapy have been developed that the field has become diverse and eclectic. Behavior therapists tend to be pragmatic and ingenious in trying new methods, and they select and combine techniques to fit individual clients. New methods are constantly being developed and tried. We will cover a few of these.

Multimodal behavior therapy, now called *broad spectrum therapy*, represents a systematic eclecticism. It is an assessment and therapy framework that encompasses elements of all the above behavioral methods as well as cognitive-behavioral therapy and rational-emotive therapy. It is associated with the work of Lazarus (1976, 1981). Psychological disorders are viewed in terms of seven modalities—behavior, affect, sensation, imagery, cognition, interpersonal relationships, and drug/biological aspect—which result in the clever acronym BASIC ID. Clients are assessed as to their functioning in each of the modalities, and a specific treatment plan is made for each of the seven. For example, a shy client may show passivity and compliance in behavior, for which assertion training is prescribed; anxiety and fear in affect, for which desensitization is prescribed; images of helplessness and ridicule in imagery, for which coping imagery exercises are taught; perfectionism in cognition, for which cognitive disputation (described in Chapter 12) is done; avoidance and withdrawal in interpersonal relations, for which risk-taking assignments are given; and excessive eating and coffee drinking in the drugs/biology aspect, for which diet and exercise are prescribed.

Lewinsohn and his colleagues (Lewinsohn, Clarke, & Hoberman, 1989; Lewinsohn & Hoberman, 1982) have developed a behavioral model for working with depressed people, including the elderly depressed (Zeiss & Lewinsohn, 1986) and other special populations, called the *Coping with Depression model*. It involves a multimodal, group psychoeducational treatment method. In the group, depressed individuals are taught problem-solving skills, including analyzing a problem, discovering and evaluating new approaches, and developing strategies for implementing these approaches. The emphasis in group is on problem solving, cognitive restructuring, and social skills training. Daily monitoring of pleasant and unpleasant events in relation to mood, relaxation training, homework, and role playing may also be utilized. The goal is to increase both the activity (behavior emitted) and the rewards for activity in formerly withdrawn, negativistic, depressed people. Rather than the "learned helplessness" seen in depression, "learned resourcefulness" is taught.

Francine Shapiro's (1995) *Eye Movement Desensitization and Reprocessing* (EMDR) therapy is another relatively new behavioral technique. EMDR is a desensitization procedure, but instead of relaxation, therapist-led eye movements performed by the client are paired with images of what frightens or disturbs the client. Clinical evidence suggests that EMDR is a quick, highly effective treatment for posttraumatic stress disorder, although published studies do not always support this conclusion (Shapiro, 1995). In addition to whether it works, controversy occurs over how it works. While it may work like other desensitization methods, Shapiro (1995) proposes that EMDR actually changes the way the brain processes the traumatic experience and memories of it. As with many behavior therapies, whether and how EMDR works requires further research.

POSTMODERN BEHAVIOR THERAPY

As behaviorist Neil Miller did nearly half a century earlier (Dollard & Miller, 1950), postmodern behavior therapists have recast the usual sorts of therapeutic interventions into behavioral terms. A group known as radical behaviorists (Hayes et al.,

1995; Jacobson, 1994; Kohlenberg & Tsai, 1991, 1994; Linehan, 1993) have called for behavior therapy to return to B. F. Skinner's experimental analysis of behavior. Not only do they criticize behavior therapy as just a collection of techniques that no longer have much to do with behaviorism, they also argue that Skinner has been misrepresented and misunderstood by behavior therapists in the past. Contrary to common beliefs about Skinnerian behaviorism, radical behaviorists place importance on understanding thinking and feeling (called private behaviors) not just on "observable" (public) behavior, seriously consider genetic determinants of behavior, and are interested in early childhood determinants of behavior.

In the radical behaviorists' view, behavior therapy can never be a method that is applied to everyone, but rather, it must be idiographic. Each behavior therapy intervention must be designed for a specific individual, because behavior is a function of learning history, genetics, and the situational context, all of which will vary greatly among different people. Even when two people appear to be in the same environment to an outside observer, they are actually in different environments because they have different learning histories and so experience the context differently. A therapeutic intervention can be designed only by a *functional analysis* of all of these variables as they affect a specific person.

A functional analysis examines the function of a behavior in its particular context, rather than examining the behavior itself. For example, a radical behaviorist would not focus on the avoidance behavior in phobias, but would analyze the function of a specific individual's phobic behavior in its situational and historical contexts. As another example, there can be no universal definition of social skills in radical behaviorism. A behavior is socially skilled if it *functions* as a skill in a specific situation in relation to certain others when performed by an individual with a specific learning history.

In traditional behavior therapies, therapists use similar rewards such as money or praise for everyone. By doing so, they are using reinforcement that is chosen by the therapist and may be experienced as arbitrary by any one individual. Radical behaviorists argue that reinforcers will vary from person to person, and they emphasize natural reinforcement and the contingencies that occur in "the real world." They observe which therapist behaviors and which situational factors reinforce the desired behaviors of a specific individual in therapy and then use those as reinforcers. By consciously using their own genuine behavior that they have already actually observed strengthening desired client behaviors, radical behavior therapists claim to be using "natural," rather than "arbitrary" reinforcement.

Although our review of radical behaviorism necessarily simplifies a complex theory and cannot cover it all, we will look at one other concept. Skinner originally made the distinction between direct contingency control versus rule-governed behavior. Traditional behavior therapies emphasize the first one: public "observable" behavior that is rewarded or punished by an external stimulus, such as temper tantrums being rewarded by parental attention. Radical behaviorists have reemphasized the importance of the second distinction. Also called indirect contingency or verbal control (Hayes et al., 1995), rule-governed behavior refers to behavior that is guided by verbalized thoughts or feelings. Recall that radical behaviorists consider thoughts and feelings to be behavior like any other, only private, and therefore governed by the same principles as all behavior. Thus, thoughts and feelings are learned, and they can be verbalized to one's self (i.e., kept private) or to another person (i.e., made public). Depending on the situational and historical context, these verbalizations can become rules that influence observable behavior. For example, a woman may have learned "Girls are afraid of snakes" and be likely to develop a snake phobia, while another woman may have learned "Snakes make fun pets" and be likely to handle snakes. The behavior of avoiding or handling snakes is said to be rule-governed. On the other hand, the snake-avoiding behavior of people who live in a jungle infested with poisonous snakes is said to be under direct contingency control (i.e., controlled by external reinforcers). The concept of rule-governed behavior allows radical behaviorists to account for individual differences, for the effects of cognitions and emotions on behavior, and for the effectiveness of verbal therapy.

After this brief review of radical behaviorism, let us now turn to some of the treatments developed by radical behavior therapists. Each has its own name, leading to an "alphabet soup" of acronyms. Functional Analytic Therapy (FAP) emphasizes an intense, emotional relationship between client and therapist that functions both to elicit and to reinforce relevant client behaviors. Acceptance and Commitment Therapy (ACT) encourages client acceptance of difficult or disturbing feelings and thoughts, not by altering these private behaviors, but by placing them in a new context. Dialectical Behavior Therapy (DBT) is designed to treat borderline personality disorder by behaviorally teaching clients to modulate their extreme reactions. As discussed in Chapter 14, Integrative Behavioral Couple Therapy (IBCT) teaches couples to accept each other, rather than engaging in self-defeating behaviors such as trying to change the partner. As you will see, and as radical behaviorists ironically note, their therapeutic interventions appear to be more similar to psychodynamic, client-centered, existentialist, and other interpersonal therapies than to traditional behavior therapies.

Functional Analytic Psychotherapy (FAP)

Because Kohlenberg and Tsai's (1991) Functional Analytic Psychotherapy (FAP) emphasizes an intense, emotional relationship between therapist and client as the vehicle for behavioral change, it is best suited for people with difficulties in close relationships or other interpersonal problems. The context of therapy is designed to elicit the client's problematic behaviors, and these behaviors are changed by the natural reinforcers of the therapist's reactions in the therapy session. FAP opposes the use of arbitrary reinforcers chosen by the therapist; rather, genuine reactions of the therapist are used to reinforce improvements in client behavior as they occur. For example, FAP would not address shyness by teaching assertive behavior and rewarding it with therapist praise. Rather, in the context of therapy that fosters closeness and trust, a FAP therapist's behavior would naturally evoke shy behavior, which in FAP would be called socially avoidant behavior and would be dealt with as discussed below, and any assertive behavior that occurred would be shaped and reinforced by the therapist's genuine reaction, such as "I feel close to you when you tell me what you really want."

FAP requires the therapist to pay attention to clinically relevant behaviors (CRBs) as they occur in the therapy session. There are three types of CRB. The first are behaviors related to the client's presenting problem; for example, a person who complains of social anxiety avoids eye contact during the session. The second type of CRB are improvements in client behaviors that occur in the session; for example, this socially avoidant client asks for an extra session. The third type of CRB refers to clients' talking about their own behavior and what seems to cause it, as when they make interpretations on their own; for example, this same client may say, "I freeze up when other people look me in the eye and I think they are going to judge me."

FAP recommends five "rules" for therapist behavior to help develop the therapist's own rule-governed behavior. The first one, to watch for CRBs, is the core of FAP. In therapy, the main consequence of client behavior is the therapist's reaction. By attending to CRBs, the therapist can react naturally to them and thus promote the necessary genuine, intense, emotional relationship between client and therapist.

The second rule is to evoke CRBs. Depending on the client's presenting problem, the therapist can do a variety of things to elicit the clinically relevant problematic behavior during therapy. When that behavior occurs in session, the therapist can then react according to the fifth rule, described below, to help the client deal with it then and there. The therapist should also provide for the development of improved clinically relevant behavior. Any technique from free association to homework assignments that provides the opportunity for the client to try out an improved behavior is acceptable in FAP.

The third rule is to reinforce improvements in CRB as they occur in session. The therapist must be alert to the significance of even small behavior changes as potential improvements for specific clients. For example, a socially anxious client requesting an extra session may be inconvenient for the therapist, but a FAP therapist would recognize the significance of this particular client making a direct request as an improvement in CRB and so would reward the assertive behavior by readily agreeing to an extra session. On the other hand, the same request by a client whose problems include demanding, overly dependent behavior would not be reinforced.

The fourth rule is to observe the potentially reinforcing effects of therapist behavior in relation to client CRBs. Following this rule involves the therapist making a functional analysis along the lines of observing which of his or her own behaviors strengthen which client behaviors and which have the opposite effect. For example, a therapist may observe that when she responds warmly and enthusiastically to her socially anxious client's self-disclosing statements, the client changes the subject. With this particular client at this time in therapy, warmth is not reinforcing the improved clinically relevant behavior of talking about feelings. The therapist may find that listening neutrally leads to more self-disclosing statements by this client.

The fifth rule is to give interpretations of variables that affect client behavior. Statements of functional relationships between the client's behavior and other variables help clients become aware of problematic clinically relevant behavior and what brings it about. In addition, giving such interpretations models the third type of CRB, those that involve making observational statements of one's own behavior, for the client. For example, a therapist may interpret, "When I make a positive remark about you, you look away and change the subject." This interpretation points out the first type of CRB and models the third type of CRB. It will also lead to an intense interpersonal discussion that may evoke the second type of CRBs, improved behaviors.

If followed, the rules of FAP lead to the intense relationship required for developing and reinforcing therapeutic change. This therapy then looks more like interpersonally based psychodynamic therapy or client-centered therapy than like traditional behavior therapy.

Acceptance and Commitment Therapy (ACT)

As with other radical behavior therapy, the Acceptance and Commitment Therapy (ACT) of Hayes and his colleagues (Hayes et al., 1995) requires a strong therapeutic relationship between therapist and client. Within this context, the goal of ACT is to support the client's acceptance of unacceptable or disturbing thoughts and feelings without needing to avoid, escape from, or control them. Recall that thoughts and feelings are (private) behaviors like observable (public) behaviors. Trying to avoid certain thoughts and feelings may lead to self-defeating behavior in specific individuals in certain contexts. While most adult psychotherapies deal with clients' thoughts and feelings, ACT does not try to alter these private behaviors, but rather, to place them in a different context. There are five phases in this treatment.

The first phase of ACT involves "creative hopelessness." The therapist confronts clients with the hopelessness and futility of their past attempts to avoid or change their unacceptable or disturbing thoughts and feelings. In the second phase, clients are encouraged to examine their own experiences to identify how self-defeating it is to try to control their thoughts and feelings. This part of ACT is similar to strategic therapy's observation that the solution is the problem (see Chapter 14 for details of strategic therapy); that is, the client's "solution" to unacceptable feelings, trying to avoid experiencing them, actually becomes the problematic avoidance behaviors.

In the third phase of ACT, the goal is to help people distinguish between themselves and their behavioral reactions. To the extent that people can separate the "I" from what "I do, think, and feel," the more they can allow themselves to experience unacceptable feelings without feeling threatened. For example, clients are encouraged to say "I am having the thought that I am stupid and cannot give my oral report," rather than "I am stupid and can't give my oral report."

In the fourth phase of ACT, "letting go of the struggle," clients are encouraged to experience rather than avoid negative thoughts and feelings. Interventions that look like the reflections of client-centered therapy or the paradoxes of strategic therapy are used to achieve this goal. In the fifth phase, the emphasis on committing to and implementing changes most closely resembles traditional behavior therapy.

Dialectical Behavior Therapy (DBT)

Marsha Linehan (1987, 1993) has developed a program of behavior therapy for people with borderline personality disorder. Called Dialectical Behavior Therapy (DBT), it is grounded in the assumption that social interactions and personal growth are a result of a dialectical process, which involves an action leading to a reaction resulting in a synthesis. However, it is assumed that borderlines are stuck in going back and forth between extremes of emotion and behavior without ever learning a new synthesis, or middle ground. She contracts with borderlines to attend her program for a year and then the contract is renegotiated, but generally, therapy with border-lines is very long term, because they need a great deal of help. She tries to establish a collaborative, consultative relationship between the therapist and client, with an emphasis on problem solving so that the client's needs are met and the therapist's needs (for client improvement) are also met.

There are three components to DBT. Clients attend a weekly psychoeducational group, which teaches behavioral skills, assertion, affect regulation, cognitive restructuring, problem solving, and coping, typical behavioral techniques we have described earlier. The second component of the treatment program is telephone contact, and clients phone the therapist when they need help with applying the skills learned in group to the real world. On the telephone, the therapist focuses the client, who, like most borderlines, is in a state of perpetual crisis, on how to solve the current problem by asking the client to define the problem, describe what led up to it, review the skills that can be applied to the situation, and then decide what to do about it.

The third component is weekly individual therapy. Here, the relationship with the therapist is used as a reward in shaping improved behaviors, as is done in Functional Analytic Psychotherapy. Borderline clients first agree on certain behavioral goals, and they are allowed to continue therapy only if they maintain the agreement to work on those goals. The therapist must ensure that competent and improving behaviors are rewarded with the therapist's time and attention, because it is easy to inadvertently reward incompetent or even suicidal behavior by attending to it more than to competent behavior.

In individual therapy, agreed-on target behaviors are organized hierarchically, and in each session, the therapist and client first address behaviors that have occurred in the highest target area before discussing other issues. The first therapeutic target behavior involves the elimination of suicidal and self-destructive behavior. The second is the reduction of therapy-threatening behavior, such as not attending therapy, not talking about important issues, and the like. The third target behavior on the list involves work and living skills necessary to maintain an adequate life. Fourth, core skills for emotional control are addressed. Finally, if there are no issues left in any of the previous areas, the specific goals of the individual client are discussed.

While many of the behavioral methods used in DBT are similar to those used in other behavior therapies, Linehan has developed some new techniques for use with borderline clients. One of these is **validation.** According to Linehan, borderlines have been raised in families that invalidate their experience so that genuine emotion becomes highly threatening. The therapist validates the client by listening carefully to the client's experience; by reflecting accurately to the client the therapist's observation of the client's thoughts, emotions, and behaviors; and by finding the "nugget of truth" in the client's present situation that would naturally make the client feel and behave that way. For example, if clients feel that the therapist doesn't like them, rather than invalidating their experience by denying any dislike, the therapist addresses what clients think they are doing that is unlikeable. The focus then becomes teaching clients how to elicit the behaviors, such as liking them, that they want in other people.

Evaluation of Radical Behavior Therapies

In addition to giving us a new "alphabet soup" of therapies, radical behaviorists have elucidated a number of challenging theoretical points of difference with traditional behavior therapy, and they have developed several new and intriguing intervention strategies. Research on the effectiveness of radical behavior therapies is hampered by the fact that the approach emphasizes individualized interventions for specific people in certain contexts. However, research generally supports the effectiveness of these therapies, just as it does with most other therapies. For example, Hayes et al. (1995) summarize research that has demonstrated the effectiveness of ACT in treating depression, several different anxiety disorders, and the emotional distress of families with handicapped children, a situation in which the removal of the stressor is not possible.

Radical behavior therapy may be open to the criticism that it merely gives new labels to what is usually done in interpersonal talking therapies. However, unlike traditional behavior therapies that remain very different from other forms of psychotherapy, radical behavior therapies creatively utilize techniques borrowed from therapies from psychoanalysis to cognitive-behaviorism, and they lend themselves to the possibility of theoretical integration with other therapies.

EVALUATION OF BEHAVIOR THERAPY

Behavior therapy is unique in its emphasis on research, assessment, and empirical verification of efficacy. Because of this emphasis, a large body of knowledge has developed to help in the evaluation of behavior therapy. The field has matured sufficiently to recognize its weaknesses as well as its strengths.

Criticisms of Behavior Therapy

Many criticisms of behavior therapy center on theoretical disagreements between different schools of thought. Critics claim that because their theory is the correct one, behavior therapy is wrong, not "deep enough," or just misses the point. For example, psychoanalysts criticize behavior therapy for not treating the underlying unconscious conflict, but just the superficial symptoms, as discussed in Box 10.2.

Behavior therapy is criticized as not being behavioral at all. Systematic desensitization is criticized as relying on cognitions and "imagining" the phobic stimulus. Radical behaviorists argue that what is called behavior therapy is merely a collection of behavioral techniques that have very little relationship to genuine behaviorism. Behavioral technology is applied too quickly, too enthusiastically, and with too many modifications, so that it frequently loses its ties to empirically verified behavioral principles. Precisely how is a technique such as role playing asking for a date based on behavioral principles? Pairing all the stimuli surrounding lighting up a cigarette with electric shock seems a clear case of classical conditioning and aversive therapy. However, what kind of behavioral technique is making the client chain smoke many cigarettes fast until he is exhausted and nauseous? Does giving it the name *massed practice* make it a behavioral method? Can it be considered a technique of aversion therapy? Or is it an example of reverse psychology? It may be that practitioners generalize or modify behavioral techniques without considering their theoretical or empirical rationale, until some methods do not appear to be related to the known principles of learning.

Behavior therapy is criticized for being open to incorrect applications and deliberate misuse. The principles of behavior therapy seem clear and easy to understand, but inexperienced individuals unfamiliar with the empirical foundation of behaviorism may try to apply the principles in inappropriate ways or to inappropriate problems. Attempting to extinguish depression would be an obvious example of misapplication, and we mentioned earlier how time-out is sometimes used incorrectly in schools.

Since behavior modification involves the deliberate manipulation of reward contingencies so that desirable behavior is increased and undesirable behavior is decreased, critics contend that it is or can be misused to serve merely a social control function, or to manipulate or even oppress people. Behavior therapy is accused of being coercive and manipulative, promoting social conformity, and limiting freedom of choice. Critics are concerned with who decides what is desirable behavior to be rewarded and what is undesirable behavior, since value judgments are inherent in such decisions. They also point out that behavior modification methods are often used with relatively powerless groups, such as retarded children or mental hospital patients.

Defenders of behavior modification point out that any procedure can be misused and that care must be taken to serve the best interests of the clients. Furthermore, they say, rewards are being given out in all social situations, and children and mental patients are being managed and manipulated all the time anyway. With behavior modification, the value judgments as to which behaviors to reward and which not to reward are made explicit and therefore open to criticism and change. In other words, defenders argue, behavior modification is just ordinary social behavior made conscious and deliberate and out in the open. Finally, they conclude, proper contingency management techniques are highly effective for helping individuals change in directions they themselves wish to go.

A similar criticism is made by Blechman (1984), who argues that behavior therapy may be used in support of the majority culture without considering the possibly negative consequences to certain groups, such as women. For example, parent training, although called *parent* training, is given almost exclusively to mothers. It is possible that parent training has unintended negative consequences for women by making them feel as if they are to blame for their children's problems, lowering their self-esteem, and giving them more activities to be responsible for and to organize.

Aversion therapy is especially criticized, for ethical reasons. Aversion is seen as mechanistic and dehumanizing and likely to be used as coercive enforcement of social conformity. Interestingly enough, B. F. Skinner himself argued against the use of aversives in many of his writings, for in addition to punishment being morally questionable, he thought it did not work very well. The use of aversion to treat homosexuality has been especially criticized, since homosexuality is no longer seen as a disorder or abnormality. Defenders argue that aversion therapy is given only to homosexuals who *want* to change their sexual preference. Critics counter that perhaps those homosexuals who "want" to change are merely giving in to social pressure. Behavior therapists may be helping them conform without adequately questioning the rightness of such conformity.

New applications and new forms of behavior therapy are being developed every day. Some critics believe that behavior therapies are developed and implemented without adequate research. Behaviorists' pride in their emphasis on empiricism may clash with pragmatic desires for quick, inexpensive psychological treatments.

Strengths of Behavior Therapy

A large body of research demonstrates that behavior therapy is at least as effective as other forms of therapy and possibly the most effective treatment for certain problems. (Much of this research is covered in Chapter 15, including reviews of studies that do not support this conclusion.) Behavior therapy is a cost-effective form of treatment, an aspect that becomes increasingly valued in our society. Even though behaviorists do not meet the ideal of empirically evaluating every treatment before it is implemented, behavior therapists subject their methods to empirical research far more frequently than any other group, except client-centered therapists. And this research tends to support the effectiveness of behavior therapy.

As brain–behavior connections are increasingly researched, biological evidence of behavior therapy's effectiveness may appear. A landmark study conducted at the UCLA Neuropsychiatric Institute found that *both* successful drug therapy *and* behavior therapy led to identifiable changes in the brains of people with obsessive-compulsive disorder (Baxter et al., 1992). Thus, there is evidence that effective changes in behavior can cause changes in the brain, as well as improving symptoms and disorders.

From a values orientation, a strength of behavior therapy may be that it is essentially egalitarian. Although criticized as potential social control agents, behavior therapists see themselves as "giving away" their knowledge to clients. They fully explain their procedures and their theoretical and empirical rationales. They describe the empirically verified effectiveness of their methods. They do not "interpret" their clients' questions about their methods as "resistance," but respect their clients' right to know by answering their questions fully. Once clients have their therapists' knowledge, they can use it to achieve any goal they desire.

We have already discussed various instances when behavior therapists acknowledge the importance of the relationship between client and therapist. In Functional Analytic Psychotherapy, the relationship serves as the main vehicle for modifying behavior. In addition, a large research study found that compared to other therapists, behavior therapists were equally high in warmth, empathy, and genuineness, even slightly more so (Sloane, Staples, Cristol, Yorkston, & Whipple, 1975). Behavior therapists recognize the importance of being rewarding, and being warm and empathic increases their ability to be rewarding. Trustworthiness and their egalitarian approach also make them rewarding.

IN CONCLUSION

Although not all behaviorists are egalitarian and even though it can be argued that children and mental patients do not freely choose their own therapy goals, behavior therapy at its best is essentially a cooperative enterprise between therapist and client.

The client may define the treatment goals, and the therapist may describe and explain the methods to reach them. They can mutually agree on a clear plan of action and then work together to implement the treatment plan. This egalitarian approach undoubtedly contributes to a good relationship between therapist and client. It may be the essential ingredient for behavior therapy's effectiveness.

BIBLIOGRAPHY

Ayllon, T., & Azrin, N. H. (1968). *The token economy: A motivational system for therapy and rehabilitation.* New York: Appleton-Century-Crofts.

Azrin, N., & Nunn, R. (1977). *Habit control in a day.* New York: Simon & Schuster.

Bandura, A. (1969). *Principles of behavior modification.* New York: Holt, Rinehart & Winston.

Bandura, A. (1977). *Social learning theory.* Englewood Cliffs, NJ: Prentice-Hall.

Baxter, L., Schwartz, J., Bergman, K., Szuba, M., Guze, B., Mazziotta, J., Alazraki, A., Selin, C., Ferng, H., Munford, P., & Phelps, M. (1992). Caudate glucose metabolic rate changes with both drug and behavior therapy for obsessive-compulsive disorder. *Archives of General Psychiatry, 49,* 681–689.

Bellack, A., & Hersen, M. (1985). *Dictionary of behavior therapy techniques.* New York: Pergamon.

Berglas, S., & Levendusky, P. G. (1985). The Therapeutic Contract Program: An individual-oriented psychological treatment community. *Psychotherapy, 22,* 36–45.

Blechman, E. (1984). *Behavior modification with women.* New York: Guilford.

Bouton, M. E., & Swartzentruber, D. (1991). Sources of relapse after extinction in Pavlovian and instrumental learning. *Clinical Psychology Review, 11,* 123–140.

Cipani, E. (Ed.). (1989). *The treatment of severe behavior disorders: Behavioral analysis approaches.* Washington, DC: American Association on Mental Retardation.

Dangel, R., & Polster, R. (1984). *Parent training: Foundation of research and practice.* New York: Guilford.

Dinsmoor, J. (1992) Setting the record straight: The social views of B. F. Skinner. *American Psychologist, 47,* 1454–1463.

Dollard, J., & Miller, N. (1950). *Personality and psychotherapy.* New York: McGraw-Hill.

Eckman, T., Wirshing, W., Marder, S., & Liberman, R. (1992). Technique for teaching schizophrenic patients in illness self-management: A controlled trial. *American Journal of Psychiatry, 149,* 1549–1555.

Eysenck, H. J. (1967). *The biological basis of personality.* Springfield, IL: Thomas.

Eysenck, H. J., & Martin, I. (Eds.). (1987). *Theoretical foundations of behaviour therapy.* New York: Plenum.

Forehand, R., & McMahon, R. (1981). *Helping the noncompliant child: A clinician's guide to parent training.* New York: Guilford.

Franks, C., & Barbrack, C. (1983). Behavior therapy with adults: An integrative perspective. In M. Hersen, A. Kazdin, & A. Bellack (Eds.), *The clinical psychology handbook.* New York: Pergamon.

Gewirtz, J., & Baer, D. (1958). Deprivation and satiation of social reinforcers as drive conditions. *Journal of Abnormal and Social Psychology, 57,* 165–172.

Glynn, S. M. (1990). Token economy approaches for psychiatric patients. *Behavior Modification, 14,* 383–407.

Griest, D., & Wells, K. (1983). Behavioral family therapy with conduct disorders in children. *Behavior Therapy, 14,* 37–53.

Harris, B. (1979). Whatever happened to Little Albert? *American Psychologist, 34,* 151–160.

Hayes, S. C., Follette, W. C., & Follette, V. M. (1995). Behavior therapy: A contextual approach. In A. S. Gurman & S. B. Messer (Eds.), *Essential Psychotherapies: Theory and Practice.* New York: Guilford Press.

Jacobson, E. (1938). *Progressive relaxation.* Chicago: University of Chicago Press.

Jacobson, N. S. (1994). Behavior therapy and psychotherapy integration. *Journal of Psychotherapy Integration, 4,* 105–119.

Jones, M. (1924). The elimination of children's fears. *Journal of Experimental Psychology, 7,* 383–390.

Kiraly, J., & McKinnon, A. (1984). *Pupil behavior, self-control, and social skills in the classroom.* Springfield, IL: C. C. Thomas.

Klein, R., Hapkiewicz, W., & Roden, A. (1973). *Behavioral modification in educational settings.* Springfield, IL: C. C. Thomas.

Kohlenberg, R. J., & Tsai, M. (1994). Functional analytic psychotherapy: A radical behavioral approach to treatment and integration. *Journal of Psychotherapy Integration, 4,* 175–201.

Kohlenberg, R. J., & Tsai, M. (1991). *Functional analytic psychotherapy: Creating intense and curative therapeutic relationships.* New York: Plenum Press.

Lazarus, A. (1976). *Multimodal behavior therapy.* New York: Springer-Verlag.

Lazarus, A. (1981). *The practice of multimodal therapy.* New York: McGraw-Hill.

Levendusky, P., Berglas, S., Dooley, C., & Landau, R. (1983). Therapeutic contract program: Preliminary report on a behavioral alternative to the token economy. *Behavior Research and Therapy, 21,* 137–142.

Lewinsohn, P., Clarke, G., & Hoberman, H. (1989). The Coping with Depression Course: Review and future directions. *Canadian Journal of Behavioural Science, 21,* 470–493.

Lewinsohn, P., & Hoberman, H. (1982). Depression. In A. Bellack, M. Hersen, & A. Kazdin, (Eds.), *International handbook of behavior modification.* New York: Plenum Press.

Linehan, M. (1987). Dialectical behavior therapy: A cognitive behavioral approach to parasuicide. *Journal of Personality Disorders, 1,* 328–333.

Linehan, M. (1993). *Cognitive-behavioral treatment of borderline personality disorder.* New York: Guilford.

Linehan, M., Armstrong, H., Suarez, A., Allmon, D., & Heard, H. (1991). Cognitive-behavioral treatment of chronically parasuicidal borderline patients. *Archives of General Psychiatry, 48,* 1060–1064.

Lovaas, O., & Simmons, J. (1969). Manipulation of self-destruction in three retarded children. *Journal of Applied Behavioral Analysis, 2,* 143–157.

Mahoney, M. (1972). Research issues in self-management. *Behavior Therapy, 3,* 45–63.

Mahoney, M., & Thoresen, C. (1974). *Self-control: Power to the person.* Monterey, CA: Brooks/Cole.

McMahon, R., Tiedemann, G., Forehand, R., & Griest, D. (1984). Parental satisfaction with parent training to modify child noncompliance. *Behavior Therapy, 15,* 295–303.

Mowrer, O. (1947). On the dual nature of learning—A reinterpretation of "conditioning" and "problem-solving." *Harvard Educational Review, 17,* 102–148.

Mowrer, O., & Lamoreaux, R. (1946). Fear as an intervening variable in avoidance conditioning. *Journal of Comparative Psychology, 39,* 29–50.

Mowrer, O., & Solomon, L. (1954). Contiguity vs. drive-reduction in conditioned fear: The proximity and abruptness of drive-reduction. *American Journal of Psychology, 67,* 15–25.

O'Leary, K., & O'Leary, S. (1977). *Classroom management.* New York: Pergamon.

Patterson, G. (1973). Reprogramming the families of aggressive boys. In C. Thoresen (Ed.), *Behavior modification in education.* Chicago: University of Chicago Press.

Patterson, G., & Chamberlain, P. (1994). A functional analysis of resistance during parent training therapy. *Clinical Psychology, 1,* 53–70.

Patterson, G., & Gullion, M. (1976). *Living with children: New methods for parents and teachers.* Champaign, IL: Research Press.

Rachman, S. (1991). Neo-conditioning and the classical theory of fear acquisition. *Clinical Psychology Review, 11,* 155–173.

Rapee, R. (1991). The conceptual overlap between cognition and conditioning in clinical psychology. *Clinical Psychology Review, 11,* 193–203.

Rescorla, R. (1988). Pavlovian conditioning: It's not what you think it is. *American Psychologist, 43,* 151–160.

Shapiro, F. (1995). *Eye movement desensitization and reprocessing.* New York: Guilford Press.

Skinner, B. F. (1938). *The behavior of organisms.* New York: Appleton-Century.

Skinner, B. F. (1971). *Beyond freedom and dignity.* New York: Knopf.

Sloane, R., Staples, F., Cristol, A., Yorkston, N., & Whipple, K. (1975). *Psychotherapy versus behavior therapy.* Cambridge, MA: Harvard University Press.

Stampfl, T., & Levis, D. (1973). *Implosive therapy: Theory and technique.* Morristown, NJ: General Learning Press.

Watson, J. (1913). Psychology as the behaviorist views it. *Psychological Review, 20,* 158–177.

Watson, J., & Rayner, R. (1920). Conditioned emotional reactions. *Journal of Experimental Psychology, 3,* 1–14.

Wolpe, J. (1958). *Psychotherapy by reciprocal inhibition.* Stanford, CA: Stanford University Press.

Wolpe, J. (1982). *The practice of behavior therapy* (3rd ed.). New York: Pergamon.

Zeiss, A., & Lewinsohn, P. (1986). Adapting behavioral treatment for depression to meet the needs of the elderly. *Clinical Psychologist, 39,* 98–100.

11

Behavioral Medicine and Hypnosis

Sandy S., a 53-year-old married woman with two grown children, suffers from cardiovascular disease. With only a tenth-grade education, she has worked for many years without any possibility of advancement as a file clerk in a large business. At home, she is responsible for all cooking and housework. Her husband works hard as a machinist, but spends his time at home tinkering with his hobbies or watching sporting events on TV. Sandy does not report feeling depressed, but she is "upset" over her physical problems.

In the worry and strain of modern life, arterial degeneration is not only very common but develops often at an early age. For this, I believe that the high pressure at which men live and the habit of working the machine to its maximum capacity are responsible rather than excesses in eating and drinking. (Osler, 1892, p. 14)

Psychologists are beginning to discard the old belief that hypnosis transforms a person into some strange, passive, dominated new creature. Instead they are beginning to realize that hypnosis can be used and should be used to elicit the natural and innate behavior and reactions of the subject, and that through such a measure human behavior can be studied in a controlled and scientific manner. (Milton Erickson, 1941, reprinted in Rossi, 1980, p. 18)

Behavioral medicine and hypnosis are related and fascinating fields, because they deal with the age-old question of the relationship between the mind and the body. Both demonstrate that the mind-body split is, in fact, artificial, that mind and body are a unity, each affecting the other. With behavioral medicine, behavioral changes can lead to changes in disease processes affecting the body. With hypnosis, verbal suggestions can induce physiological reactions in the body, as well as changes in health and behavior. Although psychotherapy has long recognized and medicine is beginning to recognize the importance of the mind–body connection, it is the crux of behavioral medicine and hypnosis.

If behavior therapy was the result of the application of scientific behavioral theory and methods to psychopathology, then behavioral medicine began as the application of scientific behavioral theory and methods to physical pathology. Because of its use in behavioral medicine, there has been a renewed interest in hypnosis. It is interesting that the most mentalistic of techniques, hypnosis, is now often considered a behavioral method.

FOUNDATIONS OF BEHAVIORAL MEDICINE

As a rather recently recognized specialty in professional psychology, behavioral medicine has sometimes been called health psychology, clinical health psychology, medical psychology, behavioral health, and other names. It can be said that behavioral medicine is the application of psychological principles to problems and disorders that have been traditionally labeled medical. In many instances, these medical problems seem to involve significant psychological factors, which suggests that psychological techniques may be useful in treating them. Some scholars distinguish between health psychology, as the application of behavioral principles to prevent disease and promote health, and behavioral medicine, as the application of behavioral principles to the diagnosis, treatment, and rehabilitation of disease. However, there is a great deal of overlap between the two, and we will use the term *behavioral medicine* as the general name for this field.

Schwartz and Weiss (1978) define behavioral medicine as follows:

> The interdisciplinary field concerned with the development and integration of behavioral and biomedical science, knowledge, and techniques relevant to health and illness and the application of this knowledge and these techniques to prevention, diagnosis, treatment, and rehabilitation. (p. 250)

Matarazzo (1982) defines health psychology as follows:

> The aggregate of the specific educational, scientific, and professional contributions of the discipline of psychology to the promotion and maintenance of health, the prevention and treatment of illness, and the identification of etiologic and diagnostic correlates of health, illness and related dysfunction, and to the analysis and improvement of the health care system and health policy formation. (p. 4)

Other than one claiming to be an interdisciplinary field and the other a psychological field, the difference between these two rather broad definitions is not great. To add another distinction, Millon, Green, and Meagher (1982) define clinical health psychology as follows:

> The application of knowledge and methods from all substantive fields of psychology to the promotion and maintenance of mental and physical health of the individual and to the prevention, assessment, and treatment of all forms of mental and physical disorder in which psychological influences either contribute to or can be used to relieve an individual's distress or dysfunction. (p. 9)

Furthermore, distinctions are made between the *disease,* as what is objectively wrong with the person; *illness,* as the person's subjective experience of the objective disease; and *illness behavior.* Illness behavior includes adopting the role that people expect an ill person to play, defining and evaluating symptoms, seeking help, altering life routines, and the like. The psychological components of illness behavior are obvious, and it is easy to see that psychology could be important in illness, too. Evidence has accumulated that psychological factors affect the physical disease process as well.

At present, in the United States and other developed nations, the major killer of humans is not disease caused by viruses and other pathogens but rather, harm to the body caused by the individual's behavior. At the turn of this century, infectious diseases were the leading cause of death, but by mid-century the leading cause of death became chronic disease. Leading causes of death, illness, and injury include incorrect eating habits (too much food, too much fat, too much salt), drug and alcohol abuse, lack of exercise, vehicular accidents, and cigarette smoking. It is estimated that one-fifth of U.S. deaths are related to smoking alone. In terms of improving public health in the United States, the focus has shifted from controlling external factors such as germs and poor sanitation to changing individuals' behaviors, such as their eating habits or reactions to stress. It is only logical that psychology should be in the forefront in the treatment of these problems.

Psychologists have a large body of proven skills for changing behaviors, including all of the principles of learning and techniques of behavior change described in Chapter 10. The same emphasis on the scientific method, objective assessment and empirical verification of efficacy, and the assumption that all behaviors are lawful responses to identifiable and changeable learning conditions comprise the foundations of behavioral medicine. Just as behavior therapy has become eclectic and diverse, behavioral medicine utilizes behavior change methods from other schools of thought, as well as learning theory.

As the field has conducted research and gained clinical experience, the philosophical underpinnings of both behavioral and biological medicine have evolved to an integrative, holistic view. Disease is seen as multifaceted and multidetermined. Not only do the behavior, cognitions, and emotions of the individual interact with and influence the physiological, neurological, and immunological systems of the body, but the individual also interacts with and is affected by interpersonal, social, and environmental contexts. This view, known as **reciprocal determinism,** implies that intervention at any of these levels affects all the others, because they function in an ongoing process of mutual interaction and influence.

The old mind–body dualism allowed for psychology as a discipline to apply the scientific method to the study of the mind, but it also limited psychology to the "mental" realm and impeded the development of a holistic view of human functioning. While the philosophy of biomedicine and all science has become more holistic, health care practice and policies are still dominated by mind-body dualism. Hospitals and health agencies are divided into departments of psychology, departments of internal medicine, departments of surgery, and so forth. Almost all health insurance policies divide coverage between mental health and medical-surgical health benefits, generally with lower coverage for the former than for the latter, although national legislation to require equal coverage of mental and physical disorders was introduced in 1996 and 1997. These divisions make it difficult to determine who is responsible for biofeedback treatment of surgically induced incontinence, for example. These "real world" divisions run counter to the increasing tendency of science to integrate and synthesize knowledge.

Interestingly, science is beginning to pinpoint the exact nature of the link between the mind and the body (and it is *not* the pineal gland, as Descartes thought!). The emerging field of psychoneuroimmunology studies the relationship between the immune system and psychosocial stressors, which appear to directly affect the functioning of the hormonal, autonomic, and immune systems of the body (Cohen & Williamson, 1991; Volhardt, 1991). Research with animals has demonstrated that stress can affect the immune system so that it cannot effectively fight microorganisms, toxins, or even tumors (Laudenslager, Ryan, Drugan, Hyson, & Maier, 1983; Kiecolt-Glaser & Glaser, 1992; Visitainer, Volpicelli, & Seligman, 1982). Furthermore, it has been demonstrated experimentally that the immune system itself may be open to suppression or enhancement through classical conditioning, so that modifiable learning may be of importance to immunocompetence (Ader & Cohen, 1985). If so, psychology may have more than emotional support and coping skills to contribute to the treatment of allergies, AIDS, and other immune system disorders.

The Very Brief History of Behavioral Medicine

Since Roman times, some physicians have speculated that the mind affects the course of an illness, even whether an individual becomes ill. By this century, it was generally accepted that at least in the case of the so-called *psychosomatic illnesses,* such as ulcers and hypertension, the individual's psychological state was an important determinant of the disease. Parallel to the changes of viewpoint in clinical psychology, the first psychological interpretations of psychosomatic illness were psychoanalytic. It was thought, for example, that unmet, unconscious oral and dependency needs led to ulcers (Alexander, 1950). The growth of behavior therapy in the 1950s and 1960s led psychologists working in medical fields to turn from psychoanalytic to behavioral views of illness.

The usefulness of the behavioral view was promoted in the late 1960s, when it was discovered that biofeedback (discussed in the next section) could be used to help treat some medical disorders. Once biofeedback legitimized psychology's entrance into the medical field, many other behavioral techniques, including hypnosis, were applied to a variety of medical problems. Although the term *behavioral medicine* has been used at various times in the past, psychological involvement in health care grew into a definably separate field by 1978, when the Society of Behavioral Medicine was organized, the APA established a new Division of Health Psychology (38), and the *Journal of Behavioral Medicine* began publication.

The specialty has continued to grow since then. Division 38 was the second–fastest-growing division in the APA, with a 195 percent increase in membership from 1980 to 1990 (DeAngelis, 1992). Its growth has been attributed to three factors. First, there was the "discovery" of the behavioral components of disease. Second, there is the growing emphasis on "self-care." Once people are ill, the reality is that their health care is mostly self-care, and psychologists can help them take better care of themselves. The third trend pushing behavioral medicine is the high cost of traditional health care.

Biofeedback

Because biofeedback is so often identified with behavioral medicine and was its first important method of intervention, we will cover it first. The use of biofeedback is now recognized as a separate, specialized *skill,* and professional psychologists, as well as physicians, physical therapists, and others can seek certification in its use from the Biofeedback Certification Institute of America.

Biofeedback is a treatment technique in which people are trained to improve their health by using signals from their own bodies. It is a system of recording information about individuals' ongoing physiological responses and displaying the information so they can perceive second-by-second changes in their functioning. It makes ordinarily nonconscious, nonvoluntary, automatic bodily responses evident by the electronic display of information taken from mechanical or electrical sensors. For example, ordinarily, your heart beats at a certain rate or changes its rate automatically without your awareness. When you are hooked up to an EKG machine, your heart rate becomes available to your conscious awareness. You can watch and listen to the tracing and bleeps that represent your heartbeats. You are given immediate, ongoing visual and auditory feedback about the biological activity, hence the name biofeedback.

Biofeedback was first developed by academic psychologists researching certain controversial questions about the nature of learning. Research psychologists such as Neil Miller (1985) were astonished to find that people could apparently learn to raise or lower their heart rate when they got biofeedback about the rate. They also found that many other nonconscious, automatic physiological responses, such as blood pressure, muscle tension, and brain waves, which had been thought to be nonvoluntary, appeared to be modifiable by learning. The early research suggested that biofeedback resulted in true learning curves and the acquisition of a new response. Subsequent research has suggested that this is incorrect and that biofeedback enhances a person's ability to make relatively small voluntary changes in physiological responses through increased awareness alone, but more research is needed.

Rather than wait several decades as they did with other academic behavioral discoveries, clinical psychologists immediately saw that if such physiological responses could be modified, then perhaps patients could learn to control health-threatening physiological responses. Biofeedback technology has been used to treat several types of medical disorders. Biofeedback of blood pressure has been used to treat hypertension, migraine headaches, Raynaud's disease (a circulatory disorder that causes uncomfortably cold hands); biofeedback of muscle tension to treat headaches, backache, vaginismus, and stress; biofeedback of brain waves to treat stress and teach relaxation; and biofeedback of heart rate to treat anxiety and cardiac rate disorders, to give just a few examples.

It now appears that in many cases, biofeedback alone results in a degree of permanent change in the physiological response, such as blood pressure, that is too small to be clinically significant in controlling the condition, such as hypertension (Blanchard & Young, 1974). Roberts (1985) concluded that the research does not justify the use of biofeedback alone in therapy: it must be accompanied by other techniques. Nevertheless, patients and professional psychologists alike report that biofeedback, when used in combination with other behavioral methods, is effective in the treatment of many disorders.

The interesting question remains, how does biofeedback work? Some scholars believe that the positive effects of biofeedback, if any, are mediated through a generalized relaxation effect and through cognitive factors. Biofeedback may simply enhance people's ability to relax, and relaxation itself improves their health and well-being. Several cognitive processes are hypothesized to be an important part of biofeedback. It may increase individuals' sense of self-efficacy, that is, they become more confident that they can have an effect on their disorder, and so they do. Once people believe they have control over their problems, they feel less anxious and stressed.

Interventions in Behavioral Medicine

Although biofeedback was behavioral medicine's first recognized intervention method, it is now a relatively small part of the field. Behavioral medicine encompasses intervention in a wide variety of disorders with a wide variety of behavioral methods, including many new cognitive-behavioral methods covered in Chapter 12. The following list gives an idea of the range of activities of psychologists in behavioral medicine: assessment of candidates for back surgery or penile prosthesis surgery; desensitization of fears of medical and dental treatments; teaching skills to cope with pain; interventions to control vomiting associated with pregnancy and chemotherapy; cardiac rehabilitation; memory retraining for cognitive impairments due to strokes; consultation to improve health and safety at the work site; psychosocial services for oncology patients; psychoeducational self-management programs for asthma; coping strategies for rheumatoid arthritis; hypnosis for irritable bowel syndrome; and many more (Belar, Deardorff, & Kelly, 1987; Blanchard, 1992). Health psychologists conduct research in these areas and others as well. A more detailed description of one type of behavioral medicine treatment is given in Box 11.1.

The various behavior therapy methods that may be considered part of behavioral medicine can be grouped according to three major purposes. First, behavioral techniques are used to change physiological responses or learned symptoms that constitute or contribute to threats to health. Second, behavioral medicine contributes to the

B O X   1 1 . 1

Behavioral Treatment of Headache

To demonstrate the specifics of treatment in behavioral medicine, we will discuss the headaches of Jan N. as an example. Jan is a 39-year-old Caucasian American, the single mother of very active, 7-year-old twin boys. She also works 50 hours per week as a stockbroker in a high-pressure investment firm. Jan has suffered from debilitating headaches all of her life, but since the birth of her sons, they have increased in intensity and frequency so that she cannot function at least one day per week. Over the years, she has sought medical help to no avail. The last physician she consulted recommended that she see a psychologist, Dr. Diane R. Although skeptical, Jan is desperate and makes an appointment.

There are certain basic steps in any behavioral treatment program, beginning with assessment and diagnosis. Diane and Jan will proceed through these typical steps. Note the similarity of these steps to problem-solving training and behavior therapy.

Step 1: Define the Problem

Generally, as part of one or two initial interviews, the therapist will ask the client to define the problem. The information collected will include current symptoms, precipitating events, pain history, assessment of physiological functioning (often from physicians' reports), assessment of psychological functioning, and thoughts and beliefs about headache.

There are two main types of headaches for which behavioral treatment is sought. Migraine, or vascular, headaches are attributed to a two-step process of a prolonged constriction of arteries in the head, followed by a rebound dilation of the arteries associated with the onset of pain. Muscle-contraction, or tension, headaches are attributed to excessive, sustained contraction of the back, shoulder, and neck muscles. Some believe this distinction is questionable and argue that all headaches involve excessive muscle contraction, with migraines simply being more severe.

As Jan describes her headaches, they do not appear to be migraines, and in fact, previous physicians have ruled out that diagnosis. She reports a life full of stress and that her headaches generally occur at the end of the week. She believes they are due to the pressure at work, but she also believes that she is being punished for success at work, that once the pain begins she is doomed, that she can never be a good mother to her sons because of her pain, and other anxiety-provoking beliefs. Diane observes that Jan does not sit in a relaxed manner, but rather exhibits hunched shoulders and a wrinkled forehead. She begins the process of educating Jan about the nature of tension headaches and how they can be modified.

Step 2: Generate Alternatives

The next step in behavioral medicine is for the therapist and client to work together to generate alternative conceptualizations of the problem and alternative ways of intervening. The therapist generally elicits information about strategies the client has used before and how effective they were. The therapist gives information about alternatives, explaining the rationale, research on effectiveness, and appropriateness of each for the client's particular problem. Clients are encouraged to employ existing skills, develop untapped resources, and learn new methods of coping.

In exploring alternatives with Jan, Diane discovers and points out to Jan that several things she tried in the past did in fact work. When she used to take a break to meditate in the afternoon, her headaches were less frequent. Diane suggests that the relaxation involved in meditation reduced Jan's muscle tension and that since Jan has skills in that direction, relaxation training might be appropriate.

Besides relaxation training, other interventions have been found to be effective with headache, and Diane discusses them all with Jan. Hypnosis is useful for suggesting pain control and pain reduction and for teaching relaxation. Biofeedback is often used with headache. It might educate Jan about the level of muscle tension in her neck and shoulders and teach her how to reduce it. It may also facilitate "physiological insight" so she learns there is a connection between psychological and physiological processes.

Stimulus-control modification may help Jan identify and avoid the exact situations that bring on her headaches. If they cannot be avoided, then cognitive-behavior therapy may help her modify her anxiety-provoking and tension-raising thoughts about those situations. A thought-stopping technique may help her stop the vicious cycle of feeling a bit of head pain and thinking she is doomed and a terrible mother, thoughts that increase her muscle tension, which leads to more pain and more thoughts and so on.

Diane also suggests stress-coping group training, in which Jan would attend a small, educational, weekly group in order to learn coping strategies for stressful situations at work. The group would cover techniques for identifying cues that trigger tension, evaluating thoughts and responses to the cues, and correcting, modifying, and stopping thoughts that increase pain and instituting thoughts that are incompatible with further stress and tension.

Step 3: Evaluate Alternatives

The therapist alerts the client to typical advantages and disadvantages of each intervention strategy. Treatment recommendations will reflect the state of knowledge at that point. The client will be encouraged to anticipate the consequences of change.

BOX 11.1 *(continued)*

Among all the alternatives, Diane points out to Jan that because of her experience with meditation, she may be able to use hypnosis and biofeedback effectively. Diane cites a study by Andreychuk and Skriver (1975), who found that both hypnosis and biofeedback were more effective in the treatment of headache of individuals high in hypnotizability. Diane also cites a study by Lisspers and Ost (1990), who followed up 60 patients for six years. They had been treated for headache with biofeedback and applied relaxation training. They reported a reduction in number of headaches, use of medication, and self-ratings of pain after treatment, and this improvement was maintained for six years. Diane also describes a study on stress-coping group treatment by Holroyd and Andrasik (1980), who followed up headache patients given such group treatment and found they continued to be significantly improved. Furthermore, 63% reported decrements in symptoms other than headache. Diane is trying both to describe the empirical efficacy of the alternative treatments and to instill hope and trust in Jan.

Step 4: Choose Alternatives And Implement
The client's level of commitment and the support available in the client's environment must be evaluated at this point. Several factors will determine the choice of treatment.

Because biofeedback and hypnosis do not seem to Jan to demand as much time and energy as the other alternatives discussed, and because she hopes for a quick solution, she prefers them to the others.

Diane begins with a series of biofeedback sessions, hooking Jan up to a special EMG machine, which through painless electrodes attached to the skin detects muscle contraction and turns it into a high-pitched sound. This procedure helps Jan become aware of the level of muscle tension in her head, neck, and shoulders. By relaxing her muscles, she is able to lower the pitch of the machine's sound. After three sessions of biofeedback, Diane adds hypnosis to the sessions. These sessions include suggestions that Jan will be successful in lowering the tone in biofeedback, that she will be able to detect the cues that bring on headaches before they begin, that she will be able to relax her muscles and prevent the headaches, and that she will substitute a relaxing scene of a flower-filled meadow for her usual anxiety-provoking thoughts.

Step 5: Monitor Progress and Reevaluate
The therapist and client may need to evaluate the choice of treatment strategies based on the client's new experiential knowledge. Changes in treatment strategy may be necessary. Long-term follow-up contact may be necessary to refresh client skills.

After a few weeks of treatment, Jan reports some welcome relief of her headaches. However, she has a very bad one again and returns for treatment. Diane incorporates relapse prevention into the program, and tells Jan that occasional headaches do not mean the program is failing. She tells Jan of another study, by Andrasik and colleagues (1984), which described the usefulness of booster treatments for long-term maintenance of improvement.

Jan thinks she might like the stress-coping group after all. She also reports an unanticipated consequence of fewer headaches: she has to spend more time with her sons. She feels overwhelmed and inadequate with their activity and demands. Diane begins again with Step 1, now working on a definition of the problem as one of difficulty coping with the stress of parenting. She goes through the steps to recommend parent training and other alternatives. She and Jan will continue the process as long as it leads to effective interventions and worthwhile changes for Jan.

improvement of health care delivery. Third, behavioral medicine or health psychology addresses known risk factors, that is, behavior that is known to increase risks to health.

Interventions in Disease-Related Behavior One purpose of behavioral medicine is to intervene in the disease process itself. Psychologists are involved in the assessment, diagnosis, treatment, and rehabilitation of those aspects of diseases seen in behavior. Some medical disorders are a result of some sort of physiological response. Tensing the muscles of the head and neck may cause headaches, producing too much stomach acid helps create ulcers, breathing incorrectly intensifies some forms of asthma. The research on biofeedback suggests that people can, to a degree, control such physiological responses when they become aware of them, and so it is possible they may be able to alleviate the resulting disorder. Other interventions can alter the course of disease. For example, cancer patients often develop food aversions to anything they eat before their nausea-inducing treatments. If, as a result, they eat less or restrict their diet, their ability to fight the disease is impaired. Deconditioning their food aversions and teaching coping skills will directly affect the course of their illness.

Rehabilitation is an important part of behavioral medicine. It may not alter the disorder, but it helps people change their behavior so they can deal with the disorder. For example, behavioral therapists work with patients who have brain injuries as a result of accident or stroke. They retrain the patients' memories and teach them cognitive coping strategies. They may use biofeedback of muscle tension to retrain control over muscles paralyzed by a brain injury.

As another part of behavioral medicine, psychologists intervene in "illness behavior" or "sick role behavior." It is possible that some people are rewarded with attention and sympathy for being in pain or for being sick. Called secondary gain, the attention and sympathy people receive for their symptoms may serve as a powerful reward for those symptoms. In that sense, symptoms are learned. Furthermore, patients may become socialized or trained by the medical bureaucracy to fall into sick roles that may become chronic. In such cases, behavior therapy techniques may help improve the medical problem.

Biofeedback, systematic desensitization, classical conditioning, operant conditioning, hypnosis, contingency management, and other methods have been used alone and in combination to treat migraines, headaches, back pain, other chronic pain, cancer, alcoholism, drug abuse, hypertension, asthma, insomnia, Raynaud's disease, arthritis, gastrointestinal disorders, incontinence, enuresis, encopresis, anorexia, bulimia, irritable bowel syndrome, seizures, ulcers, vomiting, nausea, bruxism, head injuries, scoliosis, hives, and other disorders. In addition, stress, sleep, exercise, and diet are clinically modifiable behaviors of importance to immunocompetence. As already mentioned, it has been demonstrated experimentally that the immune system itself may be open to suppression or enhancement through classical conditioning, so that the behavioral treatment of allergies and other immune system disorders, including AIDS, is a possibility worthy of future research.

Interventions in Health Care Delivery   Behaviorists can assist in the improvement of health care delivery in several ways. Psychologists are involved with increasing patient compliance with medical regimens. Patient compliance is an interesting problem for medicine. All the diagnostic tests and medical advances in the world won't help if patients don't follow doctors' orders. Some surveys suggest that over half of patients do not take prescribed medicines correctly—they take them too much, not enough, or not at all. Patients often fail to keep follow-up appointments.

Certain disorders involve difficult regimens to follow. The best example is diabetes, which may require a special diet and a strict regimen of medications for all of the patient's life. Teenagers are especially resistant to the treatment necessary for diabetes. Education, group therapy, contingency management, and other techniques are used to increase patient compliance.

Behavioral medicine can help patients cope with medical procedures, some of which are frightening, painful, or nauseating. Education, modeling, and role playing can prepare patients for procedures. Simply knowing exactly what is going to happen to them can reduce patients' anxiety. Explanations, discussions, slide shows, and demonstrations help adults. Some therapists use special dolls and puppets to demonstrate surgical and treatment procedures for children. The children's fears and questions can be addressed through playing out a doctor-patient scene. Some therapists use modeling through films showing children undergoing the same medical procedure as the patient.

Behavioral techniques can help patients control their pain when they must have painful diagnostic tests or treatments. Dental treatments, spinal taps, angiograms and the like are often painful. Systematic desensitization, relaxation, guided imagery, hypnosis, and other techniques can help patients reduce or at least control their response to the pain. The same techniques can help patients reduce or control the nausea and vomiting that are the side effect of some chemotherapy for cancer.

Health psychologists often become involved in public policy related to health care. Conducting research on the many causes of illness, educating the public regard-

Using Systematic Desensitization to Treat Medical Noncompliance in Pets.

ing these causes, and working in medical settings lead to the observation that, at times, the health care system itself gets in the way of effective treatment. Behavioral psychologists gain evidence and ideas for how to improve the entire health care delivery system and, consequently, the health of individuals. Psychologists thus become involved with public policy and political activities, in court cases, in legislation regarding health insurance companies, in training and licensing requirements, and other issues. For example, if psychotherapy is proven to be cost-effective for treating somatizing patients, individuals with diabetes and asthma, and patients recovering from surgery and heart attacks, as VandenBos and DeLeon (1988) claim, then changes are required in the way we regulate hospital admitting authority, prescription privileges, health insurance reimbursement, and other health care delivery issues, to be discussed in Chapter 18. It is also possible that if it seems evident that the way our society is organized creates health-endangering stress for some groups, psychologists must become involved in social action to change society (Ewart, 1991).

Disease Prevention and Health Promotion   Behavioral medicine includes preventing illness and promoting wellness, although some consider this the province of health psychology. If research reveals that certain behaviors increase the probability of developing certain diseases, then it is clearly cost-effective and good public policy to reduce those behaviors and prevent the development of illness in the first place. If certain changes in behavior can be made and maintained, the amount of human suffering can be greatly reduced.

Health psychologists intervene in known risk factors. Certain behaviors, such as smoking and overeating, have been demonstrated by research to increase the risk of painful, disabling, and fatal diseases such as lung cancer, emphysema, and cardiovascular disorders. It follows that modification of these behaviors would decrease the health risks. A quick glance at the titles of articles in recent clinical psychology journals will show that obesity is the single disorder most frequently mentioned, with smoking a close second. The treatment of these two risk factors is a rapidly growing field.

Smoking and overeating are extremely difficult habits for some people to modify. In the past, failure and relapse rates have been unacceptably high. Behavioral medicine has entered the fray. A combination of behavioral techniques, including aversion therapy, relaxation, identification of signaling stimuli, negative practice, imagery, self-reward, contingency management, group therapy, exercise, hypnosis, and whatever else creative therapists think of, seems to be equally or somewhat more effective in modifying smoking and eating behavior than traditional methods of stopping these behaviors.

Besides the modification of smoking and eating behaviors, other known risk factors targeted by behavioral medicine include the so-called Type A personality, stress, and lack of education regarding the prevention and early detection of diseases. The traditional Type A or coronary-prone personality exhibits a set of behaviors that include hostility, time pressure, trying to do several things at once, competitiveness, driving ambition, and the inability to relax. Hypnosis, education, group therapy, biofeedback, and behavioral techniques, such as coping skills and contingency management, have been used with some degree of effectiveness to change these behaviors, assuming that this, in turn, will reduce the person's likelihood of having a heart attack in the future (Thoresen & Powell, 1992).

Stress inoculation methods and stress management programs continue to grow in popularity. It is assumed that if people can learn to control their reactions to stress, they will reduce the likelihood of developing stress-related diseases, such as hypertension, ulcers, headaches, and heart disease. Behavioral techniques are used to teach individuals to recognize the signs of stress, learn to relax, alter their priorities, and organize their time better. In addition to relaxation training, hypnosis, guided imagery, desensitization, exercise, group therapy, assertion training, and role playing, biofeedback is often used to teach people how to relax their muscles, lower their blood pressure, lower their heart rate, or induce certain kinds of relaxing brain waves.

Behaviorists are involved in educating the public regarding the prevention of health problems in the first place. The 1979 U.S. Surgeon General's report indicated that as much as half the mortality in the United States may be due to unhealthy behavior. It also stated that of the 10 leading causes of death, at least seven of them could be substantially reduced if people altered just six habits: poor diet, smoking, lack of exercise, alcohol abuse, maladaptive responses to stress, and failure to use appropriate antihypertensive medications (U.S. Surgeon General, 1979). Widespread changes in these six behaviors would substantially reduce morbidity and mortality due to heart disease, neoplastic disease, stroke, arteriosclerosis, emphysema, diabetes, cirrhosis of the liver, and psychological disabilities. Furthermore, even bacterial or viral diseases such as AIDS may be spread and controlled primarily by the behavior of individuals.

Part of prevention is the early detection of disease. Psychologists teach the importance of self-examinations of the breasts and testicles in order to detect cancer in its earliest, most curable stages. The importance of proper diet, exercise, and rest in preventing disease is taught, along with specific techniques to increase the likelihood that individuals will begin and continue to engage in exercise or good diets. Teaching people to announce their plans to exercise or diet publicly, to enlist the support of friends, to reward themselves for meeting their goals, and to structure their environment to support their goals are some of the ways that behaviorists can help people with disease prevention.

Health psychologists are sometimes involved in "wellness," the promotion of optimal health. Rather than only preventing disease, the active promotion of excellent health and general well-being is emphasized. Maintaining low weight and eating a moderately low-fat, low-salt, low-sugar diet are important in wellness, but the greater emphasis is generally on exercise. Research suggests that regular aerobic exercise has numerous benefits, from reducing weight, improving cardiovascular functioning, and increasing physical strength, to reducing depression, improving mood, raising self-esteem, and increasing energy levels, as well as lowering the risks of certain diseases, such as heart disease, diabetes, osteoporosis, and chronic pain (Dubbert, 1992). With so many things in its favor, it is perhaps surprising that regular exercise is so difficult for so many Americans. Education, group support, and contingency management techniques are used to teach and maintain regular exercise programs.

Some psychologists argue that we should be pursuing psychological wellness, in addition to physical wellness. Cowan (1991) suggests that psychological wellness is promoted through competence, resilience, social system modification, and empowerment. These concepts again suggest that psychologists become involved in public policy and social action in order to modify the social system and empower people for the sake of health and wellness.

Evaluation of Behavioral Medicine

Not everyone is enthusiastic about the possibilities for using behavioral methods to treat medical disorders and psychologists' potential movement into being primary health care providers. While many physicians welcome psychology's contributions to medical care, many oppose the entrance of psychologists into the field on the grounds that they are "practicing medicine without a license." Obviously, concerns over professional territory prompt this charge, as well as a desire to protect the public from inappropriate interventions. As the line between the mental and physical aspects of medical problems continues to blur, we can expect that psychologists will continue to develop effective behavioral techniques for helping sick people and that this controversy will also continue. The role of psychologists in the new U.S. health care systems developing in the 1990s is becoming a subject of endless debate and great contention, as we shall discuss in Chapter 18.

Some critics charge that the effectiveness of behavioral methods in this context is not proven and that insufficiently researched techniques are rushed into application.

Applying unproven techniques to medical problems is often considered especially risky and ethically questionable, although we fail to see why it should be worse than applying unproven techniques to psychological problems. Fortunately, the behavioral tradition in psychology emphasizes a process of research and verification of efficacy.

Other criticisms of behavioral medicine involve philosophical and ethical disagreements with certain interventions. For example, some people argue that "fat is a feminist issue." It is true both that the most frequently researched and treated behavioral medical problem is obesity and that far more women than men seek treatment for obesity. It is argued that both of these facts reflect our culture's unrealistic overemphasis on women being thin in order to be considered attractive and socially acceptable. Furthermore, in the cases of moderate overweight generally treated, some research suggests that dieting and being concerned with weight actually induce overweight (Brownell, 1982). It also seems possible that a dieting process that leads to several weight losses and gains is more dangerous to the health of the individual woman than simply remaining at a constant but somewhat higher than average weight. Critics argue that psychologists should not be involved in "treating" moderate obesity, but rather, should direct their efforts toward increasing the acceptance of somewhat higher than average weight in the women seeking treatment themselves and in society at large.

Some critics believe that the increasing emphasis on psychological causes of illness leads to a tendency to "blame the victim." If it is believed that certain behaviors cause certain illnesses and if society begins to emphasize personal responsibility for illness, then it is a short leap to blaming people for failing to take the steps necessary to change their behaviors and thereby failing to prevent their illnesses. It is even possible that fiscal conservatives and health insurance companies could use the belief in personal responsibility for health as a reason to cut funding for behavior-related illnesses. Health psychologists must educate the public regarding the distinction between encouraging personal responsibility for behaviors that are modifiable and not blaming people for being unable to change some behaviors or for becoming sick in spite of good health practices. After all, altering health risk behaviors changes only the *risk* or likelihood of illness—it does not guarantee health.

A great deal of research has been done on the effectiveness of behavioral interventions in health, and it generally supports the effectiveness of behavioral medicine. It is impossible to summarize this large body of research here, but some examples can be cited. The evidence on headache has already been discussed in Box 11.1. A study comparing psychological therapy and conventional medical treatment for irritable bowel syndrome found a significantly greater reduction in symptomotology in those who received therapy than in those who received conventional medical treatment, and the improvements remained 12 months after treatment (Svedlund, Sjodin, Ottosson, & Dotevall, 1983). A longitudinal study on irritable bowel syndrome found that almost all the patients treated with progressive muscle relaxation, biofeedback, and cognitive therapy improved, and the improvement was maintained for four years after treatment (Schwartz, Taylor, Scharff, & Blanchard, 1990). Many more studies along these lines have been done with many other illnesses, and these are reviewed extensively in Blanchard (1992).

Strengths of behavioral medicine include its interdisciplinary orientation, its incorporation of the new scientific holistic view, and its emphasis on scientific empiricism. Although these factors are philosophically valuable, it is probably behavioral medicine's cost-effectiveness that will ensure its place in American health care. The United States' annual per capita spending on health care is the highest in the world, yet our mortality rates and other measures of health are far from first in comparison to other developed countries. Physicians complain of being overburdened, and patients complain of lack of attention. Psychologists can address these problems by developing more effective and less costly health treatments, by preventing disease in the first place and saving those costs, and by doing some of the important educational and emotionally supportive interventions that physicians don't have the time or ability to do. All that remains is for behavioral medicine to gather and present the evidence of its cost-effectiveness to the public and the funders of health care so that they will support its inclusion in the changing U.S. health care system.

FOUNDATIONS OF HYPNOSIS

Hypnosis is a remarkable phenomenon. Two people in a special relationship, one the hypnotizer and the other the hypnotizee, engage in a conversation in which the hypnotizer tells the other to concentrate, close eyes, relax, and the like, and then gives suggestions for a variety of changes, including physiological responses, and they happen. While engaged in the activity labeled hypnosis, individuals can undergo physically painful experiences without reacting, alter other physiological responses such as blushing, "cure" palsied movements, and make seemingly difficult behavioral changes.

Hypnosis is extremely difficult to define, measure, and investigate. After many years of research and controversy, there is still little agreement as to what hypnosis is. Whether it is an altered state of consciousness, a trance, or simply deep relaxation is not known for certain. Most writers in the field of hypnosis settle for defining it simply as a heightened state of suggestibility.

How is that state of heightened suggestibility achieved? The techniques for inducing hypnosis and those used once the client is hypnotized vary tremendously, and creative therapists invent new ones every day. Hypnotic inductions may be direct or indirect, administered by a therapist or self-administered by the client. They may take a few moments or a half an hour. Induction may involve a quiet room, sitting comfortably, the hypnotist's soothing voice, and suggestions to relax and concentrate. For example, the hypnotist tells the client to stare at a certain point up on a wall and then says, "Your eyes are getting tired." Well, of course they would! However, it is believed that the client experiences the hypnotist's words as making an accurate prediction or as making a suggestion that must be obeyed, thus increasing the client's suggestible state. After several such inevitable suggestions, the client soon enters a state that both the hypnotist and the client consider to be hypnosis. It is believed that when clients successfully follow a series of suggestions to close their eyes, breathe deeply, and concentrate on certain stimuli, they are then more open to following other therapeutic suggestions.

There are a number of misconceptions about hypnosis, for example, that people can be made to do things against their will. One of the reasons for its questionable reputation may be that hypnosis is used for entertainment, such as in night club acts, when people do absurd things seemingly without awareness or will. It is debatable whether volunteers for such acts are "really" hypnotized. Rather, it appears that entertainers are experienced at selecting cooperative volunteers and persuading them to go along with the act. Hypnosis has also been negatively portrayed in horror films, making it appear that people can be made to murder or commit other terrible acts against their will. Research, of course, indicates that this portrayal is entirely inaccurate, but the negative impact of the films still exists.

Hypnosis has been used to help people recall experiences for the purposes of criminal investigations and court testimony, as well as in therapy. Not all courts have allowed such testimony, but some have, so there may be an increase in use of hypnosis in legal proceedings.

Hypnosis, despite its presentation in films and the press, is no more dangerous than other forms of therapy. A hypnotist cannot force people to do things, for hypnosis is basically a cooperative enterprise. Hypnosis cannot induce amnesia either, unless the person wants to forget. A layperson often views hypnosis as coercive, with the powerful or mysterious hypnotist forcing the hypnotized person to do things against his or her will. Even scientists fall into this sort of bias when they label people with high ability in being hypnotized with pejorative terms that imply passivity or "weakness," such as "suggestible" or "susceptible" to hypnosis. In fact, it is possible to view the ability to become hypnotized as a skill, with some individuals more able than others to enter into the hypnosis process.

Hypnosis is now considered by many to be a behavioral technique, a special skill to be utilized in a number of helpful ways. Therapists and other professionals such as dentists and physicians may seek special training and certification in hypnosis, available from a number of organizations.

A Long History Briefly Told

Hypnosis has been used for centuries by everyone from shamans and entertainers to physicians and midwives, and it has wavered in and out of respectability over the years. The formal use of hypnosis in medical treatments began early in the last century, in Europe, when it was popularized by Mesmer. Then known as mesmerism, hypnosis was used in obstetrics as early as 1831 (Chertok, 1981) and in surgery even earlier (Spanos & Chaves, 1989). Freud originally used hypnosis in psychoanalysis, but dropped it in favor of his own technique of free association. Mesmer eventually fell into disrepute, and his methods were ignored by the medical community for many decades. In recent years, hypnosis was reintroduced in behavioral medicine, where it was used with success, and as a result, it is now used in dentistry, medicine, and psychotherapy. It has again gained respectability and popularity.

Theoretical Explanations of Hypnosis

There seems to be sufficient evidence from well-controlled studies to conclude that, at least for people who are responsive to hypnosis, it is very effective in treating a variety of problems and disorders. There is much more controversy over why it works. There are many different theoretical explanations for hypnosis, but they can be grouped into two predominant views. One is that hypnosis constitutes a special state different from ordinary consciousness. In this view, hypnosis is an altered state of consciousness or trance brought about by the hypnotic induction procedures. Many who hold this view believe that the hypnotic state creates or is a product of a dissociation between different parts of the mind in that parts are "split off" from consciousness and volitional control, thus allowing suggestions for change to be effective.

The second major view of hypnosis is that it is not a special state, but simply a subset of everyday social and cognitive behaviors. Holders of this view argue that the empirical evidence indicates that hypnosis can be accounted for with the same concepts that are used to study behavior in other social situations (Kirsch & Lynn, 1995). For example, it is hypothesized that the "demand characteristics" of the hypnosis situation require a person to cooperate with the hypnotic suggestions, because everyone "knows" that that is how a hypnotized person is "supposed" to act. It is also possible that some people feel less threatened by and therefore less resistant to therapeutic suggestions when they cognitively attribute their obedience to the hypnosis and not to simply obeying someone else's advice. In the hypnosis situation, people may shift their perspective from an objective, possibly rigid position to an uncritical, accepting, possibly flexible perspective. They may become more open to new information and new ways of understanding things, but their behavior can be explained with the same psychological principles that explain all social behavior.

It seems that professional psychologists more frequently hold the view that hypnosis is a special state requiring a special theoretical rationale and that academic psychologists more frequently believe that hypnosis can be explained with the usual principles of social, behavioral, and cognitive psychology. We will focus on one well-known contemporary example of each view. The theory of Milton Erickson will represent the special state view (Erickson & Rossi, 1979; Rossi, 1980), and the work of Nicholas Spanos and his colleagues will demonstrate the cognitive-behavioral perspective (Spanos & Chaves, 1989; Spanos, 1991).

Milton Erickson's Theory of Hypnosis

Probably the most famous hypnotist in the world, Milton Erickson died in 1980 without leaving a comprehensive written summary of his theories and methods, although he wrote numerous scientific articles. He was a very charismatic and effective hypnotist and therapist, and he greatly influenced many of today's prominent therapists, such as Haley and several others. Although Erickson's work was not widely accepted when he was alive because hypnosis was not regarded as "scientific" then, his complex ideas are popular today.

Erickson believed that all forms of psychotherapy are based on suggestion and hypnosis. Hypnosis is related in Erickson's framework to the therapeutic paradox, as discussed in Chapter 14. The paradox inherent in all psychotherapies is as follows. The implicit message is that the therapist will help the client change (after all the therapist is taking the client's money for that purpose!). However, most therapists explicitly state that the client is ultimately responsible for change and the client can change only if he or she wants to. So if clients change, they are obeying the therapist's implicit message (to change), and if they don't, they are obeying the explicit message (not to change unless they want to). Once clients obey the therapist at all, and under the therapeutic paradox they cannot help but obey one message or the other, then they are hypnotized in the sense that their suggestibility has increased and they are more willing to follow other helpful suggestions.

Despite professing a pragmatic, atheoretical stance, Erickson developed a complex theoretical rationale as to why hypnosis and indirect suggestions work. Based on his detailed and extensive observations of people's behavior, he believed that normal humans are composed of at least two "minds" or systems of knowing and experiencing the world. He called these the "conscious" and the "unconscious" (or "subconscious") minds, although he meant something quite different from Freud's use of these words. The "conscious" mind is composed of those thoughts, emotions, perceptions, and memories in awareness. It has its own needs and goals and ways of knowing and communicating. It is logical, slow to react, and thinks in a linear cause-and-effect fashion. The "unconscious" mind consists of an entirely different set of thoughts, emotions, perceptions and memories, with its own needs and goals, which are not immediately available to conscious awareness. It is holistic, intuitive, quick to react, and, according to Erickson, wiser and more objective (although more literal and simplistic) than the conscious mind.

To Erickson, the "conscious" is the source of resistance and difficulties in life, while the "unconscious" contains valuable learnings and objective, experiential knowledge. For example, the unconscious knows how to walk—you walk every day without awareness. As long as walking remains outside of awareness, it is done perfectly well. When you become aware of how you walk, as when you become self-conscious about how you look to others, you start to have trouble doing it. As Erickson noted, his ideas about the conscious and unconscious minds are similar to present ideas about right and left brain functioning. The logical, linear-reasoning left hemisphere of the brain is similar to Erickson's conscious mind, and the holistic, intuitive, reactive, right hemisphere is similar to his unconscious mind (Erickson, Rossi, & Rossi, 1976). In fact, hypnosis may be seen conceptually as a way to confuse the logical left hemisphere so the therapist can directly access the right hemisphere, thus solving the therapeutic problem of access to the part of the personality that is organized to accept change, as discussed in Chapter 16.

Erickson defined hypnosis descriptively "as an artificially enhanced state of suggestibility resembling sleep wherein there appears to be a normal, time-limited and stimulus-limited dissociation of the 'conscious' from the 'subconscious' elements of the psyche" (quoted in Havens, 1985, p. 249). This definition implies all the points of Erickson's theory of hypnosis. Like other definitions of hypnosis, Erickson's includes a state of increased suggestibility, which is different from other such states in that it is artificially enhanced, through hypnotic inductions. Note also that it allows the "unconscious" (or "subconscious"—he called it both) mind to separate from the "conscious." In everyday functioning, the conscious mind dominates the way people experience and function, and it cannot solve difficulties such as anxieties and symptoms. Hypnosis is time-limited and stimulus-limited; that is, it occurs only for a certain period of time and under certain circumstances. Furthermore, Erickson considered hypnosis to be a "normal" state, and in fact, he said that some of our best behavior (such as safe freeway driving) is done while we are hypnotized.

Thus, Erickson believed that hypnosis and suggestion "worked" in therapy because they circumvented the troublesome "conscious" and spoke directly to the wiser "unconscious." Hypnotic inductions confuse the logical "conscious," sort of putting it out of commission, allowing the "unconscious" to respond. By being illogical, vivid, and literal, hypnotic techniques allow the therapist to deal with the unconscious mind directly. Since Erickson considered the unconscious to be healthier and more sensible than the conscious, hypnosis enlists the patient's better self in the change process. The unconscious is able to solve problems that the conscious cannot, and it wants to change in positive directions, so it will follow therapeutic suggestions that the conscious mind may resist.

The Cognitive-Behavioral View of Nicholas Spanos

The belief that hypnosis is not a special state is almost as old as hypnosis. Unusual events appear to happen with hypnosis, and most people assume that unusual events require special explanations. Early in the last century, Mesmer claimed that his procedures worked because of changes in "animal magnetism" and the like. The nineteenth-century physicians who tried to discredit him (and succeeded) argued that there was no such thing as "animal magnetism" and that mesmerism could be explained as merely the effect of suggestion and expectancy.

By the mid-twentieth century, psychologists began subjecting hypnosis to empirical investigation. A great deal of scientific research has failed to demonstrate that hypnosis is a special state. Two major types of studies have been done. First, there are many studies in which the behavior of people subjected to a hypnosis procedure is compared to that of people not hypnotized. The vast majority of such studies find little difference in the behavior of the two groups. For example, people who are told while hypnotized that they can bear a painful procedure and people who are simply told they can bear it report similarly reduced levels of pain. Second, there are many studies in which hypnotized people make certain claims, but indirect measures suggest these claims are not accurate. For example, individuals hypnotized to forget certain words claim they cannot remember them, but they show changes in their galvanic skin response when presented with them. (These example studies and many more are reviewed in Spanos and Chaves, 1989.) From such research it seems that the most parsimonious explanation of hypnosis is not that it is an altered state of consciousness, but rather, that it is continuous with other types of complex social behavior (Kirsch & Lynn, 1995).

T. R. Sarbin (1950) was the first modern theorist to explicitly reject the idea that hypnosis is a special state. Using a theatrical metaphor, he viewed hypnosis as role enactment. In the minidrama of the hypnosis situation, the hypnotist and client act out their roles based on their perceptions, attitudes, and expectations about what is supposed to occur in hypnosis. Thus, hypnosis is dependent on the social and historical context.

Like Sarbin, T. X. Barber (1969) explicitly rejected the idea of hypnosis as an altered state of consciousness, and throughout the 1960s, he conducted an enormous amount of empirical research that demonstrated the ordinariness of hypnosis. His experiments repeatedly showed that the behavior of hypnotized and nonhypnotized people in response to suggestions did not differ significantly. Another researcher, M. T. Orne (1962) argued that the "demand characteristics" of the hypnosis situation explained why a person would comply with the suggestions of the hypnotist.

More recently, Nicholas Spanos and his colleagues (Spanos & Chaves, 1989; Spanos, 1991) have researched the cognitive-behavioral view of hypnosis. Like Sarbin and Barber, Spanos believes that hypnosis is not an altered state of consciousness requiring any special explanation. Rather, hypnosis is historically rooted, context-generated, goal-directed, motivated, interpersonal behavior. Hypnosis behavior is a strategic response to the odd hypnotic situation and does not reflect dissociation. Individuals respond to hypnosis according to their attitudes, expectations, and interpretations of the ambiguous hypnotic situation. Susceptibility to hypnosis is not a trait, but a skill that can be enhanced with training. Basically, according to Spanos, there is no evidence that a hypnotic trance exists at all apart from the meaning it has acquired in our culture.

All of the supposedly unusual aspects of hypnosis can be explained with cognitive-behavioral principles. For example, a great deal of psychological research demonstrates that perceptual sets or expectations profoundly affect what people see and how they behave. This principle can be used to explain the supposed involuntariness of hypnosis, for instance. In our culture, most people expect to feel passive and to do things involuntarily in situations that are labeled hypnosis. They also hold situational representations or schemas about what is supposed to happen in hypnosis, such as involuntarily closing their eyes and the like. They have self-schemas, too, and some individuals, who are "susceptible" to hypnosis, may value cooperation or "letting go."

As another example, let us look at the effect of hypnotic suggestion on reducing pain. In the cognitive-behavioral view, the individual is seen as an active agent who can engage in various types of cognitive activities in order to reduce or minimize the effects of noxious stimuli. Many studies demonstrate that nonhypnotized people can make use of such coping strategies as self-distraction, positive imagery, or positive self-statements to significantly increase their pain tolerance. Hypnosis merely encourages individuals to make use of these ordinary coping strategies.

Spanos and his colleagues also emphasize the social psychological principles of role enactment, self-presentation, and impression management. All people enact roles, such as student or spouse; all people actively present themselves in the best light; and all try to manage the impressions they make on others to affect the course of interpersonal interactions. Individuals seeking hypnotic treatment are motivated to enact the role of a hypnotic subject; they try to present themselves as good, hypnotizable clients; and throughout the hypnosis situation, they try to manage the impression they are creating as someone "under hypnosis." As a result, given our cultural expectations that people "under hypnosis" behave involuntarily and can be made to do unusual things such as bear pain or hold their arms very stiff, they may well comply with helpful suggestions for changes in their cognitions and behaviors.

Hypnosis Interventions

Today, hypnosis is used for many therapeutic purposes, from its many uses in behavior medicine, described earlier, to uncovering painful memories and reducing symptoms in other forms of psychotherapy. As with other behavioral methods, the first step in any treatment involving hypnosis is assessment. Assessment as to the suitability of hypnosis for the individual and her or his problem may involve an interview or a more comprehensive evaluation. Since there is evidence that hypnosis is more effective with individuals who are skilled in being hypnotized, there are several scales for measuring a person's hypnotizability. For example, the Stanford Hypnotic Susceptibility Scale: Form C is a standardized procedure that samples a person's ability to follow specific suggestions, as is the Hypnotic Induction Profile (Pettinati, Kogan, Evans, Wade, Horne, & Staats, 1990). There are also questionnaire and group hypnotizability scales, such as the Harvard Group Scale of Hypnotic Susceptibility, Form A (Kirsch, Council, & Wickless, 1990).

Like other therapists, hypnotherapists must establish rapport with the client, explain the rationale for hypnosis, describe and discuss the intervention alternatives, and with the client, decide on a treatment plan and how to evaluate it. These steps should create a positive attitude toward hypnosis, relieve anxiety, foster a client's sense of control over the process, and engender hope and an expectation of change.

Hypnotic techniques can vary according to how direct or indirect they are. Indirect hypnotic inductions include techniques that increase the client's suggestibility without explicitly labeling them hypnosis. This form of induction may be successful with very resistant clients, those who insist they can never be hypnotized. For example, as the master of indirect suggestion, Milton Erickson would breathe with the same rhythm as a client until they were breathing in synchrony; then he would gradually change his breathing rhythm until the client was following his lead; and then he would make his therapeutic suggestions. Indirect inductions may also be given in the way the therapist uses language, for language has the interesting quality of containing both explicit messages (what is said) and implicit messages (what is not said but is logically implied). For instance, a therapist may ask a client when he would prefer to give up his symptom, on Wednesday or Thursday. While discussing the explicit message about which day, the client must accept the implicit message that the symptom is under his control and it is possible to give it up. It is very difficult for clients to resist these unspoken suggestions, and their indirectness may increase the client's willingness to follow them. More direct inductions include the more well-known orders to stare at a certain point, to close the eyes, to concentrate on certain situations, and so on.

Hypnosis has many uses in behavioral medicine, some already mentioned. For example, it has been used to treat the symptom of chronic pain when other forms of medical treatment do not help. The relaxation may help control the pain, and new reactions to pain are suggested. If the pain cannot be removed, it can sometimes be moved to a less debilitating spot or reduced. Under hypnosis, the client is taught to experience chronic back pain, for example, as a pink spot that can be moved to the head or to the lower arm, where it does not hurt as much.

As a behavioral technique, hypnosis has helped remove a variety of symptoms, including phobias, tics, anxiety, chronic pain, enuresis, and bruxism. Similar to systematic desensitization, the hypnosis treatment for phobias, for example, includes suggesting that the client will not feel fear when near the feared object or situation and suggesting an alternative feeling, as described in Box 11.2.

Besides symptom removal, hypnosis helps change or control problem behaviors such as smoking, overeating, drug abuse, or gambling. Interventions may include direct commands to stop the offending behavior, the use of guided imagery for increasing desired behavior, and suggestions that the client will not feel like doing the

BOX 11.2

Hypnotic Treatment of Bird Phobia

In the hypnotic treatment of a bird phobia, the therapist will first explain the procedure, establish rapport, obtain informed consent, and then perhaps begin treatment with an induction such as the following:

> I'd like you to find a comfortable position in your chair, one in which you won't feel physically restricted in any way. Get comfortable, and you will probably want to close your eyes. And simply breathe, deeply, at your own rhythm, and as you do, as you inhale, imagine that you are drawing all the tensions in your body into your lungs, and then as you exhale, you expel all those tensions out of your body. Keep breathing, keep expelling tension, until you feel deeply, completely relaxed. Simply breathe, and listen to my voice, and no extraneous sounds will bother you. You'll begin to feel very relaxed and heavy, as though you were sinking down into a warm, safe place, deeper, and more completely relaxed. And as you find your breathing slowing, you'll also discover that you enjoy being in this place somewhere between sleep and consciousness, and you can let go, really let go, and slowly relax, even more with every breath. When you feel comfortable and fully ready, I'd like you to focus on a point on your right knee. Good. Now I'd like you to focus completely on a point on your right hand. When you've done that I'd like you to focus on a point in the middle of your forehead, and imagine that your entire being is focused and relaxed. You feel comfortable in your body in every way, you simply exist, deeply relaxed, unburdened, and totally free. You are very deeply, deeply relaxed and comfortable.

After the bird-phobic client is sufficiently relaxed and suggestible, the therapist may say,

> You are sitting in the peaceful meadow we talked about before. You see a bird, a beautiful red bird, singing sweetly in the sunshine, and you look at it calmly, you feel happy listening to its song, you enjoy watching its beauty. When you leave my office, you will see many birds, and they will remind you of the beautiful red bird, and you will feel glad to see them, glad that there are singing birds in the world.

More suggestions may be given, and at the end of the session the therapist may say,

> Now, as soon as you are ready, you will stop thinking about this good feeling, and bring your attention back to the present. You will feel rested, refreshed, and energetic. You will be able to remember all of this session that you wish to. When you are ready, open your eyes.

The similarity of this approach to systematic desensitization as described in Box 10.3 is evident.

offending behavior anymore, that he will be able to control himself easily by doing specific suggested behaviors or thoughts, that he will do some alternative behavior. As an example, the treatment of overeating may involve a direct command to not feel hungry, the suggestion that the sight of food will lessen the urge to eat or make the client feel like doing something else such as drinking water, or the use of guided imagery to change the client's image of himself as a pig to one of himself as a greyhound as a metaphor for the goal of therapy. The same techniques can be used to change bad habits such as procrastination or nail biting. The similarity of this approach to cognitive behavior therapy will be evident in Chapter 12.

Hypnosis appears to be useful in teaching relaxation and stress management. Hypnotic induction itself relaxes the client, and once the client learns how to use hypnotic techniques to relax, she can use them whenever needed. Besides directly teaching relaxation, hypnosis helps clients manage stress by suggesting alternative behaviors, thoughts, or emotions to experience when under stress. Rather than feeling rage in a traffic jam on the freeway or during a confrontation at work, the client may be taught to retrieve the image of a peaceful place, such as a beach or meadow, at stressful times and to substitute the peaceful feeling the scene induces for the anger or anxiety being felt.

Hypnosis is also used in conjunction with other types of psychotherapy, and part or even all of the therapy is conducted with the client under hypnosis in order to enhance the effectiveness of the therapy. However, the success of treatment is not attributed to the hypnosis, but rather to the theoretical principles of whatever type of therapy is being done. If a phobia is being treated with systematic desensitization and hypnosis is used to speed up the learning of deep muscle relaxation, the effectiveness of the treatment depends on the correct application of the behavior modification principles of systematic desensitization, not the hypnosis. Hypnosis has been used as an additional technique in almost all types of therapy, from psychoanalysis to the family systems approach.

Hypnosis was used when psychoanalysis first began, and today, psychodynamic therapists sometimes make use of hypnosis in their psychotherapy. Simply put (see Chapters 6 and 7 for details), the goal of psychodynamic therapy is the reconstruction of the personality, and this goal is achieved by working through unconscious conflicts, fears, and memories in order to achieve catharsis and insight. Hypnosis can facilitate these processes. If an analytic patient has difficulty retrieving early memories or resists important issues, hypnosis may be used to enhance memory, unblock resistance, or elicit unconscious material. Sometimes, memories of early traumatic events can be discovered by regressing the patient to younger ages. Such regression is accomplished by a variety of hypnotic methods, such as the "elevator" technique. The hypnotized patient is told to imagine herself in an elevator that is at the 30th floor, the patient's age; as the elevator descends, the patient will become younger; when the elevator reaches the fifth floor, the doors open and there is an important scene from the patient's fifth year; and so on. This brief description only hints at the complexity and creativity of psychodynamic therapists using hypnosis.

Self-hypnosis is often useful. It is possible for individuals to learn to self-induce hypnosis. Some people discover self-hypnosis by themselves (as a child, one of us used to go into a trance by lying in a warm bath and staring at the drain), but therapists may teach clients self-hypnosis as part of therapy. The therapist may tape record an induction session with a client, and the client can later use the tape for self-hypnosis. The therapist may also teach the client a specific cue under hypnosis, such as suggesting that the client will be able to enter into a deep, relaxing trance by concentrating on a point on the forehead or by saying certain words to herself, and the client can then use the cue for self-hypnosis any time she wishes. The uses of self-hypnosis are similar to those of ordinary hypnosis, but responsibility for trance induction and awakening is transferred to the client.

Finally, hypnosis may be used for personal growth. Hypnosis is useful for many types of self-exploration, from regression to retrieve early experiences to imagining conversations with important others. Some people believe hypnosis can enhance artistic expression, allowing an individual's full creativity to emerge. Some people believe hypnosis can help with spiritual growth by, for example, accessing the "cosmic unconscious" (personally, we have always tried to access the "comic unconscious"). In short, hypnosis is used for many different purposes.

Evaluation of Hypnosis

Although hypnosis has gained respectability in recent years, a number of controversies about it continue. The controversy over what hypnosis is, especially whether it is an altered state of consciousness, remains unresolved. While most people experience it as an altered state of consciousness, it has not yet been possible to demonstrate empirically that it is significantly different from ordinary, relaxed consciousness. Assuming hypnosis involves an altered state of consciousness called a trance, hypnotists disagree about the importance of the "depth" of the trance. Hypnotists may agree that they can observe when someone has entered a trance by that person's slack muscles, lowered eyelids, slow breathing, and pale skin, but they do not appear to agree on what constitutes a "deep" trance. Many therapists argue that depth of trance is not important, because effective work can be accomplished in light trances. Related to these issues is that of faking hypnosis, and again, some therapists argue that whether the client is faking a trance or not, effective work can still be accomplished.

The issue of control is important in hypnosis, and this issue surfaces in several controversies. After years of disagreement and research, it appears that individuals do vary in the ease with which they enter the hypnotized state (Kirsch & Lynn, 1995). Some people are more open to suggestion than others, and several assessment instruments have been developed to measure "hypnotizability" in order to select clients who will best respond to hypnotherapy.

Hypnosis is criticized for being manipulative in its direct attempts to control the client's maladaptive behavior, but the obvious reply is that all therapies try to change the client and hypnosis only does so explicitly. Control also becomes an issue between the client and therapist during treatment, especially with resistant clients, and the use of indirect techniques to circumvent resistance is sometimes criticized as controlling and manipulative. Finally, there is the issue of whether people can be made to do things against their will under hypnosis. While research is inconclusive on this point, it appears that people who do not ordinarily engage in immoral or illegal behaviors will not do so under hypnosis. Furthermore, Erickson argued that hypnosis was time-limited and stimulus-limited so that individuals would immediately leave the hypnotized state if they were told to do something against their will (Erickson & Rossi, 1979).

Of interest to many people is the issue of the "truth" of what goes on under hypnosis. Are memories recalled under hypnosis any more or less accurate than ordinary memories? Do people manufacture memories to please the therapist? Many therapists argue that the accuracy of recalled information is irrelevant, because even if invented, the memories experienced under hypnosis are psychologically important to the individuals who create them and can be used to benefit clients in therapy. Related to this issue is that of amnesia. Can people be made to forget what goes on under hypnosis or to forget important parts of their lives? Again, research is inconclusive regarding amnesia, but many therapists include suggestions in hypnosis for clients to recall the therapy or to recall any parts of it whenever they wish.

Despite years of research, hypnosis remains a fascinating theoretical enigma. Substantial evidence of its effectiveness tempts many therapists and clients to try hypnosis, but hypnosis is not for everyone. Not all clients are sufficiently cooperative or able to enter hypnosis, and hypnosis is clearly not appropriate for some clients, such as psychotics. Not all therapists are equally comfortable or competent with hypnotic techniques. However, it appears that hypnosis, like biofeedback, has achieved sufficient clinical success, especially in behavioral medicine, that it is once again a respected therapeutic technique. In the hands of a master hypnotherapist such as Milton Erickson, hypnosis is a powerful and effective method for treating intractable problems in a short period of time. Even among ordinary therapists, hypnosis is a useful and effective therapeutic technique with individuals who are ready and willing to use it.

IN CONCLUSION

The growing scientific and public awareness of the interconnectedness of the psychological and physical aspects of human beings ensures the future growth of health psychology and behavioral medicine. Therapeutic techniques such as hypnosis and biofeedback demonstrate the mind–body connection vividly. Research that demonstrates the effectiveness of behavioral interventions, including research suggesting that changes in behavior bring about observable changes in the brain and its functioning (Baxter et al., 1992), indicate that psychology has many contributions to make to the field of medicine and public health. These contributions may include social action to change the causes of disease, as part of psychology's involvement in prevention. As we discuss the future in Chapter 18, we will consider the possibility that psychologists will become primary health care providers along with other professionals when it becomes "common knowledge" that mind and body are one.

BIBLIOGRAPHY

Ader, R., & Cohen, N. (1985). CSN-immune system interactions: Conditioning phenomena. *Behavioral and Brain Sciences, 8,* 378–395.

Alexander, F. (1950). *Psychosomatic medicine.* New York: Norton.

Andrasik, F., Blanchard, E. B., Neff, D. F., & Rodichok, L. D. (1984). Biofeedback and relaxation training for chronic headache: A controlled comparison of booster treatments and regular contacts for long-term maintenance. *Journal of Consulting and Clinical Psychology, 52,* 609–615.

Andreychuk, T., & Skriver, C. (1975). Hypnosis and biofeedback in the treatment of migraine headache. *International Journal of Experimental and Clinical Hypnosis, 23,* 172–183.

Barber, T. (1969). *Hypnosis: A scientific approach.* New York: Van Nostrand.

Baxter, L., Schwartz, J., Bergman, K., Szuba, M., Guze, B., Mazziotta, J., Alazraki, A., Selin, C., Ferng, H., Munford, P., & Phelps, M. (1992). Caudate glucose metabolic rate changes with both drug and behavior therapy for obsessive-compulsive disorder. *Archives of General Psychiatry, 49,* 681–689.

Belar, C., Deardorff, W., & Kelly, K. (1987). *The practice of clinical health psychology.* New York: Pergamon Press.

Blanchard, E. (Ed.). (1992). Special issue on behavioral medicine: An update for the 1990s. *Journal of Consulting and Clinical Psychology, 60,* 491–643.

Blanchard, E., & Andrasik, F. (1982). Psychological assessment and treatment of headache: Recent developments and emerging issues. *Journal of Consulting and Clinical Psychology, 50,* 859–879.

Blanchard, E., & Young, L. (1974). Clinical applications of biofeedback training: A review of evidence. *Archives of General Psychiatry, 30,* 573–579.

Blumenthal, J., & McKee, D. (Eds.) (1987). *Applications in behavioral medicine and health psychology: A clinician's source book.* Sarasota, FL: Professional Resource Exchange.

Brown, B. B. (1984). *Between health and illness: New notions on stress and the nature of well-being.* New York: Bantam.

Brown, B. B. (1978). *Stress and the art of biofeedback.* New York: Bantam.

Brown, D., & Fromm, E. (1987). *Hypnosis and behavioral medicine.* Hillsdale, NJ: Lawrence Erlbaum Associates.

Brownell, K. (1982). Obesity: Understanding and treating a serious, prevalent, and refractory disorder. *Journal of Consulting and Clinical Psychology, 50,* 820–840.

Chaves, J. (1994). Hypnosis: The struggle for a definition. *Contemporary Hypnosis, 11,* 145–146.

Chertok, L. (1981). *Sense and nonsense in psychotherapy: The challenge of hypnosis.* New York: Pergamon Press.

Cohen, L. (1985). What's in a name: Clinical psychology, medical psychology, health psychology . . . *American Psychologist, 38,* 29–32.

Cohen, S., & Williamson, G. (1991). Stress and infectious disease in humans. *Psychological Bulletin, 109,* 5–24.

Cowan, E. (1991). In pursuit of wellness. *American Psychologist, 46,* 404–408.

DeAngelis, T. (1992, April). Health psychology grows both in stature, influence. *APA Monitor,* pp. 10–11.

Dubbert, P. (1992). Exercise in behavioral medicine. *Journal of Consulting and Clinical Psychology, 60,* 613–618.

Erickson, M., & Rossi, E. (1976). Two level communication and the microdynamics of trance and suggestion. *American Journal of Clinical Hypnosis, 18,* 153–171.

Erickson, M., & Rossi, E. (1979). *Hypnotherapy: An exploratory casebook.* New York: Irvington.

Erickson, M., Rossi, E., & Rossi, S. (1976). *Hypnotic realities.* New York: Irvington.

Ewart, C. (1991). Social action theory for a public health psychology. *American Psychologist, 46,* 931–946.

Fromm, E., & Nash, M. (Eds). (1992). *Contemporary hypnosis research.* New York: Guilford Press.

Havens, R. (1985). *The wisdom of Milton H. Erickson.* New York: Irvington.

Holroyd, K., & Andrasik, F. (1980). Do the effects of cognitive therapy endure? Paper presented at the 14th annual convention of the Association for Advancement of Behavior Therapy, New York.

Kiecolt-Glaser, J., & Glaser, R. (1992). Psychoneuroimmunology: Can psychological interventions modulate immunity? *Journal of Consulting and Clinical Psychology, 60,* 569–575.

Kirsch, I., Council, J., & Wickless, C. (1990). Subjective scoring for the Harvard Group Scale of Hypnotic Susceptibility, Form A. *International Journal of Clinical and Experimental Hypnosis, 38,* 122–134.

Kirsch, I., & Lynn, S. J. (1995). The altered state of hypnosis: Changes in the theoretical landscape. *American Psychologist, 50,* 846–858.

Laudenslager, M., Ryan, S., Drugan, R., Hyson, R., & Maier, S. (1983). Coping and immunosuppression: Inescapable but not escapable shock suppresses lymphocyte proliferation. *Science, 221,* 568–570.

Lisspers, J., & Ost, L. (1990). Long-term follow-up of migraine treatment: Do the effects remain up to six years? *Journal of Consulting and Clinical Psychology, 50,* 313–322.

Lynn, S., & Rhue, J. (Eds.) (1991). *Theories of hypnosis: Current models and perspectives.* New York: Guilford Press.

Matarazzo, J. (1982). Behavioral health's challenge to academic, scientific, and professional psychology. *American Psychologist, 37,* 1–14.

Miller, N. (1985, April). Rx: Biofeedback. *Psychology Today,* pp. 54–56.

Millon, T., Green, C., & Meagher, R. (Eds.). (1982). *Handbook of clinical health psychology.* New York: Plenum.

Orne, M. (1962). On the social psychology of the psychological experiment with particular reference to demand characteristics and their implications. *American Psychologist, 17,* 776–783.

Osler, W. (1892). *Lectures on angina pectoris and allied states.* New York: Appleton.

Pettinati, H., Kogan, L., Evans, F., Wade, J., Horne, R., & Staats, J. (1990). Hypnotizability of psychiatric inpatients according to two different scales. *American Journal of Psychiatry, 147,* 69–75.

Prokop, C., Bradley, L., Burish, T., Anderson, K., & Fox, J. (1991). *Health psychology.* New York: Macmillan.

Roberts, A. (1985). Biofeedback: Research, training, and clinical roles. *American Psychologist, 40,* 938–941.

Rossi, E. (Ed.). (1980). *The collected papers of Milton H. Erickson on hypnosis: Volume III. Hypnotic investigation of psychodynamic processes.* New York: Irvington.

Sarbin, T. (1950). Contributions to role-taking theory: I. Hypnotic behavior. *Psychological Review, 57,* 255–270.

Schwartz, G., & Weiss, S. (1978). Behavioral medicine revisited: An amended definition. *Journal of Behavioral Medicine, 1,* 249–251.

Schwartz, S., Taylor, A., Scharff, L., & Blanchard, E. (1990). Behaviorally treated irritable bowel syndrome patients: A four-year follow-up. *Behaviour Research and Therapy, 28,* 331–335.

Spanos, N. (1991). A sociocognitive approach to hypnosis. In S. J. Lynn & J. W. Rhue (Eds.), *Theories of hypnosis: Current models and perspectives.* New York: Guilford Press.

Spanos, N., & Chaves, J. (Eds.). (1989). *Hypnosis: The cognitive-behavioral perspective.* Buffalo, NY: Prometheus Books.

Svedlund, J., Sjodin, I., Ottosson, J.-O., & Dotevall, G. (1983). Controlled study of psychotherapy in irritable bowel syndrome. *Lancet, 2,* 589–592.

Thoresen, C., & Powell, L. (1992). Type A behavior pattern: New perspectives on theory, assessment, and intervention. *Journal of Consulting and Clinical Psychology, 60,* 595–604.

Turk, D., Meichenbaum, D., & Genest, M. (1983). *Pain and behavior medicine: A cognitive-behavioral perspective.* New York: Guilford.

United States Surgeon General. (1979). *Healthy people: The Surgeon General's report on health promotion and disease prevention.* Washington, DC: U.S. Government Printing Office (Publication No. 79–55071).

VandenBos, G., & DeLeon, P. (1988). The use of psychotherapy to improve physical health. *Psychotherapy, 25,* 335–343.

Visitainer, M., Volpicelli, J., & Seligman, M. (1982). Tumor rejection in rats after inescapable or escapable shock. *Science, 216,* 437–439.

Volhardt, L. (1991). Psychoneuroimmunology: A literature review. *American Journal of Orthopsychiatry, 61,* 35–47.

Wagstaff, G. (1991). *Hypnosis, compliance and belief.* New York: St. Martin's Press.

CHAPTER
12

Cognitive Approaches to Psychopathology and Psychotherapy

We take the stand that there are always some alternative constructions available to choose among in dealing with the world. No one needs to paint himself into a corner; no one needs to be completely hemmed in by circumstances; no one needs to be the victim of his biography. (Kelly, 1955, p. 15)

Change is mediated through cognitive processes, but the cognitive events are induced and altered most readily by experiences of mastery arising from successful performance. (Bandura, 1977a, p. 79)

Suppose a parent tells his young child that he is not allowed to draw on the walls of his room with his crayons. Later, the parent discovers the child drawing on the living room walls. The parent becomes angry and spanks the child. Asked why he became angry, he says, "He knew better. He was drawing on the walls because he was deliberately being naughty." Asked why he chose spanking as a method of discipline, he replies, "I spanked him because if you spare the rod, you spoil the child. It'll probably whip some sense into him."

How would a cognitive psychologist explain this anger at the child and the choice of spanking as a method of discipline? First, the cognitive psychologist would assume that the anger is based on the parent's perception and interpretation of the situation. From a cognitive perspective, anger is a response to the perception that the other person could have controlled his actions (Weiner, 1982).

Thus, the feeling of anger is based on the interpretation that the child was "deliberately being naughty" and that he "knew better." But perhaps he didn't. Little children often are quite literal, and they do not necessarily interpret things as we do. The child may not have known that he was doing anything wrong, believing that he had been told only not to draw on his own walls. If the parent had interpreted the situation this way, he probably would not have felt quite as angry.

The action of spanking was also based on the father's interpretation of the situation. Believing the child's actions were deliberately naughty, he concluded that severe measures were called for. He may have said to himself: "He must not be allowed to act defiantly that way. That is an awful way to act." His choice of spanking came out of his beliefs about appropriate methods of discipline, and these beliefs were probably based on his own experience as a child. The choice may also have been influenced by his perceptions of self-efficacy, that is, his self-perception of his ableness or competence to handle the situation effectively. He may have perceived himself as unable to influence the child's behavior in other ways, for instance, through dialogue. In sum, a person's actions in a situation are determined by his perceptions of the situation, his ideas about the best way to handle the situation, and his perceptions about his own skills and competencies in the situation. In addition, interpretations and cognitions influence how a person feels about the situation.

Generalizing this to abnormal behavior, the cognitive perspective sees cognition as mediating or causing both psychopathological feeling states and behavior. Psychotherapy becomes, directly or indirectly, the attempt to modify these cognitions. Cognition includes our perceptions and interpretations of situations, our behavior schemes for handling situations, our values and beliefs, and our perceptions of ourselves and of our own competencies. As you shall see, cognitions do not necessarily have to be conscious, and some perspectives give cognition a place of more central importance than others. For instance, social learning theory does not see the direct modification of cognition through verbal communication as a particularly effective therapeutic strategy. In contrast, both Aaron Beck's cognitive therapy and Albert Ellis's rational-emotive therapy rely extensively on verbal communication as a therapeutic approach.

Cognitive therapies are rapidly becoming the most influential set of approaches at the present time. Many cognitive therapies include behavioral ideas and techniques and are often referred to as *cognitive-behavior* therapies. They are becoming so influential because (a) they are brief and efficient; (b) they are highly structured and systematic; (c) cognitive-behavior therapists spend a considerable amount of effort researching their approaches and demonstrating empirically that they work; and (d) cognitive-behavior therapies are typically developed as highly structured, specific treatments for specific disorders. Thus, they fit well with the current health care climate.

We will first look at the work of George Kelly. Kelly was a pioneer in applying cognitive ideas to understanding personality and to psychotherapy. Because he died before the "cognitive revolution" took place, his work is less influential than it deserves to be. We will then consider social learning theory, attribution theory, Aaron Beck's cognitive therapy for depression and personality disorders, Albert Ellis's rational-emotive therapy, and Donald Meichenbaum's cognitive-behavioral therapy.

We will also review examples of some of the specific cognitive-behavioral treatments developed for specific disorders, such as Borkovec's approach for generalized anxiety disorder and Barlow's approach for panic disorder.

KELLY'S CONSTRUCT THEORY

George Kelly was a clinical psychologist and college professor. He also coached the college drama club. As a clinician interested in behavior change, Kelly noticed that some drama students permanently changed their behaviors as a result of playing certain roles in plays. Kelly decided to apply role playing as a therapeutic method with students who sought counseling. To account for the changes he observed using this method, Kelly developed the first comprehensive cognitive theory of personality and therapy. He also developed an assessment device, called the repertory grid, to detect individuals' cognitive structures. Kelly published his ideas in 1955, then died a few years later. His work did not become well known in the United States. However, his theory has become popular in Britain, where Bannister, Fransella, and others continue to use some of his ideas.

Kelly's theory of personality begins with his fundamental postulate: A person's processes are psychologically "channelized" by the ways in which he or she anticipates events. The construction corollary is that a person anticipates events by construing their replications. What these statements mean is that individuals make sense of the world by developing cognitive categories that they can then use to try to predict, that is, anticipate, events. Furthermore, these cognitive constructions of the world determine behavior, or, in Kelly's words, "psychologically channelize" people's "processes." For example, the young child is confronted with complexity and chaos when she first notices the world around her. However, certain events repeat themselves; there are regularities even in the complexity of reality. Children may notice that there are big people and little people. Big people smile, say goo-goo, and give food and help; little people play, yell, hit, or grab things. It becomes useful for survival and comfort to notice this difference between big people and little people. Children develop a cognitive category of adult versus peer. They can then use this category to anticipate help from adults and no help from peers. They will then behave in help-seeking ways toward adults and not toward peers. Their behavior is "channelized" or determined by the way they construe events.

Kelly elaborated an entire personality theory about these cognitive constructs. There are individual differences. People will construe the same events differently, and they will develop different numbers and types of cognitive constructs, which can be organized in different ways. A person's construct system is organized with some all-embracing categories such as "good" versus "bad" and some subordinate categories such as "morally good," "esthetically good," "sensately good," and so on. While the cognitive construct system is always organized, it may be well organized or poorly organized (or fragmented), with some constructs incompatible with others. It may also be permeable (open to change) or impermeable (rigid). People are motivated to extend and define their cognitive systems. They are motivated to elaborate the system they use to make sense out of the world in order to be better able to predict and control what happens to them.

As implied above, some cognitive construct systems are better than others at helping people cope with reality. Several characteristics of cognitive constructs lead to behavior problems or mental disturbance. A simplistic system, with few cognitive constructs, will lead to trouble, because the person will constantly be confronted with new data that cannot be understood or anticipated with the system. For example, a person who sees the world in simplistic black-and-white or good-versus-evil terms will have difficulty dealing with the multitude of grays in life. There are just too many events that are not clearly good or evil. Similarly, a cognitive system that is too rigid will cause difficulties when it cannot account for everything. A paranoid person who rigidly sees everyone as untrustworthy will not be able to determine who to relate to or who can be trusted. On the other hand, a system that is too permeable will not help the person make sense out of the world at all. Psychosis, with its intruding and confusing thoughts and its lack of contact with reality, is an example of too permeable a cognitive system of constructs.

Kelly developed the repertory grid to assess what an individual's cognitive constructs are and how they are organized. The repertory grid consists of the names of people important to the individual with spaces for descriptions of these people. The examiner asks the client to describe these people and then to compare pairs of them, asking how they are alike and how they are not alike. The examiner gradually elicits the cognitive constructs the client uses to make sense out of the behavior of the people around him. By analyzing these responses, the examiner can determine what in the client's construct system is causing problems. For instance, a young man having difficulty relating to women may discover that his construct system divides people into kind and frightening, and trustworthy and untrustworthy, with females always seen as frightening and untrustworthy. To relate to women, this young man will have to change his construct system so that the male-female dimension is independent of his other categories.

Kelly prescribed a form of behavior therapy in order to change such troublesome cognitive construct systems. He believed that the individual develops a particular construct system because his particular life experiences make these constructs useful. In the case of the young man, perhaps his mother and other important female figures were unkind, withholding, and unreliable. However, now his cognitive constructs get him into trouble. If he anticipates that women are going to be unkind to him, he will behave toward them as he would toward any unkind, frightening people—defensively and perhaps with hostility. This behavior may then induce women (who may or may not be kind, but who won't understand his hostility) to be unkind and hostile in return. Then his cognitive constructs will be validated, and he will continue to avoid or be hostile to women. Kelly would try to get this young man to behave in such a way that his old cognitive constructs will be invalidated by new data; new experiences will force him to develop new cognitions.

Kelly's technique was to write out a role for a client to play in his everyday life for a couple of weeks. He emphasized that it was "just role playing," just an experiment, so the client wouldn't become anxious over performing correctly or failing. He made the role just slightly different from the way the client usually acted. The role could not be so different that the client wouldn't be able to do it or to make sense out of the new data it generated. However, it had to be different enough so that others would perceive the client's behavior as different and behave differently toward him than they had in the past. This would provide invalidating experiences for the old construct system and force the development of new constructs. The client was supposed to play the role with everyone for a couple of weeks. Specific behaviors in specific situations might also be assigned as homework from time to time. The client then discussed the resulting experiences with Kelly, who helped the client integrate the new data and the old cognitions.

Let us use the young man as an example. Kelly might have written a role such as this for him: "You are a strong, self-confident, but gentle man, especially protective and kind to women. You help women in conversations by asking them questions about their interests, listening carefully to their answers, and showing concern for their difficulties. You also like to have fun, and can occasionally tell a joke." If this young man even partially succeeds with this approach to women, he will elicit warm and kindly behavior from them, rather than the hostile and defensive behavior he provoked before. These new experiences provide new data that do not fit his old constructs of women being unkind and mean. He will be forced to construe women differently, which will change his behavior toward them.

Kelly's approach was novel for its time and anticipated many of the recent developments in cognitive therapy and such behavioral techniques as assertion training. He reported great success with it among his young, changeable college student population. Research in England suggests that the repertory grid is a useful assessment procedure in clinical and research settings and that variations of Kelly's therapy are suitable for many types of problems. In recent years, there has been a resurgence of interest in Kelly's approach. This has been because personal construct theory intersects with the idea of **constructivism** (Feixas, 1990; see Chapters 14 and 17) and can provide a basis for psychotherapy integration (Neimeyer, 1988). That is, it can be argued that we experience the world through our constructs, and that different approaches to therapy work primarily by changing our construct systems.

SOCIAL LEARNING THEORY

Perhaps the best way to introduce social learning theory is to compare it to behaviorism. Behaviorism assumes that learning is the automatic association of a stimulus with a response. Such an automatic association is "strengthened" by reinforcement, and behavior is a function of the consequences. In order for learning to occur, a behavior must be performed and reinforced. Learning is essentially a trial-and-error process, in which an organism emits a variety of behaviors until one is reinforced.

Bandura (1986) takes this view to task. He asserts that all learning is cognitively mediated. A stimulus comes to be associated with a response because it comes to have predictive value. If a shock is repeatedly paired with a light, a person avoids the light, not because the light itself has become aversive, but because it has become predictive of shock and pain. Thus, what people learn are expectancies. They do not develop conditioned responses to stimuli unless they are aware of the relationship between the stimulus and response, that is, unless they are aware that the stimulus predicts the onset of reinforcement or punishment.

Furthermore, Bandura argues that the idea that reinforcement "strengthens" associations between stimulus and response is a metaphor and not literally true. He suggests that reinforcement leads to learning because reinforcers are information givers and incentives. For instance, many social reinforcers, such as good grades on tests or teachers' approval, are reinforcing in part because they give the information that the student is on the right track. In addition, good grades are associated with other rewards and opportunities, so they have some incentive value. If a person is told that shock is a signal for a correct response, shock will function as a positive reinforcer (see, for instance, Dulany, 1968). In general, Bandura says that behavior is more a function of its anticipated consequences than of its immediate, real consequences.

Bandura goes on to point out that most important human learning is **vicarious learning.** People do not learn most of the important skills in life by performing trial-and-error responses until one is reinforced. They would not be likely to survive long if that was the way they learned. It would be a highly inefficient way to train surgeons or automobile builders, for instance, if they had to do things by trial and error until they finally got them right. Instead, most important learning takes place through observation and instruction. People learn through watching others' behavior, reading books or gathering information from other media, and receiving instructions.

People learn both how to interpret situations and what to do in a given situation. Bandura was one of the first investigators to note the relationship between being abused as a child and becoming a child abuser as an adult (Bandura & Walters, 1959). An abused child might learn that when a person with more power gets angry at a transgression by a person with less power, the person with more power has the right and obligation to use the infliction of physical pain as a punishment. No one explicitly verbalizes this as a rule, but it is modeled by the parent's actions. When the abused child becomes an adult, she may enact this same pattern of behavior. If she becomes a leader of a country, she may use it as a principle of national policy.

Situational Specificity of Behavior

A key concept for many social learning theorists is that of the situational specificity of behavior. Traditional views of the person, such as psychoanalysis, believe that each individual has an enduring personality structure made up of an organized pattern of character traits. A person might be described, for instance, as having the traits of cleanliness, friendliness, conscientiousness, optimism, extraversion, and assertiveness. Such a view assumes that this person's behavior is primarily determined by her character traits, that is, she is generally expected to be friendly, assertive, extraverted, and clean.

However, many social learning theorists believe that behavior is situation-specific. Behavior is guided by the expectancies in a specific situation. If a person acts assertively in some situation, it is not because she has an internal trait of assertiveness, but because she has learned to expect that assertiveness is effective in that situation. Because her behavior is guided by what she has learned to expect in different situations, she might act quite differently in a different situation. If she had learned to expect that quiet deference is the most effective behavior in a different situation, she would probably act deferentially.

Therefore, many social learning theorists do not believe that people will necessarily exhibit consistency of behavior in different situations. Bandura describes an autistic child who was calm, well behaved, considerate, and cooperative when the child's father was home, but at other times was destructive and undisciplined (Moser, 1965, as reported in Bandura, 1977a, p. 86). Now, which is the "real" child? According to social learning theory, both are, because the child's behavior is different in different situations.

Most people are aware of the fact that their behavior varies from situation to situation, but tend to overlook that fact to believe in stability in personality. They are aware that the teacher who seems friendly in class may be distant outside of class, the man who is beloved at work may be a tyrant at home, the child who is a "little angel" at home may be a demon at school, the person who seems distant and unfriendly at a party may be warm and caring in a one-to-one conversation. Yet because of people's beliefs in the stability of personality, they tend to discount these examples as exceptions.

The idea of situational specificity can explain why psychologists, psychiatrists, and other mental health professionals have difficulty predicting violent behavior. Often, they are asked to predict if an individual in a prison or mental hospital is likely to be violent if released. Typically, such predictions are based on the idea of personality character structure: Does this individual still exhibit character traits of a violent nature or not? Examples of violent crime committed within days of release by someone who was judged nonviolent by professionals support the idea that the situational specificity of behavior is often more important than the individual's personality structure in predicting what he or she will do.

Therefore, many social learning theorists are skeptical of explanations of behavior that rely on concepts such as personality trait and character structure. They prefer more "microanalytic" understanding of the factors involved in *why* a person characteristically acts a certain way in certain situations. Thus, they would not expect a person diagnosed as borderline personality disorder to characteristically act as if he had a fear of being alone in all the situations of his life. Instead, they would be interested in doing a detailed analysis of why he exhibits a fear of being alone in certain key situations (such as being at home alone on a Saturday night). Such a microanalysis might reveal, for instance, that the person has low self-efficacy perceptions (i.e., lacks self-confidence) concerning making friends, and feels bad when he is alone on a night when others are often engaged in social pursuits.

There are, however, theorists who adopt social learning ideas who do believe that there are ingrained, pervasive patterns to personality. Millon's (1981) "biosocial-learning" approach is one example. Millon is one of the foremost theorists of personality disorders. He believes that there are characteristic "types," such as "dependent" or "narcissistic" personalities. He argues that such enduring kinds of personality organizations develop largely through learning processes described by social learning theorists, such as extensive patterns of modeling and reinforcement in childhood.

Self-Efficacy

Bandura's (1996) concept of self-efficacy is like self-esteem in some respects, but is specific to situations. **Self-efficacy** is a person's self-perception of competence to enact a behavior or to handle a given type of situation. For example, some of you may have a sense of self-efficacy as an auto mechanic and others may not. In our example of the parent who spanked his son for writing on the walls, we suggested that he may have chosen spanking because he felt he could not influence his son through dialogue. If this was because he perceived himself as not good at verbal persuasion, then we would say he had a perception of low self-efficacy as a communicator.

Bandura has argued that an increase in self-efficacy is the common underlying dimension of effectiveness of psychotherapy (1977b). A perception of low self-efficacy has a number of negative consequences. It leads to avoidance. People are likely to avoid situations in which they feel incompetent. Thus, if you believe that if you go outdoors, you will be overwhelmed by a panic attack that you cannot manage, you will stay indoors. Defensive behavior, then, is a response to perceived low efficacy. People act defensively when they believe they cannot handle something. In essence, then, defensiveness is the converse of a feeling of mastery.

Along with avoidance, low self-efficacy leads to a tendency to give up too soon. As a result, a person does not persist long enough to find out if she can master a situation. In addition, low self-efficacy leads to a tendency to self-monitor in a self-destructive manner. The person observes her own efforts to cope with a situation and engages in negative self-evaluation. Such self-conscious rumination has a tendency to further disrupt behavior. A person who is absorbed in thoughts of how badly she is performing is no longer focusing on the situation and therefore cannot respond to it adequately. For example, if you feel sexually inadequate, you may focus on how well you are doing, not on your partner or the stimuli that make sex pleasurable. As a result, you may do things mechanically, and you are not likely to respond adequately to your own or your partner's sensations and reactions. Low self-efficacy can be seen to relate to a variety of disorders including phobias, substance abuse, depression, and anxiety disorders. We will further consider the impact of **negative self-monitoring** later in the chapter.

Related to the idea of low self-efficacy is the idea that behavior problems may be based on a lack of skills to handle situations. If a person does not have adequate assertion skills, the feeling of being "stepped on" by employers or intimates may generate depression or anxiety. Someone who lacks effective stress management skills may engage in dysfunctional stress reduction procedures, such as the use of alcohol or drugs. A person who does not have effective communication skills may be unable to establish and maintain nurturing interpersonal relationships. Someone lacking effective parenting skills may have to resort to outbursts of anger and child abuse to try to control children's behavior. Consequently, many social learning theorists have been interested in social skills training (already discussed briefly in Chapter 10).

Social skills training (Wine & Smye, 1981) is based on the idea that if psychopathology is a result of a lack of skills, training good social skills is therapeutic. Aside from assertion training, there are communication skills programs, stress management programs, and comprehensive programs that include a whole range of skills

(Goldstein, Gershaw, & Sprafkin, 1984). One study (Paul, 1981) found that a social skills training program was considerably more effective in helping hospitalized patients than typical hospital regimens, such as group or milieu therapy.

Contributions to Psychotherapy

Bandura has argued that raising the level of perception of self-efficacy is the most potent therapeutic change event and that verbal persuasion is probably the least effective way to do this. He states quite forcefully that "performance-based" therapeutic interventions are more effective than verbal ones. While verbal persuasion can be useful in modifying fears that have not been reinforced by direct experience and that are primarily a matter of misinformation, it is relatively ineffective in modifying fears that have been learned through direct experience or that have been heavily reinforced. Basically, Bandura argues that direct experience is a much more potent teacher than words delivered in a therapeutic setting. For this reason, he believes therapy must include situations in which individuals actually engage in successful mastery experiences, and the therapist must arrange therapeutic tasks so that mastery experiences occur. This can be done with the aid of therapist guidance and modeling or through the use of carefully graduated steps. Sex therapy, for instance, often includes what could be called graduated mastery experiences. The client starts out learning to enjoy sensual play without attempting intercourse. As the client learns to respond to sensual experience, he or she gradually engages in behaviors more directly related to intercourse and orgasm. By the time he or she attempts intercourse, the client has usually acquired a sense of competency and mastery at being sexually responsive.

Bandura states that a potent way of learning, in addition to direct experience, is observation. Both direct performance and observation are considerably more experiential than verbal persuasion. Most of us can sense the difference between being told "Snakes aren't dangerous" and seeing someone like us learn to overcome his or her fear of snakes. Bandura has demonstrated that observing someone else overcoming fears helps the client overcome his or her own fears.

ATTRIBUTIONAL APPROACHES

Primarily a social psychological theory, **attribution theory** (Jones et al., 1972) is based on the assumption that humans are "naive scientists." In order for people to predict and control what happens to them, they must figure out the causes of the behavior of others and their own behavior. The causes they perceive partially influence how they act. For example, if a friend has repeatedly failed to live up to his obligations to you, you may doubt the next promise he makes. You may attribute his making that promise to a momentary desire to please you, rather than to a sincere desire to live up to his obligations. On the other hand, if you attribute his prior failures to meet his obligations to unfortunate circumstances, then you may be willing to believe him the next time he makes a promise.

Since people cannot directly perceive other people's feelings, thoughts, motives, or character traits, they infer them from their behavior. Many attribution theorists assume that people do not have direct internal knowledge of the causes of their own behavior, thoughts, and feelings and therefore make similar inferences about themselves. Character traits, for instance, are inferences from patterns of behavior. I can have no direct internal knowledge of a trait of "friendliness." Instead, I attribute this trait to myself if I observe myself frequently acting in a friendly manner or if I am told by others that I am friendly.

If people attribute negative traits to themselves and negative causes to their own behavior, they may self-destruct. One of the contributions of attribution theory to understanding psychopathology is the insight that individuals sometimes interpret their own behavior in negative ways (Valins & Nisbett, 1972). Weiner and his associates (Weiner et al., 1972) have found that certain individuals act in self-defeating ways in achievement situations. When they succeed on a task, they attribute the cause of their success either to luck or to the ease of the task. When they fail, however, they attribute their failure to their own lack of ability. In contrast, people who perform well in achievement situations attribute success to their own efforts or to their ability, and attribute their failures to a lack of effort or the difficulty of the task. Those who act in self-defeating ways see the causes of their own success or failure in such a way that they are defeated before they start. If they succeed, it is not because they have any ability. If they fail, it is because they lack ability. Such a pattern is liable to lead to a lack of trying, which will, in turn, lead to a further lack of success.

Weiner's views have been incorporated into a model of depression by Martin Seligman and his associates (Abramson, Seligman, & Teasdale, 1978). They hypothesize that depression is caused by seeing oneself as the cause of something negative in one's life and then extending that perception to making a global negative attribution to one's whole character. In other words, the depressive sees herself as being at fault for her difficulties and in addition, believes that she is at fault because of some fundamental flaw in her character. Therefore, she not only sees herself as being at fault for her difficulties, but she also feels helpless to do anything to change or to control negative events.

More recently, Seligman (1990) has argued that adopting an optimistic explanatory style is more functional than adopting a pessimistic one. Optimists tend to take credit for their successes, and do not blame themselves for their failures. When something goes wrong, they do not generalize from that to assume that things will never go right. Seligman cites a number of research studies suggesting that optimistic baseball teams do better than pessimistic ones, presidential candidates who espouse optimistic philosophies tend to win, and optimism can enhance immune system functioning.

Several therapeutic approaches have been based on attributional ideas. Försterling (1985) has reviewed several programs designed to retrain people who are self-defeating in achievement situations in how they make attributions. The programs appear promising in getting such individuals to make less self-defeating attributions. Seligman (1990) presents a self-help program for training oneself to be an optimist that includes many of the ideas of other cognitive therapists to be considered later in this chapter.

A group of approaches, called **misattribution procedures,** are based on the idea that individuals make negative attributions to themselves, and then these attributions cause anxiety, which disrupts behavior. For example, a person who sees himself as shy may particularly notice his pounding heart and high pulse rate in a new social situation and say to himself, "Oh, no! I'm getting scared again!" This negative self-perception then increases feelings of fear and actually leads to shy behavior. In a study by Brodt and Zimbardo (1981), some extremely shy individuals were told that they would be bombarded with loud noise and that the noise would be the cause of their pounding heart and increasing pulse rate. The hypothesis was that since shy individuals would misattribute the cause of their symptoms to the loud noise, instead of to their shyness, they would not worry so much about their shyness. They would then be able to act in a more socially appropriate manner. In fact, such subjects did act in an essentially "normal" fashion in a new social situation. Shy subjects who had not been given this misattribution treatment acted in a noticeably shy manner.

Misattribution is based on the idea that individuals observe themselves exhibiting behavior they do not like (a pounding heart) and then make negative attributions to themselves ("Oh, gad! Here I go acting shy again!"). We have already discussed how perceptions of low self-efficacy can lead to such negative self-monitoring. If a person feels incompetent in a particular situation, he may begin to observe himself critically, looking for signs of dysfunction, and because he is no longer focused on the situation, acts less competently. When you are doing something, it is disruptive to continually focus your attention on yourself rather than on the task and on your behavior. Such self-consciousness can also intensify negative mood states (Buss, 1980).

Bandura (1986) suggested that there are ways to use self-monitoring effectively. Effective self-monitoring does not focus on what momentary success or failure means in terms of personality, self, or future. Rather it focuses on the situation and task: "What does this situation demand?" "What did I just do? Did it work? If not, why not?" "What resources do I need for my next task?" As you shall see, Meichenbaum's cognitive-behavioral therapy is an attempt to replace disruptive self-monitoring processes with more effective ones. Sex therapy also does this by trying to deflect the client's attention from self-evaluation to enjoyment of the activity. Attempts to modify dysfunctional, self-focused attention are also parts of Ellis's and Beck's cognitive approaches.

BECK'S COGNITIVE THERAPY

The single most influential cognitive approach is that of the psychiatrist Aaron Beck. Beck's work was originally on depression (Beck, Rush, Shaw, & Emery, 1979), and it has been expanded for use with a wide range of psychological problems including anxiety disorders (Beck, Emery, & Greenberg, 1985) and personality disorders (Beck, Freeman, & Associates, 1990). We shall review Beck's approach to depression in some detail, and then briefly consider the cognitive approach to personality disorders.

Cognitive Therapy for Depression

Some people, we say, look at the world through rose-colored glasses. Beck's cognitive view of depression assumes that the depressive's glasses are of a somewhat more dusky hue. Beck holds that the symptoms of both depression and anxiety are a result of the client's cognitions about the world. In particular, a **cognitive triad** characterizes the depressive's thinking: a negative view of herself (low self-esteem), a negative view of her personal future, and a negative view of her current experiences. For instance, one of us had a young woman client who was convinced that things would "never get any better" for her. That was because she was "all screwed up as a person." If she was asked how her week was she would say, "Terrible."

Depressives also exhibit basic errors in information processing that contribute to their negative perceptions. They tend to magnify negative things and minimize positive things. For instance, every week the client mentioned above would begin her session by reporting that her week had been "terrible"; she would then be asked to review her week day by day. It was invariably discovered that she had had both negative and positive experiences that week. When she said her week had been "terrible," what she had done was magnify the negative and minimize the positive. One week the big "negative" was that her mother had insulted her, while the positive experience, which had not even been mentioned at first, was that she had been promoted on her job.

Depressives also overgeneralize. For example, if your relationship breaks up, you may conclude (if you are good at depressive thinking) that "No one will ever love me." Still another depressive error is selective abstraction, in which a detail is taken out of context and then overgeneralized. Thus, in a whole conversation with someone there is perhaps one moment when things don't go well. A depressive will focus on that moment, take it out of the context of the rest of the conversation, and conclude that she made a fool out of herself and that the conversation went badly.

A predisposition toward depressive thinking is learned in early childhood. Beck assumes that children think in global, absolute, either/or ways and that in depressives, these primitive ways of thinking are carried forward into adulthood. In particular, they are maintained in the form of primitive, simplistic schemas learned in early childhood, such as "In order to be happy, I have to be successful in whatever I undertake"; "To be happy, I must be accepted by all people at all times"; "If I make a mistake, it means that I am inept"; and "I can't live without you" (Beck, Rush, Shaw, & Emery, 1979, p. 246).

Therapeutic Goals   Cognitive therapy is a systematic, structured, problem-solving approach. It is generally time-limited and rarely exceeds 30 sessions. Each therapy session has an agenda, in contrast to the free format of psychoanalysis or client-centered therapy. Beck believes the therapist should be warm, empathic, and genuine, as does Carl Rogers (see Chapter 8). However, in contrast to Rogers, he does not see these conditions as sufficient for therapy to take place. Rather, the therapeutic relationship is important because it is the source of learning. Among other things, the therapist is a model of what he or she is trying to teach. If the therapist is judgmental or moralizing, that will merely reinforce the primitive, judgmental thoughts of the client.

The ultimate goal of cognitive therapy is to identify dysfunctional cognitions, see how they trigger and generate depressive feelings and behavior, and learn to modify them. It is important to note that Beck is not as interested in what the client thinks as in how he thinks. Beck even admits that on occasion, a depressive cognition may be accurate (for instance, somebody may ignore you because they really don't like you).

Beck is not interested in teaching "positive thinking." He sees positive thinking as potentially as destructive as negative thinking. The issue is not whether the client likes or dislikes himself. The issue is whether he thinks in a mode of either "I am good" or "I am bad" depending on what happens. If he is stuck in this mode of thinking, he will say, "I am good" when things go right. But of course, that just sets him up for "I am bad" when he makes a mistake or things go wrong. It's better for him not to think in terms of "I am good" or "I am bad," depending on what happens, but rather to focus on what he does: "Did I do this well or not?"

Similarly, life, for Beck, is not the pursuit of happiness. Happiness is a by-product of activity. Though Beck has been accused of being a "positive thinker" (Hazleton, 1984), you can see that this is inaccurate. Beck does not think it is better to see a glass as "half full" than as "half empty." Instead, it is better to see it as containing four ounces of water (Beck, Rush, Shaw, & Emery, 1979).

Beck wants his clients to learn to test hypotheses. Even though occasional depressive cognitions may be accurate, depressives generate their depression through their dysfunctional errors in information processing and the cognitive triad. Beck attempts to teach clients to treat these ideas as hypotheses rather than as facts and then to test them against the evidence. The development of this hypothesis-testing attitude will lead to a much more flexible, nonjudgmental cognitive system that can handle an occasional negative cognition that is supported by the evidence. In initial sessions, Beck explores the client's difficulties and formulates a plan of action. The link between thoughts and feelings is demonstrated to the client, with examples. Then, two general lines of attack are used to combat dysfunctional cognitions. They are behavioral techniques and cognitive techniques.

Behavioral Techniques   Behavioral techniques are used first with more severely depressed clients. Severely depressed clients may have difficulty processing ideas and information. Therefore, cognitive interventions are often ineffective with them. For example, one client one of us worked with could barely say more than "This is stupid. I've got to get over this and get back to work." Trying to get her to explore her feelings and thoughts was unsuccessful. She would elaborate slightly, but then lapse back into "This is stupid. I've got to get over this and get back to work."

For such clients, behavioral interventions are used to help lift the depression. Getting the client to act counters cognitions such as "I can't do anything" or "I'm a vegetable." In addition, the therapist can get the client to begin to test his dysfunctional cognitions while engaging in the behavioral activities. As these interventions gradually help lift the depression, the client becomes open to cognitive interventions.

Beck does not believe that behavioral interventions can cure depression by themselves. The underlying negative cognitions that generated the depression need to be attacked as well or the depression will return. Nevertheless, doing something is a good "cure" to lift the depression temporarily.

Beck utilizes several behavioral interventions. The *daily activity schedule* is an hourly record kept by the client of all his activities, no matter how trivial. It helps counter the dysfunctional cognition that "I never do anything." In addition, the client is often asked to rate each activity for the amount of pleasure and the amount of "mastery" it gives him. The amount of mastery is the sense of accomplishment one gets from doing something. This also often gives the therapist insight into the client's dysfunctional cognitions. For instance, one client's daily activity record (Beck, Rush, Shaw, & Emery, 1979, p. 130) rated wallpapering the kitchen as 0 for mastery and pleasure and rated getting up, getting dressed, and eating as 1. How could wallpapering provide even less of a sense of mastery than getting up? The answer lies in this depressed client's distorted, perfectionist perceptions of his achievement (see Box 12.1), which the therapist was able to explore with the help of the mastery-pleasure ratings.

Another behavioral intervention Beck uses with depressed clients is a series of *graduated task assignments*. A client for whom getting out of bed is an accomplishment may be assigned the task of brushing his teeth and shaving. After he has mastered that, he may be assigned the task of fixing himself breakfast and going for a walk. The next week, the assignment may include reading the paper and looking at the want ads. The strategy is to pick activities that slowly and gradually return the depressed client to full functioning. However, it is important to pick tasks that are within the client's grasp. To say to a seriously depressed client who can barely get out of bed, "You'll feel better if you go look for a job," will probably contribute to his depression rather than help it. It is too big a leap to go from getting out of bed to looking for a job. In addition, Beck stresses that the goal of the activity is the doing of it, rather than the accomplishing of it. The client is told that no one accomplishes everything he or she sets out to do and that the important thing is to treat the activity as a learning experience.

Another behavioral technique is *cognitive rehearsal*. Severely depressed clients often cannot handle a complex task assignment, because they have difficulty in concentrating and thinking. As a result, they will "self-destruct." They will forget directions or they will fail to anticipate crucial prerequisites to getting the task accomplished. For instance, a client whose task assignment is to go look for a job may forget to get clothes washed the day before, or may forget to arrange for transportation. These things may only dawn on the client at the moment when the client is preparing to leave. Without clothes or transportation the client cannot carry out the task assignment and the experience becomes another failure, confirming the client's self-perception of incompetence. To counter this, the therapist has the client rehearse the task, that is, to go through the task step by step to discover what he will need to do to accomplish it. Such pitfalls are then discovered in advance, and the client can take steps to overcome them. In addition, the therapist can give the client suggestions as to how to handle unexpected pitfalls.

Another technique used by cognitive therapists is *role playing*. Beck has found that depressed clients are often more critical of themselves than of others in the same situation (Beck, Rush, Shaw, & Emery, 1979). He has clients role-play what they would say to someone else who had their problem. In the example in Box 12.1, Beck does this when he asks the client how he would feel about his wallpapering job if someone else had done it for him. One of us used this technique with a religious young man who felt guilty about masturbating. He had given it up and had been absolved by the elders of his church, who told him that the important thing was not to dwell on his past transgressions, but to try to do better in the future. Yet he still felt guilty and anxious. In therapy, he was asked to pretend to counsel another young man with the same problem. He was much more forgiving toward this imaginary man than he was toward himself. When he realized this, his guilt and anxiety subsided.

BOX 12.1

Cognitions Involved in Mastery and Pleasure Ratings

Below is a sample of a dialogue between a depressed man who had rated his achievement in wallpapering a kitchen as providing no sense of mastery or pleasure. Note Beck's questioning technique to first uncover and then attack the dysfunctional cognitions involved.

THERAPIST: Why didn't you rate wallpapering the kitchen as a mastery experience?

PATIENT: Because the flowers didn't line up.

T: Your kitchen?

P: No. I helped a neighbor do his kitchen.

T: Did he do most of the work?

P: No. I really did almost all of it. He hadn't wallpapered before.

T: Did anything else go wrong? Did you spill the paste all over? Ruin a lot of wallpaper? Leave a big mess?

P: No, no, the only problem was that the flowers did not line up.

T: So, since it was not perfect, you get no credit at all.

P: Well . . . yes.

T: Just how far off was the alignment of the flowers?

P: (Holds out fingers about an eighth of an inch apart) About that much.

T: On each strip of paper?

P: No . . . on two or three pieces.

T: Out of how many?

P: About 20 to 25.

T: Did anyone else notice it?

P: No. In fact, my neighbor thought it was great.

T: Did your wife see it?

P: Yeah, she admired the job.

T: Could you see the defect when you stood back and looked at the whole wall?

P: Well . . . not really.

T: So you've selectively attended to a real but very small flaw in your effort to wallpaper. Is it logical that such a small defect should entirely cancel the credit you deserve?

P: Well, it wasn't as good as it should have been.

T: If your neighbor had done the same quality job in your kitchen, what would you say?

P: . . . Pretty good job!

Source: Beck, Rush, Shaw, & Emery, 1979, pp. 130–131.

Cognitive Techniques   Once the depression has lifted sufficiently, the therapist can begin to concentrate on cognitive techniques. The first thing necessary is to make the client aware of the connection between his thoughts and his feelings. In order to do this, the client is given the assignment of keeping a *daily record of automatic thoughts.* Every time the client notices himself feeling depressed, he is to attempt to recover the thoughts that immediately preceded the onset of the depressed feelings. He is to record the objective situation, the thoughts he had, and the feelings they led to. For example, you are sitting in class and you suddenly begin to feel depressed. You realize that you had just noticed the attractive person near you who acts as if you don't exist. You record the situation: sitting in class, noticing the attractive person. You also record your thoughts: That person acts as if I don't exist. I'll never get a date. And you record your mood.

Initially, people often report that the depressed mood came on them without any thoughts. Beck believes that in these cases, there were thoughts present, but they occurred so quickly that the client was unaware of them. These are called **automatic thoughts,** and they are the cognitive therapist's equivalent of the unconscious (Meichenbaum & Gilmore, 1984). Automatic thoughts are thoughts that have become so habitual that when they are triggered by some situation, they flit through the client's mind too rapidly for him to notice. Yet they stimulate depressive feelings. The daily record helps clients become aware of the automatic thoughts that precede their depressive feelings and can be used by the therapist to help clients modify their dysfunctional thinking pattern.

An additional assignment, besides the daily record of dysfunctional thoughts, is often made. Along with recording the situation, thoughts, and feelings, the client is asked to write down alternative, less dysfunctional ways of perceiving the situation. This has the effect of helping the client realize that he or she has been locked into one way of seeing the situation and that there are other ways. Generating alternative views of the situation encourages the hypothesis-testing attitude that Beck is trying to teach.

The main cognitive technique used by the therapist is *questioning.* Questions are designed to help the client explore and test dysfunctional cognitions. Note in the dialogue about wallpapering in Box 12.1 that the therapist explores the possibility that the client's perception of failure as a wallpaperer might have a real basis—he made a mess, wasted wallpaper, and so on. It is clear in this example that the client's perception of failure is based instead on his perfectionist attitude. The therapist helps the client realize this through questioning. However, even if the client had made a mess, the cognitive therapist could then have explored the dysfunctional cognitions based on that situation, such as "I never do anything right," "I'm inept," and so on. Cognitive therapists use three general kinds of questions (Beck, Emery, & Greenberg, 1985): "What's the evidence?" "What's another way of looking at the situation?" and "So what if it happens?"

It is important to point out that Beck uses questions rather than attempting to argue the client out of dysfunctional cognitions. Why doesn't he try to logically persuade the client that his beliefs are incorrect? People often react to depressives in everyday life by saying, "You did fine! I'm sure your neighbor didn't care about the misaligned flowers. Don't be so hard on yourself. Everyone likes you. You have to have more confidence in yourself!"

The depressive might respond with a short-lived good feeling or argue back, "But you don't really know me. Maybe the misaligned flowers aren't so bad in themselves, but they're just a symptom of the generally sloppy, careless way I live my life. Besides, you're just trying to cheer me up." After a few rounds of this the friend will go away feeling angry and frustrated. The friend may go say to another friend, "Oh, he just likes to be depressed. He wants everyone to feel sorry for him." Anyone who has argued with a depressive has probably come away with such feelings. The perception that the depressive likes being depressed then becomes a further problem for the depressive, who begins to be rejected by the people around him, who no longer want to listen to him complain or to attempt to lift his depression. In yet another way, depression becomes a vicious cycle.

Trying to argue someone out of a deeply entrenched point of view is usually quite fruitless. Some research (Nisbett & Ross, 1980) has shown that people with deeply committed beliefs simply explain away or assimilate information contradictory to their belief system and paradoxically end up believing in it more than ever. Even if depression is based on a dysfunctional belief system, presenting contradictory evidence will have little effect. This is true for all of us whenever we have a deeply committed belief, be it religious, political, or psychological. Imagine trying to use logical argument and evidence to convince a committed Republican to be a Democrat or vice versa! Because it is difficult to argue a person committed to a belief system out of it, it is inaccurate to accuse depressives of "wanting to be depressed" when arguments fail. Beck holds that depressives would love to get out of the binds they're in if they could. They do not counter arguments because they want to stay depressed; they counter them because they are locked into a depressive belief system that they would be only too happy to escape from if they saw a way.

Beck uses a questioning technique to get the depressed person to challenge her own depressive cognitions. In Plato's *Dialogues,* Plato's philosophy is articulated through the main character of Socrates. Socrates does not expound or argue. What Socrates does is ask skillful questions to make the person he is talking to think it out until he arrives at Socrates's perspective. Arguing leads to defensiveness. People will often hang on to a point of view in an argument just to justify themselves and defend their own autonomy. The therapist who argues with a depressive may put him in the position of having to defend and justify his negative perspective. This can be circumvented by using the Socratic method—by asking questions to get the client to think it out so that he arrives at a less depressive view. In addition, it mobilizes the patient's cognitive resources and trains the patient in a method that he can use at other times.

Beck's questioning technique, then, mobilizes depressives to challenge their own cognitions. Even so, the challenges must be repeated over a period of time before they sink in. One disconfirmation of a dysfunctional belief is rarely enough to change it. The insight must be acquired over and over again before the belief system will finally change.

In addition, Beck gives *homework assignments* so that dysfunctional cognitions can be tested against direct experience. A client may be instructed to test out the belief "My boss will never give me a raise" by asking for a raise. (If the boss does not give the client a raise, the dysfunctional cognitions generated by the client from that will be dealt with, and so the experience will be a productive learning one either way.)

Role of Emotion in Cognitive Therapy

Cognitive therapy has never ignored emotion, contrary to what some have believed. Cognitive therapists do respond empathically to client emotion. However, in recent years, emotion has become more emphasized as an important component of cognitive therapy. It has come to be believed that cognitions that are activated in the context of emotion are more easily changed than cognitions that are not so activated. That is, a person's negative cognitions about himself will be more readily challenged and changed when they are dealt with in the presence of the actual negative emotions generated by such cognitions. This has led to the idea of "hot cognition" (Safran & Greenberg, 1982), that is, cognitions that are associated with emotions. In regard to this, cognitive therapists will now more actively work to elicit emotions in the belief that the activation of emotions makes the accompanying cognitions more available for challenge and reprocessing. With anxiety, for instance, the therapist may encourage the client to hyperventilate in order to recreate some of the anxious experience. At that moment, dysfunctional cognitions such as "Oh God! I'm having a heart attack," or "I'm having a panic attack and I'll totally self-destruct" can be challenged.

Cognitive Therapy for Personality Disorders

A recent extension of cognitive theory has been to the treatment of personality disorders (Beck, Freeman, & Associates, 1990). Beck and his colleagues believe that personality disorders, such as dependent personality disorder or paranoid personality disorder, are learned dysfunctional interpersonal strategies or schemas. These interpersonal strategies or schemas get triggered in various situations. As an example, whenever a problematic situation arises the dysfunctional schema or interpersonal strategy "I need help" gets triggered in dependent personality disorders (Beck, Freeman, & Associates, 1990, p. 32).

These dysfunctional schemas have been learned in childhood and chronically influence a person's behavior. For instance, the paranoid personality disorder is one in which the individual typically views other people with suspicion, and often tends to react in a negative and aggressive way to others. This disorder is based on schemas in which such individuals portray themselves as righteous and mistreated by others, and their schematic views of others see others as basically mistrustful. This leads such individuals to be continually on the alert for signs of mistreatment and slights from others.

The goal of the cognitive therapist treating personality disorders is to change these dysfunctional schemas. Many of the same techniques used in cognitive therapy of depression and anxiety are utilized with personality disorders. However, to totally change such schemas is very time-consuming, and often a therapeutic strategy is not to totally eliminate them, but to alter them so that they are less rigidly dysfunctional. With a paranoid personality disorder, the therapist might encourage the client to learn to trust some people in some situations, or to test her dysfunctional beliefs more, so that she is not rigidly ruled by them.

One new strategy of note is in working with personality disorders. Beck and colleagues (1990) point out that sometimes these long-standing dysfunctional interpersonal patterns cannot be modified without working with childhood experience. Childhood experiences are not worked with as extensively as in psychoanalysis.

However, the cognitive therapist may have the client-role play an encounter with his mother or father, if that parent seems to be a major source of the learning of the dysfunctional schemas. In cognitive therapy, the client does not merely relive early childhood traumatic experiences, but during role play is asked to practice more functional, adult ways of responding to the person in question. In essence, this allows the client to reevaluate the childhood experience from an adult perspective and to relinquish old, dysfunctional attitudes that had been developed from it. Once again, this can be seen as an extension of the idea of "hot cognition" mentioned previously: dysfunctional beliefs are best modified when their relevant affective, experiential aspects have been activated and are "alive."

ELLIS'S RATIONAL-EMOTIVE THERAPY

We have noted that one depression-causing cognition begins "I'll never. . . ." So when your third or fourth relationship doesn't work out, you say, "I'll never have a good relationship." You might even go further and say, "I'll never have a good relationship because I'm unlovable." We have shown how Beck would treat this. He would get the client to evaluate the evidence for these propositions and encourage the client to see that even a series of failures does not prove that his relationships will never work out. It is also obvious that it would be difficult to find evidence proving that he is unlovable. But there is another way to proceed. For Albert Ellis, founder of rational-emotive therapy, the important question is "So what if you never did have a good relationship?" (Beck stresses this question in therapy for anxiety.) For Ellis, a client's answer to the question can be something depressing to him only if he makes it mean something depressing. For example, most people answer the question "What if I never have a good relationship?" by insisting "I must have a good relationship in order to be happy." In other words, if people didn't set such an absolute philosophical condition on their lives, the thought that they might never have a good relationship would not be threatening or depressing.

Causes of Psychopathology

Ellis claims that this kind of **musturbatory thinking,** that is, this setting of an absolute standard for behavior and life, is at the basis of most personal difficulty. Ellis (1979b) lists three groups of such ideas that "virtually all humans hold to some degree but which disturbed individuals hold more intensely, extensively, and rigidly."

> I must be competent, adequate, and achieving, and I must win the approval of virtually all the significant people in my life. It is awful when I don't. I can't stand failing in these all-important respects. I am a rotten person when I don't do what I must do to act competently and to win others' approval.
>
> Others must treat me kindly, fairly, and properly when I want them to do so. It is terrible when they don't. I can't bear their acting obnoxiously toward me. They are damnable, worthless people when they don't do what they must do to treat me satisfactorily.
>
> I need and must have the things I really want. The conditions under which I live and the world around me must be well ordered, positive, certain—just the way I

want them to be. I must gratify my desires easily and immediately, without having to deal with too many difficulties or hassles. It is horrible when conditions are not this way. I can't tolerate their being uncomfortable, frustrating, or merely not ideal. The world is a rotten place and life is hardly worth living when things are not as they should be in this respect. (pp. 3–4)

These ideas are what Ellis calls irrational beliefs. They are absolute, rigid, intolerant, and demanding. But they are beliefs. Ellis is fond of quoting Shakespeare's Hamlet: "There's nothing either good or bad, but thinking makes it so." Ellis is especially interested in what people think they must have in order to be happy, how they must act in order to be a good person, what the world should be like, and how others ought to be. When Ellis holds that beliefs are irrational, he means that they cannot be empirically or scientifically verified. He says, "They can all be easily exposed and demolished by any scientist worth his salt; and the rational-emotive therapist is exactly that: an exposing and nonsense-annihilating scientist" (Ellis, 1973, p. 173).

Where do irrational cognitions come from? Ellis believes that all people are born with tendencies toward rational and irrational thinking as well as self-actualization. We all have them, even educated academics and intellectuals. People are born with a tendency to learn self-defeating behavior more easily than life-enhancing behavior, to remain attached to beliefs that do not work in various ways, to need to prove themselves superior to others, to demand rather than to want, to be overcautious, to be lazy, to be undisciplined, to have low frustration tolerance, to prefer the easiest way out of situations, and to be shortsighted. Though general tendencies to think irrationally may be inborn, specific irrational thoughts are learned from the person's culture. Even if they are learned in early childhood, however, they are kept alive because people continually reindoctrinate themselves.

According to Ellis, it is a person's cognitions about events that determine behavior, not the events themselves. The effect of cognition on behavior is represented by Ellis's famous A-B-C model. A is the objective event, B is the person's interpretation of the event, and C is the person's emotional or behavioral reaction. Most people tend to think that A causes C, but Ellis believes that while A contributes to C, B is the most important determinant of reactions. For instance, clients with borderline personality disorder feel they "cannot stand" being alone. But is it really true that they can't stand being alone? Or is that merely a self-perception on their part? Their perception is that A ("I am alone") leads to C (feelings of depression or panic). Ellis would suggest that this happens only because of intervening cognitions: "I do not like being alone," "I must not be alone," "I can't stand being alone." It is this set of intervening cognitions that causes the borderline's reactions of depression or panic, not being alone itself. Ellis suggests that the borderline person has made a nonsequitur. He has followed a rational (sane) sentence, "I do not like being alone," with an irrational (insane) inference, "I must not be alone," leading to the perception "I cannot stand being alone" and feelings of depression.

Ellis also says people create problems by turning preferences into needs. There is a difference between the rational statements that I prefer to have a good income, to have a good relationship, to be attractive and well liked, and the irrational beliefs that I must have a good income, I can't stand to be without a loving fulfilling relationship,

I must be attractive, and I deserve to be well liked. Ellis generally does not believe that "shoulds" and "musts" exist in nature and that people would behave much more sanely and rationally if they stayed at the level of their wants and preferences. Sounding very existential, he holds that the world just "is" and that people would be better off to accept that, rather than to make demands that the world be fair or just according to their perceptions. This is also true of the self. Ellis has argued that self-evaluation is probably the major cause of personal distress, along with musturbatory thinking. Positive self-esteem is just as bad as negative self-esteem. It is better not to judge or evaluate the self at all. In this, he agrees with Beck that it is rational to evaluate actions, but not the self.

Ellis illustrates the destructive consequences of self-evaluation, rather than behavioral evaluation, in the case of Myra, a woman who came to therapy feeling inadequate because she was unable to have an orgasm. He asks Myra to recount what she is thinking as she tries to achieve orgasm. It turns out that not only is she trying to have an orgasm, but she is also thinking that if she doesn't have an orgasm "wouldn't that be terrible, what a lousy sex partner I'd be . . . all that effort for nothing . . . how awful . . . how unfair . . . while so many other women have one so easily, with no effort at all!" (Ellis, 1979a, p. 71). A person dwelling on such thoughts cannot possibly be focusing on the pleasurable aspects of sex. Thus, the self-evaluation becomes a self-fulfilling prophecy. Ellis also talks about "disturbance about disturbance" (1979d, p. 48), which is thinking less of oneself for having problems. In addition to Myra's contributing to her own lack of orgasmic responsiveness, she also criticized herself and felt guilty for not being able to have an orgasm: "I must get orgasms like other women do, and I don't get them; that's awful! I can't stand it! I must be something of a turd for being so inferior to most other women!" (1979a, p. 69).

Therapeutic Methods

In terms of therapeutic practice, rational-emotive therapy is relatively short term (usually not over 50 sessions) and utilizes techniques from a wide range of approaches. Rational-emotive therapists will use operant conditioning techniques, desensitization, assertion training, role playing, interpersonal skills training, modeling, imagery, shame-attacking exercises (see below), and bibliotherapy (the use of reading material).

However, its central technique is **disputing**. As the name implies, disputing is the logical challenging of irrational beliefs. Ellis believes that he can identify and begin attacking a client's irrational cognitions within the first few minutes of the first session. An example of his technique is given in Box 12.2. Ellis (1973) describes this method thus:

> The rational-emotive practitioner mainly employs a fairly rapid-fire active-directive-persuasive-philosophic methodology. In most instances, he quickly pins the client down to a few basic irrational ideas which motivate much of his disturbed behavior; he challenges the client to validate these ideas; he shows them that they are extralogical premises which cannot be validated; he logically analyzes these ideas and makes mincemeat of them; he vigorously and vehemently shows why they can't work and

---

BOX 12.2

Ellis Disputes

This is the first part of an initial interview with a 25-year-old female client complaining of guilt, unworthiness, depression, and insecurity, among other things.

T: All right, what would you want to start on first?

C: I don't know. I'm petrified at the moment!

T: You're petrified—of what?

C: Of you!

T: Because of what I am going to do to you?

C: Right! You are threatening me, I guess.

T: But how? What am I doing? Obviously, I'm not going to take a knife and stab you. Now, in what way am I threatening you?

C: I guess I'm afraid, perhaps, of what I'm going to find out—about me.

T: Well, so let's suppose you find out something dreadful about you—that you're thinking foolishly or something. Now why would that be awful?

C: Because I . . . I guess I'm the most important thing to me at the moment.

T: No, I don't think that's the answer. It's, I believe, the opposite! You're really the least important thing to you. You are prepared to beat yourself over the head if I tell you that you're acting foolishly. If you were not a self-blamer, then you wouldn't care what I said. It would be important to you—but you'd just go around correcting it. But if I tell you something really negative about you, you're going to beat yourself mercilessly. Aren't you?

Source: Ellis, 1984, pp. 215–216.

---

will almost inevitably lead to renewed disturbed symptomatology; he reduces these ideas to absurdity, sometimes in a highly humorous manner; he explains how they can be replaced with more rational, empirically based theses; he teaches the client how to think scientifically. (p. 185)

Ellis has noted, however, that disputing alone is frequently insufficient for psychotherapeutic change to occur. Most clients also require active, experiential exercises in order to test out their irrational cognitions. Because of the biological tendency to think irrationally it is difficult to correct irrational habits. One "insight" into irrationality will not suffice to change such an ingrained pattern of thinking.

It is important to note that Ellis's therapy involves an attitude of unconditional acceptance toward the client. The therapist does not judge the client as a person, even though he may vigorously attack some of the client's behavior and ideas. Ellis (1979a) points out that his client, Myra, occasionally irritated him:

> Not that I wasn't tempted, on several occasions, to really tell her off. But, with the use of RET (rational-emotive therapy), I kept reminding myself that she was not a louse even though her behavior was quite lousy. And I actually got myself to believe this and to convey my belief to her! (p. 83).

Furthermore, Ellis (1979c) states that the rational-emotive therapist respects the client's value system and does not impose his value system on the client. It is not the values themselves that are attacked, but rather their absolute, musturbatory quality. For instance, if a client does something contrary to his own values, he will feel depressed, anxious, or guilty only if he believes that he is "an awful person" because of what he did. A more rational way of responding would be "I would prefer not to act that way. I'll try to do better next time." The rational-emotive therapist would not attack the person's values, but his rigid way of using his values.

In addition to disputing in therapy sessions, the therapist often gives the client the homework assignment of disputing his or her own beliefs. For instance, Myra worked at disputing the beliefs that she must have sex enjoyment easily and quickly and that she should have orgasms as other women do. She realized that although it would be highly desirable if she could, there was no evidence that she should, and that she was not a bad person because she was the way she was.

Many of the techniques that rational-emotive therapists will use, such as the behavioral techniques, are discussed elsewhere in this book. We will briefly mention two others here. The first is the **shame-attacking exercises.** Because Ellis believes that shame is the essence of many disorders, he has clients attack this feeling. In these exercises, the clients deliberately make fools of themselves. Myra, for instance, was given the assignment of walking a banana down the street on a leash. Despite feeling foolish at first, she soon realized that nothing bad happened to her, and she actually began to enjoy the experience.

The use of imagery is another technique. It is based on the work of Maultsby (1975). Myra, for instance, was to imagine a scene of sexual failure. She was to imagine trying hard to have an orgasm, failing, and her husband's being critical of her. As she imagined these things, she experienced shame and depression. Her assignment was to imagine these scenes repeatedly, but to practice experiencing the more rational feelings of sadness and disappointment. Gradually, she learned that she could experience these feelings instead.

Comparison of Ellis and Beck

You may have noticed that the approaches of Beck and Ellis are similar. Although Ellis considers his therapeutic approach to be scientific, we believe that Beck places more emphasis on a scientific attitude than Ellis, and Ellis places greater emphasis on philosophical analysis. Both believe that clients make logical errors that lead to dysfunctional conclusions. However, Beck emphasizes testing hypotheses. Are the

Using Rational-Emotive Therapy with Pets.

client's ideas true or false? Are they overgeneralizations? Can they be backed up by evidence? If the client says, "I will never have a relationship," the main thrust of Beck's approach is to demonstrate that this conclusion does not have any evidence to back it up. Ellis may do this also, but his main emphasis is on what the client believes to be the consequences of the statement, whether it is verifiable or not: "Even if it were true, does that mean you cannot enjoy life?"

As therapists, their methods differ also. Beck is certainly active in asking questions, structuring the therapy hour, and suggesting assignments and techniques, but he is relatively nondirective in his approach to the client's cognitions and beliefs. Beck never tells the client his beliefs are irrational or which beliefs to modify. Rather, he ultimately lets the client draw his own conclusions. Ellis is much more directive. He tells the client which beliefs are irrational and need modification. The technique of disputing by its very name implies this more confrontational approach.

MEICHENBAUM'S COGNITIVE BEHAVIOR MODIFICATION

Do you talk to yourself? If you do, you probably do it privately and might be embarrassed to be caught at it. You might even wonder if you were a little crazy. According to Donald Meichenbaum (1977), however, you not only have nothing to worry about, but how you talk to yourself is crucial in determining how you behave and feel. Meichenbaum points out that children talk to themselves all the time as they play and practice new skills. It is through such self-guiding speech that people learn to direct and control much of their behavior. For example, when you first learned how to drive, you most likely guided your first attempts with self-speech. Others guided your behavior at first with their instructional speech, but you then began to guide yourself, silently or out loud, saying, "Now, first put the clutch in—no—step on the brake and release the emergency brake. Start the car. Now put the clutch in. Put it in gear. Now let the clutch out—not too fast . . ." Talking to yourself is actually quite adaptive, if you say the right things. And that is the crux of Meichenbaum's cognitive-behavioral therapeutic approach.

Self-speech can be maladaptive and contribute to psychological problems in two ways. First, some individuals engage in dysfunctional self-speech. They say things to themselves that are disruptive and distressing. Someone who says "I can never do anything right. What's the use?" may give up on tasks or engage in dysfunctional behavior, such as drinking, to avoid the tasks. Second, the absence of adaptive self-speech makes dysfunctional behavior more likely. If a person does not have effective self-guiding strategies for handling a situation, then she is likely to employ ineffective, maladaptive coping methods.

Self-guiding speech is initially learned through internalizing what others say and by conscious practice, but eventually, it becomes automatic and nonconscious. After a while you no longer say to yourself: "Now put in the clutch . . ." when you go driving. Beck defines automatic thoughts as habitual thoughts that occur so rapidly that we are not even aware of having thought them. Meichenbaum says that they are thoughts that occur with very "low intensity" and so are not easily noticed. One of Meichenbaum's general therapeutic strategies is to retrain how clients talk to themselves. The retraining attempts to eliminate dysfunctional self-speech and to increase adaptive self-speech. In some of Meichenbaum's original work, this was done quite systematically. First, the therapist models the kind of self-speech the client is to learn to use. This, as with each of the succeeding steps, may be done several times. The client then practices the self-speech aloud, then whispering, and finally silently. The practice is repeated until the desired type of self-speech becomes habitual.

This general model of self-instructional training, modified appropriately to fit each particular disorder, has been used to treat many kinds of problems, including hyperactivity in children, anxiety, schizophrenia, and anger control. It has also been used to teach creativity and stress management.

Meichenbaum's early work was with hyperactive, impulsive children. Following is an example of self-speech the therapist models for a child (Meichenbaum & Goodman, 1971):.

> Okay, what is it I have to do? You want me to copy the pictures with the different lines. I have to go slowly and carefully. Okay, draw the line down, down, good; then to the right, that's it; now down some more and to the left. Good, I'm doing fine so far. Remember, go slowly. Now back up again. No, I was supposed to go down. That's okay. Just erase the line carefully . . . Good. Even if I make an error I can go on slowly and carefully. I have to go down now. Finished. I did it! (p. 117)

The speech models the skills necessary to solve the task. More importantly, however, the speech models self-reinforcement ("Good, I'm doing fine so far") and what to do if a mistake is made (not "I goofed! That's terrible! I'll never get this right!").

Thus, three skills are being learned: the task skills themselves, self-reinforcement skills, and coping with failure skills.

An extensive body of research by Meichenbaum and others (reviewed in Meichenbaum, 1977) supports the efficacy of this strategy. It must be emphasized that it is effective only when the self-speech is practiced enough to become habitual. No magical results can be achieved with only a few rehearsals. If you go and try this after reading this chapter, you will not find that you can magically make your anxiety go away because it has not become a habit for you.

The need for such repetition of the model may give the impression that Meichenbaum's training requires almost robotlike behavior. However, this is not the case. Meichenbaum emphasizes flexibility during training. He says, "In using self-instructional procedures, it is important to insure that the child does not say the self-statements in a relatively mechanical, rote fashion without the accompanying meanings and inflection" (Meichenbaum, 1977, p. 89). In addition, the therapist attempts to vary the self-statements when he models them. The goal is to have a person learn not a rigid, mechanical set of self-statements, but a flexible set of coping strategies to guide behavior.

In a "regular" psychotherapy session with an average client, Meichenbaum (1986) does not appear to follow so formally the model of therapy as we have described it above. First, Meichenbaum is quite active in attempting to provide support and validation for the client. Second, Meichenbaum tries to elicit the client's self-speech, but then, through posing questions, tries to get the client to think through the possibility of new alternatives. The processes of effective self-regulation are informally encouraged and modeled throughout the therapy session, rather than being systematically and formally modeled as in the above examples.

SPECIFIC COGNITIVE-BEHAVIORAL TREATMENTS FOR SPECIFIC DISORDERS

One of the advantages of cognitive-behavioral therapies is that they can be specifically designed to specific disorders. Thus, if a therapist is seeing a client with a particular type of problem, there may be a particular cognitive-behavioral treatment designed specifically for that disorder. Further, because cognitive-behavioral treatments consist of specific combinations of cognitive and behavioral strategies, it is possible to write **treatment manuals** that outline the specific treatment for a particular disorder. So far, cognitive-behavioral treatments have been developed for depression, generalized anxiety disorder, panic disorder, social phobia, irritable bowel syndrome, bulimia, chronic pain, chemical dependency, suicide, marital problems, obsessive-compulsive disorder, schizophrenic hallucinations and delusions, and personality disorders (Beck, 1995; Chambless et al., 1996). We shall consider two examples.

Borkovec and his colleagues have developed a cognitive-behavioral treatment for generalized anxiety disorder. Generalized anxiety disorder is characterized by pervasive anxiety not specifically tied to environmental events or cues. In one research study (Borkovec & Costello, 1993), in the behavioral part of the treatment, clients learned to monitor their reactions, and to disrupt anxiety with the use of a variety of relaxation responses and by learning to focus attention on present experience. In the cognitive part of the treatment, clients first practiced imagining themselves using their anxiety-reducing relaxation skills to control their anxious feelings in various situations. In addition, they learned various skills of cognitive restructuring, such as how to identify and combat dysfunctional, anxiety-arousing cognitions. The research study found that the cognitive-behavioral treatment was superior to a "nondirective" approach patterned after early client-centered therapy in helping reduce symptoms of generalized anxiety disorder.

Panic attacks are full-blown, intense anxiety attacks that include bodily symptoms such as a racing heart, dizziness, sweating, and so forth. In Barlow's (1988) cognitive-behavioral treatment for panic disorder, clients engage in activities that induce paniclike symptoms in the therapy session. These include engaging in exercises to stimulate the experience of cardiovascular symptoms, and hyperventilation to stimulate some of the respiratory symptoms. Engaging in such exercises, clients expose themselves to the panic symptoms, and the behavioral part of the treatment is that exposure itself can help clients get over anxiety symptoms. Then, in addition, cognitive procedures are used in which clients learn to identify the catastrophic thoughts that occur when they have these bodily symptoms. They learn to reinterpret these experiences as normal bodily processes. They also learn to challenge other, more basic cognitive errors. Research has shown this procedure to be successful in eliminating or reducing panic attacks in most clients.

RECENT THEORETICAL ADVANCES

Cognitive approaches are becoming theoretically more integrative. Beck's cognitive therapy integrates and overlaps with ideas from a variety of approaches (Alford & Norcross, 1991). Meichenbaum (1995) considers the modification of meaning as the most important therapeutic event, and sees the therapist as a "co-constructivist" who not only helps clients combat dysfunctional cognitions and improve problem-solving skills, but who also helps them develop new narrative theories of their problems (see Chapter 17) and new ways to view themselves and the world.

A particular recent innovation in cognitive therapy is Safran and Segal's (1990) interpersonal approach. These authors state that most dysfunctional beliefs are inherently interpersonal, having been learned in interpersonal contexts and having interpersonal consequences, as George Kelly said years earlier. Their approach to cognitive therapy particularly emphasizes the interpersonal interaction between the therapist and the client. They assume that the client's dysfunctional beliefs about interpersonal interactions can hook the therapist into dysfunctional interpersonal interaction patterns. A dependent personality, for instance, may be able to hook the therapist into a cycle of taking care of the client. Or it may hook the therapist into feeling alienated by the client's dependency, which may exacerbate the client's tendencies to cling and try to establish dependency.

Safran and Segal place greater emphasis on the use of therapist empathy than is typical in cognitive therapy. They believe that empathy not only establishes a relationship, but also helps in accessing client's dysfunctional interpersonal beliefs. In addition to typical cognitive techniques, an important therapeutic goal is for the therapist to "unhook" from the client's dysfunctional interaction cycle. The therapist must consciously refrain from engaging in the dysfunctional behaviors that are being elicited by the client's dysfunctional belief system. The therapist may then give the client feedback on the behaviors that are contributing to the therapist's reactions. For these therapists, therapy is a kind of "learning laboratory" in which dysfunctional cognitions will actually be activated and challenged in the "live" context of the therapeutic relationship. In this respect, Safran and Segal's approach is an integrative cognitive therapy, including aspects of both client-centered and other humanistic approaches, as well as psychodynamic concepts.

EVALUATION OF COGNITIVE APPROACHES

Effectiveness of Psychotherapy

In general, the evidence for the effectiveness of cognitive approaches to therapy is quite positive. Smith, Glass, and Miller (1980) found an effect size of 0.68 for Ellis's rational-emotive therapy, which places it with psychodynamic, gestalt, and client-centered approaches in terms of effectiveness. A more recent meta-analysis of 70 studies also provides support for rational-emotive therapy (Lyons & Woods, 1991).

The evidence for Beck's cognitive therapy of depression has been encouraging. In perhaps the most thorough and extensive research study ever done on psychotherapy, cognitive therapy and another approach, interpersonal therapy (not reviewed in this book), were compared to medication in the treatment of depression (Elkin et al., 1989). Generally, this study found that both approaches to psychotherapy were effective, and equal in effectiveness to medication in treating depression. Other research also shows cognitive therapy to be effective for depression, as well as for panic attacks and generalized anxiety disorder (Hollon & Beck, 1994).

With regard to cognitive-behavioral approaches in general, Smith, Glass, and Miller (1980) report the largest effect sizes found, along with that for hypnotherapy, for cognitive-behavioral treatments. The recent report on "empirically validated treatments" put out by a task force of a division of the American Psychological Association listed 12 cognitive-behavioral treatments as having received sufficient empirical support to be considered as "efficacious" or "probably efficacious" (Chambless et al., 1996). In sum, cognitive-behavioral treatments appear to be efficacious for a wide range of disorders.

Theoretical Evaluation

To what extent is it true that cognitions cause psychopathology, as Beck, Ellis, Seligman, Meichenbaum, and others suppose? This is a complicated issue and we cannot fully evaluate it here. However, research has shown that the relation between cognition and psychopathology is more complex than cognitive theories have held them to be. Hammen (1985) argues that the research on depression has failed to support the idea that depression is associated with either internal or stable attributions, as Seligman has argued. However, depression is itself a complex phenomenon, and there are probably multiple forms. Abramson, Metalsky, and Alloy (1988) have proposed a specific subtype of depression—hopelessness depression—for which the attributional model holds. Hammen (1985) has also concluded that there is little support for the idea that depressive cognitions or depressive cognitive styles precede the development of depressive states. Instead, depressive cognitions seem to develop along with depressive states. Thus, while depressive cognitions may serve to maintain a depression, it has yet to be proved that depressive cognitions cause depression.

Further, cognitive theories have tended to suppose that depressives distort reality in a negative direction. Several studies have found that depressives do indeed focus on the negative more so than do nondepressives. However, research has shown that it is nondepressed "normals" who often distort reality (Taylor & Brown, 1988). Normals tend to believe they have more control over their fates than they really do, while depressives are more realistic in their assessments. Normals also see themselves more positively than others see them, while depressives are once again more realistic in their assessments. In other words, while depressives may be more negative, they may also be more realistic! In general, it appears that the processing of all individuals, not just depressives, is biased by their schemas (Dykman & Abramson, 1990).

Another difficulty is that the hypothesis that cognitions cause emotions may not be entirely true. While cognitions can cause emotions, there is some evidence that emotions can cause cognitions (Bower, 1981). Some findings suggest that depressive mood, for instance, can reduce the number of positive memories that an individual can recover. Overall, it is now believed that cognition and emotion reciprocally influence one another (Brewin, 1988).

None of this means that cognition plays no role in the development of depression. However, neither the depressed, distorted cognitions of Beck and Ellis nor the negative attributions of Seligman may be associated with the development of depression. Instead, Hammen (1985) mentions that depression may be associated with people's perceptions of whether they can cope with a negative situation (Bandura's self-efficacy, for example). In addition, depression may be associated with what are called "self-schemas" (Markus, 1980). Hammen mentions some evidence suggesting that people with dependent self-schemas (those who define themselves in terms of their dependency on others) are likely to become depressed when they suffer a negative interpersonal event, but not when they suffer a negative achievement event. Individuals with self-critical self-schemas (those who define themselves in terms of how successful they are) are likely to become depressed when they suffer a negative experience related to achievement. Beck's (1987) work takes such differences into account.

One of the most important criticisms of cognitive approaches has been made by Sampson (1981). Basically, Sampson argues that cognitive approaches try to adjust the individual to fit in with social reality. The cognitive approach assumes that a client's problems are, so to speak, all in his head. If an individual is depressed, it is because he is distorting or engaging in musturbatory thinking. The possibility that his situation is objectively depressing is not taken seriously. Thus, cognitive therapists have little to say about unjust or oppressive social conditions that may cause abnormal behavior. The client needs to adjust his cognitions, and then everything will be fine.

The dangers in this seem obvious. If all of people's problems lie in how they conceive of events, then all that is necessary is for them to think differently about things. Should people change their cognitions in such a way that they will be happy? If a man is a guard in a Nazi concentration camp, feeling guilty every time he puts another person into the oven, can he change his cognitions in such a way that he not only no longer feels guilty, but finds his work interesting and enjoyable? This is an extreme example, but the point should not be dismissed because of that. Perhaps depression, for instance, is a legitimate reaction to certain situations. Neither Beck nor Ellis appear to grant this as a possibility. A lower-class African American woman with few job skills, trying to support a family by herself, has reason to become depressed. The belief that she might never get out from under racism and poverty may not be distorting. The belief that she needs more money, not just that she would prefer to have more money, is not a distortion, either. The point is that cognitive approaches, in assuming that everything is in how people construct reality, leave no basis for making judgments. If "there is nothing good nor bad but thinking makes it so," why shouldn't we only think what will make us happy? How can we decide?

We would particularly like to discuss this and related difficulties in regard to Ellis's rational-emotive therapy. Ellis believes it is more rational to say, "I prefer to be a success" than it is to say "I must be a success." We agree that the former is certainly a statement that makes life more easily lived than the latter. But is it more "rational"? We would argue that this is not true. We believe that Ellis is proposing a value system. As a value system, it is neither rational nor irrational (at least in the strict sense of these words). To say "I must be a success" is to make a value statement. To say "I prefer to be a success" is to make a different value statement. It may well be that in most instances, values stated in terms of preference lead to a more flexible, adaptive way of living than values stated in terms of musts and shoulds. But they are not more rational. For instance, we can think of a number of must statements that do not strike us as so "irrational": "I can't stand what Hitler did to the Jews," "I can't stand racial prejudice," "I will not tolerate child abuse," "People must not enslave other people." Stating these as preferences does not capture the absolute, strong nature of the value: "I would have preferred it if Hitler hadn't murdered 6 million Jews," "I would prefer it if you didn't sexually abuse your child." Ellis (1981) has recently claimed, in answer to a similiar criticism by Meehl (1981), that he is not opposed to all shoulds, only to those associated with neurotic beliefs. But this seems to beg the question. What is a neurotic belief? It seems to us that it is a belief that Ellis has previously defined in terms of its musturbatory quality.

Ellis, along with many others, attacks **shouldism.** Humanistic therapies are also often interpreted as being "anti-should." Ellis says that shoulds are not found in nature. Nature just "is," therefore shoulds are irrational. The implication seems to be that the healthy person lives in accord with reality and does not demand anything of it. This is supported by the contention that the neurotic is someone who demands that the world be fair, when in fact, it is neither fair nor unfair. But "should" we do away with shoulds? It seems to us that one of the qualities of being human is the ability to stand outside of one's life situation and imagine it otherwise. The concept of should is a kind of imperative to correct "real life" to our image of what might or could be. Involved in our image of what might be are our concepts of justice and right and wrong. Thus, we can look at children and say they should not be subjected to sexual abuse. To do away entirely with shoulds would be to accept whatever is, but we can certainly wonder if that is desirable.

Thus, it is not clear that shoulds are bad in and of themselves. Rather it may be how we apply shoulds that is the issue. Are they used and applied rigidly? Or do we think through whether a should is helping us meet our goals in a particular situation? Wessler (1990) goes so far as to suggest that guilt is not necessarily bad. We ought to feel guilty if we do something to violate our own standards. The issue is to (a) live up to our standards if they are reasonable and (b) evaluate and change our standards if they are not.

Ultimately, many of the criticisms of cognitive therapy can be subsumed under a general philosophical critique of the idea that one can say whether or not certain ideas are "true" or "false," rational or irrational, as if there were simple, objective ways of deciding such things. Kruglanski & Jaffe (1988), for instance, have pointed out that a person's beliefs are ultimately incapable of being proved true or false. They conclude that "no belief is inherently dysfunctional; it is dysfunctional only to the extent that it represents an unattainable goal" (p. 281). They also point out that many of the things Beck considers "cognitive errors" cannot truly be considered errors. For instance, they note that whenever we form any abstraction, we are being "selective." Therefore, there is no such thing as selective abstraction as a cognitive error in contrast to other kinds of presumably less erroneous forms of abstraction.

In sum, there are some difficulties with cognitive theory in its belief that certain kinds of beliefs can be said to be either rational or irrational. Perhaps, as several psychologists have pointed out, more important is the rigidity with which the belief is held, its unattainability, and how it is used by the person. As an example of this, Norem (1989) has found that "defensive pessimism" can be functional for college students. Defensive pessimists are those who catastrophize as they prepare to study for an exam, presuming that they are going to fail, and so on. Yet they use this catastrophizing to motivate themselves to study, and generally do quite well. This is different than the kind of pessimistic thinking that leads to feelings of hopelessness and paralyzes effort. In sum, even pessimism is not inherently dysfunctional.

A final criticism of cognitive therapies is that they treat psychological problems like "noise in the system" to be eliminated. A person's dysfunctional thinking is merely dysfunctional thinking to be corrected and "cognitively restructured." A person holding a very strong "should" is simply thinking irrationally and must learn not to think in terms of shoulds. A person experiencing panic or generalized anxiety is merely overattending to and misinterpreting bodily cues. What these accounts leave out is the possible functional significance of dysfunctional cognitions, shoulds, and misinterpretations. For instance, a person experiencing generalized anxiety may be overattending to bodily cues because he is feeling very vulnerable as he struggles with a difficult life choice concerning his career (Chapter 9) or because she has had a childhood that makes her feel highly vulnerable about herself (Chapter 7). A person may be thinking dysfunctionally because he is trying to be honest with himself and make himself face up to what may be the bleak reality of life (e.g., "I'll never have a good relationship"). A person may have difficulty letting go of a should because it represents a deeply held personal value for her. In our experience, there are clients who do not want to simply get over their worry by learning to relax in the presence of bodily cues. Rather, they prefer to explore what the anxiety means to them. Such a concept is not taken into account in cognitive theories.

IN CONCLUSION

Cognitive therapies and theories will continue to exert a large amount of influence in the twenty-first century. They have provided therapists with powerful, effective, and fast-acting methodologies. Their constructs are much more easily understood by people without professional training than the rather esoteric concepts of psychoanalysis and humanistic approaches. This means that the therapist is able to explain the therapeutic approach and goals to the client more thoroughly and quickly. Cognitive therapies, like the behavioral approaches, have the virtue of being systematic, planned, and structured, but they are more flexible than the behavioral approaches. In this respect, they may provide one of the most fruitful grounds for future integration of all therapies. Both Beck and Ellis are eclectic in their use of techniques in therapy. In addition, theorists such as Meichenbaum are providing theoretical models that may help integrate the contributions of many approaches. In sum, cognitive therapies will continue to be "major players" on the psychotherapy stage for years to come. Further cognitive ideas, such as that of the "schema," are now used by therapists of many persuasions, including psychodynamic and humanistic. It is possible that a cognitive "language" for talking about therapy will become the dominant theoretical language for the field.

BIBLIOGRAPHY

Abramson, L. Y., Seligman, M. E. P., & Teasdale, J. D. (1978). Learned helplessness in humans: Critique and reformulation. *Journal of Abnormal Psychology, 87,* 49–74.

Abramson, L. Y., Metalsky, G. I., & Alloy, L. B. (1988). The hopelessness theory of depression: Does the research test the theory? In L. Y. Abramson (Ed.), *Social cognition and clinical psychology: A synthesis* (pp. 33–65). New York: Guilford.

Alford, B. A., & Norcross, J. C. (1991). Cognitive therapy as integrative therapy. *Journal of Psychotherapy Integration, 1,* 175–190.

Bandura, A. (1977a). *Social learning theory.* Englewood Cliffs, NJ: Prentice-Hall.

Bandura, A. (1977b). Self-efficacy: Toward a unifying theory of behavioral change. *Psychological Review, 84,* 191–215.

Bandura, A. (1986). *Social foundations of thought and action: A social cognitive theory.* Englewood Cliffs, NJ: Prentice-Hall.

Bandura, A. (1996). *Self-efficacy: The exercise of control.* New York: W. H. Freeman.

Bandura, A., & Walters, R. H. (1959). *Adolescent aggression.* New York: Ronald.

Barlow, D. H. (1988). *Anxiety and its disorders.* New York: Guilford.

Beck, A. T. (1987). Cognitive therapy. In J. Zeig (Ed.), *The evolution of psychotherapy* (pp. 149–163). New York: Brunner/Mazel.

Beck, A. T. (1995). Cognitive therapy: Past, present, and future. In M. J. Mahoney (Ed.), *Cognitive and constructive psychotherapies* (pp. 29–40). New York: Springer.

Beck, A. T., Emery, G., & Greenberg, R. L. (1985). *Anxiety disorders and phobias: A cognitive perspective.* New York: Basic Books.

Beck, A. T., Freeman, A., & Associates. (1990). *Cognitive therapy of personality disorders.* New York: Guilford.

Beck, A. T., Rush, A. J., Shaw, B. F., & Emery, G. (1979). *Cognitive therapy of depression.* New York: Guilford.

Borkovec, T. D., & Costello, E. (1993). Efficacy of applied relaxation and cognitive-behavioral therapy in the treatment of generalized anxiety disorder. *Journal of Consulting and Clinical Psychology, 61*, 611–619.

Bower, G. H. (1981). Emotional mood and memory. *American Psychologist, 36*, 129–148.

Brewin, C. R. (1988). *Cognitive foundations of clinical psychology.* Hillsdale, NJ: Erlbaum.

Brodt, S. E., & Zimbardo, P. G. (1981). Modifying shyness-related social behavior through symptom misattribution. *Journal of Personality and Social Psychology, 41*, 437–449.

Buss, A. H. (1980). *Self-consciousness and social anxiety.* San Francisco: Freeman.

Chambless, D. L., Sanderson, W. C., Shoham, V., Johnson, S. B., Pope, K. S., Crits-Christoph, P., Baker, M., Johnson, B., Woody, S. R., Sue, S., Beutler, L., Williams, D. A., & McCurry, S. (1996). An update on empirically validated therapies. *The Clinical Psychologist, 49*, 5–18.

Dulany, D. E. (1968). Awareness, rules, and propositional control: A confrontation with S-R behavior theory. In T. R. Dixon & D. L. Horton (Eds.), *Verbal behavior and general behavior theory.* Englewood Cliffs, NJ: Erlbaum.

Dykman, B. M., & Abramson, L. Y. (1990). Contributions of basic research to cognitive theories of depression. *Personality and Social Psychology Bulletin, 16*, 23–41.

Elkin, I., Shea, M. T., Watkins, J. T., Imber, S. D., Sotsky, S. M., Collins, J. F., Glass, D. R., Pilkonis, P. A., Leber, W. R., Docherty, J. P., Fiester, S. J., & Parloff, M. B. (1989). National Institute of Mental Health Treatment of Depression Collaborative Research Program: General effectiveness of treatments. *Archives of General Psychiatry, 46*, 971–983.

Ellis, A. (1973). Rational-emotive therapy. In R. Corsini (Ed.), *Current psychotherapies.* Itasca, IL: Peacock.

Ellis, A. (1979a). The practice of rational-emotive therapy. In A. Ellis & J. M. Whiteley (Eds.), *Theoretical and empirical foundations of rational-emotive therapy.* Monterey, CA: Brooks/Cole.

Ellis, A. (1979b). Rational-emotive therapy as a new theory of personality and therapy. In A. Ellis & J. M. Whiteley (Eds.), *Theoretical and empirical foundations of rational-emotive therapy.* Monterey, CA: Brooks/Cole.

Ellis, A. (1979c). Toward a new theory of personality. In A. Ellis & J. M. Whiteley (Eds.), *Theoretical and empirical foundations of rational-emotive therapy.* Monterey, CA: Brooks/Cole.

Ellis, A. (1979d). The theory of rational-emotive therapy. In A. Ellis & J. M. Whiteley (Eds.), *Theoretical and empirical foundations of rational-emotive therapy.* Monterey, CA: Brooks/Cole.

Ellis, A. (1981). Is RET ethically untenable or inconsistent? A reply to Paul E. Meehl. *Rational Living, 16*, 11, 38–42.

Ellis, A. (1984). Rational-emotive therapy. In R. Corsini (Ed.), *Current psychotherapies* (3rd ed.). Itasca, IL: Peacock.

Feixas, G. (1990). Personal construct theory and systemic therapies: Parallel or convergent trends? *Journal of Marital and Family Therapy, 16*, 1–20.

Försterling, F. (1985). Attributional retraining: A review. *Psychological Bulletin, 98*, 495–512.

Goldstein, A. P., Gershaw, N. J., & Sprafkin, R. P. (1984). Structured learning therapy: Background, procedures, and evaluation. In D. Larson (Ed.), *Teaching psychological skills: Models for giving psychology away.* Monterey, CA: Brooks/Cole.

Hammen, C. L. (1985). Predicting depression: A cognitive-behavioral perspective. *Advances in cognitive-behavioral research and therapy* (Vol. 4). New York: Academic Press.

Hazleton, L. (1984). *The right to feel bad.* New York: Ballantine.

Hollon, S. D., & Beck, A. T. (1994). Cognitive and cognitive-behavioral therapies. In A. E. Bergin & S. L. Garfield (Eds.), *Handbook and psychotherapy and behavior change* (pp. 428–466). New York: Wiley.

Hollon, S. D., & Garber, J. (1990). Cognitive therapy for depression: A social cognitive perspective. *Personality and Social Psychology Bulletin, 16,* 58–73.

Jones, E. E., Kanouse, D. E., Kelley, H. H., Nisbett, R. E., Valins, S., & Weiner, B. (Eds.). (1972). *Attribution: Perceiving the causes of behavior.* Morristown, NJ: General Learning Press.

Kelly, G. A. (1955). *The psychology of personal constructs: A theory of personality* (2 vols.). New York: Norton.

Kruglanski, A. W., & Jaffe, Y. (1988). Curing by knowing: The epistemic approach to cognitive therapy. In L. Y. Abramson (Ed.), *Social cognition and clinical psychology: A synthesis* (pp. 254–294). New York: Guilford.

Lyons, L. C., & Woods, P. J. (1991). The efficacy of rational-emotive therapy: A quantitative review of the outcome research. *Clinical Psychology Review, 11,* 357–369.

Markus, H. (1980). The self in thought and memory. In D. M. Wegner & R. R. Vallacher (Eds.), *The self in social psychology.* New York: Oxford University Press.

Maultsby, M. C. (1975). *Help yourself to happiness.* New York: Institute for Rational-Emotive Therapy.

Meehl, P. E. (1981). Ethical criticism in value clarification: Correcting cognitive errors within the client's—not the therapist's—framework. *Rational Living, 16,* 3–9.

Meichenbaum, D. (1974). *Cognitive behavior modification.* Morristown, NJ: General Learning Press.

Meichenbaum, D. (1975). Enhancing creativity by modifying what subjects say to themselves. *American Educational Research Journal, 12,* 129–145.

Meichenbaum. D. (1977). *Cognitive behavior modification: An integrative approach.* New York: Plenum.

Meichenbaum, D. (1986). Cognitive behavior modification. In E. L. Shostrom (Producer), *Three approaches to psychotherapy: III* (film). Corona Del Mar, CA: Psychological and Educational Films.

Meichenbaum, D. (1995). Changing conceptions of cognitive behavior modification: Retrospect and prospect. In M. J. Mahoney (Ed.), *Cognitive and constructive psychotherapies* (pp. 20–26). New York: Springer.

Meichenbaum, D., & Gilmore, J. B. (1984). The nature of unconscious processes: A cognitive-behavioral perspective. In K. S. Bowers & D. Meichenbaum (Eds.), *The unconscious reconsidered* (pp. 273–298). New York: Wiley.

Meichenbaum, D., & Goodman, S. (1971). Training impulsive children to talk to themselves: A means of developing self-control. *Journal of Abnormal Psychology, 77,* 115–126.

Millon, T. (1981). *Disorders of personality.* New York: Wiley.

Moser, D. (1965, May 7). Screams, slaps, and love. *Life,* pp. 90a–101.

Neimeyer, R. A. (1988). Integrative directions in personal construct therapy. *International Journal of Personal Construct Psychology, 1,* 283–298.

Nisbett, R. E., & Ross, L. (1980). *Human inference: Strategies and shortcomings of social judgment.* Englewood Cliffs, NJ: Prentice-Hall.

Norem, J. K. (1989). Cognitive strategies as personality: Effectiveness, specificity, flexibility, and change. In D. M. Buss & N. Cantor (Eds.), *Personality psychology: Recent trends and emerging directions* (pp. 45–60). New York: Springer-Verlag.

Paul, G. L. (1981). Social competence and the institutionalized mental patient. In J. D. Wine & M. D. Smye (Eds.), *Social competence* (pp. 232–260). New York: Guilford.

Sampson, E. E. (1981). Cognitive psychology as ideology. *American Psychologist, 36,* 730–743.

Safran, J. D., & Greenberg, L. S. (1982). Eliciting "hot cognitions" in cognitive therapy. *Canadian Psychology, 23,* 83–87.

Safran, J. D., & Segal, Z. V. (1990). *Interpersonal process in cognitive therapy.* New York: Basic Books.

Seligman, M. E. P. (1990). *Learned optimism.* New York: Knopf.

Smith, M. L., Glass, G. V., & Miller, T. I. (1980). *The benefits of psychotherapy.* Baltimore, MD: Johns Hopkins University Press.

Taylor, S. E., & Brown, J. D. (1988). Illusion and well-being: A social-psychological perspective on mental health. *Psychological Bulletin, 103,* 193–210.

Valins, S., & Nisbett, R. E. (1972). Attribution processes in the development and treatment of emotional disorders. In E. E. Jones, D. E. Kanouse, H. H. Kelley, R. E. Nisbett, S. Valins, & B. Weiner (Eds.), *Attribution: Perceiving the causes of behavior.* Morristown, NJ: General Learning Press.

Weiner, B. (1982). The emotional consequences of causal attributions. In M. S. Clark & S. T. Fiske (Eds.), *Affect and cognition: The Seventeenth Annual Carnegie Symposium on Cognition.* Hillsdale, NJ: Erlbaum.

Weiner, B., Frieze, I., Kukla, A., Reed, L., Rest, S., & Rosenbaum, R. M. (1972). Perceiving the causes of success and failure. In E. E. Jones, D. E. Kanouse, H. H. Kelley, R. E. Nisbett, S. Valins, & B. Weiner (Eds.), *Attribution: Perceiving the causes of behavior.* Morristown, NJ: General Learning Press.

Wessler, R. I. (1990, July). [Untitled Presentation]. Workshop on "Working with the Internal Critic: A Therapeutic Commonality," presented at the Conference of the Society for the Exploration of Psychotherapy Integration, London.

Wine, J. D., & Smye, M. D. (1981). *Social competence.* New York: Guilford.

PART **SIX**

Relational Approaches

CHAPTER
13

Group Approaches to Treatment

[Group therapy is] a psychosocial process wherein a specially trained professional . . . utilizes the emotional interaction in small, carefully constructed groups to effect amelioration of personality dysfunctions in individuals. (Scheidlinger, 1984, p. 3)

Human beings live in groups. All individuals participate daily in numerous small and large groups, from families and friends, cliques and clubs, to work groups and political organizations. A great deal of research demonstrates the power of a group of people to influence the behavior of any one individual. These group forces may be used to bring about therapeutic behavior and personality changes in individuals.

GROUP THERAPY

Group therapy is used extensively in the United States, and there is some indication that it may be the most important method of providing mental health care in the future (Dies, 1992).

Some of the advantages of group therapy are that it is time- and cost-effective compared to individual therapy. More individuals can be seen and can receive treatment. Second, groups provide a context for interpersonal learning. Since most individuals' problems involve interpersonal relationships, at least to some degree, individuals can directly experience these problems in the presence of others in a group, and therefore have an "alive" context within which to work them out. Group experiences are more likely to approximate the day-to-day reality of clients than individual therapy (Dies, 1992). This is especially true for children and adolescents. Groups, therefore, provide greater opportunities for interpersonal interaction and experimentation, as well as for feedback. In that sense, they offer opportunities for learning that either may not exist, or may exist to a lesser extent, in individual therapy. For some clients, groups may be the treatment of choice instead of individual therapy. Below, we shall consider how different therapeutic approaches utilize groups, some of the processes that occur in groups, and how groups are used with different populations and different problems. Finally, we shall consider the self-help group movement and its implications for the treatment of mental health problems in the future.

Forms of Group Therapy Based on Individual Approaches

Almost every form of individual psychotherapy has its parallel group approach. The aim of the therapy is the same in both. Since both assume that the cause of psychopathology is to be found within the individual, treatment focuses on changing something within the individual's personality. The difference is that treatment is done in groups. However, even these groups focus on interactions in the group to achieve these aims (Yalom, 1985).

Psychoanalytic Groups   Group psychotherapy as we know it today actually began in the psychoanalytic tradition. Group analysis was seen as a way to treat greater numbers of patients. Some consider only psychoanalytic groups to be real group psychotherapy, categorizing all other types as merely "therapeutic groups," that is, groups "oriented toward providing emotional support, developing self-esteem and social skills" (Scheidlinger, 1984).

Group analysis may be combined with individual analysis for some patients. Since the disturbance in the individual's internal functioning leads to difficulties relating to others, analysis in groups may foster more or faster insights. Psychoanalysts assume that groups develop a transference relationship with the therapist and a sibling transference with group members. The therapist interprets both transference relationships. Patients free-associate to each other and report dreams, and both therapist and group members interpret the dreams and the resistances. Group members reinforce the analyst's interpretations of individuals by agreeing with the interpretation and citing examples of it from the group's interactions.

Wolf and Kutash (1986) note the power of the group setting for bringing early childhood issues alive in the present. The group symbolically becomes each individual patient's "family" psychologically, and transference relationships get played out with vivid emotional intensity. For instance, one group member may begin to feel jealous of the attention the therapist is giving another group member, and that may vividly evoke childhood experiences of having been the unfavored child. Thus, insight is attained in an emotionally "alive" context.

Structure   Psychoanalytic groups are relatively unstructured in that the therapist does not suggest exercises for the group to engage in. Nor does the therapist set specific goals for the group members to attain, as in other groups we discuss later. While there are structured activities, such as dream analysis and analysis of transferential relationships in the group, these are dealt with by the therapist as they emerge in the process of the group's interaction.

Role of Therapist or Leader   In psychoanalytic groups, the role of the therapist is similar to the role played in psychoanalytic therapy. The therapist's role is primarily to offer interpretations and to confront resistance. The leader rarely self-discloses and tends to maintain a "professional" stance. An important task of the leader is to make sure that the group does not evolve to become a "dysfunctional family," and the leader must immediately confront and interpret any tendencies in that direction.

Tavistock Psychoanalytic Groups   The Tavistock Institute in London, England, founded by Freud's daughter, Anna, is an internationally recognized training center for psychoanalytic therapy. Analysts there developed the first theory and methods for psychoanalytic group therapy, and they continue to develop and train therapists in innovative group formats. Tavistock groups range from the traditional small group of six to ten people meeting weekly with one or two analysts to large groups of 50 to 100 people meeting with two to six or more analysts for weekly sessions, intensive weekends, or two- or four-week workshops. With these very large groups, the analysts also meet with smaller subgroups for developing issues to bring to the entire group. At the risk of simplifying the analytic rationale for the Tavistock group method, it can be said that the emphasis in all Tavistock groups, regardless of size or format, is on group interpretations. While the analysts leading these groups occasionally make individual interpretations and process comments, the leaders are supposed to intervene as little as possible, so that the group must learn to rely on its own resources, and to make only group interpretations. The group therapists point out group behavior and how individual behavior is part of group behavior, and they interpret this group behavior as reflecting group transference, group resistance, group defensiveness, unconscious group emotions, group wishes to depose the leaders, and the like. Disagreements within the group may be interpreted as transferred sibling conflict, as splitting, as aspects of group ambivalence, or as reflecting internal conflict or different parts of conscious or unconscious functioning. It is argued that the Tavistock group method can bring the benefits of genuine psychoanalysis to large numbers of people.

Client-Centered Therapy   The goal of a client-centered group is to provide a warm, supportive, and empathic emotional context within which individuals can explore their relationships with themselves and with each other. A greater emphasis is placed on the process of interpersonal relating in client-centered groups than in psychoanalytic groups. Individuals are thought to learn through the process of opening up to others, confronting each other's misperceptions, and learning to trust themselves in the context of others. For instance, person A may perceive person B as "a bully." Through the process of the two talking to one another (and through the process of other members offering their feedback), these two members directly experience the process of opening up to one another, listening, being misunderstood, struggling with being misunderstood, learning how to communicate better in order to be understood, learning how to communicate in a more open, prizing way, and

Using Group Therapy with Pets.

learning how to solve an interpersonal problem. The client-centered therapist helps this process by tuning in to each party and empathically helping them "say" their personally felt meanings in ways that become more "hearable" both by themselves and by others.

Structure   The client-centered group is relatively unstructured. There is no agenda and exercises are not typically used. Since learning is thought to occur through the process of the group itself, it is important to allow that process to occur naturally, rather than trying to "force" it through structured exercises. Through the process of communicating within a "safe" group climate, members gradually struggle with themselves and come to tune in to their feelings.

Role of Therapist or Leader   The therapist is not a leader in a traditional sense and may initially start the group off (and provide a little bit of structure) by making a few general comments about what she hopes will happen in the group. After that, however, the therapist operates primarily by example. That is, the therapist tries to empathically understand each group member and tries to effectively be genuine herself. The therapist tries to relate as an equal in the group, self-disclosing and sharing her own feelings and reactions, but always trying to do so in a facilitative, effectively communicative way. Client-centered therapists believe there is a "wisdom of the group" just as there is a wisdom of each individual. Therefore, client-centered groups are democratic in that members may suggest exercises or activities for the group to do, and the process of decision on the direction the group takes is democratic. However, the leader's main task is to provide the therapeutic conditions of warmth, empathy, and genuineness. The leader hopes that by modeling these conditions through her activity, she can help group members learn to respond to one another with the same therapeutic conditions.

Gestalt Groups   As run by Fritz Perls, gestalt groups could not be said to be "proper groups" at all. Perls's groups did not really work with the interaction between members of the group. Perls's primary method was to work with individuals—only in a group format. Perls would have an individual come up and sit on the "hot seat" and work in front of the group. The rest of the group functioned as a kind of Greek chorus and Perls utilized them as a part of working with that individual. For instance, if a person felt like all others in the group were critical of him, Perls might have that person go around the group and stare at each individual member. This exercise of staring at others would have the goal of the person "taking back" his own ability to make judgments himself.

More recently, other gestalt therapists have begun to stress the interaction among group members more so than did Perls. The goal of a gestalt group is to help individuals be fully present in the moment; to be able to make full, open contact with the self and with others; and to take responsibility for themselves. How a person is presently feeling is stressed as that person interacts with others. A gestalt group could therefore be seen as a "learning laboratory" in that people learn to be fully aware of their own experience *as they live it* in interaction with others in the group.

Structure   Gestalt groups are unstructured in that gestalt leaders do not come in with preset formats or agendas for how the group should operate. However, gestalt therapists often utilize structured exercises to facilitate the learning-exploration process. These exercises are introduced spontaneously by the gestalt therapist in a given moment. For instance, during an interaction, a person may be asked to track her nonverbal body language and what it might be expressing. Or she may be asked to rephrase what she is saying from "I can't" to "I won't" to see if she can get a feel for how she is blocking herself from doing or saying something.

Role of Therapist or Leader   Gestalt therapists tend to be relatively active in groups, compared to both psychoanalytic and client-centered leaders. They are more likely to actively structure interactions, create experiments, or interrupt interactions that are taking place if they feel that doing so will lead to learning and awareness. Similar to client-centered therapists, gestalt therapists will attempt to "be real" themselves in the group and will self-disclose their own reactions, though they try to self-disclose in ways that are therapeutic and communicative.

Existential Groups   The goal of existential groups, as with individual existential therapy, is to help individuals become more authentic, and to realize their own implicit potential, which they have been blocking by playing roles and following rules and shoulds they have acquired from parents and society. In order to do this, the focus in an existential group is on here-and-now interactions. Insight is acquired in terms of how a person is presently relating. "How am I blocking myself from being more fully authentic with you right now?" would be an issue explored in an existential group. Past issues and issues with individuals outside the group are dealt with by "bringing them into" the group. For instance, if a member is having problems with her husband, she will be asked if she is experiencing any similar problematic feelings toward any member of the group, and those feelings will be worked with in the here and now.

Structure   Existential therapists could practice in any number of ways. Some might be relatively more client-centered in their approach; others might be more active, as a gestalt therapist would. There is no typical existential group structure, except that problems are dealt with by bringing them into the here and now. However, like client-centered and gestalt therapists, existential therapists do not enter the session with a specific agenda, as might a behavior therapist.

Role of Therapist or Leader   Once again, existential therapists might function more like client-centered or gestalt leaders. That is, the therapist might be more active in structuring interaction and encounters or simply function more as a member of the group. In general, existential therapists are willing to self-disclose their own reactions, as are client-centered and gestalt therapists.

Behavioral Groups   The goal of behavior therapy conducted in groups is the learning of new skills and the unlearning of old, dysfunctional behavior. Behavioral techniques such as exposure methods, skills training, parent training, stress innoculation, and coping can all be utilized in group formats.

Structure   A behavioral group is likely to be highly structured. For instance, groups are often formed specifically for the purpose of teaching assertion skills, and the leader will have a format of exercises that the group will engage in in order to learn those skills. A group of agoraphobics will practice relaxation together and may engage in group desensitization, where they imagine slowly and gradually confronting their fears of going out into open spaces.

Behavioral groups do not ignore group interaction or feelings (Rose, 1989). However, members are likely to be coached in the communications skills necessary for effective interpersonal relating.

Role of Therapist or Leader   The therapist's role is more like that of a teacher in a behavioral group. The therapist provides structured activities for learning, conducts discussions to foster that learning, gives feedback, may engage in role playing, gives lectures and demonstrations, and so on. In general, the behavior therapist would be unlikely to emphasize the sharing of his own personal feelings or reactions as a way of "being authentic or genuine" in the therapeutic interaction, as might an existential, gestalt, or client-centered therapist. However, the behavior therapist might share feelings and reactions in order to model how clients can effectively self-disclose using "I" statements.

Cognitive Groups   Cognitive groups typically include the use of behavioral techniques as well. However, they focus on confronting and dealing with clients' dysfunctional cognitions. Cognitive therapists give homework assignments and then explore clients' reactions to those homework assignments in terms of their dysfunctional cognitions. For instance, a client may have an assignment to practice assertion skills. Perhaps the client's attempt at being assertive was not successful, and he returns to the group saying "I'll never be able to do this." At that point, the group can help the client confront his own dysfunctional cognitions. Dysfunctional cognitions also spontaneously arise in group interactions.

Structure   Cognitive groups are typically structured to pursue specific goals for specific clients. The approach is flexible, but businesslike. Often, individual clients are encouraged to set goals for themselves, and structured exercises are utilized to help them achieve those goals. These exercises can include assertion training and training in other coping skills, structured homework assignments in which clients confront their fears or try out new skills in everyday life. Clients may also be given structured homework assignments to practice confronting their dysfunctional cognitions. In the group itself, clients learn to confront their own and their fellow group members' dysfunctional cognitions.

Role of Therapist or Leader   As with behavior therapy, the cognitive therapist's role in a group is more like that of a teacher or a coach. The therapist models the skills of challenging dysfunctional thinking, facilitates individuals' confronting their own dysfunctional thinking, and encourages other members of the group to learn how to challenge dysfunctional thinking. The therapist may also have guest speakers come in, assign homework, or provide structured exercises.

Group-Based Forms of Group Therapy

Some forms of group therapy began in the group format and developed somewhat separately from those based on the individual therapy approaches.

Psychodrama   **Psychodrama** was developed by J. L. Moreno (1934), and it stresses insight and catharsis through the acting process. Clients act out scenes of conflict from their childhood or present life. Group members help each other by acting the necessary parts in an individual's scene. If a depressed client has had trouble with his mother, another member of the group plays his mother. Coaches or "alter egos" stand behind the actors and suggest what to say and do. The members may switch roles, or the alter egos may play out a scene. As in gestalt, the client may be asked to play the role of the person with whom he had the conflict. However, in contrast to gestalt, the client's role would often then be taken by another group member. This way, the client can gain insight into how she appears to others.

Structure   Psychodrama is highly structured. In the warm-up phase before the actual psychodrama, clients talk about any problems that have been bothering them recently, and it is often from this discussion that a client is selected to work on his or her problem. Then that client is placed in a structured situation, such as having a dialogue with the person or persons involved. Other members of the group are utilized to either play the other roles, such as other members of the client's family, or to play alter egos. The therapist directs the encounter, pausing it at various times to restructure the interaction to highlight and explore certain issues. For instance, if the client is having trouble expressing herself to her mother, another member of the group may be used as an alter ego to stand behind the client and speak for her.

After the psychodrama, the reactions of other members of the group are solicited, particularly those who resonate with the experience of the client who was the focus of the psychodrama.

Role of Therapist or Leader The therapist plays the role of "director." He structures the action, assigns roles, and decides at various points if other members of the group are to be called in to play new roles. In this sense, the leader is highly active and directive.

Transactional Analysis Eric Berne (1964, 1966) developed **transactional analysis (TA)** in the 1950s. As the name implies, this form of therapy has a strong interpersonal basis. Although it is now also used with individual clients, it is most frequently done in group settings. TA analyzes the transactions between people rather than the inner conflicts of the individual. While social in emphasis, it takes from psychoanalysis the ideas of a tripartite division of the personality and the importance of early experience in forming the personality. The therapist interprets the client's way of interacting with other people in order to clarify these early experiences and the effect they have on current relationships. TA is also instructive; clients are taught how the personality is formed and how relationships work.

Berne named his three "ego-states" or parts of the personality the Child, the Adult, and the Parent. Each ego-state represents conscious and unconscious ways of feeling about and behaving toward others, and each has both positive and negative qualities that are learned in childhood. The Child is similar to the id, and it contains the childish and childlike impulses and ways of behaving. The Child is immature, dependent, demanding, and helpless (childish), but it is also playful, creative, and genuine (childlike). The Adult, similar to the ego, is rational, independent, and responsible, but also unfeeling and perhaps not much fun. The Parent, similar to the superego, can be nurturant, caring, and helpful, but also domineering, guilt inducing, critical, and controlling.

Each ego-state is appropriate to certain types of relationships. For example, it is appropriate for a parent to operate in the Parent ego-state toward a child. Such a way of relating usually works, and the relationship goes fairly smoothly. Problems enter when the ego-state is not appropriate to the relationship. If an individual operates in the Parent ego-state toward his or her spouse, when the Adult is more appropriate, problems arise. The spouse may be induced to behave in the Child ego-state, which may appear to make the relationship work. However, such a relationship will eventually create dissatisfaction, especially if the Child spouse tries to act like an Adult, or if the Parent spouse wants to give up the burdens of that role.

Berne also discussed the concept of **games.** Games are orderly transactions with rules that conceal ulterior motives. They generally serve as a way of avoiding getting close to people. Berne gave descriptive names to the games he observed. For example,

"Yes, But" involves playing helpless and eliciting advice from others, but always having a reason why that advice won't work or can't be done. "Yes, I should be firmer with my kids, but that always makes them angrier." In group therapy, players of "Yes, But" can keep the attention of others for hours without ever having to risk being genuinely vulnerable. Berne (1966) described the rules of several such games and the ways therapists can intervene with game players.

The life script is another TA concept. Berne believed that based on early life experiences, people "unconsciously" write a script for themselves to play all their lives. Abused children see themselves as victims and compose a life script with themselves in the permanent role of victim. Because destructive relationships in which they are victimized fit their script, they may "unconsciously" seek them out. Berne believed that if clients became aware of their scripts and roles, they could rewrite them. He also believed that people's favorite fairy tale from childhood was an indication of their life script.

Structure   While people may play a fairly permanent role in relation to others, most often, they move back and forth among ego-states as they communicate. They may begin a rational conversation as Adult, make a joke as Child, then start an argument as Parent. The other person may respond to the Adult conversation with a flippant Child disagreement, to the Child joke with a Parent criticism, and to the Parent argument with a reasonable Adult answer. Therapists interpret such social transactions for the client, pointing out the ego-state that is operating in each transaction and the effect it has on others. Therapist and client may also role play certain ego-states to analyze their effect on the transaction.

Role of Therapist or Leader   Like the psychoanalyst, the TA therapist interprets how the client behaves toward her, but in terms of the client's transactions in the Child, Adult, and Parent ego-states. Most interpretations are of interactions between group members. In addition to helping clients with relationships, TA tries to increase the client's acceptance of all the internal ego-states so the client can relate more appropriately and flexibly to others. A disowned (unconscious) Child will cause trouble, and the client is taught that it is acceptable and appropriate to be a Child sometimes.

Transactional analysis has found wide application in education and business. It is also used in marriage, family, and group therapy. Its popularity may be due to its vivid, easy-to-understand terminology and its optimistic view of relationships. It gives people a handy frame of reference for dealing with each other. A wife can deal with a critical husband by saying, "That's your Parent talking," which is likely to have a more beneficial effect than many other possible responses, such as anger, whining, or counterattack. TA's nonjudgmental attitude ("I'm OK—you're OK," Harris, 1969) may be one of the factors that makes it popular.

Structured and Time-Limited Groups   As theory and research on group processes has grown into a substantial body of knowledge, group therapists have developed many variations of group therapy. Some therapy groups are very structure, with therapists following planned agendas. Time-limited groups, which are likely to be also structured, focus on specific issues to be covered in a set number of sessions, thus capitalizing on people's tendency to work harder as a deadline approaches. We now turn to an examination of factors common to all groups.

GENERAL FACTORS OF GROUP STRUCTURE AND PROCESS

As among individual therapies, there is little consensus in the group therapy field as to theory and practice. However, group therapies share certain features. Most groups meet once a week, sometimes twice a week in the case of group psychoanalysis. Group sessions tend to be an hour and a half to two hours long. There are 6 to 12 group members, with 8 to 10 generally considered an ideal number. Some group therapists believe a carefully constructed group of equal numbers of men and women with different but complementary problems is best, while others prefer groups composed of people all with the same problem or characteristics. A lot of talking goes on in most group therapies. There may be one or two leaders.

Group Dynamics

The degree to which therapists of different persuasions take group dynamics into account is an important dimension of group therapy practice. Group dynamics have been most extensively studied by social psychologists. Below we briefly discuss some of the major issues of group dynamics and how they can affect the practice of group therapy.

Norms   All groups develop norms. **Norms** are rules about what is and is not acceptable or appropriate behavior in the group. They may also have to do with what is desirable or optimal behavior in groups. A norm common to most therapy groups is that of the need for self-disclosure (Lieberman, Yalom, & Miles, 1973; Yalom, 1985). Other norms may encourage the expression of feelings, being honest, being nondefensive, and so on. Some groups may have norms that encourage a here-and-now focus (such as in gestalt or existential groups). Attempts to talk about one's experience outside of the group or one's childhood experiences will be met with either overt or covert disapproval from the group. Norms typically reflect the theoretical orientation of the therapist running the group. For instance, in a psychoanalytic group, there may be norms concerning reporting dreams and exploring one's here-and-now relationship to therapist and other group members in terms of recollections of one's childhood experiences. In cognitive groups, there will be norms concerning challenging dysfunctional cognitions. Virtually all groups will have norms concerning confidentiality, attendence, and respecting the rights of others. The norms of some groups may encourage high levels of expression of anger, while the norms of other groups may discourage high levels of anger expression and, instead, encourage empathic support.

Norms can be either *explicit* or *implicit*. Explicit norms are usually set by the therapist, though in some groups, such as client-centered groups, the whole group may decide on a norm. Explicit norms may include rules concerning taking responsibility for oneself, attendance, not coming to group on drugs, and so on. Implicit norms are norms that may evolve through the group process itself. For instance, in a group one of the authors was in as a graduate student, there was an implicit norm that one should be comfortable touching others (for example, by giving one another hugs), and anyone who was uncomfortable with such activities was judged as "uptight." This norm was never stated explicitly, yet was clearly present and influenced how group members who did not conform were perceived.

Group norms can either be functional or dysfunctional. Group norms are functional if they provide structure to the group, while being flexible, and if they are explicit so that everyone can be aware of them and their effects. They can be dysfunctional if they are implicit and lead to pressures toward uniformity. We shall talk about pressures toward uniformity below.

Cohesiveness   Cohesiveness has to do with the degree to which members are attracted to or bonded with the group. Cohesiveness also has to do with the degree to which members of the group identify with the group, a "we" feeling. Cohesiveness has been found to be associated with change: Groups that are high in cohesiveness are more likely to produce positive change (Yalom, 1985). Cohesive groups are more likely to be able to provide rewards for "appropriate" behavior from group members, or, put another way, to provide support for them in their efforts to confront their problems and to try out new ways of being and behaving.

Pressures Toward Uniformity and Deviates   Highly cohesive groups will be able to bring more pressures to bear on those who deviate from group norms to conform. This can be positive or negative. For instance, in highly cohesive groups, pressure in the form of positive attention and support may encourage clients to open up and confront their problems. Thus, a highly cohesive group may be able to bring a positive kind of "pressure" to bear on clients who are resistant to confront and explore their problems. Pressure here need not be thought of as something coercive. Rather, the pressure is positive in that it provides rewards through support, interest, and acceptance; conforming to norms such as those of self-disclosure, exploring one's feelings, confronting one's problems, trying out new behaviors; and so on.

However, pressures toward uniformity can also be dangerous, especially if the leader is unaware that such pressures exist, and can create conformity. Some encounter groups during the 1960s and 1970s fell prey to this problem (see Lieberman, Yalom, & Miles, 1973, for some examples). These were often groups led by charismatic leaders who were able to create a kind of "true believer" following among group participants. In these groups, members who did not conform to group norms and standards were "confronted" in critical, hostile ways, and were rejected by the group if they did not conform. We know of colleagues in some gestalt groups in the 1970s who felt there was an implicit norm that "healthy people are those who are able to express a great deal of emotion in an energetic manner." Those who were best able to express strong emotion were treated as the "stars" in the group; those who were not able to were seen as "uptight." Clearly, such implicit group norms, combined with pressures toward uniformity, can create the opposite of a healthy, growthful group climate.

There is some evidence that those who deviate from group norms are at higher risk to be rejected, and, further, at higher risk to be damaged by the group process

(Lieberman, Yalom, & Miles, 1973). In sum, group norms, cohesiveness, and pressures toward uniformity can be used to the benefit of group members, or can be harmful to growth.

Importance of Group Dynamics   Different approaches place more or less emphasis on the importance of group dynamics in the group experience. For instance, in some psychoanalytic groups, there is relatively little emphasis on the dynamics of the here-and-now group itself and how that is influencing members' present behavior. The focus is primarily on helping each individual understand his or her here-and-now reactions in terms of concepts such as the past, transference, and resistance. In Fritz Perls's gestalt groups, there was virtually no attention paid to group dynamics. Other therapists will pay more attention to the dynamics of the group itself and how they influence members' perceptions of one another. For instance, the leader may call attention to how the operation of a norm is influencing members' reactions to a person who is deviating from the norms.

Along with this, some group therapists see the group as a system in its own right, rather than as merely the setting in which they work with individuals. Interactions among the members are used as a particularly potent source of learning, and therapists help the group understand how various forces and pressures in the group itself influence behavior. Yalom (1985), for instance, believes that all problems outside the group, with bosses, spouses, and family, can be dealt with inside the group by focusing on how the group member interacts with other group members.

Curative Factors in Groups

Yalom (1985) has provided a list of "curative factors" that seem to be common to all effective group therapies, despite apparent differences. These include the following:

Imparting information. Group members give each other advice and other information.

Instilling hope. The fact that some group members have learned to deal with their problems gives hope to others.

Universality. Group members learn that they are not alone in thinking and feeling the way they do. They lose their "pluralistic ignorance"—the idea that they are the only person who feels insecure or whatever.

Altruism. Being helpful to other group members increases a person's feeling of confidence, competence, and self-worth.

Interpersonal learning. Group members have an opportunity to interact with others in deep, open, and honest ways.

Corrective recapitulation of the primary family. In the supportive, intimate, emotionally intense "family" of the group, members learn new ways of viewing and relating to their family members and to others.

Catharsis. Expressing emotion helps group members feel better. It also helps develop trust, closeness, and honest communication.

Group cohesiveness. Developing closeness to the group enhances feelings of self-worth through group acceptance.

Development of socializing techniques. Groups provide opportunities for learning social skills.

Imitative behavior. Individuals learn through behaviors modeled by other group members, including the leader.

Existential factors. Individuals recognize that life is sometimes unfair, they have to face the fact of death and of their ultimate aloneness, and they have to take responsibility for themselves. All this can be openly discussed in the group.

Special Uses of Group Therapy

Groups are used for many different kinds of problems, in many different settings. Groups are used extensively in hospitals, clinics, correctional institutions, student counseling centers at universities, and so on. Dies (1992) estimates that millions of people in the United States are in groups each week. Below, we shall consider some of the uses of different forms of group therapy.

Group Therapy with Children   With children, group therapy is most often group *play* therapy. That is not to say that a group of children may not be encouraged to talk. However, children cannot usually sit still talking for long periods of time. Play is used as a structure to "hang" talking, exploring, and learning on. A range of toys and materials is presented, and the children play. Groups are usually small, say, three to five children. Learning is encouraged in the context of play. For instance, children may be encouraged to stage interpersonal encounters with puppets or dolls. This may be used to explore their feelings. The therapist may even ask explicitly "How does that make you feel?" if another person's doll or puppet acts in one way or the other. Thus, play may be used to help the children explore their feelings.

In addition, play may be used to help children learn how to problem solve. The context of an interaction between puppets or dolls may be used to help the children discuss better ways to handle problem situations.

Group therapy has also been used with children who have suffered specific traumatic experiences. For instance, groups have been run for children whose parents are undergoing a divorce (Corey & Corey, 1987). In such groups, children are encouraged to talk about and share their feelings. This allows them to explore their fears ("I'll be all alone and abandoned," "Daddy won't love me anymore"), their guilt (it is not uncommon for a child to feel responsible for the breakup), and practical concerns ("Where am I going to live?"). Dysfunctional beliefs ("I caused the breakup") can be confronted. Children also learn they are not alone in their feelings.

Such groups may also include films to provide information and various kinds of exercises, such as role playing, to help children explore and learn how to problem solve.

Groups with Adolescents   Adolescents are in the somewhat paradoxical position of simultaneously being one of the populations for which group therapy may be the most effective, yet also being one of the populations that presents the most problems in group therapy. The reason for this paradox is that adolescents, especially younger adolescents, are highly sensitive to what others think of them. Developmental psychologists even have a name for this. They call it the adolescent's "imaginary audience" (Elkind, 1978).

This exquisite sensitivity to what others think makes adolescents especially open to feedback and influence from other group members. This is why group therapy can have such a powerful effect on adolescents. At the same time, this exquisite sensitivity to what others think makes it difficult for adolescents to open up and self-disclose. Further, it makes it difficult for adolescents to engage in exercises, such as role playing, where they might worry about appearing "silly." Adolescents who are referred for therapy are often there against their will and are motivated to act in a rebellious manner toward the therapist. This may be exacerbated in a group of adolescents, where no adolescent may want to appear to be a "wimp" who is conforming to what the authority figures want.

Leaders of adolescent groups need to be especially good at providing warmth, empathy, and genuineness (see Chapter 8). Leaders must really demonstrate that they are open to hearing the adolescents' side of things. Leaders do not play the role of the professional who is there to make the adolescent conform. It is important that they form a collaborative relationship with the adolescents, so that the adolescents come to understand that self-disclosure, role playing, and the like are actually in the adolescents' best interests.

At the same time, the group leader must provide structure and set limits so that effective learning can take place. Being warm, empathic, and genuine does not mean that the leader lets "anything go." Nor does it mean that the leader may not provide informative feedback, *as well as* empathizing with the adolescent's point of view. Providing active structure through a set of activities is particularly effective. If everyone has to participate in the structured activity, then the individual adolescent will feel less foolish doing it. Further, having structure takes the burden off adolescents of "having to produce" on their own.

Thus, adolescent groups will often provide structured activities such as helping adolescents think through and form new goals, explore their values, and learn new skills. Learning new skills may be a particularly important activity in an adolescent group. Role playing and practice may be used to help adolescents learn communication skills, dating skills, job interviewing skills, assertion, and "just saying no" skills.

For example, Corey and Corey (1987) cite groups for unwed teenage fathers. These groups provide structured activities in which adolescents learn how to become more self-accepting. In addition, they learn about their legal rights and responsibilities, how to identify options, how to make sound decisions, how to explore and learn about resources available, and more about pregnancy and contraception. Thus, the group includes a multifaceted set of activities designed to help the teenager better cope with life on a variety of fronts.

Groups for Substance Abuse Problems   Group therapy is one of the most important vehicles for working with substance abuse problems. One of the most successful methods for dealing with alcohol, Alcoholics Anonymous, is essentially a large self-help group (we consider self-help groups later). Virtually all treatment programs for substance abuse include group therapy. This is not merely because it is more cost-efficient than working with individuals alone, it is also because of the powerful learning effects in groups. For instance, overcoming denial is more likely to "stick" when done in front of a group of others than when done in front of one other (e.g., the therapist). There is something about publicly admitting one's problems in front of a group that seems to be a particularly important part of the process of coping with a substance abuse problem.

Because substance abuse appears to be a problem in which the impairment of self-awareness is particularly involved, feedback from a group of people is especially useful. Various reasons have been offered for this impairment in self-awareness. Perhaps the most common is that of denial. That is, substance abusers deny the existence of a problem. They will blame circumstances, they will say that they can manage the problem on their own, they will say they can "cut down," and so on. An interesting example of this is a retired older man one of us knows who had a drinking problem. He used to sit in his chair and watch television all day, drinking vodka and orange juice. Now that he is no longer drinking he notes how he "kidded himself" by mixing his vodka with orange juice, arguing to himself that as long as he was drinking it with something healthy like orange juice, it was okay!

Another possible reason for the impairment in self-awareness is the effects of the substance itself. Over time, this may lead to a chronic impairment in cognitive functioning. For instance, this same older man now gets out and exercises during the day, reads, and rarely watches television. As he looks back on sitting in front of the TV day after day he says, "I was in a daze most of the time."

A third possible reason for lack of self-awareness is that when abusers are "high," they are especially unaware of how they are acting. It is for these reasons, among others, that group procedures with alcohol abusers appear to be helpful. For instance, an "intervention" is used to help confront an alcoholic who is refusing treatment. In an intervention, a group of people who are involved in the alcoholic's life are brought together. An expert on alcoholism is enlisted, and the group is coached in how to give feedback to the alcoholic. Often, in a manner not unlike a surprise party, the alcoholic is suddenly confronted with this group, which may consist of his wife, children, boss, friends, and so on. The group gives him concrete feedback on incident after incident in which his drinking has negatively affected their lives. The coaching by the expert is done so that the feedback is given in as loving and nonjudgmental a form as possible. Yet words are not minced in describing the toll taken on the lives of the people involved with the alcoholic. The alcoholic, who may have been only dimly aware of what he had done when drunk, now is made vividly aware. Further, while he may have heard many of these incidents before, he heard about them one at a time. Now he is confronted with an irrefutable pattern of evidence. Often, after such an intervention, the alcoholic is willing to enter a treatment program, and is usually taken there straightaway, before he can begin to work to refute or dismiss the evidence and return to old patterns of denial. The intervention is a particularly good illustration of the power of a group to induce change.

Another advantage of using groups with alcoholics is that it is often easier to see things in *others* before one sees them in oneself. Therefore, the group situation provides a particularly powerful learning environment for the substance abuser. The group will be able to identify patterns of denial and self-evasion in a given patient and provide feedback to that effect. At the same time, as the members notice these patterns in others, a context is prepared in which they can come to notice them in themselves.

Groups for substance abusers have similar goals and procedures to many of the other groups we have discussed. First, the major goal is to become aware of one's problem and to accept its existence. Second, efforts are made to explore the feelings that underlie the problem. Through that, feelings of low self-worth are often accessed, and the group situation is utilized to help abusers come to prize themselves more. In some groups, childhood roots of the problem may be explored and discussed (especially, for instance, experiences of child abuse). Third, such groups help abusers develop and identify more positive values and goals. Fourth, they help substance abusers begin to develop better coping skills. This may include helping them develop good communication skills, better problem-solving skills, and better skills for dealing with their feelings.

One note is warranted on how different groups cope with the issue of denial. It is certainly true that many substance abusers deny the existence of a problem long after it has become painfully obvious to others that a problem exists. Different groups handle denial in different ways, though most handle it by confronting it in one way or another. In some groups, denial is confronted quite brusquely. A person may simply be told "That's denial!" or "You're in denial!" In other groups, confrontation may be given more gently and respectfully, as is often done in interventions with the alcoholic. That is, "I don't believe you are seeing what you are really doing. I think you're avoiding something." Opinion differs on how forcefully a substance abuser must be confronted, with some holding that it must be done quite forcefully and "in your face" in order to break through the denial. On the other hand, there are those that believe that such aggressive confrontation is a violation of the person.

Groups for Eating Disorders   Another set of problems often treated with group therapy are eating disorders, such as **bulimia** and **anorexia nervosa.** These groups engage in many of the procedures utilized in substance abuse groups. First, there is an educational component. Members are given information on diet, eating, and health. Second, various coping skills are taught, such as how to challenge dysfunctional cognitions when one is feeling depressed or lonely, and how to deal with stress. It is believed that knowing how to deal with stress and with depressive feelings will help bulimic clients avoid using food as a way of coping. A third, important aspect is noted by one of our colleagues, Colleen O'Toole, who works with eating disorders. She says the group must help the client "get a life." That is, a major goal of the group is to focus clients on positive, productive activities to make their lives more meaningful. Along with this, there is an attempt to help clients learn to base their self-esteem on things other than their appearance, and links between self-esteem and body image are explored. Family dynamics are also considered, since many believe that eating disorders are associated with problems of separating and differentiating from one's family. Finally, O'Toole notes that it is important to focus clients *away* from talking about food and eating. Many clients in groups for bulimics enjoy telling horrific stories about their "throwing up" experiences, and if the group leader is not careful, the group can become a positive experience in which members mutually reinforce and reward one another by telling and listening to these horrific stories. In fact, if the leader is not careful, such groups sometimes deteriorate into the members "swapping recipes" on *how* to throw up! Instead, it is important to focus members away from food onto things that will help them develop more rewarding ways of living.

OTHER KINDS OF GROUPS

There are many other groups for different purposes. For instance, women's consciousness-raising groups have been very important in helping women break out of oppressive sex role stereotypes and develop more positive, potent, self-affirming identities. Men's consciousness-raising groups have emerged, which are designed to help men explore their identities and find ways to go beyond traditional stereotypes. There have been groups for couples, groups to train individuals in relaxation and assertion, and so on. Below, we consider three other kinds of groups.

Sensitivity Training Groups

Sensitivity training groups or "human relations laboratories" (or "T-groups") originally arose from the work of social psychologist Kurt Lewin in the late 1940s. An organization, the National Training Laboratory, was founded to help develop the T-group approach. Basically, T-groups developed to serve several purposes. However, they were primarily used in business and in government to help clarify and resolve interpersonal problems, facilitate communication, and foster openness and creativity within organizations. T-groups were often organized, for instance, among administrators in a business or among administrators and employees. The members of T-groups were asked to observe and learn about group process through the experience of being in a group. Thus, members would learn about various aspects of group dynamics that might play a role in obstructing effective communication in their work setting. In addition, the group was seen as an important source of interpersonal learning—individuals received feedback on how they interacted and related, with the goal of helping them to relate more effectively. Finally, individuals had the opportunity to experiment with and practice new and more effective ways of communicating. For instance, they might have the opportunity to practice giving negative feedback to another in such a way that it would be heard and utilized, rather than defensively blocked out.

The focus of sensitivity training groups was and is primarily on the here and now. Further, it is primarily on developing interpersonal awareness: How do I present to others? Do I relate effectively? What are some of the group processes and group dynamics that can affect my and others' behavior? Sensitivity training groups are used primarily with people who are not experiencing any particular major psychological problem, and they are not usually thought of as *therapy* groups.

Encounter Groups

The encounter group, or human potential movement, developed in the 1960s, primarily in California, and then spread to the rest of the nation. It was an outgrowth of the sensitivity training movement, but began to incorporate many ideas from the area of psychotherapy. Some leaders believed that such groups could be used for more than increasing interpersonal awareness and interpersonal skills. Individuals often left sensitivity training groups not only having learned about interpersonal skills, but also feeling that they had had an experience of authenticity missing in everyday life.

Encounter groups, therefore, were born as "therapy for normals," that is, they were groups in which anyone could have the opportunity to drop social masks, more deeply explore themselves, and practice relating to others on a more "authentic" basis. They came to be seen as a way of expanding human potential. The hope was that individuals would participate in such groups, get a deeper sense of their own potential to be authentic and genuine, and to relate in a more truly intimate manner, and they would then carry this back into their everyday lives.

Many people began to jump on the encounter group bandwagon, and soon encounter groups were being held in high schools, universities, churches, and many other contexts. Encounter group leaders came from many theoretical orientations. Some encounter groups were relatively unstructured and gentle. The emphasis was on safety and empathic understanding, as well as on self-disclosure. Few techniques were used. On the other hand, there were encounter leaders who used many techniques, and a whole armamentarium of encounter techniques evolved, enough to fill several published books. Some evidence (Lieberman, Yalom, & Miles, 1973) suggested that encounter groups could be dangerous if leaders engaged in high-risk practices. This research also showed that encounter groups could be helpful, and many individuals carried away positive benefits from them. Eventually, the interest in encounter groups began to diminish.

Encounter groups are still around and can still be quite useful. However, they did not turn out to be the magic change agent that many in the 1960s had hoped they would be. The lesson that potential group leaders can learn from them is that intense expression of emotion, intense feelings of intimacy, and so on, while very stimulating and exciting, do not by themselves constitute real change experiences. Lieberman, Yalom, and Miles (1973) found that cognitive learning played an important part in benefitting from an encounter group experience, as did work and practice afterward in putting what was learned into operation.

Carl Rogers (see Chapter 8) was one of the first major figures in the area of psychotherapy to embrace the encounter group movement. He believed that most people live lives in which their own potential to be themselves has been blocked by their need to play social roles in order to fit in. He believed that encounter groups would not only give individuals an opportunity to get to know themselves more deeply, but could also lead to a social revolution, challenging the rigid, stultified ways most people relate to one another in everyday life. Thus, Rogers came to see the encounter group as an important change agent for society as well as for individuals, and he worked primarily in a group format for the latter part of his life.

Rogers and his colleagues extended the small encounter group experience in two directions. First, he and his colleagues began to experiment with large group, "community" experiences in which groups of several hundred individuals would come together without any preimposed structure. The goal was to see if the group could form an open, accepting, democratic structure. They discovered that this did not always work, but it often did, leading to unique experiences in which individuals seemed to find ways of transcending dichotomies such as "either I am myself and don't conform to the group, or I go along with the group and lose myself," by finding ways of being themselves *and* being connected to the group (O'Hara & Wood, 1983; Wood, 1984).

The other direction Rogers took his work in encounter groups was toward the facilitation of world peace. Rogers believed that if politicians and people from warring factions could meet as *individuals* in an encounter group, where they could open up and discuss their feelings, they would discover the humanness in one another and that would provide common bases from which to work out conflicts. Rogers and Ryback (1984) noted that it was when President Jimmy Carter began to talk with Menachem Begin about his feelings concerning his own grandchildren that the Camp David accords between Israel and Egypt finally were worked out. Rogers and his colleagues ran a number of encounter groups between warring factions in various places in the world, such as South Africa. Rogers did not believe that these groups by themselves would create world peace. Rather, he hoped they would provide a model of the kinds of processes that would have to happen if one wished to actually work toward human peace.

Self-Help or "Mutual-Support" Groups

Self-help or "mutual-support" groups are groups typically organized around the need to cope with some particular problem. The groups are run for and by the members. Usually, they are leaderless. The prototypical self-help group is Alcoholics Anonymous. There are now nearly 200 distinct problem categories for which there are self-help groups (Jacobs & Goodman, 1989). There are self-help groups for different kinds of substance abuse problems, for parents who have lost a child to suicide, for women who have had mastectomies, for adult children of alcoholics, for survivors of child abuse, for survivors of cancer, for individuals afflicted with AIDS or herpes, for parents with problem teenagers, and so on. As of 1987, it was estimated that over 6 million Americans were in some kind of self-help group (Jacobs & Goodman, 1989), and the number is growing.

Goodman and Jacobs (1994) tried to rechristen "self-help groups" as "mutual-support groups." This latter term distinguishes such groups from self-help books and better emphasizes the true nature of such groups. However, because self-help is the more traditional term, we shall continue to use it in this chapter.

Jacobs and Goodman have termed the typical self-help group a "miniature mental health democracy" (1989, p. 537). They point out that power resides in the membership, there are equal rights within the group, and leaders are there at the pleasure of the group. Members and group processes rely on collective, experiential knowledge rather than on professional expertise. The self-help movement has arisen for a variety of reasons, including the erosion of the traditional family as a source of social support and the unavailability of needed mental health services.

Goodman (personal communication, July 1991) has argued that self-help groups represent a form of psychotherapy integration, in that many of the processes fostered by traditional psychotherapies occur spontaneously in these groups. Within the groups, members provide empathic support for one another, understanding, new interpretations, and advice and guidance. As with other groups, one of the most important and helpful experiences is finding that one is not alone and that others understand what one is going through. A particular benefit of self-help groups is the sense of empowerment that comes from the fact that the members are getting help on their own. They are not being "helped" or "fixed" by a professional.

Jacobs and Goodman predict that self-help, mutual-support groups will become the major treatment method in mental health care. First, they are inexpensive compared to groups run by mental health professionals. Second, there may be something intrinsically more helpful about exchanging intimate help with those who are in similar predicaments than in seeking help from professionals. Goodman (personal communication, July 1991) has said he thinks that self-help groups may ultimately make psychotherapy the "secondary method for mental health care" by the early twenty-first century.

How does the massive self-help movement fit in with the profession of clinical psychology? There is an uneasy tension between the two. First, some mental health professionals look on self-help groups as a kind of "poor person's" substitute for psychotherapy. In other words, these professionals believe that self-help groups are an inferior approach to treatment compared to psychotherapy. On the other side, many members of self-help groups are suspicious of professional bias, commercialism, and the need to take over passive patients. A number of self-help group members have been in treatment with professionals and have not felt helped. Some in the self-help movement see the many competing schools of psychotherapy as an industry protecting its turf from encroachment by new developments. The irony here is that in 1993 more Americans used self-help groups than psychotherapy (Goodman & Jacobs, 1994).

On the other hand, many mental health professionals refer their clients to self-help groups as adjuncts to psychotherapy. Furthermore, many mental health professionals have played roles in the creation of self-help groups in the form of initially providing leadership and training. At the present time, many self-help groups have utilized some kind of professional assistance.

Jacobs and Goodman (1989) dispute the idea that self-help groups are a kind of inferior psychotherapy. They believe that as further data are accumulated, it will become apparent that self-help groups are quite effective. Certainly this argument is not implausible. Given the research findings (see Chapter 15), which suggest that all therapies are approximately equally effective, it is not implausible to assume that there may be some common factors that operate in all forms of therapy and that these may also operate in self-help groups.

For instance, one of the most important functions of a self-help group is to provide a support network for individuals who are struggling with some kind of problem. A good deal of research by community psychologists has supported the idea that a good social support network reduces the likelihood of individuals developing problems such as depression and anxiety. Individuals without good support networks are more likely to develop psychological problems than individuals with good support networks.

One of the biggest differences between many self-help groups and formal, professional therapy groups is that they are available on an as needed basis and therefore serve more as a part of a person's support network. For instance, with Alcoholics Anonymous, members may attend meetings every night of the week if they wish. In fact, during initial stages of recovery, alcoholics *are* encouraged to attend virtually every day for several months. In the sense that they may provide an ongoing source of social support, self-help groups may offer benefits and advantages that professional groups do not. In this regard, Gendlin (1970) suggested that in the future, there would be a group available for everyone to be a part of, in the belief that having such groups is good for everyone's mental health. Based on this idea, Gendlin (1984) and his colleagues (Boukydis, 1984) formed an organization in Chicago called Changes, which was a kind of self-help center where people could drop in at any time to socialize or to talk over their problems with others.

Despite the antipathy between some self-help group members and some professionals, it is advantageous for the two to work together. First, many self-help groups would welcome professional advice and assistance, as long as it was offered on a consultantlike basis (Jacobs & Goodman, 1989). In that regard, the California Self-Help Center at the University of California, Los Angeles, headed by Gerald Goodman and Marion Jacobs, developed a series of training tapes that self-help groups could use to develop their listening, helping, and supporting skills. Second, professionals can assist in setting up self-help groups and then gradually phase themselves out. Third, they can offer themselves as consultants to self-help groups to assist if problems occur that outstrip the group's capacities to cope with them. Fourth, professionals can do research on self-help groups and use that research to consult with self-help groups so that they may be more efficient. Finally, professionals can refer their individual therapy clients to self-help groups while they see them in individual therapy.

In sum, self-help groups may be an important mode of mental health treatment in the future. Professionals will work in tandem with self-help groups for the benefit of their clients.

IN CONCLUSION

Group therapy may be one of the waves of the future. Some psychologists believe it simply makes sense. Most psychological problems are interpersonal, not just intrapsychic, so group therapy may be a superior form of treatment. It is clearly more economical than individual therapy. Greater numbers of people can be treated in less time with fewer therapists. The present and future emphasis on cost-effectiveness by institutions that pay for psychological treatment (the government and private health insurance) almost certainly ensures the increasing use of group therapy. Furthermore, some research (Kaul & Bednar, 1986) supports its general effectiveness, though there is little specific data on what approaches help what clients in what ways. Data also generally favor the conclusion that group approaches are at least as effective as individual approaches. On the other hand, research needs to be done to explore when and for whom groups may be better than individual therapy.

As therapy and self-help groups can be effective, they also have the potential to be harmful. Charismatic group leaders can create group climates in which those who do not conform are criticized and ostracized in ways that are psychologically harmful (Lieberman, Yalom, & Miles, 1973). Pressures toward uniformity, implicit group norms of which group members are not explicitly aware, and other factors can push groups in dysfunctional directions. Groups can create their own "realities," which can then get imposed on individual members to their detriment, often in the guise of "helping" them face up to themselves. An extreme example of the destructive power of such group processes can be seen in the mass suicide of the members of the Heaven's Gate group in 1997.

Given this amazing power of the group, group therapists must remain aware of the danger of a group consensus to put pressure on individual members to conform. Leaders have to be particularly careful to respect the different personal truths of the group members. Their goal is to utilize the power of the group in the service of the members and to establish therapeutic group norms. Then group therapy can fulfill its potential to help large numbers of people effectively and efficiently.

BIBLIOGRAPHY

Berne, E. (1964). *Games people play.* New York: Grove Press.

Berne, E. (1966). *Principles of group treatment.* New York: Oxford University Press.

Boukydis, K. M. (1984). Changes: Peer counseling supportive communities as a model for community mental health. In D. Larson (Ed.), *Teaching psychological skills: Models for giving psychology away* (pp. 306–320). Monterey, CA: Brooks/Cole.

Corey, M. S., & Corey, G. (1987). *Groups: Process and practice* (3rd. ed.). Monterey, CA: Brooks/Cole.

Dies, R. R. (1992). The future of group therapy. *Psychotherapy, 29,* 58–64.

Elkind, D. (1978). Understanding the young adolescent. *Adolescence, 13,* 127–134.

Gendlin, E. T. (1970). A short summary and some long predictions. In J. T. Hart & T. M. Tomlinson (Eds.), *New directions in client-centered therapy* (pp. 544–562). Boston: Houghton Mifflin.

Gendlin, E. T. (1984). The politics of giving therapy away: Listening and focusing. In D. Larson (Ed.), *Teaching psychological skills: Models for giving psychology away* (pp. 287–305). Monterey, CA: Brooks/Cole.

Goodman, G., & Jacobs, M. K. (1994). The self-help, mutual-support group. In A. Fuhriman & G. Burlingame (Eds.), *Group psychotherapy.* New York: Wiley.

Harris, T. A. (1969). *I'm ok—you're ok.* New York: Harper & Row.

Jacobs, M. K., & Goodman, G. (1989). Psychology and self-help groups: Predictions on a partnership. *American Psychologist, 44,* 536–545.

Kaul, T. J., & Bednar, R. N. (1986). Research on group and related therapies. In S. N. Garfield & A. E. Bergin (Eds.), *Handbook of psychotherapy and behavior change* (3rd ed., pp. 671–714). New York: Wiley.

Lieberman, M., Yalom, I., & Miles, M. (1973). *Encounter groups: First facts.* New York: Basic Books.

Moreno, J. L. (1934). *Who shall survive?* New York: Nervous and Mental Disease Publishing.

O'Hara, M. M., & Wood, J. K. (1983). Patterns of awareness: Consciousness and the group mind. *The Gestalt Journal, VI,* 103–116.

Rogers, C. R., & Ryback, D. (1984). One alternative to nuclear planetary suicide. In R. F. Levant & J. M. Shlien (Eds.), *Client-centered therapy and the person-centered approach: New directions in theory, research, and practice* (pp. 400–422). New York: Praeger.

Rose, S. D. (1989). *Working with adults in groups.* San Francisco: Jossey-Bass.

Scheidlinger, S. (1984). Group psychotherapy in the 1980's: Problems and prospects. *American Journal of Psychotherapy, 38,* 494–504.

Wolf, A., & Kutash, I. L. (1986). Psychoanalysis in groups. In I. L. Kutash & A. Wolf (Eds.), *Psychotherapist's casebook* (pp. 332–352). San Francisco: Jossey-Bass.

Wood, J. K. (1984). Communities for learning: A person-centered approach. In R. F. Levant & J. M. Shlien (Eds.), *Client-centered therapy and the person-centered approach: New directions in theory, research, and practice* (pp. 297–316). New York: Praeger.

Yalom, I. D. (1985). *The theory and practice of group psychotherapy* (3rd ed.). New York: Basic Books.

CHAPTER
14

Marriage, Family, and Child Counseling

Marsha and George have been married for seven years. They have two children: Jane is 5, and the second, Mark, is 3. Marsha and George have felt that they have been growing apart in recent years. They do not spend as much time together. Their sex life is not as good as it once was. George is occasionally having difficulties obtaining erections and Marsha does not seem to be "in the mood" as often as she once was. In addition, Mark, who is in preschool, has been acting somewhat shy and withdrawn.

How should these problems be treated? Where should a therapist start? In general, the problems of this family fall under the purview of the specialty called marriage, family, and child counseling, a profession now licensed by a number of states. In addition, there are many other mental health professionals, such as psychiatrists, psychologists, or clinical social workers, who also practice in the general area of marriage, family, and child counseling. A subspecialty in these areas is that of sex therapy.

The couple above have problems that could be treated by any one of the four approaches we consider in this chapter. If they decided to focus on the problems of their 3-year-old, they might take him to a therapist who specializes in working with children. If they decided to focus exclusively on their sexual relationship they might seek out the services of a sex therapist. If they decided to focus on their couple issues, they might seek out marital counseling. If it was decided that their problems involved the whole family in some way or other, they might receive family therapy.

These four specialties are considered together in this chapter because they are often interrelated, and practitioners who specialize in one often specialize in the others. Sometimes sexual problems are a result of couple or family problems. Perhaps the stresses and strains of dealing with the children have affected both George and Marsha, either directly making them less interested in sex or decreasing the level of intimacy between them, which then resulted in sexual problems. Sometimes problems with children are a result of family or couple problems. Perhaps problems between George and Marsha have affected the family, resulting in Mark's acting shy and withdrawn at preschool. Other times, children's problems are entities in their own right. Perhaps Mark is a genetically shy child who needs special attention in order to thrive.

We shall consider each of these four approaches in turn. Before we start, we should note is that the principles we allude to in doing both sex therapy and treating couples can be used (with appropriate modifications) with any couple. That is, we focus on the "normative" American couple: heterosexual and married. However, both sex and couples therapy can be used with unmarried couples and with gay and lesbian couples. Similarly, when we discuss "families" we use the "normative" model of a family: a father, mother, and children (and possibly dog). However, this normative family is becoming increasingly nonnormative in the United States. Once again, the general principles of family therapy, with appropriate modifications, can be applied to the many other forms that families take in our current culture besides the traditional one.

PSYCHOLOGICAL INTERVENTIONS WITH CHILDREN

Almost every school of therapy has a version for use with children. While the theories may be seen as equally applicable to children and adults, the methods of intervention must be altered for children. Children differ from adult clients in two ways. First of all, children almost never voluntarily request psychotherapy, and so children participate in therapy under at least some degree of duress. More importantly, children differ profoundly in their cognitions, perceptions, and emotions at different developmental stages, and they lack the maturity and cognitive development to benefit from interventions that rely on verbalization and self-examination. Most forms of therapy with children have substituted play for the largely verbal activities required of adults in therapy.

Psychological interventions for children have been developed to treat a wide variety of problems in a wide variety of settings. A distinction may be made between clinical child psychology, which deals with disorders, and pediatric psychology, which deals with child rearing and educational issues, but as with many specialities, there is a great deal of overlap in the types of problems addressed. Children may be treated for such disorders as phobias, anorexia and bulimia, childhood schizophrenia, autism, depression, mental retardation, asthma, headaches, or the aftereffects of child abuse or other trauma. Psychologists may also be consulted for such childhood issues as toileting, sibling rivalry, lack of friends, nightmares, and tantrums.

Psychoanalytically Oriented Therapy

It is probably not surprising that the historical development of child therapy began with psychoanalysis, during the 1920s in the United States. While Sigmund Freud treated a child called Little Hans by advising his father, it was left to two women analysts to develop methods for use specifically with children. Anna Freud (1928, 1946) and Melanie Klein (1955) are credited with establishing a theory and methodology of psychoanalysis to use with children. While both allowed play to substitute for free association, Klein emphasized the symbolic meaning of play and Freud its ability to enhance the relationship with the therapist. Another early analyst, Levy (1939), used play to recreate and work through specific traumatic situations experienced by the child. About the same time, Alfred Adler (1930), an ex-follower of Sigmund Freud, developed his Individual Psychology for use with children and their families. His treatment emphasized allying with the child, teaching the child to compensate for deficiencies in the self and the family, and educating the family in better parenting methods. Many educators and child therapists continue to use Adlerian concepts today.

As with adults, the child analyst will interpret the meaning of dreams, daydreams, fantasies, and play activities, in terms of both transference issues and symbolic meanings about early or traumatic experiences and the child's family. The goal is to help the child negotiate the developmental stage according to the psychoanalytic theory of development and to increase the child's self-understanding and conscious control of behavior. Except for specialized private practice, psychoanalytic treatment of children is not common today in the United States, although psychodynamic concepts are used by many types of therapists.

Client-Centered Therapy

As with adult therapy, the next historical development in child therapy involved the Rogerian school. During the 1940s and 1950s, nondirective techniques were used with children, most often as a part of play therapy, discussed below. Virginia Axline (1947a,b) attempted to apply client-centered therapy to the treatment of children with reading and other problems. Agreeing with Carl Rogers that human beings are born with the capacity for prosocial behavior and self-realization, client-centered child therapists provide unconditional positive regard for their clients in an attempt to undo the damage caused by the parents' conditions of worth on the child's natural good qualities, and they reflect feelings in order to help the child connect with those tendencies. The emphasis is on the accepting, trustworthy relationship between the therapist and child, rather than on any specific techniques or theorized causes for problems in child development.

Play Therapy

Although Axline began in the client-centered school, play therapy soon became recognized as a special form of child therapy in itself. There are now many types of play therapy, including one based on Jungian theory, which utilizes special fantasy play figures in sand trays. Play therapy is sometimes criticized as a vague collection of assorted techniques, without a systematic guiding theory, but there are at least two major types of play therapy at present.

Classical Play Therapy   In classical play therapy, conducted in a moderate-sized play room with a variety of toys and play and art materials, the therapist focuses on developing a warm, caring relationship with the child. The therapist accepts the child as she is, allows the child to take the lead in the sessions, and does not try to change the child or intervene in or direct the child's play in any way. The therapist creates a safe and permissive atmosphere so that the child feels free to express herself. The therapist attends to, accepts, and reflects the child's feelings in a manner that helps the child develop self-understanding. The therapist does not otherwise "help" the child, but rather, allows her to solve problems in her own way. The therapist sets limits only when required for safety and to help the child accept appropriate responsibility. In classical play therapy, it is believed that if the therapist consistently behaves in these ways, a therapeutic process will be generated in which the child's natural tendency toward growth will be enhanced. The emphasis is on the relationship and generating this process, rather than on specific therapeutic objectives or outcome goals. The general goals of classical play therapy are to help the child develop self-esteem, responsibility, and self-acceptance, to experience a sense of control, and to become more self-directed, as well as more socially appropriate.

Structured Play Therapy   Many modern child therapists believe that classical play therapy takes too long, is inefficient and vague, and most importantly, may collude with the child in avoiding facing difficult issues. Earlier beliefs that children should never be pressured to express certain feelings or discuss certain topics and that with trust and safety, feelings will be expressed spontaneously are now considered likely to be seen by the young child as permission or even encouragement not to talk about certain issues, especially socially taboo topics such as child sexual abuse.

Structured play therapy, while acknowledging the importance of establishing an accepting, safe relationship between therapist and child, emphasizes specific therapeutic objectives. The therapist is active in directing and structuring the child's play, often arranging a specific activity for each session in order to accomplish specific goals within a certain time range. The therapist utilizes planned stories, metaphor, drawing activities, dolls, and puppet play to raise and explore specific issues with the child. Once the issue has been raised for discussion, the therapist may direct the child's exploration of feelings about the issue, explain that other people feel the same way, teach specific problem-solving or coping behaviors, or make other active interventions.

The traumatic experiences of a sexually abused child, for example, may never come up in classical play therapy, yet the abuse is the major reason for the child's disturbed behavior. Sexually abused children are motivated to keep their problem secret for several reasons, including the molester's threats about what will happen if they tell, a fear of disrupting the family, shame, and society's denial of the problem. In structured play therapy with a sexually abused child, the therapist may tell a story about an abused child or animal and ask the child what the person or creature in the story may feel or should do. The therapist may ask the child to draw a picture of a scared person and then ask a series of questions about the drawing, such as "What could be scaring this person?" Puppets can be used to talk about abuse indirectly, or dolls can be used to demonstrate what happened to the child. Abused children often find it possible to talk about the abuse as if it has happened to someone else—a doll, or a puppet—when they tend to deny and retract if asked about abuse directly. Once the abuse can be discussed, then the therapist will direct an exploration of the child's feelings of helplessness, shame, fear, and rage and help the child understand, accept, and redirect these feelings. Specific coping behaviors are also taught. Although this description of structured play therapy with sexually abused children is necessarily superficial, it is easy to see how different it is from classical play therapy.

Behavior Therapy

Behavior therapy is often used with children, generally in special classrooms or in family therapy, as described in Chapter 10. Almost all special education classes and treatment facilities for disturbed children utilize behavioral methods to a greater or lesser extent. Rewards, points, or tokens are given for desired behaviors, such as sitting still, paying attention during a short lesson, or completing work, and time-out is commonly used for undesired behaviors. Critics argue that time-out is widely misunderstood and misapplied, with children spending long periods of time in unhelpful isolation. If so, it is possible that educators need improved training in behavioral principles. Teachers may also use behavior therapy with certain individuals in a regular classroom, especially if the child is involved in behavior therapy with the family.

Although children can be taught to self-monitor and change their own behaviors, more frequently, parents are taught to use behavioral methods with their children instead of the ineffective or aversive methods they have been using. Parents can be taught to specify clearly the behaviors they desire, to reward those behaviors appropriately, to ignore mild misbehavior, and to set appropriate limits for specific problem behaviors. Limit setting may include the use of time-out. Although designed to address specific behaviors, behavior therapy with children also enhances their feelings of self-esteem and competence. Similar changes are often observed in the parents.

Behavioral Medicine and Hypnosis

A variety of behavioral and child therapy methods have been found to be beneficial in children's medical treatment. Children can be taught to use imagery or self-hypnosis in order to cope with painful medical procedures. Puppet or doll play to explain surgical procedures is useful in reducing children's fears and enhancing the outcome of surgery. Classical play therapy may help hospitalized children express themselves and retain a positive outlook through the stress of a debilitating illness. Behavior therapy can increase compliance with difficult diets or other medical regimens. Just as behavioral medicine with adults is a growing field, new methods of intervening in the medical treatment of children are being developed every day.

Hypnosis is also used with children. For example, hypnosis has occasionally been used to help anxious and hyperactive children calm down and learn to calm themselves. Now available for children are audiotapes that contain a soothing hypnotic induction, which children can use to help themselves go to sleep or deal with other problems. The use of self-hypnosis in helping children cope with painful medical procedures has already been mentioned.

Cognitive-Behavior Therapy

Cognitive-behavior therapy is beginning to be used with children to treat such problems as impulsivity, hyperactivity, conduct disorder, and even reading disability. In the latter, the aim is to stop the child's self-defeating self-speech and automatic thoughts and to replace them with coping thoughts. Typically, these children say to themselves things such as, "This is too hard. I'll never get it. See, I made a mistake. It's ruined. I may as well give up." The therapist may model a writing assignment by saying out loud, "Let's see, copying these words is difficult, but I can manage it. I'll start with the first letter. It's an A. I begin here and make this line go like this. Oh, I made a mistake, but it's good enough. I'll keep going. Now I need to make a line like this." By acknowledging the difficulty but reassuring the self that it can be done, by breaking the task down into its component parts, and by accepting mistakes, the therapist teaches reading-disabled children to modify their self-defeating thoughts and behaviors.

Psychopharmacological Interventions

Although children are sometimes medicated for anxiety and depression, most frequently, children are given drugs for attention-deficit/hyperactivity disorder. The use of these drugs remains controversial. Drugs such as Ritalin may have negative side effects such as inhibiting growth, although research is resulting in improved drugs. Critics argue that children are drugged for the convenience of teachers and parents and that treated children misattribute their improvement to the drug and not to themselves. Defenders argue that these children suffer from a biologically based brain disorder and that it is unethical to deny them a needed biological intervention. Because drugs appear to be effective and quicker and cheaper than psychological interventions in the treatment of attention-deficit/hyperactivity disorder, their use is likely to continue and to grow.

Family Therapy

In some child guidance clinics in recent years, the family is required to participate as part of therapy for the child. Many therapists reject the notion that a child can have a problem or be treated for it in isolation from the familial context of that problem. A child is frequently the **identified patient** when a family becomes dysfunctional. In such cases, family therapy, as described later in the chapter, would be the treatment of choice.

Parents may be involved in therapy with children in other ways. For example, in behavior therapy, they may be taught to apply behavioral methods to modify undesired behaviors in their children. Even in classical play therapy, the parents (usually the mother) meet occasionally with either the child's or another therapist to discuss the child's behavior and to enhance the parent's support of the child's changes.

Group Therapy

As with adult therapy, children may be treated in groups of three to eight under the different models of therapy. For example, in psychoanalytic groups for children, interpretations of parental transference to the therapists or sibling issues between the children may be made. In behavior therapy, small groups of anxious, socially inhibited children may be taught assertive, sociable behavior. Play therapy is often quite effective in groups. In structured play therapy for sexually abused children, for example, two or three therapists with four to six children may meet for planned, guided play exercises directed to the issues of such abused children. The advantages of group therapy in such cases include modeling revealing the secret, the ending of the "pluralistic ignorance" of each child thinking that abuse has happened only to her or him, a reduction of shame and guilt, and the ability to practice problem-solving and coping behavior with both peers and adults.

SEX THERAPY

Sex therapy as it is practiced today is a relatively recent development. For a long time, it was assumed that sexual problems were symptoms of deeper personality disturbances, and they were treated with in-depth psychotherapy. However, with the work of Masters and Johnson (1970) in the late 1950s and 1960s, treatment of the sexual dysfunctions themselves was developed. This is not to say that sex therapists ignore the possibilities that a person's sexual problems may reflect underlying personality difficulties or that they may be secondary to problems in a relationship. These may be taken into account. However, there are now treatment procedures specifically for the sexual dysfunctions themselves. In this respect, sex therapy resembles a behavioral approach to therapy more than a psychoanalytic or humanistic approach.

In most cases treated with sex therapy, one member of a couple has an identifiable sexual dysfunction, such as erectile dysfunction, premature ejaculation, orgasmic dysfunction, or vaginismus (painful involuntary muscle spasms when intercourse is attempted). Though we are including sex therapy in a chapter that deals with therapy with more than one individual, an individual may seek sex therapy even though he or she is not a member of a couple.

After education about normal sexual functioning, a first step in sex therapy with couples is to take the burden of blame from the identified patient and to define the sexual dysfunction as a couple problem. A second step is to forbid sexual intercourse until the therapist gives permission, an order that some theorists see as a "paradoxical intervention," which we discuss later in this chapter. Masters and Johnson claim this restriction reduces "performance pressure." According to their theory, sexually dysfunctional people are so anxious about their performance and their possible failure that the anxiety interferes with their ability to perform or enjoy sex. Such individuals also engage in **spectatoring** (watching and judging their own sexual performance) so they lose touch with their **sensate focus** (what actually feels good sexually). Many of the exercises in sex therapy are supposed to teach people to regain their sensate focus.

The assigned exercises and homework in sex therapy are similar to a gradual desensitization procedure (see Chapter 10). Ethical sex therapists do not touch their clients sexually or observe their clients' sexual behavior. Exercises are always done in private with the partner, or possibly with a "sexual surrogate" (though surrogates are not used very often anymore because of AIDS). The first exercises may be to touch, hug, and kiss with their clothes on. The next day (in Masters and Johnson's program) or the next week (in weekly, outpatient sex therapy) the couple reviews what happened with the therapist. If the exercise went well and did not elicit much anxiety, the next assignment may be touching and fondling with clothes above the waist removed. Part of the touching may involve a sensate focus exercise in which partners take turns massaging each other while the person being massaged directs the massager on what to do. The receiver of the massage also says what feels good where. This is educational for both partners and also increases communication. The next assignment may be touching with all clothes off. Subsequent exercises are specific to the type of dysfunction being treated. While erotic activities are encouraged during sex therapy, sexual intercourse is specifically prohibited until the therapist gives permission. If it is successful, the therapy has worked. However, if the couple is not successful at intercourse, the therapist accepts responsibility for failure, and they go back to earlier exercises.

If the problem is erectile dysfunction and it has been determined that the problem is largely or exclusively psychological, the exercises are designed to help the man obtain and sustain an erection, and intercourse is gradually introduced. If the problem is premature ejaculation, a stop-start technique may be used. The couple start intercourse, and when the man feels he may ejaculate, he stops until he feels he has regained control. If the problem is psychological orgasmic dysfunction in the woman, she is taught to have orgasms through manual stimulation, and then intercourse is gradually introduced. If the problem is vaginismus, she is induced to have orgasms with nothing in the vagina. Then a small object such as a finger is inserted, working gradually up to orgasm with a penis in the vagina.

Recently, sex therapists have increasingly encountered sexual desire disorders. With the "sexual revolution" that occurred in the 1960s, it became increasingly fashionable to be sexual. Now sex therapists are encountering individuals who, for various reasons, find their level of sexual desire lower than they would like. Among the possible psychological causes of this are pressure to conform to societal norms to be sexual; couples' problems; discrepancies between partners' level of interest in sex; stress; and repressive or traumatic childhood experiences. It has been estimated that as many as 40 percent of couples who come in for sex therapy complain of this problem (Leiblum & Rosen, 1988). Depending on what the problem is, the sex therapist will proceed in different ways to deal with this problem. For instance, resolving problems in the relationship between the partners may be the treatment of choice if, for instance, one partner is experiencing low desire because he or she is angry at the other partner. If there is discrepancy in desire, facilitating dialogue toward compromise may be the solution. If the problem is primarily pressures to fit a model of what society deems as "normal," sex education in which individuals are acquainted with the idea that there is an enormous diversity in "normal" sexual behavior may be utilized. Finally, if early childhood sexual abuse or a severely repressive upbringing are the problems, intensive longer-term psychotherapy might be used.

Though sex therapy is most frequently done with couples, there are methods for working with individuals alone. Zilbergeld (1992) presents methods that can be used by a male to cope with erectile dysfunction or premature ejaculation. One of Zilbergeld's most important contributions is helping the client be aware of his "conditions for good sex" and of myths about male sexuality (for instance, "Sex equals intercourse," "Sex requires an erection," "A man always wants and is ready to have sex"). Similarly, Barbach (1975) presents exercises women can do by themselves to become orgasmic. She also discusses the many conflicting and contradictory messages about sex that a woman in our culture receives. For example, she is taught to turn off sexual feelings all through adolescence, and then, when she is married, she is suddenly expected to "emerge as a turned on passionate woman" (p. 39).

Sex therapy has been criticized for being so limited in focus that it can be effective only for couples whose problem is solely sexual and who have a good relationship otherwise. However, most sex therapists are not so naive as to concentrate exclusively on the sexual dysfunction without making some attempt to assess its relation to other individual or relationship problems and to include those problems in the therapy if necessary.

Sex therapy has also been criticized by feminists on the grounds that it has been used to enforce cultural norms of the right way to have sex, and these cultural norms are usually masculine. For example, the goal of women's attaining orgasm through intercourse may meet men's expectations and desires, but it may not be practical for women. Some research indicates that women attain orgasm more easily through oral or manual stimulation than through intercourse, and indeed, it may be difficult for many women to attain orgasm through intercourse, even with sex therapy.

MARITAL AND COUPLES COUNSELING AND THERAPY

A marital or couples counselor's initial assumption is that problems of the individuals in the couple are caused by the malfunctioning of the couple as a unit, rather than solely by emotions or personality structures within either or both individuals. A couples therapist makes a point of defining clients' difficulties as a couple dysfunction, even if the couple enters therapy because of the disorder of one partner.

In other words, most marital counselors assume that psychological problems lie between individuals, rather than solely within one partner or the other, though the couple's problems may manifest in the individual symptoms of one of the partners. Many theorists therefore view marital therapy as a subset of family therapy, and many of the ideas discussed in this section are similar to those of the family therapists discussed later.

Most marriage therapists focus on the communication between the spouses. It is assumed that part of the couple's dysfunction is their inability to communicate clearly what they think, feel, and want to each other. There are several reasons: Their parents may not have taught them how to communicate, their childhood experiences may have taught them to ignore or repress certain dangerous feelings or issues, or they may fear the spouse's reaction if they reveal their real feelings. Because they don't communicate what they want, they don't get what they want, and the resultant hurt and anger contribute further to their problems. As long as important feelings and beliefs are kept hidden or are communicated indirectly, the couple will not be able to solve their conflicts and misunderstandings.

Here is a typical example. The wife wants the husband to take out the trash. In her childhood family, the man took out the trash, and it was a part of how he showed he cared for his wife. When her husband fails to take out the trash, she feels hurt and rejected. Perhaps she is unaware of these feelings, or perhaps she is afraid or ashamed to reveal them, but she does get hurt and then angry when he does not take out the trash.

In the husband's childhood family, perhaps the woman took out the trash, or perhaps there was a constant battle over the trash and the loser had to take it out. When his wife asks him to take it out, he feels pressured and threatened, and he experiences the request as an unreasonable demand, demeaning of his role as head of the family. However, he is also unaware or afraid or ashamed of these feelings, and he just feels angry.

How does this situation affect their communication? She, feeling hurt and let down, says, "Why didn't you take out the trash?" He, feeling nagged by this unanswerable question, says, "I didn't see it." She, feeling frustrated and further enraged at this evasion of her real message, shouts, "Are you blind? It's right by the back door where you left it all week!" He, feeling attacked, screams, "Are you crippled? Take it out yourself!" It goes on. She yells, "You never help, you worthless bum," and he returns, "Shut up, you bitch," or worse, "There's no need to get so irrational." You can see they won't be able to solve the conflict this way.

Couples therapy involves techniques to help clarify communication. They focus on the precise nature of the problem and its accompanying experience. In therapy, the wife may cry, "He never contributes. He never helps." The therapist tries to narrow this blanket condemnation down to a specific example of nonhelping. Perhaps the wife remembers that he didn't take out the trash the night before. The therapist tries to elicit her version of what happened and how she experienced it: What was she thinking and feeling at each point? Her underlying feelings of hurt and rejection may be brought out. The therapist elicits the husband's version and his experience, with his underlying feelings of hurt and criticism. The spouses are usually surprised to learn what the other one really thought and was trying, however indirectly, to say. The therapist's next task may be to teach or elicit alternative ways of communicating about this issue.

Much of marital therapy involves teaching the couple social skills. The therapist tries to model clear, direct, nonjudgmental, effective communication when talking to the couple and may also employ specific techniques to teach communication skills. One such technique is sometimes called mirroring. The husband is asked to tell his version of a conflict, and the wife is directed to listen carefully. She is then asked to say as precisely as possible what she heard her spouse say. He is asked if she got what he was trying to say and, if not, to say it again. It is surprising how frequently spouses cannot do this task. Even when they are given the specific assignment of listening carefully so they can repeat the message, they get caught up in thinking of a defense to what the spouse is saying or hear an attack when none is intended or simply are unable to hear anything other than their own projections or expectations. In other cases, the communicating spouses do not say clearly what they want to. If they can be made aware of their spouses' misunderstanding, they may be able to restate or explain what they want and gradually learn to communicate more directly and clearly.

When a couple's communication skills are improved by these methods, their difficulties often seem to disappear, or they are able to solve their problems on their own with their new ways of communicating. Sometimes the therapist must continue to help the couple. Even with clear and honest communication, some conflicts are difficult to resolve. There may be profound differences in sexual desire or values about religion or child rearing. Compromises can be negotiated or tolerance for each other's differences can be taught.

Finally, some couples decide to divorce when the nature of their conflict is clarified. Whether marital therapists should always work to save a marriage or accept divorce as a reasonable alternative solution is a controversy we will not address here. Also, it should be unnecessary to note that the principles of marital therapy apply to all intimate couples, married or not, heterosexual or not.

Psychodynamic Marital Therapies

Although most couples therapists work to improve communication and reduce blame and coercion (Greenberg & Johnson, 1988), they approach this in different ways. Therapists influenced by psychoanalytic theory try to help couples clarify the projections and expectations each partner is placing on the other, which have been carried forward from early childhood experiences. It is believed that individuals often choose as partners people who unconsciously fit into their dynamics from childhood: they tend to recapitulate their childhoods in one way or the other. Psychoanalytic therapists believe that these projections must be explored and clarified in order to facilitate positive, proactive communication.

A variant of psychodynamic theory—ego analysis (Wile, 1981)—takes a different tack. Wile believes that individuals act dysfunctionally with their spouses because they do not feel entitled to their feelings. While this may have originated in childhood, it is very much a here-and-now experience. For instance, a husband may not feel entitled to feeling angry because his wife is so busy at work that she does not spend as much time with him as she used to. Not feeling entitled to the anger, the feelings may either leak out in hidden, passive ways, or may come out in rigid, defensive explosions. Even individuals who, on the surface, are apparently acting as if they feel entitled to their feelings, by constantly expressing anger in a "definite" tone of voice at high volume, are likely experiencing self-disapproval at some level, which is why their expressions of anger seem rigid and exaggerated. Wile's goal is to help each partner reduce self-criticism and come to accept their and each others' feelings. When this occurs, couples are able to "have" their feelings in more functional ways, and communicate more effectively. Basically, Wile tries to get each partner to be on the other's side, and when this happens, there is no need to "negotiate" compromises, because compromises will often spontaneously occur.

Behavioral and Cognitive Marital Therapies

Behavioral and cognitive methods have been adapted for use with couples, resulting in a number of different approaches.

Behavioral Marital Counseling   Behavioral marital counseling (Jacobson & Margolin, 1979) has two aims: to reduce or eliminate problem behaviors and to increase positive and effective behaviors. Usually, the goal of increasing positive behaviors is considered first. Partners are asked to list all the positive behaviors they would like the other person to perform. They are told initially to exclude positive behaviors they would like the other to perform, but that are a source of conflict. Then the partners work on increasing the frequency of these behaviors. For instance, they may have "caring days": one spouse tries to maximize the positive experience of the other, and spouses are encouraged to surprise one another with positive experiences.

A key part of this is training and encouraging partners to show their appreciation for the positive behaviors of the other. In addition, the partners monitor the rates of pleasing events and keep records of daily levels of satisfaction.

The second part of counseling is aimed at reducing problems. This is attacked by teaching the partners effective problem solving. Problem solving breaks down into two phases: problem definition and problem resolution. To define their problems, clients are taught to state their complaints in brief, specific, nonblaming ways. They are also taught to state their feelings, to admit their own role in the problem, and to paraphrase the other person's viewpoint, even if it is not consistent with their own. An example of an effective problem definition, which includes a statement of feelings, is "When you let a week go by without initiating sex, I feel rejected" (Jacobson & Margolin, 1979, p. 230).

To resolve problems, clients are encouraged first to brainstorm, to come up with as many possible solutions as they can. They are to suspend judgment of the various options until as many have been generated as possible. Then they consider and evaluate each option. Finally, they are taught to negotiate and compromise until a solution is arrived at. This solution is recorded in writing.

Sometimes a contract is included. A contract may be set up with specific reinforcers or consequences associated with the performance or nonperformance of the behaviors involved. Thus, if one partner wants more sex and the other wants more affection, the provision of these may be made contingent on the performance of other behaviors that each desires in the other person, such as taking out the trash or not nagging so much. However, there is some controversy over the use of contracts and reward contingencies with marital problems (Christensen, 1983), and they are not used in all cases.

A general goal of the behavioral approach is to teach these problem-solving skills so that the couple can use them on their own. Couples are encouraged to set aside certain specified times to engage in problem solving and to refrain from attempting problem solving when they are in the midst of an emotional conflict.

Integrative Behavioral Couple Therapy (IBCT)   Christensen, Jacobson, and Babcock (1995) describe an integrative approach to behavioral couples therapy, in which the idea of acceptance, typically found in humanistic and psychodynamic approaches, is incorporated along with behavioral techniques. Integrative Behavioral Couple Therapy (IBCT) is one of the radical behavior therapies, discussed in Chapter 10. Like those therapies, it emphasizes acceptance. It is trying to change unacceptable feelings and thoughts that leads to problematic behavior in individuals, and trying to change one's partner is seen as the source of a couple's difficulties. Acceptance involves "letting go of the struggle" to change one's partner. Acceptance also encourages couples to use their problems as opportunities for developing a closer relationship, rather than to try to "solve" or avoid the problems.

IBCT develops individualized strategies for each couple based on a **functional analysis** (see Chapter 10) of their attempts to communicate and attain intimacy within the therapy session, rather than assuming, as does traditional couples therapy, that there are universal criteria for good and bad communication in marriage. IBCT attempts to promote improved behaviors by creating intimacy-enhancing experiences in the therapy sessions and by ensuring that natural rather than arbitrary reinforcers follow when these behaviors occur.

There are four categories of acceptance-focused interventions in IBCT. In "empathic joining around the problem," methods to promote compassion and empathy toward the partner's formerly unacceptable behavior are used. In interventions that "turn the problem into an 'it'," couples are encouraged to join together against the problem and to view it as something outside of themselves about which to commiserate. Third, tolerance-building techniques are designed to prepare couples for the inevitable conflicts in their relationship and to desensitize them to conflict. Finally, self-care techniques teach people how to take better care of themselves so they are less dependent on their partners for giving them what they want.

For example, a couple battling over whose fault it is that they "never talk anymore" might be treated in the following way. Instead of arguing about whether the husband withdraws or the wife nags (a typical pattern addressed in traditional marital therapies), IBCT would encourage acceptance and focus on examples of intimate communication in the session. The couple might be encouraged to empathize with each other about how sad they are and how they miss their old conversations. "Not talking" is seen as something that has happened to them, not as something one person does or does not do to the other. The therapist may use the tolerance-building technique of pointing out the positive aspects of not talking. Of course, all the while, the couple actually *are* talking in the therapy session, and the therapist ensures that the natural reinforcer of feeling closer will increase the likelihood of their engaging in more talk outside the session.

Cognitive Approaches Many behavioral approaches have increasingly incorporated cognitive techniques. Cognitive-behavioral marital therapy might include many of the previously mentioned exercises, but will also help members of the couple identify and challenge dysfunctional cognitions and expectations. Cognitive approaches to marital therapy (e.g., Dattilio & Padesky, 1990) utilize many of the same cognitive challenging techniques discussed in Chapter 12. There are three basic aspects to cognitive therapy with couples. First, the cognitive therapist tries to modify unrealistic expectations in the relationship. Second, the cognitive therapist tries to modify the making of faulty attributions to one another (e.g., "you don't *really* care for me"). Third, partners are taught procedures, such as the behavioral ones we have previously discussed, to avoid destructive interactions.

Experiential-Humanistic Approaches

The experiential-humanistic approach of Greenberg and Johnson (1988) focuses on the elicitation and expression of clients' subjective experience, particularly what they call "primary emotions." They believe that members of couples act defensively toward one another because they don't feel safe. The emotions they do feel and express are secondary emotional reactions, that is, defensive emotional reactions. For instance, a partner who frequently gets angry because he feels his spouse is not paying enough attention to him is using anger as a kind of defensive reaction to try to protect himself. Underneath the anger is a more primary emotion, such as fear or vulnerability. The goal of emotionally focused therapy is to help each member of the couple access these more primary emotions. Accessing primary emotion changes the nature of the couple's interaction. When the husband is able to express vulnerability and acknowledge how much he wants and needs his partner in a nondemanding, nondefensive way, the partner finds it easier to open up and share her primary emotions. Eventually, better collaborative communication is facilitated.

Another experiential-humanistic approach is that of Relationship Enhancement (Guerney, 1984). It is derived from client-centered therapy and is not only a form of therapy, but also a form of training that can be used to prevent problems in the first place. It can be used for a variety of relationships, such as for parents and children or for groups of individuals, and is not limited to couples. Some of the goals of Relationship Enhancement are: to help individuals understand their emotions, wishes, goals, and conflicts better; to help them learn how to better understand others; and to help them learn how to understand and resolve problems between themselves and others better. Relationship Enhancement is essentially a skills training approach, and is therefore actually an integration of client-centered and behavioral ideas. Couples are taught the skills of effective expression, such as learning to show understanding for the other before you immediately fire off your response. They are also taught the skill of being empathic, which includes learning how to listen intently, sense and "absorb" the other's mood, concentrate on the other's internal world, put oneself in the other's place, and then express one's tentative understanding in a functional manner. Along with these and other skills, couples are also taught problem-solving skills, in a manner similar to behavioral marital therapy.

FAMILY COUNSELING AND THERAPY

Most forms of family counseling and therapy view the family as a system. A system is a pattern of interrelationships among elements, such that each element of the system both determines and is determined by the other elements in the system. The behavior of any part of a system reflects the overall organization of the system and feeds back into the system itself. Furthermore, systems have often been thought to evolve toward a state of equilibrium, or "homeostatic balance," although with respect to family systems, many theorists are now questioning this notion.

From a systems view, problems of individuals are seen, in part at least, as reflecting some kind of malfunction in the whole system. If a system has achieved homeostatic balance, and something threatens that, the system may adjust to return it as close to equilibrium as possible. Thus, if a problem between husband and wife threatens to destroy a whole family system, a child may develop either a psychological or physical problem as a way of restoring balance. This is not consciously done by the child, but rather is a response to the pressures and strains in the family system itself.

The child's developing a problem may deflect the couple's attention from their problems, and thereby serve to restabilize the system, at least to some degree.

Some family systems theorists believe that, therefore, families "need" their problems. If a therapist works only with the individual with the problem, say, the child who is acting dysfunctionally at school, this may not help. In fact, as the child gets better, someone else in the family may begin to develop a problem. One of our colleagues worked for some time with a family in which the members "rotated" problems. The father would periodically drink heavily, the daughter would periodically become rebellious and do things such as ditch school, and the mother would periodically become depressed. When the father was drinking heavily, the mother and the daughter would be problem-free. If, through therapy, the father began to reduce his drinking, either the mother or the daughter would begin to have a problem. When that problem abated, another member of the family would develop a problem. This went on for quite a while until the family system itself finally changed. The goal of family therapy, therefore, ultimately becomes that of reorganizing the family system so that it does not "need" a problem.

Returning to our example at the start of this chapter, it is possible that any one (or all) of the problems in this family represent a systems problem in the whole family. The spouse couple problem may be some subtle reflection of stresses and strains in the whole family system itself, as may be their sexual problems. The 3-year-old child's problems may similarly reflect a subtle dynamic in the family system itself. Family therapists would want to work with the whole family in this case to help fix things. Many family therapists believe that to work only with the individuals involved (say, the child) is useless, or worse than useless. They argue that the person who comes to therapy (again, perhaps the child) is merely the identified patient when the real patient is the entire family.

There are many different approaches to family therapy, corresponding to each of the major schools of therapy we have covered previously in this text. Because they are largely extensions of the ideas and principles used in individual contexts, we will not cover these approaches, but instead focus on approaches that have made new contributions to the understanding and treatment of behavioral difficulties.

Approaches to family therapy vary along a dimension from those that, while systems-oriented, also focus on individual dynamics and processes, to those that are more purely systemic. We shall first consider Murray Bowen, whose approach, while systemic, also includes many psychodynamic ideas. Next we shall consider the views of Virginia Satir, who similarly is systemic, but includes many ideas from experiential-humanistic theory. Next we shall consider approaches that are more purely systemic: Minuchin's Structural approach, and the strategic approaches of Jay Haley and Cloe Madanes, Paul Watzlawick, and Steven de Shazer.

Murray Bowen and Personal Differentiation

For Murray Bowen (1978), who was one of the first to designate his approach a family systems approach, the key issue in psychopathology is the degree of personal differentiation of each person from his or her **family of origin,** that is, the family within which he or she was raised. Therefore, even though Bowen is a systems theorist, his approach has also been heavily influenced by psychoanalysis. For Bowen, **differenti-ation** consists of the ability to remain emotionally controlled while in the context of one's family and the ability to have a clear sense of one's own values, beliefs, and re-actions separate from others. A truly differentiated person is able to think objectively about a situation and not be overwhelmed by emotion and to assert and own his or her values and beliefs without attacking or dismissing the values and beliefs of others.

For most people, there are areas in their relationships to their families where they remain undifferentiated. People remain fused or emotionally entangled with their families in various ways. The degree of lack of differentiation is an index of the indi-vidual's emotional disturbance. Bowen believes in a **multigenerational transmission process** for lack of differentiation. Lack of differentiation in the parents is transmit-ted to the children. An anxious mother who is not sufficiently differentiated herself, for instance, will project her anxiety onto a child. Bowen argues that this process may lead to progressively lower levels of differentiation generation by generation, ulti-mately resulting in the production of a psychotic child.

Lack of differentiation leads either to an inability to keep oneself separate from another or to a pathological, defensive separateness. Unresolved attachments to par-ents may be "resolved" by cutting off emotions. Thus, someone may yearn for emo-tional closeness, but defend against it. Either an inability to maintain separateness or a defensive separateness will lead to an unstable situation with a spouse. You will ei-ther be demanding things you feel you are not getting from your spouse or you will feel demands from your spouse.

In order to deal with the tension and instability, couples usually form a triangle with a third person. This means that a third person is drawn into the emotional sys-tem in order to provide a kind of stability. For instance, a wife who cannot feel close to her husband may devote herself to her child and distance herself from her hus-band. In states of relative calm, most triangles include two members who are rela-tively close to one another and one member who is an outsider, as in our example of the wife and child. Triangulation can occur because of an intergenerational instabil-ity. For instance, a son who has been overly close to his mother may marry in order to create some distance between himself and her. In states of high tension, more and more people may be included in triangles. Other siblings, relatives, and even neigh-bors may be included. Thus, a husband and wife who have been unable to deal with their tension by including one child may include more children. There may be a hus-band-wife-son triangle and a husband-wife-daughter triangle and perhaps even a wife-daughter-son triangle. One example of including members outside the family in a triangle is the extramarital affair.

Even though Bowen believes that fusion and lack of differentiation are passed down through generations and that ultimately, an individual's problems have to do with lack of differentiation from the family of origin, Bowen does not necessarily work with the whole family. He believes the therapist can work with individual members of the family, but he prefers to work with the marital subsystem.

One technique Bowen uses is constructing a **genogram** of the family. This is a dia-gram that shows the relationships of the husband and wife to their families of origin. Re-lationships are diagrammed in terms of fusion and emotional cutoff. Bowen may show the genogram to the family as a way of helping them gain insight into their difficulties.

The primary goal of Bowen's family therapy is to develop the autonomy of each family member. Part of this process is helping the spouses to become aware of how their relationships to their families of origin affect their relationships to each other and to their children. Thus, Bowen, like Satir, values insight as a growth-producing mechanism. Bowen attempts to provide an atmosphere in which such learning can occur, modeling differentiation himself. For instance, husband and wife will attempt to triangle Bowen into their problems by trying to get him to take sides in an argument. Bowen attempts to avoid this by making sure that any statements he makes are identified as his own and by not being judgmental.

Bowen also tries to model and teach observation of the family system. In other words, he attempts to model separating objective observation of what is going on from overly subjective emotional reactions. His belief is that emotional reactions of anger, blame, sadness, anxiety, and so forth result from lack of differentiation. Therefore, by keeping the emotional climate of therapy toned down and by encouraging observation, he is facilitating differentiation. This approach differs from Satir's emphasis on feelings.

Bowen provides an atmosphere that facilitates differentiation also by having each spouse talk to him rather than to each other. As the husband, for instance, talks to Bowen, the wife listens. Afterward, Bowen may ask the wife for her reactions to what she heard. Bowen might then ask the husband for his reactions. This mechanism facilitates differentiation because it keeps the spouses from falling into old, undifferentiated patterns of argument, blame, criticism, and so forth, in which emotions run high. It puts one spouse in the role of observer as the other talks. Again, Bowen differs from Satir, who encourages spouses to talk to each other.

Finally, Bowenian therapists encourage husband and wife to go back to their families of origin and confront them. They help coach the husband and wife so that they can interact with their families in different, more productive ways than before. This allows the husband and wife to engage in experiential learning in order to develop greater differentiation.

Virginia Satir and Dysfunctional Communication

Satir (1967) assumed that dysfunctional communication is a large part of families' problems. Dysfunctional communication results from the way the marital partners were raised as children and from their unrealistic, unspoken expectations of what the spouse will do for them.

Satir believed that every individual grows up with unspoken assumptions and rules learned from parents about the way families should work and how family life should run. In disturbed families, the spouses grew up with low self-esteem and chose their marital partners in the hope that the partner would supply the esteem they lack. Of course, a partner cannot do that, so these insecure people are doomed to disappointment. Furthermore, they tend to view differences with a partner as threats, as evidence that the other does not love them. However, differences are inevitable, because they come from different families with different unspoken rules. Since the rules are unspoken, disagreements about them are difficult to resolve. All of this leads to severely disturbed communication and disturbed family functioning.

Let us look at a typical case. The wife comes from a large family in which the men waited on the women. Since it was a large family, one had to be assertive and expressive to gain attention. The husband is an only child from a family in which the women waited on the men, and the men were quiet and unexpressive. When the couple first met, they were immediately attracted to one another. He, being quiet and unassertive, saw her as a fascinating, lively, mysterious creature who would love him and take care of him. She saw him as a strong, stable person who would love her and take care of her (wait on her). As the inevitable disappointment sets in, she comes to see him as a boring stick-in-the-mud, and he comes to see her as irrational, bossy, and overemotional. (It is not uncommon that the quality in a spouse that most aggravates a partner is the very quality that first attracted the partner.)

In addition to the disappointment of unrealistic expectations, this couple's low self-esteem makes them perceive differences between them as threatening to their relationship. When the husband does not talk to her or wait on her, the wife takes it as evidence that he does not love her. When she talks all the time and fails to wait on him, the husband concludes the same thing. Both their lack of confidence and the fact that they may not even be aware of their unspoken rules about family life prohibit them from discussing these rules. They are in pain, but they cannot talk about that, either. Their younger child develops symptoms: poor grades and non-compliance. The child's problems keep the family from falling apart and give the parents an issue they can agree to focus on. It is the child's symptoms that bring the family into therapy.

In weekly family therapy sessions, Satir tried to make the couple aware of all these processes. She took a family history from each spouse and pointed out how differently they were raised. She tried to elicit their unspoken assumptions and their feelings about behavior that differs from these assumptions. She helped them communicate more clearly and directly by reflecting their feelings and raising their intended meanings. She might have asked the clients to mirror one another's statements. Satir also interpreted the family's behavior as it occurred in front of her. Frequently, when the parents start to talk about a meaningful issue, the child with problems engages in distracting or symptomatic behavior. She may break things, start talking loudly about something else, twitch and squirm hyperactively, or throw a temper tantrum. Satir interpreted this behavior as the child's attempt to protect the parents from having to deal with the pain of their low self-esteem and their marital disappointments. The role of the child's symptoms in the family can thus be made clear to all.

Satir described five roles or basic modes of communication in families: placating, blaming, superreasonable, irrelevant, and congruent. In this disturbed family, the father is always superreasonable, never showing his true feelings; the mother placates him all the time, never showing her true feelings; the older child blames everything on everyone else; and the symptomatic child responds with irrelevant annoying habits and silly talk. Only congruent communication—messages that reflect a person's genuine feelings and intentions—can help solve family conflict. Satir tries to model and teach congruent communication.

Once the family has gained insight into the role the child's symptomatic behavior is playing in the family, the behavior is useless to protect the parents or to maintain family homeostasis, and it will be given up. In this respect, Satir is one family thera- pist who values the acquisition of insight. In addition, as the parents learn to commu- nicate more effectively, their sense of competence and feelings of esteem improve. They are better able to tolerate each other's differences and to explore the meaning of those differences. The child learns a new role in the family, and they all learn commu- nications and problem-solving skills. The entire family system functions better.

One significant difference between Satir's approach and other family approaches that emphasize communication is that Satir places a greater emphasis on feelings. Communication is not merely the communication of ideas and perspectives, but of feelings. Therefore, in addition to gaining access to unspoken family rules and as- sumptions, her approach focuses on becoming more aware of feelings, which are the intended meanings of most messages.

Minuchin and the Structural Approach

Salvador Minuchin (1974) is one of the founders of the family systems view of per- sonal problems. His therapy, called **structural family therapy,** is based on a view of the family as a hierarchically organized system. That means that the system has vari- ous levels and subsystems. For instance, there is the spousal subsystem (husband and wife relating to one another), the parental subsystem (husband and wife relating to one another in terms of the children and relating to the children), and a sibling sub- system. There may be other subsystems, such as ones that include grandparents or in- laws or subsystems organized by gender (female and male subsystems). These sub- systems overlap, interact, and separate as the family goes about its daily functioning.

What goes wrong in disturbed families has to do with the characteristics of the subsystems. Difficulties can develop around boundary problems. In a well-organized family, there are clear, but not rigid, boundaries between various subsystems. For in- stance, there is a clear distinction between the parental and the child subsystems. In a disturbed family, that distinction may be blurred, as in a family in which there is an alliance of a mother and child against a father, or in totally child-focused families, in which the spouses have no relationship, or in immature families, in which no one takes the role of parents or where children have too much authority. In a well-orga- nized family, the sibling subsystem is organized in a hierarchical manner appropriate to age, that is, children are given responsibilities and privileges commensurate with age. In a poorly organized family, older children may be treated like younger chil- dren, or younger children may be given responsibilities and privileges more appro- priate to older children. In families with parental substance abuse, the children may be "parentified" and take on responsible roles beyond their capacity. In the well-or- ganized system, distinctions are not too rigidly drawn. For instance, the parental subsystem is not so rigid that parents always act like parents and always put them- selves in the role of authority.

There are two major types of dysfunctional family systems. In the **disengaged family,** the subsystem boundaries are excessively rigid, and family members are dis- connected from one another. This type of family is conducive to the development of antisocial personality in children. In the **enmeshed family,** the boundaries are weak or unstable, and individuality is difficult to maintain. A disorder typical of this type of family is anorexia, which Minuchin sees as an attempt to assert autonomy and gain control over the self.

Minuchin's goal is to help families restructure their subsystems and to establish appropriate boundaries. He uses a variety of methods and takes an active and directive part in the therapeutic process. Some compare him to a freedom fighter trying to liberate the family from its destructive rules and roles. He learns the family's language and rules and joins the family system for a while. Once the therapist joins the family, it is a different system already. Minuchin may take sides in family arguments if he perceives that a family member has no appropriate allies. Sometimes he speaks for family members, putting their unspoken thoughts into words. He tries to provoke weak couples into strengthening their spousal subsystem. He may define a child as inappropriately parental and, by doing so, challenge the parents to ally with each other and to exert their authority. Minuchin directs family members to behave certain ways in homework assignments. He might put a weak father in charge of a symptomatic son for a week and tell the overcontrolling mother not to interfere. He sometimes exaggerates family patterns, for instance, by yelling in a family that yells too much.

One interesting aspect of Minuchin's method is his use of the family's seating arrangement in therapy sessions. He arranges the room so that family members have a choice of where to sit as they enter the room for the first session. How they sit is often a gauge of how the family interacts. Minuchin will actively rearrange seating to change the interaction. For instance, if overprotective mother and dysfunctional son sit together and father sits off to the side, son and father may be made to sit next to one another.

Strategic and Solution-Focused Approaches

In the early 1960s, the Mental Research Institute in Palo Alto, California, was a hotbed of innovation. Some of the biggest names in family therapy were there—Virginia Satir, Don Jackson (whom we do not discuss here), Jay Haley, and Paul Watzlawick. Collectively, their approach was known as the "communications" approach. From that base, Satir went off to develop her own communication approach, and Haley and Watzlawick went off to develop their "strategic" approaches. From them, as well as from others, developed the more recent "solution-focused" approaches, such as that of Steven de Shazer, which shares much in common with strategic approaches.

Haley and Watzlawick are two of the foremost strategic therapists, but there are others. As an example of a solution-focused approach we will mention the work of de Shazer. Another influential form of strategic therapy was developed in Milan, Italy (Selvini Palazzoli, Cecchin, Prata, & Boscola, 1978). What is common to all of these approaches is the goal to design a strategy to change the problem behavior in either a family or an individual client. The goal of therapy is to remedy the problem behavior, not to gain insight, get in touch with feelings, assume responsibility, or challenge dysfunctional cognitions. Watzlawick (1978) argues that cognitive insight is not only therapeutically useless, but may be counterproductive. Thus, each intervention is individually tailored to a particular client's or family's problem. Strategic and solution-focused therapists are content to remove the problem behavior or symptom, without worrying about the dynamics supposedly underlying them. In this regard, these approaches are similar to behavior therapy.

Another important commonality is that the approaches all derive much of their therapeutic strategy from the work of Milton Erickson. Although some therapists think that Erickson's influence equals Freud's (Dowd & Milne, 1986), he is not well known among nonprofessionals. Therefore, before we discuss strategic approaches, we will introduce Erickson's work.

Milton Erickson

We shall use a story to introduce Milton Erickson's work (Feldman, 1985; see also our discussion of him in Chapter 11). A woman spent some time studying with him and then returned to her home city. She subsequently wrote Erickson complaining about her lack of results in trying to work the way he did. In the same letter, she incidentally asked for a recipe for cinnamon pie, which she had had at his home. In his reply Erickson did not address her concerns about her work. Instead, he merely gave her the recipe for cinnamon pie, with the comment, "Of course, every good cook must adjust the seasoning to suit their own particular taste" (Dammann, 1980, p. 200).

This story illustrates the indirect way Erickson communicated his messages. The woman was not directly told, "You need to adapt what you learned from me to your personal style," but the message was implied. Erickson was one of the most colorful therapists. The things he did were often startling, uncommon, and delightful. Perhaps what is most impressive about his work is that he was a pioneer. Now, several years after his death (in 1980), he is becoming a highly influential figure. Yet, while he was alive, he worked in relative obscurity, engaging in a kind of therapy that fit no models popular at the time, for it was not Freudian, client-centered, or behavioral.

Erickson did not believe in the importance of insight or awareness for inducing personality change. Instead, he believed that the unconscious was a source of wisdom, and his therapy was designed to draw on that. In addition, Erickson believed that major change could be induced by first inducing smaller changes. Like a snowball rolling downhill, a small change could change the overall system of the personality or the family for the better.

Erickson is primarily known as a hypnotist, and that was one of his major tools. He believed that all therapy worked by suggestion. However, he devised many techniques to utilize the power of suggestion without the use of hypnosis. **Paradoxical interventions** are one example. Paradoxical interventions include **reframing** (or, "positive connotation") and *prescribing the symptom.*

Reframing is reinterpreting a behavior that a client sees as pathological in a positive way. For instance, de Shazer (1985) relates the case of a young woman whose problem was that she was unable to speak up around her fiancé. Instead of treating this as a problem, the therapist congratulated her on having learned the most important lesson in communication—how to listen. Her perception of her silence as pathological was reframed as something positive. In addition, she was told that she now had to learn another skill. She had to pay attention to her fiancé and try to detect when he was ready to listen.

With prescribing the symptom, the therapist instructs the client to perform the very symptomatic behavior the client is trying to eliminate, although not neccessarily exactly as it occurs spontaneously. In one of Erickson's most well-known cases, a husband and wife who both wet the bed were instructed to deliberately wet the bed each night before they went to bed. The bedwetting soon stopped. Watzlawick (1985) relates the case of a man who was constantly arguing with his wife. He was instructed to go out on the weekend and pick arguments with others. After trying to follow this instruction, he stopped arguing with his wife.

While reframing and symptom prescription are perhaps the best known Ericksonian interventions, there are others. One technique Erickson used was to give the client an apparent choice, but actually, the message left no choice. In addition, the message carried an indirect suggestion that the client would stop exhibiting the symptom. For instance, Erickson might say, "When are you going to stop the arguing—on Wednesday or on Thursday?" Such a message apparently presents the client with a choice, but takes for granted that the client will stop exhibiting the symptom.

Another Ericksonian technique was the use of **teaching stories,** stories that convey a message metaphorically. Cameron-Bandler (1978) used this to treat a young man for premature ejaculation. First, the man was told that nothing could be done about his problem. Later, he was placed in a hypnotic trance and told a story. The essence of the story was that one could go on a "vacation" in one of two ways. One could either rush to the destination or take the slow route, enjoying the sights along the way. The message implied should be clear, and this teaching story appeared to cure the young man's difficulties.

An example of Erickson's belief that a small change could lead to much larger changes is given in Feldman (1985). The client was a depressed, angry woman, who complained of hating Phoenix, but was reluctant to go on a vacation. While she was in a hypnotic trance, Erickson suggested to her that while on vacation, she would be curious about seeing an unexpected "flash of color." This mobilized her to look for the unexpected, and of course, she did eventually see an unexpected flash of color in the form of a redheaded woodpecker flying past a tree. After seeing this, she continued to search for "color" in her life, and she eventually became someone who enjoyed traveling and was not depressed.

Erickson believed that one could use a client's symptom as part of the solution to his problem. In other words, instead of working against the client's symptom, he worked with it and turned it to the client's favor. Actually, this is the strategy that underlies his other techniques, such as reframing and paradoxical intervention. However, we will give an example in which the technique is used directly. A hospitalized patient believed himself to be Jesus. Many therapists would presume the belief is a defense and try to remove it by helping the client acquire insight into its defensive nature. These therapists would be working against the symptom. Erickson's approach was to mobilize the symptom positively. He said to the man, "I understand that you have experience as a carpenter." Thus, part of the symptom of believing himself to be Jesus was used therapeutically. Erickson was able to get the client involved in doing productive work, thereby lessening the need for the symptom in the first place.

Modern Strategic and Solution-Focused Therapists

We will consider the work of three "teams" of modern strategic and solution-focused therapists: Jay Haley and his colleague Cloe Madanes (Haley, 1976; Madanes, 1984), Paul Watzlawick and his colleagues (Watzlawick, Weakland, & Fisch, 1974), and Steven de Shazer (1985). All are similar (though not identical) in their therapeutic strategies, and all draw on Erickson's work. They differ most in their theories of psychopathology and personality.

Jay Haley and Cloe Madanes   For Jay Haley, all behavior is communication. Humans cannot not communicate. Even remaining silent conveys a message: "I don't want to talk." Communication occurs on more than one level at once. For instance, if you ask someone for advice, she may answer by saying "You should do so and so." What she suggests you do is the content of the communication. However, she has also agreed with your definition of the relationship as one in which you are helpless and she acts as the wise helper. For Haley, in addition to conveying content, communication serves to define a relationship in terms of who has power. He sees power, "who's in charge," as a basic issue in all human relationships.

Haley analyzes interpersonal relationships in terms of power arrangements and sees psychological symptoms as metaphorical communications through which the power relationships in a family system are expressed. For instance, a wife who wishes her husband to stay home with her may develop anxiety attacks. She is not consciously in control of the anxiety attacks, but at the same time, her husband must stay home in case she has one. Therefore, the message "Stay home with me" is conveyed metaphorically in the symptom of the attacks, and the symptom also serves the purpose of exerting power over the husband.

In a family system, a pathological behavior is some metaphorical communication about the family. For Haley, as well as for Watzlawick, the question of why pathological behavior occurs is not as productive as the question of what purpose it serves. Haley and many other theorists adopt a "functionalist" view, that is, they believe that pathological behaviors serve functions in the family (Bogdan, 1986). The functions are unconsciously generated; families are largely unaware of how the symptoms function in the family.

While Haley sees the process of symptom formation as largely unconscious, he does not believe that insight and awareness are important therapeutic goals. Instead, he advocates direct manipulation of behavior as it functions within the family system. The therapist must take charge and intervene in the family in such a way as to change the dysfunctional family system. Haley, Madanes, and others have developed a large set of techniques to apply to individual cases.

Before we describe the strategies, we wish to mention how such strategies are arrived at. First, these therapists often work with a one-way mirror. One therapist sees the family, while a group of other therapists observe through a one-way mirror. The intervention strategy used is devised by the whole team. In designing a strategy, Haley (1985) points out that great care must be taken to design a strategy that the clients will comply with. Therefore, as with many of the other therapeutic interventions described in this book, it takes a great deal of skill to successfully design a strategic intervention that both will be followed by the clients and will be effective. So, if you're having problems with your husband or wife, or children, or parents, it would be better for you to try something besides paradoxical interventions or other strategies discussed here.

One set of strategies used by these therapists involves restructuring the family. In one form of restructuring, other members of the family are asked to share the symptom. For example, one family came to therapy because the middle daughter was exhibiting problem behavior. Her siblings were "model" children. The family was told that it was unfair that the middle daughter carry the burden of being the troublemaker for the whole family. The family appeared to need a troublemaker, but the burden should be shared. Each of the other children was given the assignment of being the troublemaker for a period of time. This eliminated the middle daughter's problem behavior (Madanes, 1985).

In another type of restructuring, the normal power structure in the family is reversed. If a parent is acting irresponsibly, a child may be put in charge of that parent or of that parent's happiness. In one case, a mother was accused of physically abusing her children, who were generally unruly and uncooperative. One of the most uncooperative children (who, among other things, set fires) was put in charge of making his mother's life easier. This appeared to bring out the love and caring the child felt for the mother, and her abuse of the children stopped, as did the son's disruptive behavior (Madanes, 1984).

These therapists also use reframing and paradoxical interventions. For example (Madanes, 1987), a young adult male was gambling so much he was seriously in debt and was draining the family funds. His gambling was being supported by his mother and aunt, who would give him money to help get him out of debt. The therapist, rather than telling him to stop gambling, instructed him to gamble. However, the structure under which he gambled was altered. His mother and aunt had to go with him to the racetrack, tell him which horses to bet on, and then stand in line with him while he placed his bets, warding off any friends or acquaintances that might approach. In addition, the family was to hold nightly poker games in which the mother and aunt were to coach the young man on how to play. Though the mother and aunt did not know anything about gambling, they enthusiastically agreed to learn so they could play their parts. After rehearsing these procedures in therapy sessions, the young man disgustedly told the therapist that she did not know anything about gambling, but that it did not matter, because he was going to give up gambling, get a job, and pay his debts anyway. This is what he proceeded to do.

In the paradoxical intervention in the gambler's case, the behavior prescribed differed quite a bit from the spontaneous symptom. In some cases, the change is more subtle. For instance, if a husband and wife tend to argue in one room in their home, they will be instructed to argue deliberately, but in a different room. Or the timing of the arguments might be changed. The husband and wife might be instructed to set aside 20 minutes each day to argue.

Related to the use of paradox is an intervention in which the therapist talks about all the possible negative things that might occur if the problem is solved. The therapist implies that the family could not tolerate the elimination of the problem or even that it would be disastrous for the family to eliminate the problem and that they are at the best level of adjustment they can hope for. This intervention is thought to work by mobilizing the family's resistance. In order to prove the therapist wrong, they must change for the better. (See Box 14.1.)

Paul Watzlawick and Constructivism   Paul Watzlawick is one of the foremost spokespersons for the viewpoint of **constructivism** (Watzlawick, 1984; see also Chapter 17). Briefly put, constructivism holds that there is no "one true objective reality"; rather, each individual constructs his own reality and there are, therefore, multiple possible constructions of reality. Individuals' concepts of reality are like maps. Maps are representations of reality, but no map reproduces reality. Furthermore, different maps of the same territory can be drawn, and each may be useful in its own way. A geological map of an area will not look identical to a road map.

Does this mean that any construction of reality is equally acceptable? No. While we might not be able to say that any one view is the true one, we can say that some constructions work better than others. Watzlawick (1984) gives the example of a boat captain navigating a channel at night. There may be multiple "correct" routes that will get him through the channel. However, there are also clearly wrong routes that will lead to shipwreck. Watzlawick argues that the same is true of people's views of their world. For Watzlawick, therefore, we can never talk about the validity of an idea about reality, we can only talk about its viability, that is, is the idea helpful and useful?

Constructivism is a very popular notion in the area of family therapy at the present time. In general, constructivism leads to the idea that how we use language shapes and defines our realities. Therefore, if we can shift how we talk and think about our realities, those realities will shift. Constructivists believe that one of the goals of therapy is to change how we "language" our experience. Constructivists play with words and use paradoxes and the like to help shift the personal constructions through which individuals experience their world.

Paul Watzlawick's work is a prime example. For Watzlawick, psychological problems are actually attempts at solutions to life problems. Psychological problems occur when people attempt to solve new life problems with a solution that worked in the past or for old problems, but that does not work now. Often, when the old solution strategy does not work, they try "upping the dosage." Finally, they may even break down. Solutions themselves are based on how the individual is defining or "constructing" the problem. That is, a solution is based on an implicit premise about what the reality is, and what the problem is.

Watzlawick (1985) gives the example of army ants, who have evolved a pattern of marching in a column. This strategy allows the colony of ants much greater flexibility in adaptation and survival than any one ant would have on its own. Yet, this life-enhancing strategy can become their downfall. If, by some accident of terrain, the lead ant starts to march in a circle and catches up to the last ant in the column, the ants will continue to march in a circle until they die. The strategy that evolved because of its survival value becomes a problem under the wrong conditions. The ants are "stuck."

BOX 14.1

The Function of Disruption

The therapist ushered the family into the therapy room, where an angry mother and her two oldest teenage daughters immediately sat together on a sofa and the youngest, the identified patient, sat in the chair farthest away. The mother reported that Wendy was being truant from junior high, failing several classes, lying, and stealing. As a single mother who worked full time and went to college at night, she just "couldn't take" any more disruption from her always difficult child.

Most of the therapy hour was spent eliciting each person's version of the family's difficulties, with the therapist empathizing with each individual's feelings and perceptions. The mother and two oldest daughters insisted that everything would be just fine if it weren't for Wendy. Her truancy was the final straw because the mother had to miss work to go to Wendy's school for a parent conference. Since Wendy sat far away, huddled sullenly in her chair, refusing to speak or look at anyone, the therapist empathized with how difficult it must be for her to talk with everyone against her and how distressed, embarrassed, hurt, and angry she must feel. Having made contact with each family member by validating her viewpoint, the therapist made her paradoxical intervention.

The therapist delivered this speech slowly and seriously:

As you know, I believe the reason one member of a family shows problem behavior is because the entire family is in pain. And this family certainly is in pain. Everyone is busy, stretched to the limit, and stressed out. Mrs. G works, goes to college, raises a family alone. Each daughter goes to school, helps run the household, does chores and homework, tries to have a social life. It's just too much. But only Wendy acts out the family pain by doing bad things. She saves the rest of you from having to look at the kind of stress and pain you live under by being the bad one. In fact, she is sacrificing herself to save you, her loved ones, from having to experience your own pain. And she is sacrificing herself, because after all, she's the one who will have to pay. She must really love all of you a lot.

But I don't want you to change too fast. If Wendy suddenly started being good, you'd all have to face your own pain, and you might not like that. So Wendy, during the next week, I want you to be truant as much as possible and continue lying. In fact, tell at least three really good lies. I want you to continue to sacrifice yourself and protect the rest of your family. Okay, I'll see you all next week at this time.

The effect of this intervention on the family was electric. They all immediately sat straight and listened carefully. Wendy sat up, leaned forward, and looked at the therapist as if she were crazy. The others looked between Wendy and the therapist in confusion. The mother started to

---

BOX 14.1 *(continued)*

protest that she didn't want Wendy to sacrifice herself in that way, but the therapist ushered them out of the room with promises to see them next week.

The next week, quite a different family entered the therapy room. Three cheerful daughters sat comfortably on the sofa together, and a beaming mother sat in a chair beside them. They reported that they couldn't understand it, but they'd had a great week together. For some reason Wendy went to school and did not lie or steal. They all got along well together and even had some fun together. No one could explain it. The therapist said that she was glad to see the family handling their issues so well and that they could call her in the future if they needed to. The family did not request another appointment for over a year.

For Watzlawick, therefore, the problem is that the individual, couple, or family is stuck in a construction of reality that is blocking them from finding creative, new solutions. It is as if they are looking at the world through blue-colored glasses, and therefore do not notice other colors that might help them resolve their problem. They are stuck, trying to do the best they can, rather than unconsciously trying to maintain their symptoms because their symptoms are unconsciously gratifying, as some other perspectives hold.

This distinction between "stuck" versus "gratified" is an important one and deserves a few more comments before we move on to further consider Watzlawick's views. Wile (1981), whose psychodynamic perspective on working with couples we have previously considered, also embraces the idea that psychopathology involves being "stuck." He points out that traditional psychoanalysis, some family views, some behavioral views, and some humanistic views hold that a person acts psychopathologically because in some way, he is gaining gratification from the pathological behavior. For instance, a depressive may be seen as trying to gain attention through her depression. Wile, like Beck, Rogers, and the constructivists, holds that the depressive remains depressed because she is stuck. The solutions she is using simply get her mired deeper. We can think of someone in quicksand, whose "solution" is to struggle, which makes things worse. Depressives react to a failure by setting higher standards for themselves, as if they are trying to motivate themselves to succeed. However, this solution is actually dysfunctional, since it only increases the chance of failure, which is followed by increased depression (Simon, 1979, in Bandura, 1986, p. 360).

For those who believe pathology is maintained by gratification, therapy involves either making the client aware of how his symptoms are providing unconscious gratification or removing the gratifications. For those who believe the client is repeating unproductive solutions because he does not know better, therapy involves helping the client get unstuck.

How does Watzlawick propose to get a client unstuck? How would you help the ants? Would you put the lead ant on a couch and help it gain insight into its past?

Would you have it focus on its feelings or felt meanings? Would you wonder what dysfunctional cognitions the ant has? Or would you simply place a stick strategically so that the circular pattern is broken up, allowing the ants to march forward once again?

For Watzlawick, therapy is a matter of using some intervention to break up the circle in which the client is stuck. He (1987) argues that insight is irrelevant to change and that change occurs all the time in everyday life without insight. If the old system is broken up, new, forward-moving behavior will take its place, and engaging in a new behavior can change a whole personal system for construing reality. This is a crucial point because Watzlawick believes that a simple change can result in a major, pervasive, personal change. In contrast, psychoanalysis, for instance, believes that changing one's personal construct system takes years of reviewing of its roots in early childhood.

One of Watzlawick's key ideas is the distinction between **first order change** and **second order change.** People get stuck because they operate out of unquestioned assumptions about the nature of reality and, in particular, about the nature of the problem situation they are dealing with. For some "traditional" husbands, it is practically "bred in the bone" that the husband is supposed to be dominant; the wife is supposed to stay at home and not work. All people have these unquestioned assumptions. They form part of their first order reality. When individuals attempt to solve problems, they operate out of those assumptions, without realizing they are assumptions. Then, when things go wrong, they do not question the assumptions underlying their actions, goals, and perceptions, but simply try to refine their strategies or actions in accord with those same old assumptions. For instance, someone sinking in quicksand may not question his assumption that some kind of vigorous action is needed to get out. So even when thrashing about does not help, he shifts to another kind of vigorous action (perhaps trying to swim and kick with his feet), rather than questioning his assumption that vigorous activity is an appropriate solution.

Watzlawick argues that what is needed is not a first order change, in which one simply tries new ways to solve the problem from the same old assumptions. What is needed is a second order change, in which the assumptions themselves are overthrown. The person has to be able to step outside of the old frame he puts on situations, to see them in a new way. A simple illustration of this is given in Figures 14.1 and 14.2.

The therapist's task, then, is to induce second order change. This will get the system "unstuck" and moving again. Let us consider an example of someone who

Figure 14.1   The problem is to connect all nine dots by drawing four lines without lifting the pencil from the page. See Figure 14.2 for the solution.

Figure 14.2   People have trouble with this problem because they see the nine dots as a square. They have to change that assumption and see the dots in a different way to solve the problem.

attempts to solve a problem by instituting first order changes. One of us knows of a family in which the wife, because of her own traumatic family background, is overprotective toward her teenage daughter. Because the woman was somewhat wild as a child, she is concerned about her daughter's becoming wild. So she is highly restrictive concerning her daughter's curfew time and her daughter's friends. If you think in terms of a system, you can imagine what might happen next. Such overprotectiveness generates rebellion in the daughter. She begins to exhibit some of the very behaviors the mother has been so worried about: cutting school, hanging around with people the mother dislikes, and acting rebellious at home. This convinces the mother that she was on the right track all along—the daughter is in danger of going down the wrong path. The mother therefore redoubles her efforts to control the daughter and becomes even more restrictive. Thus, her solution is to do "more of the same." This is the first order change she attempts. The basic premise underlying all her attempts to control her daughter is never questioned. A second order change in this mother's case might be to facilitate a shift in perspective so that she "sees" that focusing on the positive with her daughter, and building a positive relationship with her, in addition to or instead of trying to control her, might lead to better outcomes. Thus she might be told "It is important that you persist in your efforts to monitor your daughter. However, in order for you to know her better so that you can do this more effectively, we believe you need to spend more time carefully listening to her. So we suggest the following. . . ."

How does Watzlawick propose to initiate second order change? Watzlawick argues that there are two languages. The verbal, logical, analytic language of the left brain and the language of image, metaphor, synthesis, and totality of the right brain. According to Watzlawick, "This language of the right brain does not explain; it creates, it evokes" (1978, p. 58), and it is in this language that therapists must speak. This is the language of strategic interventions, the language of concrete imagery, indirect suggestion, metaphorical communication, paradox, and jokes. It is this language that can create second order change.

Watzlawick's approach to therapy is quite brief, with the average being about six sessions per client (Watzlawick, 1985). The Watzlawick group uses many of the techniques we have already encountered (Watzlawick, Weakland, & Fisch, 1974). Among others mentioned by Watzlawick (1985) is the therapeutic double bind. The client is given an instruction that puts her in a paradoxical position. A woman client who said she "couldn't say no" was instructed to go around to each person in the room and say no to them. She said, "No! I can't do that!" Of course, by saying no to the intervention, she was saying no.

Watzlawick phrases his communications in such a way as to make "every success theirs" and "every failure ours." After a successful change the client might be told, "Amazing! You must have done something different. What did you do to make it a success?"

Steven de Shazer   De Shazer's approach is one of those called "solution-focused." The emphasis in solution-focused therapies is on the future: finding ways of helping people get where they want to go. Correspondingly, there is little or no emphasis on the past in terms of what "caused" the problem. In order to create solutions, solution-focused therapists rely on client strength and creativity, and in this regard, they share Carl Rogers's faith in the self-healing capabilities of people (Miller, Duncan, & Hubble, 1996). One of their most basic strategies is to help clients notice what they are doing right, or to remember when things were going the way they wanted them to go. In essence, solution-focused therapists believe that clients often already know how to solve their problems; they are just not paying attention to the ways to make things go better that they already know how to do, or were doing at one time.

De Shazer (1985) shares the idea that problems are most often the outcomes of attempts at solution, and he would agree with Watzlawick (1987) that pathology is a system that has run out of ways of dealing with a problem. On the development of the causes of the problem, the de Shazer position is compatible with other theoretical perspectives covered in this book. For instance, it could be that a problem has complex roots in the past. However, de Shazer believes that just because a problem is complex does not mean that it demands a complex solution. One could think of the story of Alexander the Great and the Gordian Knot, which no one could untie. Alexander's solution was to take his sword and cut it apart. There may well be solutions to problems that are quite simple, though the problem itself is quite complex.

De Shazer does not believe that the solution must exactly match the problem. As a skeleton key can be used to unlock a variety of locks, therapeutic solutions can unlock a variety of problems or complaints. In this respect, therapeutic solutions work by "unsticking" the client. They break up the old system, and de Shazer believes, as does Milton Erickson, that the clients actually then resolve the problem with new, creative solutions the therapist could never have anticipated or planned.

A key theoretical point of de Shazer's (1985) is a rejection of the traditional concept of clients' unconscious resistance to change. He says,

> I became more and more convinced that clients really do want to change. Certainly some of them found that the ideas about how to change did not fit very well. However, I found it difficult to label this as "resistance" when it seemed to be a message the clients were sending in an effort to help the therapist help them. . . . Over and over I found people sent to me by other therapists . . . to be both desperate for change and highly cooperative. (p. 15)

The implication is that resistance may be as much a function of the therapist's interventions as it is a function of the client. Perhaps clients resist intervention techniques that do not fit them well. The de Shazer group works to minimize resistance and elicit clients' cooperation by complimenting clients on what they are already doing to try to solve their problem.

Many of the interventions used by the de Shazer group are based on the work of Milton Erickson and are shared by other strategic and solution-focused therapists. We will mention some we have not previously covered. De Shazer respects the reality of each client. If two clients give differing views of the problem, the therapist stays neutral and does not take sides. Rather, the therapist may mirror the conflict. However, it may be done in such a way as to put the couple in a "positive double bind," as Watzlawick does. In one example, a husband and wife were treated for cocaine abuse. They also were concerned about problems in the marriage. One partner believed the real problem was not the drug abuse, but their fights and arguments. The other thought it was the drugs that were causing the marital problems. The intervention given by the de Shazer group to the couple is described below. We will not reproduce the rather complex theoretical logic for this intervention here (de Shazer, 1985), but it is based on the fact that each member of the couple was seeing the problem in either/or terms.

> You've got a problem. It seems to us, Ralph, that your marital problems are being exacerbated by the drugs, or fogged over by the drugs, or perhaps even created by the drugs. Perhaps you need to, stop the drugs, just to see what is going on. But, on the other hand, we agree with you, Jane, that if you two were to stop the drugs, then there might be nothing there. And, you might not have time to create anything before the marriage broke up. In short, we don't know what the . . . you are going to do.
>
> I suggest you think about what I just said, and decide what actions you are going to take . . . first. (p. 52)

The interesting thing is that this intervention resulted in a two-thirds reduction of drug use by the next session and complete elimination of drug use by two weeks later, along with the development of new, positive marital activities. Follow-ups at six months and one year indicated no further drug use and infrequent arguments. In other words, a substance abuse problem and a marital problem appeared to be "cured" in two sessions!

Another intervention, similar to one used by the Watzlawick group, is to have the clients concretely and specifically define what they would like changed. Most clients come in and say things such as "We want our marriage improved" or "I want to get over being depressed" or "I want to stop being anxious so much." These are global, vague goals. Clients are asked to try to imagine concrete behavioral differences that could be used as an index of change for the better. For instance, for people who want their marriage "improved" it might be "spending one night together sharing a pleasant activity without fighting." For the depressive it might be "feeling calm and content while sitting at home on a Saturday night watching TV." For the anxious person it might be "stepping outside the door and feeling calm." The interesting thing is that the simple act of developing and defining such concrete goals is therapeutic. Clients find ways of bringing them about that are unique, creative, and not predictable by the therapist.

De Shazer, following Erickson, believes that change is not only possible, it is "inevitable," and this attitude is conveyed to the client. For example, the client may be asked "What will you do when you have changed?" or "When do you think you will be over this problem—by next week or the week after?" A specific intervention is to tell a client to "pay attention to what you do when you overcome the urge . . ." (1985, p. 132). This may be used, for instance, with overeating. The client is told to pay attention to what he or she does when he or she overcomes the urge to eat. There are two parts to this intervention. First, it implies that the client can change, that is, she can overcome the urge to eat. Second, it focuses the client's attention on the positive moments when he or she succeeds and counteracts either/or thinking. De Shazer points out that things in life are rarely "always" or "never" and that always/never thinking is an example of the either/or thinking that is often involved in dysfunctional behavior. Overeaters often say "I always overeat" or "I never can control my appetite," yet this is rarely true. Most dieters do overcome their urges to eat, frequently. They may fail at other times, but they do not always fail.

Summary of Strategic and Solution-Focused Approaches   Despite their differing theoretical orientations, the therapists we have examined all share a belief that the therapist's task is to intervene in such a way that the old, dysfunctional system is disrupted, freeing the system to develop and move forward in positive ways. They all believe that small, seemingly irrelevant changes can have a ripple effect, resulting in major and lasting changes within the individual client or the family system. They believe that instead of pitting themselves against the client's or family's problems, which could mobilize resistance, they should work with the symptoms in some way. Therefore, interventions frequently do not proscribe the symptom, but rather, place it in a different context. They also agree that insight into the causes of the symptoms is not necessary or important for change.

Finally, there is a fundamental shift in orientation among many of the strategic and solution-focused approaches toward strengthening and enhancing positive functioning rather than trying to "fix" negative functioning. Because they believe that negative functioning is simply a result of a system getting stuck on a negative track, they believe that one can get the system back on a positive track by enhancing positive behavior. Essentially they believe that clients get stuck in a negative vicious cycle. Therapy can create a positive "vicious cycle." Negative vicious cycles get created by clients' dwelling on the negative and by using the same old solutions that have not worked previously. One way to break out of this is to have clients concretely imagine and remember how they have done things successfully in the past. O'Hanlon and Weiner-Davis (1989), for example, continually emphasize asking clients to focus on what they were doing when things were going well.

Along with this, these approaches emphasize the future more so than the past. "The future is more important than the past in determining present behavior," (Shlien, 1988), to quote a phrase that strategic therapists would agree with. They try to get clients to imagine positive outcomes because anticipating positive outcomes feeds back to influence present behavior to move in that direction. If one imagines negative outcomes, the feedback system will operate to have the negative image feed back and increase the probability of negative behavior. In sum, strategic therapists are suggesting ways of doing therapy that represent fundamental "paradigm shifts" from most of the more traditional ways of approaching psychological problems.

EVALUATION OF MARRIAGE, FAMILY, AND CHILD THERAPY

Evaluation of Child Therapy

Reviews of previous research (Casey & Berman, 1985; Kazdin, 1994; Vernberg, Routh, & Koocher, 1992; Weisz, Weiss, Alicke, & Klotz, 1987) indicate that psychological interventions with children are effective. Similar to the findings with adults, children who undergo psychotherapy show improvement on a number of outcome measures significantly more frequently than comparison groups of untreated children. Research now focuses on the question of what methods work with children at specific developmental stages with specific problems in specific situations.

Given the apparent increase in child abuse and child sexual abuse in the United States in the past decades, psychological services for children are much needed. In fact, a poor economy both increases the incidence of these problems and leads to cuts in the services needed to treat them, so that in most of the country, child service agencies are overwhelmed. Prevention would appear to be more cost-effective, and many programs for the prevention of child abuse have been developed and demonstrated to be effective. Furthermore, the increasing number of children born to drug-abusing mothers and to mothers with AIDS means even greater demand for psychological services for children in the future. Again, an emphasis on prevention seems both humane and cost-effective, but the young casualties of our social problems still deserve help and effective treatment.

Modern child therapies are briefer, more directive and structured, and more goal-oriented than earlier ones. Almost all require the participation of the parents as part of the treatment. The necessity of combining knowledge of the child's developmental changes in cognition, emotion, and perception with the utilization of therapeutic interventions means that therapy must change as knowledge of child development improves. Future research must address the issue of how interventions made at one age are construed by the child at a later age and how early interventions can be made to "last" through the developmental changes of the growing child. Vernberg, Routh, and Koocher (1992) propose the concepts of "developmental psychotherapy" and "healthy versus deviant pathways" to deal with this issue. The focus in their model is on the therapist intervening to help a child regain his footing on a developmental pathway more likely to lead to adequate adaptation in later stages of life.

Evaluation of Marital and Family Therapy

Gurman, Kniskern, and Pinsof (1986) reviewed research on marital and family therapy and drew the following conclusions. First, nonbehavioral marital and family therapies are effective and produce beneficial outcomes in two-thirds of cases. Second, marital therapy is more likely to be successful when both spouses are treated than when only one spouse is treated. Third, the positive benefits of both behavioral and nonbehavioral approaches can usually be achieved in less than 20 sessions. Fourth, family and marital approaches appear to work better than individual therapy in treating family-related problems.

Gurman et al. (1986) conclude that the strongest evidence overall is for approaches based on behavioral methods. For many other approaches, there is simply little reliable empirical evidence available, either positive or negative. A more recent review of marital and family therapy (Alexander, Holtzworth-Munroe, & Jameson, 1994) does not substantially alter the conclusions of Gurman and colleagues.

In particular, behavioral methods have been shown to be promising or helpful for family work with schizophrenia, substance abuse, anxiety disorders, juvenile delinquency, conduct disorders, and marital discord. There is some evidence for the effectiveness of psychodynamic approaches with marital discord, a combined strategic-structural approach with substance abuse (Stanton et al., 1982), and the structural approach for psychosomatic disorders. The experiential-humanistic approach of Greenberg and Johnson (1988) for couples therapy has been shown to be effective for working with marital problems, as has the Relationship Enhancement approach (Guerney, 1984).

Several reports support the effectiveness of Minuchin's approach. Rosman, Minuchin, Liebman, and Baker (1978, as reported in Prochaska, 1984) report results on the treatment of 53 anorexics; they found that 86% achieved normal eating patterns. These writers also report successful outcomes for 17 chronic asthmatics and for the reduction of stress effects on children with diabetes. As with the research noted previously, there were no control groups, however.

Informal evaluations of the effectiveness of strategic therapies have been carried out by those who practice it. Weakland, Fisch, Watzlawick, and Bodin (1974) reported complete relief or significant improvement in 72% of their cases using the Watzlawick brief therapy approach. A follow-up on many of these, as well as other cases, found similar results (62% improvement), indicating that the changes wrought by this approach persist for some time after treatment. There was some evidence that there were positive changes in areas other than the specific presenting problems. However, their data do not meet stringent research standards. Success rates are largely based on clients' subjective reports, and no control groups were used. The de Shazer group tends to follow up their clients for six months to a year, and they report a similar figure of 72%. However, their results are subject to the same criticisms.

Despite the paucity of evidence for many approaches, Gurman, Kniskern, and Pinsof (1986) conclude that it is too early to dismiss any approach. In sum, the research is supportive of the effectiveness of marital, family, and strategic approaches. However, much of the data are not scientifically rigorous and must be treated with caution.

While there is little well-controlled empirical evidence on strategic approaches in general, there have been a number of studies on the effectiveness of paradoxical interventions in particular. A recent tabulation by Orlinsky, Grawe, and Parks (1994) of 13 studies on paradoxical intervention found that all 13 showed positive results. This is better than the results for any other technique from any other therapy. Hill (1987) has done a meta-analysis of earlier research on paradoxical interventions. On the average, clients who received paradoxical interventions were better off than 84% of clients in untreated control groups, and better off than 72% of clients who received placebo treatments (see Chapter 15). There was also tentative support for paradoxical interventions being more effective than nonparadoxical interventions. Hill holds that the evidence is particularly strong for the effectiveness of positive reframing, somewhat less so for symptom prescription. Positive reframing is more helpful with depression, and many therapists believe that symptom prescription should not be used with depression. Hill's conclusions are based on a small number of studies (15) on a limited number of disorders (insomnia, depression, agoraphobia, procrastination, and stress). Therefore, it is not clear for what populations paradoxical interventions are appropriate, but the evidence is strong that they can be useful.

Theoretical Evaluation

Because the marital, family, and child approaches constitute a diverse collection, we will not evaluate them as a whole. However, there are criticisms that have been leveled specifically at strategic approaches that need to be considered. Many systems theorists believe that an individual client's symptom serves some functional significance in the family. In other words, the symptom is an unconscious strategy for dealing with some family issue. However, criticisms of such a view can be made (e.g., Bogdan, 1986). First, it is no more than an assumption or an indirect inference that the presenting complaints of the identified patient are meeting some family need. This is not directly observable.

Second, there are certain inconsistencies in the idea. For example, an adolescent's school problems might be assumed to serve to bring father and mother, who have intimacy problems, closer together. But if we assume that all family problems are an attempt to resolve some family imbalance, then what imbalance is the parents' intimacy problems attempting to resolve? This leads to an infinite regress.

Third, this viewpoint can be questioned from an "ecological" view of systems. In an ecological system, a balance among all forces present will evolve. For instance, in an area in which rabbits eat grass and coyotes eat rabbits, a balance evolves in which the number of rabbits is controlled by the amount of grass available and by the number of coyotes around. The number of coyotes is controlled by the number of rabbits available, and indirectly by the amount of grass available, and so on. It is true that changes in one part of the system lead to adjustments in other parts (e.g., a drought affecting the amount of grass will affect both rabbits and coyotes). But to argue that one element of the system changes in order to keep the system in balance would be like arguing that coyotes eat rabbits in order to keep the ecological system in balance. But that is not why coyotes eat rabbits. They eat rabbits because they are hungry, and their eating rabbits keeps the system in balance because the whole system interactively evolved that way. Bogdan (1986) prefers an ecological metaphor and argues that problems often evolve in family systems accidentally. Arguing from the work of Watzlawick and his colleagues, Bogdan suggests that problems evolve because "ordinary life difficulties are mishandled. And they persist because no one realizes that it is the mishandling that perpetuates the problem" (p. 35).

In a similar manner, the functionalist perspective can be criticized for minimizing the role of individual psychological variables. The assumption is that pathological behavior is always the result of the family system and not the result of any individual process. This perspective was originally developed in family theories of schizophrenia, in which it was argued that schizophrenics were actually the identified patients in pathological families. Case histories were given suggesting that families of schizophrenics were more disturbed in many ways than normal families. However, the functionalist perspective overlooks an alternative possibility. It is possible that having a disturbed family member, such as a schizophrenic, disturbs the family. Patterns of disturbance similar to those found in families of schizophrenics have also been found in families of children with other serious illnesses, such as leukemia. Having a sick child may affect the way the whole family functions. It would be most peculiar to argue that a child developed leukemia in order to bring his mother and father closer together. An ecological system point of view could handle the fact that an individual member of the system could be disturbed, and that disturbance could then disturb the rest of the system. This could then become an accidental dysfunctional feedback loop.

Furthermore, the systems theory depends on the idea that each element of the system has some identity of its own independent (at least partially) of its place in the system. A system with coyotes and rabbits will be different from a system with sheep and raccoons. Some systems theorists seem to discount the idea that each individual in the family system has his or her own personality, which plays its role in the overall family system. To really understand a family system, one has to take into account the individual characteristics of the members of that system, just as one must know that an ecological system has rabbits and coyotes in it instead of sheep and raccoons. There is nothing fundamentally incompatible between the ideas that family members have their individual personalities (and problems) and that they are part of an interactive system.

Another major criticism of strategic approaches has to do with their manipulativeness. Strategic therapists do not value insight. They do not believe that change occurs by making clients aware of their own problems so that clients can consciously initiate and control their own changes. Instead, it could be said that the therapists institute change by playing tricks on clients.

The therapists might reply that all therapy interventions are manipulations, so why not do them consciously and deliberately? This is an argument that behaviorists used to make in response to criticisms that they were manipulative. Haley (1985), who has been openly assertive about the therapist's using manipulation to help the client, has made fun of the idea that if a therapist does something without deliberately trying to manipulate and it works, that is somehow all right, while if the same thing is consciously done as a manipulation, it is not. Furthermore, it could be argued that these manipulations work. People are better off afterward and with a lot less investment of time and trouble than with so-called insight therapies.

An argument against manipulative intervention is that it does not empower people. One of the important current movements in psychology is the idea of "giving psychology away" (Larson, 1984). The idea is to develop techniques that people can use to manage their own lives. Strategic therapy may eliminate symptoms, but it does not empower individuals to change their lives on their own if further problems arise. It seems to imply that people must be "operated on" when they are stuck, rather than unstick themselves. Psychoanalytic and humanistic approaches do not merely wish to get the client unstuck, to get rid of symptoms, but to develop the client's own self-management skills. Perhaps that is why they take longer.

While all strategic and solution-focused therapists plan their interventions and use paradoxical techniques, not all of them accept the manipulative model of theorists such as Jay Haley. They use the techniques not to manipulate the client into some specific outcome, but to free the client to solve the problem creatively. De Shazer points out that the actual solutions clients come up with to their problems are unique, developed by the clients themselves, and not predictable by the therapist.

Another criticism is leveled at the range and permanence of strategic approaches. Advocates of other approaches sometimes question whether changes brought about in such a brief time, using such noninsight methods, can have any enduring quality. They argue that in such a short time, these approaches cannot cause change that persists and that they will not work with enduring characterological problems, such as addictions and personality disorders. Certainly, cures of substance abuse that appear to take place in two sessions, as with the case of de Shazer's we reviewed earlier, will be greeted with skepticism by those who believe that psychological problems represent ingrained behavior patterns.

In response, Watzlawick (1985) has pointed out that even if it were true that a client might eventually have to return to treatment with a new problem or a recurrence of the old, that does not invalidate the treatment's success. He notes that no one expects medical doctors to effect cures of infections so that the patient will never get another infection. Furthermore, there is no evidence that the changes wrought by analytic or humanistic approaches are any more permanent. In fact, not only does analysis take years, but people frequently return to it with recurrent or new problems. Finally, strategic therapists point to cases of supposedly chronic characterological problems that they have helped, such as bulimia, substance abuse, and antisocial behavior in adolescents.

However, individual case histories do not prove that the strategic approach is generally effective with such problems, and strategic therapists do not present any systematic evidence showing that it is. Though it may be true that they have helped individual cases of substance abuse, personality disorders, or other problems that are typically seen as longstanding and difficult to treat, further research will have to demonstrate that these approaches can be generally effective with such problems.

Finally, bear in mind that published successes achieved by these approaches have usually taken place under unusual circumstances. They have occurred at institutes, such as Watzlawick's brief therapy institute in Palo Alto, California, or de Shazer's institute in Milwaukee. In these institutes, families or couples are typically seen by one therapist, while a team of other therapists watch through a one-way mirror. The intervention given to the family or couple is one designed by the whole team. We know of colleagues who trained in the strategic or solution-focused approach, but have found it more difficult to put into operation in private practice where one does not have a team of colleagues watching through a one-way mirror. Under these circumstances, these colleagues have reported that it becomes more difficult to use such interventions with the degree of success reported by these institutes, and these colleagues report having to resort to other approaches in addition to strategic ones.

IN CONCLUSION

Aside from the contributions of specific procedures and approaches for working with sexual difficulties and with families, couples, and children, the two major contributions of family and couples perspectives that will continue to be influential in the twenty-first century have to do with viewpoints. The first is the recognition that people exist in and are influenced by larger relational units (e.g., the system idea). Systems ideas offer an important corrective to the highly individualistic biases of most traditional psychological theories. The idea that, at least in part, "you are who you are with" implies a major shift in how we are to view human beings. Family systems theorists were the first to advocate this idea. Now they are being joined by multicultural, feminist, psychodynamic, and humanistic theorists who are arguing that interpersonal relationships, and, at a larger level, cultural relationships play an important role in defining who individuals are and in influencing how they function. It is as yet unclear how this is going to play out in practice, but it would seem likely that new models will evolve that take both individual and systemic factors into account.

The second major viewpoint comes from strategic and solution-focused therapies. These therapies have given us a totally new view on how to provide treatment. First, they hold that to focus on finding the causes of a person's problems is simply irrelevant. Instead, we should be focused on finding solutions. Second, in order to do this, we should not be focusing on pathology, but rather on strength. We should focus on the positive about people, and locate and enhance their strengths. Focusing on strengths often leads to individuals finding solutions to their problems much more quickly than they would if the focus were on pathology. Along with this, strategic and solution-focused therapists have provided a whole armamentarium of procedures that seem in many cases to facilitate change quickly. In this sense, strategic and solution-focused therapists have been a major force in the development of brief psychotherapy. Especially because of its fit with the modern health care climate, which requires brief psychotherapy, it seems likely that strategic and solution-focused viewpoints and methods will continue to exert an influence.

The third viewpoint contributed by family systems theorists is that of constructivism, which, while not totally a creation of family systems theorists, has been given major impetus by them. We discuss constructivism further in Chapter 17.

BIBLIOGRAPHY

Adler, A. (1930). *Guiding the child on the principles of individual psychology.* New York: Greenberg.

Alexander, J. F., Holtzworth-Munroe, A., & Jameson, P. B. (1994). The process and outcome of marital and family therapy: Research review and evaluation. In A. E. Bergin & S. L. Garfield (Eds.), *Handbook and psychotherapy and behavior change* (pp. 595–630). New York: Wiley

Axline, V. (1947a). Non-directive therapy for poor readers. *Journal of Consulting Psychology, 11*, 68–75.

Axline, V. (1947b). *Play therapy: The inner dynamics of childhood.* Boston: Houghton Mifflin.

Bandura, A. (1986). *Social foundations of thought and action: A social cognitive theory.* Engle-wood Cliffs, NJ: Prentice-Hall.

Barbach, L. G. (1975). *For yourself: The fulfillment of female sexuality.* New York: Signet.

Bogdan, J. (1986). Do families really need problems? *The Family Therapy Networker, 10,* 30–35, 67–69.

Bowen, M. (1978). *Family therapy in clinical practice.* New York: Aronson.

Cameron-Bandler, L. (1978). *They lived happily ever after.* Cupertino, CA: Meta.

Casey, R., & Berman, J. (1985). The outcome of psychotherapy with children. *Psychological Bulletin, 98,* 388–400.

Christensen, A. (1983). Intervention. In H. H. Kelley, E. Berscheid, A. Christensen, J. H. Har-vey, T. L. Huston, G. Levinger, E. McClintock, L. A. Peplau, & D. R. Peterson (Eds.), *Close relationships.* New York: Freeman.

Christensen, A., Jacobson, N. S., and Babcock, J. C. (1995). Integrative behavioral couple ther-apy. In N. S. Jacobson & A. S. Gurman (Eds.), *Clinical handbook of couple therapy* (pp. 31–64). New York: Guilford.

Dammann, C. (1980). Family therapy: Erickson's contribution. In J. Zeig (Ed.), *Ericksonian approaches to hypnosis and psychotherapy.* New York: Brunner/Mazel.

Dattilio, F. M., & Padesky, C. A. (1990). *Cognitive therapy with couples.* Sarasota, FL: Profes-sional Resource Exchange.

de Shazer, S. (1985). *Keys to solution in brief therapy.* New York: Norton.

Dowd, E. T., & Milne, C. R. (1986). Paradoxical interventions in counseling psychology. *The Counseling Psychologist, 4,* 237–282.

Feldman, J. B. (1985). The work of Milton Erickson: A multisystem model of eclectic therapy. *Psychotherapy, 22,* 154–162.

Freud, A. (1928). *Technique of child analysis.* New York: Nervous and Mental Disease Pub-lishing Company.

Freud, A. (1946). *The psychoanalytic treatment of children.* New York: International Universi-ties Press.

Greenberg, L. S., & Johnson, S. (1988). *Emotionally focused therapy for couples.* New York: Guilford.

Guerney, B. G., (1984). Relationship Enhancement therapy and training. In D. Larson (Ed.), *Teaching psychological skills: Models for giving psychology away* (pp. 171–206). Mon-terey, CA: Brooks/Cole.

Gurman, A. S., Kniskern, D. P., & Pinsof, W. M. (1986). Research on marital and family thera-pies. In S. L. Garfield & A. E. Bergin (Eds.), *Handbook of psychotherapy and behavior change* (3rd ed., pp. 565–626). New York: Wiley.

Haley, J. (1976). *Problem-solving therapy: New strategies for effective family therapy.* San Francisco: Jossey-Bass.

Haley, J. (1985, December 11). *Strategic family therapy* (Video and discussion). Presented at the Evolution of Psychotherapy Conference, Phoenix, AZ.

Hill, K. A. (1987). Meta-analysis of paradoxical interventions. *Psychotherapy, 24,* 266–270.

Jacobson, N. S., & Margolin, G. (1979). *Marital therapy: Strategies based on social learning and behavior exchange principles.* New York: Brunner/Mazel.

Kazdin, A. E. (1994). Psychotherapy for children and adolescents. In A. E. Bergin & S. L. Garfield (Eds.), *Handbook of psychotherapy and behavior change* (pp. 543–594). New York: Wiley.

Klein, M. (1955). The psychoanalytic play technique. *Journal of Orthopsychiatry, 25,* 223–237.

Landreth, Garry L. (1991). *Play therapy: The art of the relationship.* Muncie, IN: Accelerated Development Inc.

Larson, D. (Ed.). (1984). *Teaching psychological skills: Models for giving psychology away.* Monterey, CA: Brooks/Cole.

Leiblum, S. R., & Rosen, R. C. (Eds.). (1988). *Sexual desire disorders.* New York: Guilford.

Levy, D. (1939). Release therapy in young children. *Child Study, 16,* 141–143.

Madanes, C. (1984). *Behind the one-way mirror: Advances in the practice of strategic therapy.* San Francisco: Jossey-Bass.

Madanes, C. (1985, December 13). *Strategic therapy* (Video and discussion). Presented at the Evolution of Psychotherapy Conference, Phoenix, AZ.

Madanes, C. (1987). Advances in strategic family therapy. In J. Zeig (Ed.), *The evolution of psychotherapy* (pp. 47–54). New York: Brunner/Mazel.

Masters, W., & Johnson, V. (1970). *Human sexual inadequacy.* Boston: Little, Brown.

Miller, S. D., Duncan, B. L., & Hubble, M. A. (1996). *Escape from babel.* New York: Norton.

Minuchin, S. (1974). *Families and family therapy.* Cambridge, MA: Harvard University Press.

O'Hanlon, W. H., & Weiner-Davis, M. (1989). *In search of solutions: A new direction in psychotherapy.* New York: Norton.

O'Hara, M. M., & Anderson, W. T. (1991, September/October). Welcome to the postmodern world. *The Family Therapy Networker,* pp. 19–25.

Orlinsky, D. E., Grawe, K., & Parks, B. K. (1994). Process and outcome in psychotherapy—noch einmal. In A. E. Bergin & S. L. Garfield (Eds.), *Handbook of psychotherapy and behavior change* (pp. 270–378). New York: Wiley.

Prochaska, J. O. (1984). *Systems of psychotherapy.* Homewood, IL: Dorsey Press.

Rosman, B., Minuchin, S., Liebman, R., & Baker, L. (1978, November). *Family therapy for psychosomatic children.* Paper presented at the annual meeting of the American Academy of Psychosomatic Medicine, Atlanta, GA.

Satir, V. (1967). *Conjoint family therapy.* Palo Alto, CA: Science and Behavior Books.

Selvini Palazzoli, M., Cecchin, G., Prata, G., & Boscola, L. (1978). *Paradox and counterparadox.* New York: Aronson.

Shlien, J. M. (1988, September). *The future is more important than the past in determining present behavior.* Paper presented at the 1st International Conference on Client-centered and Experiential Psychotherapy, Leuven, Belgium.

Simon, K. M. (1979). *Effects of self comparison, social comparison, and depression on goal setting and self-evaluative reactions.* Unpublished manuscript, Stanford University, Stanford, CA.

Stanton, M. D., Todd, T. C., & Associates. (1982). *The family therapy of drug abuse and addiction.* New York: Guilford.

Vernberg, E., Routh, D., & Koocher, G. (1992). The future of psychotherapy with children: Developmental psychotherapy. *Psychotherapy, 29,* 72–80.

Wachtel, E., & Wachtel, P. (1986). *Family dynamics in individual therapy.* New York: Guilford.

Watzlawick, P. (1978). *The language of change: Elements of therapeutic communication.* New York: Basic Books.

Watzlawick, P. (Ed.). (1984). *The invented reality: How do we know what we believe we know?* New York: Norton.

Watzlawick, P. (1985, December 13). *Brief therapeutic interventions.* Paper presented at the Evolution of Psychotherapy Conference, Phoenix, AZ.

Watzlawick, P. (1987). If you desire to see, learn how to act. In J. Zeig (Ed.), *The evolution of psychotherapy* (pp. 91–99). New York: Brunner/Mazel.

Watzlawick, P., Weakland, J., & Fisch, R. (1974). *Change: Principles of problem formation and problem resolution.* New York: Norton.

Weakland J., Fisch, R., Watzlawick, P., & Bodin, A. (1974). Brief therapy: Focused problem resolution. *Family Process, 13,* 141–168.

Weisz, J., Weiss, B., Alicke, M., & Klotz, M. (1987). Effectiveness of psychotherapy with children and adolescents: A meta-analysis for clinicians. *Journal of Consulting and Clinical Psychology, 55,* 542–549.

Wile, D. B. (1981). *Couples therapy.* New York: Wiley.

Zilbergeld, B. (1992). *The new male sexuality.* New York: Bantam.

PART **SEVEN**

*Empirical
and Theoretical Issues*

Research
in Psychotherapy

Psychotherapy has existed as a formal practice for about 100 years. For nearly 50 of those years it was not studied scientifically, until Carl Rogers began recording and studying therapy sessions in the 1940s. Even then, research on psychotherapy remained controversial for many years, so much so that we felt a need to justify the importance of researching psychotherapy in the two previous editions of this book. Now, however, as we approach the millennium, the importance of psychotherapy research has never been greater. Demands from health care agencies and those who pay the bill for psychotherapy for accountability have raised the need to know more about the effectiveness and usefulness of psychotherapy to new levels. In this chapter, we consider basic issues involved in conducting research on psychotherapy, give a general overview of findings to date, and conclude by discussing current controversies and political pressures affecting how psychotherapy research is conducted and how evidence is evaluated.

WHY WE NEED TO STUDY PSYCHOTHERAPY EMPIRICALLY

There has been a continuing debate over research on psychotherapy. Because of the difficulty of the task, many practitioners have dismissed attempts to study the effectiveness of psychotherapy scientifically. Guntrip (1973) makes one typical argument. He says that psychotherapy is so individualized that it is difficult, if not impossible, to study it using normal experimental methods. Similarly, Simkin and Yontef (1984) said, "Gestalt therapists are singularly unimpressed with . . . nomothetic research methodology. No statistical approach can tell the individual patient or therapist what works for him" (p. 306). They go on to say that each gestalt session is an experiment, and so constant research is being done on each individual client. As we shall see, there are those who agree that normal experimental methods may not be the ideal empirical method for studying psychotherapy. But even if this were true, that does not mean research on it cannot be done. And, at the present time, mainstream opinion in psychology is that psychotherapy *can* be studied (and typically is) using experimental methodologies.

Those who argue that psychotherapy is too difficult to study empirically also typically argue that empirical research is not needed because the truths of psychotherapy have been experienced by people over and over for themselves through the countless times people have been in psychotherapy. For instance, both psychoanalysts and gestalt therapists have sometimes argued that anyone who doubts the truth of their viewpoint will discover the truth if he or she undergoes analysis or gestalt therapy. The basis of this type of argument is that you can learn "truths" from direct experience that you cannot gain from books or empirical research. One psychoanalyst has asserted that the view that later psychological difficulties are caused by events in early childhood "is not a theory; it is an empirical finding confirmed in every psychoanalysis" (Arlow, 1984, p. 24). Guntrip (1973), another analyst, said, "I have stated that much of Freud's clinical observation of psychic experiences as verifiable matters of fact, turning up again and again in the widest variety of persons, has proved to be of permanent validity" (p. 7). From a gestalt perspective, Fritz Perls said, "We present nothing that you cannot verify for yourself in terms of your own behavior" (Perls, Hefferline, & Goodman, 1951, p. 7).

But is seeing believing? It is often on the basis of experiences in therapy that people become firm believers in a particular theoretical approach. Psychoanalysts become convinced that problems are based on repressed feelings from early childhood. Behaviorists become convinced that problems are a matter of conditioning. Humanists become convinced that problems stem from a lack of self-acceptance and the fragmentation of the person into intellectual and emotional sides. And cognitive-behaviorists become convinced that problems depend on what clients think to themselves. The experience of seeing an apparent cure may be so vivid that the therapist believes that what he has seen verifies the "truth" of his theory.

How valid and trustworthy is experience in therapy for supporting the truthfulness of particular theoretical beliefs? Not very valid at all! It is one of the purposes of this chapter to make you aware of how deceptive "seeing is believing" can be.

Let's say that you're about to work with your first client. He enters your office, complaining of chronic and pervasive anxiety. You've decided from reading this book that a short-term psychoanalytic approach to therapy makes sense to you. You look for a recurring relationship theme related to events in his early childhood. You discover that he was criticized a lot as a child by his father. You see that he now chronically expects criticism. Underlying that is a lot of unconscious resentment and hostility. You help him become aware of this pattern. As you do this, he gets in touch with his anger and resentment toward his father. After several sessions, he reports that he feels better, and soon the anxiety seems to have diminished to a manageable level. You are amazed at the efficacy of your method, you stand a picture of Freud on your mantle, and put fresh flowers before it daily.

Or you prefer the behavioral approach. You help your client examine his life and find that he becomes anxious in situations in which he must assert himself, though he had not previously noted the connection. Since he is a traffic policeman, you realize that he is likely to feel anxious frequently. You create a series of hierarchies of situations in which he feels anxious. You teach him deep relaxation. You have him imagine these situations in a state of relaxation and you practice assertion skills with him. After 10 to 20 sessions the client happily reports that he rarely feels anxious. You are highly impressed with your behavioral approach and begin to carry a picture of Joseph Wolpe in your wallet.

Depending on your point of view and how you worked with the client, you might become convinced of either the "truths" of the psychoanalytic or of the behavioral approach. Experience can be a powerful persuader. Yet, in reading the two examples above, you may already have seen the problem in claiming that "facts" about personality and psychotherapy can be learned from therapy sessions. If many of Freud's observations are "facts," why are they repeatedly confirmed in psychoanalytic sessions, but not in behavioral sessions? If the behavioral view is correct, why is it not confirmed in psychoanalytic sessions? If we can discover "facts" through our direct experience in psychotherapy, then how come Carl Rogers, Joseph Wolpe, Albert Ellis, Aaron Beck, Carl Jung, Alfred Adler, and Fritz Perls all started out doing psychoanalytically oriented psychotherapy, but later developed theories that have little in common with psychoanalysis, or with one another? It should be obvious that the kinds of experiences therapists and clients have in therapy, no matter how vivid and compelling, do not provide a scientifically reliable basis for knowledge. Seeing may be believing, but neither seeing nor believing is necessarily knowing.

Why are conclusions drawn from the therapy experience not scientifically reliable? One reason is that people tend to "see" what they expect to see. There is reason to believe that Freud had already developed a belief in the sexual basis of neurosis before he began to "see" it in his clients. Freud developed the idea that problems are based on early childhood, and analyst after analyst carried that idea into therapy with them. Theorists carrying different preconceptions did not "see" the things that Freudians claim are empirical truths. Analysts encourage their clients to talk about early childhood and then, when change occurs, attribute the change to reviewing early childhood. Cognitive therapists have their clients talk about their dysfunctional cognitions and then attribute change to that. Client-centered therapists focus on clients' feelings, so assume it is something about that process that creates change.

Therapist preconceptions also probably shape the kind of material that the client brings out. It has been argued (Hobbs, 1968) that Freudian clients get Freudian insights, Jungian clients get Jungian insights, and so on. Over the course of many sessions, a good deal of material compatible with the therapist's point of view will be highlighted and discussed. It is not surprising that both the therapist and client become convinced that what they have discovered is the "truth."

But what about the client? Change experiences, when you gain an insight and suddenly feel transformed, are powerful, and experiences that include a lot of emotion are also compelling. If people experience a great deal of emotion, they tend to believe that somehow something important must be happening. Yet these experiences are not reliable scientifically. Let us take an example from psychoanalysis. Guntrip (1973, pp. 176–177) reports a case of a client who came to therapy for treatment of depression. In addition, he had a chronic sinus condition. Through the analysis process, he remembered that he had been left alone to nurse his dying mother, but the day of her death remained a total blank. One night, the forgotten memory of her death burst into his consciousness. He remembered that she had gone mad at the end and had died cursing him. This memory had been so horrible he had repressed it. When the memory was recovered, his sinuses opened, and the fluid poured out.

Such an experience is quite dramatic. Both therapist and client are likely to conclude that the repression of the memory "caused" the sinus condition and the recovery of the memory "cured" it. But is that true? There is no obvious connection between his blocked sinuses and his mother's madness. But even if there were (suppose she had yelled at him, "You're so stuffy!"), would that have proven that the repressed memory caused the sinus condition? Would the clearing up of the sinus condition after recovery of the memory prove that recovering the memory was the cure of the sinus condition? The answer to both is no.

Any highly emotional experience, in the proper context, might have a direct impact on the body. The specific content of the memory may have had nothing to do with the physical effect, except to make it seem more plausible. What may have been important was the emotional impact of recovering the memory. Intense emotional experiences are often associated with change, regardless of the belief system they are associated with. It is not implausible to imagine that this same man goes to a Christian evangelist, has a highly emotional conversion experience, is told by the preacher that his sinuses will open, and, lo and behold, they do. Or he goes to a primal therapist, "recovers" some primal pain from early childhood, and his sinuses open.

Still another possibility is the power of suggestion. The client recovers this emotionally charged memory and says to himself, "This must be it!" Unconsciously, he convinces himself that this was the cause, and the power of suggestion causes his sinuses to open.

We are not saying that these alternatives (and there are others) are the correct ones. We simply want you to see that you cannot conclude that it was specifically the recovery of the particular repressed memory that was therapeutic. (Again, we are using psychoanalysis to illustrate a point that applies to any of the therapy systems.) In addition, we do not even know for sure that it was the therapy that caused the memory to surface into consciousness. Perhaps some random event happened that day to bring the memory to consciousness. So we may not conclude that the therapy was responsible for the sinuses opening.

Further, you cannot conclude that the repressed memory caused the problem, either. Suppose there is an apparent connection between the memory and the clogged sinuses; the mother did say, "You're so stuffy!" There is certainly a similarity between this experience and the client's symptom of a stuffy nose. But because two things are similar does not mean that one caused the other. It is easy to find past experiences that "fit" current problems in retrospect. Probably all of us can find some experience in our childhood that is like some problem we are having now. But that does not mean that those experiences caused the present-day problems. It is tempting to conclude that I dislike myself now because my father was overly demanding, but there is no inevitable connection between the two. Many people who had an overdemanding father do not dislike themselves as adults.

The fact that it is easy to search one's past and find things that "explain" one's present was demonstrated in one research study (Ross, Lepper, Strack, & Steinmetz,

1977). Students were given the history of a person. Some were told that he went on to have a career as a politician, while others were told that he went on to commit suicide. Neither group had any difficulty in finding things in the history that "explained" the eventual outcome, though both groups were working with identical past histories for the person.

It is possible that what is therapeutic about an insight or explanation in therapy has nothing to do with the truthfulness of that insight or explanation. Jerome Frank (1974, 1982) suggests that therapy operates by combatting demoralization. Insights and explanations help if they make the client's experience seem sensible. An insight or explanation need not be true if it gives a person some hope and if it suggests some things the person can do to manage his or her life. Suppose you "learn" in therapy that your low self-esteem was "caused" by your father's constant put-downs. It does not even matter if this is true. If you believe it is true, you may decide, "Well, I don't have to put myself down just because he did." Or, "That was his opinion, and he was pretty screwed up himself." In other words, the explanation may be therapeutic anyway. Spence (1982), a psychoanalyst, argued that psychoanalytic interpretations are therapeutic because of their coherence-making qualities, not because of their truth. Kelly (1963) found that plausible-sounding interpretations, based on no theory, were often therapeutic. So, just because an interpretation is therapeutic does not mean it is true, and just because it isn't true does not mean it won't be therapeutic.

We hope by now you see that you cannot draw reliable conclusions from experience in therapy about whether therapy works, what in therapy works, or what the causes of psychological problems are. Therapy sessions are an important source of ideas and hypotheses, but they do not provide reliable evidence as to what works and why. Next we consider some of the issues involved in obtaining more reliable evidence.

METHODOLOGICAL ISSUES IN PSYCHOTHERAPY RESEARCH

Ultimately, scientific research involves being able to establish the existence of relationships in the real world with a certain degree of reliability. One wants to be able to say that *x* is reliably associated with *y*, for example, "psychotherapy helps people feel better," and "insight in psychotherapy is useful." There are two general approaches to science used to establish the reliability of relationships among variables. The first, more well-established way, is to use traditional experimental designs. In psychotherapy, this has typically involved the use of **control groups.** More recently, a second approach, called **qualitative research,** has gained favor with some who believe that traditional experimental designs are either inappropriate or incomplete for capturing the phenomena of psychotherapy. We will first discuss the use of control groups in research, and then we will briefly consider qualitative research.

Control Groups

Suppose someone goes to therapy and gets better. In order to say that the therapy worked, a researcher would like to be able to say that it was the therapy that helped her get better. However, it is possible that something else going on in the client's life caused the change, not the therapy. A client may improve when she gets a job or when her husband recovers his love for her. Many of the changes in children are simply due to the maturation process. It is even possible that certain disorders have their own natural course, like a cold or the flu, and the client would eventually get better even without therapy. There is some evidence that this is true for many cases of depression.

The most common way of demonstrating that it is the form of therapy that is associated with the production of the change is to use a control group. One group of clients receives the therapy, and another group (the control) does not. A bare outline of the procedure is to have, for example, 40 depressed patients, with 20 assigned to the treatment group and 20 to the control group. The assignment is done randomly, so that the chances are pretty good that the two groups are approximately equal, that is, that one group does not differ in any systematic way from the other group. Change in the individuals in both groups is measured at the end of treatment. If the clients in the therapy group have changed more than those in the control group, it is concluded that something about the therapy caused the change.

The procedure is not as simple as the outline sounds. First, there are ethical problems in putting people in a control group because they are being denied treatment that they may need. Second, it may be difficult to get a group of patients who are similar in diagnosis, age, sex, and other variables. There are ways to handle this, which we will not go into here, but such matching methods make the research design more complicated. Third, control groups often do not remain untreated. Individuals who are not receiving the therapy being researched may go to some other therapist or talk to a friend, doctor, or minister (some of whom have had counseling training).

One of the ways devised to handle some of these problems is the waiting list control group. Since there are waiting lists at many clinics anyway, there is nothing unethical about placing some clients in the waiting list control group. Clients are randomly assigned either to available therapists or to the waiting list control. After the research treatment period, people on the waiting list are given treatment. People on waiting lists may be less likely to seek treatment elsewhere, so the waiting list control group may remain somewhat more pure. One problem with the waiting list is that clients will not wait indefinitely. It cannot be used, for instance, in studies of a two- or three-year psychoanalysis. The treatment studied must be relatively brief.

Even if it is found that the treatment group does improve more than the control group, can it be concluded that it was really the therapy that caused the improvement? No. It could simply be that the attention given the clients or the power of suggestion or their belief that they would get better was the agent of change. One way some psychologists have attempted to compensate for these possibilities is to try to use **placebos.** The issue of placebos has received extensive attention in both medicine and psychotherapy (Shapiro & Morris, 1978). In medicine, placebos are regularly used in research. In testing a new drug, for example, some patients are given the drug and others are given an inactive sugar pill, but are told they are being given the drug. In many studies, placebos have been found to cause some improvement. Pill placebos have been used in some studies of psychotherapy, for instance, on depression. In other studies, a placebo control group might be given a pseudo-treatment, a treatment that is really expected to do nothing, but is given as if it is a real treatment. However, a problem with placebo pseudo-treatments is that they are difficult to design when we are not sure what elements make therapy work. Some have even argued that the powerful elements in therapy are the placebo effects: the power of suggestion and hope.

There has even been controversy over whether placebos are meaningful or necessary for psychotherapy research (Critelli & Neumann, 1984; Parloff, 1986). An alternative to a placebo design is a **comparative design** (Basham, 1986; Parloff, 1986). In a comparative design, known treatments are compared to one another. For instance, Borkovec and Costello (1993) compared their cognitive-behavioral treatment for generalized anxiety disorder to a simple form of nondirective therapy (essentially an early form of client-centered therapy), as well as to a no-treatment control group. Basham argues that this type of design is preferable to the use of only no-treatment control groups.

Meaning and Measurement of Change

Defining Change   Suppose you have an untreated control group or a placebo group being compared to a therapy treatment group. Now you have to decide how you are going to measure change. To do that, you have to decide what you mean by change. And this turns out to be perhaps even more complex than the issue of controls.

What is change in therapy? How could you tell if your client had improved? Perhaps the most obvious answer is by noting an improvement in the client's presenting complaint. If a client came to therapy because she was drinking too much, change might be if she is no longer drinking, that is, if there is symptom removal. However, many therapists have more grandiose goals for their clients than the clients themselves have (Bergin & Lambert, 1978). They want to "reorganize the personality" or "get the client to trust his feelings, take responsibility," and "think rationally." Many therapists assume that symptoms are the result of a more pervasive, underlying disorder. Substance abuse may reflect difficulties with self-esteem or interpersonal relationships. Anxiety may reflect a distorted cognitive style or a denial of one's potential. Conversion disorders may represent attempts to manage fear. Most psychological disorders, such as schizophrenia, personality disorders, conversion disorder, substance abuse disorders, and so on, are generally thought to represent organized patterns of symptoms, not collections of isolated symptoms (only the behavioral view has systematically questioned this). If symptoms are believed to represent some underlying disorder, therapists will not be interested in symptom improvement, but in changes in personality traits, emotional experiencing, self-esteem, and cognition.

Another difficulty with looking at change in terms of symptom removal is that often, there is no simple, clear symptom. There may be multiple symptoms, and therapy may help some, but not others. For instance, the borderline personality syndrome consists of several symptoms, including impulsiveness, difficulty being alone, boredom, identity problems, anger, and depression. Or the presenting complaint may not be a clear-cut symptom, such as "drinking" or "fear of going out of the house." For example, a client may complain of being depressed, feeling that life is meaningless, or having difficulties in managing children, relating to a spouse, or relating to superiors at work.

One of the consequences of this is that what therapists see as change depends on their theoretical viewpoint. A behaviorist might focus on symptom removal and behavior change; a humanist on increased self-acceptance, responsibility taking, and emotional experiencing; a cognitive behaviorist on progress toward a flexible, differentiated cognitive system.

In addition, what is considered a positive change varies. Generally, the therapist has a set of values about change derived from his or her theory of therapy. The client may have another. And relatives and friends of the client may have still another.

You, as a therapist, are not only interested in change per se; you are also interested in positive change. And what you define as positive change depends in part on your values. Therefore, it is possible that people with different values will see change differently. Your client is a depressed, middle-aged woman who has spent her adult life being a housewife and mother, and starts therapy complaining of depression. Her children are now leaving home, and her life feels empty. Through therapy, she begins to feel that she has spent her life living for others and that she wants to do something in the way of a career herself. As she begins to make these realizations, her depression lifts. Both she and the therapist see these changes as positive, but will her traditional husband who believes that a woman's place is in the home? Or a 17-year-old boy is referred to therapy because his parents are worried that he does not show proper interest in girls. The therapist discovers that he is gay, and therapy consists of helping him accept this side of himself. This may or may not sit well with the parents if they hold traditional values.

It has generally been accepted that change in therapy is multidimensional (Bergin & Lambert, 1978). Different therapies concentrate on different types of change in the personality or behavior, and change looks different from different vantage points in the person's life. In fact, Stiles, Shapiro, and Elliott (1986) have argued that psychological normality is heterogeneous, in contrast to physical health. Different therapies have differing definitions of psychological health, and they may all be right for different individuals.

At the same time, there is currently pressure to define change in terms of the alleviation of specific problems, particularly as defined in the DSM-IV. Agencies that fund psychotherapy research, perhaps responding to the demands of the marketplace and to those who pay for mental health care, are increasingly interested primarily in research studies that explore the effectiveness of therapies in alleviating DSM disorders (Goldfried & Wolfe, 1996).

Measuring Change   In the days when psychoanalysis ruled the roost in psychotherapy, change was usually defined in terms of change in personality structure. Thus, someone who wished to demonstrate that therapy worked would use various personality tests to measure change. Since client-centered therapy emphasizes self-acceptance, research on therapy conducted by client-centered therapists used measures of self-acceptance, such as self-esteem scales. With the ascendancy of the behavioral perspective in the 1960s, an increasing emphasis was placed on behavioral measures. It was argued that changes in personality structure and self-acceptance were meaningless unless they manifested themselves in observable behavior change, and so, behavioral measures were favored over personality measures (Lambert, 1983).

Behavioral measures, self-acceptance measures, and personality tests are ways of measuring change. For instance, one way to measure change is to use a client's self-report before and after therapy. The client may be asked to rate the degree to which he has improved on the target symptoms that brought him to therapy. Or he may rate his behavior in various areas, such as in functioning socially and at work. Or he may rate himself on self-acceptance or on various personality traits. There are simple personality inventories in which the client checks off adjectives that he believes describe him.

If the client provides one source of measurement of change, the professional psychologist provides another. In research studies, it is common to have the therapist rate the client's progress, often making the same kinds of ratings the client might be asked to make about himself. Or a professional psychologist assesses the client's personality from tests such as the MMPI, Rorschach, and TAT administered before and after therapy. They interpret results of the projective tests (for example, to see if ego strength has increased or tendencies toward denial and repression have declined) and look at changes in scores on objective test scales. For instance, Rogers, Gendlin, Kiesler, and Truax (1967) found that clients with therapists high in warmth, empathy, and genuineness showed reductions on the "schizophrenia" scale of the MMPI.

A professional psychologist or psychiatrist may be used as a neutral observer or rater. A common practice now in psychotherapy research is to have the client undergo a structured interview with a neutral psychologist or psychiatrist who preferably does not know whether the client was in therapy or in a control group. This neutral observer rates the client on a number of scales, for instance, how much anxiety or depression the client is exhibiting.

Another source of measurement of change is an informant's report, that is, a rating of the client made by some person in the client's life. For example, a client's wife may be asked to rate his personality or behavior before and after therapy.

Still another measurement of change involves attempts to assess behavior change directly. These may include ratings of behavior by others and more "objective" measures of behavior. We have already discussed behavioral measures in Chapter 5, but will briefly review their use in psychotherapy research. An example of an objective measure of behavior change is one that has been used in research on fears of snakes (Lang, Lazovik, & Reynolds, 1965). Before treatment with systematic desensitization, clients with fears of snakes were asked to approach a cage with a snake in at as close as they could. Some were so afraid of snakes that they were not even able to enter the room in which the cage was placed. After treatment, the same procedure was used. Most clients were able to approach the cage and look at the snake, and some were even able to pick it up.

Most behavioral measures involve direct or indirect observation of behavior. A relative may keep track of the number of times the client loses her temper or drinks or engages in whatever target behavior is being modified. In hospitals, nurses and attendants usually do the observing. They keep track of the target behaviors on some kind of behavior rating form. An indirect way of observing behavior is to use tape recorders. For example, if family interaction patterns are the target, the family may be asked to keep cassette tape recorders going. This allows direct recording of arguments and other verbal patterns of interaction. Still another behavioral observation technique is to set up role-playing situations. These are less desirable than observing behavior in real life, but sometimes observing behavior in real life can be difficult. A role-playing situation may be set up, for instance, in which a client asks his boss for a raise. The effectiveness and appropriateness of his assertive behaviors can then be rated.

Behaviorists do not rate traits such as "aggressiveness," but observe the specific situations in which the client acts aggressively and how. After therapy, ideally the person is observed in the same kinds of situations to see if the behavior has indeed been modified. Therapy researchers generally favor measurement of situation-specific behaviors as indexes of therapy effectiveness, if they can be obtained (Lambert, 1983).

We have not previously mentioned the single subject research design used by behaviorists. This strategy avoids the necessity of having many subjects to serve as treatment and control groups. Behaviorists sometimes use an individual subject as her own control. Before therapy begins, the target behaviors are observed in the situations in which they occur and a baseline of the frequency is established. For instance, before treatment starts, it is observed that on the playground, a boy commits an average of four aggressive acts per 15-minute observation period. Behavioral observations are made again after treatment is initiated. If it has worked, the rate will have changed; in this case, perhaps it drops to one incident every 15 minutes. The effect of the treatment can be further studied by withdrawing or reversing it. Suppose the treatment for the aggressive boy was reinforcing positive behavior and ignoring negative behavior. Suppose, also, that before treatment, it had been observed that the child was ignored when he acted positively and received a lot of attention (in the form of criticism and punishment) when he acted up. Upon the return to those responses to his behavior, the rate rises again to four incidents every 15 minutes. When the therapeutic strategy is resumed, once again the rate drops to one incident every 15 minutes. This demonstrates that it is the therapeutic strategy that has caused the improvement, without the use of control groups. Unfortunately, such a design is most appropriate to behavioral treatments and is far less applicable to approaches such as psychoanalysis or gestalt (how would you reverse the treatment of "insight into the past"?).

Objective records can be used as a measurement of change in psychotherapy. Some studies, for instance, use grade-point average in school, and several studies have found increases in the average as a result of therapy. Other objective indexes that have been used include hospitalization rates, incarceration rates, and number of clients receiving therapy who are unemployed versus unemployed control subjects.

A particularly important subgroup of objective indexes for some disorders are physiological measures, such as blood pressure, heart rate, galvanic skin response (which reflects anxiety), penile tumescence (when sexual dysfunction is the target symptom), and brain wave response. These measures are usually used when the disorder being treated involves stress or anxiety or when the treatment used includes relaxation, meditation, or biofeedback methods. Weight loss or weight gain are obvious biologically based measures when the problem being treated is either obesity or anorexia.

Since each of the many ways to measure change has its limitations, it is usually recommended that multiple measures, utilizing different sources of information, be used (Lambert, 1983). For instance, a battery of measuring devices recommended by a group of psychotherapy researchers (Waskow & Parloff, 1975) includes several client self-reports, one report filled out by the therapist, one assessment done by an independent mental health professional, two reports filled out by other people in the client's life, and one objective personality test. Most of the reports filled out by client, therapist, and independent assessor are ratings of target complaints and symptoms of psychopathology. The particular measures recommended by Waskow and Parloff have been debated (see various articles in Lambert, Christensen, & DeJulio, 1983), but the idea of multiple measures is generally accepted.

Analogue Designs

One way psychotherapy researchers attempt to cope with some of the above complexities is the use of **analogue designs.** An analogue research design attempts to scale down real therapy to a few variables that can be studied in a laboratory setting. What is gained over doing research on real therapy is precision. For instance, a technique may be studied independently of how it is actually used in a real therapy context. Studies of the gestalt empty chair technique (reviewed in Chapter 9) are examples. In each study, a subject attempts to resolve conflict feelings by using the empty chair technique. In contrast to a real therapy context, this is the only technique used, the session is short, and it is done only once. The problem of control groups is simplified because it is easy to have some subjects do nothing for an hour and serve as a control. It is also easy to design a placebo control. One might, for example, have subjects merely discuss their problem or read articles about it for an hour. Measurement problems are also simplified. Usually specific, immediate change is measured, and issues of how the person will behave in real life are avoided. Behavioral measures that can be taken in the laboratory, physiological measures of anxiety, or paper-and-pencil attitude measures may be used. Analogue studies on fears of snakes, for instance, may measure how much closer the subject will approach a snake after treatment. In the empty chair studies, various ratings of conflict resolution were taken. One study (Bohart, 1977) found that people who used the empty chair technique were less likely to be punitive toward other people on a learning task.

Analogue studies can help researchers to understand relationships between the time-limited use of specific therapeutic interventions and certain specific changes that can be immediately measured in a laboratory situation. The problem is that analogue situations are rarely similar to real therapy situations. Clients are often college undergraduates rather than "real" clients. Only one specific technique is usually used, in contrast to actual therapy, in which a variety of approaches may be used over several sessions. You may question whether analogue situations tell us much about how real therapy works. On the other hand, there is no proof that analogues do not tell us about what goes on in real therapy (Kazdin, 1980). Furthermore, they can be helpful in understanding specific therapy processes. Ideally, both analogue studies and studies of actual therapy can converge to help us understand how therapy works.

Other Research Problems

We have only scratched the surface of the many problems associated with doing research on psychotherapy. Follow-up is another problem: How long after therapy should clients be followed to see if change has been maintained? Following clients for any length of time is difficult; clients may move, die, or otherwise become unavailable.

Or suppose you want to compare psychoanalysis to behavior therapy. You should probably have several psychoanalysts and several behavioral therapists in your study. But do all psychoanalysts or behavioral therapists proceed identically? What if different kinds of persons become psychoanalysts and behavioral therapists? Suppose some personality characteristic differs between these kinds of persons and suppose that affects the outcome of therapy? One of the recent answers to this dilemma is to use **treatment manuals** to standardize the way therapy is delivered. We shall discuss treatment manuals and the controversy over them later in this chapter.

By now we hope you realize that it is exceedingly difficult to provide an answer to the question: "Does the so-and-so approach to psychotherapy work?" For similar reasons, it is quite difficult to know why a therapy works in certain cases. Is it the personality of the therapist or the elements in the therapy that the particular theory claims are important? Is it factors that no one is aware of? We also hope by now that you see that believing you can tell whether a therapy works by personal experience, either as therapist or client, is quite simplistic. Return to the examples at the start of the chapter and ask yourself: Would the client have changed without the therapy? Has the client changed? If change has occurred, is it because of insight, getting in touch with feelings, combatting dysfunctional cognitions, or desensitization? Could it have been that any of those techniques would have worked because they all give the client a sense of hope? Could it have been that the therapist was a supportive, encouraging person? Are the therapist's perceptions of change accurate? How permanent and stable are the changes?

Qualitative Designs   In recent years, qualitative research designs, already used in other research areas such as sociology and anthropology, have become more popular in psychology. Some qualitative researchers have argued that experimental designs are inadequate to capture the complex interactive process that is psychotherapy. Psychotherapy is not like a medication that can be simply administered to a large group of subjects and its effects measured and compared to a placebo control group. Instead, psychotherapy is a give-and-take, back-and-forth process between therapist and client. The process that emerges is different for each therapist-client pair, and the solutions that emerge are often unique. Therefore, to compare a treatment group to a control group, as if a common "treatment" were being uniformly applied to all clients (as is the case with medication) simply is not an adequate way to learn about psychotherapy's effectiveness. Some qualitative researchers reject control group experimental designs entirely; others do not reject them, but believe they must be complemented by qualitative methods in order to achieve a full understanding of how psychotherapy works.

Qualitative research operates on a different set of assumptions than the control group design. Qualitative researchers believe that the best way to achieve a scientific understanding of psychotherapy is through intense analysis of individual cases. A qualitative researcher might collect data on a sample of clients in psychotherapy by periodically interviewing them, by having them fill out questionnaires, and/or by taping the therapy sessions. Then, using various qualitative descriptive and interpretive methods, the researcher tries to understand the experience of the clients and its relationship to the processes that occurred in therapy. Procedures are used that serve to minimize biases in interpretation. What is achieved is an intense understanding of individual cases, from which generalizations can be drawn about psychotherapy experiences in a broader sense. So far, qualitative research has been used more to study the processes occurring in psychotherapy than the question of psychotherapy's effectiveness. For instance, Rennie (1990, 1994) played tapes of therapy sessions back for both clients and therapists and asked them what they were thinking about at key moments during the process. Using qualitative methods to analyze clients' responses, Rennie has demonstrated that clients are much more active during the therapy process than most models of psychotherapy hold. Clients do a lot of thinking to themselves, privately working on their problems as they talk to the therapist, but often they do not share these thought processes with the therapist. They use their own empathic understanding of the therapist to work with or around the therapist, depending on how understood they feel by the therapist. Watson and Rennie (1994) have demonstrated how actively clients work to symbolize their experience and feelings and reflect on them to discover new meanings and make personal changes.

Qualitative designs have become increasingly accepted in recent years, and there have been attempts to establish criteria for their reliability and validity (Stiles, 1993). Qualitative designs tend to be favored by researchers studying psychotherapies that rely on more open-ended, discovery-oriented, and relational methods, such as many psychodynamic, humanistic, feminist, and constructivist approaches. However, at the present time they are not as extensively used as more traditional quantitative experimental methodologies.

THE EFFECTIVENESS OF PSYCHOTHERAPY

Despite all the problems, a good deal of research has been done on psychotherapy. There are two general kinds of psychotherapy research: outcome research and process research. **Outcome research** deals with the effectiveness of psychotherapy. **Process research** deals with the processes that go on in therapy interactions. An example of process research is a study by Brunnink and Schroeder (1979), in which they compared the verbal behavior of psychoanalytic, gestalt, and behavior therapists. As expected, there were several differences. For instance, gestalt therapists were more active in providing direct guidance and used more self-disclosure than psychoanalysts.

Process and outcome research can be linked; a study can attempt to relate differences in therapy process to therapy effectiveness. For instance, researchers could see if the differences between gestalt and psychoanalytic therapists in verbal behavior relate to differences in effectiveness. Our review of psychotherapy research below will focus primarily on outcome research.

As previously noted, it has only been in the last 50 years that intensive efforts have been made to study the question of psychotherapy's effectiveness scientifically. Perhaps the event that triggered these efforts was a report by Hans Eysenck. Eysenck (1952) searched the literature for published reports of success rates for different psychotherapies and for different psychotherapy institutes. He collated these rates for neurotic patients and found a success rate of 44% for psychoanalysis and 64% for various other approaches. In order to know if these rates meant that therapy worked or not, Eysenck attempted to find a recovery rate for neurotic patients who did not receive psychotherapy. He discovered data on two such groups of patients and calculated that they had a spontaneous recovery rate of 72%. The apparent conclusion from Eysenck's data was that at best, there was no evidence that therapy worked, and at worst, the less therapy one had, the better!

However, Eysenck's report had many scientific problems (Bergin, 1971), and its conclusions could not be accepted. Its main function was to stimulate research on the question of psychotherapy's effectiveness. During the intervening years, a large number of research studies on the effectiveness of psychotherapy have been conducted, with a wide range of patients, over a wide range of types of problems, and across different kinds of therapies. The following now appear to be generally accepted as the conclusions from this research (Bergin & Garfield, 1994).

First, it is now generally accepted that psychotherapy, on the average, is effective, and is more effective than placebo control groups. In fact, there is more research on the effectiveness of psychotherapy than on any medical treatment (Messer, 1994). Second, on the average, there appears to be no general difference in effectiveness among the different approaches to psychotherapy that have been studied. That is, research has generally supported the approximately equivalent effectiveness of the cognitive, behavioral, psychodynamic, and humanistic therapies that have been researched. This particular finding has been called the "dodo bird" verdict, based on *Alice's Adventures in Wonderland* in which the dodo bird judges a race and proclaims that everyone has won and all must have prizes. A cautionary note here is that there are varying estimates that there are over 250 to 400 different therapy approaches in use today, and many of these approaches have not been researched. It is important to bear in mind that the conclusion that "all psychotherapies are equivalent" bears only on those therapies that have been researched. Separate research studies have shown the effectiveness of various marital and family therapies (Gurman, Kniskern, & Pinsof, 1986).

Another set of findings is that the biggest contributor to the successful outcome of therapy is the client (40% of the outcome variance). The second biggest contributor is the therapeutic relationship (30%). Techniques and differences among therapy approaches only contribute 15%, with 15% unaccounted for (Lambert, 1992).

Finally, psychotherapy is not equally effective for all problems or for all clients. Generally, it has been shown to be effective for anxiety, depression, marital problems, and various types of specific behavioral problems. It has not been generally shown to be effective for schizophrenia (although it has been shown to be helpful with selected subsets of schizophrenics), and it has at best been only modestly successful, if at all, with substance abuse problems and various kinds of antisocial behavior.

In terms of the length of therapy, most researchers believe that the evidence has not supported the idea that *generally* long-term therapy is more effective than short-term, as traditional psychoanalysts have held. Howard, Kopta, Krause, and Orlinsky (1986) conducted a meta-analysis on research on over 2,400 clients. Their analysis showed that approximately 50% of patients are measurably improved by the eighth session of therapy, and 75% are improved by the twenty-sixth session. This evidence supports the recent shift in the field toward brief psychotherapy. There is even evidence that a number of patients have benefitted from a single session of therapy, leading to the development of single session therapies (Rosenbaum, Hoyt, & Talmon, 1990). However, it must be noted that such relatively rapid improvements most likely take place in less disturbed patients with less serious problems (Lambert, Shapiro, & Bergin, 1986).

On the other hand, a *Consumer Reports* survey (Seligman, 1995) found that people who reported staying in therapy longer also reported receiving more benefit. In addition, Blatt and Ford (1994) have provided evidence that long-term, intensive, psychoanalytically oriented treatment can be effective, especially for clients who were more concerned with issues of self-definition, self-worth, and self-control, than for clients more concerned with relationship issues. The *Consumer Reports* study has been criticized for its methodological limitations (Jacobson & Christensen, 1996), but these two studies taken together do suggest that the rush to briefer and briefer forms of psychotherapy may be a bit premature (Miller, 1996).

Meta-Analysis

We have repeatedly referred to the meta-analysis of Smith, Glass, and Miller (1980) in earlier chapters. Meta-analysis is a statistical procedure that is applied to the results of all available studies on a certain topic. From the procedure, an effect size is calculated. An effect size is something like a standard deviation. It is a way of calculating how much the average effect due to a particular treatment is above the mean or average effect of those who are not given the treatment. The numbers given for effect sizes are not easily interpretable by themselves, but we can give you an approximate idea of what they mean. Smith, Glass, and Miller (1980) located 475 studies in which some kind of therapy was compared to some kind of control group. The overall effect size for psychotherapy was 0.85. This means that the average person who received therapy was better off than 80% of the persons who did not. For comparison's sake, the effect size for nine months of instruction in reading in elementary school in improving reading scores is 0.67 (Smith, Glass, & Miller, 1980, p. 88). The effect size for cigarette smoking increasing the probability of getting lung cancer is 0.60 (APA Commission on Psychotherapies, 1982, p. 137).

In terms of specific approaches, cognitive therapies, hypnotherapy, and systematic desensitization at first appeared to be the most effective. Psychodynamic, client-centered, gestalt, rational-emotive, transactional analysis, behavior modification, and various eclectic behavioral treatments were around the average in effectiveness. Despite the apparent superiority of some of the cognitive-behavioral therapies, Smith, Glass, and Miller conclude that on closer analysis, there is no evidence that cognitive and behavioral therapies in general are superior to verbal therapies in general. They reach this conclusion for a variety of reasons, including the fact that behavioral treatments used different kinds of measures of effectiveness than verbal therapies and in studies where the two were pitted against one another directly, there was no clear superiority.

There has been controversy over the Smith, Glass, and Miller meta-analysis, and several subsequent meta-analyses have been done (Wierzbicki, 1993). Results are not entirely consistent, but in general, the conclusions of Smith, Glass, and Miller continue to be, with some exceptions (see our discussion of empirically validated treatments below), accepted by the profession at large (see Bergin & Garfield, 1994).

We will briefly review one particular research study that exemplifies the above conclusions. The study by Sloane, Staples, Cristol, Yorkston, and Whipple (1975) compared psychoanalytically oriented psychotherapy to behavior therapy. A group of patients with diagnoses of either personality disorder or neurotic disorder were randomly assigned to psychoanalytically oriented treatment, behavioral treatment, or a waiting list control group. Three psychoanalytic therapists and three behavioral therapists were used. Attempts were made to get experienced, outstanding representatives of each approach (two of the three behavior therapists were Joseph Wolpe and Arnold Lazarus). Patients were treated for four months. Attempts were made to define what would be included as behavior therapy and as psychoanalytic therapy. Patients were assessed right after the end of treatment, and again a year after beginning treatment. Assessment of therapeutic outcome included several personality inventories, ratings by patients, therapists, and informants, assessment by an independent assessor, and analysis of target symptoms.

On target symptoms, both therapy groups improved more than the control group. On assessments of more global improvement, the two therapies were again rated as generally equal, though there were some instances in which behavior therapy appeared to be superior. No specific patient characteristics appeared to relate generally to therapeutic outcome, but there was some evidence that "acting-out" patients did better in behavior therapy.

Recent Developments in Psychotherapy Research: The Search for Specificity

As of the late 1980s, most psychotherapy researchers had generally accepted the conclusion that all of the major psychotherapies worked about equally well. The question then became why. Was it because there were basic common factors in all the therapies that were responsible for their effectiveness? Or was it possible that different therapies and techniques worked better for different psychological conditions, but when averaged together, they all looked about equally effective? Still another response to this finding was to begin to focus on specific processes in therapy and to try to understand in more detail how change occurred. We review each of these three possibilities below.

The Therapeutic Alliance as a Common Factor   A large number of common factors in different therapies have been proposed (see chapter 16). However, few have been researched. The one for which there is the most suppport is the therapeutic relationship, or, as it is now called, the *therapeutic alliance*. The therapeutic relationship appears to be the single most important curative factor in therapy, outweighing the importance of techniques or of differing approaches (Lambert, 1992). Some research (Horvath, 1995; Luborsky, McLellan, & Woody, 1985) found that measures of the alliance between therapist and client were the strongest predictors of whether the therapy would be successful. Other research has found that even in the case of prescription of antidepressant medication, the relationship between physician and client made a powerful difference in whether the medication was helpful (Krupnick et al., 1996).

It was Carl Rogers who originally proposed that the therapeutic relationship was a primary curative agent. As noted in Chapter 8, his further claim that it is three general therapist qualities—warmth, empathy, and genuineness—which make the difference has only partially been supported by the data. They are important, but the evidence does not support the claim that they are necessary and sufficient. Modern conceptions of the therapeutic alliance focus on three aspects of the relationship—the bond, the goals of therapy, and the tasks of therapy. A good therapeutic alliance includes a strong bond between therapist and client (and this is where warmth, empathy, and genuineness play a role). In addition, it includes an agreement between therapist and client on the goals to be pursued in therapy and the procedures and tasks to be used to attain these goals.

The therapeutic alliance is not seen as something the therapist establishes alone, but rather as a product of the collaboration between therapist and client. Thus, both client and therapist contribute. In this regard, Henry, Schacht, and Strupp (1986) found that greater therapist levels of "helping and protecting" and "affirming and understanding" were associated with positive therapeutic outcomes. However, they also found evidence that client behaviors contributed to how well a therapist was able to provide good therapeutic conditions. For instance, client behaviors of "disclosing and expressing" were related to the therapist's being more helping, affirming, and understanding, while client behaviors of "walling off and avoiding" were more associated with negative and hostile therapist behaviors. The most intriguing finding of this study was that the same therapist, using the same techniques, could come across with one client as "affirming and understanding" and with another as "blaming and belittling." This suggests that the presence of helpful behaviors in the therapist is partially dependent on the behavior of the client.

Differential Treatments for Different Problems   With regard to the hypothesis that perhaps different therapies are effective for different conditions, on the whole, with a few exceptions, research findings have tended to contradict this idea (Bergin & Garfield, 1994). For instance, a wide range of therapies seem to be of approximately equal effectiveness for the treatment of depression, including medication, cognitive therapy, and client-centered therapy. In a study by *Consumer Reports* magazine, data was collected from readers who had been in therapy. No differences were reported in effectiveness among differing approaches for any problems (Seligman, 1995). On the other hand, there are cases in which specific approaches seem to be differentially effective. One study by Stiles, Barkham, Shapiro, and Firth-Cozens (1992) found that clients' problems that are vaguely formulated or unfocused responded better to interventions of a psychodynamic or humanistic variety, while well-formulated, specific, and focused problems responded better to more prescriptive (cognitive-behavioral) interventions.

One possibility is that different treatments may not typically be differentially effective for different *problems*, but different treatments may work better with different *types of individuals*. This is the strategy pursued by Larry Beutler and his colleagues (e.g., Beutler & Clarkin, 1990). In a series of studies, Beutler has shown that clients who are highly "reactant" (i.e., highly autonomous and resistant to perceptions that others are trying to control them) do better with more nondirective treatments, while more dependent clients do better with more directive treatments.

As you will see below, the issue of whether different treatments are needed for different problems is far from settled. It is likely that both sides of the controversy are right: For many problems, it may not matter which approach to therapy is used, while for others, it may matter greatly.

Understanding the Process of Change Traditional psychotherapy research focused primarily on the issue of outcome: Is therapy A effective compared to a control group, and/or is therapy A more effective than therapy B? This kind of question, while important, has not been of particular use to the practicing clinical psychologist, and most practicing clinical psychologists have not found research findings very useful in terms of their actual therapeutic practice (Cohen, Sargent, & Sechrest, 1986; Morrow-Bradley & Elliott, 1986). Most clinicians find consultation with colleagues and their own experience in doing therapy to be more influential on their practice than research findings. With findings apparently indicating that all therapies worked about equally well, research efforts in the 1980s began to turn more to the question of what specifically contributed to therapeutic change.

Believing that a more fine-grained analysis of what happens in therapy would be of use to clinicians, a number of researchers have begun to do intensive analyses of the process of psychotherapy. Two of the newer approaches to trying to understand the process of change are those of Rice and Greenberg's (1984) task analysis, and the idea of "discovery-oriented" research (Elliott, 1984; Mahrer, 1988). Both of these approaches attempt to identify important events in the psychotherapeutic process, and then to study what actually occurs in a therapy intervention.

Task analysis, for instance, starts by developing a model of the change process on a specific therapeutic "task." Then, a number of actual "performances" are studied to see how well they fit the model. The model is revised to fit with what has been learned from studying these actual performances. Then the model is once again compared to new examples to see how well it fits. Greenberg (1984) has used this approach to study the process of resolution in the gestalt "two-chair" procedure. The client "task," for instance, is to resolve a "split." A **split** is an experience in which the client feels at odds with herself. For instance, part of her may be wanting to leave her marriage, and the other part may be criticizing her for that. In the gestalt two-chair exercise, the client role-plays the conflict. In one chair, she acts out the role of the "internal critic," in this case, the side that is saying "you should stay in the marriage." Then she switches chairs and acts out the role of the "want" side, in this case, the side that wants to leave the marriage. She continues back and forth, switching sides, until some resolution is reached. Greenberg (1984) notes that several studies have found that this procedure is effective in helping the client with the "task" of resolving a conflict. By studying a number of actual "performances" of this task, Greenberg was able to develop a model of how the process goes when it results in successful resolution. Among other things, the process seems to work best when the "critic" side "softens" in its approach to the "want" side. Consistent with the point we made above, a perusal of Greenberg's (1984) work provides a good deal of concrete information that practicing clinical psychologists can actually incorporate into their practice.

One of the most important ideas to come out of Rice and Greenberg's (1984) work on task analysis is the idea of a "therapeutic marker." Their general strategy is to try to identify "markers," that is, behavioral signs exhibited by the client that suggest that the client needs to work on a certain therapeutic task. For instance, the marker for the use of the two-chair technique is that the client is expressing a split—"I feel like leaving my marriage, but then I feel like I'm a bad person for wanting that. I should stay in it." The presence of a marker that the client is struggling with a specific kind of problem in a specific way at a specific time can then be used to choose a particular therapeutic intervention that will be of assistance at that moment. In other words, identifying a therapeutic marker helps the therapist to make effective moment-by-moment decisions. Greenberg, Rice, and Elliott (1993) have identified several other therapeutic markers which suggest that the therapist use specific interventions at specific moments. A number of other researchers have now begun to try to identify other therapeutic markers relevant to their approaches (e.g., Safran & Segal, 1990).

A related development has been that of "discovery-oriented" research (Elliott, 1984; Mahrer, 1988). Mahrer (1988), for instance, has suggested that therapists try to identify what they believe are significant events in therapy sessions. They collect many instances of that kind of event, and then look for patterns. The researcher can then begin to identify the kinds of therapist operations and procedures that bring about this kind of event, and the relationship of that event to ultimate therapeutic outcome. Mahrer and Nadler (1986), for instance, have identified a list of what different therapists have considered to be good moments in therapy, that is, moments that are hypothesized to be important in creating therapeutic change. These can include such things as the client exploring and expressing emotions, expressing insight or understanding, expressing feelings toward the therapist, or talking about personal, self-related material. In subsequent research, good moments in psychotherapy have been researched by Mahrer and his colleagues. For instance, Mahrer, White, Souliere, Macphee, and Boulet (1991) found that the therapist telling the client to describe, show, express, and "be" an emotion when the client was having difficulty accessing emotions helped facilitate a good moment of expressing emotion. Recently, Mahrer, Gagnon, Fairweather, and Cote (1992) have begun to identify criteria that denote whether a therapy session has been a "very good one" or not.

Elliott (1984) has suggested that an important process for learning about what actually happens in therapy is the use of "interpersonal process recall" (Kagan, 1984). Elliott identified moments in therapy when clients made "insight" statements, following therapist interpretations. These sessions were taped, and the client and the therapist later listened to the segment of therapy that includes the insight statement and talked about what they were experiencing at the time. From this, Elliott was able to develop a model of an "insight event." For instance, an insight event appeared to run through three phases: the client begins to process the information offered by the therapist; the insight occurs; and the client experiences a sense of newness, relief, accuracy, and helpfulness, and the insight leads to further exploration and new learning.

Research from the events paradigm seems to offer concrete, helpful information for practicing therapists. As of the late 1980s, it appeared that this would be the direction in which psychotherapy research would be heading: toward a more detailed, fine-grained, intensive understanding of how in-session processes facilitated change. However, under pressures to be described below, psychotherapy research has made an abrupt about-face, and is returning to the study of the question of whether specific treatments work for specific disorders.

CURRENT RESEARCH CONTROVERSIES AND ISSUES: POLITICS AND PSYCHOTHERAPY

As health care has increasingly come to be paid for by the government and by insurance companies, there has been an increasing demand for health care service providers to be able to demonstrate that the treatments they are providing work as they say they do. Along with this has come a call for the development of treatment guidelines in both medicine and mental health care. Treatment guidelines specify what treatments are to be used for particular disorders. For instance, an agency of the federal government, The Agency for Health Care Policy and Research, is busy developing treatment guidelines for a wide range of medical and psychological disorders. In 1993, this agency published treatment guidelines for depression. Treatment guidelines, ideally, are based on the best empirical evidence available for treating a particular disorder. However, those who develop treatment guidelines always have their own point of view, and interpret evidence in terms of that point of view. As a result, politics and science commingle in ways that lead to controversy in the current health care arena.

Health care agencies and insurance companies have not been happy with the general statement that "all psychotherapies work about equally well." If they are to pay for psychotherapy for a particular disorder, they want to know *which* specific psychotherapy treatment has been shown through research to work for that disorder. Further, many clients themselves want to know if a particular treatment is going to help them with their particular problem. The result has been increased pressure on psychotherapists to demonstrate that particular psychotherapy treatments work for particular disorders. This has changed the face of psychotherapy research (Goldfried & Wolfe, 1996). Research has swung away from the study of psychotherapy processes back to a study of questions such as: "Does cognitive-behavior therapy work for eating disorders?" "Does client-centered therapy work for depression?" "Does brief psychodynamic therapy work for anxiety attacks?" Proponents of each of the major therapies are setting out to "empirically validate" their approaches for the treatment of specific disorders in order that they not become obsolete, excluded from treatment guidelines and, therefore, from compensation by those who pay the bill for mental health treatment. In general, in both the United States and Europe, there are movements afoot to develop guidelines for the practice of "evidence-based" psychotherapy, that is, using psychotherapy only in ways that are supported by empirical research. Below we consider some of the developments with respect to this general trend.

Treatment Guidelines and the American Psychological Association Template

We previously mentioned the guidelines for the treatment of depression published by an agency of the federal government. These guidelines are a perfect illustration of how science has become completely mixed up with politics in the current health care arena. This governmental agency, under the influence of medical thinking, concluded from its review of the research that the use of medication was the treatment of choice for severe depression, and that depression was a "chronic illness." Many psychologists would not only contest the idea that depression is a chronic illness, but also would hold that the available evidence indicates that psychotherapy alone is equally as effective as medication, and does as well as psychotherapy and medication combined. Further, psychotherapy has a lower relapse rate than medication. This suggests that making medication the treatment of choice for depression is not compatible with the research evidence and unduly favors medication over psychotherapy.

In order to counter what psychologists saw as a biased reading of the evidence on the treatment of depression, the American Psychological Association developed a template for evaluating and constructing treatment guidelines (Task Force on Psychological Intervention Guidelines, 1995). This template provides empirical criteria for deciding whether a given set of guidelines for therapeutic practice is justified by the data. The template's criteria include both *efficacy* and *effectiveness* of psychotherapy. *Efficacy* has to do with what we described earlier in the chapter: doing careful experiments using control groups. These studies must be done, in essence, by studying specific treatments for specific disorders. In addition, the template mandates that the *effectiveness* or *utility* of the psychotherapy must be studied, that is, the effectiveness of the therapy must be studied under real-life conditions.

The reason for the distinction between efficacy and effectiveness or utility is that many carefully controlled experimental studies of psychotherapy are done in ways that have little to do with the conditions under which psychotherapy is practiced in real life. For instance, in real life, if a client comes to a therapist complaining of feeling anxious all the time, the therapist works with the client regardless of whether the client perfectly meets the criteria for the diagnosis of generalized anxiety disorder, and regardless of whether the client has other problems (e.g., depression, personality disorder). Yet in many of the carefully controlled research studies on therapy, clients are excluded from participating unless they meet strict criteria. Thus, in one study on a cognitive-behavioral treatment for generalized anxiety disorder, of the over 500 clients who were referred to the researchers for possible inclusion in the study, nearly 450 were rejected as not meeting the researchers' criteria (Borkovec & Costello, 1993). These researchers found that their cognitive-behavioral treatment was effective. However, one can ask how useful such information is to a practicing clinician, given that nearly 90% of the clients referred for the study (presumably because they were feeling anxious) were not included. That this is a genuine concern is illustrated by the findings of Weisz, Weiss, & Donenberg (1992) that psychotherapy with children practiced in the field was not as effective as psychotherapy practiced under carefully controlled research conditions.

The APA template thus encourages us to take a broader look at the scientific evaluation of psychotherapy, by looking at both questions of efficacy (can the psychotherapy be demonstrated to work under carefully controlled conditions?) and effectiveness (how well does it work under real-life conditions?). However, the template itself has been criticized by proponents of psychotherapies whose methods and purposes do not easily fit into a model of psychotherapy as a specific "treatment for a disorder." There are still many therapists who believe that diagnosis and treatment of specific problems is not the proper goal therapy. Instead, their goal is to promote deeper relational connections, self-awareness and insight, and deeper levels of a capacity to experience self and life. This includes many psychodynamic and humanistic therapists, feminist therapists, and constructivist therapists. Many of them believe that the template's criteria favor psychotherapies that can easily be evaluated using traditional experimental research methodologies, and they worry that the template might ultimately be turned against their preferred approaches. They are now lobbying to have nonexperimental and qualitative research methods, which fit their approaches better, included in the template's criteria.

Empirically Validated Treatments

Recently, a task force of Division 12 of the American Psychological Association published a set of guidelines for deciding which psychotherapy treatments had been empirically validated (Task Force on Promotion and Dissemination of Psychological Procedures, Division of Clinical Psychology of the American Psychological Association, 1995), along with a list of treatments that had met their criteria. In order to be included on this list, a particular psychotherapy had to be shown to be effective for the treatment of a particular disorder in two different control group or analogue studies in which the treatment was either compared to a placebo control group or to another treatment of known effectiveness.

However, the task force also had two additional new requirements for conducting a psychotherapy research study. First, the treatment had to be *manualized*. Manualization means that the procedures to be used to treat a particular disorder are described in fairly intensive detail in a "treatment manual." A treatment manual is meant to insure that therapists in a research study all practice the therapy in the same way. Many psychotherapy studies in recent years have used treatment manuals. The task force held that manualization was good not only for research purposes, but for the training of therapists.

Second, the therapy was essentially required to be studied using a population of clients who all had the same disorder. This is in marked contrast to many earlier studies of psychotherapy in which the treated group of clients might have included a wide range of disorders. From the perspective of a health care agency, a study showing that cognitive therapy works on a group of clients with different diagnoses does not tell very much about how it works for any *specific* diagnosis. Therefore, studies need to demonstrate how it works for a specific problem or diagnosis, and thus, the client population receiving treatment must be carefully specified in terms of what kind of problem is being treated.

Using these criteria, the task force came up with a list of specific psychotherapies used to treat specific disorders that met its research criteria. These were called "empirically validated treatments," and other approaches to therapy that did not meet its criteria were labelled "experimental." Further, because many of the research studies on psychotherapy done in earlier years had not been manualized and had not been on specific treatments for particular disorders, the task force essentially concluded that these studies were null and void under the new criteria. They then stated that the old conclusion that all therapies were about equally effective could now be discounted. The task force went on to recommend that its empirically validated treatments be taught in graduate programs. Some other writers who support the idea of empirically validated treatments have suggested that eventually, if therapists do not use empirically validated treatments, they will be subject to malpractice suits.

Controversy over Empirically Validated Treatments   The publication by the task force of Division 12 of the American Psychological Association of its list of empirically validated treatments was met with immediate controversy (e.g., Bohart, O'Hara, & Leitner, in press; Garfield, 1996; Goldfried & Wolfe, 1996). Many criticisms were made, some of which we mention. First, the list of empirically validated treatments was almost exclusively cognitive-behavioral, with only a very few psychodynamic and humanistic treatments included. This is not surprising because of the task force's criteria: Cognitive-behavioral treatments are easily manualized and easily studied as treatments for specific disorders, while psychodynamic and humanistic therapies are typically more open-ended. Further, under the task force's criteria, many therapies, such as client-centered therapy, which had substantial empirical evidence to back up their effectiveness under the old research criteria, now found themselves banished to the group of "experimental" (i.e., empirically unsupported) therapies.

Second, many clinicians worried that the list would supercede their use of their own clinical judgment as to what was best to use with their particular clients. They would be forced to apply an "empirically validated treatment," for instance, to a particular client with panic disorder, when their own clinical judgment might suggest doing something else. They further worried that this document would give health care agencies ammunition in further being able to tell clinicians what to do with their clients.

Third, many argued that the task force's conclusions were not justified by the empirical evidence available. For instance, many of the studies on the task force's list could be criticized as being irrelevant to how psychotherapy is practiced in the real world because they were done under carefully controlled research conditions (see the discussion of efficacy versus effectiveness in the previous section on the American Psychological Association template). In fact, cognitive behavior therapy for generalized anxiety disorder is on the task force's list, and we noted above how one of the studies supporting it excluded nearly 90% of the kinds of clients who might seek out such a therapy in real life. In this regard, Goldfried and Wolfe (1996) reported a story of one psychotherapy researcher joking that the first law of psychotherapy research is not to use real clients.

Fourth, many object to the requirement of the manualization of therapy. Manualization of therapy has been criticized by a number of writers. It has been held that manualization of therapy makes therapy a "paint-by-numbers" process (Silverman, 1996), negating the necessary flexibility that the therapist must have to be effective. In real life, therapists do not follow manuals; they try one thing, and if it doesn't work, they try another (Seligman, 1995). Therapy is a complex, interactive process. Manualization, it is held by some, destroys therapist spontaneity and fails to capture the most important quality in therapy—that of the relationship.

Fifth, even though the task force did not specifically require that research studies use DSM diagnoses, it did require that they "carefully specify" the types of clients being treated. By this they meant that the therapy had to be studied as a treatment for a particular kind of disorder or problem. This, too, does not fit with how therapists practice in real life. A client may come in with one problem, but during therapy, the problem may shift, and new goals may emerge. Or the therapy may work on multiple problems at the same time. Many therapies are not specifically focused on problem removal in any case.

Finally, as with the American Psychological Association template, it has been argued that the criteria for deciding that a therapy is empirically validated favor psychotherapies that are designed along the lines of the medical model, that is, as specific treatments for specific disorders, and discriminate against therapies that are not so conceived. Qualitative research methods and findings from qualitative studies, for instance, are not given much weight in the task force's criteria. Further, the whole idea of ever "validating" a therapy has been criticized. It has been noted that at best, all one can ever do is gather data that empirically *supports* the use of a given therapy, but there is always more that can be known about how a therapy works and who it works for. Thus, "validation" is an ideal never to be achieved.

Defenders of the task force's work have argued in reply that the guidelines were never meant to be used to dictate what clinicians did in actual practice. Further, they have argued that all therapies can be manualized and that treatment manuals are important to make sure that therapy is provided in a standardized and competent way. However, treatment manuals are never meant to be followed rigidly to the exclusion of what is happening with a particular client. Finally, they have suggested that those who complain that their favorite therapies are not on the list get busy doing the research to empirically validate them. They argue that therapies will need to be empirically validated in the future to remain viable.

Whether or not the attempt to establish a list of empirically validated treatments ultimately succeeds, it is likely that there will be increasing pressure for therapists to show that what they do is "evidence-based." However, there are alternatives to the empirically validated treatment approach. For instance, Grawe's (1997) "research-informed psychotherapy" does not favor any one approach to therapy over any other. Instead, Grawe tries to sort out four factors of therapeutic effectiveness that have been supported by the research, and to argue that *all* the traditional approaches to psychotherapy are limited in that they tend to favor only one or two of these four factors. He argues that therapy should use all four. His four factors are: helping clients to have real-life experiences of mastering their problems; clarification of meaning (e.g., learning to articulate feelings, gain insight); problem actualization (helping clients actually experience the problem while they learn to master it or gain insight into it); and utilization of clients' own change potential and resources. For Grawe, sensitive and skillful utilization of these four factors with individual clients constitutes effective, research-informed psychotherapy practice.

Measuring Outcome in Clinical Practice

The trend toward demanding specific evidence on effectiveness is filtering down to the level of the individual practitioner. There are increasing demands that individual practitioners be able to document their effectiveness in working with different types of disorders. Some managed care companies already require therapists to periodically administer questionnaires to their clients to monitor therapy progress. Various proposals for how to do this have been given. Some have suggested using individualized scales with which clients rate their progress toward the goals that have been set at the start of therapy. Others have suggested using standardized tests. In either case, it is likely that at least in some contexts, practitioners will be required to measure how much each of their clients has improved, keep records, and be able to demonstrate their effectiveness in working with different types of problems. This, too, is fraught with difficulty, since it could lead to some therapists unfairly being seen as less effective than other therapists because the clients diagnosed "borderline" that they happened to have seen are simply more difficult to work with than the clients diagnosed "borderline" that some other therapists happened to have seen.

IN CONCLUSION

The state of psychotherapy research is in great flux. There is increased pressure to do research demonstrating psychotherapy outcome—that is, that specific treatments work for specific disorders—at the same time as many believe that a more fruitful research avenue to follow would be to forget about studying different approaches to psychotherapy and instead study the specific change processes that occur. The threat of empirically validated treatments is that clinicians may be required to only or primarily use such treatments in their everyday practice by outside health care agencies that pay for mental health care. Yet these treatments may lack validity in terms of the real-life conditions of everyday psychotherapy practice. The promise of using psychotherapies that have been supported by empirical research is that consumers can be offered treatments that have shown some reliability in alleviating the problems that have brought them to therapy. It seems important, as well as ethical, to study psychotherapy and to discover what is most helpful and efficient. Different research methods and criteria are favored by different researchers, but methods and criteria that may be optimal for some approaches to psychotherapy may not be optimal for others. We hope that three trends will develop. First, researchers will stay "methodologically open," allowing different therapies to be studied with methods appropriate to their structure and purposes. Second, any who hold that a particular approach to psychotherapy works will support, encourage, or conduct research on that approach. Third, research will be used to guide and inform their practice by all clinicians, but it will not be used to constrain and dictate what they do in working with their partner in the whole enterprise—the individual client.

BIBLIOGRAPHY

APA Commission on Psychotherapies. (1982). *Psychotherapy research: Methodological and efficacy issues.* Washington, DC: America Psychiatric Association.

Arlow, J. A. (1984). Psychoanalysis. In R. Corsini (Ed.), *Current psychotherapies* (3rd ed., pp. 19–64). Itasca, IL: Peacock.

Basham, R. B. (1986). Scientific and practical advantages of comparative design in psychotherapy outcome research. *Journal of Consulting and Clinical Psychology, 54,* 88–94.

Bergin, A. E. (1971). The evaluation of therapeutic outcomes. In A. E. Bergin & S. L. Garfield (Eds.), *Handbook of psychotherapy and behavior change.* New York: Wiley.

Bergin, A. E., & Garfield, S. L. (1994). Overview, trends, and future issues. In A. E. Bergin & S. L. Garfield (Eds.), *Handbook of psychotherapy and behavior change* (4th ed., pp. 821–830). New York: Wiley.

Bergin, A. E., & Lambert, M. J. (1978). The evaluation of therapeutic outcomes. In S. L. Garfield & A. E. Bergin (Eds.), *Handbook of psychotherapy and behavior change: An empirical analysis* (2nd ed.). New York: Wiley.

Beutler, L. E., & Clarkin, J. F. (1990). *Systematic treatment selection*. New York: Wiley.

Blatt, S. J., & Ford, R. Q. (1994). *Therapeutic change: An object relations perspective*. New York: Plenum.

Bohart, A. C. (1977). Role playing and interpersonal-conflict reduction. *Journal of Counseling Psychology, 24,* 15–24.

Bohart, A., O'Hara, M., & Leitner, L. (in press). Empirically violated treatments: Disenfranchisement of humanistic and other approaches. *Psychotherapy Research*.

Borkovec, T. D., & Costello, E. (1993). Efficacy of applied relaxation and cognitive-behavioral therapy in the treatment of generalized anxiety disorder. *Journal of Consulting and Clinical Psychology, 61,* 611–619.

Brunnink, S., & Schroeder, H. (1979). Verbal therapeutic behavior of expert psychoanalytically oriented, Gestalt and behavior therapists. *Journal of Consulting and Clinical Psychology, 47,* 567–574.

Cohen, L. H., Sargent, M. M., & Sechrest, L. B. (1986). Use of psychotherapy research by professional psychologists. *American Psychologist, 41,* 198–206.

Critelli, J., & Neumann, K. (1984). The placebo: Conceptual analysis of a construct in transition. *American Psychologist, 39,* 32–39.

Elliott, R. (1984). A discovery-oriented approach to significant change events in psychotherapy: Interpersonal process recall and comprehensive process analysis. In L. N. Rice & L. S. Greenberg (Eds.), *Patterns of change* (pp. 249–286). New York: Guilford.

Eysenck, H. J. (1952). The effects of psychotherapy: An evaluation. *Journal of Consulting Psychology, 16,* 319–324.

Frank, J. D. (1974). Psychotherapy: The restoration of morale. *American Journal of Psychiatry, 131,* 271–274.

Frank, J. D. (1982). Therapeutic components shared by all psychotherapies. In J. H. Harvey & M. M. Parks (Eds.), *Psychotherapy research and behavior change*. Washington, DC: American Psychological Association.

Garfield, S. L. (1996). Some problems associated with "validated" forms of psychotherapy. *Clinical Psychology: Science And Practice, 3,* 218–229.

Goldfried, M. R., & Wolfe, B. E. (1996). Psychotherapy practice and research: Repairing a strained alliance. *American Psychologist, 51,* 1007–1016.

Grawe, K. (1997, April). *Research-informed psychotherapy*. Plenary address at the convention of the Society for the Exploration of Psychotherapy Integration, Toronto, Canada.

Greenberg, L. S. (1984). A task analysis of intrapersonal conflict resolution. In L. Rice & L. Greenberg (Eds.), *Patterns of change* (pp. 67–123). New York: Guilford.

Greenberg, L. S., Rice, L. N., & Elliott, R. (1993). *Process-experiential psychotherapy: Facilitating emotional change*. New York: Guilford.

Guntrip, H. (1973). *Psychoanalytic theory, therapy, and the self*. New York: Basic Books.

Gurman, A. S., Kniskern, D. P., & Pinsof, W. M. (1986). Research on marital and family therapies. In S. L. Garfield & A. E. Bergin (Eds.), *Handbook of psychotherapy and behavior change* (3rd ed., pp. 565–626). New York: Wiley.

Henry, W. P., Schacht, T. E., & Strupp, H. H. (1986). Structural analysis of social behavior: Application to a study of interpersonal process in differential psychotherapeutic outcome. *Journal of Consulting and Clinical Psychology, 54,* 27–31.

Hobbs, N. (1968). Sources of gain in psychotherapy. In E. Hammer (Ed.), *Use of interpretation in treatment.* New York: Grune & Stratton.

Horvath, A. O. (1995). The therapeutic relationship: From transference to alliance. *In Session, 1,* 7–17.

Howard, K. I., Kopta, S. M., Krause, M. S., & Orlinsky, D. E. (1986). The dose-effect relationship in psychotherapy. *American Psychologist, 41,* 159–164.

Jacobson, N. S., & Christensen, A. (1996). Studying the effectiveness of psychotherapy: How well can clinical trials do the job? *American Psychologist, 51,* 1031–1039.

Kagan, N. (1984). Interpersonal process recall: Basic methods and recent research. In D. Larson (Ed.), *Teaching psychological skills: Models for giving psychology away* (pp. 229–244). Monterey, CA: Brooks/Cole.

Kazdin, A. E. (1980). *Research design in clinical psychology.* New York: Harper & Row.

Kelly, G. A. (1963). *A theory of personality.* New York: Norton.

Krupnick, J. L., Sotsky, S. M., Simmens, S., Moyher, J., Elkin, I., Watkins, J., & Pilkonis, P. A. (1996). The role of the therapeutic alliance in psychotherapy and pharmacotherapy outcome: Findings in the National Institute of Mental Health Treatment of Depression Collaborative Research Project. *Journal of Consulting and Clinical Psychology, 64,* 532–539.

Lambert, M. J. (1983). Introduction to assessment of psychotherapy outcome: Historical perspective and current issues. In M. J. Lambert, E. R. Christensen, & S. S. DeJulio (Eds.), *The assessment of psychotherapy outcome.* New York: Wiley.

Lambert, M. J. (1992). Psychotherapy outcome research. In J. C. Norcross & M. R. Goldfried (Eds.), *Handbook of psychotherapy integration* (pp. 94–129). New York: Basic Books.

Lambert, M. J., & Bergin, A. E. (1994). The effectiveness of psychotherapy. In A. E. Bergin & S. L. Garfield (Eds.), *Handbook of psychotherapy and behavior change* (4th ed., pp. 143–189). New York: Wiley.

Lambert, M. J., Christensen, E. R., & DeJulio, S. S. (Eds.). (1983). *The assessment of psychotherapy outcome.* New York: Wiley.

Lambert, M. J., Shapiro, D. A., & Bergin, A. E. (1986). The effectiveness of psychotherapy. In S. L. Garfield & A. E. Bergin (Eds.), *Handbook of psychotherapy and behavior change* (3rd ed., pp. 157–212). New York: Wiley.

Lang, P. J., Lazovik, A. D., & Reynolds, D. J. (1965). Desensitization, suggestibility, and pseudotherapy. *Journal of Abnormal Psychology, 70,* 395–402.

Luborsky, L., McLellan, A. T., & Woody, G. E. (1985). Therapist success and its determinants. *Archives of General Psychiatry, 42,* 602–611.

Mahrer, A. R. (1988). Discovery-oriented psychotherapy research: Rationale, aims, and methods. *American Psychologist, 43,* 694–702.

Mahrer, A. R., Gagnon, R., Fairweather, D. R., & Cote, P. (1992). How to determine if a session is a very good one. *Journal of Integrative and Eclectic Psychotherapy, 11,* 8–23.

Mahrer, A. R., & Nadler, W. P. (1986). Good moments in psychotherapy: A preliminary review, a list, and some promising research avenues. *Journal of Consulting and Clinical Psychology, 54,* 10–15.

Mahrer, A. R., White, M. V., Souliere, M. D., Macphee, D. C., & Boulet, D. (1991). Intensive process analysis of significant in-session client change events and antecedent therapist methods. *Journal of Integrative and Eclectic Psychotherapy, 10,* 38–55.

Messer, S. B. (1994). Adapting psychotherapy outcome research to clinical reality: A response to Wolfe. *Journal of Psychotherapy Integration (Newsletter Section),4,* 280–282.

Miller, I. J. (1996). Time-limited brief therapy has gone too far: The result is invisible rationing. *Professional Psychology: Research and Practice, 27,* 567–576.

Morrow-Bradley, C., & Elliott, R. (1986). Utilization of psychotherapy research by practicing psychotherapists. *American Psychologist, 41,* 188–197.

Parloff, M. (1979). Can psychotherapy research guide the policymaker? A little knowledge may be dangerous. *American Psychologist, 34,* 296–306.

Parloff, M. (1986). Placebo controls in psychotherapy research: A sine qua non or a placebo for research problems? *Journal of Consulting and Clinical Psychology, 54,* 79–87.

Perls, F. S., Hefferline, R. F., & Goodman, P. (1951). *Gestalt therapy.* New York: Julian Press.

Rennie, D. L. (1990). Toward a representation of the client's experience of the psychotherapy hour. In G. Lietaer, J. Rombauts, & R. Van Balen (Eds.), *Client-centered and experiential therapy in the nineties* (pp. 155–172). New York: Guilford.

Rennie, D. L. (1994). Storytelling in psychotherapy: The client's subjective experience. *Psychotherapy, 31,* 234–243.

Rice, L. N., & Greenberg, L. S. (Eds.). (1984). *Patterns of change.* New York: Guilford.

Rogers, C. R., Gendlin, E. T., Kiesler, D., & Truax, C. B. (1967). *The therapeutic relationship and its impact: A study of psychotherapy with schizophrenics.* Madison: University of Wisconsin Press.

Rosenbaum, R., Hoyt, M. F., & Talmon, M. (1990). The challenge of single-session therapies. In R. A. Wells & V. J. Giannetti (Eds.), *Handbook of the brief psychotherapies* (pp. 165–189). New York: Basic Books.

Ross, L., Lepper, M. R., Strack, F., & Steinmetz, J. L. (1977). Social explanation and social expectation: The effects of real and hypothetical explanations upon subjective likelihood. *Journal of Personality and Social Psychology, 35,* 817–829.

Safran, J., & Segal, Z. (1990). *Interpersonal process in cognitive therapy.* New York: Basic Books.

Seligman, M. E. P. (1995). The effectiveness of psychotherapy: The *Consumer Reports* study. *American Psychologist, 50,* 965–974.

Shapiro, A. K., & Morris, L. A. (1978). The placebo effect in medical and psychological therapies. In S. L. Garfield & A. E. Bergin (Eds.), *Handbook of psychotherapy and behavior change: An empirical analysis* (2nd ed.). New York: Wiley.

Silverman, W. H. (1996). Cookbooks, manuals, and paint-by-numbers: Psychotherapy in the 90's. *Psychotherapy, 33,* 207–215.

Simkin, J. S., & Yontef, G. M. (1984). Gestalt therapy. In R. Corsini (Ed.), *Current psychotherapies* (3rd ed.). Itasca, IL: Peacock.

Sloane, R. B., Staples, F. R., Cristol, A. H., Yorkston, N. J., & Whipple, K. (1975). *Psychotherapy versus behavior therapy.* Cambridge, MA: Harvard University Press.

Smith, M. L., Glass, G. V., & Miller, T. I. (1980). *The benefits of psychotherapy.* Baltimore, MD: Johns Hopkins University Press.

Spence, D. P. (1982). *Narrative truth and historical truth: Meaning and interpretation in psychoanalysis.* New York: Norton.

Stiles, W. B. (1993). Quality control in qualitative research. *Clinical Psychology Review, 13,* 593–618.

Stiles, W. B., Barkham, M., Shapiro, D. A., & Firth-Cozens, J. (1992). Treatment order and thematic continuity between constrasting psychotherapies: Exploring an implication of the assimilation model. *Psychotherapy Research, 2,* 112–124.

Stiles, W. B., Shapiro, D. A., & Elliott, R. (1986). Are all psychotherapies equivalent? *American Psychologist, 41,* 65–180.

Task Force on Promotion and Dissemination of Psychological Procedures, Division of Clinical Psychology of the American Psychological Association (1995). Training and dissemination of empirically-validated psychological treatments: Report and recommendations. *The Clinical Psychologist, 48,* 3–23.

Task Force on Psychological Intervention Guidelines. (1995). *Template for developing guidelines: Interventions for mental disorders and psychosocial aspects of physical disorders.* Washington DC: American Psychological Association.

Waskow, I. E., & Parloff, M. B. (Eds.). (1975). *Psychotherapy change measures.* Washington, DC: Department of Health and Human Services.

Watson, J. C., & Rennie, D. L. (1994). Qualitative analysis of clients' subjective experience of significant moments during the exploration of problematic reactions. *Journal of Counseling Psychology, 41,* 500–509.

Weisz, J. R., Weiss, B., & Donenberg, G. R. (1992). The lab versus the clinic: Effects of child and adolescent psychotherapy. *American Psychologist, 47,* 1578–1585.

Wierzbicki, M. (1993). *Issues in clinical psychology: Subjective versus objective approaches.* Boston: Allyn & Bacon.

CHAPTER 16

Psychotherapy Integration: Convergence in Psychotherapy

Recent surveys have found that the majority of practicing clinical psychologists perceive themselves as eclectic (Norcross & Prochaska, 1982; Prochaska & Norcross, 1983), that is, they use techniques and concepts from a variety of theoretical sources. One of the reasons for this may be research findings that suggest that each of the major approaches to psychotherapy is approximately equivalent in effectiveness to the others. Knowing that differing approaches can all be effective, practitioners have been more likely to borrow what is useful from each one.

Along with the tendency toward eclecticism in practice, there has been a growing interest in finding commonalities among differing approaches and ways of integrating them. Prior to the 1970s, there had been sporadic efforts in this direction. Dollard and Miller (1950) attempted to translate Freudian concepts into behavioral terminology. Gendlin (1996) proposed that all therapies worked by influencing the client's experiencing process. Frank (1961) was among the first to propose that there were nonspecific factors common to the effectiveness of the various approaches.

The movement toward integrating approaches to psychotherapy has been mushrooming in recent years. There is now an international society for the study of psychotherapy integration: the Society for the Exploration of Psychotherapy Integration. There is also a professional journal devoted to the topic. The Society for the Exploration of Psychotherapy Integration currently has over 800 members, and holds conventions each year. Over the last 15 years, more than 50 books have been published presenting various integrative and eclectic views of psychotherapy.

TYPES OF PSYCHOTHERAPY INTEGRATION

Recent interest in integrating approaches has taken several directions. There are generally considered to be three different orientations toward psychotherapy integration: technical eclecticism, common factors, and theoretical integration (Arkowitz, 1992). However, another approach, assimilative integration (Messer & Warren, 1990), has also been identified. We will briefly review each of these major approaches to psychotherapy integration. Then, we will consider what we perceive as some of the emerging convergences in the field of psychotherapy.

Technical Eclecticism

The term *technical eclecticism* refers to the idea that the therapist will be eclectic, that is, he or she will borrow or use techniques and procedures from different approaches. Technically, eclectic therapists believe that what the therapist does should primarily be guided by what works rather than by a theoretical perspective. Perhaps the most well-known advocates of the technical eclectic approach to psychotherapy integration have been Arnold Lazarus, Larry Beutler, and John Norcross (Lazarus, Beutler, & Norcross, 1992). In general, they hold that the therapist should assess what the client's problem is and choose whatever intervention or approach will work best with that problem.

Many therapists who adopt this approach place a strong emphasis on research to discover what approaches work the best with what problems for what types of individuals. For instance, rather than "prescribe" empathy for everyone based on a theoretical perspective such as that of either client-centered therapy or self psychology, Beutler, Crago, and Arizmendi (1986) note that research has found that active provision of empathy with highly suspicious clients may be counterproductive. With this in mind, technically eclectic therapists have recently argued that even the therapeutic relationship should be tailored to fit with clients (Norcross, 1993). With some clients, the therapist should be more active and directive; with others, the therapist should be more passive and nondirective. With some clients, the therapist might adopt a more informal interactive style; with others, the therapist might need to be more formal and businesslike.

One can be technically eclectic and still adhere to a theory. Arnold Lazarus, for instance, generally adheres to a social learning point of view. There are many cognitive and client-centered therapists who are technically eclectic in the procedures they utilize in therapy, but they ground these procedures in their particular theoretical perspectives. However, for true technically eclectic therapists, theory is secondary to what works.

An example of technical eclecticism is a book by Beutler and Clarkin (1990) entitled *Systematic Treatment Selection*. In this book, these authors use research findings to structure therapy. They suggest that prior to therapy, therapists assess such factors as clients' expectations about treatment, clients' levels of coping skills, their motivation, their problem severity, their personality style, their environmental stressors, and their environmental support systems. These plus other factors are taken into account in developing a treatment plan. A series of decisions are made on whether the client is treated in an individual, group, or family therapy format; treatment duration (short- or long-term); how to structure the relationship; and what techniques to use. For instance, one needs to decide whether intense eye contact between therapist and client is either indicated or contraindicated by various client variables (such as the client's personal sense of boundaries).

As examples of how to choose techniques, if the client is dealing with unidentified feelings, the therapist might choose to use client-centered reflection as a technique. If challenging a client's dysfunctional cognitions is important, one may use various cognitive techniques.

Several other theorists have tried to provide models of how various therapies can be incorporated into an eclectic treatment model. Egan (1982), for instance, has argued that therapy can be broken down into three general stages. First is the *exploration* stage, during which skills such as those used in client-centered therapy are most appropriate. Second, after exploration, comes the stage of *interpretation,* when a formulation of the problem is made. During this stage, psychodynamic and cognitive approaches are most helpful. During the third stage, *action* is emphasized. Here, action strategies, homework assignments, and so on are stressed. In this stage, behavioral approaches are most appropriate. A related model, that of Beitman (1987), postulates stages of engagement in the therapeutic process, *pattern search* (i.e., identifying important patterns related to clients' problems), *change,* and *termination.*

Prochaska, Norcross, and DiClemente (1994) have argued that there are six general stages in the change process. The first stage is the *precontemplation* stage. Clients in this stage are not generally aware that there is a problem. The second stage is the *contemplation* stage. Here, the client is aware of the problem, and is engaging in self-examination. However, the client still does not have a good formulation of the problem. The third stage is *preparation,* which involves getting ready to change and making a commitment to change. The fourth stage is *action.* Here, the client is aware of the problem and has developed some formulation of it, and is therefore ready to take action. The fifth stage is *maintenance,* that is, maintenance of change once it has been achieved. This stage can include the awareness of the possibility of relapse and the willingness to recycle through the earlier stages if necessary. The sixth stage is *termination,* in which the person is totally confident of his ability to maintain the change (this last stage may be an ideal achieved by only a few).

For Prochaska, Norcross and DiClemente, different therapies appear to be most appropriate at different stages. For instance, when clients are in the precontemplation stage, that is, they are unaware that they have a problem, are not engaging in self-examination, or whatever, strategic therapies or psychodynamic therapies might be the treatment of choice. During the contemplation stage, when clients are actively engaged in exploration of the problem, cognitive therapies or existential therapies might be most appropriate. During the action stage, behavior therapy, gestalt therapy, or structural therapy might be most appropriate. Finally, for maintenance, behavior therapy may be most appropriate.

Still another model of the process of therapy is the "assimilation of problematic experience" model of Stiles and his colleagues (1990). These authors believe that an experience is problematic because it creates emotional disequilibrium until it is productively assimilated. A scale has been developed for modeling this process of assimilation.

At the lowest end of the scale (stage 0) a problematic experience is warded off and the client is unaware of it. At the next stage (stage 1), unwanted thoughts about the discomfort begin to break into awareness. Unwanted thoughts may also be associated with various negative feelings, such as anxiety, fear, or anger. In the next stage (stage 2), the client begins to acknowledge the existence of the problematic experience, but is unable to formulate the problem clearly. In stage 3, the client is now able to make a clear statement of the problem. In stage 4, some understanding and insight are gained. This leads to stage 5, in which the understanding is used to actively work on the problem. In stage 6, the client achieves some successful resolution of the problem. In stage 7, this resolution is generalized to other problems.

In terms of prescribing treatment, these authors suggest that when the problem is warded off, or is vague and unclear (e.g., stages 0 to 2), psychodynamic or humanistic approaches are most appropriate because of their exploratory nature. Once a clear problem formulation has been reached (stage 3 and above), a more prescriptive approach to therapy, such as a cognitive-behavioral approach, is more appropriate. One research study (Stiles, Barkham, Shapiro, & Firth-Cozens, 1992) found that therapy proceeded more smoothly when exploratory approaches preceded prescriptive approaches, rather than vice versa.

Common Factors

In our years of teaching, we have often had the experience of students studying the different approaches to psychotherapy and concluding "they're all talking about the same thing!" This observation by students is consistent with the approach to psychotherapy integration called "common factors." Those who follow this approach believe that there are common factors that appear in the differing therapies. They cite the fact that research has repeatedly failed to find significant differences in effectiveness among the differing approaches as evidence that there could be common underlying factors at work in the different therapies.

Jerome Frank (1982) was one of the first to suggest that there were some common dimensions to therapeutic change. He has suggested that one underlying dimension of all therapies is that they combat demoralization. In addition, they provide an emotionally charged, confiding relationship; a healing setting (such as hospital, clinic, office); a rationale or conceptual scheme to help the client make sense of his or her experiences; and a ritual to restore health that both client and therapist believe in. These function to provide a therapeutic relationship that combats alienation and demoralization, expectations of help, new learning experiences, arousal of emotions, enhancement of the client's sense of self-efficacy or mastery, and opportunities to practice new learning.

Goldfried (1980b) has noted the following common features: a facilitative therapeutic relationship, creation of client expectancy of help, encouragement of reality testing of client ideas and perceptions, provision of corrective experiences through which faulty ideas and behaviors may be modified, and provision of an external or objective perspective.

Marmor (1987) has suggested that most therapies provide a facilitative relationship, opportunities for release of emotional tension in an atmosphere of expectation and hope, cognitive learning, repeated reality testing and practice, and corrective emotional experiences. Furthermore, most therapies rely on operant conditioning, reinforcing some behaviors and not others, even if only by talking about them in therapy. Also, whether they explicitly acknowledge it or not, most therapies provide opportunities for identifying with and modeling after the therapist. Finally, all therapies work partially through suggestion and persuasion, again, even if this is not explicitly acknowledged.

In an issue of the journal *Cognitive Therapy and Research* (Goldfried, 1980a), therapists of differing orientations were asked for their opinions on the importance of various elements of the therapy experience. Almost all agreed on the importance of a good therapeutic relationship, the provision of new, corrective experiences, the provision of direct feedback on thinking, emotion, and behavior, and the utilization of cognition and awareness. Some research has supported both the use of corrective experience as a therapeutic commonality (Drozd & Goldfried, 1996) and facilitation of awareness (Castonguay et al., 1995). However it has also been found that the *kinds* of awareness facilitated by cognitive therapists is different than the kinds of awareness facilitated by psychodynamic therapists (Castonguay et al., 1995).

Recently, Bohart and Tallman (1996; in press), synthesizing ideas from a wide range of sources and other writers, have argued that perhaps the most important therapeutic commonality is the active agency of clients themselves. They have argued that the best solution to the question of why all psychotherapies seem to work about equally well, despite wide differences in methods and philosophies, is that clients are the agents of change in therapy, more so than therapists. Clients are able to use widely differing approaches, coming from widely different philosophical bases, to manufacture change for themselves. Further evidence for this thesis comes from studies that have shown that self-help approaches to therapy and activities such as journaling often work as well as professionally provided therapy (Christensen & Jacobson, 1994; Segal & Murray, 1994). Bohart and Tallman suggest that what all therapies have in common is that they provide a safe and supportive "work space" where clients can do the work of thinking through their problems and engaging in self-change and self-healing. Such a work space is not usually available in everyday life, where clients are too stressed and overwhelmed to think clearly and creatively, and where friends and relatives are not adept at listening and responding in ways that promote productive thinking, exploring, and self-healing. Therapists facilitate change through (a) providing such a safe work space, and (b) providing "tools" (e.g., ideas, suggestions and techniques) that clients can use in manufacturing their own solutions.

The common factors approach to psychotherapy integration is intuitively appealing, and our approach to psychotherapy integration, presented later in this chapter, is based on it. However, it has had its critics. For one thing, different theorists identify different common factors. Second, so far, there is only a little research to support the idea of common factors. Third, Mahrer (1989) has argued that many of the common factors proposed are at such a general level of description that they are not very helpful. For instance, the fact that all therapies provide for cognitive learning, or for corrective feedback does not tell us very much about the specifics of how these work or don't work in the different therapies.

Theoretical Integration

Perhaps the most difficult and challenging approach to psychotherapy integration is the attempt to come up with a unifying theoretical view that transcends the traditional views presented in this book. This is difficult, because the assumptions of the major approaches to psychotherapy are so different (Messer, 1986). Below, we consider some incompatibilities among varying perspectives.

Psychoanalysis tends to focus on defense against and avoidance of painful feelings, experiences, and conflicts as a major theoretical construct. If a patient thinks dysfunctionally, a psychoanalyst assumes that such thinking is really a symptom of deeper, underlying avoidance mechanisms. On the other hand, behavior therapy and cognitive therapy focus on learning. Pathological thoughts and behaviors are bad habits that have been learned and can be unlearned. Thus, for a cognitive therapist, a client who thinks dysfunctionally is simply misled. There is no assumption that the dysfunctional thinking is serving purposes of avoidance at deeper personality levels.

Both psychoanalysts and cognitive therapists emphasize rationality as the sine qua non of effective human functioning, and both strive to "strengthen the ego" or the ability to think and behave rationally. Both tend to assume that "nonrational" aspects of the personality, such as emotion and motivation, are "irrational" (not "nonrational"), and can interfere with rational functioning. In contrast, client-centered and gestalt therapists, as well as many family systems therapists whose ideas have been influenced by Milton Erickson, believe that the "nonrational" feeling side of the personality can often be the source of deep creativity. It is often precisely an overdeveloped, exclusive reliance on rational functioning that interferes with the utilization of this more intuitive, organismically wise side of the person. Carrying this further, cognitive therapists see their job as replacing dysfunctional cognitive schemas with functional ones, while client-centered therapists see the job as loosening rigid dysfunctional cognitive aspects so that a person's creativity may operate.

Finally, family systems theorists believe that behavior is heavily influenced by the immediate interpersonal systems of which people are a part. This view is compatible with behavioral and social learning views, which emphasize the importance of immediate situational influences on the person, such as reinforcers. These views tend to de-emphasize internal personality characteristics, in contrast to the typical psychodynamic view of the person, which emphasizes a relatively fixed, set personality structure laid down in childhood.

The point of all this is that these differences make theoretical convergence difficult. But you might say, "All of these are true! People are influenced by their past, they do have personalities, and their current interpersonal relationships affect them. People do need to become more rational, and they need to learn to trust their more intuitive side. People have often simply learned bad habits, and sometimes people are avoiding things they don't want to face. There! Now, can't we come up with a unifying theory of the human being, and get on with it?"

The problem with this is: how do we weight each of these factors? It is precisely here that theorists of various orientations differ. A psychodynamicist might agree with the above but argue that the most important factors are the tendency to avoid painful experience and the impact of the past. A family systems therapist might agree that personality exists, but believe that the here-and-now family system is the most important factor influencing behavior. A client-centered therapist might agree that humans avoid painful issues, but believe that the most important factor is the human capacity to change and grow creatively.

At the present time, we are a long way from being able to properly assign weights to these different factors. We simply do not know enough about human behavior to do this with any degree of accuracy. As a result, claims that any one theory can be used to integrate all psychotherapy are premature. It is unlikely that any one theory would be able to please individuals who have allegiances to any of the traditional viewpoints (Bohart, 1992).

As a result, theoretical integration is the approach to psychotherapy integration that is most fraught with potential problems. There are those who do not even believe that it is a useful one. Beutler (1989) believes that theories are primarily reflections of individually held values. They are more like philosophical "world views" and have little to do with actual therapy practice. Therefore, it is more fruitful to concentrate on the empirical question of what works best with what problems than on unifying theory. On the other hand, there are those such as Arkowitz (1989) who believe that theoretical integration is ultimately important because it helps practitioners to frame and understand the use of various techniques, as well as to develop new techniques.

Several approaches we have covered in other chapters are actually attempts at theoretical integration, such as the process-experiential approach of Greenberg, Rice, and Elliott (in Chapter 8), and the interpersonal cognitive approach of Safran and Segal (in Chapter 12). In addition, there have been several other interesting "first attempts" at theoretical integration. Paul Wachtel (1977) has tried to integrate behavioral and psychodynamic ideas. Wachtel holds that early childhood experiences set the stage for adult dysfunction. However, he believes that these early childhood experiences create adult dysfunction in "cyclical" unconscious, self-fulfilling prophecy ways. That is, they lead the person to behave in a way that then brings reinforcement from the here-and-now situation for the pattern of behavior carried forward from childhood. Thus, both childhood and here-and-now reinforcement play a role in the maintenance of adult pathological behavior. Suppose a person unconsciously learned to be submissive to her parent as a way of avoiding her anger toward a parent she perceived as mistreating her. Now, as an adult, she acts in a timid, deferential way, all the while repressing her anger. It is likely that she will actually elicit mistreatment from others, thereby reinforcing the dysfunctional behavior pattern. The more mistreated she is, the more deferential she becomes. In psychotherapy the goal is not only to help her gain insight into her unconscious patterns and anger, but also to get her to behave differently in the here and now. Either can break the dysfunctional pattern.

Mahoney (1991) has proposed an integrative developmental cognitive model. Mahoney adopts the constructivist position that reality is relative and that each individual constructs his or her reality. There is no "one" objective reality that can be said to be the correct one. Therefore, one cannot talk about the rationality or irrationality or the truthfulness or falsity of constructions. One can only talk about whether a person's construction of reality works or is viable. This also implies that ideas about reality are never perfect or finished, but continue to be modified with experience. Learning and development involve elaborating, differentiating, and refining ideas about the world. These ideas or constructions exist to a large extent at a tacit or nonconscious level. Some of these constructions may have been developed early in life. People resist rapid change in their core constructs because they strive to protect the integrity and coherence of their world views.

In contrast to some cognitive theorists, Mahoney emphasizes the importance of affect or emotion. He sees emotions as powerful, knowing processes. He also emphasizes the unity of thought, feeling, and action.

For Mahoney, psychological difficulties represent discrepancies between challenges and capacities. In other words, difficulties arise when coping skills cannot match the challenges of reality. Furthermore, pathological responses often represent behavior patterns that were adaptive in some prior life situations. Therapy for Mahoney includes utilizing cognitive insight, exploring affective responses, utilizing behavioral methods, working with rather than against resistance, and providing a safe, caring therapeutic relationship as a context that facilitates change.

Mahoney's approach draws on psychodynamic, humanistic, cognitive, behavioral, and systems perspectives. In this respect, it represents one of the first truly eclectic theoretical attempts at integration.

Another comprehensive attempt at theoretical integration is that of Andrews (1990). Andrews's model is based on the idea that humans are motivated to preserve their self-concepts. Psychological problems are the result of clients' being stuck in dysfunctional patterns of behaving, acting, and feeling based on the need to maintain consistency with their self-concepts. Different approaches to therapy operate at different points to break up these patterns and to allow new feedback in.

Finally, Bohart (1992) has proposed an integrative theory based on the idea of process. First, he suggests that psychopathology is not primarily a matter of misconstruing, distorting, or misperceiving. Nor is it primarily a matter of behaving inappropriately. In fact, if you think back on your previous week, you will probably be able to remember at least one incident when you misperceived something and one incident when you behaved in a way that was either not very effective or was inappropriate. Bohart suggests that such misperception and misbehavior are a part of life. Psychopathology occurs when the person fails to learn from feedback and therefore fails to modify misperceptions or dysfunctional behavior.

To put it another way, the issue is not "why am I chronically misperceiving myself as no good," but rather "why am I not learning from feedback that this misperception is not helping me deal with life effectively?" Put this way, psychopathology becomes a matter of a failure to learn. Life is complex and humans are like explorers, trying things out and learning from feedback. Encountering problems is a part of life.

Throughout their lives people are continually challenged to alter perceptions and be-liefs so as to more comprehensively, adaptively, and flexibly cope. They are also con-tinually challenged to learn and refine behavior so that it becomes more fine-tuned and adaptive. Failure, frustration, and loss are a part of life, and learning how to learn from them and to move on is the key to effective functioning. Psychopathology is a function of how people cope when they fail, confront loss and despair, or experience blocks and obstacles in their life path.

All therapies operate by helping the client learn how to learn, that is, by helping the client function more intelligently. The therapy process itself models the very skills that are needed to learn creatively. First, in order to master problematic experi-ences, a person must be able to "stay with" these experiences, which means tolerating and acknowledging the unpleasant emotions, such as anger, anxiety, despair, or fear, that accompany them. Therapists model and encourage this process of tolerating and staying with these emotions in order to learn about the problematic experiences. This is modeled by psychodynamic, humanistic, and cognitive therapists. Even behavior therapists, by encouraging their clients to keep records of when and where they feel negative emotions, implicitly encourage attending to the emotion in order to learn about it rather than avoid it.

Second, therapists model the idea that people must continually check abstrac-tions about self, others, and life in general, against data and experience. This allows them to learn and modify abstractions to better fit their experiences of reality.

Third, therapists encourage clients to broaden their range of attention. Clients are often failing to find new solutions to life problems because their attention span is overly constricted. They fail to notice information available either in the environ-ment or in themselves. Both psychodynamic and humanistic therapists encourage clients to track the flow of their inner experience, that is, to pay greater attention to internal information. Cognitive and behavior therapists encourage a broader atten-tion span with respect to external information. Cognitive therapists encourage clients to notice exceptions to the generalized dysfunctional rules and beliefs they are using to guide their lives. Behavior therapists encourage clients to pay attention to when and where problems occur.

Next, most therapies encourage the client to pay more attention to the process of struggling with a problem rather than to the product or outcome. They encourage an exploratory attitude, that is, individuals must try things out, learn and explore. And part of that exploratory process is that there will be stops and starts and setbacks as a person moves toward resolution.

Assimilative Integration

Even if no one had become interested in actively fostering the integration of the dif-fering approaches to psychotherapy, there is ample evidence that a movement toward psychotherapy integration has been happening anyway. Messer and Warren (1990) have discussed assimilative integration. This means that integration may happen as a given approach begins to integrate within itself insights from the other approaches.

Assimilative integration appears to be happening on all fronts. In the area of psy-chodynamic theory, object relations theory is moving toward a rapprochement with cognitive theory, as it begins to focus on the idea that our behavior is driven by internal cognitive representations of our relationships with people. Self psychology is really an integrative theory, comprising aspects of both psychodynamic and humanistic theory (Tobin, 1990). Cognitive approaches (see Alford & Norcross, 1991) have integrated insights and techniques from both behavioral and humanistic approaches. We have already mentioned that many cognitive theorists are now incorporating ideas from psychodynamic attachment theory. Existential-humanistic approaches have begun to integrate insights from cognitive theory and from psychoanalytic attachment theory (e.g., Greenberg, Rice, & Elliott, 1993; Greenberg, Safran, & Rice, 1989), as well as from self psychology (Tobin, 1990). A recent existential-humanistic integrative model shows how existential therapists can fruitfully use cognitive, behavioral, and psychodynamic approaches within an existential framework (Schneider & May, 1995). Finally, most modern psychodynamic, humanistic, and cognitive theorists take the idea that people are affected by their current interpersonal systems quite seriously. And there have been several attempts to integrate family systems theory itself with ideas from other psychotherapeutic approaches (Allen, 1988; Feldman, 1992; Wachtel & Wachtel, 1986).

Objections to Psychotherapy Integration

Not everyone necessarily supports the movement toward integration and convergence. Landsman (1982) suggests that behaviorism and humanism have much to learn from one another while preserving their separate identities. Franks (1984) believes that behavior therapy and psychoanalysis are conceptually incompatible and that integration even at the level of clinical practice has drawbacks. Bohart (1991) has argued that while self psychology and client-centered therapy have much in common, there are still important differences.

Stiles, Shapiro, and Elliott (1986) argue that different approaches to psychotherapy are actually different pathways to mental health, and that there are different ways of being mentally healthy. In a sense, the argument of Stiles and colleagues is similar to technical eclecticism, only perhaps we could call it theoretical eclecticism, in that they are arguing that different psychotherapeutic theories represent different models of mental health. The implication of this is that different clients might "thrive" with different approaches. That is, some clients might benefit more from pursuing a psychodynamic path to mental health, others from pursuing an existential-humanistic path, and so on.

Certainly if we take the ideas of multiple realities, constructivism, and cultural diversity seriously, then it may well be that there are a variety of ways to be mentally healthy, and that each of the traditional theories is a model of one possible way. Different theories may fit different clients. Perhaps some clients simply live in a psychodynamic reality better than a behavioral reality. Our experience has been that different students seem to resonate with different theoretical stances. Showing films of therapists of varying persuasions in class reinforces this: No therapist is uniformly liked by all students, and there is usually much diversity in their responses to them. If this is the case, then it may make sense to keep the diverse theoretical models. Each may represent a "world view" that is more compatible for some clients than for others.

If this were the case, trying to collapse all these models into one overarching model might be misguided, or at least premature. What might be needed instead is a "model of models," that is, an overarching theory that can explain how people utilize different models of reality in order to live effectively, and how a therapist might need to understand, respect, and work within the client's model of reality in order to facilitate growth from within it.

OUR VIEWS ON INTEGRATION AND CONVERGENCE

In the previous two editions of this text we presented our version of a "common factors" approach to psychotherapy integration. We believe there do appear to be a number of factors that are common to differing approaches. Below, we present an updated version of our view.

We suggest that all therapies are based on an attempt to solve a common underlying problem, that of access. We will look at their differing conceptualizations of that problem, and their procedures for circumventing it. Then we will look at commonalities among views of what is psychopathological and what changes will lead to more effective functioning. Finally, we will look at the therapeutic procedures that are supposed to lead to changes.

The Basis of All Therapies: The Problem of Access

In a sense, all therapies exist because people's attempts to control their own or others' behavior and feelings by rational argument, persuasion, command, and analyzing frequently fail (see Rachman, 1981, for a similar suggestion). Suppose you have a friend named Sue. Sue is involved with Bill, but Bill constantly mistreats her. He goes out on her, is inconsiderate and self-centered, and has even hit her on occasion. All of Sue's friends tell her that Bill is no good for her. She will even say that she knows that he is no good for her. Yet this knowledge seems to have no effect on her feelings. She loves him nevertheless.

At the same time, there is Ron. Ron is kind, considerate, faithful, and reliable. Everyone tells Sue that Ron would be perfect for her. Intellectually, Sue believes this also. But knowing that Ron is right for her seems to have no effect on how she feels. She just doesn't feel attracted to him.

We will give one other example. You are about to go on a job interview. You begin to feel anxious. You tell yourself there is nothing to fear. You may even try to argue rationally with yourself: "It is in my better interest to be relaxed at the job interview." Yet, perversely, against your own better interest, you find your pulse racing, you're sweating, and your voice may be quavering as you begin the interview.

People may know intellectually what they should do or what would be best for them, but find themselves unable to act or feel accordingly. When they dislike some way they are behaving or feeling, they may try different intellectual means to change. They may self-engineer (Gendlin, 1964), that is, decide how they should behave and command themselves to act accordingly. They may argue rationally with themselves, marshalling evidence for why they ought to change their behavior. Or, they may hunt for reasons why they aren't acting the way they believe they ought—they speculate that there may be underlying reasons for their behavior. They play detective and gather clues for various possibilities. Maybe they are staying in a dysfunctional relationship because they have an underlying need for security. Or perhaps they eat too much because they are compensating for dissatisfaction in their love life. Or maybe they have an underlying need to fail. But such deductions do no good. They still don't change. Thus, it could be said that people try to cognitively control their behavior either through rational argument, command, and persuasion, or through attempts at self-analysis. Underlying these attempts to change behavior are usually expectations of how people think they should be in order to be happy.

People use similar methods to try to control or change others' behavior. Parents say, "Eat your spinach. It's good for you." They warn adolescents of the dangers of drug abuse. They present a friend with rational arguments in favor of leaving a destructive relationship.

From Freud on, therapists have been aware of the impotence of such purely cognitive attempts to change behavior. For instance, Beck (1979), working with a client, suggests the following insight: "Do you see any connection then between your trying to make things go well with the men and your futile attempts to make things go well with your mother?" And the client replies, "Yes, I can see it. . . . I understand it in my head but somehow I haven't been able to digest it emotionally and get to the point where I can not involve myself in these negative relationships."

If behavior and feeling states could be controlled consistently through conscious, rational means, we would not need therapists. People would simply explain to themselves and others logically why they should act or feel in such and such a way and they would do it. But people come to therapy when such efforts fail. They come when they are unable to persuade themselves not to be depressed or that there is nothing to fear if they go outdoors. They come because they cannot control their drinking or change the pattern of arguing in their marriage. They come because they have physical illnesses that are inexplicable and do not respond to medical treatment. They are sent by parents or the legal system, who have failed to persuade them to comply with society's norms.

We conceive of the person as an organized system of behaviors, thoughts, perceptions, motives, beliefs, and emotions. The problem of access is: Why does direct rational, intellectual information fail to gain access to the system of the person and facilitate change? For instance, why doesn't it work when a person says to herself, "I can control my impulses to eat if I try," but it does work when a therapist, utilizing Erickson's techniques, says, "Pay attention to what you do this week when you control your urge to eat." The message "I can control my impulses to eat" is implied in both, but the less direct communication somehow gains access and works, while the more direct communication does not get through.

Put another way, the access problem has to do with the fact that one part of the person can know what is needed to change, but that knowledge somehow does not affect other parts of the person. Different therapies have different theories of why direct, conscious, rational communications do not have an immediate impact on the person. Different therapies also have their own ways of gaining access. In fact, most therapy techniques could be viewed as different methods of communicating or generating information so that it gets through and facilitates change. We will first look at general strategies for facilitating access and then at each major perspective and how it deals both theoretically and practically with this problem.

Strategies for Facilitating Access

Experiential Methods   Cognitive learning and consciousness raising have been postulated as common underlying dimensions in psychotherapy, yet, as we have repeatedly pointed out, no approach relies on cognitive learning alone. All, in one way or another, include an experiential component to increase the effectiveness of cognitive learning (Bohart, 1993). The importance of experiential learning has also been cited as a common dimension by Goldfried (1980b), Gendlin (1996), and Arkowitz and Hannah (1989). However, we wish to point out the interrelatedness of cognitive and experiential learning. That is, sheer cognitive learning alone seems to be ineffective. However, cognitive learning plus an experiential component seems to be one of the ways of gaining access. There are at least three different, but overlapping, ways in which experiential learning is utilized to facilitate access: direct experience, experiential articulation, and experiential evocation.

Direct Experience   Many approaches rely on direct experiential learning. Behavioral approaches are perhaps the best example of this. Behavior modifiers reinforce or extinguish behavior at the moment it is occurring. Meichenbaum and Bandura provide direct modeling of individuals learning how to cope with various problem situations and then encourage practice of the behaviors involved. Assertion training and social skills training programs involve direct behavior rehearsal. Conditioning techniques, such as systematic desensitization, attempt to modify directly emotional reactions to real or imagined stimuli.

The cognitive-behavioral approaches of Beck and Ellis include homework assignments in which clients are instructed to test their cognitions directly against experience. Beck also believes that the therapeutic relationship itself is an important source of learning. The client can learn how to challenge dysfunctional cognitions from watching the therapist. George Kelly's cognitive approach included having clients act out roles in real life to try out different behaviors that would lead to different experiences and evidence to correct faulty cognitive constructs.

From a client-centered perspective, Gendlin (1967) has argued that direct experiential interaction in the therapeutic relationship is a potent source of learning. Clients learn how to be self-accepting, how to listen to themselves, and how to be genuine through interaction with an accepting, empathic, genuine therapist.

Recent psychoanalytic approaches, such as those of Kohut and object relations theory, see the therapeutic relationship as a situation in which the client can directly experience the distorting aspects of primitive childhood constructions of reality. Change takes place through a corrective emotional experience as much as through cognitive insight.

Strategic therapists also use exercises involving direct experience. For instance, a client may be coached in how to woo his wife (Madanes, 1985). Other techniques encourage the client to engage in certain behaviors in the hopes that they will break up the client's old system. Once the system is broken up, new, more adaptive behaviors may be creatively discovered through action, without the necessity of cognitive learning or insight. Finally, gestalt therapy also relies on direct experiential learning. Rather than talk about conflict resolution, gestalt therapists will have clients roleplay the various sides of the conflict to experience direct learning (Greenberg, 1984).

Experiential Articulation Many approaches value the acquisition of some kind of insight, or the generation of new, useful self-knowledge. In psychoanalysis, insights may be acquired by the client's own processes of introspection or may be given by the therapist. In client-centered therapy, the process of finding just the right words to formulate what is implicitly known or sensed at the experiential level "carries forward" the growth process (Gendlin, 1964). In both cases, the formulation of this new knowledge in words is not therapeutic unless it articulates or matches the client's experiential state.

Psychoanalytic interpretations are effective only if the proper affective context has been established, that is, the relevant concrete memories and feelings must be close to consciousness. It is like discussing a movie: You are most likely to "gain insight" into the movie when it is "fresh" in your mind. Similarly, insights only work when the problem is "hot," "present," or "alive," rather than cold. At that point, an insight can articulate or connect with a host of bodily aspects of the problem: vivid memories, feelings, or bodily reactions. In the words of one of our colleagues, therapy may connect "feelingless words" with the experiential feeling and "wordless feelings" with meanings (Beverly Palmer, 1987, personal communication).

Client-centered reflections or experiential responses are also attempts to articulate what is currently being felt at the experiential level. Gendlin (1964, 1968) says that words are therapeutic if they come from the client's experiential sense of the problem, rather than being cognitively generated and applied to experiential sense. Thus, a client may say, "I feel really bothered by my wife," and a client-centered therapist may articulate that sense of being bothered more fully, "You feel like she never lets you alone."

Something like experiential articulation also plays a role in Beck's cognitive therapy. For instance, a cognitive therapist could say to a depressed client, "You generate your own depression by interpreting events in a negative way." Such an abstract cognitive insight would probably have little effect on the depressive. What Beck has the client do is keep a daily record of dysfunctional thoughts. At the moment the client is experiencing depression associated with some dysfunctional thought, he attempts to capture that thought in words and write it down, along with an objective description of the situation. The abstract cognition that the client generates his own depression through his cognitions is now matched to a vivid, concrete experiential example.

Finally, de Shazer (1985), a strategic therapist, also uses a kind of experiential articulation. A client who is having trouble dieting may say, "I never can control my eating." De Shazer points out that clients often phrase their complaints in terms of "always" or "never," but things are rarely "always" or "never." However, it would be useless to tell the client, "Oh no. It's not true that you never control your eating. Sometimes you do." It is more effective to instruct the client to "pay attention to what you do when you control your urge to eat," because there will almost always be times that the client does control the urge. The client thus learns concretely and experientially that self-control is not a matter of "always" or "never." We will have other occasions to consider this intervention, as there is more to it than the client's matching of cognitive insight to experience.

All this suggests that cognitive articulation can be useful if it is done in relation to the relevant, directly felt experience. While Beck has his clients keep daily records of dysfunctional thoughts primarily for data-gathering purposes for later discussion and evaluation, psychoanalysis and client-centered therapists believe there is an immediate, direct benefit of experiential articulation. For psychoanalysts such articulation is an emotionally experienced insight that leads to change. For client-centered therapists, experiential articulation leads to a directly felt change in the problem, a sense of integration, clarification, and closure.

It is possible that formulation or articulation of an experience at the moment it is "fresh" consolidates or facilitates learning from it. Consider the example of talking over a movie with friends when you have just seen it and it is fresh. As you attempt to put your reactions into words, you clarify, integrate, and consolidate your impressions of it. Another example might be recording your impressions of a situation as you observe it. Your articulation of what you observe will help you to organize and consolidate learning from the observations (see, for instance, Bandura, 1986). Trying to articulate your impressions later when the situation is not fresh is more difficult and will probably have less of an impact on learning.

There is a question as to whether experiential articulation creates change or merely consolidates it. Psychoanalysis assumes that gaining insight causes change. Gendlin (1964) has argued that insight actually follows change. For example, by the time a person can articulate her anger toward her father, a change has already taken place to make that anger consciously available. Repression has already been overcome. The formulation of the anger in words may serve only to consolidate and integrate this change into the personality structure.

Experiential Evocation in Therapy   In order for new meanings to be developed and learned in an experiential context, therapy may have to evoke the relevant experiential reactions. This can be done through the use of words, images, or exercises. Techniques may be used to evoke vivid memories, images, relevant feelings, "felt meanings" (Gendlin, 1964), or other whole body experiences associated with a problem situation. Or there may be a specific focus on the evocation of strong emotional reactions.

Evocation of Experiential Reactions   There are various ways therapists attempt to evoke experiential reactions in therapy. One way is to use vivid, everyday language. Concrete language is more likely to evoke an experiential reaction than abstract jargon. Some research (Nisbett & Ross, 1980) has suggested that we are more influenced by vivid information than by "pallid," abstract information. Most therapy orientations advocate the use of concrete, vivid language.

To make information vivid and concrete, therapists of many schools attempt to get clients to "flesh out" vague, abstract characterizations of their problems with concrete details. Polster (1985), from a gestalt perspective, has suggested that clients often come into therapy only with "titles" of their stories ("My wife and I don't get along"), and the job of therapy is to supply the concrete details. Fleshing out abstractions is also an integral part of Beck's cognitive therapy.

Fleshing out abstractions partially allows hypothesis testing. The client is able to see if generalizations such as "I can never control my hunger" or "I always fail" are accurate. In addition, however, recalling a concrete example of when the client failed or when he had difficulty controlling his hunger will be more likely to evoke the bodily feelings and experiences associated with the abstract statement. This is an explicit part of Rice's reformulation of empathic and experiential responding in client-centered therapy (Rice & Saperia, 1984). The client is asked to imagine herself in the specific situation in which she experienced the problem. Then exploration takes place with that specific situation as a constant referent. The gestalt role-playing technique also reevokes the concrete experiential components of a problem.

Exercises designed to be experientially evocative are a part of many encounter groups. Participants may engage in a "blind walk," in which they are blindfolded and led around by another participant. The issue of trust is not merely talked about, but actively experienced. Guided imagery or guided fantasy exercises are also used. Presumably, imagery and fantasy evoke more of the full body response to a situation than mere words. For instance, participants might be asked to imagine how it would feel to be a "lost, lonely child in the woods."

Imagery is also used in the cognitive therapies of Beck and Ellis, and therapy approaches based on Erickson's work, such as strategic therapy, often use stories or metaphors. Such stories probably work both because they convey the meaning in an experientially evocative context and because their indirect nature bypasses the "negative self-monitor" (discussed below).

Arousal of Emotion   Some approaches to therapy, such as primal therapy, focus explicitly on the arousal of strong emotion. The belief is that certain emotions, usually anger or sadness, are so repressed by society, and thus by the individual, that they "build up" like fluids inside the person, causing psychological problems. This is often called the "hydraulic model" of emotions. These approaches attempt to evoke these emotions and to cause them to be discharged through expression, called "emotional catharsis."

While catharsis therapies and techniques may often be effective, the idea that emotions are like fluids that need to be vented and discharged is debatable. Gendlin (1984), for instance, has pointed out that merely "feeling the feeling" is not, by itself, therapeutic. People often fully experience and express their anger without undergoing any change or resolution of their problems. Beck (Beck, Rush, Shaw, & Emery, 1979) has noted that crying and the expression of sadness in cognitive therapy sometimes make clients feel better, but often do not.

Bohart (1980), summarizing research literature on anger, has concluded that the hydraulic model of emotions does not fit the data, and that catharsis or expression of feelings alone is not therapeutic. Sometimes anger expression makes people feel more angry rather than less, and again, though crying sometimes makes people feel better, frequently, it does not. He suggests that what is therapeutic about approaches that stress emotional arousal and expression is that such approaches provide experiential opportunities for cognitive insight or working through. Without such an insight or working-through process, the sheer expression of feelings will not be therapeutic. In other words, to relate it to our current topic, it is likely that emotional arousal and expression evoke the whole range of bodily experiences and memories associated

---

B O X   1 6 . 1

Are Emotions Like Fluids to Be Discharged?

You are angry at your professor because you feel you were unfairly graded on a test. Is your anger like a fluid that can be drained off through expression? It may depend on where and how you express it. If you talk over your feelings with an empathic friend, you may indeed feel better. If you express your anger to the professor, and he admits his mistake and changes your grade, you will feel still better. But is it the expression of the feelings in these two cases that would make you feel better or the communication with someone who helped you work through the issues involved in your anger?

Bohart (1980) suggests it is more likely to be the latter. Instead of talking to a friend or a responsive professor, suppose you scream in the middle of a field. Do you think your anger would be drained away, and you would no longer feel angry about how unfairly you were treated? Or suppose your professor is unresponsive to your feelings. Do you think your expression would drain off the anger in that case? It would be quite unadaptive if we could eliminate feelings of anger regarding some injustice by simple expression without doing anything to modify the unfair situation.

If emotions are like fluids, and we can drain them away through expression, what about love and happiness? Do we reduce our level of love by expressing it? Do we become less happy if we shout for joy?

Sheer emotional expression by itself is not necessarily beneficial. It needs to be accompanied by some sort of cognitive working-through process (see also Nichols & Efran, 1985).

---

with a conflict situation. It is not merely the emotional expression itself that happens. In addition, the whole experiential context of the problem is made available for cognitive reworking (see Box 16.1).

Beck (1987) has said that cognitive therapy works better when affect is aroused. It is easier to work on a client's anxiety or depression when the client is experiencing these feelings. However, this is not because the emotions are being expressed and drained off, but because when the client is feeling anxious or depressed, the associated dysfunctional cognitions are more available and more readily modified.

One other reason for the therapeutic efficacy of emotional arousal has been suggested by Frank, Hoehn-Sarie, Imber, Liberman, and Stone (1978). They suggest, on the basis of some research findings, that emotional arousal makes the client more likely to adopt the suggestions and cognitive framework being advocated by the therapist.

Experiential Components in Therapy   All these various uses of an experiential component in therapy suggest that therapy must ultimately have an impact at the bodily or experiential level. Sheer cognitive insight, especially if couched in abstract terms, seems to have little impact at the bodily or experiential level. Therefore, some therapists attempt to work directly at that level. They reinforce behavior changes. These behavior changes presumably include the bodily cues and schemas that direct and control the behavior. Or they attempt to teach new behavior schemes or to directly condition emotional responses.

Other approaches attempt to modify these bodily reactions and schemes through cognitive reconstruction. They may help the client to gain insight, or they may convey a new way of looking at something in a story. In either case, such cognitive insights are useless unless the relevant bodily, experiential cues are present. There must be a match between bodily experience and cognition for the cognition to influence or consolidate behavior change. Experiential evocation, then, may make bodily cues available for reworking and reprocessing. Cognitively talking about and articulating one's experience as one is experiencing it may create change at the bodily level. In a similar manner, observing someone do something is a direct visual experience, and learning may be facilitated if one articulates to oneself the relevant factors being demonstrated.

This would explain why abstract, cognitive insight is frequently useless. Such abstract cognitive insights by themselves do not evoke the relevant concrete bodily reactions. If they are to be useful at all, they need to be timed to when such cues are present.

Some social psychological research is relevant. At least under some conditions (see Collins, 1970), attitude change is facilitated by having people role-play the attitude the therapist would like them to adopt. For instance, a person may be instructed to write an essay in favor of a certain position. To write an essay, the person needs to think, remember, and rehearse, and any bit of experience relevant to the position being argued may be dredged up. Under some conditions (and what conditions these are continues to be controversial), such role playing does indeed cause attitude change.

We should also point out that the relevant variable is the presence of experiential cues, not necessarily emotional cues. Many therapies have focused on emotion or affect. But emotion is actually a subset, or one kind, of experience. It is likely that emotional focus in therapy is helpful because it evokes experiential reactions. When a client gets in touch with his childhood anger toward his father, this usually also evokes vivid visual memories and other bodily reactions. The therapeutic learning probably involves all the bodily components of the experiential reaction, not just the emotional ones, just as learning to drive a car evokes and involves experiential reactions that are not necessarily emotional.

We will conclude this section with a relevant story of a friend. When this friend was a young woman she was in a play. Her role was of a pregnant woman considering an abortion. Until our friend played this role she had never really "worked out" her own feelings about abortion. Oh, sure, she had heard pro and con arguments. But, as we have seen, most such arguments tend to be abstract, and they often do not have an impact on people because they are not "meaningful" or "relevant" at the time. How often do you hear people say: "They were just words until it happened to me"? In terms of what we have been saying, the arguments do not have an impact, they are "just words" because the person is not having the relevant bodily experience. For our friend, arguments for and against abortion had been just words until she played the role of someone struggling with the issue. She found that through playing this role, the issue became much more concrete and real to her, and she had to work through her own feelings about it. When, sometime later, she accidentally became pregnant and had to face the issue for herself, she found that her prior experience in the play had helped her clarify her choices. She was able to decide fairly confidently on the right thing to do for her.

Practice and Habit   Practice to develop new habits also plays a role in creating experiential change. There are at least two reasons for this. The first is evidential, that is, people are not going to give up a belief system simply because of one or two disconfirmations of it. Even though Beck could demonstrate that a client's failure at wallpapering wasn't really a failure (see Chapter 12), the client will need repeated demonstrations before he is willing to give up his general belief that he is incompetent. People want good, stable evidence (i.e., repeated experience) before they are willing to change their beliefs.

Secondly, it is through practice and experience that people often come to understand what abstract formulations really mean. Suppose you are learning to drive and your instructor gives you directions: "Let out the clutch slowly as you step on the accelerator." While this may seem fairly specific, it is actually an imprecise, abstract description of what you are to do. How slowly? How much do you step on the accelerator? When do you coordinate the two events? You jarringly find out that the instruction is only a rough guide to what you are to do as you lurch forward wildly or stall the car. The words of the instruction are abstract because they do not precisely tell you (nor could they) the specific bodily movements and events involved. You have to use the words as a rough guide and then practice. Eventually, you learn at the bodily level the specific reactions and movements involved and no longer need to guide yourself with the imprecise words. When you finally get it right, you may even find that the vague and abstract words now make concrete bodily sense. "Oh, I see! Let the clutch out as I step on the accelerator!" (See Goldfried, 1979, for a similar suggestion.)

Practice with any cognitive abstraction may eventually cause bodily change. The abstract generalizations guide the learning of specific bodily skills. Suppose I challenge myself every time I catastrophize: "It's not awful that I didn't get an A on the test, although I would have preferred an A." I may eventually change the bodily schemas associated with the catastrophizing in a manner similar to my learning to work a clutch. Eventually I may no longer need to verbalize to myself. Suddenly I may find that the words make more sense to me: "Oh, I see! I would have preferred to get an A, but it isn't awful that I didn't!"

We have given examples of habit as a method of creating access for certain cognitive insights. Of course, habit is also a key component of behavioral approaches, in which repeated practice facilitates direct experiential learning.

Neutralizing the Effects of Negative Self-Monitoring   One of the most important abilities that human beings have is to monitor their own actions, thoughts, and feelings. They not only respond to stimuli, perform behaviors, think, and feel, but watch themselves do these things and use their observations to change if they are not responding adaptively. It has been argued that virtually all dysfunctional behavior involves dysfunctions in self-monitoring (Bohart, 1992). An integrative approach to psychotherapy by Ryle (1982) is based on a similar idea. All of us have mistaken ideas about reality from time to time and occasionally behave in ways that are not adaptive. However, most of the time, we are able to correct this behavior, while in cases of dysfunctional behavior, the person fails to correct or modify mistaken ideas or maladaptive responses.

In psychotherapy, we suggest that there are various ways clients have of monitoring themselves and others that contribute to the access problem. Information can result in change only if it is fully and accurately heard. However, this does not always occur in therapy because people tend not to listen to the information being given, but instead evaluate it in ways that seem to interfere with its therapeutic function. We call this *negative self-monitoring*. For instance, clients may find ways of discounting or misusing the information they receive. They may hear feedback as criticism and use it to further devalue themselves. Clients may discount positive feedback because they believe the therapist is being paid to "say nice things," or they may resist input because they perceive it as a threat to their autonomy or to unconscious maintenance of repression. Or, as part of how they monitor themselves, they may use their perceptions of what is wrong to implement dysfunctional methods of fixing things. For example, they may try to fix a sexual arousal problem by trying to become aroused, which may instead make matters worse. Two methods that therapies use to solve the problem of negative self-monitoring are the adoption of the phenomenological attitude and the use of indirect communication.

Phenomenological Attitude Many therapies attempt to get the client to suspend critical evaluation. For instance, psychoanalysis encourages the client to free-associate. In normal social conversation, a person evaluates the thoughts that pop into his mind. Those that are seen as irrelevant or morally or socially inappropriate are censored by the person and not verbalized. With free association the client is to report whatever comes to mind.

Psychoanalysts believe there is an unconscious censor that critically evaluates both internal and external information. It screens out of consciousness forbidden wishes, impulses, and thoughts. It also leads the person to distort, deny, or otherwise misuse information from outside, such as communications by the therapist. Getting the client to consciously suspend the censor and simply listen to whatever comes to mind nonevaluatively gradually allows forbidden material to appear. As this happens more and more, the client's conscious "observing" ego becomes strengthened, and the client has less and less need to evaluate and screen out or distort information. In some sense, the goal of psychoanalysis is to enable the client to listen nonevaluatively to all his thoughts, feelings, and fantasies, no matter how primitive.

Client-centered therapists similarly encourage a nonevaluative attitude. They do this through their own nonjudgmental acceptance of the client and through attempts to intuit a human, understandable motive behind behavior, even if the behavior is dysfunctional or repugnant. Gendlin (1964) emphasizes that attempts at self-monitoring and self-regulation "from above" are untherapeutic and that the client needs instead to wait and listen to his experiential self. A person cannot therapeutically hear what is in her experiencing if she is critically evaluating what ought to be there.

Gestalt therapists have argued that "pure awareness" is therapeutic. They encourage attempts to simply observe and be aware of what is, without analyzing what it means or judging how it ought to be or whether it is good or bad, appropriate or inappropriate, adaptive or maladaptive.

We call this the use of the phenomenological method in therapy. The phenomenological method was originally a philosophical approach developed by Edmund Husserl (1964). The goal of the phenomenological method is to "get back to pure experience" by suspending preconceptions. Therapeutically, this means the client should try to simply observe something without attempting to figure out what it "means" at an underlying level, or without judging it or evaluating it as good, bad, adaptive, maladaptive, appropriate, or inappropriate. This also means that the client suspends the way he already views and interprets the world and his experience. Only by doing this can new learning occur.

The phenomenological method is used in its purest form in meditation. Washburn describes receptive meditation as "the practice of open, nonreactive attention. Experience is witnessed nonselectively and without interference or interpretation" (1978, p. 46). Variants also appear in both cognitive and behavior therapy. Behavioral approaches to habit control include having clients keep a diary of when and where they engage in the habitual behavior. Keeping such a record makes clients observe their own behavior and reactions and the situations that seem to elicit them. Reinforcement procedures can be utilized to modify the behavior. However, simply keeping the diary itself is often helpful, perhaps because of clients' increased awareness.

Beck's cognitive treatment for depression includes keeping records of when and where depression occurs and the dysfunctional cognitions present. This employs the phenomenological method because the client is learning to separate the situation itself from his analysis and evaluations of it. Beck has clients practice writing alternative interpretations of the situation. This further reinforces the client's learning to perceive a situation independently of his preconceptions. Ellis's A-B-C model, in which A is the situation, B the interpretation, and C the emotional or behavioral reaction, also encourages the client to observe nonevaluatively.

Finally, de Shazer (1985), a strategic therapist, also uses a variant of the phenomenological method. As we have shown, a client with a dieting problem may be encouraged to pay attention to what he does when he resists the urge to eat. The intervention is to simply pay attention to these things, not to try to make them happen.

Adopting the phenomenological attitude encourages the client's "gaining distance" from the problem. Mahoney (1985) lists "distanced manifestation" as one method of problem resolution. He says it "entails a joint effort to allow the problem to manifest itself fully while one simultaneously disidentifies from it" (p. 30). This can be seen to operate in various therapeutic approaches. For instance, psychoanalytic free association allows parts of the problem to become "fully manifest" and the client learns to "disidentify" with the unconscious impulses: "I am not identical to my primitive incestuous desires. There is more to me than that."

From a client-centered perspective, Gendlin (1982) has described what happens as clients learn to listen nonevaluatively and focus on felt meanings: "In learning to put problems down one learns a specific relation to problems: sensing them but not being in them. . . . That distance enables one to relate to the problem as a whole, *from a spot a little outside it"* (p. 27, italics Gendlin's). From a cognitive perspective, Beck, Rush, Shaw, and Emery (1979) say, "As situations and cognitions are recorded, the patient gains some distance from their effect. The therapist's goal is to increase the patient's objectivity about his cognitions" (p. 164).

Indirect Circumvention   These techniques are used primarily by therapists who have been influenced by Milton Erickson. They include indirect suggestion, communication through metaphorical stories, reframing, and paradoxical interventions (see Chapter 13). The intervention we have considered several times previously is an example of indirect suggestion. A client who wants to diet is not directly told "You can control your eating." Instead, the message is indirectly suggested: "Pay attention to what you do when you control your urge to eat."

Paradoxical interventions and reframing apparently encourage the persistence of symptoms and problem behaviors. A contentious client may be told to deliberately get in arguments. A couple who continually fight may be told that their fighting is a sign of how much they love one another. They may even be told that to stop fighting would be disastrous for their marriage. How do such paradoxical interventions work?

There are a variety of theories as to why they do work (Riebel, 1984). We suggest that one reason is that they circumvent or turn off critical self-monitoring. The activity of criticizing themselves for problem behavior such as arguing is disrupted if people are told to do it, or if they are told that it would be disastrous if they stopped. Similarly, the activity of trying to self-engineer, control, and demand that they act differently is also disrupted.

Therapeutic Value of Suspending Self-Monitoring   But why is it therapeutic to turn off these activities? Why is it therapeutic to cease self-criticism, conscious intellectual self-analysis, and self-engineering? Why is it therapeutic to observe and listen nonevaluatively, that is, to receptively self-monitor?

We have suggested that critical self-monitoring can get in the way of therapy. Gendlin (1984) has pointed out that we often try to solve our own problems by playing therapist with ourselves. "Our usual conscious self is the therapist, often a crudely directive one who gets in the way. . . . That therapist frequently attacks in a hostile way . . . claims to be smarter . . . takes up time with distant inferences and interpretations" (p. 83). Similarly, Rice and Saperia (1984) suggest that what often gets in the therapist's way is "the tendency of clients to react to their own reaction and focus on how irrational or undesirable it had been, expanding on their own childishness or irrationality or on the undesirable consequences" (p. 40).

One positive result of suspending critical, analytic, and evaluative monitoring is that new information can get through and facilitate change. For instance, if you continually evaluate your behavior and feelings in terms of shoulds and oughts, you may distort them. If you think you should not be behaving in a certain way, you may either deny the existence of this behavior or misrepresent it. You may "repress," "deny," or "split off" your feelings or other parts of yourself. I may also misrepresent or distort messages from outside. Information then fails to have an impact and facilitate change.

Similarly, if clients' existing ways of interpreting the world are inadequate, then any self-analysis they engage in will reflect these inadequacies and will merely perpetuate the problem. Depressive thinking is a good example. Even information that most people see as positive fails to change a depressive because it is evaluated in terms of the depressive's existing negative conceptions. Similarly, a depressive critically monitors his own behavior and sees it as inappropriate, bad, or maladaptive. He does not merely receive information, but interprets it to conform to his view of the world and himself. Because of this monitoring, any internal or external communication loses its therapeutic potential.

Social psychological research on attitude change (Collins, 1970) shows that information will best facilitate attitude change if monitoring activity can be neutralized. For instance, people are more likely to be influenced by a speaker who presents both sides of the argument, not just the side he is advocating. Their critical monitor then says, "He is trying to be fair," and they allow themselves to trust the information more. Similarly, people are more likely to be influenced by something they overhear than by the same thing said directly to them. The critical monitor says, "He doesn't know I'm listening, so he's not trying to impress or please me, so he must really mean it." The fact that overheard communications get through better than communications made directly to the person recalls the use of indirect suggestion and related therapeutic techniques.

Critical self-monitoring may interfere with information processing because it mobilizes resistance. Many people resist being influenced by others, even if resisting is to their disadvantage. Brehm (1966) has suggested that people sometimes resist attempts to influence them to protect and demonstrate their freedom and independence. For instance, if they comply with a suggestion made directly to them, they may feel as though they are compromising their autonomy.

People also resist internal behavioral and emotional prescriptions. If I critically tell myself I ought to diet, I may experience my freedom as being restricted and rebel. This may be particularly true if I perceive dieting as a demand internalized from my parents and society. It is for this reason that gestalt and client-centered approaches are so interested in getting clients to choose their shoulds and oughts as their own or discard them.

There are other reasons for resistance. The critical monitor may evaluate information as a threat to repression and therefore distort or deny it. Similarly, information that is evaluated as a threat to existing ways of viewing the world and the self may be interpreted and modified to be compatible with the existing schemes (Kuhn, 1970; Nisbett & Ross, 1980). The information's potential for causing change is therefore neutralized. Resistance may also be generated by internal conflict (Arkowitz, 1991)—one part of the self wants to change and another doesn't. In this case, information will once again not be utilized therapeutically.

Another way self-monitoring may interfere therapeutically is that there appear to be times when a person is more likely to change if she does not try. Perhaps the best example is modifying sexual behavior. If clients are busy trying to change behavior, they are less available to experiencing the pleasurable, self-corrective aspects of the activity. In this case, monitoring behavior and trying to self-engineer become part of the problem and interfere with natural self-regulatory processes. De Shazer (1985) and Watzlawick (1987) point out that a person's attempts at solution often perpetuate or magnify the problem. This is particularly true if these attempts grow out of the person's way of viewing the problem and the world, and these views are dysfunctional.

For instance, suppose a husband and wife both believe that "If you love me, you will make no demands on me. You will be sensitive to my needs." The husband comes home from work and does not want to talk. The wife, who has been at home with only a 3-year-old to talk to all day, wishes to talk. She interprets the husband's wish not to talk as a sign that he doesn't care about her. Her solution to this is to criticize and accuse him of not caring about her. Similarly, he feels that if she cared about him, she would not demand that he talk. His solution is to criticize her. Then they both see the arguing as a further sign of the other's lack of caring. So both become increasingly guarded and defensive, looking for further signs of lack of caring and responding with further criticism. In other words, they try to solve the problem by criticizing each other, but the attempt at solution itself becomes a part of the problem.

Disrupting the clients' attempts to try to solve the problem, then, may facilitate solution ("Don't just do something. Stand there!"). If arguments are reframed as "showing love," then people will not worry so much if an argument occurs. They will not interpret the argument as a sign of difficulty. They will then not get so defensive and be so vigilant for further signs of lack of caring or "insensitivity" or whatever. And the relationship will become less of a battleground.

Paradoxical interventions also suspend trying. Suppose the couple is assigned the task of noticing and responding to anything that appears to be a slight. They have been assigned to try to do what they have apparently already been doing. But actually, what they had previously been trying to do was fix up the marriage by noticing apparent slights and challenging them. Now they have been assigned to try to be critical and defensive, rather than to try to save the marriage. Thus, the paradoxical intervention suspends their attempts to save the marriage. This may interfere with their interpreting apparent slights as threats to the marriage. If they are busily on the lookout for slights because they are supposed to notice them and defend themselves, they are less likely to be thinking that a slight means "My spouse doesn't love me." As they no longer worry so much about whether they love each other, the tension may ease. Put another way, the paradoxical intervention may disconnect the occurrence of an argument from the interpretation that "This means that you don't love me." The cessation of trying leads to an increase in acceptance, and, as we have seen, many therapies advocate acceptance, especially self-acceptance, as a therapeutic goal.

Mahoney (1985) has said,

> Contemporary western ideologies continue to reflect an impatient preoccupation with increasing the boundaries of personal causation. . . . We long to control our feelings, our actions, and our lives. . . . The net message . . . is to try harder. Little wonder, then, that we appear to lead the world in dysphoria and stress-related diseases." (p. 31)

Oddly enough, ceasing to try seems to contradict the injunction of many therapies to "take responsibility for oneself." However, it is really gaining control by giving up attempts to control things that are uncontrollable.

Finally, we believe that methods of dealing with negative self-monitoring partially work by shifting the client's attentional focus; that is, by either defocusing or refocusing the client's attention. Clients partly create their problems by dysfunctionally focusing attention on aspects of their own behavior and the environment, which feed back and maintain their problematic reactions. For instance, according to Beck's cognitive theory, depressives overfocus on aspects of their experience that are negative. At the same time, they neglect positive aspects. All that a person might see in a particular situation is its potential for failure, rather than noticing the potential available for success. Psychoanalytically, someone who has failed to develop a stable sense of separation and individuation as a child will overfocus on aspects of relationships that involve autonomy or dependency. Such a person might focus only on a prospective romantic partner's apparent ability to provide a merging experience, and therefore may neglect to focus on other things relevant to a good relationship. Encouraging clients to adopt the phenomenological attitude encourages them to defocus or decenter (Safran & Segal, 1990) their attention. Instead of paying attention to only selected aspects of their experience, they are encouraged to "stand back." This may lead to their noticing previously neglected aspects, and may by itself cause a shift in the way they view things.

Indirect methods appear to work in part by shifting attentional focus. For instance, reframings shift the focus of the client's attention away from the failure aspects of an experience to more positive ones. If the client is not overfocusing on failure aspects, he or she may now be free to notice aspects of the situation that can lead to new, positive behavior or to solutions. Paradoxes may also do this. Suppose a husband and wife who argue are ordered to argue at 5:00 o'clock p.m. every day. Knowing they are going to argue at that time, they may find their attention free to flow to other aspects of their relationship at other times, rather than continually looking out for potential conflicts between them. They may begin to focus on positive aspects and find ways of compromising so that by 5:00 p.m. they have nothing to argue about.

Theoretical Reasons for the Access Problem

Now that we have considered the various ways therapies attempt to deal with the access problem, we will briefly look at some theoretical explanations for its existence. In one way or another, they all involve a lack of conscious awareness.

Our whole consideration of the problem of access was based on the observation that people frequently cannot change problem behavior or feeling through abstract, cognitive self-commands or self-analysis. Nor are such commands and information from others necessarily useful by themselves. In considering different therapeutic solutions to this problem we have encountered a variety of therapeutic techniques in which cognitive formulation of insight is irrelevant. Behavioral approaches may work whether or not the client formulates a cognitive, verbal insight about what is going on. Metaphorical stories may convey meaning and initiate change even though the individual cannot consciously state how she has been changed. Similarly, paradoxical techniques may instigate change without the client's being consciously aware of how the change has occurred. Watzlawick (1987) has said that change occurs all the time in everyday life without insight.

Thus, it is not clear that in order to change, the client needs to be able to formulate the problem or its presumed cause or what needs to be done. Yet the issue of awareness or its lack is involved in each theoretical perspective on the access problem. These theories either assume that conscious, rational self-direction doesn't work because of a lack of awareness of the relevant factors involved or that the human is built in such a way that cognition is simply impotent to modify behavior.

For psychoanalysis, conscious, rational self-control is normally impotent because the real causes of behavior have been repressed and are unconscious. In therapy, conscious insights work only if they are timed to coincide with the availability to awareness of the relevant previously repressed concrete memories and affects. For client-centered therapy, conscious, rational self-control often does not work because it consists of shoulds and oughts learned from society and directed at the person. The result is that the individual's experiential organismic wisdom is ignored or denied. In therapy, verbally formulated self-knowledge can be therapeutic if it arises from listening to the experiential, organismically wise bodily level, rather than simply being cognitively derived. For gestalt, conscious, rational self-control frequently fails because it has been split off from ongoing organismic awareness. Words and symbolizations can create behavior change if they arise from the ongoing stream of organismic awareness. Cognitive behavioral approaches assume that behavior is often controlled by automatic thoughts of which the client is unaware, or by cognitions that are conscious but that are not recognized as dysfunctional or irrational.

Each of the above approaches assumes that lack of awareness—of repressed material, experiential bodily wisdom, automatic thoughts, or dysfunctional cognitions—plays a role in dysfunctional behavior and is why people cannot consciously control such behavior. In various ways they suggest that cognitive awareness, under the proper circumstances, can effect change. Many other approaches also see a lack of awareness as important in causing dysfunctional behavior, but are skeptical that cognitive awareness under any conditions is therapeutic. Behavior therapy is one example. Most problem responses are seen as being learned at a subcortical level and are therefore simply not modifiable by conscious, cognitive activity. Many family systems theorists believe that problems arise from the dynamics of the family system, and family members are not aware of these dynamics. Even family therapists may not have direct knowledge of these dynamics, but may have to infer them. Furthermore, many such therapists do not believe that increasing awareness of these dynamics is particularly therapeutic. They believe that therapeutic interventions must work to change the system directly. Increased awareness is irrelevant.

What is common to practically all the theoretical perspectives is the suggestion that psychopathological behavior is at least partially created by a lack of awareness. Put another way, behavior is at least partially controlled by factors that lie outside of conscious awareness. To what extent is it plausible that behavior can be controlled by factors outside of awareness?

Nonconscious Information Processing   The idea that extensive information processing happens nonconsciously is now commonly accepted. Nisbett and Ross (1980) have argued that while people have conscious awareness of their thoughts, they are not aware of the processes that generate them. Similarly, while people may be aware of their emotions, they are often not aware of their causes (Maslach, 1979). Shevrin and Dickman (1980), after reviewing a variety of models of consciousness, suggest that all information processing occurs first at the nonconscious level and only later and secondarily do some aspects show up as conscious ideation. Fischer and Pipp (1984) have even argued that consciousness is a construction in the sense that knowledge is at first unconscious and people "become conscious" in certain areas only when knowledge in that area becomes sufficiently developed and complex.

Information can be detected and processed nonconsciously (Shevrin & Dickman, 1980; Lewicki, 1986). We can, for instance, meet a new person, interact with them, and develop a "like" or "dislike" reaction to them, without being aware of how we do it (Zajonc, 1980). Therefore, theories that suggest that people are unconsciously influenced by family dynamics and therapy techniques that rely on indirect communication seem plausible. It is unclear how "wise" nonconscious information processing can be. Some (Greenwald, 1992) hold that it is not very wise. Others believe that it can be wise. Gendlin (1984) has argued that one reason people sometimes have problems putting feelings into words is that nonconscious, preconceptual experience is more finely ordered and more complex than the rather crude words can handle. Mahoney (1985), based on the work of Hayek (1978), has argued that nonconscious processes may actually be too complex for consciousness and that is why they are unavailable to consciousness.

With respect to this, Polyani (1966) has argued that people "know more than we can say." Recent evidence (Bowers, 1984; Reber, 1976) suggests that people can "know" things intuitively, though others (e.g., Greenwald, 1992) debate this. Sometimes people even do better trying to solve a problem intuitively than in a strictly cognitive, analytic way. Similarly, Shweder, Turiel, and Much (1981) have done research demonstrating that children have greater intuitive moral understanding than they can verbalize.

We will give two examples of "knowing more than we can say." First, it is often reported that Einstein said that he was "guided by a feeling" in his pursuit of resolving the problems that ultimately led to the development of relativity theory. Apparently, his ideas originated in visual imagery, and only from that was he able to derive the words and mathematical expressions needed to develop the theory (Gardner, 1983). Second, it has been pointed out that no one understands how outfielders in baseball catch fly balls (Shirley, 1984). How does an outfielder "know" to turn his back and run to where the fly ball is coming? He only has an instant after the ball is hit to make his appraisal and then act. Not even physicists seem to be able to understand how this is done.

In reference to feelings and affect, Zajonc (1980) has argued that feelings are generated by processes that lie outside of conscious awareness. He proposes that there are two parallel, partially independent mental systems: the affective and the cognitive. Zajonc locates the affective system in the right hemisphere of the brain, which is spatial, holistic, and nonverbal in its functioning. He points out that affective judgments are basic. People have like and dislike reactions quickly and immediately in many situations before they are able to figure out reasons for the reactions. Affective reactions are not subject to conscious, cognitive control, and they may persist long after the evidential base for them is discredited. Zajonc concludes by characterizing the affective system as relatively quick in its responsiveness but stereotyped, while the cognitive system is slow but flexible.

Zajonc's views have been challenged, and more recent perspectives on emotion postulate a more complex, interconnected relationship between it and cognition (e.g., Greenberg & Safran, 1987). However, Zajonc's point that affective reactions are not usually under immediate conscious control is another example of how factors outside of awareness can influence a person's reactions.

Other models (e.g., Bucci, 1995; Martin, Paivio, & Labadie, 1990) of why verbal knowing does not necessarily create change at the bodily, nonverbal level have proposed that there are two fundamentally different *knowing systems,* a verbal one and a nonverbal one (Paivio, 1986). These models have argued that therapy must work to build "bridges" connecting verbal knowing to knowing that has been achieved through primarily nonverbal, imagistic means. Only when such bridges are built will full therapeutic change take place.

These suggestions are in accord with a "modular" view of the access problem, which we describe below. Much is unknown about nonconscious processes and feelings. However, recent research and theorizing by experimental psychologists appear to be compatible with many of the observations of clinical psychologists that factors outside of awareness do influence behavior.

A "Modular" Explanation of the Access Problem   Recent decades of brain research provide us with a possible neurological model for the problem of access. Many students are familiar with mass media presentations about right-brain and left-brain functioning as a result of split-brain research. As a last-ditch effort to treat severe epilepsy, some individuals have had the commissure, which connects the right and left hemispheres of the brain, surgically cut so that the two hemispheres function entirely separately. Research on these split-brain patients indicates that there are at least two different "minds" within each individual, each "mind" with its own way of thinking, knowing, experiencing, feeling, and with its own goals and motives.

Split-brain research suggests that the following characteristics and functions are preferentially organized in the left hemisphere of most people's brains: logical, sequential reasoning; analytic and abstract reasoning; linguistic processing; analysis; a long reaction time; and perhaps the "negative self-monitor" we discussed earlier. The following appear to be preferentially organized in the right hemisphere: emotional and evaluative reactions; holistic, inferential, intuitive reasoning; literal, concrete, nonverbal functioning; a short reaction time; spatial relations ability; and recording literal properties of the physical world. It is important to remember that the functioning of normal, non–split brains may not be accurately demonstrated in split brains, but the view that there is a neurological basis for different "minds" may provide an explanation for the problem of access.

While normal brains function as a unit, it can be said that in our culture, the left brain is more highly valued or "dominant," because most of our conscious thoughts and social transactions are conducted through language. It is therefore easy to access the part of the personality that is verbal, but it is not easy to access the nonverbal, possibly right-brain parts of personality. Verbal insight occurs in the easily accessed left hemisphere, but it does not effect change.

Famous split-brain researcher Michael Gazzaniga (1985) argues that the brain is composed of several (not just two) "modules" functioning as a "loose federation." Each module, whether in the left or right hemisphere, has its own way of acting and reacting. All modules except one (the language one) are nonverbal, expressing themselves through overt or covert actions. These modular activities frequently operate apart from our conscious verbal selves.

However, we do not experience ourselves as a loose federation of independently acting modules. Rather, we usually experience ourselves as one self acting in a unitary fashion. Because the split-brain findings fly in the face of our usual experience of ourselves, Gazzaniga argues that the left brain has a special component that he calls the "interpreter." This interpreter accommodates and instantly constructs a theory to explain why any behavior occurs. This creates the experience of unitary consciousness, even though brain processes are modular. Just as we attribute motives to others (as in attribution theory), we do the same for our "other selves," our behavior from different (unconscious or nonverbal) brain modules.

Many therapists observed the phenomena Gazzaniga describes, decades before split-brain research. They have given that other, nonverbal part of the mind different names, such as unconscious, subconscious, or organismic valuing process. But they have all recognized that the problem for therapists and clients trying to change neurotic behavior is accessing this different part of the mind. Some therapists have claimed that this other part of the mind contains nonverbal "wisdom" that might help people change.

Milton Erickson (see Chapters 11 and 14) was the most explicit about the existence of at least two different "minds," each with its own way of experiencing and processing. He stated clearly that the subconscious contains "wisdom" and that hypnosis allows the therapist to speak directly to the subconscious. Hypnotic techniques are designed to bypass the logical conscious and access the wise subconscious so that the client can then change in a healthy direction. He also argued that paradoxical techniques are effective because they confuse the logical mind so that it gives up and allows the subconscious to work. The way Erickson wrote about the conscious mind makes it sound very similar to left-brain functioning, and the way he described the subconscious sounds similar to right-brain functioning.

Freud also recognized different "minds" in the same person. There are the conscious and the unconscious and also the id, ego, and superego, each with its own motives and perceptions. Unlike Erickson, Freud saw the unconscious as problematic and the source of difficulties, not as wise. However, like Erickson, he recognized the importance of accessing the unconscious. Techniques such as free association were supposed to get around the conscious and gradually allow unconscious elements into awareness. Gazzaniga would prefer to "correct" Freud by calling the unconscious "coconscious but nonverbal mental modules." Repression may be viewed as right-brain or nonverbal modular experience that cannot get into or be interpreted by the left-brain or verbal module(s).

Carl Rogers's view also fits in with this neurological model of the problem of access. His "organismic valuing process" can be equated with right-brain or nonverbal brain modules. He saw psychopathology as being out of touch with or incongruent with this process. Psychotherapeutic techniques such as reflection and accurate empathy were supposed to help access this part of experience. Like Erickson, Rogers believed that there was "organismic wisdom" and that accessing this part of personality functioning, helping the client get in touch with it, would bring about therapeutic change.

There are many interesting parallels between different theories of psychotherapy and the findings of split-brain research. The concept of brain modules, some verbal (conscious) and some nonverbal (not conscious), provides a useful model for explaining the problem of access in psychotherapy and the failure of verbal knowledge alone to change neurotic behavior. A variety of therapeutic techniques from paradox to empathy can be viewed as ways of avoiding the verbal (left) brain module(s) and accessing the nonverbal (right) brain module(s). This line of reasoning represents an attempt to describe a possible neurological basis for one converging aspect of differing approaches to psychotherapy.

Even family therapists have tried to utilize neuropsychological models. Boscolo, Cecchin, Hoffman, and Penn (1987) wrote,

> When we look for an intervention, we try to find a logic that will appeal to the family. The content of the intervention can be crazy, but formally it must have a logic. And we can speculate that the logic of the intervention will be directed to the left brain of the family (if you want to think like that) and the crazy part of the intervention will go to the right brain. (p. 34)

Furthermore, Gazzaniga's concept of an "interpreter module" to create a sense of unitary consciousness out of the loose federation of different brain modules may also be useful in explaining psychopathology and integrating psychotherapy theories. For example, there may be individual differences in the competence of the interpreter module. An interpreter that fails to unify consciousness may be exhibited in multiple personality disorder. An overactive interpreter may create rigidity in the face of conflicted emotions. A critical interpreter could be the negative self-monitor. It is possible that therapists must avoid the interpreter in order to access other parts of the personality or to improve the interpreter module's ability to function.

The Importance of Self-Acceptance

The problem of access is a common theme in recent approaches to psychotherapy. Another common element is their concern with self-acceptance. In previous chapters and in the discussion of negative self-monitoring, we pointed out some negative effects of low self-evaluation. Individuals with feelings of low self-efficacy may pay so much attention to evaluating themselves that they pay less attention to the demands of the task and, as a result, perform less well than they could have. Similarly, focusing on the self may magnify negative feelings and lead to attributing negative character traits to the self.

Theorists such as Ellis, Rogers, and Beck have pointed out the dysfunctional aspects of making negative self-attributions. They suggest that while it may be functional to make process evaluations of how one is performing on a task ("Is this behavior that I am engaging in working or not?"), it is not functional to generalize from specific behavioral failures to one's whole self. It is one thing to say, "I am not under-standing this material" and another to conclude, "therefore I am stupid and no good."

Self-acceptance, however, does not necessarily mean having a positive view of oneself. We have already seen that Ellis, Rogers, Beck, and others believe that at-tributing global positive traits to oneself may be as dysfunctional as attributing global negative traits. Ellis and Beck suggest that nonevaluative acceptance is healthier than either positive or negative self-evaluation. Ellis has perhaps been most forceful of all in arguing that one would simply be better off never making generalizations about one's whole self from one's behavior. It is better to focus on evaluating one's behav-iors and actions.

A common goal of psychoanalytic, humanistic, and cognitive approaches is to fa-cilitate client self-acceptance. Each attempts to get the client to believe that "I am not an overall bad person because I have primitive incestuous wishes and fantasies" (psy-choanalysis); "I have certain thoughts, feelings, or perspectives that do not agree with the 'shoulds' I have been taught" (humanistic); or "I have not behaved perfectly or my life does not match my perfectionistic, rigid either/or schemas" (cognitive approaches).

Recently, acceptance in a broader sense has become a major variable in radical behavioral approaches (Hayes, Follette, & Follette, 1995; Linehan, 1997). For in-stance, in couples therapy, it has been recognized that it is as important to promote partners' acceptance of one another as it is to try to change each partner's behavior so that it please the other partner (Christensen, Jacobson, & Babcock, 1995). Linehan (1997) notes the essential paradox between the necessity of accepting clients as they are (and thereby promoting self-acceptance), while encouraging them to change. She argues that it is precisely the therapist's ability in negotiating a continual balance be-tween these two contradictory demands that is involved in the promotion of change.

Rigid Schemas as a Major Cause of Psychopathology

The idea that it is people's interpretations of events that cause problems, rather than the events themselves, is a common theme in psychoanalytic, humanistic, and cogni-tive therapies. Virginia Satir, a humanistically oriented family therapist, said, "I think if I have one message . . . it would be that the event does not determine how to re-spond to the event" (quoted in Krier, 1986).

More particularly, these diverse theoretical approaches see psychopathology as the result of rigid, repetitive constructions or world views that are imposed on real-ity. Psychoanalysis holds that the diversity of the real world is reduced by the client to a repetitive reliving of perceptions and interpretations developed in early child-hood. Humanistic therapies address how the client boxes reality into rigid shoulds and oughts learned in childhood. Feelings that do not fit the boxes may be disowned or ignored. Gestalt suggests that the client splits experience into rigid categories, such as "good and evil," "mind and body," and then treats these rigid categories as more real than the reality they were meant to describe.

Beck's cognitive therapy is based on the assumption that both depression and anxiety are in part the result of dysfunctional cognitive interpretations of reality. These interpretations are based on schemas learned in early childhood and are held rigidly by the client.

Finally, many family systems therapists (Watzlawick, 1987; de Shazer, 1985) hold that problems are caused by the individual's perception and construction of events. They argue that therefore what is needed in therapy is a second-order change, in which the individual's way of construing the world is fundamentally reorganized.

Solving a problem from within an established way of construing the world is a first-order change. Second-order changes involve reorganizing clients' basic premises for dealing with the world and would seem to be the goal of most therapies. For instance, psychoanalysis is not interested in helping clients cope from within their rigid childhood-based way of construing the world. Instead, it hopes to cause a fundamental reorganization in this system, so that new, more flexible and accurate solutions to their problems appear.

Rigid schemas have a primitive either/or quality. De Shazer (1985) has said that construing problems in either/or terms is itself part of the problem. For psychoanalysis, the primitive construct systems developed in early childhood include a number of simplistic, either/or ways of construing reality: "Mommy loves either me or daddy, but not both", "Mommy is either all good or all bad." Some constructions are so primitive that, according to object relations theory, the child does not separate himself from the mother.

Therapy as the Development of a Hypothesis-Testing Attitude

If psychopathology is based on the rigid application of a primitive interpretation of reality, then therapy must involve an attempt to change this interpretation. But most therapists are not interested in merely changing the client's existing way of interpreting reality. They are also interested in developing a hypothesis-testing attitude toward reality. In other words, they do not want the client to recognize her interpretation as limited and simply replace it with another interpretation that is applied the same way. They want the client to realize that any interpretation of the world is a construction, or hypothesis, and that it should be subjected to continual and lifelong evaluation. Carl Rogers said a goal of therapy is to get the client to "hold his constructs tentatively." Beck teaches his clients the method of empirically testing and evaluating cognitions. Similarly, Ellis wants his clients to dispute their irrational cognitions. Finally, Schafer (1978) has argued that a key event in psychoanalytic therapy is not merely learning that one has been interpreting the world through primitive childhood constructions, but that such interpretations *are* constructions and are therefore modifiable.

Therapy as the Reorganization of Personal Meaning

Therapy, therefore, is the reorganization of the client's personal meaning system (Mahoney, 1985). In particular, therapy can be seen as including the differentiation and integration of meaning (Rice & Saperia, 1984; Wexler, 1974). A good example would be object relations theory. Object relations theory holds that borderline personalities construe people in rigid ways as either "all good" or "all bad." Part of therapy is learning to develop a more differentiated view of people, that there are gradations of good and evil and that a person may be a combination of both. This leads to the person developing a more integrated view, that people are complex creatures containing both good and bad qualities. Then, if someone does something "bad," the person does not see him as "all bad." Client-centered, gestalt, and cognitive therapies similarly attempt to create more differentiated and integrated ways of construing the world.

Mahoney (1985) has argued that therapy often works not by eliminating a problem behavior, but by consolidating it into the personality in a more functional way. Something that is currently maladaptive is integrated into the personality in such a way that it loses its destructive qualities and may even come to possess functional qualities. For instance, rebelliousness that may be causing a person difficulty at a job may be "tamed" or integrated into the personality in such a way that it comes to have adaptive uses. When the person learns when, where, and how to express her rebelliousness, it may become useful in fighting injustice or in challenging rigid, conformist ways of doing things.

Similarly, a client who is "oversensitive" to signs of rejection may not eliminate that oversensitivity, that is, he may still notice the subtle cues that he previously interpreted as rejection. But he may learn that his interpretations are not necessarily correct and become able to engage in reality testing. His oversensitivity may become adaptive in that he notices subtle cues others don't, and this quality may make him more effective with other people.

Reframing may work in part by facilitating consolidation and integration (see Chapter 14). The ultimate in reframing is R. D. Laing's view of schizophrenia as a growth process instead of a disease. Regardless of whether or not schizophrenia is a disease, reframing it as a growth experience may be therapeutic. First of all, it will encourage the schizophrenic to no longer view part of herself as bad or socially undesirable. Therefore, it should raise her self-esteem. This should lead to a reduction in anxiety and an increase in effective functioning. In addition, it should encourage the schizophrenic to "use" her schizophrenic experiences in adaptive, prosocial ways. For instance, she may learn to "tame" them and use them artistically. Reframing the experience of being paralyzed in an automobile accident in such a way as to find some meaning may help patients cope. This has been called the use of "interpretive secondary control" (Fiske & Taylor, 1984), in which a person "controls" an event by extracting meaning from it. The person may then reorganize the priorities in his life.

Insights into the past also are ultimately therapeutic only if they can be consolidated and reframed. To know that you are the way you are because your father mistreated you may be of little help if all that does is leave you feeling angry. However, if you can reframe the experience and learn to forgive him or see him as an imperfect human being who made mistakes, then the experience can be consolidated into your personality. As you forgive him, you forgive yourself and others, so you take a more flexible, differentiated view of others. You may even be able to use your own experience of being mistreated to empathize with others or to gain a sense that you can triumph over tragedy.

Self-Empowerment

Another common theme among the various therapy approaches is that they all try to give the client a sense of control or "empowerment," a sense of "I can . . ." or "I am able. . . ." We have chosen the term empowerment as an umbrella term for several related concepts: overcoming a sense of helplessness, gaining a sense of self-efficacy, taking responsibility for oneself, becoming able to choose, and becoming autonomous. While empowerment is a goal of several approaches, they differ somewhat in how it is to be achieved.

In psychoanalytic theory, a sense of empowerment develops as a result of reclaiming disowned parts of the self. As people are able to acknowledge what has been repressed, they become able to control, coordinate, and integrate their own functioning. Bettelheim's (1982) retranslation of Freud states it well: "Where 'it' was shall 'I' be." In other words, something that felt separate from the person and not controllable ("it") becomes part of the self ("I") and under control. A similar goal is found in client-centered therapy, gestalt, and other humanistic approaches in their emphasis on owning, choosing, or becoming response-able.

In social learning theory and social skills training, the goal is expressed as increasing feelings of self-efficacy. Self-efficacy is the perception that one is able to enact certain behaviors, and it usually increases as one learns effective skills.

One of Ellis's goals of therapy is for the client to take responsibility for choices. This occurs as the client learns to challenge his or her rigid, absolute, musturbatory tendencies.

Research has shown that those who have an "internal locus of control," that is, who feel able to control what happens to them, generally exhibit greater adaptive behavior than those who have an "external locus of control," who feel their fate is not in their hands, though there are complications and exceptions (Phares, 1976). Seligman (1990) believes that feeling helpless is associated with various maladaptive psychological and physical responses. Langer and Rodin (1976) found that having a sense of responsibility for themselves was physically beneficial to people in an old-age home.

In a similar vein, Frank (1982) argues that one of the main things therapy does is help clients to overcome feelings of demoralization. And Bandura (1977) thinks that the ultimate outcome of all therapies is to increase feelings of self-efficacy. Both overcoming demoralization and increasing feelings of self-efficacy lead to a sense of hope. And research on the placebo effect suggests that believing one has a chance of improving increases the likelihood of improving (Shapiro & Morris, 1978).

We have also noted that trying to control oneself is, at times, counterproductive. There are times when receptive acceptance seems to be more therapeutic than attempts at control. However, this may be because active attempts at control do not work, whereas receptive acceptance is the best way to control the situation. Rothbaum, Weisz, and Snyder (1982), have suggested that giving up attempts at control is sometimes more adaptive than continuing attempts to control. They call this "secondary control," which we mentioned in our discussion of therapy as differentiation and integration of meaning.

Mahoney (1985) comments on our culture's overemphasis on personal control:

> Embedded in our desperate quest for control is a metatheory of personal and public freedom. And much of that freedom is libertarian in flavor—it seeks freedom from its contexts rather than freedom within them . . . the net message . . . is to try harder. . . .
> The eastern alternative to effort is "surrender," a kind of passive intentionality that

attempts to integrate and utilize the contrasting powers of internal and external influence. . . . The practical implications of the effort/surrender issue merit our close attention. To me, its relevance seems most apparent in disorders that involve sympathetic/parasympathetic conflicts—anxiety, insomnia, and several sexual dysfunctions. Here it is clear that there are times when effort seems to get in the way of progress. Here I am comfortable encouraging patience, gentleness, and some kind of self-trust. (pp. 31–32)

Beck, Emery, and Greenberg (1985) prescribe acceptance of anxiety as part of their treatment program for anxiety disorders. The old maxim that wisdom is controlling what can be controlled, accepting what cannot be controlled, and knowing the difference seems relevant.

The Interpersonal Nature of the Human Being

An important, emerging common factor across different approaches is an increasing emphasis on the interpersonal nature of the human being. Psychological problems are increasingly coming to be viewed as primarily interpersonal in nature by all theorists from the systems, humanistic, cognitive-behavioral, and psychodynamic camps. Systems theory, of course, always held this. Some humanistic theorists, such as client-centered theorists, also held that psychological problems developed primarily in an interpersonal matrix and could be cured in an interpersonal matrix (e.g., through the provision of warmth, empathy, and genuineness). Some early psychodynamic theorists such as Harry Stack Sullivan emphasized the interpersonal nature of psychopathology and psychotherapy. However, it is only recently that all approaches have come to place the interpersonal in the forefront. Now in the psychodynamic area, object relations theory, attachment theory, and self psychology hold that psychological problems are primarily a matter of disturbed relationships with other people, and therapy is primarily a matter of repairing such relationships. Cognitive therapists such as Aaron Beck see personality disorders as dysfunctional interpersonal strategies that have been learned in an interpersonal matrix. And in the humanistic camp, gestalt theory has moved away from Fritz Perls's highly individualistic emphasis to a more interpersonal focus.

Carrying this further, there are signs of a "paradigm revolution" occurring in how we view the nature of the human being. In Chapter 17, we note that the Western view of the self as separate, autonomous, bounded, and directed from within is both masculine and culture-specific and does not fit the experience of many other groups of people in the world. For many other cultures, as well as for women, the self is a "self-in-relation." That is, self exists and has meaning in terms of its relationships, rather than by virtue of its separateness and autonomy.

The emphasis on a view of the self as a self-in-relation has been most forcefully promulgated by feminist (Jordan, Kaplan, Miller, Stiver, & Surray, 1991) and multicultural theorists. However, it fit with new developments in client-centered therapy (Bohart, 1995), gestalt therapy (Wheeler, 1991), and self psychology (Stolorow, 1992). Stolorow, for instance, holds that the person does not exist apart from an interpersonal matrix. That is, the person is always constituted in terms of whom the person is relating to. One cannot understand an individual's experience in a given moment without reference to the "intersubjective field" of which the person is a member. This is a fundamentally radical shift in how we view human beings, suggesting that our subjective experience, far from being something entirely within us, is fundamentally, in some sense, between ourselves and another person or persons.

Gestalt theory always held to a view of human beings that would be compatible with this shift toward viewing people as fundamentally interconnected (Wheeler, 1991). Client-centered theory, similar to gestalt, always implicitly held to a more intersubjective view, yet emphasized autonomy and individualism. Recently, from a client-centered perspective, Holdstock (1990) and O'Hara (1992) have begun to emphasize a more interconnected, intersubjective view.

From a cognitive perspective, Martin Seligman (1990) has argued that our culture's overemphasis on individuality has left the individual all alone, a fragile, separate, tiny speck in the universe. He argues that to ultimately overcome our culture's current high rate of depression, people must begin to reidentify with causes larger than themselves.

In sum, there may be a paradigm revolution occurring in how we view the nature of the human being—a shift from seeing the human as fundamentally separate to seeing the human as fundamentally interconnected. On the other hand, there are those who disagree with this trend. Anspach (1991) argues that there are many cultures in the world that are aspiring toward the individualistic model of the self in Western societies. Therefore, it is too early to know the outcome of this possible paradigm revolution: It is unclear whether this new, emerging view of the human being will ultimately replace the old, individualistic view.

IN CONCLUSION

When we were completing the 1994 version of this text, we were convinced that psychotherapy integration would be the wave of the future. We expected that most practitioners would be eclectic, borrowing from different approaches and using whatever worked. We envisioned the particular clinical psychologist choosing what would work best with a particular client from a host of possible procedures and philosophical ideas. Based on this, we even contemplated doing away with or significantly shortening our discussion of the major traditional theoretical approaches in this edition. However, these expectations were premature. The influence of managed health care on the field of psychotherapy is changing its face (see our discussion in Chapter 18). There have been renewed demands for research showing that specific treatments work for specific disorders. This has led to a shift away from the study of common elements in psychotherapy to a renewed focus on so-called "pure-form" psychotherapies (e.g., cognitive-behavioral, psychodynamic, humanistic) and how they can be specifically designed to be used to treat depression, panic, generalized anxiety disorder, eating disorders, and so on. Under managed care, it is as possible that the individual clinician may be required in the future to use a manualized (see Chapter 15) version of a pure-form psychotherapy for a client with a particular disorder as it is that the therapist would be allowed to eclectically choose what might work best for that client from a host of procedures and ideas. In accord with this, many therapists are devoting their attention to developing manualized versions of brief forms of psychodynamic, cognitive-behavioral, and experiential-humanistic therapies in order to subject them to empirical test. Correspondingly, energy is being diverted away from psychotherapy integration.

Nonetheless, the psychotherapy integration movement remains vigorous and alive. Researchers and theoreticians continue to work on studying eclectic therapeutic practice, common factors, and theoretical integration. In keeping with the push for therapy practice to be based on empirical evidence, evidence-based approaches are being developed that are integrative in nature (e.g., Beutler & Clarkin, 1990; Grawe, 1997). Additionally, we believe that what is going to happen (and what is already happening) is that efforts to empirically validate specific therapies for specific disorders will ultimately lead the field to the same place it has been in the past—back toward psychotherapy integration. We will find that for most of the problems people bring to therapy, resourceful clinicians will have been able to design brief, manualized versions of their favorite pure-form psychodynamic, humanistic, or cognitive-behavioral approaches such that each approach works equally as well as other approaches. This has already happened with respect to depression, for there is now evidence that cognitive-behavioral, psychodynamic/interpersonal, and client-centered approaches all work equally well. After several years of research, clinicians will be faced with the situation of having an empirically validated psychodynamic therapy for generalized anxiety or for posttraumatic stress disorder, an empirically validated cognitive-behavioral treatment, and an empirically validated experiential/humanistic treatment. Then, once again, efforts will shift toward the question of how to integrate these different approaches. In the meantime, clinicians interested in psychotherapy integration will have continued to develop integrative models, and to research them, and many therapists in private practice will have continued to develop their own integrative and eclectic ways of doing therapy.

BIBLIOGRAPHY

Alford, B. A., & Norcross, J. C. (1991). Cognitive therapy as integrative therapy. *Journal of Psychotherapy Integration, 1,* 175–190.

Allen, D. (1988). *Unifying individual and family therapies.* San Francisco: Jossey-Bass.

Andrews, J. D. W. (1990). *The active self in psychotherapy.* Boston: Allyn & Bacon.

Anspach, M. S. (1991). Is a change in the theory of the person necessary? A note on Sampson's discussion of individuality in the post-modern era. *Theoretical and Philosophical Psychology, 11,* 111–115.

Arkowitz, H. (1989). The role of theory in psychotherapy integration. *Journal of Integrative and Eclectic Psychotherapy, 8,* 8–16.

Arkowitz, H. (1991, August). *Psychotherapy integration: Bringing psychotherapy back to psychology.* Invited address at the Convention of the American Psychological Association, San Francisco, CA.

Arkowitz, H. (1992). Integrative theories of therapy. In D. K. Freedheim (Ed.), *History of psychotherapy: A century of change* (pp. 261–303). Washington, DC: American Psychological Association.

Arkowitz, H., & Hannah, M. T. (1989). Cognitive, behavioral, and psychodynamic therapies: Converging or diverging pathways to change? In A. Freeman, K. Simon, L. Beutler, &

H. Arkowitz (Eds.), *Comprehensive handbook of cognitive therapy* (pp. 143–168). New York: Plenum.

Bandura, A. (1977). Self-efficacy: Toward a unifying theory of behavioral change. *Psychological Review, 84,* 191–215.

Bandura, A. (1986). *Social foundations of thought and action: A social cognitive theory.* Englewood Cliffs, NJ: Prentice-Hall.

Beck, A. T. (1979). *Cognitive therapy of depression* (Live demonstration of interview procedures). New York: BMA Audio Cassettes, Guilford.

Beck, A. T. (1987). Cognitive therapy. In J. Zeig (Ed.), *The evolution of psychotherapy* (pp. 149–163). New York: Brunner/Mazel.

Beck, A. T., Emery, G., with Greenberg, R. L. (1985). *Anxiety disorders and phobias: A cognitive perspective.* New York: Basic Books.

Beck, A. T., Rush, A. J., Shaw, B. F., & Emery, G. (1979). *Cognitive therapy of depression.* New York: Guilford.

Beitman, B. (1987). *The structure of individual psychotherapy.* New York: Guilford.

Bettelheim, B. (1982). *Freud and man's soul.* New York: Vintage.

Beutler, L. E. (1989). The misplaced role of theory in psychotherapy integration. *Journal of Integrative and Eclectic Psychotherapy, 8,* 17–22.

Beutler, L. E., & Clarkin, J. F. (1990). *Systematic treatment selection.* New York: Brunner/Mazel.

Beutler, L. E., Crago, M., & Arizmendi, T. G. (1986). Research on therapist variables in psychotherapy. *Handbook of psychotherapy and behavior change* (3rd ed., pp. 257–310). New York: Wiley.

Bohart, A. (1980). Toward a cognitive theory of catharsis. *Psychotherapy: Theory, Research and Practice, 17,* 192–201.

Bohart, A. (1982). Similarities between cognitive and humanistic approaches to psychotherapy. *Cognitive Therapy and Research, 6,* 245–250.

Bohart, A. (1991). Empathy in client-centered therapy: A contrast with psychoanalysis and self psychology. *Journal of Humanistic Psychology, 31,* 34–48.

Bohart, A. (1992). Un modelo integrador de proceso para la psicopatologia y la psicoterapia. *Revista De Psicoterapia, 3,* 49–74.

Bohart, A. (1993). Experiencing: The basis of psychotherapy. *Journal of Psychotherapy Integration, 3,* 51–67.

Bohart, A. (1995). The person-centered therapies. In A. Gurman & S. Messer (Eds.), *Modern psychotherapies.* New York: Guilford.

Bohart, A., & Tallman, K. (1996). The active client: Therapy as self-help. *Journal of Humanistic Psychology, 36,* 7–30.

Bohart, A., & Tallman, K. (in press). *The client as active self-healer.* Washington DC: American Psychological Association.

Boscolo, L., Cecchin, G., Hoffman, L., & Penn, P. (1987). *Milan systemic family therapy.* New York: Basic Books.

Bowers, K. S. (1984). On being unconsciously influenced and informed. In K. S. Bowers & D. Meichenbaum (Eds.), *The unconscious reconsidered* (pp. 227–277). New York: Wiley.

Brehm, J. W. (1966). *Response to loss of freedom: A theory of psychological reactance.* New York: Academic Press.

Bucci, W. (1995). The power of the narrative: A multiple code account. In J. W. Pennebaker (Ed.), *Emotion, disclosure, & health* (pp. 93–124). Washington DC: American Psychological Association.

Castonguay, L., Raver, P., Wiser, S., & Goldfried, M. (1995, April). *Challenging client's view: Similarities and differences between cognitive-behavioral and psychodynamic-interpersonal therapies.* Paper presented at the Convention of the Society for the Exploration of Psychotherapy Integration, Washington, D.C.

Christensen, A., & Jacobson, N. (1994). Who (or what) can do psychotherapy: The status and challenge of nonprofessional therapies. *Psychological Science, 5,* 8–14.

Christensen, A., Jacobson, N. S., and Babcock, J. C. (1995). Integrative behavioral couple therapy. In N. S. Jacobson & A. S. Gurman (Eds.), *Clinical handbook of couple therapy* (pp. 31–64). New York: Guilford.

Collins, B. (1970). *Social psychology.* Reading, MA: Addison-Wesley.

de Shazer, S. (1985). *Keys to solution in brief therapy.* New York: Norton.

Dollard, J., & Miller, N. E. (1950). *Personality and psychotherapy.* New York: McGraw-Hill.

Drozd, J. F., & Goldfried, M. R. (1996). A critical evaluation of the state-of-the-art in psychotherapy outcome. *Psychotherapy, 33,* 171–180.

Egan, G. (1982). *The skilled helper* (2nd ed.). Monterey, CA: Brooks/Cole.

Feldman, L. B. (1992). *Integrating individual and family therapy.* New York: Brunner/Mazel.

Fischer, K. W., & Pipp, S. L. (1984). Development of the structures of unconscious thought. In K. S. Bowers & D. Meichenbaum (Eds.), *The unconscious reconsidered* (pp. 88–148). New York: Wiley.

Fiske, S. T., & Taylor, S. E. (1984). *Social cognition.* Reading, MA: Addison-Wesley.

Frank, J. D. (1961). *Persuasion and healing.* Baltimore, MD: Johns Hopkins University Press.

Frank, J. D. (1982). Therapeutic components shared by all psychotherapies. In J. H. Harvey & M. M. Parks (Eds.), *Psychotherapy research and behavior change.* Washington, DC: American Psychological Association.

Frank, J. D., Hoehn-Saric, R., Imber, S. D., Liberman, B. L., & Stone, A. R. (1978). *Effective ingredients of successful psychotherapy.* New York: Brunner/Mazel.

Franks, C. M. (1984). On conceptual and technical integrity in psychoanalysis and behavior therapy: Two fundamentally incompatible systems. In H. Arkowitz & S. B. Messer (Eds.), *Psychoanalytic therapy and behavior therapy: Is integration possible?* (pp. 223–248). New York: Plenum.

Gardner, H. (1983) *Frames of mind: The theory of multiple intelligences.* New York: Basic Books.

Gazzaniga, M. (1985). *The social brain: Discovering the networks of the mind.* New York: Basic Books.

Gendlin, E. T. (1964). A theory of personality change. In P. Worchel & D. Byrne (Eds.), *Personality change.* New York: Wiley.

Gendlin, E. T. (1967). Therapeutic procedures in dealing with schizophrenics. In C. R. Rogers, E. T. Gendlin, D. J. Kiesler, & C. B. Truax (Eds.), *The therapeutic relationship and its impact: A study of psychotherapy with schizophrenics.* Madison: University of Wisconsin Press.

Gendlin, E. T. (1968). The experiential response. In E. F. Hammer (Ed.), *Use of interpretation in treatment.* New York: Grune & Stratton.

Gendlin, E. T. (1982). An introduction to the new developments in focusing. *The Focusing Folio, 2,* 24–35.

Gendlin, E. T. (1984). The client's client: The edge of awareness. In R. F. Levant & J. M. Shlien (Eds.), *Client-centered therapy and the person-centered approach: New directions in theory, research, and practice.* New York: Praeger.

Gendlin, E. T. (1996). *Focusing-oriented psychotherapy.* New York: Guilford.

Goldfried, M. R. (1979). Cognition and experience. In P. C. Kendall & S. D. Hollon (Eds.), *Cognitive-behavioral interventions: Theory, research, and procedures* (pp. 141–146). New York: Academic Press.

Goldfried, M. R. (Ed.). (1980a). Special issue: Psychotherapy process. *Cognitive Therapy and Research, 4,* 271–306.

Goldfried, M. R. (1980b). Toward the delineation of therapeutic change principles. *American Psychologist, 35,* 991–999.

Grawe, K. (1997). Research-informed psychotherapy. *Psychotherapy Research, 7,* 1–20.

Greenberg, L. S. (1984). A task analysis of intrapersonal conflict resolution. In L. N. Rice & L. S. Greenberg (Eds.), *Patterns of change.* New York: Guilford.

Greenberg, L. S., Rice, L. N., & Elliott, R. (1993). *Facilitating emotional change: The moment-by-moment process.* New York: Guilford.

Greenberg, L. S., & Safran, J. D. (1987). *Emotion in psychotherapy.* New York: Guilford.

Greenberg, L. S., Safran, J. D., & Rice, L. N. (1989). Experiential therapy: Its relation to cognitive therapy. In A. Freeman, K. Simon, L. Beutler, & H. Arkowitz (Eds.), *Comprehensive handbook of cognitive therapy* (pp. 169–187). New York: Plenum.

Greenwald, A. G. (1992). New look 3: Unconscious cognition reclaimed. *American Psychologist, 47,* 766–779.

Hayek, F. A. (1978). *New studies in philosophy, politics, economics, and the history of ideas.* Chicago: University of Chicago.

Hayes, S. C., Follette, W. C., & Follette, V. M. (1995). Behavior therapy: A contextual approach. In A. Gurman & S. Messer (Eds.), *Essential psychotherapies* (pp. 182–225). New York: Guilford.

Holdstock, L. (1990). Can client-centered therapy transcend its monocultural roots? In G. Lietaer, J. Rombauts, & R. Van Balen (Eds.), *Client-centered and experiential psychotherapy in the nineties* (pp. 109–122). Leuven, Belgium: Leuven University Press.

Husserl, E. (1964). *Cartesian meditations: An introduction to phenomenology.* The Hague: Martinus Nijhoff.

Jordan, J. V., Kaplan, A. G., Miller, J. B, Stiver, I. P., & Surrey, J. L. (Eds.). (1991). *Women's growth in connection: Writings from the Stone Center.* New York: Guilford.

Krier, B. A. (1986, February 12). Virginia Satir: Making psychological connections. *Los Angeles Times,* Section V, pp. 1, 12–13.

Kuhn, T. S. (1970). *The structure of scientific revolutions* (2nd ed.). Chicago: University of Chicago Press.

Landsman, T. (1982). Not an adversity but a welcome diversity. Reprinted in M. R. Goldfried (Ed.), *Converging themes in psychotherapy: Trends in psychodynamic, humanistic, and behavioral practice.* (1982). New York: Springer.

Langer, E. J., & Rodin, J. (1976). The effects of choice and enhanced personal responsibility for the aged: A field experiment in an institutional setting. *Journal of Personality and Social Psychology, 34,* 191–198.

Lazarus, A. A., Beutler, L., & Norcross, J. (1992). The future of technical eclecticism. *Psychotherapy, 29,* 11–20.

Lewicki, P. (1986). *Nonconscious social information processing.* New York: Academic Press.

Linehan, M. (1997). Validation and psychotherapy. In A. Bohart & L. S. Greenberg (Eds.), *Empathy reconsidered* (pp. 354–392). Washington DC: American Psychological Association.

Madanes, C. (1985, December 12). *Advances in strategic family therapy.* Paper presented at the Evolution of Psychotherapy Conference, Phoenix, AZ.

Mahoney, M. J. (1985). Psychotherapy and human change processes. In M. J. Mahoney & A. Freeman (Eds.), *Cognition and psychotherapy* (pp. 3–48). New York: Plenum.

Mahoney, M. J. (1991). *Human change processes.* New York: Basic Books.

Mahrer, A. (1989). *The integration of the psychotherapies.* New York: Human Sciences Press.

Marmor, J. (1987). The psychotherapeutic process: Common denominators in diverse approaches. In J. K. Zeig (Ed.), *The evolution of psychotherapy* (pp. 266–273). New York: Brunner/Mazel.

Martin, J., Paivio, S. C., Labadie, D. (1990). Memory-enhancing characteristics of client-recalled important events in cognitive and experiential therapy: Integrating cognitive experimental and therapeutic psychology. *Counselling Psychology Quarterly, 3,* 239–256.

Maslach, C. (1979). Negative emotional biasing of unexplained arousal. *Journal of Personality and Social Psychology, 37,* 953–969.

Messer, S. (1986). Eclecticism in psychotherapy: Underlying assumptions, problems, and tradeoffs. In J. C. Norcross (Ed.), *Handbook of eclectic psychotherapy* (pp. 379–397). New York: Brunner/Mazel.

Messer, S., & Warren, S. (1990). Personality change and psychotherapy. *Handbook of personality* (pp. 371–398). New York: Guilford.

Nichols, M. P., & Efran, J. S. (1985). Catharsis in psychotherapy: A new perspective. *Psychotherapy, 22,* 46–58.

Nisbett, R. E., & Ross, L. (1980). *Human inference: Strategies and shortcomings of social judgment.* Englewood Cliffs, NJ: Prentice-Hall.

Norcross, J. C. (Ed.). (1993). The relationship of choice: Matching the therapist's interpersonal stance to individual clients (Special Section). *Psychotherapy, 30,* 402–426.

Norcross, J. C., & Prochaska, J. O. (1982). A national survey of clinical psychologists: Affiliations and orientations. *The Clinical Psychologist, 35,* 1, 4–6.

O'Hara, M. (1992, April). *Selves-in-context: The challenge for psychotherapy in a postmodern world.* Invited Address at the Conference of the Society for the Exploration of Psychotherapy Integration, San Diego, CA.

Paivio, A. (1986). *Mental representations: A dual coding approach.* New York: Oxford University Press.

Phares, E. J. (1976). *Locus of control in personality.* Morristown, NJ: General Learning Press.

Polster, E. (1985, December 12). *The storyline in psychotherapy* (Live demonstration). Presented at the Evolution of Psychotherapy Conference, Phoenix, AZ.

Polyani, M. (1966). *The tacit dimension.* New York: Doubleday.

Prochaska, J., & DiClemente, C. (1986). The transtheoretical approach. In J. C. Norcross (Ed.), *Handbook of eclectic psychotherapy* (pp. 163–200). New York: Brunner/Mazel.

Prochaska, J. O., & Norcross, J. C. (1983). Contemporary psychotherapists: A national survey of characteristics, practices, orientations, and attitudes. *Psychotherapy: Theory, Research and Practice, 20,* 161–173.

Prochaska, J. O., Norcross, J. C., & DiClemente, C. (1994). *Changing for good.* New York: Morrow.

Rachman, S. (1981). The primacy of affect: Some theoretical implications. *Behavior Research and Therapy, 19,* 279–290.

Reber, A. S. (1976). Implicit learning of synthetic languages: The role of instructional set. *Journal of Experimental Psychology: Human Learning and Memory, 2,* 88–94.

Rice, L. N., & Saperia, E. (1984). Task analysis of the resolution of problematic reactions. In L. N. Rice & L. S. Greenberg (Eds.), *Patterns of change: Intensive analysis of psychotherapy process.* New York: Guilford.

Riebel, L. (1984). Paradoxical intention strategies: A review of rationales. *Psychotherapy, 21,* 260–272.

Rothbaum, F., Weisz, J. R., & Snyder, S. S. (1982). Changing the world and changing the self: A two-process model of perceived control. *Journal of Personality and Social Psychology, 42,* 5–37.

Ryle, A. (1982). *Psychotherapy: A cognitive integration of theory and practice.* New York: Grune & Stratton.

Safran, J., & Segal, Z. (1990). *Interpersonal process in cognitive therapy.* New York: Basic Books.

Schafer, R. (1978). *Language and insight.* New Haven, CT: Yale University Press.

Schneider, K. J., & May, R. (1995). *The psychology of existence: An integrative, clinical perspective.* New York: McGraw-Hill.

Segal, D. L., & Murray, E. J. (1994). Emotional processing in cognitive therapy and vocal expression of feeling. *Journal of Social and Clinical Psychology, 13,* 189–206.

Seligman, M. (1990). *Learned optimism.* New York: Knopf.

Shapiro, A. K., & Morris, L. A. (1978). Placebo effects in medical and psychological therapies. In S. L. Garfield & A. E. Bergin (Eds.), *Handbook of psychotherapy and behavior change: An empirical analysis* (2nd ed.). New York: Wiley.

Shevrin, H., & Dickman, S. (1980). The psychological unconscious: A necessary assumption for all psychological theory? *American Psychologist, 35,* 421–434.

Shirley, B. (1984, August 7). Judging fly balls puzzles fielders, physicists. *Los Angeles Times,* Section III, p. 4.

Shweder, R. A., Turiel, E., & Much, N. C. (1981). The moral intuitions of the child. In J. H. Flavell & L. Ross (Eds.), *Social cognitive development: Frontiers and possible futures.* Cambridge: Cambridge University Press.

Stiles, W. B., Barkham, M., Shapiro, D. A., & Firth-Cozens, J. (1992). Treatment order and thematic continuity between contrasting psychotherapies: Exploring an implication of the assimilation model. *Psychotherapy Research, 2,* 112–124.

Stiles, W. B., Elliott, R., Llewelyn, S. P., Firth-Cozens, J. A., Margison, F. R., Shapiro, D. A., & Hardy, G. (1990). Assimilation of problematic experiences by clients in psychotherapy. *Psychotherapy, 27,* 411–420.

Stiles, W. B., Shapiro, D. A., & Elliott, R. (1986). Are all psychotherapies equivalent? *American Psychologist, 41,* 165–180.

Stolorow, R. D. (1992). Closing the gap between theory and practice with better psychoanalytic theory. *Psychotherapy, 29,* 159–166.

Tobin, S. A. (1990). Self psychology as a bridge between existential humanistic psychology and psychoanalysis. *Journal of Humanistic Psychology, 30,* 14–63.

Wachtel, E., & Wachtel, P. (1986). *Family dynamics in individual therapy.* New York: Guilford.

Wachtel, P. L. (1977). *Psychoanalysis and behavior therapy: Toward an integration.* New York: Basic Books.

Washburn, M. (1978). Observations relevant to a unified theory of meditation. *Journal of Transpersonal Psychology, 10,* 45–65.

Watzlawick, P. (1987). If you desire to see, learn how to act. In J. Zeig (Ed.), *The evolution of psychotherapy* (pp. 91–99). New York: Brunner/Mazel.

Westen, D. (1990). Psychoanalytic approaches to personality. In L. A. Pervin (Ed.), *Handbook of personality* (pp. 21–65). New York: Guilford.

Wexler, D. A. (1974). A cognitive theory of experiencing, self-actualization, and therapeutic process. In D. A. Wexler & L. N. Rice (Eds.), *Innovations in client-centered therapy.* New York: Wiley.

Wheeler, G. (1991). *Gestalt reconsidered.* New York: Gardner.

Zajonc, R. B. (1980). Feeling and thinking: Preferences need no inferences. *American Psychologist, 35,* 151–175.

PART **EIGHT**

Contemporary Issues

The Psychologist and Contemporary Society: Diversity and Postmodern Issues

Western clinicians must incessantly ask themselves these cross-cultural ethical questions: Is my intervention a pernicious form of missionary work? Are my therapeutic goals mere proselytization? Does my effect on this family—on this culture—differ significantly from that of colonialism? (Landrine, 1992, p. 414)

The "social revolution" of the 1960s was more than just people protesting the war in Vietnam, wearing flowers in their hair, and listening to the Beatles. In psychology, it marked the beginnings of an important change from an exclusive focus on the individual psyche to a greater awareness of the human in society. A general consciousness that individual psychological problems and their treatment were intimately and intricately bound up with society as a whole arose. Feminists began to assert that many problems suffered by women reflected society's sexism rather than individual flaws in a woman's character. Ethnic minority groups began to argue that many of the mental health problems they suffered were caused or exacerbated by such factors as racism and poverty. Gays and lesbians similarly began to challenge society's definition of their lifestyles as "deviant." In a broader sense, the advent of the community psychology movement in the 1960s argued that *all* psychological problems are embedded in social factors.

Traditional models of treatment were also challenged. It was argued that individual psychotherapy too often laid the blame for the client's problems at the client's doorstep and ignored important social factors that played a role. It was also argued that therapists tended to impose a model of mental health on the client that reflected an implicit White male view of what constitutes healthy functioning, while ignoring the unique experiential backgrounds of women, people from other cultures, and gays and lesbians.

Further social change currently requires psychology to reexamine its assumptions. Population trends in the United States are such that it is estimated that by about the year 2050, the average person in the United States will *not* be descended from White Europe (Comas-Díaz, 1992). Diversity will become an increasingly important issue for psychologists to face, and the theories and models on which they have traditionally based their practice will be increasingly challenged.

Multicultural and feminist psychology present the challenge of fundamentally different ways of thinking to professional psychology and society. To a society that emphasizes individualism, relationships based on hierarchical differences in power, and linear logic, feminist and multicultural psychology offer a view that values community, egalitarian relationships, and holistic thinking. The benefit of this challenge is that it encourages psychologists to analyze their therapies and their relationships with clients in terms of what they may be doing to replicate and reinforce the very social structures that are causing the clients' problems. This analysis will lead to new types of therapy, more effective psychotherapy, and improved services to clients.

Besides diversity, professional psychology is responsive to many other social issues. Due to consumer and third-party payer demands for low-cost help, psychology has developed new treatment modalities that emphasize brief therapy and self-help. Diversity and social change have profoundly influenced psychology, and we now turn to a detailed examination of these effects.

THE CHALLENGE OF DIVERSITY

Many have argued that most of the theories we have considered in this book—psychoanalysis, object relations theory, humanistic and existential theories, cognitive and behavioral theories, and systems theories—have largely been the product of White males and reflect Western cultural values. Most of these theories emphasize an individualistic perspective. That is, the healthy individual is self-sufficient, separate, controls and is in charge of him- or herself, takes responsibility, is not enmeshed with others, has good boundaries, has a clear, solid sense of self and identity, and so on. Psychological dysfunction is seen as some deficit in the ability to be an individual, and a general goal of most therapies is to increase individuation. Therapists do not want to tell the client what to do, for instance, because that will foster or perpetuate dependency, rather than encourage self-sufficiency and autonomy.

But are these theories *universal* theories of human nature? What if they are culture-specific and reflect distinct cultural biases? What happens when these theories, and the therapists who practice using these theories, encounter people who do not share these values?

This is the problem professional psychology has begun to face in the last 20 years. Initially, the solution was for therapists to be aware of and empathic to differences. A good therapist would be aware of the cultural differences in working with an Asian American or Hispanic American family or individual. A good (male) therapist would be aware of differences in experience and values based on gender when working with a female client.

Typically, it was argued that the therapist should be empathic to the client's situation and take the client's background into account in planning a treatment strategy. However, this version of multiculturalism was often advocated in a "technically eclectic" way (see Chapter 16). That is, the therapist would take the client's cultural background into account only as a *treatment strategy*. Empathy would be used as a strategy to create a context in which the therapist's interventions could be utilized. With an Asian American client or family, for example, the therapist would respect the clients' needs for a therapist who was directive. While respecting these differences, however, the goals of therapy remained basically the same: to enhance autonomy, to "de-enmesh" families, and so on. The therapist simply "blended" his or her techniques with the client's cultural background so that the same old therapy goals could be achieved.

However, in recent years, this solution to the problem of dealing with diversity in therapy has begun to be challenged. It is argued that multicultural therapy is not merely modifying our therapeutic procedures in order to take ethnic differences into account so that traditional therapy goals, which would effectively reduce ethnic differences, can be achieved. Rather, we need to be truly open to the meaning of cultural differences and fundamentally reexamine the very bases of our theories and views of healthy functioning in response to the challenges of diversity. We need new theories, new goals, and new ways of achieving them.

As an example of how diversity can affect psychotherapy, consider the practice of psychotherapy in India (Rosenbaum, 1992). In India, the boundaries of the self tend to be much more diffuse than in the United States. Rosenbaum (1992) reported that when he first arrived in India there was a sign on the door of the head of a clinical psychology program that said "Please Do Not Knock." Thinking that this meant that the man did not want to be disturbed, Rosenbaum did not enter. However, later, he found out that in India this meant "Please walk right in; don't bother knocking first."

In many parts of India people just walk right in on others if they are familiar with them. The message in India is, "Being with others is more important than achieving a planned goal." This attitude affects the practice of therapy as well. Therapists do not adhere to the standard "50-minute hour," and family members may drop in on the therapeutic work at any time. Boundary limits, such as on confidentiality, which are rigidly adhered to in the United States, are not respected in India. A therapist may call a client's employer or visit the family, without the client's permission. This is not seen as intrusiveness, but rather, as connectedness and caring.

In India, family togetherness is greatly valued and there is less of an emphasis on individual needs. The family is a open system, and when one member of the family is invited somewhere, all members may go. Indians find the Western idea of the parents leaving the children home with a babysitter while going out to be somewhat odd. Because individual desire is not emphasized as it is in the West, the values and goals of therapy are different. Indians tend to see the Western emphasis on autonomy and privacy as somewhat "sick."

In sum, it can be seen that our cultural assumptions are just that, cultural assumptions, and not objective truth. Our goals and how we practice therapy have been heavily dependent on these cultural assumptions.

The Self Across Cultures

The healthy self in most Western psychological theories is a separate, autonomous self. It is a self that has its own separate, private universe of its own values, beliefs, goals, and desires. Having a firm, stable sense of identity is important. A healthy self has a well-developed, separate sense of identity that it "owns," which is its alone. From this perspective, individuals who are not self-sufficient, who are dependent on others, who do not have clearly defined and articulated stable senses of themselves, or who have difficulty separating their own wishes, values, and desires from those of others around them, are seen as pathological. Borderline personality disorder is one of the best examples. A person who feels identityless and abandoned unless she is in a relationship is seen by object relations theory as suffering from a major defect in ego structure going back to the most formative period of early childhood.

Having a separate and autonomous self is related to having self-control. The healthy self controls itself. It is not swept away by its emotions or passions. Its intellect is in charge of itself. It manages its own emotions, solves its own problems, sets its own goals, and directs its own life. It does not blame its problems on external forces. It does not see itself as externally controlled. It accepts responsibility for itself. The ability to take care of itself and self-manage are therefore also healthy qualities of this self. This emphasis on self-control may be so extensive that individuals may believe they can control virtually anything if they only adopt the right psychological attitudes and take responsibility for themselves. Recently, this idea has even extended into the area of physical health, as discussed in Chapter 11, and some may assert that people are responsible for contracting illnesses.

All of these models of healthy and pathological behavior are based on a particular view of the nature of the self. This can be called the "Western" self, and it is also more particularly a *masculine* self. In this view of the self, there is a clear and unequivocal distinction between the self and the not-self (Landrine, 1992). The boundaries of the self end at the skin of the individual. It is important to have clear boundaries. The self is separate and is controlled from within. Ideally, it is free of all contexts and self-sufficient. It is an autonomous entity so it has rights, such as the right to privacy (Landrine, 1992). Development is the process of moving this self, which is initially dependent, toward self-sufficiency and autonomy.

These ideas are not advocated only by psychoanalytic and humanistic points of view. Cognitive and behavioral perspectives have also advocated many of the same ideas. Healthy individuals, according to Beck and Ellis, do not need relationships in order to be happy. Effective people regulate their own lives through rational thinking. Behaviorism has similarly emphasized the development of various self-management techniques, including strategies of self-reinforcement. In family systems theories, one of the major ideas is that psychopathology is due to such factors as "lack of differentiation," "enmeshment," and so on. These concepts all imply that healthy families promote individuality and independence. Having diffuse or poor boundaries in a family is seen as pathological. It is healthy to have good, solid (but not too rigid) boundaries.

Feminists and multiculturalists attack the model of the separate, autonomous self. Multiculturalists point out that this model of the self is highly culture-specific. In other cultures, the boundaries of the self are extended to include one's family and even one's social group. The belief in a separate, context-free self is simply not held. For instance, in our culture, because we believe in a context-free self, we have the concept of *personality trait,* that the self has characteristics independent of contexts. We describe individuals as "shy," or "friendly," as if these traits exist within them, independent of different social contexts. In contrast, in other cultures, individuals are described in terms of their relationship to their contexts (O'Hara, 1984). An individual may be described as "friendly at social gatherings," instead of "friendly." Similarly, individuals are often identified in terms of their relationships. In many cultures, an individual may be called by a name that means the "son of X" or the "mother of Y," rather than having a separate autonomous name (Triandis, 1989).

For these cultures, the self is truly a "self-in-relation" (O'Hara, 1992). For women, the self is also primarily a self-in-relation (Jordan et al., 1991). In such cultures or for such groups, *interdependence* is stressed, rather than *independence.* For instance, in many cultures, duty and obligation to one's social group are valued over individual self-actualization. One "actualizes" *through* strengthening one's bonds with others, rather than by breaking free from those bonds.

Contributions of Diverse Views of the Self

Adopting such a different view of the self has important implications for doing psychotherapy. For instance, theorists at the Stone Center in Wellesley, Massachusetts, have published a book entitled *Women's Growth in Connection* (Jordan et al., 1991). The title suggests the radically different perspective being advocated by feminists and multiculturists.

First, clients' experiences are viewed differently. As an example, a colleague of ours was seeing a woman who was devoting herself to her ill mother in a way that was interfering with her own life. Rather than seeing this as "codependent" or "pathological," the therapist validated the value of interpersonal connectedness. This was vastly relieving to the client, who had experienced a good deal of shame from other therapists who had told her that she was "enmeshed," "dependent," and so on. In our culture, it is pathological to sacrifice oneself for another. But validating the positive thrust in this client's behavior paradoxically gave her life meaning and purpose. She no longer felt shame at what she was doing.

Similarly, Linehan (1989) has argued that many borderline women define themselves in terms of their relationships and to try to get them to be *independent* is to work against their deepest sense of identity. Rather than trying to get them to be independent, Linehan's strategy is to try to teach them to be more "healthily" *dependent,* that is, to learn how to be dependent without destroying the very relationships they are dependent on. She goes on to argue that our society needs to provide more vehicles for healthy dependency rather than trying to force everyone to conform to the cultural model of independence.

Both O'Hara (1992) and Jordan and colleagues (1991) have spelled out some of the implications of the connectionist view of the self as a self-in-relation for doing psychotherapy. First, they argue that the therapist must respect the individual experience of the client. That is, the therapist must be willing to listen to this client's experience *as this client's experience,* rather than seeing the client through the lenses of the therapist's own cultural biases. Therapy must be *particularized,* and therapists cannot apply a generalized model to a client. Therapy is the specific "meeting of persons." Second, the therapist and the client must establish an egalitarian relationship. Hierarchical therapeutic relationships in which the therapist has power and is the expert are eschewed. Instead, the therapist and the client share a *mutual* relationship. A mutual relationship means that the therapist must be willing to be open and self-disclosing as well as the client. Empathy is highly valued and prized. And it is the *relationship* that is the primary source of growth. That is, problems are understood as being matters of relationship, growth is seen as learning how to be more effectively in relationship, and therefore, the therapeutic relationship itself is the "learning laboratory" for growth. As therapist and client deal with ruptures and difficulties in the therapeutic relationship itself, the client learns how to be in and grow through relationships. An essential part of this view is that the *therapist* is as much changed by the therapy process as the client is.

POSTMODERN TREATMENT APPROACHES

In response to the challenge of diversity, psychology both as a science and as a practice has had to incorporate the idea that there is no one, universal "Truth." Science cannot "discover" an objective, absolute truth, because humans conduct and create science in a specific historical and environmental context. Just as there is no absolute truth in science, there can be no single definition of mental health for therapists.

This view is part of an intellectual movement called postmodernism, which holds that "truth" is relative. Modernism held that there is a fixed objective reality. Through appropriate scientific and intellectual methods, one can come to know the one objective truth about the world. Modernism led psychology to the belief that there are universal laws and truths about human beings. Modernism also led to the belief that there are objectively "right" and "correct" ways to be. Modernist ideas in psychology have typically privileged the values and beliefs of dominant groups, such as those of Western, White, heterosexual males.

Postmodernists, in contrast, hold that the experience of different groups of people constitute different personal realities, and there is no one objective truth about human nature (O'Hara & Anderson, 1991). Each culture creates its own way of viewing and experiencing reality, as do individuals. Typically, postmodernists argue that people must be understood in their own terms, rather than compared to a dominant group's "objective" standards. Therapy, then, must be conducted in terms of the perspectives and values of the individual client and the client's cultural background. Furthermore, contemporary treatment approaches must consider psychology's place in the power structure of the larger society. It is possible that the modernist approach of considering the dominant group's view to be "objective truth" replicates that power structure and thereby exacerbates the client's problems.

In response to these views and to several social forces, professional psychology has developed a number of treatment alternatives to traditional psychotherapy. All of these approaches challenge professional psychology and society, because they involve shifts in fundamental assumptions about the nature of psychological problems, such as changing from seeing problems as existing in individuals to placing them in the situation or social context. This and other issues are raised in the following contemporary treatment approaches.

Multicultural Counseling

In doing therapy with members of diverse cultural groups, the same general principles as are discussed above in working from a self-in-relation perspective are advocated (Comas-Díaz, 1992). Multicultural therapists avoid stereotyping and encourage clients to explore their full potential, while realistically acknowledging social barriers to their aspirations. The same sorts of guidelines for therapists working with women, discussed below and in Box 17.1, are useful for those working with different ethnic groups. Furthermore, Comas-Díaz (1992) has noted that the general APA guidelines for doing therapy include recognizing ethnicity and culture as significant parameters. This awareness includes being respectful of the roles of family members, community structures, values and beliefs, religious and spiritual beliefs, and so on.

Therapists must be aware that many of the assumptions of Western culture we have previously considered may not be held by members of other cultures. For instance, members of other cultural groups may not share the emphasis on internalized control shared by Western civilization. They may emphasize the role played by destiny or fate in their lives and assume that individuals cannot control everything, but only a portion of the events in their lives. Secondly, many members of other cultures place a greater emphasis on religion and spirituality than do Western psychotherapeutic cultural values. Psychological problems are often seen as an imbalance between the spirit and the body, and the neglect of one's spirit is seen as unhealthy. The result is that spiritual beliefs and practices are often valued as an important part of life and of change. Other values may be different as well.

As an example of these points, Heide (1989) describes the treatment of a young Asian American female college student who was suicidal because she was not achieving well in school. A typical cognitive intervention with such a client would be to challenge her dysfunctional thoughts that she is "no good" because she is not doing well in school. However, this intervention failed to help her, because it did not take account of her cultural background, in which to do poorly in school is shameful to the family. Modifying the intervention to get her to consider which would be more shameful, doing poorly in school or killing herself, was effective when she realized that suicide would be even more shameful.

Treatment Issues in Multicultural Counseling   A useful distinction when working with multicultural clients has been pointed out by López and colleagues (1989), who have argued that therapists need to take into account both culture-specific and culture-general factors. Culture-general factors are common to all humans across

BOX 17.1

APA Guidelines for Therapists Working with Women Clients

1. The conduct of therapy should be free of constrictions based on gender-defined roles, and the options explored between client and practitioner should be free of sex role stereotypes.
2. Psychologists should recognize the reality, variety, and implications of sex-disciminatory practices in society, and should facilitate client examination of options in dealing with such practices.
3. The therapist should be knowledgeable about current empirical findings on sex roles, sexism, and individual differences resulting from the client's gender-defined identity.
4. The theoretical concepts employed by the therapist should be free of sex bias and sex role stereotypes.
5. The psychologist should demonstrate acceptance of women as equal to men by using language free of derogatory labels.
6. The psychologist should avoid establishing the source of personal problems within the client when they are more properly attributable to situational or cultural factors.
7. The psychologist and a fully informed client mutually should agree upon aspects of the therapy relationship such as treatment modality, time factors, and fee arrangements.
8. While the importance of the availability of accurate information to a client's family is recognized, the privilege of communication about diagnosis, prognosis, and progress ultimately rests with the client, not with the therapist.
9. If authoritarian processes are employed as a technique, the therapy should not have the effect of maintaining or reinforcing stereotypic dependency of women.
10. The client's assertive behaviors should be respected.
11. The psychologist whose female client is subjected to violence in the form of physical abuse or rape should recognize and acknowledge that the client is the victim of a crime.
12. The psychologist should recognize and encourage exploration of a woman client's sexuality and should recognize her right to define her own sexual preferences.
13. The psychologist should not have sexual relations with a woman client nor treat her as a sex object.

Source: American Psychological Association (1978).

cultures, while culture-specific factors are unique to a given culture. López and colleagues (1989) have pointed out that therapists need training in appropriately discriminating culture-specific from culture-general factors. Initially, therapists often overlook the culture-specific and "see" culture-general factors in their clients, such as a poor sense of identity or relationship problems. As they become sensitive to culture-specific factors, they may begin to overfocus on those. For example, in working with a woman from a ghetto family who was exhibiting borderline symptomatology, the therapist assumed that this was probably the result of her living in a poor, chaotic family situation (a culture-specific factor), when actually, it may have been due to the fact that the woman lacked the development of an ethnic identity (the development of a sense of identity is more of a culture-general factor). Only with further experience do therapists finally achieve a balanced perspective between focusing on and identifying culture-specific and culture-general factors.

Two related and particularly important issues in working with multicultural clients are the formation of a positive ethnic identity and *acculturation* versus *biculturation*. There appear to be stages in ethnic identity development, of which there are several models (Bustamente, 1992). In a typical model, individuals begin with their original cultural identity, and they may have to struggle to accept themselves when the larger society demeans them. They have often internalized the negative evaluations of the dominant culture and may be trying to assimilate into that culture. As they mature, they may go through a stage of embracing their original culture and angrily rejecting the majority culture that rejects them. Finally, they integrate aspects of both cultures into their unique positive ethnic identity. The process of forming a positive ethnic identity is similar to a dialectical process in which a thesis (original devalued cultural identity) leads to an antithesis (new aggressively valued cultural identity), which leads to a new synthesis (integrated, accepting cultural identity).

Acculturation is defined as the degree to which the ethnic individual attempts to assimilate to the dominant culture. For instance, does a Latino attempt to become "like" the larger Anglo culture in terms of values, beliefs, and behaviors? Basically, many models of the development of ethnic identity see either acculturation, in which the individual relinquishes his or her cultural identity to assimilate, or the opposite, when the individual refuses to acculturate at all, as stages along the way to developing a fully integrated cultural identity. In bicultural models of ethnic identity formation, the individual develops an integrated bicultural identity, which involves building a bridge between his or her cultural background and the larger culture, while relinquishing neither. Biculturalism involves, as Bustamente (1992) has pointed out, realizing that there are good and bad things in both cultures and helping clients sort out their own stance on acculturation and biculturation.

A Theory of Multicultural Therapy   Derald Wing Sue and his colleagues (D. W. Sue & D. Sue, 1990; D. W. Sue, Ivey, & Pedersen, 1995) have developed a theory of Multicultural Counseling and Therapy (MCT), based on six assumptions. First, MCT is a metatheory, or a theory about theories, that offers an organizational framework for understanding all helping approaches, including the worldviews of Western psychotherapy and non-Western helping models. Second, treatment must focus on the multiple levels of experiences (individual, group, and universal) and contexts (individual, family, and cultural) that affect the identities of both counselor and client. Third, the identity development of both counselor and client is a major determinant of their attitudes and behaviors, and the level or stage of ethnic or cultural identity of each will determine what they believe to be appropriate counseling goals and processes. For example, a bicultural therapist should be sensitive to the different treatment strategies that would be necessary for a culturally different client whose identity involves assimilation to the majority culture as opposed to one whose identity development seems to be in the stage that completely rejects the majority culture.

The fourth assumption of MCT is that no one helping approach is effective for all populations. The effectiveness of MCT is enhanced when the therapist intervenes in ways that are consistent with the life experiences and cultural values of the client. Fifth, MCT stresses multiple helping roles, including systems interventions and prevention. For example, an African American student referred for fighting in school may be the victim of racist comments from other students. In this case, the therapist will have a better understanding of how to help by visiting the student's environment and observing it directly. The therapist may have to play the roles of advisor, advocate, environmental change agent, and educator, as well as counselor, in order to help this student.

Finally, MCT emphasizes the liberation of consciousness of both therapist and client. Competent multicultural counselors must constantly develop attitudes, knowledge, and skills related to an awareness of their own values and biases, an understanding of the worldviews of culturally different clients, and culturally appropriate interventions. Since MCT is contextual, the therapist will also change and grow as a result of treating the culturally different and attempting to help them deal with issues of identity, power, oppression, and liberation. Ideally, the research and theories of professional psychology will also change and grow as a result of MCT.

Need for Multicultural Therapists   There is a great need for multicultural therapists, given the population shifts in the United States. Surveys conducted in 1980 and 1991 revealed some progress in the training of those working with ethnic minorities, but noted that cultural competence, not just cultural awareness, was still needed, as was a significant increase in the numbers of minorities entering the field (Bernal & Castro, 1994). Until enough non-White individuals become trained as psychologists, the need for multicultural Caucasian therapists remains. There is also a great need for bilingual therapists, including therapists who can use sign language with the deaf. When therapists are unable to learn the needed language, it is possible to use interpreters or to collaborate with bilingual and bicultural nonprofessional counselors. Some therapists encourage the use of indigenous healers or other community authorities as adjuncts to therapy.

Landrine (1992) proposes a *cultural triage model* of intervention for those working in different cultures. In this approach, a Western clinician, an indigenous healer or other community authority from the culture, and the family of the individual with a psychological problem consult and agree on several conceptualizations of the problem and attempt a multicultural/multilevel treatment by the Western clinician, the indigenous healer, and the family. For example, when Southeast Asian children in

Trying to Take a Multicultural Approach with Pets.

Stockton refused to return to school after their classmates were shot by a sniper in 1990, therapy failed until this approach was utilized by having an indigenous healer remove the spirits of their murdered friends through a culturally appropriate ritual.

The ethnic distributions of therapists and the population mean that for the fore-seeable future, many Caucasian therapists will have to attempt multicultural therapy. Because cultural beliefs are unconscious and feel "right," Caucasian therapists must work hard to increase their awareness of their own cultural assumptions, in addition to educating themselves about the values of other cultural groups. In fact, D. W. Sue and D. Sue (1990) urge Caucasian therapists to become aware of the formation of white identity, especially as it overprivileges them. At a minimum, they must be careful not to impose their cultural beliefs on others, and ideally, they should remain open to the value of others' beliefs even for their own lives. They must try not to replicate the power structure of dominance of other ethnic groups by Caucasians.

Feminist Therapy

As with multicultural counseling, feminist therapy presents the challenge of a fundamentally different way of thinking to professional psychology and society. To a society that emphasizes individualism, relationships based on hierarchical differences in power (with Caucasian men in the dominant position), and "masculine" linear logic, feminist psychology offers a view that values community and connectedness, egalitarian relationships based on sharing power, and holistic thinking. The early feminist slogan, "The personal is political," is at the heart of the feminist critique of traditional therapy that it decontextualizes people's problems. That is, a therapy that emphasizes individual problems and individual solutions fails to recognize the degree to which women's limited gender role, devalued status, and lack of power contributes to their frustration, depression, low self-esteem, and other problems such as unassertiveness. Feminist therapy challenges psychologists to analyze their therapies and their relationships with women clients in terms of what they may be doing to replicate and reinforce the very social structures that are causing the women's problems. The following case history illustrates these points.

Mildred came to see one of us in therapy (the *male* of us, by the way). Mildred was a 48-year-old woman, in a program in nursing. She was doing well in school and had been active in the nursing club, where she had ascended to the position of president. Her goal was to go on to become a licensed nurse. She came to therapy because she was troubled by nagging doubts from a previous experience.

Mildred was divorced. She recounted that she had been married to a businessman for many years and had had several children, all of whom were now adults. This businessman had neglected her emotionally and kept her in a subservient role. He had controlled all the finances in the marriage. As her children grew older and she became bored in her exclusive role as housewife, she wanted to go back to school. He was opposed to this and put considerable pressure on her to stay at home, telling her that that was her place, and so on. Because he controlled the family purse strings, she was dependent on his cooperation to go back to school. In the face of this resistance, she soon gave up her plans and subsequently lapsed into a depression.

Her husband arranged to have her treated by a traditional psychiatrist who assumed that her depression reflected both a biochemical flaw in her and psychological ego weaknesses based on early childhood experience. She was hospitalized, pumped full of medication, and essentially told that her problems were due to unconscious anger toward men based on early childhood experiences, which she was turning inward on herself as depression.

This went on for several years, and she was repeatedly told that her depression reflected exclusively her own inadequacies. Finally, by some miracle (and we are often amazed at the resiliency of the human spirit), she dragged herself out of this situation. She mustered enough strength to initiate a divorce, even though both her husband and psychiatrist continued to label her as the problem. The husband, with his considerable resources, managed to make sure that as the divorce proceeded, Mildred ended up with very little.

After Mildred started back to school, her depression began to lift. However, this experience had left its mark: She continued to worry that she was indeed "flawed." While she was doing all right, this continual fear was undermining her ability to utilize her full capabilities.

Therapy was brief and consisted primarily of allowing Mildred to recount in detail the horrors of this experience. The therapist encouraged Mildred to evaluate for herself her husband's and the psychiatrist's claims that the problem was in her, and in the supportive atmosphere provided, she was able to begin to see how oppressed she had been. The therapist himself also validated her point of view, helping her to see how her problems reflected a social issue rather than an individual, intrapsychic deficit.

Early Roots of Feminist Therapy   Although the beginnings of feminist thought can be traced back to ancient times, as in the Greek play *Lysistrata,* the modern women's movement in the United States began in the last century with the struggle for women's suffrage. After American women won the right to vote in 1920, feminist activism died down until the general political activism of the 1960s. The lessons of the civil rights movement led women to begin reconsidering their own unequal status in society. Women began meeting in consciousness-raising groups to discuss and analyze their common problems and the social and political contexts of them. Such meetings were often therapeutic, and there was a fruitful exchange of ideas between feminists and therapists so that by the late 1970s, feminist versions of most of the other schools of therapy had been developed.

Between the two waves of feminist activism, women psychoanalysts, such as Helene Deutsch, Marie Bonapart, Jeanne Lampl-de-Groot, Joan Riviere, and Frieda Fromm-Reichmann, struggled with issues of female sexuality and feminine identity. Karen Horney and Clara Thompson developed the theories that differed with Freudian theory most. Horney pointed out that women did not envy men's penises, but rather, their greater social and economic power. She also theorized that male envy of women's childbearing ability was at the root of their devaluation of women. Thompson and Horney both examined the role of women's economic dependence and restricted opportunities on their development. Although later feminists objected strongly to psychoanalysis for devaluing, restricting, and pathologizing women, it was women psychoanalysts who continued feminist theorizing during the 1930s, 1940s, and 1950s.

Because its egalitarian philosophy eschews identified leaders or authority figures, there is no one precise feminist therapy. Nevertheless, there is a professional identity for the field of feminist therapy, as seen in a number of journals, such as *Women and Therapy,* the *Journal of Feminist Family Therapy,* and others, as well as a number of organizations, such as Division 35 (Psychology of Women) of the APA and the Association for Women in Psychology. During the 1970s, psychologists interested in women's issues developed a set of guidelines for therapists working with women clients, and they were accepted and published by the APA in 1978, as shown in Box 17.1. The APA was the first to support such a set of special guidelines, and they have served as the basis for similar guidelines for therapists working with lesbians and gay men or with different ethnic groups. A code of ethics for feminist therapy has also been developed (Lerman & Porter, 1990).

Types of Feminist Therapy   As already noted, there are feminist versions of most types of therapy, although most of these focus on deconstructing and reducing the sexism inherent in them. Sometimes a distinction is made between therapies that are nonsexist but still focus on the individual and radical feminism, which holds that social change and political action are necessary for the healing of the individual.

Feminist psychoanalysis (an oxymoron to some) has developed out of the work of Nancy Chodorow (1978), who drew on object relations theory and Marxist social theory to place analytic ideas about the family into its sociocultural context. Therapists and researchers at the Stone Center continue to develop feminist-based psychodynamic theories and methods (Jordan et al., 1991). Feminist psychoanalysis rewrites the account of feminine development in an affirmative, woman-centered way, with the emphasis on early experience leading to an identity rooted in relationships and other strengths.

Feminist behavior therapy, like other behavior therapies, asserts that dysfunctional behavior is learned from and maintained by the environment, but in addition, it identifies sex role training and factors in the environment that affect women differentially (Blechman, 1984). For example, assertion training may work well to help men attain their goals, but when women engage in the same assertive behavior, it is often met by hostility and rejection from others. Behavior therapists are urged to set goals and utilize methods that are appropriate for women.

Feminist family therapy agrees with traditional family therapy that the individuals in a family cannot be taken out of context, but they add the importance of the context of the power structure outside the family, which is replicated in the traditional family (Marecek & Hare-Mustin, 1991). The strengths and needs of the women in the family, the right of women to extrafamilial life, the forces within and without the family that impede women's movement outside the family, and nontraditional families, such as single mothers or lesbian families, are emphasized in feminist family therapy.

Core Principles of Feminist Therapy   Although there is diversity, feminist therapies share certain core principles, which have been listed by Brown and Brodsky (1992) as follows. First, feminist therapy values the diverse and complex experiences of women from all racial, class, religious, age, and sexual orientation groups. Society and other therapies have privileged the view of White, heterosexual men, and it is essential to rebalance the construction of reality so that the values and experiences of women are seen as normal and equal in value. Second, feminist therapy attends to the power dynamics in the therapy relationship, with the goal of developing egalitarian relationships and empowering the less powerful. Third, feminist therapy attends to both individual variables and the social context, especially the effects of assigned gender roles on identity, development, and mental health. Fourth, feminist therapy relies on the empirical database arising from feminist scholarship that studies disorders of high prevalence in women, such as depression, eating disorders, and the effects of abuse. Fifth, feminist therapy values a balance of both healthy autonomy and relational competence for all adults, rather than seeing healthy males as independent and healthy females as socially skilled. Sixth, therapeutic goals in feminist therapy include both intrapsychic change and a changed perspective on the social and cultural realities that affect people's lives. Rather than helping people adjust to what is, feminist therapy focuses on the empowerment of the individual, with the possible need to change society and not the person.

There are other commonalities in the feminist therapies. A major difference from other therapies is the insistence on a nonhierarchical therapeutic relationship. Therapy goals are developed cooperatively between client and therapist. Although the client and therapist have different roles to play, one exploring her life and the other offering assistance, therapy is seen as a cooperative relationship between the two. The myth of value-free psychotherapy is rejected, and feminist therapists attempt to make their own biases and values explicit so that client and therapist can deal with them.

The values and viewpoints of the therapist and client are seen as different, but equal in value.

Current Issues in Feminist Therapy   A future goal for feminist therapy may be to articulate a comprehensive theory that can encompass all the variations, although many prefer the organic process of constant change we have at present. Standards for training in feminist therapy need to be developed, and such training must be made more widely available. The ultimate goal of feminist therapy is to become widely accepted in all of psychology and to influence the direction of the entire field. Earlier feminist thought rejected the possibility of any real difference between women and men with the idea that all differences were due to cultural training and oppression of women. Recently, there has been an emphasis on research demonstrating biological differences between the sexes, such as differences in brain organization of language, in the hypothalamus, and in the corpus callosum. As Marecek and Hare-Mustin (1991) have observed, the focus on male–female differences has pushed the question of male dominance and female subordination to the periphery.

The current emphasis on biological sex differences is dangerous, as earlier feminists realized when they rejected such differences, because it is easy for differences to become differentially valued in favor of the dominant group. How the dominant group differs is seen as superior, and then the difference is used to substantiate their dominant position. "Different but equal" is apparently a difficult concept, especially for groups that value hierarchical organization. Feminist therapists must once again force attention to be paid to questions of gender, power, and equality.

Constructivism and Narrative Psychotherapies

Constructivists (see also our discussion in Chapter 14) hold that at the individual level, each of us constructs our own reality. It is impossible ever to say what is the "truth" about objective reality, because no one can ever know objective reality. We always know reality through the lens of our cognitive structures and mental representations of reality. This view does not mean that we can make the world anything we want, simply that our ideas about the world are always constructions and therefore limited and incomplete. Furthermore, our ideas about the world cannot be judged by any criteria of "objective validity," but they can be judged by their capacity to afford adaptation and development.

Constructivist therapies (Mahoney, 1991; Neimeyer & Mahoney, 1995) work with clients when their ways of dealing with the world are not working and do not lead to adaptation and development, and they help clients develop new constructions of the world that are more viable. (Note the similarity of these ideas to the earlier views of Jean Piaget and George Kelly, discussed in Chapter 12.) Therapy becomes the process not of "correcting" the client's distorted views, but of helping the client evolve her or his own unique views of the world in ways that make them more functional. The therapist is therefore not the "expert" on the client, but rather, an expert on helping clients "make new meaning" and use their already existing beliefs and experiences to develop new and more helpful ways of dealing with the world. For instance, instead of eliminating "shoulds" as a traditional cognitive therapist might, the constructivist therapist helps clients consider how such thinking functions in their lives and then helps them to evolve ways of using "shoulds" so that they promote rather than interfere with coping.

Constructivist therapists may use any number of procedures borrowed from cognitive, humanistic, family systems, or psychodynamic approaches. It is not what the therapist does so much as how the therapist does it that matters. Techniques are used to help clients explore and create meaningful new perspectives and ways of viewing the world.

Narrative therapies (Freedman & Combs, 1996; see also our discussion at the end of Chapter 6) are a form of constructivist therapy. Narrative views hold that we live our lives as if they were embodied stories (Howard, 1991). We organize our lives along storylike lines. Therapy, then, is the "restorying" of our lives. From a narrative perspective, the past is never fixed. The past's impact on the present is determined by the story we hold about our past. We can "restory" our past and then it will have a different impact on our present. To quote Keen and Fox (1973, p. 42) "What happened to you in the past has yet to be determined."

But what about someone who was sexually abused as a child? Isn't that historical fact? Yes. At the same time, the person's story about the abuse may be contributing to his present problems. For instance, the person's story about the abuse may include "I am a helpless child and I have been irreparably damaged" and even "I am responsible for what happened." This story leaves the client feeling helpless and depressed. Therapy alters these interpretations of the fact of abuse and makes a new story: "I am not responsible, I am no longer a helpless child, and I can recover from this experience and grow strong because of it." Narrative therapies help clients construct more viable and workable "life stories" that help them see new possibilities in their lives.

Narrative and constructivist approaches fly in the face of the current managed care view of psychotherapy (see Chapter 18). These therapies are open-ended and discovery-oriented. The therapist does not start with a preplanned goal about what the client needs to change in order to get well. Nor does the therapist apply a specific standardized set of treatment procedures to correct the client's "disorder." Instead, constructivist and narrative therapists try to remain open to the emerging process between themselves and their clients and to facilitate the clients' own creative "story-repair and elaboration" processes as they go.

Other Issues in Contemporary Treatment Approaches

Religion and Psychotherapy   A particularly important cultural variable is religion. As previously noted, religion is quite important in many cultural groups. Further, the majority of the population in the United States is religious. Yet psychotherapists in general have tended to minimize or ignore the influence of religion in people's lives, and the population of mental health professionals is, on the average, less religious than the average client. This has led to a state of affairs in which many religious clients are suspicious of mental health professionals, who they expect will not be empathic with their views. As a result, many religious clients seek help from their pastors and ministers rather than from mental health professionals. Yet there are those who are increasingly emphasizing the importance of therapists' understanding the role of religion in personal functioning (Bankart, Koshikawa, Nedate, & Haruki, 1992; Payne, Bergin, & Loftus, 1992). In addition, there are those who have argued that therapy must go beyond normal psychological functioning and deal with the spiritual in order to be fully effective. Below, we consider two different approaches to psychotherapy that include a religious element: approaches that utilize Eastern mysticism and Christian counseling.

Transpersonal Counseling Transpersonal approaches generally hold that full personal growth cannot be achieved through a psychological approach alone. They emphasize the necessity for a spiritual or transpersonal transformation as well. While there has always been a tradition of Christian counseling, the transpersonal view was dominated in the late 1960s and 1970s by Eastern mystical traditions. Mystical experience, meditation, and altered states of consciousness were important topics.

Eastern mystical thought tends to see the subject-object dichotomy as an illusion. In other words, the idea that the self observing the world is somehow separate from the world that is observed is an illusion. Further, the idea that the world is made up of separate things, which have fixed identities, is also an illusion. Actually, the world is an ever changing "flux" or "dance" (Zukav, 1979). Eastern mystical approaches hope to get the individual to suspend these illusory concepts about the world.

The main tool of attaining such realizations for many transpersonal psychologists is meditation. There are two kinds of meditation: concentrative and receptive. In *concentrative meditation,* the person attempts to keep attention focused on one object, usually a word, image, or phrase. In *receptive meditation* the person attempts to do what appears to be the opposite: to allow consciousness to flow freely and uninterruptedly, to let go and become a pure observer of experience. Washburn (1978) has argued that the seemingly different types of meditation ultimately have similar effects. As internal chatter is suspended, the individual becomes able to become aware of herself as the constructor of her own conscious activity. She becomes aware of the unconscious, automatic thoughts and schemas that she uses to shape and form concepts and perceptions. As these are suspended, she moves toward a state of "bare witnessing." As with hypnosis, there is controversy over whether meditation involves an altered state of consciousness.

Christian Approaches Christian approaches to psychotherapy hold that the accepting of Christ and of a Christian way of life is the ultimate healing act. Christian approaches stress human finiteness and imperfection in comparison to God. Being finite and imperfect, people should be tolerant and forgiving of themselves and others. We may ask for God's forgiveness. Forgiveness leads to a kind of living in the here and now. Instead of ruminating over past sins, the Christian focuses on how he can improve now. Instead of judging himself, since he and all other human beings are imperfect and will occasionally err, he focuses on what he can do in the future to live a better life. Christianity also values selflessness and doing away with pride. If people are able to do away with pride, then they will not need to be defensive and protect their self-esteem. They will be able to accept their failings and drawbacks with humility.

There is no one specifically Christian way of practicing psychotherapy. Existential-humanistic concepts more easily interface with Christian ideas (Payne, Bergin, &

Loftus, 1992), but attempts have been made to forge integrations between Christian beliefs and other therapy approaches as well. Christian therapists can utilize cognitive techniques, behavioral techniques, and the like. Among some of the techniques utilized are prayer and meditation, religious imagery, and the encouragement of forgiveness (Payne, Bergin, & Loftus, 1992). For instance, Propst, Olstrom, Watkins, Dean, and Mashburn (1992) gave an example of combining Christian imagery with a cognitive-behavioral therapy technique. They had a client visualize an image of his imperfections and then visualize Christ overlooking these imperfections and refusing to condemn the client. These authors found that a cognitive-behavioral approach modified to deal with religious themes in such a manner was more effective with religious clients than a standard cognitive-behavioral format.

Therapy with Lesbians and Gay Men   Many of the same principles that apply to treating members of ethnic minority groups, religious clients, and female clients apply also to treating gay men and lesbians. That is, the therapist must be aware of his or her biases, be empathic with the experience of the client, and understand the special issues and needs facing a gay or lesbian client. We will discuss some of the special treatment issues in working with gay men and lesbian clients. It is important for therapists to be knowledgeable about resources in the lesbian and gay communities. Many support groups and workshops are available, and often, a referral to these resources in addition to or instead of therapy is helpful.

In our Western, predominantly Christian cultural tradition, homosexuality has generally been looked on negatively as a "sin." This bias was reflected in psychological theories, particularly psychoanalytic theories, in which homosexuality was seen as a developmentally more immature form of sexual expression. For a long time, homosexuality was seen as a psychological disorder. It was only in 1974 that the American Psychiatric Association decided to remove a homosexual orientation from the list of mental disorders. This followed a number of research studies showing that gay men and lesbians on the average were no more psychologically disturbed in general than heterosexual men and women and that what problems they did have stemmed mostly from the negative stereotyping forced on them by society.

Despite a lack of evidence to support their position, a small number of mental health professionals still consider homosexuality to be a psychological disorder, and they practice "conversion therapy" aimed at helping people with same-sex attractions change their sexual orientation. Advocates of this position argue that therapists have abandoned people who are unhappy with their sexual orientation by blaming their unhappiness on homophobia. Critics of this position obviously disagree and question whether it is ethical to offer "therapy" that has no evidence of being effective.

The decision by the American Psychiatric Association to destigmatize homosexuality has not eliminated negative stereotypes in the culture at large, not even in the mental health profession itself as evidenced by the "conversion therapy" advocates discussed above. Gay men and lesbians still face considerable societal discrimination. For therapists working with gays and lesbians, it is particularly important to be aware of the fact that the client's problems may well have a real basis in the client's life context and of the psychological and physical dangers the client may face (Greene, 1993). It is important for therapists to disentangle characterological and personal difficulties from problems engendered by a gay and lesbian lifestyle in a hostile society (Maarse & Lyons, 1992).

Two of the most important issues faced by gays and lesbians are the connected issues of developing a positive gay or lesbian identity and "coming out." Coming out (of the closet) involves gay men and lesbians revealing their identity to the community at large, including sharing this information with their families and with those at work.

Similar to the dialectical process of developing a positive ethnic identity, the development of a positive gay or lesbian identity may take place in stages. There are several models of gay and lesbian identity development (Bustamente, 1992). In general, in these models, individuals start out struggling with the idea and perhaps denying that they might be gay. They may have their own internalized homophobia. The therapist particularly needs to be sensitive to this, and many therapists are not (Greene, 1993). That is, persons who are just beginning to confront the possibility of their gayness may be uncomfortable and unwilling to bring the issue up to a therapist. If the therapist does not ask, "Could you perhaps be gay?" or if the therapist does not support fledgling attempts to open the issue, the client's own conflicts may block its being explored. As gays and lesbians begin to assimilate their sexual orientation into their identities, they may go through a period where they are angry at or deny the larger society, identifying exclusively with the gay and lesbian lifestyle and rejecting heterosexual society. Later, they will move into an integrated stage accepting of the good and bad in both worlds.

Coming out can be a difficult, emotionally challenging, and sometimes dangerous process. Gay men and lesbians need to be helped to assess the real dangers involved and to decide who to come out to and how. Coming out, for instance, to one's family may or may not be productive, and gay men and lesbians sometimes need to face the issue of emotionally "cutting off" from their families (Maarse & Lyons, 1992). Along with this may come the issue of loss, and an important part of counseling with gay men and lesbians may be to deal with the grief over such loss. On the other hand, coming out can also be a courageous act of love and self-affirmation, and ways of making it a positive experience have been developed (Eichberg, 1990).

A major determinant of issues around coming out is the person's position in terms of the process of developing a gay or lesbian identity. During the early stage of identity formation, if the individuals try to come out, they may come out in an angry, confrontive way, possibly alienating their family and others around them. Later, as they move into a more integrative "live and let live" stage, coming out may occur more gently and integratively, taking the feelings of family and others into account (Bustamente, 1992; Eichberg, 1990).

Other issues confronted by gays and lesbians about which therapists need to be particularly sensitive are that gays and lesbians have few role models for establishing relationships and family structures, and that many gays and lesbians, alienated from their families of origin, may form "surrogate families." As with other groups, therapists have an obligation to educate themselves about the unique life experiences and views of lesbians and gays.

CONTEMPORARY TREATMENT MODALITIES

One of the most influential contemporary social forces is the reduced level of funding for mental health care from all sources. Many consumers have always been interested in quick, effective help. Health care companies have always been interested in cutting costs. Reduced funding, along with new technology and research findings, have increased the pressure for the development and acceptance of new treatment modalities, or ways of delivering therapy. Psychological services no longer have to occur within a context of face-to-face talking with a professional over several weeks, months, or years. Instead, therapy can be delivered in a short period of time, with technological assistance, or through books or other forms of self-help.

Brief Therapy

Most of the therapies covered in previous chapters are considered time unlimited, in that clients are allowed, even encouraged, to attend therapy for as long as necessary, however long that is. Throughout the history of professional psychology, beginning with Freud, who complained about "interminable analysis," there have been those who have argued in favor of brief therapy, variously called "planned short-term therapy," "time-limited therapy," "time-sensitive treatment," even "single-session therapy." There has been the moral argument that therapists have "the social responsibility to provide needed services to the many rather than many services to the privileged few" (Hoyt, 1995). There has been the theoretical argument that the prospect of a short time limit benefitted therapy because it "heightened" its intensity and impact (Davanloo, 1980; Strupp & Binder, 1984). In recent decades, reduced funding for mental health services and the cost-cutting of managed care organizations has added a pragmatic argument in favor of brief therapy.

What is "brief"? Traditional psychoanalysis can last for years, so some psychodynamic therapists consider a year of therapy to be brief. Many health plans pay for 10 sessions, with 20 possible if necessary, and that may be considered brief therapy. The brief therapy called crisis intervention, developed by community psychology, is traditionally held to be six sessions. Some psychologists have presented a model for single session therapy (Budman & Gurman, 1988; Rosenbaum, Hoyt, & Talmon, 1990; Rosenbaum, 1994). They argue that since we can never be certain that a client will come back, all therapy sessions should be treated as single-session interventions.

Although the issue may have been forced by cuts in funding for psychotherapy, brief therapies are effective, worthwhile types of interventions with a solid theoretical and empirical basis. Reviews of the research (Bloom, 1992; Rosenbaum, Hoyt, & Talmon, 1990; Hoyt, 1995; Rosenbaum, 1994) repeatedly find that short-term psychotherapy is as effective as time-unlimited therapy, regardless of diagnosis or duration of treatment. In comparing long-term and brief therapies, Hoyt (1995) notes that "the equivalence of outcomes is compelling." While it seems that the effectiveness of brief therapy might present a challenge to therapists, most of whom still follow long-term approaches, psychologists should find this conclusion comforting, because in fact, about 30 percent of people who consult a therapist come for only one session and the overall average number of sessions per client is about eight.

Theoretical Bases of Brief Therapy   Although all brief therapies share certain assumptions, the theory is largely eclectic. Since the therapy must necessarily be focused and specific to the particular client's goals, it is argued that brief therapists must have the knowledge, skill, and flexibility to use a wide range of intervention methods that may be appropriate for a particular problem. Even brief therapists who prefer a certain theory can be technically eclectic.

Some of the assumptions of long-term therapy are that change is difficult, a "cure" or "deep" change in basic character must be sought, that presenting problems are not as important as the "basic" pathology, that change occurs mainly in therapy and not in everyday life, that client resistance is inevitable and must be carefully worked through, and that therapy is good and more therapy is better. The assumptions of brief therapy challenge all of these. In line with a connectionistic philosophy and with the strategic and family systems therapies, brief therapy emphasizes the interconnectedness of life, and it assumes that a small intervention or small change can have far-reaching ripple effects. Brief therapy also assumes that change occurs all the time in everyday life. Thus, in a sense, change is easy, and the therapist needs to make just one well-timed, precise intervention to have a profound effect. A well-designed intervention need not take a long time, and the therapist is viewed as a catalyst or change-agent in the ever-changing process called life.

Rather than attending to pathology, brief therapy focuses on client strengths and resources. By believing in the client's resources, brief therapists accept the client's definition of the presenting problem as well as the client's goals, thus avoiding the problem of resistance. Brief therapy assumes that therapy may not always be good, that less is more, and that change should occur outside therapy, perhaps long after the initial intervention. In a way, brief therapies see the therapist's job as rather like nudging the client on to a more adaptive developmental path.

Although the research suggests that brief therapy is as effective as time-unlimited therapy for all diagnoses, most brief therapists believe that it is unsuitable for certain individuals, such as those with psychotic symptoms, suicidal intentions, alcohol or drug addictions, a propensity to violence, or severe character disorders. (It might be noted, however, that long-term therapy has not been demonstrated to be very effective with these problems, either.) The ideal candidate for brief therapy is suffering from anxiety, depression, other symptoms, or a situational problem, and has sought therapy or otherwise shown evidence of attempts to change. Such clients may well agree more with the assumptions of brief therapy than with those of long-term therapy, for most people seeking help want and expect immediate change. Brief therapists assume it is possible, and they focus their work to help bring it about.

Brief Therapy Methods   What the therapist actually does in brief therapy reflects these underlying assumptions. Brief therapies, whether for one session or six or more, share certain characteristics and elements. The brief therapies are pragmatic, structured, directive, goal-oriented, and focused on problem solving. The time-limited nature of the contact is made clear, sometimes through an explicit contract between client and therapist. Although brief therapies may be as varied as traditional therapies, most contain at least the following steps.

First, the therapist and client together identify a focal problem, and the therapist actively keeps the therapy focused on that. Because it is assumed that everything is connected to everything else, focusing on almost any problem and bringing about a change in it will have ripple effects on other difficulties, including possibly the "basic" pathology, whatever that may be. Throughout the session, the therapist attends to the relationship with the client, assessing what kind of relationship the client wants, and trying to create trust and a sense of safety. Client affect about the focal issue is explored and expressed, possibly as a result of therapist empathy and reflection. Then the therapist actively begins a problem-solving process, by emphasizing client resources and skills and searching for information, such as past client successes, that would help the client change. At this point, the therapist may use interpretation, suggestion, reframing, hypnosis, metaphor, or specific behavioral or cognitive methods to help the client begin to organize her or his own resources and act on the problem. Often, specific homework is assigned, in line with the assumption that change occurs outside of therapy. A fitting end to the session includes summarizing what has been accomplished in the session, client plans for further problem solving and change, and leaving open the possibility of returning for further assistance if desired. The client may be asked to describe what was accomplished to encourage memory and recall of a useful lesson.

This brief description of brief therapy cannot convey the variety of methods incorporated into the short-term or single-session structure. An example case may convey what it is like. Michael Hoyt reported the following single session (reported in Rosenbaum, Hoyt, & Talmon, 1990):

> A young married couple sought consultation, complaining of "communication problems." He referred to stresses at work, financial frustrations, and sexual dissatisfaction with the marriage. She felt depressed and unable to connect with her husband, worried he would abandon her, and wondered if she should return to her parents' house. They looked reasonably healthy, and neither had any previous psychiatric contact, but both now sat avoiding the other's eyes and appeared depressed. The room grew unpleasantly quiet.
>
> "You look like someone died," the therapist observed aloud. "What happened?"
>
> Previously unmentioned, a painful story was told: A midtrimester pregnancy had miscarried the year before. The couple had tried to bury their grief with the unborn child and had pulled back from one another to avoid the sadness that closeness brought. . . . An hour spent talking, crying, and hugging "unstuck" the grieving/healing process. No further professional psychotherapeutic intervention was needed.

Types of Brief Therapy   All of the therapies we have already covered have brief versions. Behavior and cognitive-behavior therapies are short-term to begin with, and they are highly goal-directed and offer specific remedies for specific problems. Perhaps the most contrary to stereotype are the brief forms of psychoanalysis, which psychoanalysts prefer to call short-term psychodynamic psychotherapy to distinguish it from "real" psychoanalysis.

The time-limited dynamic psychotherapy of Strupp and Binder (1984) lasts 25 to 30 sessions. The focus is on dysfunctional interpersonal relationship patterns, as opposed to early childhood sexual and agressive wishes. It is assumed that earlier difficulties with significant others have given rise to patterns of interpersonal relating that originally served a self-protective function but are now self-defeating and maladaptive. In childhood, the person experiences a disturbed pattern of interpersonal relationships, from which he develops organizing themes that form a rigid, habitual way of construing and acting in current relationships. These patterns are hidden from the self because of "the ubiquitous human tendency to hide from oneself painful experiences and their aftermath" (Strupp & Binder, 1984, p. 32). The client unconsciously believes these patterns will bring him security and nurturance in current relationships. Relationships are defensively distorted in order to protect the self as the person strives to achieve these primitive, unconscious forms of intimacy. Time-limited dynamic psychotherapy attempts to identify and concentrate on these "focal issues."

Strupp and Binder believe that these central relationship issues will manifest themselves in the therapeutic relationship and that reexperiencing them in the transference relationship will be therapeutic. The therapist attempts to help the client become aware of the symbolic meanings of his or her behavior, but this needs to be done when "an appropriate affective context exists" (1984, p. 136). At the same time, intellectual reconstruction of the past is de-emphasized. In fact, Strupp and Binder assume that it is impossible to really recover the past. The most important quality of a therapeutic relationship is that it is a human one. Learning occurs not through acquisition of abstract knowledge, but "rather it is the result of a human *experience* in which he or she feels understood and in which this understanding is given new meanings" (1984, p. 45). While it is true that transference involves bringing past relationships into the current, therapeutic relationship, Strupp and Binder assume that the client's feelings toward the therapist also include some real aspects of the here-and-now relationship. The therapist is to use her own feelings as signals of how the client is attempting to structure their relationship. Empathic listening is important, and the therapist is encouraged to engage in honest self-disclosure, if necessary and appropriate.

Luborsky's (1984) supportive-expressive psychoanalytically oriented therapy is similar. It is based on the assumption that a *core conflictual relationship theme* (CCRT) is at the center of a person's problems. This relationship theme developed from early childhood experiences, but the client is unaware of it and its connection to childhood experiences. Therapy is oriented toward increasing the client's awareness of the theme. It is assumed that the client will have better control over behavior if he knows more about what he is doing at the unconscious level. The transference relationship is important in that the CCRT will be lived out and enacted in relationship to the therapist. A supportive, empathic relationship is considered crucial, and Luborsky speculates that compared to the acquisition of insight, the relationship may be the more potent therapeutic factor.

Single-Session Therapy   Many have noted that there is a parallel between the structure of each individual therapy session and that of the overall course of treatment (Hoyt, 1995). It seems entirely possible that a precise, well-timed intervention could have a profound effect in one session. In fact, Rosenbaum (1994) argues that psychology should study single-session therapies for a picture of therapy in miniature in order to research what really works in therapy and to achieve theory integration. He also argues that the 20 to 50% of clients who attend only once should not be considered therapy dropouts, but rather, examples of single session therapy. His research and that of others indicates that people who come to therapy once rate its effectiveness just as highly as those who come for several sessions and do not differ from them on any outcome measure (Rosenbaum, 1994).

Like other brief therapies, single session therapy is focused and goal-oriented, assumes that change can occur in the moment and outside of therapy, emphasizes client strengths, accepts the client's definition of the problem, and is eclectic. The single-session therapist is active and directive, taking responsibility for keeping the session focused on the agreed-upon issue and goal. However, the choice of a single session is usually left to the client, and the therapist should be ready to work for as long as two hours in order to make it. It is also left open that the client can return at any time, so in this sense, single-session therapy is not time-limited.

Similar to the structure of many-session treatment, the single session generally covers the following steps. First, the therapist engages the client and establishes rapport. Second, therapist and client define the purpose of the meeting and agree on realistic and obtainable therapeutic goal(s). The therapist may also instruct the client about how to use therapy. The therapist creates an opportunity for the client to express thoughts, feelings, and behavior, all the while assessing the client's strengths, resources, and motivations. The therapist then makes the treatment intervention(s), assesses its effects, and adjusts her behavior accordingly. Homework may be assigned or practiced right in the session. Finally, client changes are reviewed, summarized, and rehearsed to consolidate learning.

Brief therapy has a long future. As discussed above, research repeatedly demonstrates that it is as effective as long-term therapy, and it is probably more cost-effective. Psychologists would do well to seek training in the brief therapy methods.

Technology and Counseling

Many professional psychologists, like many Americans, have fallen in love with modern technology. The possibilities for utilizing technology in all aspects of psychological services are being explored in research and practice. However, it must be pointed out that Freud was the first, as he was in many areas, to attempt to deliver psychological help through means other than face-to-face contact. He was a voluminous letter writer and sometimes delivered psychological advice and interpretations by mail, including a short dream analysis for a mid-Western American woman who wrote to him for help in 1927 (Benjamin & Dixon, 1996).

Telephones have been incorporated into attempts to help people since their invention. "Hotlines" for people suffering suicidal or other crises are well known, and some clinics offer "warmlines" for people to call during the day with less serious problems, such as parenting or health issues. Some private therapists offer counseling and brief therapy over the telephone for a fee. Individuals can call a 900 number anytime and speak with a therapist trained in this type of work. The therapy offered is, of course, brief, and it shares the assumptions and methods of brief and single-session therapies.

Some people use radio and television call-in programs in a way similar to telephone counseling. While most radio and telephone psychologists see themselves as performing an educational function, sometimes they also do brief therapy on the air and make appropriate referrals off the air.

With the development of powerful computers, the potential uses of technology have expanded. Computer-like machines were first used in psychological assessment to score personality questionnaires. Since then, computer programs have been developed that administer, score, and interpret many types of psychological tests, including the Rorschach ink blot test. Computers are also used to compose assessment reports, bill clients, keep client records, and the like. Busy professionals look forward to the day when treatment forms and records will be entirely computerized, and they can be free of some of the paper-work demands of current practice. Computerized databases can also be used to make referrals and organize services.

The most challenging and intriguing use of computer technology is in the delivery of psychological treatment. Early programs attempted to replicate traditional psychotherapy and counseling with a computer serving as the therapist. The client types what he or she wants to say directly into the computer, which is programmed to ask questions, make comments, and even give reflections or interpretations. There is some evidence that certain individuals are more comfortable communicating with the completely nonjudgmental computer than with humans (Canoune & Leyhe, 1985) and that people can find this type of "therapy" helpful (Christensen & Jacobson, 1994; O'Dell & Dickson, 1984; Zarr, 1984).

Recent computerized treatment programs involve administering specific types of therapy for specific problems, such as cognitive-behavioral interventions for phobias, and incorporating educational video and CD-ROM technology. For example, Christensen and Jacobson (1994) reviewed published computerized treatments for obesity, phobias, and depression, all of which were reported to be as effective as therapist-administered treatments. They suggested that such computerized therapy may best be called "self-administered treatment." Also similar to self-help, discussed in the next section, are on-line support groups for people with eating disorders and other problems. Furthermore, creative professional psychologists are developing and marketing CD-ROM programs to help people with parenting and communication skills and to change many other behaviors.

Critics of technological psychological services charge that telephone, computerized, or CD-ROM "therapists" may miss vital information supplied by the in-person encounter and therefore make ineffective or harmful interventions. Defenders argue that the possibility is slim and that the benefits outweigh the drawbacks. Benefits are that therapy is made available to large numbers of people and that electronic counseling is quick, convenient, and relatively inexpensive. In fact, it may reach people who would not otherwise consider therapy because of the cost or stigma and people who prefer the anonymity of the technological help. Although research so far indicates that technological psychological treatments are as effective as face-to-face therapy for some important behaviors, much more research is needed in this area as new technology develops.

Self-Help

As members of a largely individualistic culture, Americans have always liked self-help. The forms of psychological self-help are many, from self-administered computer programs to mutual support groups such as Alcoholics Anonymous and Recovery Inc. Some believe that self-help should be called "psychoeducational methods" in order to distinguish it from psychotherapy and counseling. Professional psychologists are involved in designing, marketing, supervising, consulting, and referring clients to self-help methods.

The bookstore shelves devoted to psychology and self-help books are always loaded. Some therapists recommend such books to their clients and discuss them with them, and it is possible that many people use such "bibliotherapy" alone without also seeing a therapist. For example, Eichberg's (1990) *Coming Out: An Act of Love* and Slater's (1995) *The Lesbian Family Life Cycle* can be very helpful to young gay men and lesbians and their family members. In addition to published books, some psychologists have designed various written materials, workbooks, and exercises to help clients with specific problems.

We already mentioned self-administered computerized treatment programs in the section above. With the development and marketing of computerized programs for skills training, behavior change, and treatment of specific problems, we can expect that the self-help section of CD-ROM stores will soon be comparable to that in bookstores.

Self-help and mutual-support groups have already been discussed in Chapter 13. People participate in all sorts of support groups, either informally in hospital waiting rooms and the like or formally by joining Alcoholics Anonymous or other groups. It was estimated in 1990 that 15 million Americans participated in about 500,000 self-help groups (Roan, 1991). Recovery Inc., believed to be the nation's first self-help organization, has more than 800 groups meeting weekly across the United States (Beaubien, 1996). With the reduction in traditional mental health services, these numbers can only grow. Furthermore, there is evidence (Galanter, 1988) that self-help groups are effective in helping their members in a number of ways, including reducing symptoms and increasing self-esteem and social cohesion, and as effective as traditional therapy (Christensen & Jacobson, 1994).

Mutual-support groups have gone on-line. Some so-called "chat rooms" and listservs, in which people who have called in on their computer's modem can exchange written messages on specific topics in real time or not, have probably served functions similar to mutual-support groups all along. Now therapists have designed and set up sites on the World Wide Web for the specific purpose of providing on-line mutual-support groups for people with certain disorders. For example, researchers at Stanford and San Diego State Universities developed an eight-week psychoeducational CD-ROM program with weekly assignments and e-mail messages between participants for women at risk of developing an eating disorder, and their early data suggested that it was effective by a number of measures, including significant improvements in participants' body image and reducing their drive for thinness (DeAngelis, 1997).

Although challenged by the possibility that self-help may equal professional help, psychologists can participate in self-help in several ways. "Giving psychology away" includes, after all, teaching the public how to help themselves. Some self-help books or methods are more effective than others for certain people, and psychologists can both design and research them and make appropriate recommendations. For example, one study found that externalizing, defensive clients responded better to supportive, self-directed reading therapy than to professionally administered cognitive therapy, while with internal, low-resistant clients it was the reverse (Beutler et al., 1991). Some psychologists believe psychology should research the relative effectiveness of other forms of help available in the community, including help offered by nonprofessional counselors, with the goal of educating consumers as to how to make the best use of the helping alternatives available (Christensen & Jacobson, 1994). They recommend turning away from research that compares professional treatments and focusing on research that compares self-help, mutual-support groups, and nonprofessional therapies, both for theoretical reasons and simply because many more people need mental health services than can ever be served by expensive, professional therapists.

Self-help is popular and probably as effective as professional help, so professional psychologists should work to make it as effective as possible. During the 1980s, the state-supported California Self-Help Center worked to establish needed mutual-support groups, consulted to groups that needed help to function well, and maintained a database to refer callers with almost any type of problem to appropriate support groups in their own communities throughout the state. This Center provided a model for the effective utilization of the expertise of professional psychologists combined with self-help resources so that help reached many people at a relatively low cost. In 1993, a woman who had been helped by support groups started a similar service in Los Angeles County, the Self-Help and Recovery Exchange, with a grant from the California Wellness Foundation (Johnson, 1997). Psychologists will want to know about and become involved in such resources.

IN CONCLUSION

Diversity and other social issues have challenged professional psychology and presented it with the opportunity to develop new psychotherapy theories and new treatment modalities. This challenge has not always been welcome, because these changes deal with our most profound assumptions, beliefs, and values. The change from time-unlimited to brief therapy, forced by economics, contradicts many basic assumptions of traditional therapy. In addition, the change from an individualistic, hierarchical view to a connectionistic, egalitarian one is difficult for many people. In dialectical terms, the thesis of individualism is being challenged by the antithesis of connectionism, and we trust that psychology will be part of the resulting synthesis, preserving the best of both views. The development of self-administered and technology-mediated treatments delivered through the global electronic community may be part of this synthesis.

BIBLIOGRAPHY

American Psychological Association. (1978). APA guidelines for therapists working with women clients. *American Psychologist, 33,* 1122–1123.

American Psychological Association Task Force on Sex Bias and Sex-Role Stereotyping in Psychotherapuetic Practice. (1975). *Report of the Task Force.* Washington, DC: Author.

Bankart, C., Koshikawa, F., Nedate, K., & Haruki, Y. (1992). When West meets East: Contributions of Eastern traditions to the future of psychotherapy. *Psychotherapy, 29,* 141–149.

Beaubien, G. (1996, November 13). Talking it out. *Los Angeles Times,* November 13, p. E3.

Benjamin, L. T., & Dixon, D. N. (1996). Dream analysis by mail: An American woman seeks Freud's advice. *American Psychologist, 51,* 461–468.

Bernal, M., & Castro, F. (1994). Are clinical psychologists prepared for service and research with ethnic minorities? Report of a decade of progress. *American Psychologist, 49,* 797–805.

Beutler, L., Engle, D., Mohr, D., Daldrup, R., Bergan, J., Meredith, K., & Merry, W. (1991). Predictors of differential response to cognitive, experiential, and self-directed psychotherapeutic procedures. *Journal of Consulting and Clinical Psychology, 59,* 333–340.

Blechman, E. (Ed.). (1984). *Behavior modification with women.* New York: Guilford.

Bloom, B. (1992). Computer-assisted intervention: A review and commentary. *Clinical Psychology Review, 128,* 169–198.

Bloom, B. (1992). *Planned short-term psychotherapy: A clinical handbook.* Boston: Allyn & Bacon.

Brown, L. (1990). The meaning of a multicultural perspective for theory-building in feminist therapy. In L. Brown & M. Root (Eds.), *Diversity and complexity in feminist therapy.* New York: Haworth.

Brown, L. (1994). *Subversive dialogues: Theory in feminist therapy.* New York: Basic Books.

Brown, L., & Brodsky, A. (1992). The future of feminist therapy. *Psychotherapy, 29,* 39–43.

Brown, L., & Root, M. (Eds.). (1990). *Diversity and complexity in feminist therapy.* New York: Haworth.

Budman, S., & Gurman, A. (1988). *Theory and practice of brief therapy.* New York: Guilford.

Bustamente, A. (1992, April). Beyond the DSM-III: The role of the therapist in affirming the development of a positive gay identity in lesbian and gay clients. Symposium presented at the Annual Convention of the Society for the Exploration of Psychotherapy Integration, San Diego.

Canoune, H., & Leyhe, E. (1985). Human versus computer interviewing. *Journal of Personality Assessment, 49,* 103–106.

Chodorow, N. (1978). *The reproduction of mothering: Psychoanalysis and the sociology of gender.* Berkeley, CA: University of California Press.

Christensen, A., & Jacobson, N. S. (1994). Who (or what) can do psychotherapy: The status and challenge of nonprofessional therapies. *Psychological Science, 5,* 8–14.

Comas-Díaz, L. (1991). Feminism and diversity in psychology: The case of women of color. *Psychology of Women Quarterly, 15,* 597–610.

Comas-Díaz, L.(1992). The future of psychotherapy with ethnic minorities. *Psychotherapy, 29,* 88–94.

Cowan, E. (1980). The wooing of primary prevention. *American Journal of Community Psychology, 8,* 258–284.

Davanloo, H. (1980). *Basic principles and technique in short-term dynamic psychotherapy.* New York: Aronson.

DeAngelis, T. (1997, March). Do online support groups help for eating disorders? *APA Monitor,* p. 43.

Deikman, A. (1982). *The observing self.* Boston: Beacon Press.

Eichberg, R. (1990). *Coming out: An act of love.* New York: Dutton.

Freedman, J., & Combs, G. (1996). *Narrative therapy: The social construction of preferred realities.* New York: Norton.

Galanter, M. (1988). Zealous self-help groups as adjuncts to psychiatric treatment: A study of Recovery, Inc. *American Journal of Psychiatry, 145,* 1248–1253.

Greene, B. (1993). Human diversity in clinical psychology: Lesbian and gay sexual orientations. *The Clinical Psychologist, 46,* 74–82.

Halliday, G. (1991). Psychological self-help books: How dangerous are they? *Psychotherapy, 28,* 678–680.

Hattie, J., Sharpley, C., & Rogers, H. (1984). Comparative effectiveness of professionals and paraprofessional helpers. *Psychological Bulletin, 95,* 534–541.

Heide, F. (1989, April). Negative outcome in psychotherapy. Symposium presented at the Annual Convention of the Society for the Exploration of Psychotherapy Integration, Berkeley, CA.

Howard, G. (1991). Culture tales: A narrative approach to thinking, cross-cultural psychology, and psychotherapy. *American Psychologist, 46*, 187–197.

Hoyt, M. F. (1995). Brief psychotherapies. In A. S. Gurman & S. B. Messer (Eds.), *Essential psychotherapies: Theory and practice.* New York: Guilford Press.

Johnson, T. (1997, April 18). Self-help exchange provides a base of support for support groups. *Los Angeles Times,* p. B2.

Jordan, J. V., Kaplan, A. G., Miller, J. B., Stiver, I. P., & Surrey, J. L. (Eds). (1991). *Women's growth through connection: Writings from the Stone Center.* New York: Guilford.

Keen, S., & Fox, A. (1973). *Telling your story.* New York: Doubleday.

Landrine, H. (1992). Clinical implications of cultural differences: The referential versus indexical self. *Clinical Psychology Review, 12*, 401–415.

Landrine, H. (Ed.). (1993). *Diversity in feminist psychology.* New York: Guilford.

Lerman, H., & Porter, N. (Eds.). (1990). *Feminist ethics in psychotherapy.* New York: Springer.

Linehan, M. (1989, April). What is support in psychotherapy and is it good or bad? Symposium presented at the Annual Convention of the Society for the Exploration of Psychotherapy Integration, Berkeley, CA.

López, S., Grover, K. P., Holland, D., Johnson, M. J., Kain, C. D., Kanel, K., Mellins, C. A., & Rhyne, M. C. (1989). Development of culturally sensitive psychotherapists. *Professional Psychology: Research and Practice, 6*, 369–376.

Luborsky, L. (1984). *Principles of psychoanalytic psychotherapy: A manual for supportive-expressive treatment.* New York: Basic Books.

Maarse, G., & Lyons, C. (1992, April). *Growing up gay and lesbian: Implications for psychotherapy integration.* Discussion Group at the Annual Convention of the Society for the Exploration of Psychotherapy Integration, San Diego, CA.

Mahoney, M. J. (1991). *Human change processes.* New York: Basic Books.

Marecek, J., & Hare-Mustin, R. (1991). A short history of the future: Feminism and clinical psychology. *Psychology of Women Quarterly, 15*, 521–536.

Markus, H., & Kitiyama, S. (1991). Culture and the self: Implications for cognition, emotion, and motivation. *Psychological Review, 98*, 224–253.

Mednick, M. (1991). Currents and futures in American feminist psychology: State of the art revisted. *Psychology of Women Quarterly, 15*, 611–622.

Neimeyer, R., & Mahoney, M. (1995). *Constructivism in psychotherapy.* Washington, DC: American Psychological Association.

O'Dell, J., & Dickson, J. (1984). ELIZA as a "therapeutic" tool. *Journal of Clinical Psychology, 40*, 942–945.

O'Hara, M. (1984). Person-centered Gestalt: Toward a holistic synthesis. In R. F. Levant & J. M. Shlien (Eds.), *Client-centered therapy and the person-centered approach: New directions in theory, research, and practice.* New York: Praeger.

O'Hara, M. (1992, April). *Selves-in-context: The challenge for psychotherapy in a postmodern world.* Symposium on "New Treatment Strategies for Women: Integrating Theory and Action," presented at the Annual Convention of the Society for the Exploration of Psychotherapy Integration, San Diego, CA.

O'Hara, M., & Anderson, W. (1991, September/October). Welcome to the postmodern world. *The Family Therapist Networker,* 19–25.

Payne, L. R., Bergin, A. E., & Loftus, P. E. (1992). A review of attempts to integrate spiritual and standard psychotherapy techniques. *Journal of Psychotherapy Integration, 2*, 171–192.

Propst, L., Olstrom, R., Watkins, P., Dean, T., & Mashburn, D. (1992). Comparative efficacy of religious and non-religious cognitive-behavior therapy for the treatment of clinical depression in religious individuals. *Journal of Consulting and Clinical Psychology, 60,* 94–103.

Quackenbush, R. (1991). The prescription of self-help books by psychologists: A bibliography of selected bibliotherapy resources. *Psychotherapy, 28,* 671–677.

Roan, S. (1991, June 18). Helping themselves. *Los Angeles Times,* Section E, pp. 1, 4.

Roan, S. (1992, November 24). Calling for help. *Los Angeles Times,* Section E, pp. 1, 6.

Rosenbaum, R. (1992). Psychotherapy and integration in India. *Journal of Psychotherapy Integration, 2,* 65–70.

Rosenbaum, R. (1994). Single-session therapies: Intrinsic integration? *Journal of Psychotherapy Integration, 4,* 229–252.

Rosenbaum, R., Hoyt, M., & Talmon, M. (1990). The challenge of single-session therapies: Creating pivotal moments. In R. Wells & V. Gianett, (Eds.), *Handbook of brief psychotherapies.* New York: Plenum.

Slater, S. (1995). *The lesbian family life cycle.* New York: Free Press.

Strupp, H., & Binder, J. (1984). *Psychotherapy in a new key: A guide to time-limited dynamic psychotherapy.* New York: Basic Books.

Sue, D. W., Ivey, A., & Pedersen, P. (1995). *A theory of multicultural counseling and therapy (MCT).* Invited address delivered by Derald Wing Sue at the Western Psychological Association Convention, Los Angeles.

Sue, D. W., & Sue, D. (1990). *Counseling the culturally different: Theory and practice.* New York: Wiley.

Sue, S. (1988). Psychotherapeutic services for ethnic minorities: Two decades of research findings. *American Psychologist, 43,* 301–308.

Triandis, H. C. (1989). The self and social behavior in differing cultural contexts. *Psychological Review, 96,* 506–520.

Washburn, M. (1978). Observations relevant to a unified theory of meditation. *Journal of Transpersonal Psychology, 10,* 45–65.

Wells, R., & Gianett, V. (Eds.). (1990). *Handbook of brief psychotherapies.* New York: Plenum Press.

Zarr, M. (1984). Computer-mediated psychotherapy: Toward patient-selection guidelines. *American Journal of Psychotherapy, 38,* 47–62.

Zukav, G. (1979). *The dancing Wu Li masters.* New York: Bantam Books.

CHAPTER 18

Professional Issues and the Future

In the inevitable specialization of modern society, there will become increasing need of those who can be paid for expert psychological advice . . . [and] in the end there will be not only a science but also a profession of psychology. (Cattell, 1937, p. 3)

D espite this early prediction, psychologists have to begin to ask, does professional psychology *have* a future? George Albee was saying it was uncertain at best as early as 1970. Social forces, changes in the health care system, and shifts in the economy guarantee that all the mental health professions will change dramatically in the next few years. In this chapter, we will examine some of these forces and attempt to predict how psychology will change.

First, however, we will examine professional issues that have concerned psychology since its beginning and that will undoubtedly continue to be important in the future. Some of these issues reflect clinical psychology's attempt to establish itself as an independent profession. Others reflect its response to the forces of social change. Most of these issues are interesting because they show how professional psychology and the other mental health professions interact with society as they try to define and solve social problems.

ETHICAL ISSUES

As an independent profession, psychology, like medicine and law, developed a set of ethical principles to guide its own practice and internal methods to police and discipline its members, rather than being regulated by government or any other external agency. These professions argue that only fellow professionals understand the field well enough to judge the correctness of other professionals' practices.

Ethical principles are supposed to protect the welfare of the public. The need for protection rests on the assumption that there is a disparity in power and expertise between psychologists and consumers. People seeking psychotherapy are assumed to be vulnerable and liable to be harmed by improper practices. Therapists are assumed to be more knowledgeable than clients and to hold a position of authority over them. Clients, then, must have additional protection.

Early in the development of psychology, the American Psychological Association established a set of ethical principles to guide psychologists, including professors, researchers, and clinical psychologists. The principles are all based on a concern for human rights and human welfare. The welfare of the consumer of psychological services is paramount, and the principles, such as confidentiality and competence, are designed to ensure that welfare. "Consumers" include students and research subjects (including animals) as well as therapy clients. The APA ethical principles, as revised in 1992, are summarized in the Appendix.

The APA ethical principles undergo constant revision in response to professional and social problems. The APA Ethics Committee periodically publishes proposed revisions for discussion by the profession. For example, the problem of dual relationships has come up in different forms over the years. While the ethical principles have always considered it unethical for therapists to have other types of relationships, such as friend or supervisor, with clients, early versions of the ethical principles did not explicitly prohibit sex with clients, but assumed that as a dual relationship, it would be unethical. As sex between therapists and clients became recognized as a serious social problem, the ethical principles explicitly prohibited it. The 1992 revision, presented in the Appendix, next attempted to address sex between therapists and *former* clients. This issue has been extremely controversial, and the 1992 compromise that "psychologists do not engage in sexual intimacies with former therapy patients and clients even after a two year interval except in the most unusual circumstances" led to many heated arguments.

Confidentiality and Privilege

Confidentiality is the *ethical* responsibility of psychologists to safeguard information they receive in the course of their practice (including teaching and research, as well as therapy). **Privilege** is a *legal* right of consumers of medical, legal, and therapy services to control information about themselves. Both the ethic of confidentiality and the legislated right of privilege are based on two assumptions: (1) that successful treatment of consumers of medical or therapy services rests on the full disclosure by the client of potentially embarrassing or harmful information and (2) that consumers will not disclose this important information unless they are assured it will not be revealed. Both of these assumptions are open to empirical verification, which has not been done, and are not necessarily true. However, they guide ethical practice and legislation.

Privilege is a legal right that has evolved over the centuries for people who consult priests, lawyers, and doctors. The holder of the privilege chooses whether information is revealed to others, such as the court or other professionals. The therapist may release information only with the written permission of the holder of the privilege. In the case of children or incompetents, privilege is a legal right held by their parents or guardians, although in some cases, it devolves to the therapist.

Privilege is legislated in the evidence codes of most states to apply to the people who consult mental health professionals, as well as lawyers and doctors. In 1996, the Supreme Court ruled in *Jaffe* vs. *Redmond* that licensed therapists cannot be forced to testify about confidential communications between them and their clients, so the right of privilege for clients of therapists now has national recognition.

There are several exceptions to confidentiality and privilege. In most states, privilege does not apply in certain cases, such as a child who is a victim of a crime (such as physical or sexual abuse) or a person who seeks counseling in order to commit a crime. Another important exception to confidentiality is embodied in the 1971 *Tarasoff* decision of the California Supreme Court. The court ruled in favor of parents who sought damages against a psychologist for failing to warn them that the psychologist's client was intending to (and did) kill their daughter. In its famous statement, the Court said that "Private privilege ends where public peril begins." This ruling has been interpreted to mean that therapists of homicidal patients are obliged to break confidentiality and inform the police and the intended victim(s) of their patients' intentions.

Some have argued that the *Tarasoff* case and similar court rulings place an unreasonable burden on therapists in terms of assessing and predicting dangerousness. Empirical studies have demonstrated that it is not possible to predict dangerousness based on psychological assessment alone, although progress is being made (Salekin, Rogers, & Sewell, 1996). Because psychologists and psychiatrists claim to be able to predict other things, such as the course of a mental disorder, the public expects them to predict dangerousness and becomes angry when they fail to do so. The best predictor of dangerousness is past dangerous acts, yet the police and prisons are not usually held liable when they release dangerous individuals without warning the public. Other critics of these court rulings argue that any breach of confidentiality threatens the therapeutic process and that dangerous people will be deterred from seeking the treatment they need, thus increasing the danger to the public.

One survey (Givelber, Bowers, & Blitch, 1985) found that *Tarasoff* had not greatly affected psychological practices. After all, dangerous clients are fairly rare. However, such court rulings demonstrate how the mental health professions and society are still in the process of working out the ethical obligations of therapists.

The ethical obligations of therapists with suicidal clients are not clear-cut. *Tarasoff* and the ethical obligation to prevent suicide would appear to indicate that confidentiality may be broken when a client expresses suicidal intentions. Family members or close friends (if there are no family members nearby) should be informed so that they can provide extra support to the client and be alert to indications of suicidal behavior. The suicidal client should be informed of the therapist's intention to so inform others. Some argue that breaking confidentiality may heighten the possibility of suicide by reducing the effectiveness of therapy or making the client less trusting of the therapist. Others respond that preventing the suicide takes precedence over all other considerations.

Informed Consent

The appropriate use of **informed consent** in psychology has been debated. It is argued that people cannot really consent to something unless they have been fully informed as to exactly what they are consenting to. It is well established that patients submitting to a medical procedure must be fully informed of what is to be done and all the possible side effects before they consent to it. Psychologists have worked toward developing a good informed consent procedure for psychotherapy. Most agree that before clients consent to psychotherapy, they should be informed of the limits of confidentiality, how much it will cost, their rights as clients, and the qualifications and competence of the therapist. Some psychologists believe that clients should also be informed of the type of therapy being offered, including a brief description of what is expected of the client and what the therapist will do. Some state that this should include the possible risks and benefits of therapy. Some believe that clients should be told how likely the form of therapy is to work (based on empirical studies of similar cases) and how long it will take to work. Everyone seems to agree that the process of informed consent must be documented.

One important aspect of informed consent includes telling clients of the limits of confidentiality. Therapists who do not inform clients of the limits and who later, because of *Tarasoff,* must disclose a client's dangerous intentions are liable to be sued for malpractice (if they don't break confidentiality, of course, they are liable to be sued for negligence). However, it may be frightening to clients to hear right away that confidentiality does not hold if they become homicidal or suicidal, or it may lead them to be distrustful of the therapist. A full disclosure of the limits of confidentiality may deter the very people who need therapy from obtaining it. Some recommend making informed consent an ongoing process and raising the limits of confidentiality after two or three meetings when some degree of trust has been established. These issues have not been resolved, so informed consent procedures for psychotherapy still vary greatly from one therapist or agency to another.

LEGAL ISSUES

Professional psychology becomes embroiled in legal issues in several ways. First, legislation is passed that directly or indirectly affects the practice of psychology. For example, licensing laws directly address the profession, and a variety of laws regulating health care affect professional practice. Second, psychologists may be sued for malpractice, and court decisions in such lawsuits affect the profession. The example of the *Tarasoff* court decision has already been discussed. Psychologists may also be involved in legal issues as expert witnesses and forensic psychologists, but we will not discuss these examples.

Licensing of Professional Psychologists

Licensing and certification of psychologists and other therapists were established amid controversy in the 1950s and 1960s, as noted in Chapter 1. Both the desire to protect the public from untrained and incompetent practitioners and the need to establish an independent professional identity prompted organized psychology to pressure state legislatures to pass laws to license psychologists.

A *license* is issued by a state to professionals who have demonstrated competence in their field by academic achievement and by passing certain kinds of tests or requirements set by the licensing board. The license is supposed to protect the public by ensuring that only qualified and competent persons may offer their services to the public. *Certification* is generally seen as a weaker form of control than licensure. The state merely certifies that the professional has completed the education or experience requirements for that profession. The certificate does not imply competence, while the license supposedly does. *Registration* of therapists is the minimum way to regulate the mental health professions, in that therapists merely inform the state that they are practicing. In California, for example, psychological assistants and psychologists who are not yet licensed must register with the state.

Sunset Legislation   The practice of licensing psychologists and other therapists came under attack in the 1970s as failing to protect the public and merely serving a guild function to protect the professions. Critics argued that licensing keeps the cost of psychological services high by limiting the number of practitioners and reducing competition. Some states threatened to pass "sunset laws" that would abolish licensing boards automatically every five years unless they were evaluated and specifically reenacted. In the late 1970s in Alaska, Florida, and South Dakota, the practice of psychology was unlicensed and unregulated for a period of time. The APA and state psychological organizations lobbied these states, and psychology was once again regulated in all states. However, with the movement in the 1990s to cut government, sunset legislation was reintroduced in several states and passed in California in 1994. It can be seen from these events that the professional status of psychology may still be tenuous, for no one has ever seriously suggested abolishing the licensing of physicians.

National Register of Health Service Providers in Psychology   The National Register was established in the 1970s partly in response to sunset legislation. If licensing were abolished, membership in the National Register could substitute. The National Register also serves as a guide to health care companies as to who is a licensed psychologist, that is, whose fees to pay.

Health Care Regulation

Health care companies and government regulation of them are important factors in determining the nature of psychology as a profession (see Box 18.1). What types of disorders are covered by health insurance, what types of therapy health companies will pay for, how many sessions are covered, and what types of therapists will be reimbursed are issues that have had a tremendous impact on all the mental health professions. To counter the control of health care corporations, consumers and mental health professionals have both brought lawsuits against the companies and lobbied for legislation to regulate them.

Psychologists struggled for years to force health insurance programs to cover or reimburse their fees. They argued that because there is no evidence that psychiatrists are any more effective than psychologists (see Chapter 15 for this research), the policy of insurers to cover only the fees of medical doctors constituted illegal restraint of trade. This issue was supposed to have been settled in the case of the "Virginia Blues." For years, Blue Cross and Blue Shield of Virginia required psychologists to bill for services through a physician. Assisted by the APA, the Virginia Academy of Clinical Psychologists brought an antitrust suit against the insurance company in 1978, and won on appeal in 1984.

Many states passed **freedom of choice (FOC)** legislation as a result of lobbying by both consumer groups and mental health professionals. FOC laws are supposed to guarantee patients the right to choose their own therapists by requiring health insurance programs to provide equal coverage of psychotherapy services by psychologists and psychiatrists (and sometimes social workers and other therapists as well). These laws were supposed to reduce consumer costs by increasing competition. However, under managed care, as discussed below, this point may be moot.

Legal threats to the practice of psychology appear in unexpected places, as seen in the example of ERISA, the Employee Retirement Income Security Act (1980). This federal act was designed to improve all employee benefits, but it did not require health insurance to cover mental health benefits or to provide employees freedom of choice of doctors, contrary to most state laws. Chrysler Corporation announced in late 1984 that it would no longer pay for the services of a psychologist for any of its employees nationwide, citing ERISA as the reason. However, in 1985, the U.S. Supreme Court ruled against Chrysler.

These issues are far from settled, however, because of constant changes in the health care system. The legislative and court battles of previous decades may now be replayed in relation to corporate systems of health care and proposed government controls on them. For example, in 1996 and 1997, the federal government attempted to pass laws mandating equal coverage of mental and physical disorders, as well as minimum maternity stays and other requirements. The process of corporations regulating health care and the government then regulating the corporations will remain of extreme interest to professional psychologists.

Malpractice

Even the best therapists are human, and humans make mistakes. Therapists carry malpractice insurance so that if they make a mistake, the victims of that mistake will be adequately compensated for the harm they have suffered. Malpractice insurance also protects clients if therapists knowingly do something wrong, such as practicing outside of their area of competence. In general, malpractice of therapists is difficult to prove, partly because there may be disagreement as to what constitutes "good

B O X   1 8 . 1

A Brief History of Health Care in the U.S.

The way health care is delivered in the United States has changed dramatically over the last two centuries. In the eighteenth century, health care was a matter of informal cooperation between family and community members. If someone in the community became known as good at delivering babies, pulling teeth, setting broken limbs, or whatever, then that person was consulted when the need arose. Payment, if any, was in the form of goods or returned favors, and the person performing the health service did not earn his or her living that way.

By the middle of the nineteenth century, sufficient numbers of individuals earned their living providing healing services that an identifiable profession of physicians developed, and the American Medical Association was formed in order to establish an identity and formal qualifications for the profession of medicine in the United States. By the turn of the century, other types of healers, such as community members and midwives, were almost eliminated. Physicians established and owned hospitals and clinics, which also employed doctors, and many were in private practice or partnerships. Most physicians charged a fee for each visit or service they performed, and this fee-for-service method of payment financed the system of health care delivery until about the middle of this century.

By the 1950s, several factors combined to make continuing the fee-for-service system of payment for health care almost economically impossible. Population increases and medical technology advances increased both costs and demand dramatically. In the United States, physicians responded by forming health insurance companies, and business followed suit. Health insurance spreads the costs of the health care delivery system more evenly thoughout the population, because all those covered by the insurance pay directly or indirectly for the system, but only a few people use it a great deal. With insurance, the health care system is financed in a way that is similar to taxation (everyone pays something), but since physicians and corporations own the insurance companies, they control the health care delivery system rather than consumers or citizens. Health insurance basically preserved the fee-for-service system of independent practitioners for another 40 years by making its cost bearable by spreading it out among many people.

In the 1990s, the U.S. health care delivery system underwent another revolutionary change, which some have called the industrialization of medicine. Currently, for-profit corporations are developing and marketing many types of health care systems and organizations to replace the independent practitioners supported by health insurance payments. It seems likely that by the end of this century, control of the U.S. health

BOX 18.1 (continued)

care system will shift from physicians and insurance companies to corporations, from fee-for-service payments to systems of managed care run for corporate profit.

The "alphabet soup" of current health care systems includes the health maintenance organization (HMO), the preferred provider organization (PPO), the independent practitioner association (IPA), the employee assistance program (EAP), the consumer health alliance (CHA), and others. Health care professionals join together to form HMOs as corporations offering complete health care to patients who pay monthly or annual fees to remain members of the HMO. Theoretically, HMOs should stress prevention and health maintenance over acute care after health has deteriorated, because they make more money if their members stay well. PPOs and IPAs are similar. Large corporations and businesses form EAPs or contract out for services to offer disturbed employees therapy at the place of employment, so they will become less disturbed and more productive, thus saving the company the costs of firing, hiring, and training a new employee. As a regional group of citizens, a consumer health alliance acts like a buying club to purchase health services at a negotiated (lower) price and to distribute them to members.

Health care is the third largest industry in the United States, and some psychologists are arguing that psychology should be part of it, as well as physicians and corporations. Furthermore, they contend that the mental health professions must drastically change the way they operate, or they will end up the poorly paid employees of large corporations. They must create new services and market them aggressively. For example, clinical psychologists could form their own special organizations to market specific services, such as stop-smoking clinics, and they could market them to individuals, HMOs, and corporations. They could move more persuasively into the field of health psychology and emphasize wellness, prevention, and social action. Psychologists could move aggressively into medicine's traditional territory, for some believe that clinical psychologists are competent to prescribe medication for psychological disorders (DeLeon, 1986).

There is enough business to go around. The need for care of the physically ill and mentally disordered is universal to all times and cultures. What is less clear is which professions will provide the needed services and who will control the institutions that profit by their delivery. Only by carefully attending to the changes in the health care system and responding promptly and creatively to them will psychology remain a viable, if very different profession.

practice" and partly because malpractice suits come down to the word of a supposedly mentally disturbed patient against that of a professional therapist.

In 1985, the malpractice insurance carriers for both the American Psychiatric Association and the American Psychological Association announced that they would not cover therapists who had sexual relations with their clients. Some people saw this announcement as progress, in that the insurance companies seemed to be taking a strong stand against therapist-client sexual relations. However, others saw it as a sexist way for the insurance companies to cut costs at the expense of victims. The most frequent type of malpractice lawsuit against therapists involves a complaint of sexual abuse brought by a female client against a male therapist. Certainly, a therapist's having sex with a client is malpractice—it is unethical, it is a mistake, it harms the client. Yet the insurance companies singled out this particular type of malpractice as not covered. Under this regulation, if a client sues a therapist over the malpractice of sexual contact and if the therapist is found not guilty, then the insurance companies will pay the legal expenses of defending the case. If, however, the therapist is found guilty (did have sex with the client, did harm the client), then the companies will not pay the therapist's legal fees or compensate the victim! This regulation seems to defeat the purpose of malpractice insurance.

PROFESSIONAL ISSUES

This section examines issues that are important to psychology as a profession that offers helping services to the public, issues relevant to other helping professions as well. The present and future practice of professional psychology reflects its past efforts to define itself as an independent profession in the face of opposition and competition from medicine, psychiatry, and other groups. Past controversies over ethical and legal issues, discussed above, and the definition and diagnosis of mental disorder, discussed below, mask economic and political struggles over professional territory and the right to practice. Often, these conflicts are couched in "scientific" terms or posed as efforts to "protect clients" in order to avoid facing the underlying political issues of territoriality. Currently, professional psychologists as well as physicians and all health workers are struggling to define their fields within the constantly changing U.S. health care delivery system. (See Box 18.1)

At present the majority of professional psychologists work in private practice or in separate departments of psychology within mental health institutions. They have achieved recognition from the public as independent professionals, and this status is at present substantiated in the law. However, professional psychology's status as an independent mental health profession is historically recent and remains tenuous.

Competition with Medicine

Until World War II, only psychiatrists were allowed to perform psychotherapy with adults. In spite of the pressure of the need for therapists to treat the returning veterans, the American Medical Association continued into the 1950s to claim that psychotherapy was a medical procedure to be done only by medical doctors. The increased number of trained clinical psychologists and the increased funding for mental health in the 1960s allowed clinical psychology to establish itself as an independent profession. However, in recent years competition for mental health business has increased, and there have been several attempts once again to constrain the practice of clinical psychology and other mental health professions.

As we pointed out in Chapter 1, in actual practice, psychologists and psychiatrists frequently cooperate and work well together in private practice and in hospitals and mental health agencies. Many psychologists and psychiatrists call for an end to the competition and point out that the two professions need each other, that their respective expertises are complementary (Berg, 1986), and that the resources spent on competition would be better spent on a cooperative approach to the mental health problems facing our society (Cattell, 1983).

Chapter 1 noted that psychoanalytic training used to require a medical degree. Psychologists argued that this requirement was unnecessary except for the purpose of restricting who may become psychoanalysts, and they sued certain psychoanalytic institutes over this requirement as constituting restraint of trade, that is, restraint of their right to practice their profession. While psychologists (and social workers) won the lawsuits, they still have great difficulty being accepted for psychoanalytic training.

Relations between psychology and medicine remain uneasy. At its annual meeting in 1984, the AMA passed a resolution in which it pledged "to fight incursions of nurse midwives, podiatrists, nurse practitioners, physician's assistants, psychologists, nurse anesthetists, and optometrists into medical practice via prescribing privileges, independent practice, mandated third-party reimbursement or other expansion of their scope of practice" (AMA, 1984, p. 79). The AMA agreed to provide staff to help state medical societies resist new legislation that expanded the independent practice of psychologists and others and also to support amendments to current law in order to restrict that expansion. One article concerned about psychiatry's future alleged that one of the factors threatening the existence of psychiatry is "dominance of psychotherapy by nonmedical psychotherapists" (Lesse, 1986). With its tremendous economic resources, the AMA may succeed in reversing some of the gains psychology and others have made as independent professions.

Defining and "Diagnosing" Mental Disorders

Originally an attempt to reduce the stigma of mental disorder (it seemed better to be ill than wicked or possessed), the definition of psychological disorders as "mental illness" can also be viewed as a way to establish professional territoriality. If psychological problems are viewed as biological illnesses, then they should be treated by medical doctors in clinics and hospitals with medication and prescribed treatments. By this definition, psychologists are not qualified to treat the mentally ill. However, if mental disorders are defined as psychological or behavioral in nature, then psychologists and other therapists would be qualified to treat them. The problem, of course, is that mental disorders are both physical and psychological.

The Biological Model   The view that the cause of mental illness is to be found in a disorder of the physical body is an old one, but it showed a resurgence in the 1980s as the model of choice in psychiatry. The biological view represents a challenge to professional psychology, which has long emphasized psychological, familial, and social causes of disorder. The challenge is not only to psychology's theoretical stance, but also to its right and competence to treat psychological problems.

A large number of drugs have been found to modify disordered thoughts, feelings, and behaviors. It is not certain how these drugs work, but they have been observed to have varied benefits, such as reducing anxiety, depression, or thought disorder, as well as some negative side effects. Although the ideal is to be able to prescribe a specific drug for a specific symptom in specific types of individuals, at present, such precision is not possible. Medication has been demonstrated to bring about dramatic improvements in many cases, but some patients object to its use or refuse to take it because of side effects, and some professionals believe drugs can be misused to oversedate and control difficult patients.

Another biologically based treatment, electroconvulsive shock therapy (ECT), was found to be useful in the treatment of severe depression. It was rarely used for many years after the development of antidepressant medication, partly because it resulted in injuries and some degree of brain impairment, but it is apparently regaining some degree of popularity. The technology has improved so that injuries are much less likely, and proponents argue that it works much more quickly than antidepressants and that in some resistant cases it is more effective. Critics might argue that it is still barbaric to administer shocks to the brain just because it is quicker and cheaper than protecting someone until a combination of antidepressants and intensive psychotherapy can begin to work.

Biologically based therapies have been the domain of psychiatry, but as psychophysiological research on the brain and behavior advances, psychologists may also include biological interventions in their treatment plans. Matarazzo (1992) believes that intellectual and personality assessment will also become biologically based in the near future. It may be that a holistic model emphasizing the unity of biological and psychological processes can be embraced by both psychology and psychiatry. Under this model, interventions can be made through either psychological or biological points, with similar effectiveness, since mind and body are one. The validity of this possibility is supported by research that demonstrated that successful behavioral or drug treatment of obsessive-compulsive disorder brought about similar changes in brain functioning (Baxter et al., 1992).

DSM-IV The *Diagnostic and Statistics Manual of Mental Disorders* was largely written by medical doctors, although other mental health professionals were consulted for later revisions. In spite of its careful avoidance of the term *mental illness,* the words *diagnosis, prognosis, illness,* and *disease* appear throughout the DSM-IV, reflecting its medical assumptions. Since third-party payers and managed care providers require DSM diagnoses, all mental health professionals must use it, reinforcing the medical definitions of psychological disorders.

Professional Competence

As part of their attempt to attain professional parity with psychiatry, clinical psychology determined that the Ph.D. degree was a necessary part of training, as were so many hours of supervised practice. In fact, the Ph.D. in clinical psychology may take more years to complete than medical school, and the amount of training in treatment and psychopathology is probably greater than that for psychiatrists. Nevertheless, psychiatry still argues that psychologists are not competent to treat certain groups of people, because they are not trained in medicine and pharmacology.

Certification   Certification in specific skills is offered by many training programs. Different from state certification, these certificates are available in alcoholism counseling, hypnotherapy, hospital practice, marriage counseling, and other proficiency areas. Some consumers and health care companies are demanding certification of specialized therapists, and some psychologists have complained that certificates have become more important than doctoral degrees in psychology. Because of the demand for certification, the APA began offering certificates itself in 1992 as part of its continuing education programs in order to prevent control of certification from devolving to other groups. In 1995, the APA College of Professional Psychology was established to serve as a certificate granting body. The first proficiency certificate the College offered was in the treatment of alcohol and other psychoactive substance use disorders. In the future, psychologists may find they need both a license and certification in a proficiency or specialty.

Continuing Education   Ethical therapists maintain their competence and keep their skills up to date by taking continuing education courses. Some believe that specific continuing education should be required by law for the maintenance of the license. For example, California requires all therapists to take courses in child abuse, human sexuality, and alcohol and drug abuse, as well as 18 hours of approved continuing education per year in order to maintain their licenses.

Hospital Privileges

Until 1984, only psychiatrists and medical doctors were allowed hospital privileges and the right to hospitalize their clients. The Joint Commission on Accreditation of Hospitals (JCAH) accredited only hospitals that allowed only psychiatrists and medical doctors to admit their private patients and to treat hospitalized patients. Due to pressure in the form of a lawsuit brought by the psychological community (*Capp* v. *Rank*), in 1984, the JCAH agreed to accredit hospitals that extend hospital privileges to licensed psychologists, although physicians would still determine patient care. However, it was entirely up to individual hospitals whether to include psychologists, and since hospitals are governed almost exclusively by medical doctors, few hospitals extended staff privileges to psychologists.

This situation may change, since states are beginning to pass laws that require hospitals to accept applications for hospital privileges from psychologists. For example, as of 1997, the state of California requires state-owned and state-operated hospitals to accept psychologists on staff. However, in most states, psychologists may not commit patients to mental hospitals or psychiatric wards, whether they can admit them or not.

Prescription Privileges

Because some believe that biologically based interventions or a combination psychobiological model is the wave of the future, psychologists have been considering trying to gain a new legal right, that of prescribing medication, since about 1985. They are discussing limited prescription writing privileges, and proposed laws and training programs are already under consideration in several states. There is precedent for nonphysician prescription privileges, in that nurse practitioners may prescribe medication in many states and psychologists may prescribe medication in the Indian Health Service. The evidence is that nonphysicians can be trained to prescribe medication competently (DeLeon, Fox, & Graham, 1991).

Arguments in favor of prescription privileges for psychologists include enhancing their ability to address certain societal needs, such as excessive medication of the elderly, quality care for the chronically mentally ill, and rural and other underserved populations. Psychologists need prescription privileges because of their increasing identification as practitioners in a health discipline and to increase the breadth of available treatment options. Arguments against prescription privileges include a divisive, potentially expensive legal battle that may alienate consumers. Furthermore, some believe that what distinguishes psychologists is their ability to treat problems without "resorting" to medication. They argue that prescription privileges would buy into and reinforce biological and medical views of mental illness.

It seems clear that psychologists *can* be trained to prescribe medication and that they are perfectly capable of doing so competently and to the benefit of patients. Many psychologists already have extensive knowledge of psychopharmacology because of their work experience. Whether psychologists gain this right will depend on other factors, such as territoriality and competition with psychiatry. It is even possible that in the future, institutions may prefer to contract with psychologists to dispense medication for psychological disorders rather than with the more expensive psychiatrists.

Treatment Manuals and Empirically Validated Treatments

The development of treatment manuals and the APA Task Force on Empirically Validated Treatments (EVTs) were described in Chapter 15. Many see the reduction of psychotherapy to standardized methods that can be be listed in a manual as part of the growing power of the medical model. Manuals force the use of diagnosis in order to know which manual to use. Therapy comes to resemble how a physician proceeds. The client comes in and the doctor conducts an intake interview to gather information for the purpose of making an accurate diagnosis of the person's problems. Then, based on that diagnosis, a treatment plan is taken from a manual to alleviate this client's specific symptoms. The treatment is then applied to the client. Such treatments are highly symptom-focused and do not deal with issues of meaning in an individual's life. For example, anxiety problems are seen as reflecting problems of internal overattention to physiological signals, and clients are taught to use relaxation when they notice these internal signals, rather than addressing whether this anxiety has any meaning in terms of how they are conducting their lives.

As discussed in Chapter 15, many object to this model and the use of treatment manuals. First, there is the issue of the reliability and validity of diagnosis, especially diagnosis based on DSM. Diagnoses may not be of much value in deciding what to do with a unique individual in a unique social context. Second, there is a body of research that indicates that these types of treatments do not work for everyone and that a substantial number of people are helped only by long-term, exploratory psychotherapy (Roth & Fonagy, 1996). Third, some people desire traditional psychotherapy. We know of a head of a major Health Maintenance Organization who paid out of pocket for exploratory humanistic therapy rather than try any of the therapies in the HMO. Research should be directed to determining the types of people for whom long-term and intensive psychotherapy services are indicated, in addition to developing treatment manuals for specific symptoms.

In terms of professional psychology, the advent of treatment manuals has several implications. It is possible that there will be a major split in the profession. Some may remain involved in the implementation of the manualized approach, working within the changes in the health care system brought about by corporate control of it, as discussed in the next section. Others may choose to practice outside the health care establishment so they can practice the kinds of therapy they and some clients prefer (O'Hara & Anderson, 1991). One famous therapist, for instance, has begun to call himself a "human development consultant" and to accept only fee-for-service payments from clients rather than be paid by insurance or managed care companies. Because therapists who work outside the health care establishment may not use manuals or EVTs for DSM disorders, some psychologists who favor the EVT approach have suggested that those who do not could be subject to malpractice suits (Austad, 1996). However, as long as there are standards of practice developed by a professional body for a particular way of practicing, it is not likely that a practitioner would be accused of malpractice. There are now movements to develop treatment guidelines for the responsible and professional provision of exploratory-oriented therapies, such as Guidelines for the Practice of Humanistic Psychotherapy (1997).

PSYCHOLOGY AND CORPORATE CONTROL OF THE HEALTH CARE SYSTEM

A profound threat to psychology as an independent profession (and to medicine and all the mental health professions) has been the shift in the U.S. health care system to control by corporations (see Box 18.1 for the history). In the United States today few people pay directly for their own medical care, only the very poor or the very rich. By 1990, about 85% of all American health care (DeLeon, VandenBos, & Kraut, 1984; Flanigan, 1991) was covered by some form of government insurance, private insurance, health maintenance organizations, or other corporate health care systems. Thus, corporate-owned health care systems and insurance companies wield tremendous power in determining the nature of health care in the United States and thus, the practice of the mental health professions. Furthermore, the failure of the U.S. government to reform the health care system in the early 1990s solidified corporate power over the system.

The potential for conflict between the interests of for-profit corporations and those of consumers and citizens is great. Corporations are interested in profits, and not all forms of health care are profitable, but may still be needed. It is argued that the corporate health care system is not responsive to the special characteristics of people needing psychological help or to the mental health professions, other than psychiatry with its emphasis on hospitalization, biological causes, and drug treatments (Kiesler, 1992). The changes in the health care delivery system may threaten the hard-won gains of psychology to be recognized as an independent profession.

Accountability and Peer Review

Corporations and states demand accountability from their health service providers. As a result of increasing costs, procedures to make the mental health professions more accountable for their claims and services have been introduced into all health care delivery systems. In order to continue to receive funding, providers of psychotherapy must now demonstrate that their services accomplish what they claim.

Peer review was seen as a way for clinical psychology to become accountable while retaining the professional independence to judge its own performance. Peer review is the examination of an individual psychologist's cases by other psychologists to see if the treatment provided is appropriate, competent, and necessary. It is rather like supervision, and, done correctly, it should help therapists with their difficult cases. Many mental health agencies instituted their own peer review programs in the 1970s before it was required by their funding sources. Now, many health care companies require peer review of certain cases before they pay for the costs of the treatment, and some require it of all cases after as few as four to ten sessions.

Cost-Effectiveness

Along with general accountability, there have been increased demands that psychology demonstrate that its services are cost-effective, that its services or solutions to problems both work *and* cost less than other methods of treatment or doing nothing. Many studies demonstrate that psychological services can be very cost-effective. Providing certain patients with psychotherapy can reduce overall health costs by decreasing utilization of other, more expensive medical services. Alcoholism treatment programs save companies more money than they cost by reducing lost workdays and the costs of training new employees. Relatively inexpensive stop-smoking programs save enormous amounts of money that would otherwise be spent on expensive cancer treatments or wasted on lost workdays and reduced productivity due to illness. People must be convinced that psychotherapy is worth it. Forceful and persuasive education and marketing is needed, including empirical demonstrations of cost savings.

On the other hand, an emphasis on cost-effectiveness may cause psychology and society at large to lose touch with other worthwhile goals. For example, a study by O'Farrell et al. (1996) compared the cost-benefit of behavioral marital therapy with or without 15 additional relapse prevention sessions in the treatment of alcoholism. For both treatments, the cost savings in reduced health and legal system utilization were greater than the costs of delivering the therapy. Adding the relapse prevention sessions led to less drinking and better marital adjustment than behavioral marital therapy without them, but it did not lead to greater cost savings. Nevertheless, reduced drinking and improved marital adjustment are worthwhile goals, whether we can put a monetary value on them or not. It is important for psychology to persuade the public that cost-effectiveness is not the only measure of the value of psychological services.

Cost-Cutting and Rationing

In order to cut costs, corporations have turned to "managed care," a system that essentially restricts the way employees may utilize medical services. By such strategies as reimbursing fees of only certain low-cost physicians, contracting for specific services, and negotiating the price, corporations both contain costs and ration health care. In addition, state governments have been trying to cut public health costs for years. Whether to increase corporate profit or to reduce state spending, managing and rationing health care to reduce costs affects everyone, including psychology and the mental health professions.

Another strategy for containing costs, started by Medicare and some prepaid medical plans, is the use of prospective payment systems (PPS) and diagnosis-related groups (DRGs). Hospitals and health care professionals are paid a flat fee based on the average cost of care for a patient's diagnosis, whether that actual patient's case is treated quickly or develops complications. If treatment costs are less than the set fee, the savings go to the provider as profit, but if the costs are more, then the provider takes the loss. It is especially difficult to predict the course of a mental disorder, and the use of DRGs may lead to inappropriate discharge of patients and financial risks to those who treat more severe cases. As of 1996, psychology and psychiatry had successfully fought the imposition of PPS and DRGs in the mental health area, because, they argued, it is so difficult to predict what a specific individual will need. However, a challenge for psychologists now and in the future will be to adapt to these changes in the health care system and to demonstrate that their services save money by enhancing mental and physical health (Cummings, 1986).

Another way to cut costs is to eliminate coverage for certain types of practitioners or certain types of treatment. In fact, health care corporations may begin to *demand* certain kinds of treatment, such as using only specific treatment manuals. Many consider this outcome to be one of the dangers of the APA Task Force on Empirically Validated Treatments, as discussed above and in Chapter 15.

The increased unwillingness of taxpayers to fund mental health programs and the ever-present desire of managed care companies to increase profits and cut costs will probably mean that demonstrating and convincing the public of the importance and cost-effectiveness of psychological services will be essential to the survival of professional psychology. Working within this framework may be based on the assumption that resources are always going to be limited and we must learn how to ration them, rather than working to direct and increase resources to mental health. All of this sounds terribly money grubbing. Whatever happened to helping people in distress, to the sense of community responsibility for the less fortunate members of society, to the desire to enhance human functioning and improve our society? These American ideals can probably be elicited, especially if it is shown that it saves money to act on them.

THE PROFESSION AND SOCIETY

What is the relation between psychology and society at large? What should that relation be? Psychologists and other therapists are citizens and members of their society, and their professions exist in a certain historical and social context. Clinical psychology came into being in the United States at a time when science and individualism were highly valued. Should professional psychology try to remain neutral, accept society as it exists, encourage society to change, or work actively to bring about social change? If being an agent of change is an acceptable role, what social changes should be worked toward?

Clinical psychology is in the business of changing people, yet it is often accused of preserving the status quo. Like any established profession or interest group, it tends to resist change and to see its self-interest in keeping the advantages it has. If psychologists are comfortable in private practice, they will resist the drastic changes in the health care system. If professionals make their living by "treating" certain types of people, they will resist anything that redefines those people or reduces their numbers (i.e., prevention). And, like any science, psychology must view the world through its own cultural values.

Change Versus Adjustment

Continuing controversy occurs over the issue of whether people should change to adjust to society or society should change to fit the needs of individuals. Many critics have argued that the goal of most psychotherapy is to make people fit into what exists, so they don't rock the boat. We even refer to how "adjusted" people are. These critics contend that it is the situation (the way society is organized) that is the problem, not the "maladjusted" individuals (Albee, 1996). If society is organized in an unhealthy or inhumane way, then people will naturally become disturbed. It is both immoral and futile to help these people adjust without changing the conditions that lead to maladjustment. Otherwise, helping people "adjust" is just another way of shoring up the status quo.

Many writers have recognized the social control functions of the mental health professions and criticized them for serving as the "soft police." Some behaviors have been defined differently over the years, so that different social control agents have been brought to bear on them. Excessive drinking behavior was once a sin, railed against by preachers and temperance organizations. Then for a few years it was a crime, and excessive drinkers were arrested and imprisoned. Recently, excessive drinking behavior has become a disease, treated by doctors and therapeutic programs. In this sense, alcoholism doctors and counselors are now the soft police—the social control agents for excessive drinking behavior.

Feminist critics regard much of the practice of psychotherapy as incorporating the sexism and stereotypes of the current society. Mostly male therapists try to get mostly female clients to "adjust" to their gender role, their stereotype, their oppression. A woman who dislikes the female role and its lack of power may not be suffering from "penis envy" or a gender identity disturbance. She may simply be realistic about her role in society. By helping women "adjust" to unjust conditions, therapists are both preserving the status quo and perpetuating the oppression of women. Psychology has been responsive to these criticisms, for the American Psychological Association has established guidelines for therapy with women that encourage therapists to locate the cause of women's distress in their situation, not as something wrong with them (see Box 17.1). The same principles would apply to those treating other oppressed groups, such as gays and lesbians and certain racial and ethnic groups.

Some see a growing tendency for our society to "medicalize" intractable social problems such as drug abuse. Since physicians and therapists are not likely to resist new categories of patients and potential income, this trend will probably continue. Medicalization of social problems is also supported by citizens and taxpayers, because it may be a way to avoid the harder task of dealing with the conflicting values and socioeconomic factors that underlie these problems and to avoid the necessity for difficult social change.

Misuses of Mental Health Concepts

The most widely criticized misuse of mental health concepts is the so-called insanity defense. John Hinckley's attempt to assassinate President Reagan and his subsequent acquittal due to insanity enraged many people and brought the issue to the public's attention. Arguing against the insanity defense for decades, Szasz (1961) documented that the insanity defense once resulted in miscarriages of justice in the sense that those being adjudged "innocent by reason of insanity" served longer periods of incarceration in mental hospitals than they would have if sentenced to prison (this is no longer the case since prison sentences were lengthened during the 1980s). Szasz argued that since "mental illness" is a myth and, therefore, professionals often disagree on whether a defendant was insane at the time of the offense, trials should be conducted solely on the basis of whether the person committed the alleged criminal act or not. Defenders of the insanity defense contend that abolishing it would also result in grave injustice, for each case must be assessed individually and the accused's state of mind, intentions, and capability of making rational decisions must be taken into account.

Other misuses of mental health concepts are not as apparent, although certainly just as debatable, as the insanity defense. Two examples come to mind. Once, a stress management program for blue-collar workers was being advertised in Oakland. The billboard shouted "Stress at work? Powerlessness is bad for your health." Was this an innovative program showing workers how to organize themselves to gain power at work? No, it was a call for workers to seek counseling. Through stress management, workers would be taught to adjust to aversive working conditions, rather than organizing and demanding that their working conditions be improved (this criticism holds for stress management programs for executives as well). No longer do employers and corporations have to worry about providing appropriate working conditions—they just teach the workers (and the executives) to adjust. The source of employee distress is placed in the employee, not on the way business and work are currently organized.

Our second example has to do with a study once funded by the Department of Energy. The DOE paid a psychiatrist to determine the causes and cures of "nuclear phobia." Several psychologists attacked this study because of its methodological flaws and because of its obvious pronuclear bias. The critics claimed the study was a political use of mental illness jargon to label concerned citizens as having a phobia. Concerned citizens who disagree with the government's pronuclear energy stand and who may engage in political activities against nuclear power and nuclear weapons are just "crazy"—they've got "nuclear phobia"! Potentially, the DOE could next fund a study to "cure" nuclear phobia. Psychological methods could be used to manipulate the public for pronuclear purposes under the guise of "treating" a "mental illness." Regardless of the merits of nuclear power, most people would agree that introducing a "mental disorder" such as "nuclear phobia" into the controversy confuses the issue and renders reasonable discussion difficult. And many would agree that it is a misuse of mental health concepts.

It is not only the politically conservative who use mental health concepts to further political aims. Some liberal therapists used to argue that all anxiety and mental disorders were due to the ever-present threat of nuclear war and that the only way to treat them was to eliminate that threat. The point we are trying to make is that in our present society, social values get "medicalized." People can then argue about the nature of and payment for "treatment," rather than confronting fundamental differences in values. Psychology must guard against misuse of its concepts while still engaging itself in the solution of our social problems.

Psychological Intervention in Social Problems

How can professional psychology address social problems? In the past, psychology has lobbied for laws, such as the passage of licensing laws and laws regulating health care businesses. In addition, psychology has often used its research findings to try to affect social policy, as when psychologists testify in Congress about child development and many other areas of research that relate to proposed legislation. The APA files "friend of the court" briefings in legal cases that can be clarified by psychological research findings, such as when the U.S. Supreme Court ruled on confidentiality between therapist and client. These same interventions will be useful in the future, and many psychologists urge the field to include strong public education campaigns whenever such issues arise in order to increase public understanding and gain public support.

Where do corporations and insurance companies get their money? Directly and indirectly from almost every citizen. Most health care in the United States is covered by some form of government or corporate health insurance. Taxpayers pay for government insurance. And taxpayers pay for the private insurance, too. They pay premiums or their employers pay premiums and pay them less (an indirect cost to the employee). Any people without health insurance utilize emergency rooms, which pass the costs on to their insured patients. So virtually every citizen pays for the health care system in the United States. However, in the United States, private companies provide this service rather than the citizens through their government, as in countries with "socialized medicine" such as Great Britain. Thus, the citizens have little power to determine how the health care system is run, and much of their health care money goes for profit. Decisions about the health care system, which affect all of us and which all of us pay for, are made by the corporations. It seems inevitable that health care must be rationed, but the question is who will make the difficult decisions.

It is possible that interested parties must intervene at the corporate level. Consumers and professionals alike have vested interests in the health care corporations, and they can lobby, vote as investors, work for legislative control, and persuade and educate in relation to them. The strength of psychology is its empirical basis, and a research focus on the ways to save money and increase profits by meeting human needs may be the best way to bring about needed social change.

THE FUTURE

Many social, economic, political, and demographic trends will affect the future of professional psychology. While predicting the future is always subject to uncertainty, broad patterns of change can already be discerned. The growing emphasis on cost containment and biological bases of disorder coupled with increased demand and need for psychological services mean that growth in psychological services will be in the areas of brief and short term therapy, specialities that combine psychology and biology such as neuropsychology and psychoimmunology, and self-help. Although control of health care has shifted to corporations and their systems of managed care, both consumers and professional providers must become active in trying to determine the future availability and types of psychological services in the United States.

One important trend is the decreased availability of government money to pay for training, research, and services in mental health. The tremendous deficit spending by the federal government in the 1980s coupled with constant demands for lower taxes guarantee reduced spending by government for mental health and other programs for decades to come. The power of the corporate world to determine the nature of both medical and psychological practice will increase. The potential for conflict between the goals of the corporate world and the goals of mental health professionals and consumers is great. However, it is possible that improving the quality of life for all Americans can be shown to contribute to profits, especially in the long run.

Other changes with implications for psychology are easily discerned from the daily news. The population of the United States is shifting. All ethnic groups are increasing their proportion of the population. The aged are also increasing their percentage of the population, and this trend will continue for some decades, since the baby boomers are hitting middle age. The toll of numerous problems, such as AIDS, alcohol and drug abuse, unemployment, and homelessness, must be addressed. The use of technology in all areas of life is increasing. Although no one seems certain of the direction, it is apparent that the socioeconomic organization of the United States is in the throes of profound change, shifting from industrial production to services and information. Such drastic social changes increase people's stress and, consequently, the demand for psychological, medical, and psychiatric services.

What does all of this augur? Traditional employment opportunities for psychologists in government-funded mental hospitals, mental health agencies, and private practice will decrease, and employment will be sought in business and industry and the new systems of health care delivery. To say that therapists should consider alternatives to traditional private practice and individual psychotherapy is an understatement. It is imperative that the mental health professions develop new roles and services. It is probably equally imperative that they empirically demonstrate the effectiveness and the cost-effectiveness of these new roles and services, and then learn to market them as well (Cummings, 1986).

Changes in Professional Practice

What changes can be expected in the practice of psychology? It is easy to guess that there will be increasing use of group therapy and brief psychotherapy. The demand for bilingual, including signing for the deaf, and multicultural therapists will increase. More specialists in aging, disability, and handicaps will be needed. With the increase in AIDS, experts in immunocompetence, death and dying, and grief counseling will be needed, too.

Already it is argued that therapy must become both more eclectic and more specific so as to determine which method to use with which disorder in what types of people (Lazarus, Beutler, & Norcross, 1992). When the empirical evidence allows us to determine exactly what to do with specific problems, then treatment manuals with specific directions on how to implement the therapy can be developed, as discussed above. Then it will be possible for therapy services to be delivered by minimally trained individuals. Psychologists may do the research, develop the manuals, and supervise the delivery of services, rather than treat clients themselves. Problems with this possibility were discussed above and in Chapter 15.

A survey of 75 prominent therapists (Norcross, Alford, & DeMichele, 1992) predicted that clinical interventions would change in the United States in the next 10 years in the direction of becoming more short term, present-centered, structured, and directive, with an increase in the use of self-change techniques, problem solving, homework assignments, communication skills, cognitive restructuring, and social skills training. The same survey predicted a decrease in long-term, psychodynamic, person-centered, humanistic, and existential therapies. On the other hand, Bugental and Bracke (1992) argued that the emphasis on short-term, problem-solving therapy will ultimately stimulate a demand for humanistic therapy that addresses issues of emptiness and lack of personal meaning. Undoubtedly, however, people will have to pay for therapy that addresses such spiritual needs themselves, but there may be private practice opportunities in helping people deal with their hunger for meaning and personal growth.

Many psychologists agree that psychology as a profession must give up its traditional role of treating psychologically disordered individuals. Not only are corporations and taxpayers disenchanted with that role, but it can also be said that clinical psychologists are wasting their behavioral and research skills in that role. Their skills would be of greater benefit to society if used in dramatically different contexts, including public education and social action. So let us turn to an examination of some of the new roles proposed for professional psychology.

Future Roles for Professional Psychologists

In order for psychology to move into new roles, training and education of psychologists must change, and new definitions of the competencies required of psychologists must be developed. An example of one obviously needed change in training is to shift the emphasis from learning individual psychotherapy to including brief therapy methods. Psychologists should also be learning to apply behavioral and psychological principles to a wide variety of problems and situations.

The emphasis on accountability and cost-effectiveness means that clinical psychologists interested in research may turn to evaluation research. They have been and will be involved in the assessment of the effectiveness of mental health and other programs. Private foundations and government agencies that grant money to groups to carry out various treatment programs demand that an evaluation research component be built into the program. Corporate health care systems also demand empirical demonstration of the effectiveness of treatments before they pay for them. Clinical psychologists are qualified with their research skills and clinical experience to conduct such evaluation studies.

George Albee (1968, 1970, 1982) has long argued that professional psychology should be working to put itself out of business by focusing on the prevention of psychological disorders. He believes psychologists should stop wasting their expertise providing inefficient and costly psychotherapy to a few individuals. Furthermore, prevention should include competence promotion and social equality for disadvantaged groups, not just the reduction of risk factors for mental disorders (Albee, 1996). Prevention has been demonstrated to be more cost-effective than treatment, and further studies on this point should be done (Reiss & Price, 1996). In addition, psychology should forcefully make the case for prevention to the public and the corporations. If the cost-effectiveness of prevention can be gotten across, then many new roles for psychologists would open up, including psychoeducation, community programs, and social action.

Part of prevention and "giving psychology away" may involve the increasing use of master's level therapists and nonprofessional counselors. The use of nonprofessional counselors increases the number of counselors available and decreases costs, in addition to providing counselors similar to the clients. Leaving individual therapy to nonprofessionals, professional psychologists may become involved in the provision of the training and supervision of the nonprofessional counselors.

Many psychologists urge their profession to use behavioral skills to treat expensive social problems. Many individual behaviors lead to problems that are costly to all of us. Often, these behaviors appear to be matters of individual choice and personal freedom, and the fact that they constitute social problems that cost us all lots of money is not obvious. People cannot be forced to alter these behaviors, but the application of psychological principles can help alter them without threatening individual freedom. AIDS and alcohol and drug abuse are examples of such social problems. Smoking is another. It is not just the individual smoker's business when he gets cancer, emphysema, or heart disease. Each and every one of us pays directly and indirectly for the expensive treatments for these diseases, which are largely preventable. As experts in behavior change, psychologists may be called on to help alter or prevent such "individualistic" behaviors.

Psychologists will be involved in innovations in the delivery of services, including electronic counseling and other uses of technology. Education and prevention may involve psychologists in all the mass media.

Psychology may move into the field of behavioral toxicology and environmental health science, including research, assessment, treatment, and prevention related to environmental hazards that affect behavior (Weiss, 1983). The environment is increasingly polluted with dangerous chemicals that affect health, the brain, and behavior, and psychologists can research the behavioral and neurological effects of toxins and develop methods of treating those effects. They are also capable of designing programs to educate the public about toxins or to modify the behavior of the polluters.

Family mediation is a growing field. Family mediators help divorcing families clarify their goals, develop a workable divorce agreement, and solve problems that arise after the divorce. The goal of family mediation is to reduce the child and adult casualties of a common social event, and psychologists have the needed skills in communication, family processes, contracting, and behavior modification.

Psychologists have a great deal to contribute to the social problem of crime and its victims. Since altering crime-causing social conditions like poverty and racism is both expensive and unlikely, Siegel (1983) has suggested that society and psychology shift their attention from crime to the victims. Treating and compensating the victims of crime may well be more humane and cost-effective than building more prisons and increasing the punishments for crime.

There are many other possible future roles for psychologists, depending on the direction the current changes in health care delivery take. In one possible scenario, psychologists (and physicians) end up the poorly paid employees of corporations, with little independence. A two-tiered system of health care may well develop, with cheap managed "care" for most people and private care for the rich. In this case, a few psychologists may still engage in private practice, as psychotherapists helping to provide meaning or perhaps as psychological personal trainers, such as "executive coaches" and the like. Either way, the need for an entreprenuerial attitude and clever marketing is obvious.

On the other hand, some (Diekstra & Jansen, 1988; VandenBos & DeLeon, 1988; Ewart, 1991; Galavotti et al., 1997; Resnick, 1997) argue that psychologists should strive for a bigger role in the new systems of health care delivery, even that of primary health care provider. The biopsychological model implies that behavioral interventions will be as effective as medicinal ones, and with prescription privileges, psychologists could easily be the first person ill people would like to see.

Although the possibilities for future roles for psychologists seem numerous, it is incumbent on psychologists to demonstrate that their methods of dealing with these social problems are cost-effective, humane, and good for society and to lobby politically for recognition and payment for their professional skills. Just as the profession successfully fought to achieve the right to practice in earlier decades, psychology will handle the corporatization of health care with negotiation, regulation, litigation, and even clever marketing. Marketing psychological skills to corporations may be preferable to the costly and potentially divisive process of political and legal action. By dropping their old roles and creatively developing new ones, psychologists will both improve society and enhance the prospects for the profession.

Employment Prospects in Psychology

Students who wish to pursue a career in professional psychology may be either overwhelmed or encouraged by what we have said about the future. In fact, the services provided by the mental health professions have been and always will be needed and valuable. At present, psychology is a fluid field in a rapidly changing society. The traditional advantage of clinical psychology for someone entering the field was its diversity. The psychologist could go into research, teach at colleges and universities, do private practice, or obtain employment in a variety of clinical settings. Professional psychology will increase in diversity and provide even more different career opportunities. However, it will probably become the student's responsibility to seek out a variety of education and training experiences. Graduate training has been slow to change in the past, and there is no reason to expect it to offer many new forms of training, especially since it is not clear where the field is heading. Students will have to seek out special education, supervisors, and training experiences on their own.

Students, as well as professional psychologists needing to expand their practice, should explore several options and develop a special skill. As we have already noted, therapy will emphasize short-term and problem-oriented approaches, clients will be increasingly diverse, services will be delivered in corporate health care systems, and aggressive marketing strategies may be necessary. Specialties that seem to be growing at present include neuropsychology, behavioral medicine, and treatment of AIDS and alcohol abuse. In addition, expertise in evaluation research, a second language, multicultural counseling, aging, and, of course, computers will enhance employment prospects. Grant writing, marketing, and business administration skills are also valuable. If prescription privileges are allowed psychologists, then training in psychopharmacology will be important.

Some psychologists argue that assessment will be a highly important skill in the future. Managed care may try to contain costs by designing specific interventions based on precise assessment. Matarazzo (1992) believes that both cognitive and personality assessment will become increasingly biologically based in the future, because research on the brain will lead to the development of measurements of biological determinants of aspects of intelligence and personality. If so, special training in psychophysiology and assessment would be useful.

An advantage of psychology as a profession is that many of the psychologist's skills are "content-free," in that they can be applied in many settings. For example, methodological skills are valuable in many nontraditional job areas. In surveying psychology alumni of Claremont Graduate School, Oskamp (1988) found applied psychologists working in such nontraditional areas as health research, planning, and management; organization development; consumer and media research and marketing; computer consulting, planning, and management; educational research and curriculum planning; energy and resource use management; environmental design; legal and criminal justice research; aging research and consultation; and legislative, regulatory, and policy staff positions.

Even if all "care" gets "managed," there will still be possibilities for independent practice for psychologists with business savvy, an entrepreneurial spirit, a willingness to diversify, and an ability to market creatively. Although we cannot know or cover all future roles, a few examples should suggest the range of possibilities. A psychologist could open an animal care practice to market to veterinarians which would include services from modifying undesirable pet behavior to running bereavement groups for people whose pets have died. A practice could include evaluation for workers' compensation programs, consultation to employee assistance programs, and re-training employees that corporations wish to eliminate. "Globalization" may provide the opportunity for psychologists to develop practices devoted to conflict management for people whose behaviors, beliefs, and values are extremely different (Mays et al., 1997).

Just as professional psychology must become proactive in determining the future of the field, so must individuals contemplating entering the field take responsibility for creating a future career for themselves. They must explore options, seek special training, and consider what contributions they can make and how best to participate in psychology and society in the twenty-first century.

IN CONCLUSION

Professional psychology is exciting precisely because it is a changing field. As it always has, it is responding to important social forces in the midst of social change. Psychology interacts at many levels with individuals and society to attempt to address the crucial issues of our time and place. Thus, it is involved with determining our future, both as individuals and as a society. That makes it a fascinating field and a rewarding career.

BOX 18.2

How to Choose a Therapist

After learning about the many types of therapies and therapists available, you may wish for some more practical information about how to choose a therapist for a family member, a friend, or yourself. The plethora of possibilities is perhaps confusing. However, there are two basic pieces of advice: ask others and pay attention to what your own feelings tell you about any therapist you see.

Asking friends, relatives, and other health care professionals to recommend a therapist is a good strategy. You may already have an idea of what type of therapist is needed. If someone is depressed, possibly suicidal, and possibly in need of hospitalization, a psychiatrist would be best. You may already know whether a sex therapist, hypnotist, psychoanalyst, feminist, or behaviorist is needed or preferred. In that case, you can ask state and local professional organizations for therapist referrals. For example, you may telephone the county mental health association, the state psychological association, a psychoanalytic institute in a large city, United Way, or other groups. Get enough recommendations so you have several therapists from which to choose.

The next step is to call the therapists to ask about their services and perhaps to make an appointment. Do not hesitate to ask questions about fees, therapist training and qualifications, and therapeutic methods over the telephone. A concerned and ethical therapist will be willing to talk about such issues. Furthermore, therapists should be willing to discuss your problem and to make some statement about whether it is within their area of expertise. If you wish to know that the therapist is

BOX 18.2 *(continued)*

licensed, you may call the appropriate state licensing board. (You would also call it if you ever wanted to make a complaint against a therapist.)

After getting an idea of the therapists available and getting some information from them, you may decide to make an appointment with one or two. An initial appointment does not mean a commitment to that therapist. Many therapists encourage people who are in the process of deciding to begin therapy to "shop around," to visit other therapists, and to be sure they are comfortable with one before they decide to go into therapy. Again, you should feel free to ask the therapist anything you need to know in order to make your decision. The therapist will also ask you questions in order to assess the nature of your problem and what sort of treatment it requires.

Your own reactions to the therapist and to the therapy hour are your best guides to choosing a therapist. Did you feel comfortable? Do you now feel hopeful? Did the therapist seem competent? Do you feel some degree of trust and confidence in the therapist? Do the methods the therapist intends to use appeal to you? While it is likely that a person trying to choose a therapist feels vulnerable and confused, and while that person's problem may be inability to trust or judge others, nevertheless, a person should be able to give some thought to these sorts of questions. And certainly any strongly negative reactions would indicate that another therapist should be chosen.

You may not develop clear feelings about a therapist until you have seen her or him several times. If, after an initially positive reaction, you begin to have doubts or negative feelings, you should raise these feelings for discussion in therapy. Admittedly, this may be difficult. It is possible that these feelings are important for your therapy and they can be worked on. It is also possible that you may decide to change therapists. Most likely, however, if you have obtained several referrals from good sources and paid attention to your feelings while you interviewed several therapists, you will feel comfortable with your therapist and benefit greatly from therapy.

BIBLIOGRAPHY

Adler, T. (1992, June). Is a degree not enough? Field eyes credentialing. *APA Monitor*, p. 26.

Albee, G. (1968). Conceptual models and manpower requirements in psychology. *American Psychologist, 23*, 317–320.

Albee, G. (1970). The uncertain future of clinical psychology. *American Psychologist, 25*, 1071–1080.

Albee, G. (1982). Preventing psychopathology and promoting human potential. *American Psychologist, 37*, 1043–1050.

Albee, G. (1996). Revolutions and counterrevolutions in prevention. *American Psychologist, 51,* 1130–1133.

American Medical Association. (1984). *Proceedings of the house of delegates of the American Medical Association.* Chicago: Author.

American Psychological Association. (1992). Ethics code. *APA Monitor,* pp. 39–42.

Austad, C. (1996). *Is long-term therapy ethical? Toward a social ethic in an era of managed care.* San Francisco: Jossey-Bass.

Austad, C., & Hoyt, M. (1992). The managed care movement and the future of psychotherapy. *Psychotherapy, 29,* 109–118.

Banta, H., & Sax, L. (1983). Reimbursement for psychotherapy: Linking efficacy research and public policymaking. *American Psychologist, 38,* 918–923.

Baxter, L., Schwartz, J., Bergman, K., Szuba, M., Guze, B., Mazziotta, J., Alazraki, A., Selin, C., Ferng, H., Munford, P., & Phelps, M. (1992). Caudate glucose metabolic rate changes with both drug and behavior therapy for obsessive-compulsive disorder. *Archives of General Psychiatry, 49,* 681–689.

Berg, M. (1986). Toward a diagnostic alliance between psychiatrist and psychologist. *American Psychologist, 41,* 52–59.

Berkman, A., Bassos, C, & Post, S. (1988). Managed mental health care and independent practice: A challenge to psychology. *Psychotherapy, 25,* 434–440.

Bersoff, D. (1983). Hospital privileges and the antitrust laws. *American Psychologist, 38,* 1238–1242.

Binner, P. (1986). DRGs and the administration of mental health services. *American Psychologist, 41,* 64–79.

Birren, J. (1983). Aging in America: Roles for psychology. *American Psychologist, 38,* 298–299.

Brentar, J., & McNamara, J. (1991). The right to prescribe medication: Considerations for professional psychology. *Professional Psychology: Research & Practice, 22,* 179–187.

Brentar, J., & McNamara, J. (1991). Prescription privileges for psychology: The next step in its evolution as a profession. *Professional Psychology: Research & Practice, 22,* 194–195.

Bugental, J., & Bracke, P. (1992). The future of existential-humanistic psychotherapy. *Psychotherapy, 29,* 28–33.

Cattell, R. (1937). *The fight for our national intelligence.* London: P.S. King and Sons.

Cattell, R. (1983). Let's end the duel. *American Psychologist, 38,* 769–776.

Cheifetz, D., & Salloway, J. (1984). Patterns of mental health services provided by HMOs. *American Psychologist, 39,* 495–502.

Conrad, P., & Schneider, J. (1980). *Deviance and medicalization.* St. Louis: Mosby.

Cummings, N. (1986). The dismantling of our health system. *American Psychologist, 41,* 426–431.

Cunningham, S. (1985, January). The public and nuclear power: Scientists attack DOE attempt to reduce "phobia." *APA Monitor,* p. 18.

DeLeon, P. (1986). Increasing the societal contribution of organized psychology. *American Psychologist, 41,* 466–474.

DeLeon, P. (1988). Public policy and public service: Our professional duty. *American Psychologist, 43,* 309–315.

DeLeon, P., Fox, R., & Graham, S. (1991). Prescription privileges: Psychology's next frontier? *American Psychologist, 46,* 384–393.

DeLeon, P., & Pallak, M. (1982). Public health and psychology: An important, expanding interaction. *American Psychologist, 37,* 934–935.

DeLeon, P., Uyeda, M., & Welch, B. (1985). Psychology and HMOs: New partnership or new adversary? *American Psychologist, 40,* 1122–1124.

DeLeon, P., VandenBos, G., & Cummings, N. (1983). Psychotherapy—Is it safe, effective, and appropriate? The beginning of an evolutionary dialog. *American Psychologist, 38,* 907–911.

DeLeon, P., VandenBos, G., & Kraut, A. (1984). Federal legislation recognizing psychology. *American Psychologist, 39,* 933–946.

DeNelsky, G. (1991). Prescription privileges for psychologists: The case against. *Professional Psychology: Research & Practice, 22,* 188–193.

Diekstra, R., & Jansen, M. (1988). Psychology's role in the new health care systems: The importance of psychological interventions in primary health care. *Psychotherapy, 25,* 344–351.

English, J. (1986). Diagnosis-related groups and general hospital psychiatry: The APA Study. *American Journal of Psychiatry, 143,* 131–139.

Ewart, C. (1991). Social action theory for a public health psychology. *American Psychologist, 46,* 931–946.

Flanigan, J. (1991, September 29). U.S. health-care system getting a dose of reality. *Los Angeles Times,* Part D, pp. 1, 16.

Galavotti, C., Saltzman, L., Sauter, S., & Sumartojo, E. (1997). Behavioral science activities at the Center for Disease Control and Prevention: A selected overview of exemplary programs. *American Psychologist, 52,* 154–166.

Givelber, D., Bowers, W., & Blitch, C. (1985). *The Tarasoff controversy: A summary of findings from an empirical study of legal, ethical, and clinical issues (NIMH Summary Report).* Washington, DC: NIMH 874.

Gorenstein, E. (1984). Debating mental illness: Implications for science, medicine, and social policy. *American Psychologist, 39,* 50–56.

Hager, P. (1985, June 4). State power to mandate health benefits upheld. *Los Angeles Times,* p. 1.

Jacobs, D. (1988). Marketing psychological services in the public sector. *Psychotherapy, 25,* 377–386.

Kiesler, C. (1992). U.S. mental health policy: Doomed to fail. *American Psychologist, 47,* 1077–1082.

Kiesler, C., & Morton, T. (1988). Psychology and public policy in the "health care revolution." *American Psychologist, 43,* 993–1003.

Kiesler, C., & Simpkins, C. (1991). The de facto national system of psychiatric inpatient care: Piecing together the national puzzle. *American Psychologist, 46,* 579–584.

Kilburg, R., & Ginsberg, M. (1983). Sunset and psychology or how we learned to love a crisis. *American Psychologist, 38,* 1227–1231.

Klerman, G. (1983). The efficacy of psychotherapy as a basis for public policy. *American Psychologist, 38,* 929–934.

Lazarus, A., Beutler, L., & Norcross, J. (1992). The future of technical eclecticism. *Psychotherapy, 29,* 11–20.

Lesse, S. (1986). The uncertain future of clinical psychiatry. *American Journal of Psychotherapy, 40,* 4–16.

Lorion, R. (1991). Prevention and public health: Psychology's response to the nation's health care crisis. *American Psychologist, 46,* 516–519.

Ludwigsen, K., & Enright, M. (1988). The health care revolution: Implications for psychology and hospital practice. *Psychotherapy, 25,* 424–428.

Matarazzo, J. (1992). Psychological testing and assessment in the 21st century. *American Psychologist, 47,* 1007–1018.

Mays, V., Rubin, J., Sabourin, M., & Walker, L. (1997). Moving toward a global psychology: Changing theories and practice to meet the needs of a changing world. *American Psychologist, 52,* 485–487.

McCall, N., & Rice, T. (1983). A summary of the Colorado clinical psychology/expanded mental health benefits experiment. *American Psychologist, 38,* 1279–1291.

McGinnis, J. M. (1991). Health objectives for the nation. *American Psychologist, 46,* 520–524.

McGuire, T., & Frisman, L. (1983). Reimbursement policy and cost-effective mental health care. *American Psychologist, 38,* 935–940.

Michael, J. (1982). The second revolution in health: Health promotion and its environmental base. *American Psychologist, 37,* 936–941.

Norcross, J., Alford, B., & DeMichele, J. (1992). The future of psychotherapy: Delphi data and concluding observations. *Psychotherapy, 29,* 150–158.

O'Farrell, T., Choquette, K., Cutter, H., Brown, E. et al. (1996). Cost-benefit and cost-effectiveness analyses of behavioral marital therapy with and without relapse prevention sessions for alcholics and their spouses. *Behavior Therapy, 27,* 7–24.

O'Hara, M., & Anderson, W. (1991, September/October). Welcome to the postmodern world. *The Family Therapy Networker,* 19–25.

Oskamp, S. (1988). Nontraditional employment opportunities for applied psychologists. *American Psychologist, 43,* 484–485.

Pepe, M., & Wu, J. (1988). The economics of mental health care. *Psychotherapy, 25,* 352–355.

Reiss, D., & Price, R. (1996). National research agenda for prevention research: The National Institute of Mental Health Report. *American Psychologist, 51,* 1109–1115.

Resnick, R. (1985). The case against the Blues: The Virginia challenge. *American Psychologist, 40,* 975–983.

Resnick, R. (1997). A brief history of practice—expanded. *American Psychologist, 52,* 463–468.

Riley, W., Elliot, R., & Thomas, J. R. (1992). Impact of prescription privileges on psychology training: Training directors' survey. *The Clinical Psychologist, 45,* 63–71.

Roth, A., & Fonagy, P. (1996). *What works for whom? A critical review of psychotherapy research.* New York: Guilford Press.

Salekin, R., Rogers, R., & Sewell, K. (1996). A review and meta-analysis of the Psychopathology Checklist and Psychopathology Checklist—Revised: Predictive validity and dangerousness. *Clinical Psychology: Science and Practice, 3,* 203–215.

Savage, D. (1992, November 10). Court lets firms cut health care. *Los Angeles Times,* Section A, pp. 1, 18–19.

Siegel, M. (1983). Crime and violence in America: The victims. *American Psychologist, 38,* 1267–1273.

Szasz, T. (1961). *The myth of mental illness: Foundations of a theory of personal conduct.* New York: Harper & Row.

Teplin, L. (1984). Criminalizing mental disorder: The comparative arrest rate of the mentally ill. *American Psychologist, 39,* 794–803.

Theaman, M. (1984). The impact of peer review on professional practice. *American Psychologist, 39,* 406–414.

Tulkin, S., & Frank, G. (1985). The changing role of psychologists in health maintenance organizations. *American Psychologist, 40,* 1125–1130.

VandenBos, G., & DeLeon, P. (1988). The use of psychotherapy to improve physical health. *Psychotherapy, 25,* 335–343.

VandenBos, G., & Stapp, J. (1983). Service providers in psychology: Results of the 1982 APA human resources survey. *American Psychologist, 38,* 1330–1352.

Weiss, B. (1983). Behavioral toxicology and environmental health science: Opportunity and challenge for psychology. *American Psychologist, 38,* 1174–1187.

Woolfolk, R. (1985). What's at stake in the mental illness controversy. *American Psychologist, 40,* 468.

Zaro, J., Batchelor, W., Ginsberg, M., & Pallak, M. (1982). Psychology and the JCAH: Reflections on a decade of struggle. *American Psychologist, 37,* 1342–1349.

Zimet, C. (1989). The mental health care revolution: Will psychology survive? *American Psychologist, 44,* 703–708.

APPENDIX

American Psychological Association Ethics Code, 1992 Version

INTRODUCTION

The American Psychological Association's (APA's) Ethical Principles of Psychologists and Code of Conduct (hereinafter referred to as the Ethics Code) consists of an Introduction, a Preamble, six General Principles (A–F), and specific Ethical Standards. The Introduction discusses the intent, organization, procedural considerations, and scope of application of the Ethics Code. The Preamble and General Principles are *aspirational* goals to guide psychologists toward the highest ideals of psychology. Although the Preamble and General Principles are not themselves enforceable rules, they should be considered by psychologists in arriving at an ethical course of action and may be considered by ethics bodies in interpreting the Ethical Standards. The Ethical Standards set forth *enforceable* rules for conduct as psychologists. Most of the Ethical Standards are written broadly, in order to apply to psychologists in varied roles, although the application of an Ethical Standard may vary depending on the context. The Ethical Standards are not exhaustive. The fact that a given conduct is not specifically addressed by the Ethics Code does not mean that it is necessarily either ethical or unethical.

Membership in the APA commits members to adhere to the APA Ethics Code and to the rules and procedures used to implement it. Psychologists and students, whether or not they are APA members, should be aware that the Ethics Code may be applied to them by state psychology boards, courts, or other public bodies.

This Ethics Code applies only to psychologists' work-related activities, that is, activities that are part of the psychologists' scientific and professional functions or that are psychological in nature. It includes the clinical or counseling practice of psychology, research, teaching, supervision of trainees, development of assessment instruments, conducting assessments, educational counseling, organizational consulting, social intervention, administration, and other activities as well. These work-related activities can be distinguished from the purely private conduct of a psychologist, which ordinarily is not within the purview of the Ethics Code.

The Ethics Code is intended to provide standards of professional conduct that can be applied by the APA and by other bodies that choose to adopt them. But whether or not a psychologist has violated the Ethics Code does not by itself determine whether he or she is legally liable in a court action, whether a contract is enforceable or whether other legal consequences occur. These results are based on legal rather than ethical rules. However, compliance with or violation of the Ethics Code may be admissible as evidence in some legal proceedings, depending on the circumstances.

In the process of making decisions regarding their professional behavior, psychologists must consider this Ethics Code, in addition to applicable laws and psychology board regulations. If the Ethics Code establishes a higher standard of conduct than is required by law, psychologists must meet the higher ethical standard. If the Ethics Code standard appears to conflict with the requirements of law, then psychologists make known their commitment to the Ethics Code and take steps to resolve the conflict in a responsible manner. If neither law nor the Ethics Code resolves an issue, psychologists should consider other professional materials and the dictates of their own conscience, as well as seek consultation with others within the field when this is practical.

The procedures for filing, investigating and resolving complaints of unethical conduct are described in the current Rules and Procedures of the APA Ethics Committee. The actions that APA may take for violations of the Ethics Code include actions such as reprimand, censure, termination of APA membership, and referral of the matter to other bodies. Complainants who seek remedies such as monetary damages in alleging ethical violations by a psychologist must resort to private negotiation, administrative bodies, or the courts. Actions that violate the Ethics Code may lead to the imposition of sanctions on a psychologist by bodies other than APA, including state psychological associations, other professional groups, psychology boards, other state or federal agencies, and payors for health services. In addition to actions for violation of the Ethics Code, the APA Bylaws provide that APA may take action against a member after his or her conviction of a felony, expulsion or suspension from an affiliated state psychological association, or suspension or loss of licensure.

PREAMBLE

Psychologists work to develop a valid and reliable body of scientific knowledge based on research. They may apply that knowledge to human behavior in a variety of contexts. In doing so, they perform many roles, such as researcher, educator, diagnostician, therapist, supervisor, consultant, administrator, social interventionist, and expert witness. Their goal is to broaden knowledge of behavior and, where appropriate, to apply it pragmatically to improve the condition of both society and the individual. Psychologists respect the central importance of freedom of inquiry and expression in research, teaching, and publication. They also strive to help the public in developing informed judgments and choices concerning human behavior. This Ethics Code provides a common set of values upon which psychologists build their professional and scientific work.

This Code is intended to provide both the general principles and the decision rules to cover most situations encountered by psychologists. It has as its primary goal the welfare and protection of the individuals and groups with whom psychologists work. It is the individual responsibility of each psychologist to aspire to the highest possible standards of conduct. Psychologists respect and protect human and civil rights, and do not knowingly participate in or condone unfair discriminatory practices.

The development of a dynamic set of ethical standards for a psychologist's work-related conduct requires a personal commitment to a lifelong effort to act ethically; to encourage ethical behavior by students, supervisees, employees, and colleagues, as appropriate; and to consult with others, as needed, concerning ethical problems. Each psychologist supplements, but does not violate, the Ethics Code's values and rules on the basis of guidance drawn from personal values, culture, and experience.

GENERAL PRINCIPLES

Principle A: Competence

Psychologists strive to maintain high standards of competence in their work. They recognize the boundaries of their particular competencies and the limitations of their expertise. They provide only those services and use only those techniques for which they are qualified by education, training, or experience. Psychologists are cognizant of the fact that the competencies required in serving, teaching, and/or studying groups of people vary with the distinctive characteristics of those groups. In those areas in which recognized professional standards do not yet exist, psychologists exercise careful judgment and take appropriate precautions to protect the welfare of those with whom they work. They maintain knowledge of relevant scientific and professional information related to the services they render, and they recognize the need for ongoing education. Psychologists make appropriate use of scientific, professional, technical, and administrative resources.

Principle B: Integrity

Psychologists seek to promote integrity in the science, teaching, and practice of psychology. In these activities psychologists are honest, fair, and respectful of others. In describing or reporting their qualifications, services, products, fees, research, or teaching, they do not make statements that are false, misleading, or deceptive. Psychologists strive to be aware of their own belief systems, values, needs, and limitations and the effect of these on their work. To the extent feasible, they attempt to clarify for relevant parties the roles they are performing and to function appropriately in accordance with those roles. Psychologists avoid improper and potentially harmful dual relationships.

Principle C: Professional and Scientific Responsibility

Psychologists uphold professional standards of conduct, clarify their professional roles and obligations, accept appropriate responsibility for their behavior, and adapt their methods to the needs of different populations. Psychologists consult with, refer to, or cooperate with other professionals and institutions to the extent needed to serve the best interests of their patients, clients, or other recipients of their services. Psychologists' moral standards and conduct are personal matters to the same degree as is true for any other person, except as psychologists' conduct may compromise their professional responsibilities or reduce the public's trust in psychology and psychologists. Psychologists are concerned about the ethical compliance of their colleagues' scientific and professional conduct. When appropriate, they consult with colleagues in order to prevent or avoid unethical conduct.

Principle D: Respect for People's Rights and Dignity

Psychologists accord appropriate respect to the fundamental rights, dignity, and worth of all people. They respect the rights of individuals to privacy, confidentiality, self-determination, and autonomy, mindful that legal and other obligations may lead to inconsistency and conflict with the exercise of these rights. Psychologists strive to be aware of cultural, individual, and role differences, including those due to age, gender, race, ethnicity, national origin, religion, sexual orientation, disability, language, and socioeconomic status. Psychologists try to eliminate the effect on their work of biases based on those factors, and they do not knowingly participate in or condone unfair discriminatory practices.

Principle E: Concern for Others' Welfare

Psychologists seek to contribute to the welfare of those with whom they interact professionally. In their professional actions, psychologists weigh the welfare and rights of their patients or clients, students, supervisees, human research participants, and other affected persons, and the welfare of animal subjects of research. When conflicts occur among psychologists' obligations or concerns, they attempt to resolve these conflicts and to perform their roles in a responsible fashion that avoids or minimizes harm. Psychologists are sensitive to real and ascribed differences in power between themselves and others, and they do not exploit or mislead other people during or after professional relationships.

Principle F: Social Responsibility

Psychologists are aware of their professional and scientific responsibilities to the community and the society in which they work and live. They apply and make public their knowledge of psychology in order to contribute to human welfare. Psychologists are concerned about and work to mitigate the causes of human suffering. When undertaking research, they strive to advance human welfare and the science of psychology. Psychologists try to avoid misuse of their work. Psychologists comply with the law and encourage the development of law and social policy that serve the interests of their patients and clients and the public. They are encouraged to contribute a portion of their professional time for little or no personal advantage.

ETHICAL STANDARDS

The ethical standards consist of 102 specific rules to guide psychologists' behavior in eight areas: all types of work relationships; evaluation, assessment, or intervention; advertising and other public statements; therapy; privacy and confidentiality; teaching, training, supervision, research, and publishing; forensic activities; and resolving ethical issues. For example, the ethical standards require psychologists to maintain their expertise, prohibit sexual harassment, guide psychologists' fees, ensure that psychologists explain assessment results to clients, outline permissible advertising practices, prohibit sexual intimacies with clients, discourage sexual intimacies with former clients, describe procedures for maintaining confidentiality, prohibit deception in research, provide guidelines for publication credit, outline appropriate behavior for forensic psychologists, and require cooperation with ethics investigations. In the interest of saving space, the full standards are not reproduced here.

Glossary

Accurate empathy The therapist's ability to enter the client's world and see things from her or his point of view.

Adultomorphizing Seeing the child in terms of adult processes.

American Board of Professional Psychology (ABPP) Awards special diploma to experienced, qualified professional psychologists.

Analogue design In psychotherapy research, a brief treatment is studied that is designed to be analogous to some part of real therapy. The treatment usually focuses on one or two elements of real therapy in order to better isolate them from all the complex factors of real therapy and to study them.

Anorexia nervosa An eating disorder in which the individual eats very little or not at all, to the point that weight loss can become life-endangering.

Apperception Term used in some projective tests, such as the Thematic Apperception Test, referring to the final, clear phase of perception when there is recognition, identification, or comprehension of what has been perceived.

Assimilative integration Different approaches to psychotherapy become more integrative by incorporating ideas and strategies from other approaches.

Attachment theory John Bowlby's psychodynamic theory of development. Healthy development is based on children forming secure bonds or attachments with their caretakers. This allows the development of good working models of reality.

Attribution theory A theory in social psychology that in order for people to predict and control events, they will attribute causes to those events. It is the attribution that determines their response, not the event.

Automatic thoughts In Beck's cognitive therapy, habitual dysfunctional thoughts that occur rapidly and automatically, often without much awareness.

Aversion therapy Pairing an aversive stimulus with a previously attractive stimulus in order to create an avoidance response or to suppress undesirable behavior.

Behavioral or contingency contracting Contractual behavior therapy in which the client is fully involved in formulating a contingency management plan.

Behaviorism School of scientific psychology that emphasizes observable behavior over innate or internal variables.

Biofeedback Technique that allows people to monitor and control their own internal bodily functions by making these functions observable.

Boulder model The scientist-practitioner model for clinical psychology developed by the 1949 APA training conference held in Boulder, CO.

Bruxism Habit of grinding teeth.

Bulimia An eating disorder characterized by uncontrolled binges. May also involve efforts made by the person to regurgitate food so they do not gain weight.

Caring days In behavioral marital therapy, one spouse tries to maximize the positive experience of the other for a specific day.

Certification A way of regulating professional psychology. The state certifies that the psychologist has the claimed training.

Classical conditioning A learning procedure developed by Pavlov in which a neutral stimulus and an unconditioned stimulus are paired until the neutral stimulus evokes the same response as the unconditioned stimulus.

Classical psychoanalysis Freud's approach to psychoanalysis as opposed to modern theories such as object relations theory and self psychology.

Cognitive rehearsal A cognitive-behavioral technique used when homework is given. The client imagines every step needed to do the homework to anticipate possible glitches.

Cognitive triad The three basic components of thinking in depressives, including a negative view of themselves, their personal future, and their current experiences.

Cohesiveness Degree to which members are attracted or bonded to a group.

Common factors approach An approach to psychotherapy theory integration involving the investigation of what all therapies share.

Comparative design In psychotherapy research, two different treatments are compared to one another.

Compensation Dealing with frustration and inadequacy in one area by investing in another area.

Conditioned response A learned response that is made to a conditioned stimulus (in classical conditioning) or as a result of reward or punishment (in operant conditioning).

Conditioned stimulus A neutral stimulus that acquires the capacity to evoke a response after association with an unconditioned stimulus (in classical conditioning).

Conditions of worth In client-centered theory, parents impose "conditions of worth" on their children, that is, they make their children feel worthwhile only if they act in accord with certain parental expectations or conditions.

Confidentiality The ethical obligation of professionals to keep information obtained from a client confidential.

Congruence In client-centered theory, to be aware of one's own inner experiencing and to act so that behavior matches that experiencing.

Constructivism The philosophy that reality is a construct of each individual. There is no one true, objective reality.

Contingency management Behavior modification technique that involves setting up a system of rewards for desired behaviors and loss of rewards for undesired behaviors.

Control group In scientific research, the group of participants who do not receive the treatment under study.

Conversion disorder A psychological disorder involving one or more physical symptoms that mimic physical illness.

Coping strategies Skills taught in self-management behavior therapy.

Covert modeling In behavior therapy, learning by imagining someone else performing the behavior one wishes to learn.

Covert practice In behavior therapy, rehearsing positive skills in imagination.

Covert sensitization In behavior therapy, pairing of some aversive stimulus or negative consequence with some unwanted behavior in imagination.

Crisis intervention A therapeutic method developed for intervening to help people in crisis.

Dialectical approach The philosophical view that considers social or personal change to be a process of forming a thesis (one view of things), which produces an antithesis (the opposite of the original view), which produces a new synthesis (a combination of the two positions).

Decentering The ability to step outside of one's own perspective, guessing through imagination or logic how things would look from another person's perspective.

Defense mechanisms Habitual and unconscious psychological devices used to reduce or avoid anxiety.

Defensive pessimism Catastrophizing about the possibility of failing in order to motivate oneself to work hard.

Demonology Early belief system in demons, spirits, and possession.

Denial A defense mechanism involving the refusal to recognize the real nature of one's behavior.

Diagnostic Related Groups (DRGs) Groupings of similar disorders for which third-party payers pay a flat fee based on the average cost of care for patients with such diagnoses.

Differential diagnosis The process of distinguishing between similar disorders.

Differentiation The ability to have a clear sense of one's own values, beliefs, and reactions, separate from those of others.

Discovery-oriented research Research approaches to psychotherapy in which the researcher attempts to identify significant moments or events and explore how they actually function in therapy.

Disengaged family Family whose boundaries are rigid and in which communication is restricted or avoided between family members.

Displacement A defense mechanism involving the deflection of feelings onto a less threatening target.

Disputing Central technique of rational-emotive therapy. The therapist directly challenges a client's irrational beliefs.

DSM *The Diagnostic and Statistical Manual of Mental Disorders* of the American Psychiatric Association.

Ego In psychoanalysis, the part of the personality that is reality-oriented.

Enmeshed family Family in which boundaries are weak or nonexistent so that roles are unclear and responsibilities are confused.

Evocative unfolding Technique utilized in process-experiential psychotherapy when the therapist helps the client vividly remember a situation in which the client did something he or she feels uncomfortable with or doesn't understand.

Experiencing The bodily, "felt" way of knowing at the visceral or "gut level," as opposed to intellectual, verbal, conceptual knowledge.

Experiential articulation A formulation of a client's self-knowledge into words that match the client's experiential state.

Experiential psychotherapy (1) A generic name for a group of therapies, usually from the existential-humanistic approach, that rely on emotion and experiencing to facilitate change; (2) Gendlin's person-centered experiential psychotherapy, which emphasizes tuning into one's felt or experienced meanings; (3) Mahrer's experiential psychotherapy, which relies on the activation of strong feeling to access inner experiencing potential.

External locus of control Feeling that one's fate is in the hands of external forces.

Extinction A type of learning that occurs when rewards are no longer delivered and the response ceases.

Family of origin The family from which each spouse in the present family originally came.

First order change Trying to solve a problem from the same old assumptions, with the same old methods.

Focusing In Gendlin's person-centered experiential psychotherapy, the ability to tune in to one's felt or experienced meanings. Also, the name of a specific technique developed by Gendlin to facilitate such tuning in.

Free association In psychoanalysis, the patient is asked to say whatever comes to mind without censorship.

Freedom of Choice (FOC) State laws requiring health insurance companies to allow patients the freedom to choose their own health care providers and treatments.

Functional analysis Behaviorists analyze the context of a behavior and the function(s) it serves with that context. Functional analysis identifies the conditions that elicit a behavior and the consequences that maintain it.

Functionalism Early school of academic psychology that studied what the mind does, rather than the contents of the mind.

Fused A description of people who are emotionally entangled, and who have a difficult time distinguishing their own feelings and values from those of others.

Games In transactional analysis, orderly transactions with rules that conceal ulterior motives.

Generalization A type of learning in which a response that has been conditioned to one stimulus occurs with other, similar stimuli.

Genogram Diagram that shows the relationships of the husband and wife to their families of origin.

Gestalt An organized whole.

Good moments Alvin Mahrer's list of the kinds of events in psychotherapy that have been theorized to be associated with the facilitation of change, such as a moment of insight or heavy emotion.

Hermeneutics The philosophical idea that psychotherapy is an interpretive science, that by helping clients develop insight into the relationship of their past to their present, therapists are actually helping them develop a good working "story" about their pasts, rather than discovering any "real truth" about the past.

Horizontal interpretation A therapeutic response designed to increase client insight into patterns in the client's current behavior.

Hot cognition Cognitions associated with emotions.

Hysteria Early psychological disorder characterized by emotional excitability, excessive anxiety, sensory and motor disturbances, and the simulation of organic disorder.

Id In psychoanalysis, the part of the personality that consists of instincts and reflexes.

Idealizing needs The need to have someone to idealize in order to develop the self's own set of values and ideals.

Identified patient The person identified as the patient, the person "having" the problem, even though the "real" problem lies in the entire family, or couple.

Implosive therapy Also known as flooding, a behavioral technique in which the therapist attempts to heighten or exaggerate the client's fears in hopes that they will be extinguished.

Incomplete gestalts Uncompleted experiences.

Individuation The process of developing a unique sense of self.

Inferiority complex The set of cognitions and emotions that maintain a sense of inferiority or insecurity.

Informed consent Informing clients of all the pros and cons of therapy so they can agree to it with full knowledge.

Instrumental conditioning A learning procedure developed by Skinner in which voluntary behavior is rewarded and strengthened.

Intellectualization A defense mechanism in which repressed impulses are allowed into awareness only in an intellectual way, to avoid experiencing them.

Internal consistency A type of test reliability, also called split-half reliability, which measures the degree to which parts of a test correlate with each other.

Internal locus of control Feeling that one controls one's own life.

Interpretive secondary control Gaining control by giving up control or by accepting that one does not have control over certain things in one's life.

Introjection In psychoanalysis, the internalization of attitudes, beliefs, and values of others such as parents.

In vivo **desensitization** A behavior therapy technique in which desensitization is done with real-life stimuli rather than with imagery.

Larry P. Important California Supreme Court ruling in the case of *Larry P.* v. *Wilson Riles and the Board of Education.* The court ruled that intelligence tests were biased against non-White children.

License A way of regulating professional psychology. The state issues a license to professionals who demonstrate the required education and competence.

Life script In transactional analysis, the concept that people unconsciously write scripts in childhood for themselves to play all their lives.

Managed care Attempt by third-party payers to reduce costs of health care by negotiating prices and rationing care.

Marker A client behavior that signals that the client is struggling with a certain kind of emotional processing problem in a certain way. Can be used to signal what kind of therapeutic intervention should be used at that moment to help the client process the problem.

Mental status examination Formal part of an interview that assesses the client's current mental functioning.

Meta-analysis A statistical procedure that allows results from a variety of studies to be combined so that overall trends can be observed.

Metapsychology The implicit, underlying assumptions of a psychological theory.

Mirroring In couples therapy, a technique in which one spouse is asked to repeat as precisely as possible what the other said; in object relations theory, the response of the mother or the therapist that reflects the child's or client's experience.

Misattribution procedures A therapeutic technique in which clients are taught to attribute the causes of their problems to other factors in such a way that self-blame and worry are reduced.

Modeling Learning by observing another person perform the desired behavior. Also called observational learning.

Multiaxial model Basis for the DSM-III and DSM-IV. It takes a diagnosis on five separate scales, or axes, to make a complete diagnosis.

Multigenerational transmission process From Bowen's family systems approach, the belief that a lack of personal differentiation is passed down from one generation to another.

Multiple realities The concept that reality is relative to each person's point of view and, therefore, there is no possible way for any human to determine one "correct" view of reality.

Musturbatory thinking In rational-emotive therapy, thinking in terms of "musts" and "shoulds."

Narrative perspectives Perspectives on human behavior that argue that people live their lives in terms of the "stories" they construct about themselves and events.

Narrative truth In hermeneutics, the concept of helping clients develop good "working stories" about their lives.

National Register of Health Service Providers in Psychology Listing of licensed professional psychologists that can be used by third-party payers to determine fee reimbursement.

Negative practice A behavior therapy technique involving repeatedly doing unwanted behavior until it is aversive.

Negative reinforcement In learning theory, a reward that involves the removal of an aversive stimulus, such as turning off a painfully loud noise.

Negative self-monitoring Ways in which clients watch themselves and their own behavior and evaluate them negatively.

Neurotic paradox The fact that a learned fear does not extinguish even though the original conditions for its learning have long since passed.

Nomothetic research methodology A research methodology that looks at how groups of individuals differ along certain dimensions, in contrast to studying particular individuals.

Nonpossessive warmth In client-centered therapy, a set of therapist qualities called, variously, unconditional positive regard, acceptance, prizing, respect, caring, nonpossessive love.

Norms (in group therapy) Explicit or implicit rules or standards of behavior that guide the behavior of group members.

Norms (in psychological testing) The distribution of scores of a large number of representative, typical people. A particular individual's score on a test can be compared to the norms for an idea as to the meaning of that score.

Objective test A pencil-and-paper personality test with a structured set of limited answers.

Object relations theory Modern psychoanalytic theory emphasizing relationships between people.

Observational learning In social learning theory, learning through imitation.

Operant conditioning See instrumental conditioning.

Ordeals A psychotherapeutic strategy that makes the dysfunctional symptom too costly to maintain.

Organismic valuing process Carl Rogers's idea that humans have an inborn capacity to experience what is good for them.

Outcome research Research that deals with the outcome of psychotherapy and its relative effectiveness.

Paradoxical intervention A therapeutic technique that involves prescribing the symptom.

Personal constructs Beliefs and concepts people develop in order to make sense out of their experiences.

Person-centered Rogers's most recent name for his theory.

Phenomenological method In Husserl's philosophy, the therapeutic goal is to suspend judgments and preconceptions.

Phobia An exaggerated or unrealistic fear of a specific stimulus or situation.

Placebo In psychotherapy research, a treatment that is designed to actually be neutral. Then, if the real psychotherapy treatment is more effective than the placebo, it suggests that the effectiveness is not merely due to the client's having an expectation that he or she will get better, but rather, is due to actual components of the real psychotherapy treatment itself.

Positive reinforcement In learning theory, a reward that involves the delivery of a positive stimulus, such as giving a rat food for pressing a bar.

Primary prevention In community psychology, interventions aimed at preventing the development of psychological disorder in the first place.

Privilege The legal right of the clients of psychologists (and other professionals) to control information about them.

Problematic reaction point A therapeutic marker in which a client reports being self-critical or puzzled about something he or she has done. In process-experiential psychotherapy, the technique of evocative unfolding is used to help the client process the problem.

Problem-solving training A behavioral method for teaching people how to deal with problems by defining the problem, generating alternatives, evaluating them, acting on one, and assessing the effect of the attempted solution.

Process-experiential psychotherapy Person-centered approach developed by Leslie Greenberg, Laura Rice, and Robert Elliot. Includes the systematic use of both client-centered and gestalt psychotherapy techniques applied at specific points in therapy when clients exhibit certain therapeutic markers.

Process-oriented To see life and the self as an ongoing, changing process and, therefore, to be open to experience in order to continually learn and grow.

Process research Research that deals with the processes that actually occur in psychotherapy, rather than outcomes.

Professional model Established the Psy.D. degree and training in practice, not research, for clinical psychology. Also called the Vail model.

Projection A defense mechanism in which unacceptable motives or feelings are attributed to others.

Projective test A personality test that involves presenting ambiguous stimuli in order to elicit responses from an individual.

Psychic determinism The belief that nothing psychological happens by chance.

Psychodrama A form of group therapy in which clients act out scenes of conflict from their childhood or present life.

Rationalization A defense mechanism in which plausible and acceptable reasons for one's behavior and feelings are created in order to hide one's real motives.

Reaction formation A defense mechanism in which one behaves in a way that is diametrically opposite to what one unconsciously wants.

Reciprocal determinism The holistic view that causation is not unidirectional, but that events influence each other.

Reciprocal inhibition In systematic desensitization, the pairing of incompatible responses in order to suppress one response.

Reflection of feeling In client-centered therapy, the therapeutic response of accurately mirroring the client's experience.

Reframing The therapeutic technique of reinterpreting a behavior that a client sees as pathological in a positive way.

Registration A way to regulate the practice of psychology in which psychologists merely register their practice with the state.

Reliability The "trustworthiness" of a psychological test.

Repression The primary defense mechanism that involves removing from awareness all unwanted or threatening memories, impulses, or feelings.

Respondent conditioning See classical conditioning.

Response cost Behavior modification method involving the removal of positive reinforcers to suppress unwanted behavior.

Role playing A technique used in many therapies, including behavior therapy, psychodrama, cognitive-behavior therapy. Client or therapist or both act out a situation that is problematic for the client so that new behaviors can be tried and learned.

Scientist-practitioner model Established the Ph.D. and training in both research and practice for clinical psychology. Also called the Boulder model.

Secondary prevention In community psychology, an intervention method aimed at preventing psychological problems from deteriorating into worse conditions, as in crisis intervention.

Second-order change A shift in fundamental premises so that the problem is framed in an entirely new way, frequently leading to a creative solution.

Self-efficacy Bandura's theory that one's self-perceptions of one's competence determine behavior.

Self-empowerment Therapeutic goal of giving clients the feeling that they have the power to affect their own lives.

Self-objects In object relations theory, another person who supports one's developing sense of self by providing certain functions until the self can develop those capacities.

Sensate focus Learning to focus on the sensations that are a part of sex, rather than worrying about the outcome.

Shame-attacking exercises A therapeutic technique in which clients are instructed to do something that creates shame so they can find out that nothing objectively bad happens.

Shaping In learning theory, rewarding closer and closer approximations of the desired response.

Shouldism See musturbatory thinking.

Spectatoring Watching and judging one's sexual performance.

Split In both gestalt therapy and process-experiential therapy, when clients experience a split between what they want to do and what they think they should do. The gestalt two-chair technique is utilized to help clients resolve the split.

Splitting In object relations theory, the idea that the very young child splits positive and negative feelings and perceptions about the mother and about the self off from one another, because it is too uncomfortable to perceive mother or self as having both good and bad qualities.

Spontaneous recovery rate The rate at which people appear to spontaneously recover without undergoing psychotherapy. There is much controversy over whether there is a "real" spontaneous recovery rate that applies to everyone.

Standardization group In the development of psychological tests, the group of people on which the test is standardized, the group of people whose scores serve as the norms of the test.

Stress innoculation A behavioral treatment for managing stressful events and preventing stress responses. Practicing responses to (imaged) stressful events is assumed to innoculate or prepare clients for future stress.

Structural family therapy Minuchin's approach in which the family is viewed as a hierarchically organized system.

Structuralism An early school of academic psychology that emphasized the structure of the mind, rather than its contents or functions.

Sublimation The process of channeling repressed desires and conflicts into socially acceptable outlets.

Sunset legislation Laws passed in the 1970s that allowed the regulation of professional psychology to cease.

Superego In psychoanalysis, the part of the personality that contains the conscience as well as the ideals to which the person aspires.

System In a family approach to counseling, a system is a pattern of interrelationships among elements, such that each element of the system both determines and is determined by the other elements in the system.

Systematic desensitization A behavior therapy method in which relaxation is paired with vivid images of phobic situations or objects in order to reduce fear.

Tarasoff 1971 California Supreme Court ruling which set limits to therapist-client confidentiality and privilege. The court ruled that therapists must warn potential victims of dangerous clients.

Task analysis Research strategy developed by Laura Rice and Leslie Greenberg in which therapy is looked on as a series of emotional processing tasks for the client to engage in. The researcher defines what a given task is and studies the process by which therapist and client strive to resolve the task.

Teaching stories Stories that convey a therapeutic message metaphorically.

Technical eclecticism In psychotherapy theory integration, an approach that emphasizes the pragmatic use of techniques from different therapies, although one theoretical outlook may be maintained.

Tertiary prevention In community psychology, intervention methods aimed at fixing or "repairing" psychological disorders once they have occurred.

Theoretical integration In psychotherapy integration, the attempt to develop an integrative theory that includes ideas from differing approaches.

Therapeutic alliance The general quality of the relationship between therapist and client.

Therapeutic marker See marker.

Time-out In behavior therapy with children, an extinction procedure in which the child is briefly removed from a situation in which undesired behaviors are being rewarded.

Token economy In mental hospitals and other institutions, a reinforcement system in which patients are given tokens as reinforcers for specific desired behaviors.

Transactional analysis (TA) A form of therapy that analyzes transactions between people rather than internal conflicts of the individual.

Transference The process in which the client projects attitudes and emotions that apply to other people in his/her past onto the therapist.

Treatment manuals For purposes of research and treatment, explicit steps in doing a particular treatment for a particular diagnosis are described in a book or manual.

Triangulation In order to deal with tension and instability, or conflict between oneself and another, a two-person system draws a third person into the system in order to deflect or deal with the tension or instability.

Unconditioned response In classical conditioning, the response that "naturally" occurs to the unconditioned stimulus.

Unconditioned stimulus A stimulus innately capable of eliciting a response. In classical conditioning, it is paired with the conditioned stimulus until both elicit the response.

Unfinished business In gestalt therapy and process-experiential psychotherapy, the client is struggling with an issue from the past that is "unfinished."

Vail model The professional model for clinical psychology developed at the 1973 APA training conference held in Vail, Colorado.

Validation Technique used in dialectical behavior therapy that emphasizes the validity of the client's experience.

Validity The appropriateness of the interpretations of test results.

Vertical interpretation A therapeutic response designed to increase client insight into the connection between current behavior and past childhood determinants.

Vicarious learning Learning through watching others; also called modeling and observational learning.

Working model In object relations theory and Bowlby's psychodynamic attachment theory, the idea that a child develops a working model of interpersonal relationships and of reality in general from interactions with the caretaker. This becomes the model for later interactions with the world.

Index

A-B-C model, 354, 488
ABPP. *See* American Board of Professional Psychology
Abuse. *See* Child abuse; Substance abuse problems
Academic psychology, 28–30
    and psychoanalysis, 35–36
Acceptance
    in client-centered approach, 206–207, 214, 216–217
    versus control, 501–502
    in couples therapy, 407–408
    importance of, 497–498
Acceptance and commitment therapy (ACT), 298
Access problem, 24, 478–479
    neurological model of, 495–497
    strategies for overcoming, 480–492
    theoretical reasons for, 492–497
Accountability, 557
Acculturation, 521
Achenbach Child Behavior Checklist (CBCL), 122
    evaluation report based on, 130
Achievement tests, 81
ACT. *See* Acceptance and commitment therapy
Adjustment, versus change, 559–560
Adler, Alfred, 43, 171–172, 174, 398
Administration, in practice of psychology, 22
Adolescents, group therapy with, 385–386
Adult (ego-state), 380
Affectively meaningful knowledge, and therapy, 154–155
Age norms, 77
Aggression
    in Freud's theory, 143, 174
    in object relations theory, 175–177

Albee, George, 543, 564
Alcoholics, group therapy for, 386–388
Alcoholics Anonymous, 386–387, 393
AMA. *See* American Medical Association
American Board of Professional Psychology (ABPP), 8–9, 46
American Journal of Psychology, 29, 35
American Medical Association (AMA), 6, 552
American Psychiatric Association, 6
American Psychological Association (APA)
    versus American Psychiatric Association, 6
    clinical section within, 37
    code of ethics, 7, 544, 573–577
    counseling section within, 39
    development of, 45–49
    divisions of, 47–48
    and empirically validated treatments, 460–462
    guidelines for working with women, 520, 559–560
    on professional training, 6–7
    proficiency certification by, 554
    size of, 45–46
    and treatment guidelines, 459–460
American Psychological Society (APS), 48
Anal stage, of personality development, 147–148
Analogue research designs, 449
Analytical psychology, 172
Anima-animus (archetype), 173
Anorexia nervosa, group therapy for, 388–389
Anxiety
    existential approach to, 242–244

narrative truth and reduction of, 159
    psychopathology and, 146–147
Anxiety hierarchy, 279–280
APA. *See* American Psychological Association
APS. *See* American Psychological Society
Aptitude tests, 123–126
Archetypes, 172–173
Aristotle, 31
Army Alpha test, 37
Articulation, experiential, 481–482
Asian personality theories, 231
Assertion training, 283–285
Assessment, 54–65
    behavioral, 42, 119–123
    cost-effectiveness of, 63–64
    criticism of, 63–65
    definition of, 54
    development of, 39–43
    ethics in, 59
    future of, 566
    intellectual, 39–41, 54, 77–84
    issues in, 59–63
    methods of, 54
    neuropsychological, 42–43, 84–91
    and norms, 55
    personality, 41–42, 54
        objective, 42, 110–119
        projective, 41–42, 104–110
    in practice of psychology, 21
    process of, 57–59
    reliability of, 55–56
    and standardization, 55
    use of technology in, 62–63
    validity of, 56–57
    vocational, 123–126
Assessment report, 59
    examples of, 91–97, 126–132
Assimilative integration, 476–477
Asylums, nineteenth-century, 32
    efforts to reform, 33

Attachment theory, 194–195
Attention, as reward, 274, 277
Attribution theory, 343–345
Authenticity, in existential therapy, 244–245
Automatic thoughts, 350
Aversion therapy, 280–283
    criticism of, 301
Aversive control, 286
Awareness
    as common factor, 472
    in gestalt therapy, 250–251, 255
    lack of, and dysfunctional behavior, 493
Axline, Virginia, 398

Bandura, Albert, 273, 343
    concept of self-efficacy, 342
    social learning theory of, 30, 339–343
Barber, T. X., 325
BAT. *See* Behavior avoidance test
BDI. *See* Beck Depression Inventory
Beck, Aaron, cognitive therapy of, 345–353, 488
Beck Depression Inventory (BDI), 42, 116
Beers, Clifford, 33
Beery Buktenica Developmental Test of Visual-Motor Integration (VMI), 87
    drawings from, 88
Behavior avoidance test (BAT), 121
Behavior modification, 285–290
    cognitive, 358–360
Behavior therapy, 44, 278–300
    with children, 400
    for depression, 347–348
    enduring contributions of, 302–303
    evaluation of, 300–303
    feminist, 526
    focus of, 473
    foundations of, 268–271
    in groups, 378
    history of, 271–272
    multimodal, 294
    postmodern, 294–300
    versus psychoanalysis, 269–270, 300, 454
    theoretical foundations of, 119–120
    view of psychopathology, 275–277
Behavioral approaches, 267–305.
    See also Behavior therapy
    to marital counseling, 406–408
    phenomenological method in, 488
    and psychoanalysis, integration of, 474

radical, 294–300
Behavioral assessment, 42, 119–123
    clinical uses of, 123
    methods of, 120–121
    psychophysiological techniques in, 121
    radical, 122
    reliability of, 122–123
    validity of, 123
Behavioral medicine, 306–321
    biofeedback in, 310–311, 314
    with children, 400
    versus clinical health psychology, 13
    definitions of, 307
    development of, 45
    enduring contributions of, 331
    evaluation of, 319–321
    foundations of, 307–309
    history of, 309–310
    interventions in, 310–319
Behavioral toxicology, psychology and, 23, 564
Behaviorism, 29
    theoretical foundations of, 119–120
The Bell Curve (Herrnstein & Murray), 83
Bender, Lauretta, 41
Bender-Motor-Gestalt Test, 41, 42–43, 87
    evaluation report based on, 95–96
    personality assessment with, 107
Berne, Eric, 380–381
Biculturation, 521
Binet, Alfred, 37, 39, 77, 82
Biofeedback, 310–311, 314
Biologically based therapies, 552–553
Biosocial-learning approach, 341
Blacky Pictures, 106
Borderline behaviors, 181, 354, 445
    consistency of, 164–165
    dialectical behavior therapy for, 298–299
    early experiences and, 193, 195
    object relations view of, 196
Boston Diagnostic Aphasia Examination, 43
Boston Process Approach, 89–90
Boulder Conference of APA (1949), 6, 38, 46
Bowen, Murray, 410–412
Brain, functions of, localization of, 85, 495–497
Brain-behavior connections, 302
Brain damage
    disorders associated with, 86
    and neuropsychological assessment, 85–87
Breuer, Josef, 34–35
Brief therapy, 532–536

effectiveness of, 532
methods of, 533–534
psychoanalytic, 188–191
theoretical bases of, 532–533
types of, 534–535
Broad spectrum therapy, 294
Bulimia, group therapy for, 388–389

CAC. *See* Certified alcoholism counselor
California Psychological Inventory (CPI), 42, 116–117
California Self-Help Center, 539
Career counseling, 9–10. *See also* Vocational assessment
    historical development of, 38
    tests used in, 123–125
Case history interview, 102–103
    example of, 93
Castration anxiety, 148
    Kohut's view of, 186
CAT. *See* Children's Apperception Test
Catharsis therapies, 142, 483
CATs. *See* Cognitive ability tests
Cattell, James M., 29
Cattell, Raymond, 19
CBCL. *See* Achenbach Child Behavior Checklist
CCRT. *See* Core conflictual relationship theme
Certification. *See* Licensing and certification
Certified alcoholism counselor (CAC), 18
CHA. *See* Consumer health alliance
Change, psychological
    versus adjustment, 559–560
    defining, 445–446
    emotion and, 442
    experiential learning and, 480–486
    first-order, 423, 499
    measuring, 446–449
    neutralization of negative self-monitoring and, 486–489
    problem of, 24. *See also* Access problem
    purely cognitive attempts for, 478–479
    resistance to, 155–156
    second-order, 423, 499
    therapeutic conditions of, 154–155
    understanding process of, 456–457
Character structure, fixed versus fluid, 164–165, 517
Charcot, Jean, 34, 43
Checklists, behavioral, 121–122

Child(ren)
  behavior therapy with, 400
  behavioral medicine with, 400
  client-centered therapy with, 398
  cognitive-behavior therapy with, 401
  evaluation of therapy for, 428
  family therapy with, 401
  group therapy with, 385, 402
  hypnosis with, 400
  intellectual assessment of, 39, 58
  interventions for, 43, 397–402
  personality assessment of, 106, 110
  play therapy with, 398–400
  psychoanalysis with, 397–398
  psychopharmacological interventions for, 401
Child (ego-state), 380
Child abuse
  and borderline personality disorder, 195
  in Freudian theory, 159
  play therapy for, 399
  and repression, 163
Children's Apperception Test (CAT), 106
Choice
  in existential theory, 241–243
  in gestalt theory, 252
Christian approaches to psychotherapy, 529–530
Classical conditioning, 272–273
  therapy based on, 279–283
Classical psychoanalysis, 34
Classroom, behavior modification principles in, 288
Client-centered approach, 203–237
  acceptance in, 206–207, 214, 216–217
  with children, 398
  creativity in, 215
  current status of, 226–227
  enduring contributions of, 232–233
  evaluation of, 227–232
  experiencing in, 210–213
  experiential articulation in, 481
  and group therapy, 375–377
  individualism in, 209
  information-processing interpretation of, 224
  model of person in, 204–209
  multiple realities in, 205
  phenomenological method in, 487, 488–489
  problems with, 230–232
  process orientation in, 208–209
  to psychopathology, 212–214
  qualities of therapist, 216–221
  recent developments in, 221–226
  tentative constructs in, 207–208
  therapy based on, 214–221

Clinical child psychology, 14, 397
Clinical health psychology, 13, 307. *See also* Behavioral medicine
Clinical neuropsychology, 10–11
Clinical prediction, 61–62
Clinical psychology
  competition with psychiatry, 6, 19, 551–552
  education and training for, 6–7
  employment in, 9
  historical development of, 37–38
  licensing and certification in, 7–8
  methods of, 4
  profession of, 5–9
  and social problems, 5
  and team approach, 20
Clinically relevant behaviors (CRBs), 296–297
Cognition, 336
  and emotion, 363, 494–495
  hot, 352, 353
Cognitive ability tests (CATs), 77
Cognitive approach(es), 335–369
  Bandura's, 339–343
  Beck's, 345–353
  with children, 401
  criticism of, 363–365
  to depression, 345–351, 362, 488
  Ellis's, 353–357
  emotions in, 352
  enduring contributions of, 366
  evaluation of, 362–366
  experiential articulation in, 481
  focus of, 473
  to generalized anxiety disorder, 360–361
  group therapy with, 378–379
  hypnosis with, 325–326
  interpersonal, 361–362
  Kelly's, 337–339
  marital counseling with, 408
  to panic disorder, 361
  to personality disorders, 352–353
  recent theoretical advances in, 361–362
Cognitive assessment. *See* Intellectual assessment
Cognitive behavior modification, 358–360
Cognitive behaviorism, 30
Cognitive triad, 346
Cohesiveness, group, 383
Collective unconscious, 172
Common factors approach, to psychotherapy integration, 23–24, 471–473
Communication
  direct, limitations of, 479, 490
  dysfunctional, families and, 412–414
  levels of, 418
Communication skills training programs, 226

Community Mental Health Act (1963), 44
Community psychology, 12–13
  Adler and, 171
  development of, 45
Comparative design, in research, 445
Compensation, as defense mechanism, 145
Competition, among mental health professions, 6, 19, 551–552
Computers, use in counseling, 536–537
Concurrent validity, 56
Conditionability, genetic differences in, 277
Conditioned Reflex Therapy (Salter), 44
Conditioned response, 272
Conditioned stimulus, 272
Conditioning
  classical, 272–273
    therapy based on, 279–283
  operant (instrumental), 273
    reinforcement in, 273–275
    therapy based on, 283–293
Confidentiality, 544
  exceptions to, 545–546
Confrontation
  in existential therapy, 245
  in group therapy, 388
  as therapeutic response to resistance, 156
Construct theory, 337–339
Construct validity, 56
Constructivism, 420–425, 527–528
Consumer health alliance (CHA), 550
Contingency management, 285–290
Contracting, behavioral, 289–290
Control
  versus acceptance, 501–502
  locus of, 501
  verbal, 295–296
Control groups, 443–445
Conversion disorder, 141
Coping imagery exercises, 292
Coping with Depression model, 294
Core conflictual relationship theme (CCRT), 190, 535
Corporations, 556–558, 562
Correlation coefficient (r), 55
Cost-effectiveness
  of assessment, 63–64
  of brief therapy, 532
  emphasis on, 557–558
Counseling
  paraprofessional, 18–19
    trends in, 564
  in practice of psychology, 21
  profession of, 17

Counseling and Psychotherapy (Rogers), 38, 43, 204
Counseling psychology
  education and training in, 9
  historical development of, 38–39
  methods of, 4
  profession of, 9–10
  and social problems, 5
Countertransference, 157
Couples counseling. *See* Marital counseling
Covert modeling, 293
Covert practice, 284
Covert sensitization, 283
CPI. *See* California Psychological Inventory
CRBs. *See* Clinically relevant behaviors
Cultural triage model, 522–523
Culture. *See also* Multicultural counseling
  and boundary of self, 209
  and goal of therapy, 514–515
  and intelligence tests, 83
  and perception of self, 516–518
  and projective personality tests, 108
  and self-actualization, 231

DAP. *See* Draw-A-Person test
DBT. *See* Dialectical behavior therapy
De-reflection, 245
Death instinct, 143
Decentering, 217
Deductive approach to objective personality tests, 110–111, 115–116
Deep muscle relaxation, 272, 279, 281
Defense mechanisms, 144–145
  evidence for, 162
  gestalt view of, 252
  mature, 146
  in self-psychology, 188
  splitting as, 179–180
Defensive pessimism, 365
Demonology, 31–32
Denial
  as defense mechanism, 144
  group approach to, 388
Depression
  attribution model of, 344
  behavioral approach to, 294, 347–348
  cognition and, 362–363
  cognitive therapy for, 345–351, 362, 488
  constructivist view of, 422
  treatment guidelines for, 458–459

Desensitization
  EMDR, 294
  systematic, 272, 279–280, 281–282
  in vivo, 280, 282
de Shazer, Steven, 415, 416–417, 425–427
Determinism, psychic, 151
Developmental psychotherapy, 428
Developmental school psychologists, 12
Developmental stages
  Freud's, 147–149
  Mahler's, 178–180
Deviance
  dealing with, 31–39
  definition of, 30–31
Diagnosis, 65–73
  client-centered approach to, 231–232
  controversy over, 555–556
  criticism of, 72–73
  differential, 65
  functional, 65
Diagnosis-related groups (DRGs), 558
Diagnostic and Statistical Manual of Mental Disorders (DSM), 66–72, 553
  bias in, 69, 70–71
  criticism of, 72–73
  DSM-IV, 68–69, 71
  revising, controversies over, 70–71
Dialectical behavior therapy (DBT), 298–299
Differential diagnosis, 65
Differentiation, in family, 411
Discovery-oriented approaches, 231, 457, 527–528
Disengaged family, 414
Displacement, as defense mechanism, 145
Disputing, in rational-emotive therapy, 355–356
Dix, Dorothea, 33
Double blind, 426
Draw-A-Person test (DAP), 41, 104, 107
Drawing tests, 107
Dreams
  Freud's view of, 155
  in gestalt therapy, 256
DRGs. *See* Diagnosis-related groups
DSM. *See* Diagnostic and Statistical Manual of Mental Disorders
Dynamic-eclectic therapies, 161
The Dynamics of Vocational Adjustment (Super), 38
Dysfunctional communication, in families, 412–414

EAPs. *See* Employee Assistance Programs
Eastern mysticism, and psychotherapy, 529
Eating disorders
  behavioral therapy for, 318
  group therapy for, 388–389
Eclectic therapies, 161, 469–471
ECT. *See* Electroconvulsive therapy
Education and training, 553–554
  bachelor's-level, 18
  for clinical neuropsychology, 10
  for clinical psychology, 6–7
  continuing, 554
  for counseling psychology, 9
  for educational psychology, 11
  for psychiatry, 14–15
  for psychoanalysis, 15–16
  for school psychology, 11
  for social work, 16
Educational psychology, 11
Edwards Personal Preference Schedule, 42
Effect size, 453
Effectiveness, 451–452. *See also under specific approach*
  treatment guidelines and, 459
Efficacy, 459
Ego, 147, 149
  neo-Freudian views of, 173, 174
Ego analysis, 404
Ego-ideal, 148
Ego-states, in transactional analysis, 380
Electra complex, 148–149
Electroconvulsive therapy (ECT), 553
Elements of the Philosophy of Mind, Applied to the Development of Thought and Feeling (Secord), 29
Ellis, Albert, 353–357
EMDR therapy. *See* Eye Movement Desensitization and Reprocessing therapy
Emotion(s)
  arousal of, 483–484
  and change, 442
  and cognitions, 363, 494–495
  in cognitive therapy, 352
  as experience, 485
  primary, 408–409
Emotional catharsis, 142, 483
Emotional object constancy, 180–181
Empathy
  in client-centered therapy, 217–218
  in cognitive therapy, 361
  in existential therapy, 244
  in self-psychology, 183, 186

Empirical approach to objective personality tests, 110, 111–115
Empirically validated treatments (EVTs), 460–461, 555–556
  controversy over, 461–462
Employee Assistance Programs (EAPs), 21, 550
Employee Retirement Income Security Act (ERISA), 548
Employment
  trends in, 562, 565–567
  types of, 9, 21
Empowerment, 500–502
Empty chair technique. *See* Two-chair technique
Encounter groups, 226, 229, 389–390
Enmeshed family, 414–415
Environmental health science, psychology and, 23, 564
EPQ. *See* Eysenck Personality Questionnaire
Erickson, Milton, 327, 496
  family therapy, 416–418
  theory of hypnosis, 323–325
Erikson, Erik, 173
ERISA. *See* Employee Retirement Income Security Act
Ethics
  APA code of, 573–577
  in assessment, 59
  in professional psychology, 7, 543–546
Ethnic identity development, 521
Evaluation. *See* Assessment
Evocation of experiential reactions, 482–483
Evocative unfolding, 229–230
  as therapeutic marker, 225
EVTs. *See* Empirically validated treatments
Existential-humanistic approach, 238–239
  criticism of, 260–262
  enduring contributions of, 262–263
  to group therapy, 377–378
  personality theory of, 241–242
  philosophical background of, 239–241
  to psychopathology, 242–244
  to therapy, 244–245
Existential leap, 242–243
Experience
  articulation of, 481–482
  versus research, 439–443
Experiencing, in client-centered approach, 210–213
  research on, 228–229
Experiential knowing/learning, 210–213
  and change, 480–486
  and therapy, 154–155

Experiential psychotherapy
  Gendlin's, 223–224
  Mahrer's, 258–259
  and marital counseling, 408–409, 429
Experiential reactions, evocation of, 482–483
Exposure-based treatments, 279–283
Extinction, 273
  therapy based on, 280
Extraversion, 173
Eye Movement Desensitization and Reprocessing (EMDR) therapy, 294
Eysenck, Hans J., 277, 451
Eysenck Personality Questionnaire (EPQ), 42, 115

Face validity, 56
Factor analysis, 115
Family
  differentiation in, 411
  disengaged, 414
  dysfunctional communication in, 412–414
  enmeshed, 414–415
  function of disruption in, 421–422
  triangulation in, 411
Family mediation, 565
Family therapy, 409–428. *See also* Parent training
  with children, 401
  constructivism in, 420–425
  enduring contributions of, 433
  evaluation of, 428–430
  feminist, 526
  focus of, 473
  paradoxical interventions in, 416–417, 419
  reframing in, 416–417, 419
  restructuring in, 419
  strategic (solution-focused) approaches to, 415–428
  structural, 414–415
FAP. *See* Functional analytic psychotherapy
Feedback
  biological, 310–311, 314
  in social skills training, 284
Feminist therapy, 523–527
  challenges presented by, 513–514
  core principles of, 526–527
  current issues in, 527
  early roots of, 525
  types of, 525–526
First-order change, 423, 499
Fixation, repression and, 143
FOC legislation. *See* Freedom of choice legislation
Focusing technique, 223

Follow-up, problem of, 449
Forensic psychology, 13
Frankl, Victor, 243, 245, 261
Free association, 35, 150–151, 487
Freedom, limits and, 241
Freedom of choice (FOC) legislation, 548
Freud, Anna, 43, 375, 398
Freud, Sigmund. *See also* Psychoanalysis
  enduring contributions of, 165–166
  personality theory of, 140–149
  and psychological model of mental illness, 34–36
  seduction theory of, 143, 159–160
Functional analysis, 120, 295
Functional analytic psychotherapy (FAP), 296–298
Functional diagnosis, 65
Functionalism, 29

g factor, 82
Galton, Francis, 29
Games, in transactional analysis, 380–381
Gay men, therapy with, 530–531
Gendlin, Eugene, 206, 210, 214–215, 221, 226
  experiential psychotherapy of, 223–224, 228–229
  and group therapy, 393
General intelligence (g factor), 82
Generalization, 275
Generalized anxiety disorder, cognitive-behavioral treatment for, 360–361
Genital stage, in personality development, 149
Genuineness, in client-centered therapy, 219–221
Gestalt approach, 245–257
  effectiveness of, 259
  to group therapy, 377
  organismic self-regulation in, 249–251
  personality theory of, 246–249
  phenomenological method in, 488
  to psychopathology, 251–252
  to therapy, 254–257
Graduated exposure, 280
Grant applications, writing, 22
Greenberg, Leslie, 226
Greystone Conference (1954), 39
Group(s)
  cohesiveness of, 383
  curative factors in, 384–385
  encounter, 226, 229, 389–390
  norms in, 382–383
  pressure toward uniformity in, 383–384

Group(s) *(continued)*
  self-help (mutual-support),
    391–393, 538
  sensitivity training, 44, 389
Group dynamics, 382–384
  importance of, 384
Group therapy, 373–389
  with adolescents, 385–386
  behavioral approach to, 378
  with children, 385, 402
  client-centered approach to,
    375–377
  cognitive approach to, 378–379
  for eating disorders, 388–389
  enduring contributions of,
    393–394
  existential approach to, 377–378
  gestalt approach to, 377
  group-based forms of, 379–382
  psychoanalytical approach to,
    374–375
  for substance abuse problems,
    386–388
  for women's consciousness-
    raising, 389
Guidelines, treatment, 458–460
Guntrip, Harry, 174–175
Gut-level knowing, versus intellec-
    tual knowing, 250–251,
    261–262

Habit, and experiential change, 486
Haley, Jay, 415, 418–420, 431
Hall, G. Stanley, 29, 35, 46
Halstead-Reitan Battery, 43, 87–89
  clinical use of, 91
  validity of, 90
Happiness
  cognitive view of, 347
  existential view of, 243
  psychotherapy and, 150
Hayes, S. C., 298
Headache, behavioral treatment of,
    312–315
Health care system
  corporate control of, 556–558, 562
  history of, 549–550
  regulations regarding, 547–548
  role of psychologists in, 316–317,
    319
Health maintenance organization
    (HMO), 550
Health psychology, 13, 307. *See
    also* Behavioral medicine
Heidegger, Martin, 240
Helping methods, 3–4
Hidden meanings, 140, 149
Hippocrates, 31
Historical truth, versus narrative
    truth, 158–159
HMO (health maintenance organi-
    zation), 550

Homosexuality, and psychother-
    apy, 530–531
Horizontal interpretation, 152
Horney, Karen, 173, 525
Hospital privileges, 554
Hot cognition, 352, 353
House-Tree-Person test (HTP), 42,
    104, 107
  evaluation report based on,
    129–130
Hoyt, Michael, 534
HTP. *See* House-Tree-Person test
Human being, paradigm revolution
    in view of, 502–503
Human factors psychologists, 12
Human potential movement. *See*
    Encounter groups
Human services workers, 18
Humanistic approaches, 201–264.
    See also Existential-humanis-
    tic approach
  evaluation of, 259–262
Husserl, Edmund, 239, 488
Hypnosis, 306–307, 314
  cognitive-behavioral view of
    Spanos, 325–326
  Erickson's theory of, 323–325
  evaluation of, 330–331
  foundations of, 321–322
  history of, 43, 322
  interventions utilizing, 326–330
  neurological model of, 496
  psychoanalysis and, 150–151,
    329
  self-induced, 329–330
  theoretical explanations of,
    322–326
  use with children, 400
Hypothesis-testing attitude, 499
Hysteria, 34
  conversion, 141

IBCT. *See* Integrative Behavioral
    Couple Therapy
Id, 147, 149
Idealization, in personality devel-
    opment, 183–184
Identity development
  ethnic, 521
  gay and lesbian, 531
Illness behavior, 308, 315–316
Imagery
  Christian, use in therapy, 530
  coping exercises with, 292
  and evocation of experiential reac-
    tions, 483
  use in rational-emotive therapy,
    357
Imitation, 273
  use in therapy, 293
Implosive therapy, 280
In vivo desensitization, 280, 282

Independent practitioner associa-
    tion (IPA), 550
Indirect circumvention, 489
Indirect contingency control,
    295–296
Individual(s), and treatment types,
    455, 469
Individual Psychology, 398
Individualism
  in client-centered approach, 209,
    231
  in gestalt approach, 245–246
  as goal of therapy, alternatives
    to, 514–515
Inductive approach to objective
    personality tests, 110, 115
Industrial and organizational psy-
    chologists, 12
Inferiority complex, 171
Information processing
  client-centered approach and,
    224
  nonconscious, 493–495
Informed consent, 546
Inkblot test, 41
Inquisition, 32
Insanity defense, 560
Insight, therapeutic, 154–155
Insight event, 457
Instrumental conditioning. *See* Op-
    erant conditioning
Intake interview, 101
Integration, psychotherapy, 23–24,
    468–509
  assimilative, 476–477
  authors' views on, 478–503
  common factors approach to,
    471–473
  eclectic approach to, 469–471
  objections to, 477–478
  theoretical, 24, 473–476
  types of, 469–477
Integrative Behavioral Couple
    Therapy (IBCT), 407–408
Intellectual assessment, 39–41, 54,
    77–84
  clinical use of, 83–84
  misuse of, 64
  reliability of, 82
  validity of, 82–83
Intellectual knowing
  versus gut-level knowing,
    250–251, 261–262
  limitations of, 478–479
  versus therapeutic insight, 154
Intellectualization, as defense
    mechanism, 145
Intelligence
  definitions of, 82
  views of, 77
Interest tests, 123–126
Internal consistency, of assessment
    methods, 56

Internet, mutual-support groups on, 538
Interns, 19
Interpersonal process recall, 457
Interpersonal psychoanalytic approaches, 170–200, 502–503
  in cognitive therapy, 361–362
  enduring contributions of, 197
  evaluation of, 191–196
Interpretation(s)
  clinical versus statistical, 61–62
  horizontal, 152
  of projective tests, 109–110
  in psychoanalysis, 152–154
    effectiveness of, 161–162
  versus reflection of feeling, 219
  of tests, 58–59
  therapeutic qualities of, 443
  timing in, importance of, 153–154
  transference relationship and, 157
  vertical, 152
The Interpretation of Dreams (Freud), 35
Interrater reliability, of assessment methods, 56
Interventions. *See also under specific approach*
  changes in, 563
  for children, 43, 397–402
  development of, 43–45
  paradoxical, 416–417, 419, 489, 491–492
    effectiveness of, 429–430
Interview(s), 54, 100–104
  behavioral assessment, 120
  case history, 102–103
    example of, 93
  intake, 101
  posttest, 103
  pretest, 103
  reliability of, 103–104
  validity of, 104
Introjections, 252
Introversion, 173
Intuitive knowledge, 494
IPA. *See* Independent practitioner association
IQ tests. *See* Intellectual assessment

Jaffe v. *Redmond*, 545
James, William, 29
JCAH. *See* Joint Commission on Accreditation of Hospitals
Joint Commission on Accreditation of Hospitals (JCAH), 554
Jones, Mary Cover, 43, 271
Journal of Abnormal Psychology, 37
Jung, Carl, 37, 104, 116, 172–173

Kaufman Assessment Battery for Children (K-ABC), 41, 81
Kelly, George, 117, 207
  construct theory of, 337–339
Kinetic Family Drawing (KFD), 107
  evaluation report based on, 129
Klein, Melanie, 174, 398
Knowing
  experiential, 210–213
  gut-level, 250–251, 261–262
  intellectual, limitations of, 154, 478–479
  intuitive, 494
  verbal versus nonverbal, 495
Kohut, Heinz, 43
  personality theory of, 182–185
Kraepelin, Emil, 34, 65
Kuder Occupation Interest Survey, 124–125

Laing, R. D., 239–240, 500
Language
  experiential, 481–482
  of right brain, 424
Larry P. v. *Wilson Riles and the Board of Education*, 64
Lazarus, Arnold, 469
Learning
  biofeedback and, 310
  experiential, and change, 480–486
  observational, 273
  principles of, 272–275
  therapy and, 476
  vicarious, 340
Learning disability, neuropsychological assessment of, 88, 89–90
Learning theory. *See also* Social learning theory
  and behavior therapy, 268
Legal system, and psychology, 13, 23, 546–551
Length of therapy, 452–453
Lesbians, therapy with, 530–531
Lewin, Kurt, 389
Licensing and certification, 547
  in biofeedback use, 310
  of clinical psychologists, 7–8
  of forensic psychologists, 13
  of marriage, family, and child counselors, 17
  of psychiatrists, 15
  in specific skills, 554
Life script, concept of, 381
Lifestyle, Adler's view of, 172
Linehan, Marsha, 298–299
Logotherapy, Frankl's, 245
Luria, Alexander, 89
Luria-Nebraska Neuropsychological Battery, 43, 89
  clinical use of, 91
  validity of, 90

Machover, Karen, 41
Madanes, Cloe, 418–420
Mahler, Margaret, 174
  separation-individuation model of, 178–180
  evaluation of, 192–193
Mahoney, M. J., 475
Mahrer, Alvin, 457
  experiential psychotherapy of, 258–259
Make A Picture Story (MAPS), 106
Malpractice, 548–551
Managed care, 550, 558
Manuals, treatment, 189, 360, 460, 555–556
MAPS. *See* Make A Picture Story
Marital counseling, 404–409
  behavioral approach to, 406–408
  cognitive approach to, 408
  evaluation of, 428–430
  experiential-humanistic approach to, 408–409, 429
  psychodynamic approach to, 404–409
Marriage, family, and child counseling, 10, 396–435
  evaluation of, 428–432
Marriage, family, and child counselors (MFCCs), 17
Masochistic personality disorder, in DSM, 70
Masson, J. M., 159–160
May, Rollo, 242, 243
MBHI. *See* Millon Behavioral Health Inventory
MBTI. *See* Myers-Briggs Type Indicator
MCMI. *See* Clinical Multiaxial Inventory
MCT. *See* Multicultural Counseling and Therapy
Medical model of mental illness, 33–34, 65, 552–553
Medicalization of social problems, 5, 560
Meditation
  phenomenological method in, 488
  types of, 529
Meichenbaum, Donald, 358–360, 361
Memory
  reconstructive nature of, 158
  recovery of, therapeutic use of, 141–142, 154–155
Mental health professions (MHPs), 5–19
  competition among, 6, 19, 551–552
  cooperation among, 19–20
Mental illness
  defining, 552–553
  medical model of, 33–34, 65, 552–553

Mental illness *(continued)*
misuses of concept, 560–561
psychological model of, 34–36
and social stigma, 73
views of, historical development
of, 31–36
Mental Status Exam, 101–102
reliability of, 103
Mesmer, Franz Anton, 43, 322, 325
Meta-analysis, 453–454
Metapsychology, 142
MFCCs. *See* Marriage, family, and
child counselors
MHPs. *See* Mental health professions
Millon, Theodore, 42, 341
Millon Adolescent Personality Inventory (MAPI), 114
Millon Behavioral Health Inventory (MBHI), 114
Millon Clinical Multiaxial Inven-
tory (MCMI), 42, 114
Mind-body connection, 307, 309
A Mind That Found Itself (Beers),
33
Minnesota Multiphasic Personality
Inventory (MMPI), 42,
111–114
clinical uses of, 119
criticism of, 64–65
profile of scores, 113, 114f
reliability of, 118
Minuchin, Salvador, 414–415
Mirror, one-way, use in therapy,
418–419
Mirroring
emphatic, 183
in marital therapy, 405
Misattribution procedures, 344–345
MMPI. *See* Minnesota Multiphasic
Personality Inventory
Model Act for State Licensure of
Psychologists, 20
Modeling, 293
Modernism, 518
Moral treatment, 33, 43
Moreno, J. L., 379
Morgan, Christiana, 41
Mothering
in object relations theory, 179,
182
in self-psychology, 183
Multiaxial model, 67
Multicultural counseling, 519–523
challenges presented by, 513–514
need for therapists, 522–523
treatment issues in, 519–521
Multicultural Counseling and
Therapy (MCT), 521–522
Multimodal behavior therapy, 294
Multiple realities, in client-centered
approach, 205
Murray, Henry, 41

Musturbatory thinking, 353
Mutual-support groups, 391–393
Myers-Briggs Type Indicator
(MBTI), 42, 115–116
clinical uses of, 119

Narcissistic personality disorder,
185
Narrative therapies, 528
Narrative truth, versus historical
truth, 158–159
*National Register of Health Service
Providers in Psychology*, 8,
547
National Training Laboratory,
Bethel, Maine, 44
National Vocational Guidance As-
sociation, 38
Naturalistic observation, 120–121
Negative attention *seeking*, 274, 277
Negative reinforcement, 274
Negative self-monitoring, 342,
344–345, 487
neutralization of effects of,
486–489
Negative thinking, cognitive view
of, 347
Neo-Freudians, 170–173
NEO Personality Inventory, Re-
vised (NEO PI-R), 117
Neuropsychological assessment,
42–43, 84–91
clinical uses of, 90–91
growth in, 84–85
versus medical tests for brain
damage, 85–87
reliability and validity of, 90
Neurotic disorders, 141
Freudian approach to, 147
Neurotic paradox, 276
Nonconscious information processing, 493–495
Nonpossessive warmth, 216–217
Nonprofessional counseling, 18–19
trends in, 564
Normal symbiosis, 178
Norms
age, 77
assessment and, 55
in therapy groups, 382–383
Northwestern Conference (1951),
39

Object relations theory, 43, 170,
174–182
approach to psychopathology,
196
approach to therapy, 186–188
Objective personality tests, 42,
110–119
clinical uses of, 118–119

deductive approach to, 110–111,
115–116
external (empirical) approach to,
110, 111–115
inductive approach to, 110, 115
reliability of, 118
validity of, 118
Observation
analogue, 121
naturalistic, 120–121
participant, 121
Observational learning, 273
Observer reliability, 56
Oedipus complex, 148–149
Kohut's version of, 185–186
research evaluation of, 163
One-way mirror, use in therapy,
418–419
Operant conditioning, 273
as common factor, 472
reinforcement in, 273–275
therapy based on, 283–293
Optimism
cognitive view of, 347
solution-focused view of,
427–428
Oral stage, in personality development, 147
Organismic self-regulation, 249–251
Organismic valuing process, 213
neurological model of, 496–497
Outcome, measuring, 462–463
Outcome research, 451–452
Overeating, behavioral therapy for,
318

Panic disorder, cognitive treatment
for, 361
Paradox
neurotic, 276
therapeutic, 323–324
Paradoxical intention, 245
Paradoxical interventions, 416–417,
419, 489, 491–492
effectiveness of, 429–430
Paranoid personality disorder, 352
Paraphilic rapism, 71
Paraprofessional counseling, 18–19
trends in, 564
Parent (ego-state), 380
Parent training, 285–288
criticism of, 301
Parsons, Frank, 38
Parsons' Vocational Bureau, 43
Participant observation, 121
Patient compliance, behavioral
techniques for, 316
Patterson's behavior modification
program, 285–288
Pavlov, Ivan, 271–273
Peabody Picture Vocabulary Test,
Revised (PPVT-R), 81

Pediatric psychology, 14, 397
Peer counselors, 18–19
Peer review, 557
Penis envy, 148–149
  Kohut's view of, 186
Perls, Fritz, 245, 250–251, 253–254, 377
Perls, Laura, 245
Person-centered philosophy, 204, 221–222
Persona (archetype), 173
Personal constructs, in client-centered approach, 207–208
  in Kelly's approach, 337–339
Personal counseling, 10
Personal Data Sheet, 37, 42
Personality assessment, 41–42, 54
  objective, 42, 110–119
  projective, 41–42, 104–110
Personality disorders, 141
  cognitive therapy for, 352–353
Personality theory(ies)
  Adler's, 171–172
  Berne's, 380
  cultural differences in, 231
  existential, 238–239, 241–242
  Freud's, 140–149
    evaluation of, 162–165
  gestalt, 246–249
  Jung's, 172–173
  Kelly's, 337
  Kohut's, 182–185
  object relations, 175–177, 181–182
Personality trait, concept of, 517
Pessimism
  cognitive view of, 347
  defensive, 365
Phallic stage, of personality development, 148–149
Pharmacological interventions, psychology and, 401, 553
Phenomenological method, 239–240, 487–489
Philosophy, and psychology, 28
Phobia
  hypnotic treatment of, 328
  as learned behavior, 271–272, 276
Piaget, Jean, 30
Picture Projective Test (PPT), 106
Pinel, Philippe, 32
Placebo pseudo-treatments, 444–445
  effect of, 501
Play therapy, 398–400
  classical, 398–399
  structured, 399–400
PMDD. See Premenstrual dysphoric disorder
Politics, and psychotherapy, 458–463
Positive reinforcement, 274
Positive thinking
  cognitive view of, 347

solution-focused view of, 427–428
Postmodernism, 518
Posttest interview, 103
Power structure, in relationships, 418
PPO. See Preferred provider organization
PPS. See Prospective payment systems
PPT. See Picture Projective Test
PPVT-R. See Peabody Picture Vocabulary Test, Revised
Practice
  covert, 284
  and experiential change, 486
Predictive validity, 56
  of intelligence tests, 83
Preferred provider organization (PPO), 550
Premenstrual dysphoric disorder (PMDD), 70–71
Prescribing the symptom, 417
Prescription privileges, 555
Pretest interview, 103
Prevention
  psychology and, 564
  response, 280
Primal therapy, 210, 483
Primary emotions, 408–409
The Principles of Psychology (James), 29
Privilege(s)
  hospital, 554
  legal, 544–546
  prescription, 555
Problem-solving training, 290–292
Problematic reaction point, as therapeutic marker, 225
Process-experiential psychotherapy, 224–226
  contributions of, 233
  research on, 227
Process orientation, in client-centered approach, 208–209
Process research, 451
Product-of-behavior measures, 122
Professional model, 6
Professional organizations, development of, 45–49
Professional psychology, 3–26
  competition and cooperation within, 6, 19–20
  competition with medicine, 6, 19, 551–552
  ethical issues in, 7, 543–546
  fields in, 5–19, 564–565
  future of, 562–567
  historical development of, 27–50
  legal issues in, 546–551
  practice of, 20–23
  professional issues in, 551–556
  and society, 559–562

Projection
  as defense mechanism, 145
  gestalt view of, 252
Projective identification, 188
Projective personality tests, 41–42, 104–110
  clinical uses of, 109–110
  interpretations of, 109–110
  psychoanalytic tradition and, 104–105
  reliability of, 108
  validity of, 108–109
Prospective payment systems (PPS), 558
Psychiatric nurse, 18
Psychiatric technician, 18
Psychiatry, 14–15
  competition with clinical psychology, 6, 19, 551–552
  education and training for, 14–15
  licensing and certification in, 15
  and team approach, 20
Psychic determinism, 151
Psychoanalysis, 139–169
  and academic psychology, 35–36
  affective component in, 210
  versus behavior therapy, 269–270, 300, 454
  and behavioral approaches, integration of, 474
  brief forms of, 188–191
  with children, 397–398
  classical, 34
  effectiveness of, 160–162
  empowerment development in, 501
  enduring contributions of, 165–166
  experiential articulation in, 481
  focus of, 473
  versus gestalt therapy, 249
  goal of, 150
  and group therapy, 374–375
  hypnosis in, 150–151, 329
  interpersonal approaches to, 170–200
  interpretation in, 152–154
  and marital counseling, 404–409
  mechanics of, 158
  narrative views of, 158–159
  phenomenological method in, 487
  profession of, 15–16
  and projective tests, 104–106
  recent issues in, 158–160
  research evaluation of, 160–165
  therapy using, 150–158
  transference in, 156–157
Psychodrama, 379–380
Psychodynamic views of personality, 140
Psychoeducational school psychologists, 11

Psychological assistants, 17–18
Psychological Clinic (journal), 37
Psychological model of mental illness, 34–36
Psychoneuroimmunology, 309
Psychoneurotic Inventory of World War I, 42
Psychopathology. *See also specific psychopathology*
behaviorist view of, 275–277
client-centered perspective on, 212–214
constructivist view of, 420, 422
early experiences and, 193
existential approach to, 242–244
gestalt perspective on, 251–252
lack of awareness and, 493
object relations perspective on, 196
phenomenological approach to, 239–240
rigid schemas as cause of, 498–499
Psychopharmacological interventions, 553
for children, 401
Psychosis, 141
Freudian approach to, 147
Psychosomatic illnesses, 309
Psychotherapy by Reciprocal Inhibition (Wolpe), 44, 272
Punishment, 274
physical, reasons to avoid, 286
use in therapy, 280–283, 292–293

Q-Sort, 117
Qualitative research designs, 450–451
Questioning, in cognitive therapy, 350–351
Questionnaires, behavioral, 121–122

r. See Correlation coefficient
Radical behavioral approach
assessment, 122
to marital counseling, 407–408
therapies, 294–300
Rapprochement (developmental phase), 179
Rational-emotive therapy, 353–357
criticism of, 364
effectiveness of, 362
techniques of, 355–357
Rationalization, as defense mechanism, 145
Reaction formation, as defense mechanism, 145
Realities, multiple, 205
Reciprocal determinism, 308
Reciprocal inhibition. *See* Systematic desensitization

Recovery Inc., 538
Referral question, in assessment process, 57
Reflection of feeling, in client-centered therapy, 218–219
Reframing, 416–417, 419, 489, 492, 500
Registration, of therapists, 8, 547
Rehabilitation psychology, 12
Rehearsing
in cognitive therapy, 348
in gestalt therapy, 255
Reinforcement, 273–275
natural versus arbitrary, 295
negative, 274
positive, 274
schedules of, 275
in social learning theory, 340
Relational approaches, 373–435
Relationship(s). *See also* Interpersonal psychoanalytic approaches
focus on, 502–503
in gestalt theory, 254
neo-Freudian emphasis on, 173
power structure in, 418
psychoanalytical perspective on, 175
in self-psychology, 184–185
therapist-client. *See* Therapeutic alliance
in time-limited dynamic therapy, 534–535
Relationship Enhancement, 409
Relaxation
biofeedback and, 311
deep muscle, 272, 279, 281
Reliability
of assessment, 55–56
of behavioral assessment, 122–123
of intellectual assessment, 82
interrater, 56
of interviews, 103–104
of neuropsychological assessment, 90
of objective personality tests, 118
observer, 56
of projective personality tests, 108
split-half, 56
test-retest, 56
of vocational assessment, 125
Religion, and psychotherapy, 528–530
Repertory Grid, 117–118, 338
Repression, 141–142
and defense mechanisms, 144
and fixation, 143
lifting of, 150
neurological model of, 496
research evaluation of, 162–163
superego and, 149

Research, 439–467
analogue designs, 449
comparative design in, 445
control groups in, 443–445
current controversies and issues in, 458–463
versus experience, 439–443
importance of, 439
methodological issues in, 443–451
outcome, 451–452
placebo in, 444–445
in practice of psychology, 21–22
process, 451
professional psychology and, 4
qualitative designs, 450–451
single subject design, 448
Resistance to change/therapy, 155–156
de Shazer's rejection of, 425–426
overcoming, 187
reasons for, 490
Response cost, 290, 293
Response prevention, 280
Responsibility, in gestalt theory, 252
Restructuring, in family therapy, 419
Reward, 274
attention as, 274, 277
partial, 275
Rey-Osterrieth Complex Figure, 87
Roberts Apperception Test for Children, 42, 106
evaluation report based on, 127–129
Rogers, Carl, 38, 43, 117, 232, 455
client-centered approach of, 203–221
and encounter groups, 390–391
Role playing, 121
and attitude change, 485
in cognitive therapy, 348, 353
in construct theory, 337, 338–339
in gestalt therapy, 256–257
in social skills training, 284
Rorschach, Hermann, 37, 104
Rorschach inkblot test, 41, 104, 105
Rotter Sentence Completion Test, 107
Rule-governed behavior, 295–296
Rush, Benjamin, 32

Saroka v. *Dayton Hudson Corporation, dba Target Stores,* 65
Sartre, Jean-Paul, 240
Satir, Virginia, 412–414, 415, 498
Schemas, and psychopathology, 498–499
Schizophrenia
phenomenological approach to, 239–240

reframing as growth experience, 500
School, behavior modification principles in, 288
School psychology, 11–12
Scientist-practitioner model, 4, 6, 38, 44
Second-order change, 423, 499
Seduction theory, Freud's, 143, 159–160
Self
archetype, 173
connectionist view of, 517–518
cultural differences in perception of, 516–518
individualistic view of, 516–517
as organized structure, 176–177
Self-acceptance
in client-centered therapy, 214
importance of, 497–498
Self-actualization
in client-centered approach, 232–233
cultural differences in, 231
Self-awareness, and personal change, 166
Self-defeating personality disorder, 70
Self-disclosure by therapist, 187
versus genuineness, 220
Self-efficacy, 342, 501
Self-empowerment, 500–502
Self-help, 537–539
as common factor in therapy, 472
Self-help groups, 391–393, 538
Self-management, 290–292
Self-monitoring, 121
effective, 345
negative, 342, 344–345, 487
neutralization of effects of, 486–489
therapeutic value of suspending, 489–492
Self-objects, 182, 186
Self-psychology, 170, 182–186
approach to therapy, 186–188
Self-regulation, organismic, 249–251
Self-speech, and cognitive behavior modification, 358–360
Self-support, versus self-sufficiency, 253
Sensate focus, 402
Sensitivity training groups (T-groups), 44, 389
Sensitization. See also Desensitization
covert, 283
Sentence completion tests, 104, 107–108
Separation-individuation model, 178–180
research evaluation of, 192–193

Sex therapy, 343, 402–404
Sexuality
in Freud's theory, 142–143, 174
modern views of, 176
in object relations theory, 175–177
Shadow (archetype), 173
Shame-attacking exercises, 357
Shaping, 284
Shouldism, 364
Single session therapy, 532, 535–536
Single subject research design, 448
16PF (16 Personality Factors), 125
Skills training, 283–293
Skinner, B. F., 29, 271, 273, 295, 301
Smoking, behavioral therapy for, 318
Social history, evaluation of, 93, 102–103
Social learning theory, 30, 293, 339–343
Social problems
medicalization of, 5, 560
psychological intervention in, 561–562
Social skills training, 283–285, 342–343
Social work, 16–17
and team approach, 20
Society, and professional psychology, 22–23, 559–562
Society for the Exploration of Psychotherapy Integration, 468
Solution-focused approaches to family therapy, 415–428
enduring contributions of, 433
Spanos, Nicholas, 325–326
Spectatoring, 402
Split, as therapeutic marker, 225, 456
Split-brain research, 495–497
Split-half reliability, 56
Splitting, as defense mechanism, 179–180
Stanford-Binet Intelligence Scale, 41, 77–78
clinical use of, 83
reliability of, 82
Statistical prediction, 61–62
Stone Center, Wellesley, Massachusetts,, 517, 525
Storytelling tests, 105–106
Strangulated affect, 142
Strategic approaches to family therapy, 415–428
criticisms of, 430–432
effectiveness of, 429
enduring contributions of, 433
experiential articulation in, 481
Stress, behavioral approach to, 318
Strong Interest Inventory, 124
Structural family therapy, 414–415

Structuralism, 29
Strupp, H. H., 189–190, 534–535
Studies in Hysteria (Breuer and Freud), 35
Style of life, Adler's view of, 172
Sublimation, 144
Substance abuse problems
behavioral therapy for, 318
group therapy for, 386–388
Successive approximation, 284
Sullivan, Harry Stack, 173, 174, 502
Sunset legislation, 547
Super, Donald, 38
Superego, 148–149
Superiority, strivings for, 171
Supportive-expressive approach, 189, 190–191, 535
Symptom substitution, controversy over, 270
Systematic desensitization, 272, 279–280, 281–282
Systems change specialists, 11–12
Systems ideas, family therapy and, 416–417, 419, 433, 473

T-groups, 44, 389
TA. See Transactional analysis
Tarasoff court decision, 545
Task analysis, 229–230, 456
TAT. See Thematic Apperception Test
Teaching, in practice of psychology, 21–22
Teaching stories, 417
Team approach, to treatment of mental illness, 20
Technical eclecticism, 24, 469–471
Technology
use in assessment, 62–63
use in counseling, 536–537
Terman, Lewis, 41
Test(s). See also Behavioral assessment; Intellectual assessment; Personality assessment
administration of, 57–58
as assessment method, 54
computer administration of, 62–63
constructing, approaches to, 110–111
criticism of, 63–65
interpretation of, 58–59, 61–62
misuse of, 64
most frequently used, 60
patterns of usage, 59–61
Test-retest reliability, 56
of interviews, 104
Thematic Apperception Test (TAT), 41, 104, 105–106
validity of, 109
Theoretical integration, 24, 473–476

Theory of personality. *See* Personality theory(ies)
Therapeutic alliance/relationship, 454–455
  in brief therapy, 534
  client-centered view of, 216–221
  as common factor, 471–472
  connectionist view of, 518
  feminist perspective on, 526–527
Therapeutic markers, 225, 456–457
Therapeutic paradox, 323–324
Therapist(s)
  behavior, 302
  choosing, 567–568
  and client, relationship between. *See* Therapeutic alliance/relationship
  and empathy, 186
  qualities of, 216–221
  self-disclosure by, 187
Therapy. *See also specific therapy*
  affectively meaningful knowledge and, 154–155
  common factors in, 471–473
  culture and, 514–515
  factors affecting, 73
  goal of, 150
  integration of, 23–24, 468–509
  interpersonal focus of, 502–503
  length of, 452–453
  in practice of psychology, 21
  resistance to, 155–156
Time-limited dynamic therapy, 189–190, 534–535
Time-limited therapy. *See* Brief therapy
Time-out, 287–288
Token economies, 288–289
Top dog-underdog conflict, 256–257
Training. *See* Education and training
Transactional analysis (TA), 380–381
Transference, 35
  in psychotherapy, 156–157
  effectiveness of, 161–162
  in self psychology, 188
  sibling, in group therapy, 374
Transpersonal counseling, 529
Travistock Institute, London, England, 375
Treatment guidelines, 458
  American Psychological Association and, 459–460
Treatment manuals, 189, 360, 460, 555–556

Triangulation, in family, 411
Tuke, William, 32
Twinship, in self-psychology, 184
Two-chair technique, 225
  effectiveness of, 259
  in gestalt therapy, 256–257
Type A personality, 318

Unconditioned response, 272
Unconditioned stimulus, 272
Unconscious
  in cognitive theory, 350
  collective, 172
  Erickson's view of, 324–325, 416
  Freud's view of, 162
  Jung's view of, 172
  neurological model of, 496
Understanding, in client-centered therapy, 217–218
Unfinished business
  resolving through role playing, 257
  as therapeutic marker, 225

Vail conference of APA (1973), 6
Validation, 299
Validity, 56–57
  of behavioral assessment, 123
  concurrent, 56
  construct, 56
  controversy over, 64
  face, 56
  of intellectual assessment, 82–83
  of interviews, 104
  of neuropsychological assessment, 90
  of objective personality tests, 118
  predictive, 56
  of projective personality tests, 108–109
  of vocational assessment, 125
Values, choosing, 207–208
Verbal control, 295–296
Vertical interpretation, 152
Vicarious learning, 340
VMI. *See* Beery Buktenica Developmental Test of Visual-Motor Integration
Vocational assessment, 123–126
  clinical uses of, 125–126
  reliability of, 125
  validity of, 125
Vocational guidance. *See* Career counseling

WAIS-R. *See* Wechsler Adult Intelligence Scales, Revised
Warmth, nonpossessive, 216–217
Watson, John B., 29, 43, 271
Watzlawick, Paul, 415, 420–425, 432
Wechsler, David, 41, 78
Wechsler Adult Intelligence Scales, Revised (WAIS-R), 78
  clinical use of, 83–84
Wechsler-Bellevue test, 41
Wechsler intelligence scales, 78–81
  clinical use of, 83–84
  reliability of, 82
Wechsler Intelligence Scales for Children (WISC), 78
  WISC-III, 79–80, 80–81
    assessment report based on, 92, 94–95
Wechsler Preschool and Primary Scale of Intelligence (WPPSI), 78
Wellness, 319
Wide Range Achievement Test, Third Edition (WRAT-3), 81
  evaluation report based on, 95
Winnicot, D. W., 174
WISC. *See* Wechsler Intelligence Scales for Children
Witmer, Lightner, 37, 43
WJ-R. *See* Woodcock-Johnson Test of Cognitive Abilities
Wolpe, Joseph, 44, 271–272
Women. *See also* Feminist therapy
  APA guidelines for working with, 520, 559–560
  consciousness raising groups, 389
  discrimination against, DSM and, 69, 70–71
Woodcock-Johnson Test of Cognitive Abilities (WJ-R), 81
Word association tests, 41
World War I, and clinical psychology, 37
World War II, and development of psychology, 38, 44, 46
WPPSI. *See* Wechsler Preschool and Primary Scale of Intelligence
WRAT-3. *See* Wide Range Achievement Test, Third Edition
Wundt, Wilhelm, 29

"Yes, But" (game), 381